W9-BZF-904

MLS	master line state
MMF-PMD	multimode fiber PMD
NAC	null-attachment concentrator
NIF	neighbor information frame
NLS	noise line state
NSA	next station addressing
PCM	physical connection management
PHY	physical layer medium independent
PICS	protocol implementation conformance statement
PIXIT	protocol implementation extra information for testing
PMD	physical layer medium dependent
PMF	parameter management frame
QLS	quiet line state
RAF	resource allocation frame
RDF	request denied frame
RMT	ring management
SAC	single-attachment concentrator
SAS	single-attachment station
SBA	synchronous bandwidth allocation
SD	starting delimiter
SIF	status information frame
SMF-PMD	single-mode fiber PMD
SMT	station management
SMT-2-CS	station management-2-common services
SMT-2-IS	station management-2-isochronous services
SMT-2-PS	station management-2-packet services
SPM	SONET physical layer mapping
SRF	status report frame
THT	token holding time
TP-PMD	twisted-pair (copper) PMD
TRT	token rotation time (*r*)
TTCN	tree and tabular combined notation
TTRT	target token rotation time
TVX	valid transmission timer
UNA	upstream neighbor address
WBC	wideband channel

"Dr. Jain has produced the definitive reference on the Fiber Distributed Data Interface. It is comprehensive in both scope and depth with intuitive tutorials and informative background for those that want to understand the technologies of FDDI, helpful practice guidance for those using FDDI, and accurate models and analysis for those more interested in theoretical issues."

—Robert Grow
The Inventor of FDDI's Timed-Token Protocol

"It is a heroic document which covers the answers to questions I receive regularly. I am delighted to have such a reference document to recommend to future callers."

—Gene Milligan
Chair, ANSI X3T9.5 (FDDI) Task Group

"A serious, authoritative, and up-to-date treatment of all aspects of FDDI. Written with clarity [and] sprinkled with excellent analogies and humor, this book covers FDDI from the basics. . . Many self-test exercises (with solutions) punctuate each topic and the references are complete and current. Dr. Jain has created a superb sourcebook on a very important topic that should be on every engineer's and network manager's desk."

—Professor Ray Pickholtz
Past President, IEEE Communications Society

FDDI Handbook

FDDI Handbook

High-Speed Networking Using Fiber and Other Media

Raj Jain

Addison-Wesley Publishing Company
Reading, Massachusetts Menlo Park, California New York Don Mills, Ontario
Wokingham, England Amsterdam Bonn Sydney Singapore Tokyo Madrid
San Juan Paris Seoul Milan Mexico City Taipei

The following trademarks have been used in the book. AppleTalk and Macintosh are registered trademarks of Apple Computer Inc. ST is a registered trademark of AT&T. DECnet and VAX are trademarks of Digital Equipment Corporation. Novell and NetWare are registered trademarks of Novell, Inc. SCO is a trademark of Santa Cruz Operations, Inc. UNIX is a registered trademark of UNIX system laboratories, Inc. Micro Channel and PS/2 are trademarks of International Business Machines Corporation. NuBus is a trademark of Texas Instruments.

The publisher offers discounts on this book when ordered in quantity for special sales. For more information please contact:

Corporate & Professional Publishing Group
Addison-Wesley Publishing Company
One Jacob Way
Reading, Massachusetts 01867

Jain, Raj.
FDDI handbook : high-speed networking using fiber and other media / Raj Jain.
p. cm.
Includes bibliographical references and index.
1. Ring networks (Computer networks)—Standards. 2. Fiber Distributed Data Interface (Computer network standard) I. Title.
TK5105.72.J351994
004.6′2—dc20 93-25904
CIP

Copyright (c) 1994 by Addison-Wesley Publishing Company

All rights reserved. No part of this publication may be reproduced, stored in a retrieval system, or transmitted, in any form, or by any means, electronic, mechanical, photocopying, recording, or otherwise, without the prior consent of the publisher. Printed in the United States of America. Published simultaneously in Canada.

Cover design by Simone R. Payment
Text design by Carol Keller
Set in 10 point Times Roman by Progressive Information Technologies

ISBN 0-201-56376-2
Text printed on recycled paper.
1 2 3 4 5 6 7 8 9 10-CRW-969594
First Printing, February 1994

To my father Late Shanti Lal Jain

Contents

List of Boxes

List of Sidebars

About the Author

Raj Jain is a senior consulting engineer at Digital Equipment Corporation, where he has been involved in the design and analysis of networking and other systems since 1978. As a member of DEC's FDDI architecture team for the last eight years, he has helped analyze numerous issues related to FDDI architecture and design. He has presented tutorials on FDDI at DEC and at several conferences including the International Conference on Communications (ICC'89), ACM SIGCOMM'89, and the IEEE Local Computer Networking Conference (LCN'90).

Raj Jain received the Ph.D. degree from Harvard University and has taught graduate courses in performance analysis at Massachusetts Institute of Technology. He serves on the editorial advisory boards of *IEEE/ACM Transaction on Networking, Computer Networks and ISDN Systems, Computer Communications* (UK), and the *Journal of High Speed Networks*. He is the vice-chair of the ACM Special Interest Group on Communications (SIGCOMM). He received the "1991 Best How-to Book Systems—Advanced" Computer Press Award for his book *The Art of Computer Systems Performance Analysis* published by Wiley, New York.

Dr. Jain is known for introducing the packet train model of computer network traffic along with several congestion control and avoidance schemes. He has authored numerous papers on networking performance. He is a popular speaker, an ACM National Lecturer, and an IEEE Distinguished Visitor.

Dr. Jain is a Fellow of the IEEE. He is listed in *Who's Who in the Computer Industry, 1989, Who's Who in Writers, Editors, & Poets 1991–92*, and *Contemporary Authors 1991*.

Preface

Fiber Distributed Data Interface (FDDI) is a 100-Mbps fiber optic local area network (LAN) standard being developed by an American National Standard Institute (ANSI) accredited committee.

The *FDDI Handbook* has been designed to be a comprehensive reference book providing an easy-to-understand explanation of key aspects of FDDI. It is intended for users, buyers, managers, and designers of computer networking products and answers the following types of questions:

1. What do I need to install/manage/use an FDDI network?
2. How does FDDI work?
3. Why does FDDI work this way?
4. What other alternatives were considered for FDDI and why were they rejected?
5. What if my organization needs to use a different size, or length of fiber?
6. What should I expect in the future?

For users, it explains what features of FDDI are different from those of other popular networks such as IEEE 802.3/Ethernet and IEEE 802.5/token rings and how these features affect the applications that run on these networks. For buyers, it provides a complete list of products, what to look for, and where to find them. For network managers, it explains how to install, monitor, tune, and troubleshoot FDDI networks. For network designers and researchers, it explains what design alternatives were considered during the design of the FDDI standard and why a particular alternative was chosen.

The FDDI standard committees consist of participants from companies that are competing in the marketplace and often have very different design philosophies. The final FDDI design is an amalgamation of ideas, some of which are considered good by one set of manufacturers and not so good by others. The *FDDI Handbook* presents an objective and balanced view of both sides of the issues rather than a one-sided view.

An overview-detail-summary organization is used for each chapter and section. The first chapter of the book provides an overview of FDDI that is suitable for most nontechnical executives. Other chapters provide the details. Each chapter begins with an overview section, which provides sufficient information for speed readers, executives, and browsers. The last section of each chapter summarizes new concepts introduced in the chapter.

Entertaining sidebars and cartoons sprinkled throughout the book make it easier to understand complex technical concepts. A set of multiple-choice exercises has been added for entertainment and self-testing. You will find these useful as trivia questions during FDDI-related presentations.

Only some basic knowledge of networking concepts such as protocols and layers is required. No prior knowledge of fiber optics is needed. Familiarity with other popular protocols such as ISO, TCP/IP, and IEEE 802 will be helpful but not required.

The *Handbook* is designed for a wide audience. Therefore, it covers more topics than many of you would want to read in one pass. I suggest that you read Chapter 1, then look through the table of contents and select a few chapters to suit your interest. An extensive index will help you find the concepts you may have skipped. The index is designed to make it easy to use the *Handbook* as a reference.

If you are interested in installing an FDDI network, you may want to look in Chapters 19, 20, and 21. Chapter 21 also contains a list of issues to consider when buying adapters, bridges, routers, and other devices. Several tips in these chapters will help you save time and money by clearly understanding what different features mean and whether you need them.

Many ideas and concepts presented in the book apply not only to FDDI but to other high-speed networking technologies as well. Thus, users, managers, and designers of asynchronous transfer mode (ATM) and IEEE 100BASE-T (100-Mbps Ethernet) will also benefit from the book. For example, much of the discussion on building wiring, twisted-pair copper cable classification, fiber selection, optical components, network management, error detection, bit order, and so on applies to these other technologies as well.

This book is not meant to be a substitute for standards. Readers interested in precise details, particularly implementors, must consult the standard documents. The description here has been simplified for the sake of a clear explanation.

Some of the FDDI standards are still being developed. To keep the *Handbook* up to date, we plan to update it frequently. If you would like to know about future revisions of this book, please fill out the card at the end of this book. Also, if your company is interested in using the book or portions of it for customer or employee training, please contact the publisher regarding the availability of LaTeX sources used to produce the book.

If you notice any errors or typos, or if you have any suggestions for improvements, please contact me via electronic mail at: jain@acm.org

Littleton, Massachusetts — Raj Jain
May 1993

Acknowledgments

I would like to thank my wife, Neelu, and my sons, Sameer and Amit, for enduring lonely evenings and weekends for the last five years while I was preoccupied with this book. They had barely recovered from the absences for my previous book, *The Art of Computer Systems Performance Analysis*, and were looking forward to some time together. Instead, they learned that I had already started on the next book.

A number of my professional colleagues read drafts and helped improve the readability of the text. Special thanks to Paul Koning, Bob Grow, and Wen Pai Lu who patiently read the entire manuscript carefully and provided numerous helpful comments. Thanks are due to Bob Fink, Bill Burr, Dave Katz, Amarnath Mukherjee, E. O. Rigsbee, Ken Ocheltree, Jim Torgerson, Bill Cronin, Shirish Sathaye, Jerry Hutchison, Anil Rijsinghani, Luc Pariseau, Richard Pitkin, Chran-Ham Chang, Herman Levenson, K. K. Ramakrishnan, Ursula Sinkewic, Paul Ciarfella, Fred Goldstein, Fred Templin, Dick Stockdale, Bruce Schofield, Joe Tardo, Brian Mayo, Doug Hoeger, and Steve MacArthur for reviewing various parts of the book. Their comments have helped improve the quality of this book. Floyd Ross reviewed the original book proposal and made many constructive suggestions.

Members of our library staff have been very helpful in gathering the literature and references. In particular, Martha Sullivan has helped locate and copy hundreds of papers.

The help by the staff of Addison-Wesley is also appreciated. In particular, I enjoyed working with my editor John Wait, production editor Simone Payment, and marketing manager Kim Dawley.

The following material from American National Standards has been adapted with the permission of ANSI: Figure 2.8 and Table 2.2 from ANSI X3.139-1987; Table 3.1 from ANSI X3.148-1988; Figures 5.5, 5.7, 5.12, and Tables 5.2–5.7 from ANSI X3.166-1990; Figures 6.3, 6.4, and Tables 6.1–6.3 from ANSI X3.184-199x; and Figures 13.6, 15.4 from ANSI dpANS X3.186-199x. Copies of these standards may be purchased from ANSI at 11 West 42nd Street, New York, NY 10036.

The following material from ASC X3T9.5 contributions has been adapted with the permission of X3 Secretariat, Computer and Business Equipment Manufacturers Association (CBEMA): Figure 7.3 from ASC X3T9.5/91-277; Tables 7.3–7.8 from ASC X3T9.5/92-155; Figure 8.2 from ASC X3T9.5/92-155; Figures 10.2, 11.1, 11.3 and Tables 11.2–11.3 from ASC X3T9.5/84-49; Figures 13.11, 13.12 from ASC X3T9.5/92-297; Figures 26.1–26.3 from ASC X3T9.5/92-098; Figures 26.4–26.5 from ASC X3T9.5/92-101. For further information, contact CBEMA at 1250 Eye St, N.W., Suite 200, Washington, DC 20005. Figures 9.8, 9.13-9.15 have been adapted from ANSI T1.105-1991 with the permission of T1 Secretariat, Exchange Carriers Standards Association (ECSA) at 1200 G Street, N.W., Suite 500, Washington, DC 20005.

Figure 15.1 is based on Ichihashi, et al. (1992) published in Computer Communications, Vol. 15, No. 3. It has been adapted with the permission of Butterworth-Heinemann, Oxford, UK. Sources for other materials are acknowledged in "Further Reading" sections of various chapters.

CHAPTER **1**

Overview

FDDI stands for **Fiber Distributed Data Interface**. It is a follow-on to current local area networks (LANs) such as Ethernet and token ring. It offers a bandwidth of 100 megabits per second (Mbps), which is several times faster than 10-Mbps Ethernet, 4-Mbps token ring, or 16-Mbps token ring. FDDI's data rate is equivalent to transmitting 2500 text pages per second. It takes just 1 second to transmit four textbooks like this one.

In the 1990s, the term "FDDI" will become as common as "Ethernet" and "token ring" are today. FDDI interfaces (adapters) started appearing in 1987. Today, they are already available for all major computer systems including supercomputers, superminicomputers, minicomputers, workstations, and personal computers. According to a market survey by Rising Star Research (1992), the worldwide market for FDDI products is projected to be 1.3 billion dollars per year by 1996. In terms of number of units, the growth rate is 80% per year in 1993 and close to 100% in 1994 and 1995.

Although competing technologies are being developed for 100-Mbps networking, these technologies are far behind in their development cycle compared to FDDI, which has been standardized and incorporated in all major networking protocol suites. Products that use other competing technologies are partly proprietary and it will take several years before standards for them are finalized. FDDI products are being manufactured by hundreds of manufacturers and the intense competition is driving the prices down.

If you need bandwidth in the range of 10 to 100 Mbps, you need FDDI. Using one FDDI is cheaper than installing ten Ethernet networks, twenty-five 4-Mbps token rings, or six 16-Mbps token rings. The economies of scale in networking are such that the cost per megabit per second decreases for larger bandwidth. This is different from the economies of scale in computer systems in which buying multiple small systems is cheaper than a supercomputer of equivalent capacity.

If you are wiring a new building, it may be prudent to think about FDDI and fiber now. The speed of computer systems (for the same cost) is growing at an exponential rate. According to Gordon Bell (1992), in the near term the performance of microprocessors will improve at a 60% per year rate, providing a quadrupling of performance every three years. The increasing computation speed implies a proportional increase in the rate at which the information is produced, consumed, and communicated between these systems. Amdahl's law states that the bandwidth requirements for processors are roughly proportional to their speed. IEEE 802.3/Ethernet or IEEE 802.5/token ring networks were designed to meet the needs of processors of speed in the range of 1 to 16 million instructions per second (MIPS). Now with processor speeds commonly exceeding that limit significantly, FDDI is becoming a necessity. No wonder, FDDI interface is standard equipment on many workstations today and will be on personal computers tomorrow.

There are two scenarios in which the bandwidth requirements can exceed the capacity of current IEEE 802.3/Ethernet or IEEE 802.5/token rings. In some cases, for example, in multimedia applications, each station may need more than 10 or 16 Mbps. In others, the combined bandwidth for all stations may exceed 10 or 16 Mbps. In the first case, you need FDDI. Older LAN technologies will not be sufficient. In the second case, you have a choice. FDDI is a good solution. The alternative is to use multiple LANs, which requires you to live with the complications of configuring, managing, and troubleshooting multiple LANs and of distributing loads among these LANs.

Higher bandwidth is just one of many reasons for installing FDDI. Several other such reasons are discussed in Section 1.2. The discussion requires an understanding of some of the key technical features of FDDI, which are discussed next.

1.1 What Is FDDI?

FDDI is a set of standards developed by the American National Standards Institute's (ANSI) Accredited Standards Committee (ASC) Task Group X3T9.5. It uses a *timed token* access method to share the medium among stations. This access method, which is explained in Section 2.1, is different from the traditional token access method in that the time taken by the token to walk around the ring is accurately measured by each station and is used to determine the usability of the token.

The stations on an FDDI network are organized into a *dual ring of trees topology*, such as that shown in Figure 1.1. The main ring shown in the upper part of the figure is a dual ring since each cable consists of two fibers. The workstations connected to the concentrator in the lower part of the figure form a tree. A more general topology is presented later in Section 1.10.

An FDDI network can have a maximum of 500 stations. The socket on the station where the fiber cable is attached is called an *attachment*. Connecting one station requires at least two attachment points (one at each end of the link). The standard calls for a limit of 1000 attachments,[1] which results in the limit of 500 stations. Depending on the components used to connect the stations, the attachment limit may be reached before 500 stations are connected together. This issue is explained further in Section 1.10.

The maximum allowed length of the fiber cable between two successive stations is 2 km. This assumes a popular type of fiber called *multimode fiber*. Another type of fiber called *single-mode fiber* is also allowed, in which case the distance between stations can be as much as 60 km. The fiber modes are explained in Chapter 4. If the distance between stations is less than 500 m, lower cost optical components can be used. A standard for using twisted-pair copper cables in an FDDI network is also being designed. This is expected to reduce the cost of 100-Mbps communication to be comparable to that of lower speed LANs today. Another standard under development will allow SONET links (available from the telephone companies) in FDDI networks. SONET is explained further in Chapter 9.

The maximum allowed length of the medium in the network is 200 km. Generally, a cable has two fibers with light traveling in opposite directions. If a two-fiber cable is used, the length of the

[1]This is a simplification. Strictly speaking, most limits specified here are "default" maximums or minimums in the sense that it is possible to violate these limits provided all the default parameters are also accordingly adjusted. Because the recomputation of parameters requires considerable expertise, most users are expected to stay within these limits.

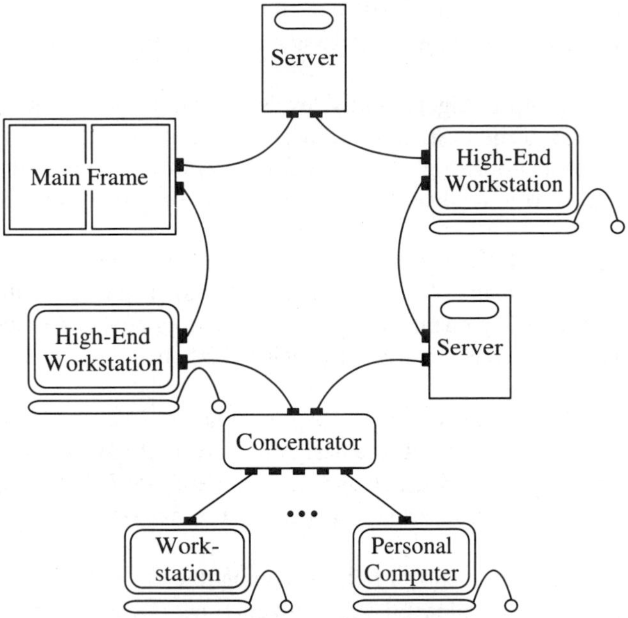

Figure 1.1 A sample FDDI network.

cable interconnecting all stations should be at most 100 km. This applies to the dual-ring topology also. In this case, the total cable on the two rings should be less than or equal to 100 km. The same limit applies if the single-mode fiber, copper, or SONET links are used. Thus, the total length of the medium cannot exceed 200 km regardless of the topology and the type of fiber. This limit is based on the time taken by the light (or electricity) to travel around the ring, which affects the ring performance as explained in Chapter 23.

Packets on FDDI are called **frames**. The maximum frame size is 4500 bytes. Since some of these bytes are used up in the frame header and trailer, the number of bytes available to FDDI users is slightly less. Generally, application level data of 4096 (4k) bytes along with the headers and trailers associated with all layers of the protocol can be easily transmitted in one FDDI frame. Since a disk sector is generally 512 bytes long, eight disk sectors can be transmitted in one frame.

FDDI's timed token access method specifically allows for two different types of traffic: synchronous and asynchronous. Synchronous traffic consists of delay-sensitive traffic such as voice packets, which need to be transmitted within a certain time interval. The asynchronous traffic consists of the data packets produced by various computer communication applications such as file transfer and mail. These data packets can sustain some reasonable delay and are generally throughput sensitive in the sense that higher throughput (bits or bytes per second) is more important than the time taken by the bits to travel over the network.

FDDI allows for two types of asynchronous traffic called *nonrestricted asynchronous* and *restricted asynchronous*. The latter mode allows two stations on the network to "mark," or restrict, the token so that other stations will not use it for asynchronous traffic. This allows the stations to transmit large quantities of data in a short time period. However, this mode is no longer used and, thus, even though there is a considerable discussion of restricted asynchronous mode in the FDDI standard documents, most manufacturers of FDDI components and most users (including the U.S. government) prohibit the use of this mode. All asynchronous traffic on FDDI is, therefore, expected to be "nonrestricted."

The standard allows for up to eight priority levels for the asynchronous traffic. The choice of the number of levels is left to the designers and users of the network. A unique scheme based on token rotation time ensures that only higher priority frames are transmitted if the load is high. Notice that the priority is assigned to individual frames and not stations. A station can transmit frames of several priority levels.

An important feature of FDDI, which is also reflected in its name, is its distributed nature. An attempt has been made to make all algorithms distributed in the sense that the control of the rings is not centralized. When any component fails, other components can reorganize and continue to function. This includes fault recovery, clock synchronization, token initialization, and topology control.

FDDI uses easily available fibers and optical components. The standard was designed to be economical to implement and, therefore, those design choices that have been proven were preferred over those that would require further research and development. All FDDI components are available and systems using the standard have started to appear in the marketplace even before the standard has been finalized.

In terms of higher layer protocols, FDDI is compatible with IEEE 802 standards such as CSMA/CD (IEEE 802.3, loosely called Ethernet), token rings (IEEE 802.5), and token bus (IEEE 802.4). Thus, applications running on these LANs can be easily made to work over FDDI without any significant changes to upper layer software.

Box 1.1 What Is FDDI?

1. FDDI stands for Fiber Distributed Data Interface.
2. It is a standard developed by the ASC Task Group X3T9.5.
3. It allows 100-Mbps communication using a timed token ring access method.
4. The stations can be arranged in a single- or dual-ring logical topology.
5. Up to 500 stations can be on a single FDDI network.
6. The multimode fibers connecting two stations are limited to a length of 2 km. With single-mode fibers, the length can be up to approximately 60 km. Lower cost optics can be used for distances less than 500 m. Standards for twisted-pair copper links and SONET links are being developed.
7. The total fiber length in the FDDI network is limited to 200 km. This is equivalent to a cable length of 100 km.
8. The maximum frame size is 4500 bytes.
9. Up to eight priority levels are allowed.
10. Three types of traffic are allowed: synchronous, nonrestricted asynchronous, and restricted asynchronous.
11. Most algorithms are fully distributed. This includes fault recovery, clock synchronization, initialization, topology control, and so on.
12. Easily available optical components and fibers are used.
13. It is IEEE 802 compatible.

Many of the FDDI specifications have been adopted by the International Organization for Standardization (ISO) and thus FDDI is now a worldwide standard and not just an American standard. Manufacturers from all over the world, including Japan, Europe, and Australia, are participating in the standards development and are producing products conforming to this standard.

The key features of FDDI are summarized in Box 1.1.

1.2 Ten Reasons to Get FDDI Now

If you are a network administrator or are involved in planning networking strategies for a corporation, the first question you face is whether you really need FDDI. The discussion in this section will help you answer that question and also help justify your choice to upper management. The circumstances under which installing FDDI makes sense are as follows:

1. *High Bandwidth*: As discussed earlier, the higher bandwidth required for higher speed computers and applications is the prime reason for using FDDI in place of older LAN technologies.

   When estimating the bandwidth requirement, the burstiness of traffic should be taken into account. The short-term load on computer networks is very high compared to the long-term average. As a rule of thumb, networks should be designed for no more than 5% long-term (daily) average utilization. Higher loading degrades response times and results in poor productivity. Thus, even if your average bandwidth requirement is 1 to 10 Mbps, you may consider installing FDDI to save people time and cost.

   In estimating the bandwidth requirements, you should also make allowance for future growth. Even if you need only 10 to 12 Mbps today, you can expect to need 100 Mbps in four to five years. Unlike computing equipment, communication equipment and wiring is harder and more expensive to replace after installation.
2. *Long Interstation Distance*: FDDI allows an interstation distance of 2 km with multimode fiber. With single-mode fiber, distances as long as 60 km can be reached depending on the quality of the fiber. These distances are sufficient to connect multiple buildings in a campus.
3. *Large Extent*: FDDI allows up to 200 km of fiber or, equivalently, 100 km of two-fiber cable. This is sufficient to cover a multicampus organization. Most other networks are limited to less than 10 km.
4. *Large Number of Nodes*: FDDI allows up to approximately 500 stations to be connected in a single network. For this reason, FDDI is particularly suitable for office environments with a large number of stations.

   In some networks, the network efficiency degrades significantly as the number of nodes sharing the medium is increased. In FDDI, some efficiency degradation occurs, but the decrease is not significant. However, for reliability and availability reasons, it is recommended that large networks be reorganized as many smaller networks connected via bridges or routers.
5. *Real-Time Traffic*: FDDI guarantees a bound on the waiting time to obtain a usable token. This service class, called *synchronous service*, is suitable for real-time applications, in which it is important that certain messages get through even during times of heavy load.
6. *Voice/Data/Video Integration*: In addition to bounded access time, synchronous service also has a reserved bandwidth. This is useful for voice and video traffic. Thus, FDDI is the preferred network for environments with multimedia traffic, such as information servers and libraries.
7. *High Availability*: Availability refers to the percentage of time the network is usable. FDDI uses a number of automatic fault recovery mechanisms, which allow the network to come back up

quickly after a failure. All links are continuously monitored. Failure of a station or a cable is quickly detected and isolated. Thus, FDDI is suitable for environments, such as air traffic control, stock market, banks, and other business applications, in which the network unavailability results in a significant loss.

8. *High Reliability*: Reliability refers to the error rates in the network while it is operating. In general, the error rates of fibers are lower than those for copper cables of equivalent length. Even copper links in FDDI have been designed to get a ring-wide bit error rate of 10^{-9}. The coding scheme and the cyclic redundancy mechanisms result in the detection of most errors. The undetected error rate is of the order of 10^{-20} or less. Thus, FDDI is suitable for networking in environments, such as air traffic control, where network errors can be expensive.
9. *High Security*: Fiber provides a secure medium because it is not possible to read or change optical signals without physical disruption. It is possible to break a fiber cable and insert a tap, but that involves a temporary disruption. For military applications, where security is of the utmost importance, FDDI that uses a fiber medium is preferred over copper-based networks, which can be tapped from their electromagnetic radiations.
10. *Noise Immunity*: In manufacturing plants, which suffer from considerable electromagnetic interference, fiber provides a noise-free medium for communication.

Box 1.2 presents a summary list of issues discussed in this section. If you do not require any of the features listed in the box, then you do not need FDDI. However, if you need one or more of the features, you need to consider the possibility of using FDDI.

Box 1.2 Ten Reasons Why You May Need FDDI

1. High bandwidth
2. Large interstation distance
3. Large network extent (periphery)
4. Large number of nodes
5. Access time guarantee
6. Throughput guarantee
7. High availability
8. High reliability
9. High security
10. Noise immunity

1.3 FDDI Network Configurations

FDDI is a versatile network that can be used in a variety of applications. Three types of computer network applications in which FDDI can be used are back-end, front-end, and backbone networks. The key characteristics of these three applications are as follows:

1. *Back-End Network*: The network used to connect a processor with storage devices is called a back-end network. These networks, generally confined to a single room, are characterized by short traffic-intensive links of typically less than 30 m. Stations may be dual-attachment stations or single-attachment stations. In either case, a physical star topology originating from a patch panel is used. The stations are frequently reconfigured. The patch panel provides this rearranging flexibility. Individual stations can be temporarily bypassed or permanently removed from the network. Optical bypassing of three or four stations is possible in this case since the resulting link still meets the length and loss requirement of a single FDDI link. The issue of bypassing is discussed further in Section 5.8.

Religions of Networking

A network architect is like the head of a religious order. Both have to design a set of rules that they feel would be good for the society. Both have a set of beliefs that they feel are true but have no means of verifying them (see Figure 1.2). These beliefs are often very strong and it is difficult, if not impossible, to make adherents of one religion agree that the beliefs of the other religions are also equally true.

I believe there is a God.
I believe network traffic needs reservation.
BIBLE
SPEC

Figure 1.2 Both religions and architecture are based on a set of beliefs.

In the world of networking, there are three major religions: connection-oriented, connectionless, and circuit-oriented. By looking at any protocol architecture, you can easily identify the religion to which it belongs. For your entertainment, we present a brief description of the three religions. It is not intended to denigrate any particular religion. It is meant to entertain you, so please read it with a sense of humor. It makes fun of all three religions.

(a) Connection-Oriented
Prior reservation
Master-slave
Central controller
Priorities
Yes, Slave!
May I speak to you, Master?
(b) Connectionless
No reservations
No priorities
Distributed control
Who is in charge here?
Everyone!
(c) Circuit-Oriented
Prior reservation
Low variance in delay
Lots of small slots
Interfaces only
Data can be lost
Our black box
Network

Figure 1.3 The religions of networking.

Architects in the connection-oriented religion believe that resources have to be reserved before they can be used. When two nodes talk, one node has to be in charge or the "master." The other node is called "slave." The master controls the communication as shown in Figure 1.3(a). When *n* nodes are on a single network, one node has to be in charge, again called the network "master." Also, since everyone on the network has a proper place in the hierarchy, there are several levels of priorities. You can recognize any protocol designed by this religion by the presence of the words *reservation, master, slave,* or *priority.*

Architects in the connectionless religion have totally opposite beliefs. They like walk-in service and would not want to make a reservation even if they have to go a long distance. When two nodes talk, they are "peers" and no one has

continued

Religions of Networking (*Cont.*)

any higher power—both have equal responsibility. When there are *n* nodes on a network, all are equally responsible and no one is in charge [see Figure 1.3(b)]. Since all nodes are equal, all communications are equal; there are no priorities and no guarantees. You can recognize any protocol designed by this religion by the absence of the words *reservation, master, slave,* or *priority*.

Architects in the circuit-oriented religion have beliefs similar to those of the connection-oriented religion but they are a bit more strong. Connection-oriented protocols have virtual circuits. Circuit-oriented protocols have real circuits that have to be reserved before communication can begin. Connection-oriented protocols switch/multiplex packets, circuit-oriented protocols switch/multiplex individual bits [see Figure 1.3(c)]. You can recognize any protocol designed by this religion by the presence of the words *reservation, master, slave,* or *priority* along with the presence of bit- or byte-level multiplexing.

During the early days of networking, the believers of these three religions couldn't compromise. That is why when IEEE 802 protocols were being standardized, the group had to be subdivided into several subcommittees. The connection-oriented camp designed the IEEE 802.5/token ring protocol. The connectionless camp designed the IEEE 802.3/Ethernet protocol. The circuit-oriented camp insisted that no LANs are required, PBX's can already provide all switching and multiplexing for voice as well as data. Why have two separate networks? All through the 1980s, adherents of one religion did not want to sell networks designed by the other religion. But they soon realized that they were each missing a large chunk of the market since there are customers whose needs are not satisfied by their religion. Now the religions are slowly disappearing and all companies sell all types of networks.

FDDI is the first networking protocol that has been designed cooperatively by all three religious camps. FDDI has several features from each of the three religions. It allows both prior-reservation (synchronous) and walk-in (asynchronous) service. It allows both master-slave and peer ports. Priorities are allowed but they are optional. Unfortunately, the union of the three religions did not last very long. The circuit-oriented camp soon realized that they were missing bit- and byte-level multiplexing and so they parted and designed FDDI-II.

2. *Front-End Networks*: The networks used to connect server hosts to client workstations are called front-end networks. These networks are typically used in office buildings, span one or more floors, and are characterized by a large number of workstations and personal computers. A single ring that uses a star layout and concentrators is typically used.

Table 1.1 Potential FDDI Applications

Industry	Why FDDI?	Configuration
Manufacturing	Noise immunity, total bandwidth, real-time response	Front-end and campus backbone
Universities	Total bandwidth, extent	Front-end, campus backbone
Financial Industries	Extent, security, availability, reliability	Multicampus backbone
Medical/Hospital	Total bandwidth, extent, availability	Campus backbone, back-end, front-end
R&D Laboratories	Bandwidth, extent	Campus backbone, back-end, front-end

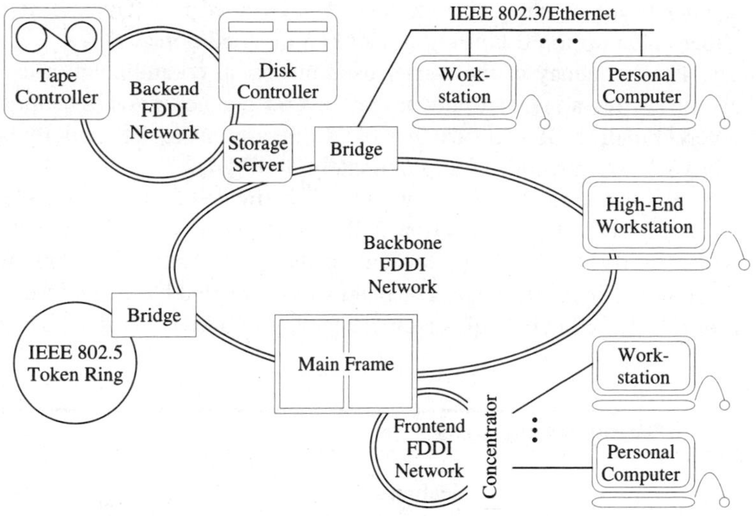

Figure 1.4 Back-end, front-end, and backbone networking applications of FDDI.

3. *Backbone Networks*: The network used to connect several networks is called a backbone network. FDDI can be used as a campus backbone to connect FDDI, IEEE 802.3/Ethernet, and/or IEEE 802.5/token ring networks in different buildings. The backbone network consists of a small number of long links. A dual ring with a ring or star layout can be used. Optical bypasses cannot generally be used because of distances involved. Multicampus backbone networks with links longer than 2 km require the use of single-mode links.

Figure 1.4 shows the use of FDDI in these three types of networks.

FDDI can be used in all segments of industry. The desired network configuration depends on the needs of the particular segment. Possible reasons and configurations for FDDI in a sample of industry segments are listed in Table 1.1.

1.4 Why Fiber?

Today optical fibers are used for all types of communication including voice, video, data, and so on. Copper cable is being replaced by optical fiber. The changeover to fiber is occurring because fiber has several advantages such as the following:

1. *Low Attenuation*: The attenuation of the fiber used in buildings today is 2 dB/km. However, fibers of attenuation as low as 0.2 dB/km are easily available (see Chapter 19) and at least an order of magnitude lower attenuation is feasible. Compare this to the attenuation of copper cables, which is generally in the range of 20 dB/km and increases for higher frequency signals. The lower attenuation of fiber means that longer distance communication is possible without

needing to regenerate the signal with repeaters. As discussed in Chapter 6, the FDDI standard allows for a fiber cable up to 60 km long under certain conditions.

2. *High Capacity*: The frequency of the carrier used in optical communication is several hundred terahertz. This allows for a signal frequency of several gigahertz (**GHz**). Optical fibers with a capacity of several hundred GHz-km are feasible. Compare this to the capacity of coaxial cables, which typically have a bandwidth of approximately 400 MHz.

   The total available bandwidth of a single fiber is estimated to be of the order of 25,000 GHz in each of the three windows (see Section 5.2). To appreciate how large this is, consider the following. The entire bandwidth now allocated by the International Telecommunications Union for radio transmission is only 275 GHz. The bandwidth allocated by the Federal Communications Commission for 68 VHF and UHF television channels is 400 MHz. With 64-kbps voice channels,

History of Optical Communications

The use of optical signals for communication can be said to have begun about 3000 B.C. when Egyptians discovered glass. This glass was not very clear and unless a piece was very thin, most of the light rays were absorbed and the glass appeared to be opaque. Today the clarity of glass is measured by the loss of optical power per unit of length. A logarithmic scale measured in decibels per kilometer (dB/km) is used (explained in Chapter 4). As shown in Figure 1.5, the Egyptian glass had a loss rate of approximately 10 dB/mm or 10^7 dB/km. This implies that the optical power was reduced to one-tenth every millimeter and after a few millimeters the power was undetectable.

Greeks are credited with using optical (fire) signals in 800 B.C. to communicate information. By about 400 B.C., they had also started using relay stations (repeaters) to extend the distance. In the next 250 years, the coding techniques were improved to the extent that alphabetic messages could be sent using these signals.

The quality of glass improved slowly and by the year 1000 A.D., the glass produced in Bohemia and Venice was much more clear with a loss rate of about 10^5 dB/km. It was still not as clear as the window glass of the 1990s, which has a loss rate of about 1000 dB/km.

In the nineteenth century, it was observed in England that light follows a narrow jet of water even around a curved path. Attempts to ex-

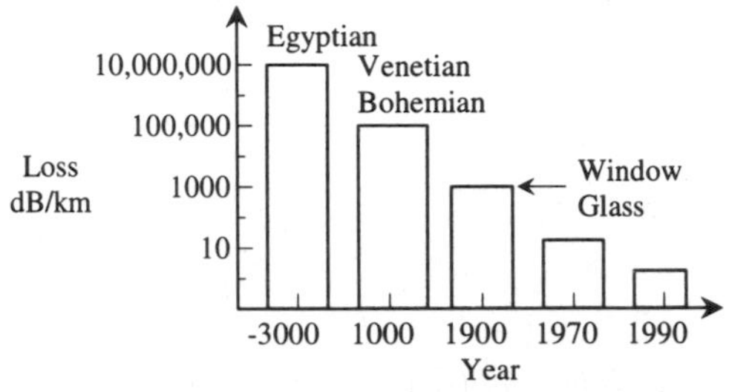

Figure 1.5 History of attenuation of light in glass.

plain this phenomenon lead to the idea of light propagation in a cylindrical medium, such as a strand of fiber. The fiber, consisting of a core and coating of different glass material, was first proposed in England in 1958. The most important revolution in optical communications began in 1960 when high-frequency laser sources were invented. Radio communication was quite common then and it was well established that a signal frequency of up to 5% of the carrier frequency could be modulated. Since the lasers had a carrier frequency of 5×10^{14} Hz, it was estimated that signal frequencies as high as 25×10^{12} Hz (25 THz) could be potentially transmitted using these laser sources. Although the optical sources were available, the medium to carry these optical signals was not available. The air as well as glass had too high a loss rate.

continued

the total busy period traffic of the current U.S. telephone network is approximately 1000 Gbps. Thus, a single fiber has a bandwidth about 90 times greater than the entire radio spectrum and about 60,000 times greater than the television broadcast spectrum. Even with inefficient modulation techniques requiring several hertz per bit, one fiber has sufficient bandwidth to carry the entire combined U.S. voice load, at least theoretically.

3. *Small Size*: The fiber is very thin. The outer diameter of a single strand of fiber is in the range of 100 μm. This is comparable to the thickness of human hairs, which have diameters close to 75 μm. Several hundred fibers can be packaged in a single cable of the same thickness as a thin coaxial cable. The number of fibers that can be accommodated in a wiring shaft is several hundred times that of the number of copper cables.
4. *Flexibility*: Unlike some coaxial cables, which are difficult to bend and hence difficult to install, fiber cables are flexible and easy to bend. Although acute bending of fiber cable is not recommended, fiber cables are easier to install.

History of Optical Communications (*Cont.*)

In 1966, two scientists named Kao and Hockham speculated that optical communication would be a feasible alternative if somehow the glass attenuation could be reduced to below 20 dB/km, which was the loss rate of copper cables used at the time. By then it was known that the attenuation was caused by impurities in the glass and so the race to produce high-purity glass began. The winner of this race was Corning Glass, which produced a so-called "low-loss fiber" in 1970. This fiber had a loss rate of 20 dB/km. Compared to today's fibers, which have a loss rate of the order of 2 dB/km, this fiber was considerably high loss, but its invention paved the way for optical fiber communications. New records continue to be established for lower loss rate and longer distance communications over fiber. Table 1.2 lists some of the recent milestones in the history of fiber communications.

Human beings are not the first among living beings to use optical communications. Several other species have been using it—even before humans began. For example, fireflies use a pulse-width modulation technique to attract members of the opposite sex during mating season (see Figure 1.6).

Table 1.2 Recent Milestones in Fiber Communications

Year	Milestone
1958	Invention of laser
1960	First practical lasers
1962	First semiconductor lasers
1966	Prediction of fiber communications
1970	First low-loss fiber and room-temperature semiconductor laser
1974	First 1 dB/km fiber
1976	System experiments and trials
1979	Fiber used in commercial service
1986	Fiber optical amplifiers

Figure 1.6 Fireflies use pulse-width-modulated optical signals to attract members of the opposite sex.

5. *Natural Abundance*: The natural supply of copper is limited and is continually being exhausted. The main ingredient required to produce fibers is silica, which is found in sand. Sand is much more abundant on this earth than copper. Silica is potentially much cheaper to produce than copper. Thus, as the demand increases, fiber prices are expected to fall much more rapidly than copper cables.
6. *No Electromagnetic Interference (EMI)*: Transmission of signals in copper cables generates electromagnetic radiation in the environment. This is an environmental pollution, which has to be limited. In most countries including the United States, government regulations limit such radiations. Light traveling through fiber does not cause EMI.
7. *No Radio-Frequency Interference (RFI)*: The radio-frequency signals that induce noise currents in copper cables have no impact on the light signal traveling through the fibers. Thus, optical communication is immune radio-frequency interference (**RFI**), which makes them ideal for use in manufacturing plants where such interference is quite common.
8. *No Crosstalk*: A side effect of electromagnetic interference is that when two or more copper wires are enclosed in the same cable or in nearby cables, the signal on one cable can interfere with that on the other. Such crosstalk is an important issue in the design of copper-based transmission systems. Although light from one fiber can leak into another fiber, such leakage is very small and can be easily prevented via proper coating. Thus, crosstalk is not a difficult design issue for fibers.
9. *Security*: The electric current traveling through a copper cable produces electromagnetic waves in the surrounding air and thus it is possible to listen to the electrical signal without touching the cable. In fact, antennas in nearby buildings are often used to eavesdrop. The light traveling through the fiber does not generate such fields and thus fibers are considered more secure. This is an important consideration in many applications such as banking and defense where security is of the utmost importance.
10. *Survivability*: A side effect of immunity to electromagnetic interference is that fiber is not affected by high-voltage surges, which commonly burn out equipment attached to copper wiring. An interesting example of this was seen recently. During a thunderstorm, lightning hit the steel guidewire between two buildings of a high-technology manufacturing concern. This caused their PBX exchange to fuse, resulting in telephone service interruption for users. Even the building security system, which used a broadband copper cable, was completely destroyed. However, the data communication system that used fiber cables continued without any interruption!
11. *Light Weight*: Fiber cables weigh much less than comparable copper cables with the same information-carrying capacity. This is particularly important in transport applications such as aircraft and automobiles.
12. *Chemical Resistance*: Copper is more chemically active than silica. Thus, chemical attacks can easily disable copper transmission lines. In particular, fiber is not damaged by water, fire, or corrosion.
13. *Temperature Sensitivity*: Temperature variations affect speed of photons and thus the velocity of light. However, the effect is small compared to that on the speed of electrons. Electrical transmission is much more sensitive to temperature variations than optical transmission.
14. *Safety*: There is no danger of shorting or sparking with fiber as is the case with copper wires when they are accidentally connected. Fiber does not attract lightning. You can safely run a fiber through areas where use of wires would be precluded; for example, through fuel tanks.
15. *Energy Efficiency*: The power levels used in fiber optic communications are extremely low compared to those in copper wire communication.

These reasons for the popularity of fibers over copper are summarized in Box 1.3.

Box 1.3 Why Fiber?

1. Low attenuation ⇒ longer distances
2. High capacity ⇒ high data transfer rate
3. Small size ⇒ more fibers
4. Flexibility
5. Natural abundance ⇒ potential economy
6. No EMI
7. Immune to RFI ⇒ high reliability
8. No crosstalk
9. Security
10. Survivability
11. High resistance to chemical attack ⇒ water, fire, and corrosion proof
12. Less temperature sensitivity
13. Safety
14. Energy efficiency

1.5 Why a Ring?

FDDI uses a ring topology. The choice of topology—ring versus bus—has been a topic of religious debate in the networking community. Because this is a book on a token-ring-based standard, a pro-ring approach is taken here. The advantages of a token ring network over contention-based bus networks are as follows:

1. *Mostly Digital Components*: In a bus network, the transmitter's signal must be receivable by all receivers on the cable. Therefore, the receiver must be capable of detecting the weakest other transmitter during its own transmission and distinguishing that other transmitter from its own echoes. This makes careful transmission system engineering necessary. The resulting design has many analog components. In a ring network, each transmitter talks to just one receiver. Thus, the analog part of the ring transceiver is relatively simple.

   To be fair, it should be pointed out that even though the analog part of the ring interface is simple, the digital part is more complex than the bus interface. In particular, the ring interface has to deal with the problems of distributed initialization and recovery and of clock synchronization. Fortunately, the design of digital circuits has advanced considerably and these problems can be easily handled.
2. *Fault Isolation*: Some failure of station attachments (transceivers) or the cable in a bus network can render the whole network inoperative. It is difficult to locate the faults in an inoperative network. The ring networks with proper wiring do not have this problem. Any one (or more) station can be isolated from the network and diagnosed for proper operation. It is much easier to isolate faults in a ring network.
3. *Extendable to Higher Speed*: The maximum obtainable throughput as a fraction of the network bandwidth is called the efficiency. For ring as well as bus networks, the efficiency decreases as the network bandwidth increases. However, the efficiency of ring networks decreases much more slowly compared to that for contention-based bus networks.

   In a contention network, at the beginning of each packet transmission, there is a period during which a risk of collision exists. This period is proportional to the length of the transmission medium since the packet is exposed to collision until its first bit reaches the farthest station. As the network bandwidth increases, the collision interval does not change (since it depends on the speed of electricity or light), but the number of bits exposed to the risk of collision increases in proportion to the bandwidth. If the packets are short, a considerable part of the bandwidth is lost due to collisions and the efficiency decreases. For example, increasing the bandwidth from 10 to 100 Mbps (without decreasing the maximum distance) in an Ethernet-like network would increase the collision-exposed portion of a packet from 64 to 640 bytes. Of course, this would not be a problem if most packets were considerably larger than 640 bytes.

4. *Applicable to Longer Distances*: The efficiency of a network decreases as the distance between nodes increases. In particular, the maximum possible distance between two nodes is called the *extent* of the network. The efficiency of contention-based bus networks decreases much more rapidly than the token ring networks. This limits the total length of the bus. For longer distances, ring networks continue to operate at acceptable efficiency.
5. *Good Performance at High Load*: At loads close to saturation, the performance of contention-based bus networks depends on the number of active nodes. If there is only one transmitter, there is no problem. But as the number of transmitters increases, the contention resolution consumes a considerable portion of the bandwidth. Ring networks are relatively less affected by the increase in the number of nodes wishing to transmit.
6. *Naturally Suited for Fiber Optic Technology*: Ring networks require point-to-point links between successive stations. This is ideal for optical fibers since it is easier to connect at the ends of the fiber than to tap in the middle. Bus networks, at least in some configurations, tap a single cable at multiple points to connect several stations. Tapping a fiber would require detecting the signal without too much loss; otherwise the system will not scale in the number of nodes.
7. *Different Media Can Be Intermixed*: In a ring network, different links can use different media. It is possible to have a ring that uses some single-mode fiber links, some multimode fiber links, and some copper links. In a bus network, separate repeaters (or signal translators) are required at each point where the medium changes. Further, the delay introduced by these repeaters will add to total propagation delay, adversely affecting the performance.
8. *Bounded Access Delay*: The access delay is defined as the time to obtain an opportunity to transmit the packet at the head of the transmit queue. Thus, it does not include the queueing delay at the station. For ring networks the access delay is typically a function of the number of nodes and the ring latency (round-trip delay around the ring). In all cases, the access delay is bounded in that a station is guaranteed to get a chance to transmit within a finite interval. In a contention-based network, every attempt to transmit could in the worst case result in a collision, so there is some chance, although it is small, that a station may not get a chance to transmit. Thus, the maximum access delay on a contention bus is unbounded.

It is obvious from this discussion that if you want to increase the speed while not reducing the distance, a contention-bus-based approach is not feasible. These arguments are summarized in Box 1.4.

Box 1.4 Why a Ring?

1. Mostly digital components
2. Easy fault isolation
3. Scalable in bandwidth
4. Scalable in distance
5. Point-to-point links
6. Easy to mix different physical media
7. Bounded access time

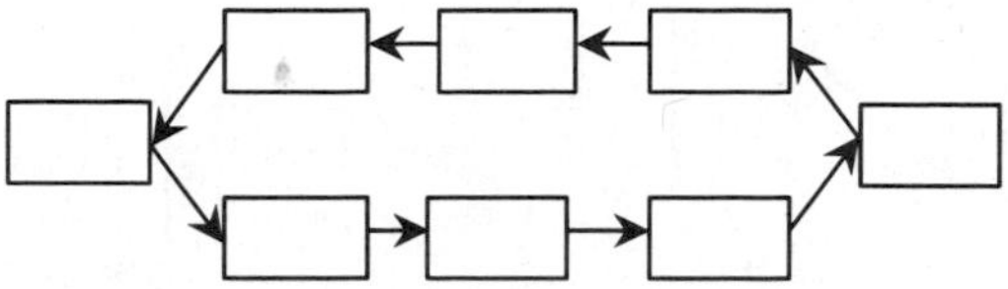

Figure 1.7 Stations connected serially are susceptible to frequent faults.

1.6 Mechanisms to Enhance Fault Tolerance

Pioneering work in token ring networks was carried out at Bell Laboratories by Farmer and Newhall (1969), who proposed and constructed a distributed "loop" network. The term "distributed" meant that no one node was responsible for controlling access to the network. A control token was passed around the loop in a round-robin fashion from node to node. Two other networks that used tokens to control access were developed by Farber et al. (1973) at the University of California, Irvine, and by Manning and Peebles (1977) at the University of Waterloo.

The first problem ring designers faced was that of fault tolerance. Strictly speaking, a ring consists of several stations connected in series as shown in Figure 1.7. The key problem with such a serial connection is the so-called "Christmas light syndrome." There is no fault tolerance. Failure of any one station can bring the whole network down. The probability of network failure increases exponentially with the number of stations. To achieve fault tolerance in ring networks, a number of techniques have been developed over the years. Of these, the following are relevant in the context of FDDI:

1. *Station Bypass*: One straightforward approach to tolerating station failures is to use electrical relays that automatically isolate the station upon failure (or shutoff). As shown in Figure 1.8, such bypass relays allow the remaining stations to reconfigure and continue operation. A similar optical mechanism, called *optical bypass*, is used in FDDI. Restrictions relating to their use are discussed in Section 1.8 and their operational requirements are discussed in Chapter 5.
2. *Dual Ring*: While bypass relays allow a ring to recover from station failures, the ring is still susceptible to the wire faults. Failure of any wire can halt ring operation. To solve this problem, Hassing et al. (1972) proposed the use of a standby wire for each wire in the network. This results in a dual-ring configuration as shown in Figure 1.9(a). The second wire was used only as a standby. Later a "self-healing" technique was proposed that allows the ring to continue operation even when both wires between a pair of neighboring stations are broken. Upon such a failure,

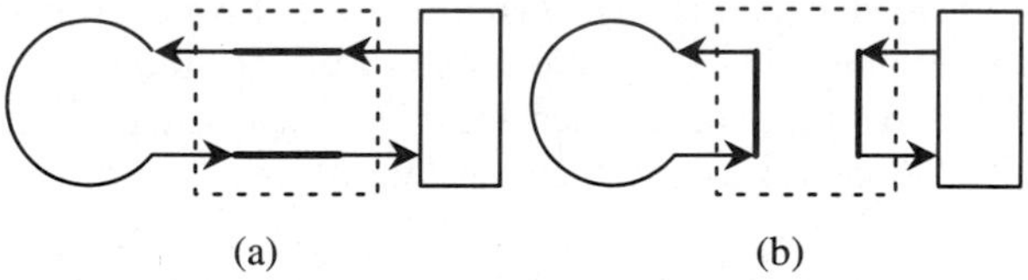

Figure 1.8 Bypass relays used in early ring networks isolate stations upon failure or shutoff.

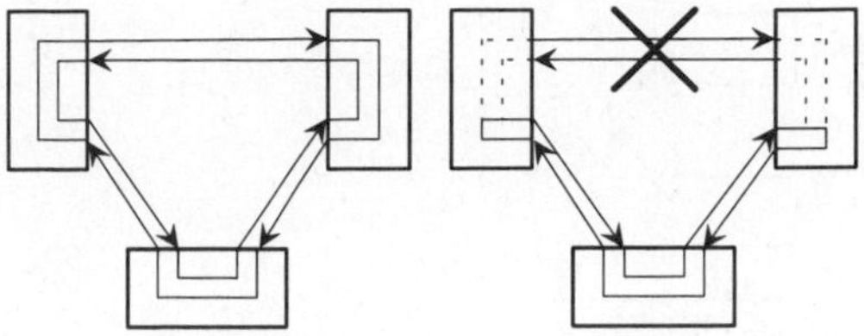

Figure 1.9 In a dual-ring topology, the operation continues even if a link failes.

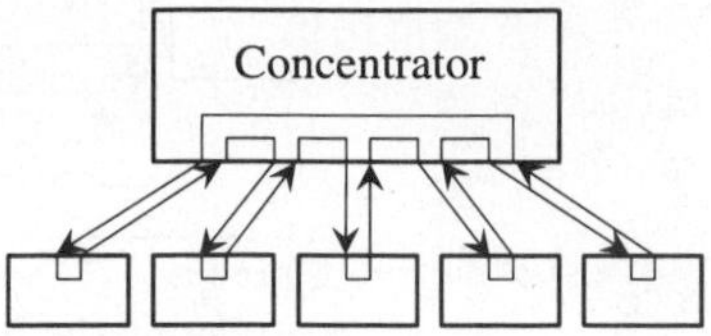

Figure 1.10 A concentrator.

the stations on the two ends of the wire reconfigure their internal paths such that the faulted wire pair is no longer used and the remaining wires form a ring connecting *all* stations. This type of reconfiguration is now called **wrapping**. According to the *American Heritage Dictionary*, the literal meaning of *wrapping* is "To arrange or fold about in order to cover or protect."

Notice that wrapping of a dual ring protects the network from only one fault. The wrapping results in a single ring. A failure of any wire used in the wrapped ring would cause the ring to **partition** such that only some subsets of (not all) stations can communicate with each other. FDDI was the first token ring standard to adopt the use of a dual ring as a fault recovery option. Now this mechanism has been adopted in other token ring standards (including IEEE 802.5/token ring).

3. *Star-Shaped Ring*: Saltzer and Progran (1980) at the Massachusetts Institute of Technology proposed the use of a star-shaped ring in which all wires from stations were brought into a centrally located wiring closet. The idea was borrowed from the telephone wiring practice of the time. Bringing all wires to one location made the fault detection and isolation considerably easier since a technician in the wiring closet could easily monitor the status of all connections and isolate the stations or cables that were found to be nonoperating. This concept has been automated and adopted in the FDDI standard in the form of a device called a **concentrator**, which continuously monitors the signals from stations attached to it and reconfigures them as necessary. This is shown in Figure 1.10. The functions and advantages of concentrators are discussed further in Sections 1.8 and 21.2.

The use of concentrators, dual rings, and station bypasses makes FDDI extremely tolerant to faults. A more complete discussion of the fault detection and isolation features of FDDI is given in Chapter 11.

1.7 FDDI Protocol Components

The ISO open systems interconnection (OSI) reference model for networking protocols consists of seven layers as shown in Figure 1.11. The bottom two layers are the physical and datalink layers, respectively. The FDDI standard has subdivided these two layers and their management into five components[2] as shown in the figure. Briefly their functions are:

[2]Only the first four of the five components are "layers" in the sense that the information is passed to the layers above or below. The fifth component, SMT, is not a layer since it communicates with all components and has no hierarchical relationship with these components.

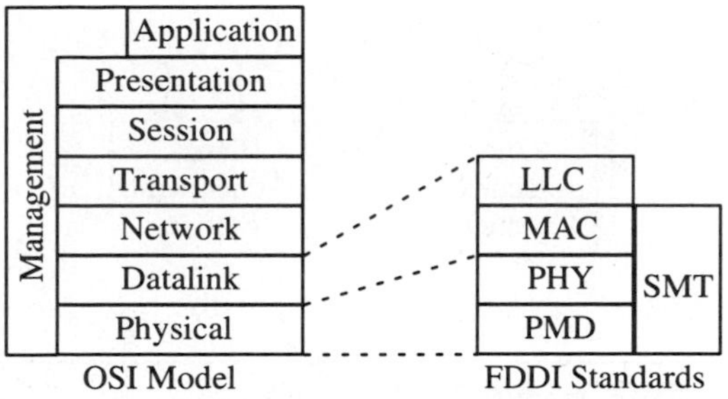

Figure 1.11 The seven layers of the ISO/OSI reference model for networking protocols.

1. *Physical Layer Medium Dependent* (*PMD*): This component of the standard deals with the optical components such as fibers, connectors, transmitters, and receivers. It also specifies the characteristics of the pulses that travel through the fiber. A number of different media are allowed in FDDI. Each medium is covered by a separate PMD standard. If a nonfiber alternative, such as copper, is used, this is the only component that will be affected. The other four components specified in this list can be used unchanged.
2. *Physical Layer Medium Independent* (*PHY*): This component deals with that part of the physical layer that does not depend on the medium. It specifies algorithms to overcome clock rate differences among the stations, to detect errors in the received bits, and to encode the information bits (data bits) into pulses (code bits) that are transmitted on the medium.
3. *Media Access Control* (*MAC*): This component specifies the rules by which all stations on the network share the medium and fairly divide the available bandwidth. It also specifies token and frame formats and rules for initializing the token.
4. *Logical Link Control* (*LLC*): This component multiplexes/demultiplexes the packets received from numerous network layer protocols. Optionally, it can provide hop-by-hop flow control and error recovery procedures. FDDI uses LLC as specified by the IEEE 802 standard.
5. *Station Management* (*SMT*): This component specifies protocols and frame formats to locate and isolate faults automatically, reconfigure the network, and initialize it.

Of the five components only four are specified by the FDDI standards. The LLC component is specified in the IEEE 802 protocols. A brief description of the LLC is given in Chapter 17. The remaining components are explained in detail in Chapters 2 through 10.

Two new components called hybrid ring control (HRC) and isochronous MAC (I-MAC) have been added in the FDDI-II standard. These components are discussed in Chapter 13.

1.8 Types of Nodes

An FDDI network consists of nodes interconnected via fiber cables. Fiber cables are passive components in the sense that they do not interpret or monitor the signals traveling through them. Nodes, on the other hand, are active components that receive the optical signal, convert it into electrical signals, decode the electrical signals into bits, ensure that the bit pattern is meaningful, and retransmit the same or possibly another bit pattern in the form of light pulses. Of the five protocol components

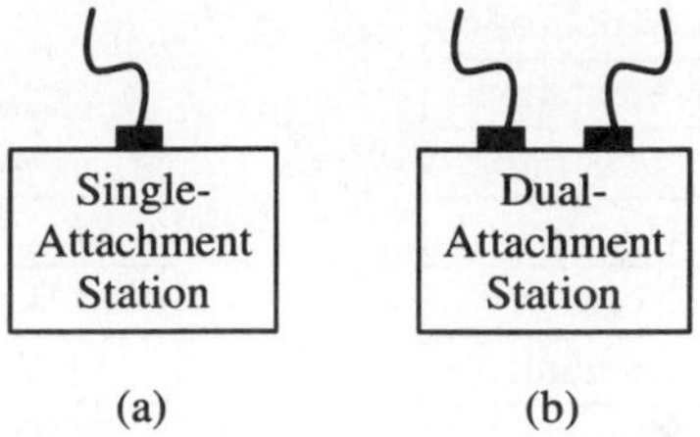

Figure 1.12 Types of stations.

discussed in Section 1.7, a node implements at least the PMD, PHY, and SMT components. It may or may not implement MAC (and LLC).

The two types of nodes are stations and concentrators. The primary purpose of a station is to transmit and receive information, while concentrators simply provide facilities to connect several stations. A station has one or more MAC. A concentrator may or may not have a MAC.

There two types of stations: **single-attachment stations (SASs)** and **dual-attachment stations (DASs)** as shown in Figure 1.12. The term "single attachment" implies that a single cable (two fibers) is used to attach the SAS to the FDDI network. It also means that a SAS is attached to only one of the two logical rings. Internally, a SAS has one PMD, one PHY, one active MAC, and one SMT component as shown in Figure 1.13.

A DAS is connected to both logical rings. It has two cables (four fibers) attached to it. Therefore, it has two PMDs and two PHYs as shown in Figure 1.14. For each attachment a PMD/PHY pair is required. A DAS has one SMT and one or more MACs. Depending on the number of MACs, it is called a single-MAC DAS or a dual-MAC DAS. Notice that the second MAC in the DAS is optional. This is because if the second ring (called the *secondary ring*) is used as a standby, no token or frames may be circulating on it and, therefore, a MAC is not required. If necessary, the internal paths inside the stations can be reorganized such that the MAC can be reconfigured to the other PMD/PHY pair. Incidentally, a PMD/PHY pair is called a **port**. Webster's dictionary defines the term *port* as "an opening in a ship's side to admit light or air or to load cargo." Ports in FDDI nodes allow a similar functionality. A port provides an external attachment to the station. It is easy to count the number of ports since each port has a connector receptacle for attachment. A DAS has

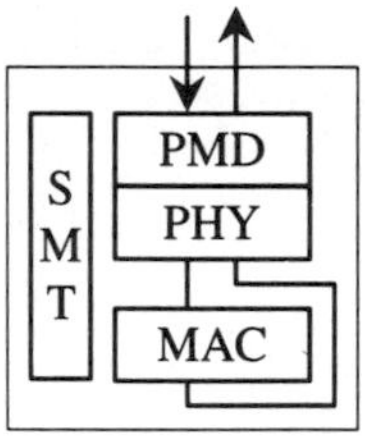

Figure 1.13 Protocol structure of a single-attachment station.

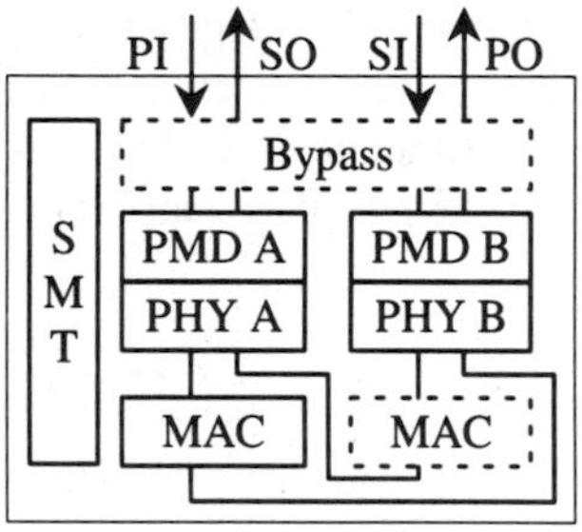

Figure 1.14 Protocol structure of a dual-attachment station.

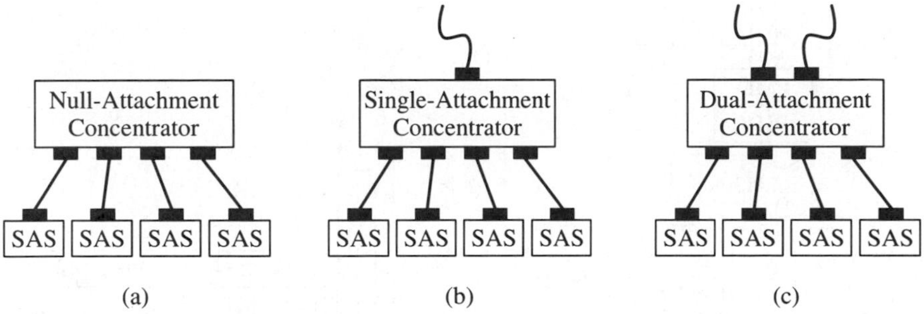

Figure 1.15 Types of concentrators.

two ports, while a SAS has one port. A dual-MAC dual-attachment station can transmit and receive frames on both logical rings.

As shown in Figure 1.14, a DAS can optionally have an optical bypass. The function of the bypass was briefly discussed in Section 1.6 and is explained further in Section 5.8.

DASs and SASs were initially also called *Class A* and *Class B* stations, respectively. However, this terminology is no longer used in FDDI standards and will not be used any further in this book.

As shown in Figure 1.15, a concentrator can have zero, one, or two attachments and is accordingly called a null-attachment concentrator (NAC), single-attachment concentrator (SAC), or dual-attachment concentrator (DAC). The protocol structure of a DAC is shown in Figure 1.16. It has two ports, which are used to connect the concentrator to the two logical rings. In addition, it has a number of additional ports, called M-ports (or **spurs**), which can be used to connect other stations to the rings. All concentrators have one SMT component. Like a DAS, a DAC can optionally have

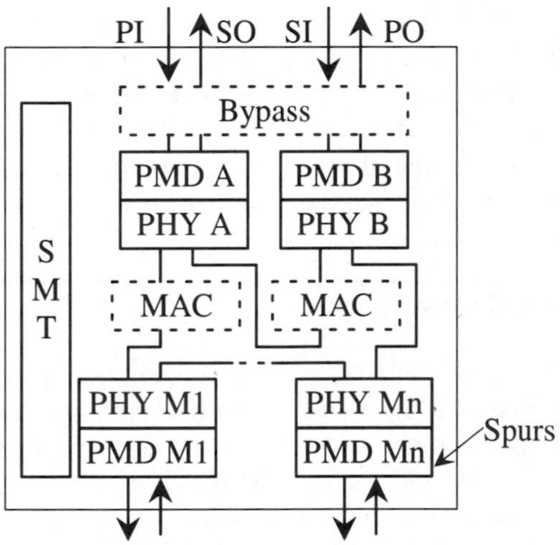

Figure 1.16 Protocol structure of a dual-attachment concentrator.

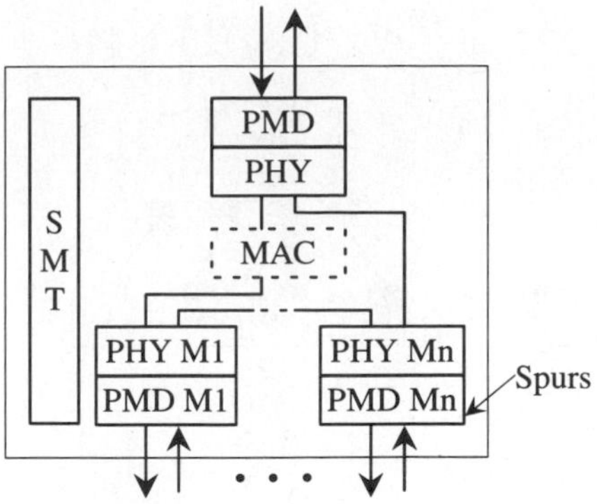

Figure 1.17 Protocol structure of a single-attachment concentrator.

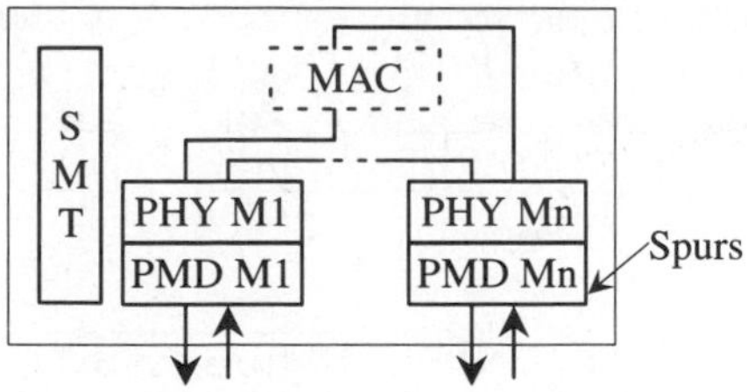

Figure 1.18 Protocol structure of a null-attachment concentrator.

an optical bypass. MACs in the concentrators are optional. Thus, a DAC may have zero, one, two, or more MACs. The protocol structures of SACs and NACs are shown in Figures 1.17 and 1.18, respectively. A SAC usually has zero or one MAC. A null-attachment concentrator is used in small ring configurations to connect a number of stations into a single ring. It may or may not have a MAC.

1.9 Types of Ports

In Section 1.8, the term *port* was defined as a PHY/PMD pair. The number of ports in a station is equal to the number of attachments. A concentrator has additional ports for connecting other stations.

A single-attachment node (SAS or SAC) has only one port called a **slave** port or S-port. As shown in Figure 1.13, the PMD and PHY components in the single-attachment nodes are said to be of type "S." Two fibers are connected to a single-attachment node. The optical signal (light) comes in on one fiber and goes out on the other. Both fibers are part of the same ring; if the incoming fiber is on the primary ring, the outgoing fiber is also on the primary. Alternately, the incoming fiber could be on the secondary ring. In that case, the outgoing fiber is also on the secondary ring.

Is a Concentrator Also a Station?

The term *node* was coined in the FDDI standards committee after considerable discussion on whether a concentrator is a station. A station's main function is to transmit and receive frames for its users. Therefore, it must have a MAC. On the other hand, a concentrator's main function is to provide attachments to other stations. Therefore, it must have such attachments (or M-ports). A concentrator may or may not be interested in frame transmission and reception. If so, a concentrator may or may not have a MAC. Thus, it was agreed that a concentrator need not be a station. The term *node* includes both concentrators and stations. A station is a node with a MAC, while a concentrator is a node with M-ports.

A dual-attachment node (DAS or DAC) is connected via two cables (four fibers) and has two ports, which are named A-port and B-port, respectively. The fibers of the cables are assigned to the primary and secondary rings in a specific manner. The port in which the primary ring signal enters (labeled *primary-in* or *PI*) is also the port on which the secondary ring signal exits (labeled *secondary-out* or *SO*). This port is the A-port. Similarly, the B-port has secondary-in and primary-out fibers. The simplest way to remember the two ports is to remember: "primary-in is A." Since a cable on the dual ring contains one fiber from both rings, secondary-out is also in the A-port. Similarly, secondary-in is B, and primary-out is also in the B-port.

Like a dual-attachment station, a dual-attachment concentrator is also connected via two ports—called A-port and B-port. The spurs on the concentrator, which allow other stations to be connected to the ring(s), are called *master ports* or M-ports. A concentrator can have any number of M-ports.

Like a SAS, the port connecting a single-attachment concentrator to the ring is called a *slave port* or S-port. In addition, the SAC has one or more M-ports.

The A- and B-ports on a dual-attachment concentrator and a S-port on a single-attachment concentrator are used for connecting the concentrator to other nodes at the same (or possibly higher) level in the physical topology. They are, therefore, also called *peer ports* or *peer attachments*. The null-attachment concentrators have no peer attachments. That is, they do not have A-, B-, or S-ports. All they have are one or more M-ports to allow connection to other stations at lower levels of the physical topology. Such concentrators are used as the roots of tree-topology networks.

1.10 A Sample Topology

Figure 1.19 shows a sample FDDI ring with one DAS, two DACs, one SAC, and seven SASs. The primary ring is shown via a sequence of solid lines and arrows. The secondary ring is shown with dotted lines. Both fibers of a cable are shown separately. The ports are labeled A, B, M, or S as appropriate.

Figure 1.19 shows a *logical* representation of the network. The fibers and the direction of signal flow are shown explicitly. Notice that there are a maximum of two counter-rotating logical rings. If you see this configuration in a computer room, normally you will not be able to see the two fibers or the signal flow inside the boxes. Physically, each piece of equipment would appear like a black box and the configuration would look something like the one shown in Figure 1.20. This is the **physical topology**. Notice that it consists of several trees hanging from a ring. This is the so-called **dual ring**

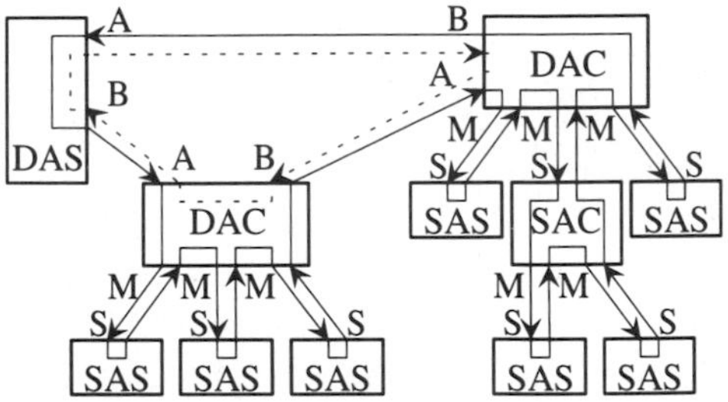

Figure 1.19 A sample FDDI network.

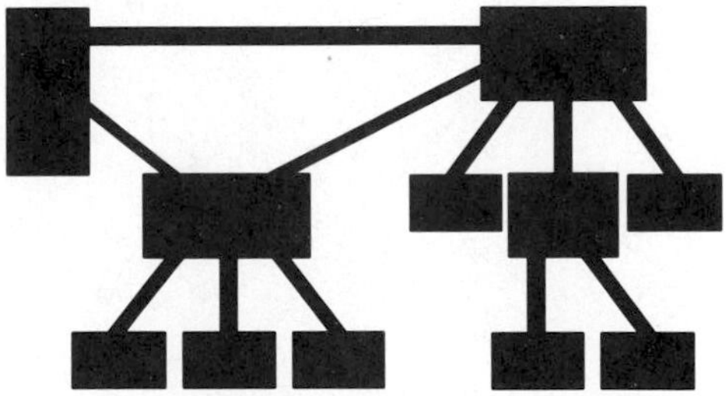

Figure 1.20 A physical representation of the sample FDDI network.

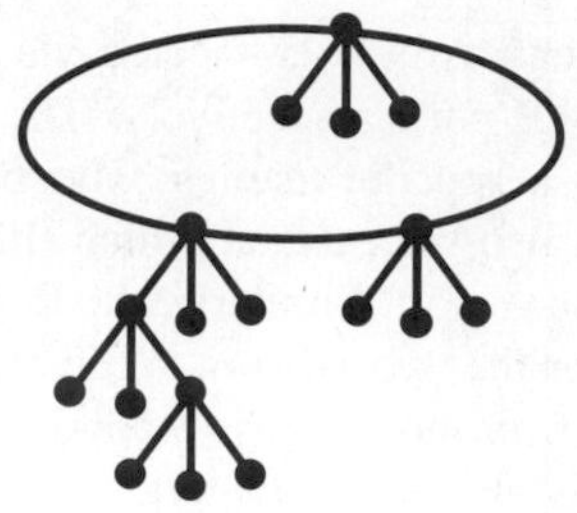

Figure 1.21 The "dual ring of trees" topology.

of trees physical topology that is allowed in FDDI. A clearer picture of the topology allowed in FDDI is shown in Figure 1.21. It consists of several trees hanging from a dual ring. The dual ring is called the **trunk ring**. Any subset of this topology is also legal. Some of these subsets, dual ring without trees, a single tree, a wrapped ring with trees, and a wrapped ring without trees, are shown in Figure 1.22.

Notice that the trees are allowed on primary as well as secondary rings. It is preferable that the trees be on a primary ring so that all (single attachment as well as double attachment) stations can be reached on the primary ring. If single-attachment stations are allowed on both rings, SASs on one ring can communicate with SASs on the other ring only if a DAS acts as a bridge or a router. Also, DASs have to keep track of the locations of various SASs. Wrapping and upwrapping of the rings complicates this tracking. Therefore, bridging or routing between the two rings of a dual ring is not done.

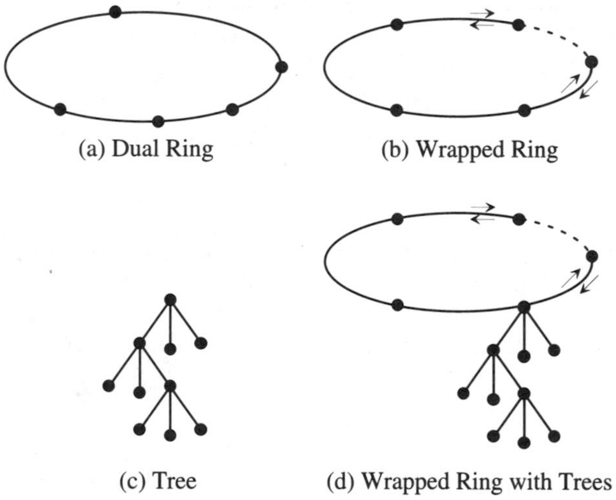

Figure 1.22 Subsets of the dual ring of trees topology.

Is FDDI a Misnomer?

The X3T9.5 Task Group was formed in 1979 to provide a high-performance I/O channel called *Local Distributed Data Interface* (*LDDI*). The idea of using optical fibers was first raised in X3T9.5 at the October 1982 meeting and subsequently the LDDI standard was abandoned and a new effort based on fiber was begun. This new standard was named *Fiber Distributed Data Interface* (FDDI).

Initially the standard was expected to be used only on a fiber medium in a fully distributed manner for data transmission. It was expected to specify only an interface similar to SCSI (small computer system interface). The features of FDDI have slowly been extended to meet diverse needs and now the name FDDI has actually become a misnomer. A more appropriate name for the current FDDI standards would be **** (four asterisks), where each asterisk stands for a wildcard in that position. FDDI is now an any-media, centralized-or-distributed, any-traffic (voice, video, or data), LAN-or-MAN-or-interface.

FDDI standards now cover nonfiber media including copper wires. FDDI-II requires a centralized master station. Since not all FDDI-II stations have the hardware necessary to become master stations, it is not a fully distributed peer-to-peer protocol.

Data were never considered to be the only traffic on FDDI. Even initial versions had features for digital voice, video, and other telephony applications.

To summarize, the logical topology of FDDI consists of a dual counter-rotating ring or its subset (single ring), while the physical topology consists of a dual ring of trees or its subsets.

1.11 Summary

FDDI is the next generation of high-speed networks. It is an ANSI standard that has been adopted by ISO and is being implemented all over the world. It allows communication at 100 Mbps among 500 stations distributed over a total cable distance of 100 km.

FDDI will satisfy the needs of organizations needing a higher bandwidth, a larger distance between stations, or a network spanning a greater distance than the IEEE 802.3/Ethernet or IEEE 802.5/token ring networks. It provides high reliability, high security, and noise immunity. It supports data as well as voice and video traffic.

FDDI can be used in back-end, front-end, or backbone networks. Most early applications of FDDI have been as a backbone network connecting several IEEE 802.3/Ethernet or IEEE 802.5/token ring networks.

Fiber is the ideal medium for backbone configurations. Because of its low attenuation it can be used for long distances at high capacity. Also, it is not affected by electromagnetic or radio-frequency interference. Therefore, it is ideally suitable for noisy environments such as manufacturing plants.

A token ring approach was selected for FDDI because it is scalable in speed and distance. The access delay is bounded and the point-to-point links are ideally suited to optical fibers. FDDI uses a number of mechanisms to enhance the fault tolerance of rings. In particular, it allows station bypasses and dual rings. Concentrators are used to provide connections to single-attachment stations.

The FDDI protocol covers the bottom two layers of the OSI reference model. It consists of five key components. PMD is concerned with the details of the physical medium. A number of PMDs have been defined for different media such as multimode fiber, single-mode fiber, low-cost fiber, copper, and so on. PHY deals with other media-independent issues of the physical layer. The rules for sharing the media among all stations are covered by MAC. Management issues related to the layers covered by FDDI are addressed by SMT. FDDI uses IEEE 802 LLC, which provides protocol multiplexing and, in some cases, flow and error control.

The two types of nodes in an FDDI network are stations and concentrators. Stations implement the MAC protocol to be able to transmit data on the medium. MAC is optional for concentrators. A node can have one or two attachments. Thus, there are dual-attachment stations, single-attachment stations, dual-attachment concentrators, and single-attachment concentrators. It is also possible to have a null-attachment concentrator, which has no further attachments for connection to higher levels of physical topology.

The attachments on FDDI nodes are called *ports*. Each port has a PMD and a PHY component. There are four types of ports: A, B, S, and M. M-ports are always on the concentrators and provide attachment points for other stations and concentrators lower in the topology tree. The port on single-attachment stations or concentrators is called an S-port. It is used to connect them to concentrators higher in the topology tree. A and B denote the ports on dual-attachment stations or concentrators that allow them to be connected to other dual-attachment stations or concentrators.

Although logically FDDI uses a dual ring, it allows a dual ring of tree physical wiring structure. The trees allow single-attachment stations to be connected to concentrators. Any subset of the dual ring of trees topology is also allowed.

An overall view of the features of an FDDI network was provided in this chapter. The remainder of this book is concerned with explaining these features and the reasons behind their selection. Several new terms have been used in this chapter. Many of these terms will be explained again in more detail. If you find a term that you could not understand, please check the index for other places where the term has been discussed in this book.

1.12 Further Reading and Historical Notes

The FDDI standard has been more than 10 years in the making. A list of some of the milestones in its development is presented in Table 1.3.

The FDDI protocols are described in a number of ANSI standards and working documents. These standards are also being adopted as ISO standards. Later, as each component of the FDDI protocol is discussed, the appropriate ANSI or ISO document for that component will be discussed.

Table 1.3 History of FDDI

Date	Milestone
October 1982	First consideration in ASC X3T9.5
December 1982	FDDI name chosen
June 1983	Detailed proposal submitted
October 1984	X3T9 technical letter ballot for MAC
July 1987	First ANSI standard for FDDI (MAC) published
February 1989	X3T9 technical letter ballot for FDDI-II
April 1989	First ISO standard for FDDI (PHY) published
July 1990	X3T9 technical letter ballot for SMT
June 1992	SMT forwarded to X3 for approval

The types of nodes, ports, and valid topologies are described in the SMT standard. Unfortunately, there is no overview document. Also, most of these standards are written for experts and are not useful to a novice.

Floyd Ross, who is vice-chair of the X3T9.5 Task Group, has written a number of overview papers. See Burr and Ross (1984), Ross and Moulton (1984), Ross (1986a, 1986b, 1987, 1989a, 1989b, 1991a, and 1991b), and Ross and Fink (1992). See also Katz (1990c) and Milligan (1988, 1989). Table 1.3 has been adapted from one of Floyd Ross's tutorials.

For a discussion of token ring versus contention bus arguments, see Saltzer, Clark, and Progran (1981).

For discussions of the history of optical communication, see Basch (1986), Tosco (1990), and Keiser (1991). Burr (1990) provides an interesting discussion on the potentials of fibers.

Table 1.1 has been adapted from Pyykkonen (1987).

For information on the FDDI market, see Rising Star Research (1992), Infonetics Research Institute (1990), and Venture Development Corporation (1988). Info Gatekeepers (1990) is a collection of FDDI-related papers presented at various conferences.

1.13 Self-Test Exercises

Note: Some exercises have multiple correct answers. See Appendix D for answers.

1.1 Which of the following apply to an FDDI ring with a null-attachment concentrator?

a. The ring has no stations.
b. The ring has no other concentrators.
c. The concentrator is broken.
d. The FDDI has no dual ring.
e. The FDDI has no trees.
f. The stations use wireless communication.

1.2 Master ports in FDDI are used

a. To connect stations on the dual ring.
b. To provide an alternate connection from dual-attachment stations.
c. To provide connections between concentrators and some stations.

1.3 What is the purpose of slave ports in FDDI?

a. To provide a cheap connection to a dual-attachment station.
b. To do all the hard work required to connect dual-attachment concentrators.
c. To allow single-attachment stations to be connected to concentrators.
d. To provide a standby connection from a concentrator.

1.4 What is the maximum number of ports that a dual-attachment node can have?

a. 2
b. 3
c. No limit

1.5 An FDDI node has two receptacles (ports) marked A and B. What is the difference between the two ports?

a. B port is used as a standby.
b. A port is used as a master and B can be used only as a slave.
c. An A port should normally be connected to a B port on another node.
d. An A port should normally be connected to an A port on another node.

1.6 Which of the following are always true for a dual ring of trees configuration?

a. There is at least one dual-attachment concentrator.
b. There are at least two single-attachment concentrators.
c. All nodes have access to both rings.
d. All nodes are dual-attachment nodes.
e. All nodes are single-attachment nodes.

1.7 Which of the following are always true for a valid FDDI configuration?

a. There are at least two rings.
b. There is at least one concentrator.
c. There is at least one tree.
d. There is at least one master port somewhere.
e. There is at least one slave port somewhere.
f. All of the above.
g. None of the above.

CHAPTER 2

Media Access Control

Media access control relates to the problem of sharing a single network medium among all the stations on the network. FDDI stations follow a set of rules to ensure that all stations get fair and quick access to the network. The rules are designed specifically for high-speed operation at 100 Mbps and are therefore different from those used in earlier lower speed Ethernet or token ring networks. The following questions are addressed in this chapter:

1. How does a station ensure that it can transmit its messages (frames) without being overrun by other stations?
2. Why doesn't FDDI use the contention mechanism used in the IEEE 802.3/Ethernet networks?
3. How is the token mechanism used in FDDI different from that used in IEEE 802.5/token ring networks?
4. How do the stations ensure that time-critical voice/video traffic meet their time deadlines while the noncritical data traffic use all available bandwidth?
5. What are the different types of frames used in FDDI and what is their format?
6. How are the frames removed from the network?
7. What happens if the token is lost?
8. Who puts the token in the network?

These and several other related issues are discussed in this chapter. The first issue, of course, is that of rules for sharing the medium, as discussed next.

2.1 Timed Token Access Method

In a local area network, several stations share a single medium, usually a bus or a ring. The stations have to follow a certain set of rules to ensure that only one station uses the medium at a time. These rules are called **access methods**.

FDDI stations use the *timed* token access method similar to that used on IEEE 802.4 token bus networks. It is different from the normal token access method used in IEEE 802.5 token ring networks. To understand why the timed token access method was invented, it is helpful to understand how the normal token access method works and why it was considered undesirable for FDDI.

In the normal token access method, a token is circulated among the stations in a round-robin fashion. A station that wants to transmit has to wait until it receives the token. It is allowed to hold

Media Access Methods

The issues of the media access method are most clearly seen when several people in a room try to communicate. The air in the room is the shared medium used to transmit and receive the voice signals among the people. What rules are required to ensure that fruitful communication takes place? The simplest method is to have no rules. This is shown in Figure 2.1(a). Everyone speaks whenever he/she likes. This was in fact the first media access protocol used in computer networking. It is called the **Aloha** (or Hello) protocol. It is easy to see that this protocol is not very efficient because many messages are lost when two or more people speak (and collide) at the same time. The probability of a successful transmission under very heavy load is zero since almost all of the messages are lost.

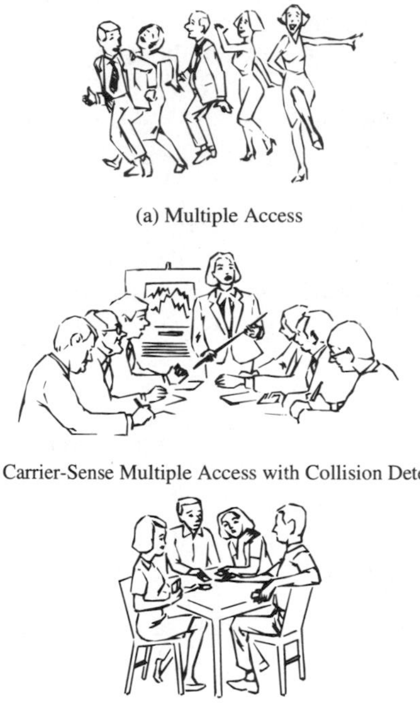

(a) Multiple Access

(b) Carrier-Sense Multiple Access with Collision Detection

(c) Token Access

Figure 2.1 Multiple-access methods.

One way to improve the efficiency of the Aloha protocol is to set a simple social rule: listen before you speak. If someone is speaking, wait until he/she finishes. This is called the **carrier sense multiple access** (**CSMA**) protocol. The term *carrier sense* refers to ensuring that there is no carrier (sound signal) in the air.

The key problem with CSMA is that as soon as someone finishes speaking, several people may start speaking. The probability of such a collision increases if the room is large so that the sound takes a significant amount of time to travel from one end of the room to another. This problem can be solved by adding another rule: listen *while* speaking (in addition to listen *before* speaking). If you hear someone else speak during your speech, let him/her know. All speakers stop and try later. This is called CSMA with collision detection (**CSMA/CD**). This protocol is used in the Ethernet and IEEE 802.3 local area networks.

A random access protocol such as CSMA/CD is ideal for the case when most of the people in the room want to listen and only a few people want to speak at a time. An example of such "bursty" traffic is a classroom with a teacher and his teaching assistants doing most of the talking. This is shown in Figure 2.1(b).

If all of the people in the room have an equal amount of talking to do, for example, in the card game shown in Figure 2.1(c), a simple protocol is to use a coin as a token, which is passed among the participants in a round-robin fashion. Anyone who wants to speak has to wait until he/she receives the token. This is the popular token access method. The amount of time a person can speak is agreed on in advance and is called the **token holding time** (**THT**).

the token and transmit its frames for a fixed interval called the token holding time (**THT**). The time between successive arrivals of the token at a station is equal to the token rotation time (**TRT**). It depends on the number of active stations and THT. An active station is one that wants to transmit.

$$\text{TRT} = \text{Number of active stations on the ring} \times \text{Token holding time} + \text{Token travel time}$$

The THT must be selected properly because it affects the response time as well as the maximum throughput of the token ring. Normally most of the stations on the ring are inactive. If a station wants to transmit a large amount of data, the station transmits for a period equal to the THT and then it has to release the token. The token goes around the ring unused. The station recaptures the token and the cycle repeats. In each cycle, the THT period is used and a period equal to the ring latency (a round trip around the ring) is wasted. The efficiency is:

$$\text{Efficiency of token access with one active station} = \frac{\text{THT}}{\text{THT} + D}$$

where D denotes the ring latency. It is obvious that for high efficiency the THT should be large. The best efficiency in this scenario is obtained by exhaustive service (THT=∞). However, a large THT is bad if the number of active stations is large. In the worst case, the TRT may be equal to the total number of stations on the ring times the THT. A large TRT implies that stations have to wait a long time before getting an opportunity to transmit. To keep TRT low, either the number of stations on the ring or THT should be kept small. Further, the TRT is highly variable since the number of active stations can vary greatly. This variability is undesirable if you want to transmit voice signals along with data on the same network. For voice signals, the token should be received within a certain prespecified bound (for example, 20 ms).

One way to overcome the problems of the normal token access method is for all stations to limit their transmissions so that the token rotation time does not exceed a preset target. The time not used by one station is used up by other stations. Once the full limit has been used, further stations do not use the token on that round. The stations agree to ensure that the token is not unduly delayed. A target token rotation time (**TTRT**) is agreed on by all the stations and they all cooperate to meet this target. Each station measures the time between successive arrivals of the token and if the measured TRT is equal to or more than the target (the token is late), it does not transmit. If the measured TRT is less than the target (the token is early), it transmits but limits its transmission so that the target is not exceeded. This is achieved by limiting the token holding time to the difference between TTRT and measured TRT.

$$\text{Token holding time} = \text{TTRT} - \text{TRT}$$

This is the method used in FDDI for data traffic that is not time critical, such as file transfers. This is asynchronous class traffic. For delay-sensitive traffic, such as interactive voice, a synchronous class is used. Synchronous traffic can be transmitted on any token (early or late). However, the duration of synchronous transmissions is small and preallocated. Each station can have a different synchronous allocation. Notice that the synchronous transmissions on a late token can cause the token rotation times to be above the target. Synchronous allocations are limited so that the worst case token rotation time is less than two times the target. In this sense, the target TRT is similar to the government budget targets. The actual TRT can be as much as twice the target.

For asynchronous traffic, FDDI stations limit their transmissions so that the token is not unduly delayed. Before beginning each new frame transmission, they check the time remaining. As long as the token is not late, they can begin a new transmission. However, if the token holding timer expires in the middle of a frame, the frame is allowed to complete. This is the so-called *yellow light rule.*

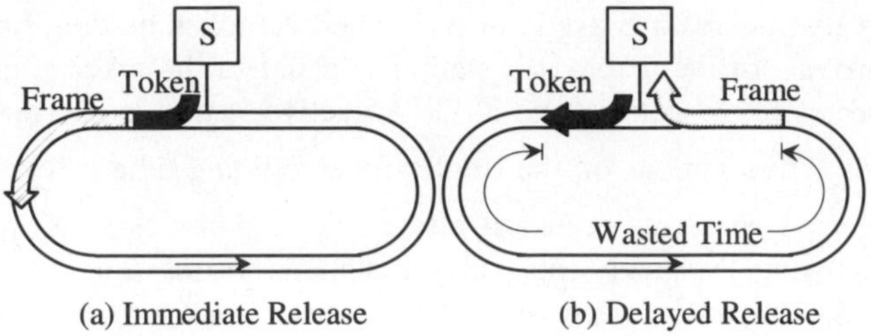

Figure 2.2 Immediate versus delayed token release.

When traffic lights turn yellow, many motorists speed up and cross the intersection. In FDDI this is legal. This phenomenon, called **asynchronous overrun**, can result in the target being exceeded by as much as the maximum frame size. As discussed in Section 22.4, this overrun is accounted for in selecting the TTRT.

Stations release the token immediately after the last frame transmission. This alternative, called *immediate token release*, was chosen in FDDI in preference to *delayed token release*, which was used in early IEEE 802.5 token rings. The two versions are shown in Figure 2.2. In the delayed version, the transmitting station waits for the first frame to arrive back at the station before releasing the token. While this waiting is an acceptable alternative at low speeds, at high speeds this results in a considerable loss of efficiency. This is discussed further in Section 2.15.

The frames go around the ring and are removed by the transmitting station. This removal is called **stripping**, which is discussed further in Section 2.11.

The TTRT is set at ring initialization. All stations on the ring bid a target value (T_Bid), and the minimum of all such requests is selected as the operational target:

$$\text{TTRT} = \min\{T\_\text{Bid}_1, T\_\text{Bid}_2, \ldots, T\_\text{Bid}_n\}$$

This is explained further in Sections 2.12 and 22.4.

For transmission of large amounts of data, FDDI provides special facilities by dividing asynchronous traffic into two classes: restricted or unrestricted. A restricted asynchronous class is used for a very large burst of data requiring several token rotations. For this purpose, the transmitting station marks the token as "restricted" (by changing a bit in the token) before releasing it. The token so marked can be used for synchronous transmissions, but it cannot be captured by other stations for asynchronous traffic. Only the stations involved in the restricted dialog can capture the token and transmit more data. This can continue for several token rotations. When the restricted dialog completes, the station that restricted the token unrestricts it. Notice that during each cycle, the dialog participants have to follow the token holding time limitations, that is:

$$\text{THT} = \text{TTRT} - \text{TRT}$$

The station restricting the token is called its **owner**. Since the address of the station is not on the token, no one other than the owner knows who restricted the token. If the owner malfunctions, the token becomes unusable. Although special watchdog mechanisms have been designed to detect such a situation, it is best not to use the restricted token option.

The token rules for FDDI are summarized in Box 2.1. The extension of these rules to multiple priorities is considered in Section 2.2.

Box 2.1 FDDI Token Rules for a Single-Priority Case

1. There are three types of traffic: synchronous, asynchronous, restricted asynchronous.
2. There are two types of tokens: restricted or nonrestricted.
3. Synchronous traffic can be transmitted whenever a station captures any token, whether early or late, restricted or nonrestricted.
4. The time for synchronous transmission is preallocated.
5. Asynchronous traffic can be transmitted if the token is early and nonrestricted.
6. The token holding time is limited so that the target is not exceeded:

   THT = TTRT − TRT

7. The last frame is allowed to complete.
8. The token is released immediately after the transmission.
9. The transmitting station is responsible for stripping all frames it transmitted.
10. Restricting a token allows a station or a group of cooperating stations to reserve the token for several token rotations.
11. Stations transmitting restricted asynchronous traffic follow the rules of timed token access.

2.2 Priorities

FDDI allows up to eight priority levels. The network administrators can choose to have none or any number of priorities up to eight. This is possible using a load-level-based priority system. In this system, low-priority messages are allowed only if the load is low; conversely, they are forbidden if the load is high.

There is one-to-one mapping of the load to token rotation time. Thus, particular priority messages are allowed only if the token rotation time is below a particular value. This is shown in Figure 2.3. At zero load, the token rotation time is equal to the ring latency D. At 100% load:

$$\text{TRT} \leq \text{TTRT} + \text{Maximum frame time} + \text{Token time} + \sum \text{Synchronous allocations} \tag{2.1}$$

The synchronous allocations are limited so that the sum of the last three terms in Equation (2.1) is less than TTRT (see Section 10.13) and, hence, the maximum TRT is less than two times the TTRT. That is:

$$\text{Maximum frame time} + \text{Token time} + \sum \text{Synchronous allocations} \leq \text{TTRT}$$

Hence,

$$\text{TRT} \leq 2 \times \text{TTRT}$$

Incidentally, if TRT exceeds the target in one rotation, the token is not used for asynchronous transmissions in the next rotation, so TRT cannot exceed the target continuously. In general, for n successive rotations, the following holds:

$$\sum_{i=1}^{n} \text{TRT}_i \leq n \times \text{TTRT} + \text{Maximum frame time} + \text{Token time} + \sum \text{Synchronous allocations}$$
$$\leq (n+1)\text{TTRT}$$

To allow $k+2$ priorities, the station manager chooses $k+1$ thresholds T_Pri0, T_Pri1, ..., T_Pri$k$,

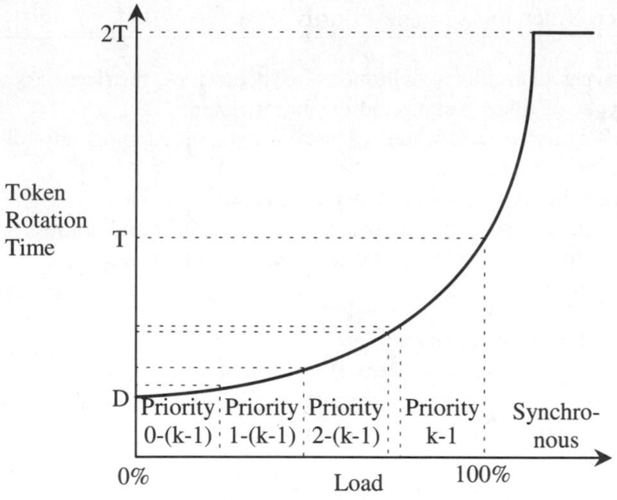

Figure 2.3 Token rotation time as a function of load.

such that:

$$D < \text{T\_Pri0} < \text{T\_Pri1} < \cdots < \text{T\_Pri}k \leq \text{TTRT}$$

The ith priority (and all higher priority) traffic can be transmitted if the TRT is less than T_Pri$i$. Further, the transmission time (THT_i) for ith priority is limited so that TRT will not exceed T_Pri$i$.

$$\text{THT}i = \text{T\_Pri}i - \text{TRT}$$

Example 2.1 Consider a three-priority system using priorities 5, 6, and 7 with T_Pri5 and T_Pri6 set at 4 and 6 ms and the TTRT (used by priority 7) set at 8 ms. In cycles in which the token is received within 4 ms, all traffic can be transmitted. In cycles with TRT between 4 and 6 ms, priority 5 traffic cannot be transmitted; only priority 6 and 7 traffic can be transmitted. If the TRT is between 6 and 8 ms, only priority 7 (highest priority) traffic can be transmitted. If TRT is more than 8 ms, no asynchronous traffic can be transmitted; only synchronous traffic can be transmitted.

If TRT is 3 ms, the priority 5 traffic's transmission time should be limited to 1 ms assuming there is no higher priority traffic at the stations. If there is higher priority traffic, that should be transmitted first. □

A number of characteristics of the FDDI priority mechanism are worth noting. First, the priority is strictly applicable only at a particular station. Since the TRTs at successive stations are different, lower priority traffic at one station may be transmitted, while higher priority traffic at another station may be denied access on the same token rotation. Also, two stations having the same priority traffic may consistently get a different share of bandwidth depending on their location. As shown in Section 23.5 lower priority stations downstream from a higher priority station get a higher share.

The reasons for the selection of this priority mechanism and its differences from the mechanism used in IEEE 802.5 token rings are explained in Section 2.15.

What Is a Frame?

For most noncomputer people, a frame is something used to enclose a painting. The framing material (wood or metal) is different from the material used for the painting (paper or cloth). In a showroom, frames help distinguish between the end of one painting and the beginning of the other. Without a frame, two or more paintings may be misunderstood to be just one painting. Computer people use the word *frame* in a similar sense. A frame is used to enclose user information so that it can be safely transmitted over network links. The special characters or symbols used to begin and end the frame are called *frame delimiters*. These delimiters help distinguish the beginning and end of the messages and prevent two or more messages from merging into each other. Generally, special control characters are used for framing. These characters are different from those used in user messages and cannot occur in the messages.

2.3 Token and Frame Formats

In FDDI, the data are transmitted in units of 4 bits (also called quartets, nibbles, or half-bytes). These 4-bit units are called *symbols*. Thus, there are 16 data symbols, which are labeled 0, 1, 2, . . . , 9, A, B, . . . , F. This is similar to expressing the data in hexadecimal. Although a data symbol consists of 4 data bits, it is transmitted on the fiber as a code consisting of 5 code bits. The details of this so-called "4b/5b" mapping are explained in Section 3.1. Here, it is sufficient to understand that 5 code bits result in 32 symbols of which only 16 are used as data symbols. The remaining 16 symbols are available for use as *control symbols*. These control symbols are labeled H, I, J, K, L, R, S, T, V, and so on. They consist of special bit patterns that cannot occur in user data. Thus, these can be used to frame the information (see Sidebar above).

A token consists of six symbols. As shown in Figure 2.4, it begins with a J-K symbol pair starting delimiter and ends with a T-T pair ending delimiter. The middle two symbols (1 byte) constitute a *frame-control field*, which can be either '$1000\ 0000_2$' or '$1100\ 0000_2$'[1] indicating a nonrestricted token or a restricted token, respectively.

The frame format is shown in Figure 2.5. Like a token, it begins with a starting delimiter of a J-K symbol pair followed by a 1-byte-long frame-control field that indicates the type of frame. The next two fields are destination and source addresses, which can each be either 16 or 48 bits long. The information field consists of an integral number of bytes (even number of symbols) followed by a 32-bit frame check sequence. The frames end with a T-symbol followed by three or more frame

Starting Delimiter	Frame Control	Ending Delimiter	
2	2	2	← Size in Symbols

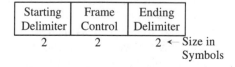

Figure 2.4 Token format.

[1]The subscript denotes the base for nondecimal numbers. In this case, the numbers are in binary.

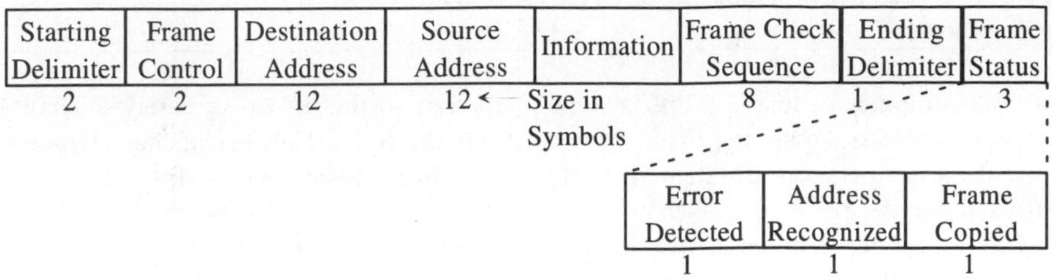

Figure 2.5 Frame format.

status indicators, each of which can have two values, S or R (set or reset). At least three indicators, called E, A, and C, are required. These show the error, address recognized, and copied status of the frame, respectively.

A bit in the frame-control field indicates whether short (16-bit) or long (48-bit) addresses are used. The address formats and the meaning of individual bits are explained in Section 2.8. Most FDDI implementations use long addresses. Short addresses are no longer used in practice and are now only of historical interest. They are even forbidden by some protocol standards. For example, RFC 1390 on IP and ARP on FDDI networks require the use of only 48-bit addresses.

The maximum length of the frame on FDDI is limited to 9000 symbols or 4500 bytes. This includes four preamble symbols and four symbols used in the ending delimiter and status indicators. A simple calculation would show that the information field in frames with long addresses is limited to 4478 bytes.

2.4 Frame Status Indicators

As discussed in Section 2.3, an FDDI frame contains several (three or more) frame status indicators. Of these, the first three are defined to be E, A, and C indicators. These reflect the error, address recognized, and frame copied status of the frame.

The E-indicator, if set, indicates that an error was detected in the frame. At the transmitting station, the E-indicator starts out as R. Each station on the ring checks the frame for validity and, if any errors are detected, it sets the E-indicator to S. Once set to S, other stations on the ring cannot reset it even if they find the frame valid. Also, other indicators (A and C) have no reliable meaning if the E-indicator is set since the source and destination addresses may be corrupted.

The A-indicator, like other indicators, starts out as R at the transmitting station. If a station on the ring recognizes the destination address as one it is supposed to receive, it sets the A-indicator. Thus, the source station can find out if the destination station is on the ring.

The C-indicator also starts out as R. If a station on the ring copies the frame, it sets the C-indicator. Generally, this station is one whose address matches that specified in the destination address field of the frame. If so, both A and C will be set. Sometimes, a bridge may copy a frame for forwarding, in which case, it may set only the C-indicator. It may or may not set the A-indicator. The rules for bridges are discussed in Section 14.4.

The FDDI standard allows additional indicators to be used. However, the total number of indicators must be odd. A T-symbol can be added if necessary to meet this requirement. This results in an integral number of bytes in the frame.

Notice that each frame status indicator is one symbol or 5 code bits long. It is incorrect to call them bits, for example, the E-bit, C-bit, or A-bit. In particular, a single noise event cannot change the indicator from R to S or vice versa.

2.5 Frame Types

The frame-control field indicates the class of the frame, length of the address field, and the type of the frame. The format of the frame-control field is shown in Figure 2.6. The 8 bits of the frame control are denoted by CLFF-ZZZZ.

The first bit denoted by C indicates the class of service. A zero indicates the asynchronous class and a one indicates the synchronous class. Unfortunately, the standard does not say anything about reception or forwarding of synchronous frames. Although the frames belonging to the two classes are usually kept in separate queues at the transmitter and are serviced separately, at the receiving end most receivers do not distinguish between the two classes. In particular, bridges do not currently provide any expedited service or synchronous transmission service for frames received with the synchronous class bit set.

The second bit denoted by L indicates the length of source and destination addresses. A zero value indicates short (16-bit) addresses, while a one indicates long (48-bit) addresses.

The next 6 bits indicate the type of frame. The frame types are listed in Table 2.1. These are:

1. *LLC Frames*: These are the most commonly seen frames on an FDDI ring. These are the frames that have been given by the LLC layer to MAC for transmission. They have an LLC header as explained in Section 17.2. All user frames received from higher layers generally come via LLC and are of this type. The FF bits in the frame control of LLC frames are 01. For asynchronous frames, the last three bits indicate frame priority. Zero is the *lowest* priority and seven is the highest. The fourth bit marked "r" is reserved and should be set to zero. For synchronous frames, there are no priorities. All four Z bits are reserved and should be zero.
2. *Tokens*: As discussed earlier in Section 2.3, the frame-control values of '1000-0000' and '1100-0000' indicate nonrestricted and restricted tokens, respectively.
3. *MAC Frames*: A number of frame types have been defined for internal use by the MAC layer. These frames are not passed to higher layers. These MAC frames are indicated by 1L00-ZZZZ in the frame-control field. The ZZZZ bits define the type of MAC frame. Two MAC frames that are used for ring initialization and fault recovery are *claim frames* and *beacon frames*. These are indicated by frame-control values of 1L00-0011 and 1L00-0010, respectively. Use of these

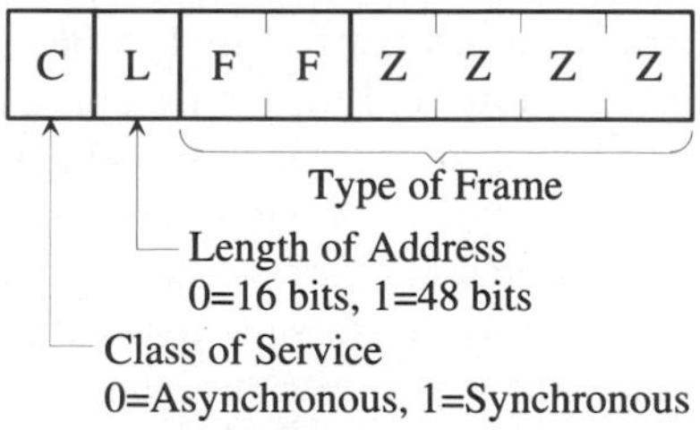

Figure 2.6 Frame-control field format.

Table 2.1 Frame Types

Frame Control	Frame Type
0X00-0000	Void frame, X = 0 or 1
0L00-0001 to 1111	Station management frame
	0100-0001 = SMT
	0100-1111 = NSA
1000-0000	Nonrestricted token
1100-0000	Restricted token
1L00-0001 to 1111	MAC frame
	1L00-0010 = beacon frame
	1L00-0011 = claim frame
CL01-rppp to rppp	LLC frame
CL10-r000 to r111	Implementor frame
CL11-rrrr	Reserved for future standardization

C = Synchronous/Asynchronous, L = Short/Long address, r = Reserved, ppp = Priority

frames is discussed further in Sections 2.12 and 2.14, respectively. The information field of MAC frames is at least 32 bits long.

4. *SMT Frames*: Station management frames are indicated by 0L00-ZZZZ in the frame-control field. The last 4 bits were originally intended to indicate the type of SMT frames. However, only two values have been defined so far. A frame-control value of '$0100\text{-}0001_2$' or 41_{16} is used for most SMT frames. The type of SMT frame is indicated by a separate field inside the frame. A value of $0100\text{-}1111_2$ or $4F_{16}$ is used to indicate **next station addressing** (**NSA**). In this case, the specified destination address is generally a group or broadcast address but the first station that is the member of the destination group is the intended destination. This member sets the A-flag in the frame status field so that other members downstream do not have to receive the frame. Next station addressing is useful in determining upstream neighbors. This is explained further in Section 10.5.
5. *Void Frames*: These frames are used as markers in several media-access-related algorithms. For example, some bridges use them to mark the end of a transmission sequence. After transmitting the sequence, these bridges continue to strip all frames until the marker frame is received. This is explained in Section 2.11. Another example of their use is in removing no-owner frames as explained later in Section 11.7.

   Void frames are tiny frames that are not required to have address, information, or frame check sequence fields. In practice, most void frames have source and destination address fields and a frame check sequence. The destination address field is ignored. These frames are not forwarded by the MAC layer to upper protocol layers nor are they forwarded by bridges to other LANs. They do reset the valid transmission timers (TVX) at all stations. Thus, if a station has captured a token but cannot start the frame transmission within a reasonable time, it can either release the token or issue a void frame to prevent other stations from timing out and reinitializing the ring. The TVX is explained in Section 2.13. The void frames used to reset TVX can be distinguished from those used for frame stripping and ring purging by looking at the destination address field. The frames used to reset TVX have a zero (null) destination address, while those used for stripping and ring purging have a destination address equal to the source address.

6. *Implementor Frames*: Frame-control values of 'CL10-rZZZ' are reserved for network implementors. Vendors can use them in whatever way they like. The *r* bit is reserved and should be zero. The use of other bits is left to the implementors. The presence of an information field is optional. The frame check sequence is ignored. Since it is not clear how different vendors can coordinate their use of these frames, such frames have not been used by anyone.
7. *Reserved Frames*: Frame-control values of 'CL11-rrrr' are reserved for future standardization. Ethernet format frames, which do not use LLC but are used commonly, are being considered for being assigned one of these reserved frame-control values.

The minimum number of bytes between the starting delimiter and ending delimiter for various frames is listed in Table 2.2. To compute the total length of the frame, add 4 bytes for tokens and 5 bytes for all other frames. This includes the size of the preamble (2 bytes), starting delimiter (1 byte), ending delimiter, and frame status (1 byte for tokens and 2 bytes for others). For example, the minimum length of an LLC frame with long addresses is 22 bytes. In practice, you may also have to add the length of the LLC header (3 bytes or more) giving 25 bytes as the minimum frame size for a valid LLC frame. Stations are required to transmit a minimum 16-symbol preamble (and not 4 symbols), thereby making 31 bytes the normal minimum frame size for an LLC frame.

Notice that all frames consist of an even number of data symbols between J-K and T. A frame is considered a valid frame if and only if it satisfies the following four *frame validity criteria*. First, there should be an integral number of bytes (an even number of data symbols) between J-K and T. Second, the number of bytes between J-K and T should be at least that specified in Table 2.2. Third, it should have a valid frame check sequence (except in void frames and implementor defined frames, where it is optional). Fourth, the error flag should be reset. If the error flag is set, the frame is considered invalid even if the FCS checks out correctly.

Table 2.2 Minimum Number of Bytes Between Starting and Ending Delimiters

Frame Control	Frame Type	Minimum Bytes
0X00-0000	Void	1
1X00-0000	Token	1
0000-0001 to 1111	SMT frames with short addresses	9
0100-0001 to 1111	SMT frames with long addresses	17
1000-0001 to 1111	MAC frames with short addresses	13
1100-0001 to 1111	MAC frames with long addresses	21
X001-XXXX	LLC frames with short addresses	9
X101-XXXX	LLC frames with long addresses	17
X010-XXXX	Implementor frames with short addresses	9
X110-XXXX	Implementor frames with long addresses	17
X011-XXXX	Reserved frames with short addresses	9
X111-XXXX	Reserved frames with long addresses	17

2.6 Frame Check Sequence

FDDI uses a 32-bit cyclic redundancy check (CRC) to ensure that the contents of a frame are error free. The CRC polynomial used is the same as that used in Ethernet, token rings, and other IEEE 802 protocols. This polynomial is:

$$g(x) = x^{32} + x^{26} + x^{23} + x^{22} + x^{16} + x^{12} + x^{11} + x^{10} + x^8 + x^7 + x^5 + x^4 + x^2 + x + 1$$

The remainder of this section is devoted to explaining how the cyclic redundancy method works. Readers familiar with CRC can skip to the next section.

The CRC method is similar to the check digit method commonly used in businesses for error detection. In the check digit method, an additional digit is added at the end of the number to be protected such that the resulting number is divisible by 9. One way to do so is to left-shift the number to be protected by one digit and then divide by 9. Discard the quotient and subtract the remainder from 9. The resulting digit is simply appended to the number. This results in a number that is an exact multiple of 9 as illustrated by the following example.

Example 2.2 Consider the three-digit number 823. Dividing 8230 by 9 gives 4 as the remainder. The difference between 9 and 4 is 5. Appending 5 to the message, we get a four-digit message 8235. This is an exact multiple of 9. Suppose this four-digit number is spoken over a noisy telephone line and the listener hears 8635. The listener divides the number by 9 and gets a remainder of 4. The listener can immediately detect the error since the received number is not an exact multiple of 9. In actual practice, the division by 9 is not necessary since the remainder can be obtained simply by summing the digits. □

This method of checking digits provides the basis for the CRC technique also. However, instead of numbers, polynomials are used. A message can be represented by a polynomial as follows. The bits of the messages are numbered sequentially from the right. The rightmost bit is called the zeroth (0th) bit. In its polynomial representation, the ith bit is used as the coefficient of x^i. In other words, the polynomial representation of an m-bit message $b_{m-1}b_{m-2}\cdots b_2b_1b_0$ is:

$$b_{m-1}x^{m-1} + b_{m-2}x^{m-2} + \cdots + b_2x^2 + b_1x + b_0$$

For example, the 5-bit number 10011 is represented by the polynomial:

$$1x^4 + 0x^3 + 0x^2 + 1x^1 + 1 = x^4 + x + 1$$

Similarly, a 10-bit message 1100110111 is represented by:

$$1x^9 + 1x^8 + 0x^7 + 0x^6 + 1x^5 + 1x^4 + 0x^3 + 1x^2 + 1x^1 + 1 = x^9 + x^8 + x^5 + x^4 + x^2 + x + 1$$

To compute an n-bit CRC the following steps are taken:

1. The first n bits of the message are complemented. This is equivalent to adding $x^n + x^{n-1} + x^{n-2} + \cdots + x^2 + x + 1$ in the leftmost n bits.
2. The message is shifted left by the n bits. This is equivalent to multiplication by x^n.
3. The resulting polynomial is divided by an n-degree CRC polynomial.
4. The remainder is complemented and placed in the rightmost n bits.

The following example illustrates these steps for a 4-bit CRC.

Example 2.3 Consider the 10-bit message 1100110111_2. Suppose we want to compute a 4-bit CRC using 10011 (or $x^4 + x + 1$) as the CRC polynomial. The message polynomial is:

$$x^9 + x^8 + x^5 + x^4 + x^2 + x + 1$$

The steps in CRC computations are as follows:

1. The first 4 bits of the message are complemented. The message becomes 0011110111_2. The resulting bit sequence is represented by the polynomial
$$x^7 + x^6 + x^5 + x^4 + x^2 + x + 1$$
2. The message is shifted left by 4 bits. Multiplying the message polynomial by x^4 we get:
$$x^{11} + x^{10} + x^9 + x^8 + x^6 + x^5 + x^4$$
3. The resulting polynomial is divided by $x^4 + x + 1$. The division is shown in Figure 2.7. The remainder is $x^3 + x^2 + x + 1$, which corresponds to 1111_2.
4. Complementing the remainder we get 0000. So the complete 14-bit message is 11001101110000. □

While the algebraic computation of CRC looks quite cumbersome, its hardware implementation is simple. As shown in Figure 2.8, a 32-bit shift register is used to maintain the coefficients of the polynomial terms. The output of the shift register sequence is fed back to intermediate points corresponding to the nonzero terms in the CRC polynomial. At the output a multiplexer is used to select whether the input bits or the complements of the shift-register bits are output. The symbol $\oplus$ represents an exclusive-or operation. After transmitting the starting delimiter (J-K pair) of the frame but just before the transmission of the frame-control field, the shift register is initialized to all 1's. The control is then held at 1 while the frame-control, destination address, source address, and the information fields of the frame are shifted into the input and the CRC is generated. Meanwhile the same bits emerging at the output are transmitted over the network. When the last bit of the information field has been processed, control is set to 0 and the complemented CRC is shifted out for transmission.

The operation at the receiving end is similar to that described previously. The shift register is initialized to all 1's. The control is then held at 1 while the incoming bits are shifted into input to

$$\begin{array}{cccccccccccccccccccccccc}
x^{11} & + & x^{10} & + & x^9 & + & x^8 & + & & + & x^6 & + & x^5 & + & x^4 & & & & & & & & \\
x^{11} & + & & + & & + & x^8 & + & x^7 & & & & & & & & & & & & & & \\
\hline
 & & x^{10} & + & x^9 & + & & + & x^7 & + & x^6 & & & & & & & & & & & & \\
 & & x^{10} & + & & + & & + & x^7 & + & x^6 & & & & & & & & & & & & \\
\hline
 & & & & x^9 & + & & + & & + & & + & x^5 & & & & & & & & & & \\
 & & & & x^9 & + & & + & & + & x^6 & + & x^5 & & & & & & & & & & \\
\hline
 & & & & & & & & & & x^6 & + & & + & x^4 & & & & & & & & \\
 & & & & & & & & & & x^6 & + & & + & & + & x^3 & + & x^2 & & & & \\
\hline
 & & & & & & & & & & & & & & x^4 & + & x^3 & + & x^2 & & & & \\
 & & & & & & & & & & & & & & x^4 & + & & + & & + & x & + & 1 \\
\hline
 & & & & & & & & & & & & & & & & x^3 & + & x^2 & + & x & + & 1
\end{array}$$

Figure 2.7 Polynomial division example.

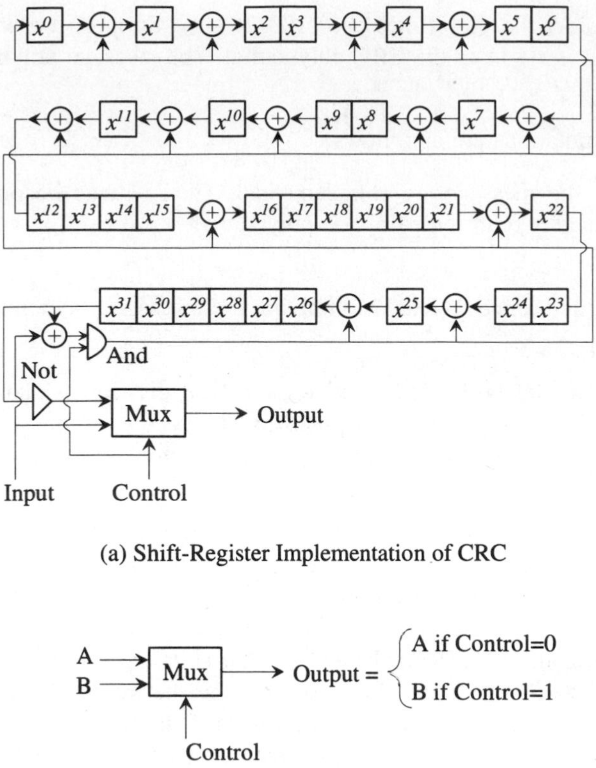

(a) Shift-Register Implementation of CRC

(b) Multiplexer Operation

Figure 2.8 CRC implementation.

generate the CRC. When the last bit of the frame (including the CRC) has been processed, the shift register should contain the following magic value:

11000111000001001101110101111011

Here, the leftmost bit corresponds to the x^{31} term of the polynomial and the rightmost bit to the x^0 term. If the shift register contains any other value, the frame is declared to have an error. Incidentally, the magic value represents the remainder when the polynomial $\sum_{i=0}^{31} x^{32+i}$ (the preloaded sequence of all 1's) is divided by the the CRC polynomial $g(x)$.

The CRC implementation shown in Figure 2.8 processes each individual bit as it is received and therefore requires a logic running at 100 Mbps. In actual FDDI MAC chips, the circuit is modified to process 4-bit symbols (or 8-bit bytes), thereby requiring a logic running at 25 Mbps (or 12.5 Mbps).

2.7 Counters

FDDI stations maintain a number of counters, which aid in monitoring the operation of the ring and diagnosing faults. These are:

- *Frames Seen*: The total number of well-formed frames seen at the receiver is counted. Notice that all well-formed frames, regardless of their destination address, source address, or type, are included in this count. The count includes the void frames, frames with good or bad CRC, and the frames stripped by the station. This counter is called Frame_ct.
- *Errors Detected*: Each station also keeps a count of frames in which it detected an error. Errors are detected by several rules including the CRC method just discussed. If a frame is received with the E-indicator reset but with an invalid CRC, the station increments the error counter (Error_ct) and sets the E-indicator. The count also includes frames that are too short, too long, have no frame status indicator, or have an odd number of symbols. Since the errors are counted at only one station, a network manager can look at all error counters and determine the location of a weak link long before it has a chance to disrupt the operation seriously.
- *Lost Frames Count*: This complements the error counter and counts the errors that prematurely end a frame. Whenever noise changes a symbol in a frame, in some cases the new symbol is such that it is obvious it was created by noise. For example, a Q, H, or V symbol appears in the frame. The MAC counts these symbol violations in Lost_ct and replaces the remainder of the frame with idles, leaving a fragment on the ring. The noise events are counted just once. A fragment ending with idle symbols is ignored by the other stations on the ring.
- *Late Counter*: In a normally operating ring, the token is expected to be seen within the target token rotation time. If the token is not seen within this period, the station increments a late counter (Late_ct). This counter is different from the other counters mentioned earlier in the sense that it is not cumulative. The late counter is cleared whenever the token is received early. Thus, Late_ct is usually zero. Whenever Late_ct becomes 2, the token is assumed to have been lost and is reinitialized using the claim process. This process is discussed in Section 2.12.

  Strictly speaking, Late_ct is not a counter in spite of its name. For example, you can use station management commands to read the value of other station counters but not Late_ct. Late_ct is simply a variable indicating the MAC state and is used for fault recovery.

2.8 Address Format

FDDI follows the IEEE addressing conventions, which are used in IEEE 802 LANs such as IEEE 802.3 (CSMA/CD), IEEE 802.4 (token bus), and IEEE 802.5 (token ring). The address length can be 48 or 16 bits. Sixteen-bit addresses are now only of historical interest. Therefore, most of the discussion in this book implicitly assumes 48-bit addresses.

The format of the addresses is shown in Figure 2.9. The first bit of the address is called the **individual/group** or **I/G** bit. In addresses belonging to individual stations this bit is 0, while for multicast addresses, which represent a group of stations, this bit is 1.

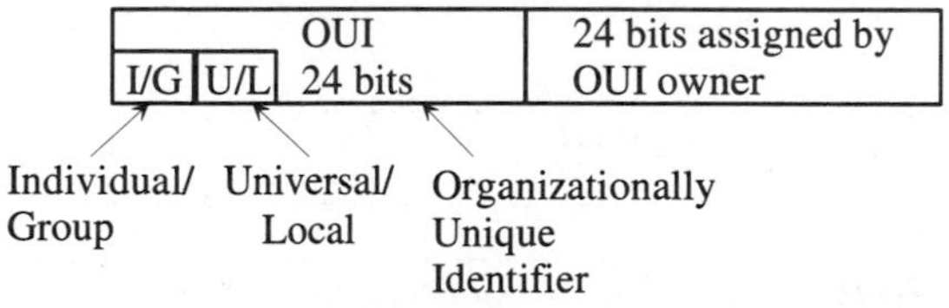

Figure 2.9 Address format.

The second bit of the address is called the **universal/local** or **U/L** bit. If this bit is 0, the address is universally unique in the sense that no other station in this universe (not just this planet) has this address. This uniqueness is guaranteed since these addresses are administered by a single organization—IEEE. Before adoption by the IEEE, this address format was used in Ethernet and address assignments were made by Xerox Corporation. IEEE honors those earlier assignments.

If the U/L bit is 1, the address is locally administered. Some network managers or network architectures use locally administered addresses for many reasons. For example, in some networks they indicate the physical location (building number, floor, pole number, and so on) of the station. In others, they indicate the logical location (network number, routing domain, and so on).

The first 24 bits of the universally administered address indicate the manufacturer of the equipment. Any manufacturer of networking equipment (or any other organization) can write to IEEE and get a block of 16.7 million (2^{24}) addresses for a nominal fee. IEEE assigns a 24-bit **organizationally unique identifier (OUI)** to the manufacturer. The OUI forms the first 24 bits of addresses of equipment made by that manufacturer. The manufacturer then assigns successive addresses from that block to its products. A complete list of OUIs can be obtained by sending a mail message to info.stds.oui@ieee.org with empty subject and message fields (both ignored). A full listing is returned to the sender via electronic mail. You can also retrieve this list via anonymous FTP from ftp.ieee.org in ieee/info/info.stds.oui file. Internet RFC 1340 also has a partial list.

Although OUI assignments are 24 bits, only the last 22 bits really identify the organization. The first (individual/group) bit is set to 0 in individual addresses and to 1 in group (or multicast) addresses assigned by the organization. The second (universal/local) bit is 0 to indicate universally

IEEE
We are here to obtain a universal address from the IEEE.

Figure 2.10 IEEE administers universal address assignment.

administered addresses. If it is 1 (local), the bits of the address have no assigned meaning. Notice the use of the word *universe*. The addresses are supposed to be unique for the entire universe not just this planet. The system allows address assignments for up to 2^{22} or 4.2 million OUIs. Since the human population of our planet is currently approaching only 5 billion, assigning OUIs will not be a problem for quite some time unless every human being asked for an OUI or living beings from another planet approach IEEE! (see Figure 2.10). Probably, in recognition of this problem, the term *global address administration* is being commonly used instead of universal address administration.

2.8.1 Group Addresses

The I/G bit of the address indicates whether it is an individual or a group address. Group addresses are also called **multicast** addresses. Frames sent to these addresses are received by all stations who are members of the group. The most commonly used group address is the **broadcast address**, which is received by all stations. The broadcast address consists of all 1's (48 1's). Even though the universal/local bit in the broadcast address is 1, it is treated as a universally assigned group address.

Some examples of group addresses are listed in Table 2.3. (A more complete list can be found in the Internet RFC 1340.) According to ISO conventions group addresses are named to indicate the destinations that are supposed to receive them. For example, frames addressed to the bridge group address are received by all bridges on a LAN.

2.8.2 Functional Addresses

A locally administered group address can have any structure for its remaining 46 bits. One particular form used on IEEE 802.5 token ring LANs is to have a special bit pattern, 1100 0000-0000 0000-0_2, in the first 17 bits and to have all but 1 of the remaining 31 bits be zero. The position of the nonzero

Table 2.3 A Sample of Group Addresses (Canonical Form)

Address	Use
01-80-C2-00-00-00	ISO/IEEE 802.1d bridge group address
01-80-C2-00-00-10	ISO/IEEE 802.1d all LANs bridge management group address
01-80-C2-00-00-11	ISO/IEEE 802.1e load server generic address
01-80-C2-00-00-12	ISO/IEEE 802.1e loadable device generic address
01-80-C2-00-00-14	ISO all level 1 intermediate systems address
01-80-C2-00-00-15	ISO all level 2 intermediate systems address
01-80-C2-00-00-16	All CONS end systems address
01-80-C2-00-00-17	All CONS SNAREs address
01-80-C2-00-00-18	IEEE 802.1b all manager stations
01-80-C2-00-00-1A	IEEE 802.1b all agent stations
01-80-C2-00-01-00	FDDI directed beacon multicast address
01-80-C2-00-01-10	FDDI status report protocol multicast address
01-80-C2-00-01-X0	Reserved for use by FDDI SMT
09-00-2B-00-00-04	ISO IS-IS all end system network entities address
09-00-2B-00-00-05	ISO IS-IS all intermediate system network entities address

Table 2.4 A Sample of Functional Addresses

Address	Use
03-00-00-00-02-00	ISO IS-IS all end system network entities address
03-00-00-00-01-00	ISO IS-IS all intermediate system network entities address
03-00-00-00-80-00	IEEE 802.1d bridge group address

bit indicates the function of the group address. A group address of this form is called a **functional address**.

Each bit in the functional address signifies the group of addresses for which it is meant. Therefore, a functional address is also called a **bit-significant** form of group addressing. This limits the number of possible functional addresses to 31 compared to 2^{24} possible locally administered group addresses. This limitation is a trade-off in order to gain the advantage of having the address recognition logic simplified considerably. The address can be recognized simply by ensuring that the address does follow the functional form and then comparing it with a mask in which bits corresponding to group addresses to be received are set. This is much simpler than the table or CAM (content addressable memory) lookup required for the normal ("flat") form of group addresses. Table 2.4 lists a few examples of commonly used functional addresses.

2.9 Bit Order

One of the most confusing issues in addressing is that of the bit order. Different networking architectures transmit the bits of a byte differently. As an example, consider the decimal number 59. Its 8-bit binary representation is 00111011. The leftmost bit, a 0 in this example, is called the **most-significant bit** (**msb**). The rightmost bit, a 1 in this example, is called the **least-significant bit** (**lsb**). While transferring this byte over some networks, you have to transmit the most-significant bit first. The successive bits seen on the network in this case would be 0-0-1-1-1-0-1-1. On other networks, you have to transmit the least-significant bit first. In this case, the successive bits seen on the network would be 1-1-0-1-1-1-0-0. These two transmission orders are known as **msb order** and **lsb order**, respectively.

Both bit orders work equally well as long as both the transmitter and the receiver follow the same order. The consensus of the IEEE 802, following the usual practice of the standard committee meetings, was to allow both systems. IEEE 802.3/Ethernet and IEEE 802.4 token bus networks follow lsb order while IEEE 802.5 token ring networks follow msb order.

Note that the bit order is a link-level issue and not a CPU or memory issue. One system, for example, an 80 × 86 system, connected to two LANs—one IEEE 802.5/token ring and the other IEEE 802.3/Ethernet—will transmit the bits of the byte differently on the two LANs. On the token ring, it will transmit 0-0-1-1-1-0-1-1 for a byte containing 59_{10} while on the Ethernet it will transmit 1-1-0-1-1-1-0-0. Conversely, identical frames received from the same source coming via different LANs to one system may be stored differently at the destination. For example, if the first 8 bits of the source address are 0010 1011, it will be stored as $2B_{16}$ when received on an IEEE 802.5 token ring and as $D4_{16}$ ($1101\ 0100_2$) when received on an IEEE 802.3/Ethernet. These two orders are also called the big-endian and little-endian bit orders, respectively (see Sidebar).

Gulliver's Travels: Little Endians Versus Big Endians

In IEEE 802 meetings, there was considerable heated discussion on the issue of bit order. In a humorous article, Danny Cohen (1981) compared the debate to a holy war described in *Gulliver's Travels*. In that war, two sides couldn't agree on the issue of which end of an egg should be broken first. Noting the similarity, Cohen borrowed the names and called the followers of msb order **big-endians** and those of the lsb order **little-endians**. These names have now become very popular.

The story described in Gulliver's Travels is as follows. In the island of Lilliput, the inhabitants are required by law to break their eggs only at the little ends. Those citizens who habitually break their eggs at the big ends are angered by this proclamation. Civil war breaks out between the Little Endians and the Big Endians, resulting in the Big Endians taking refuge on a nearby island, the kingdom of Blefuscu. Eleven thousand Lilliputian rebels die over the egg question (see Figure 2.11).

Figure 2.11 Little Endian versus Big Endian.

FDDI follows the big-endian bit order—the same as IEEE 802.5/token ring. However, on FDDI the data bits have to be converted to code bits using 4b/5b encoding (explained in Section 3.1). For example, to send 59_{10}, we first get its msb representation $0011\ 1011_2$, convert it to hexadecimal 3B, and encode individual symbols. In this case, the code bit string would be 10101 10111. This code string is then NRZI encoded before being transmitted on the fiber.

2.9.1 Address Representation

Choosing a different bit order for different LANs is not a problem except that the IEEE 802 committee wanted that one system on two LANs should have the *same* address on both LANs. There were two options—to have the same bit string *or* to have the same byte string. Choosing the same bit string on both LANs would mean different byte strings for the systems and vice versa. The committee choose to represent addresses as *bit strings*. This means that successive bits of the address when seen on the wire would be the same on both lsb and msb LANs. Note that this is different from that for the nonaddress data. For normal data the successive bits seen on the wire are different on the two types of LANs.

The most important point to remember is that *addresses are assigned as bit strings*. Their byte string representation is different on the two LANs. The following example illustrates this.

Example 2.4 Consider the SMT synchronous bandwidth allocator address. It has been assigned the following bit string:

10000000 : 00000001 : 01000011 : 00000000 : 10000000 : 00001100

Here, colons (:) have been used to indicate byte boundaries. On both IEEE 802.3/Ethernet and IEEE 802.5/token ring LANs, the successive bits seen would be as above read from left to right.

Now consider a station connected to both IEEE 802.3/Ethernet and IEEE 802.5/token ring LANs. On the IEEE 802.5/token ring LANs, it sends out the most-significant bit of the bytes first. Therefore, to send the first 8 bits, 1000 0000, the station would normally store 1000 0000 or 80_{16} in a byte. Applying the same logic to all 48 bits, we find that for MSB LANs the byte string corresponding to the above address is:

80:01:43:00:80:0C

On an IEEE 802.3/Ethernet LAN, the station sends out the least-significant bit of the bytes first. Therefore, to send the first 8 bits, 1000 0000, the station would normally store 0000 0001 or 01_{16} in a byte. Applying the same logic to all 48 bits, we find that the byte string corresponding to the above address is (in binary):

0000 0001-1000 0000-1100 0010-0000 0000-0000 0001-0011 0000

or 01-80-C2-00-01-30 in hexadecimal. □

Note that when expressing memory contents, colons (:) are used to separate successive bytes in big-endian bit order notation while dashes (-) are used for little-endian bit order.

> **Colons (:) are used to separate successive bytes in big-endian bit order notation while dashes (-) are used for little-endian bit order.**

One problem with representing the addresses as bit strings is that human beings find them hard to use. Byte strings expressed in hexadecimal are easier to use. The IEEE 802 committee recognized the need for presenting an address to human operators in a consistent form and recommended that all addresses be presented to humans in a **canonical form** or **illustrative hex**. The committee arbitrarily selected the lsb notation for this purpose due to preponderance of Ethernet stations at the time. All IEEE assignments are made using the canonical form. For example, the SMT synchronous bandwidth allocator address in canonical form is 01-80-C2-00-01-30.

For address fields FDDI uses the big-endian bit order—the same as that for all other fields. As in the case of other bits, the address has to be first represented in msb hexadecimal notation. Successive hexadecimal symbols are then encoded using 4b/5b coding. Finally, the code bits so obtained are transmitted using NRZI encoding on the fiber. The following example illustrates these steps.

Example 2.5 Consider again the SMT synchronous bandwidth allocator address:

01-80-C2-00-01-30

Its msb representation and the corresponding code bits are:

Symbols:	8	0	:	0	1	:	4	3	:
	0	0	:	8	0	:	0	C	
Code bits:	10010	11110	:	11110	01001	:	01010	10101	:
	11110	11110	:	10010	11110	:	11110	11010	

□

The rules for addresses discussed so far apply only when the addresses are transmitted/received in the source or destination address fields of a frame. Complications occur when the addresses have to be transported in the information fields of higher layer protocols. This issue is discussed in Section 18.2.

2.10 Byte Order

In the preceding discussion about bit order, we intentionally ignored the issue of byte ordering, which arises when communicating multibyte information between two computers. An example of multibyte information is a 32-bit integer quantity. This requires 4 bytes of storage. There are two ways to address (or number) these 4 bytes. In some systems, if the most-significant byte has an address n, the other 3 bytes will have the addresses $n+1$, $n+2$, and $n+3$. In other systems, the byte addressing is just the opposite. In these systems, the other three bytes will have the addresses $n - 1$, $n - 2$, and $n - 3$. These two types of systems are called **most-significant byte first** (**MSB**) system and **least-significant byte first** (**LSB**) systems. Notice that uppercase letters, MSB and LSB, are used to denote the byte ordering, while lowercase letters, msb or lsb, are used to indicate the bit order.

> **Uppercase letters, MSB and LSB, are used to denote the byte ordering, while lowercase letters, msb or lsb, are used to indicate the bit order.**

In MSB systems, the memory address of a word is that of its most-significant byte. In LSB systems, the memory address of a word is that of its least-significant byte. MSB systems are also known as systems with big-endian byte order, while LSB systems are known as systems with little-endian byte order.

Example 2.6 The 32-bit binary representation of the decimal number 4287 is:

0000 0000 0000 0000 0001 0000 1011 1111

Suppose the number is stored at memory address 0. On an MSB system, the storage contents would be:

0000 0000	0000 0000	0001 0000	1011 1111
Byte 0	Byte 1	Byte 2	Byte 3

On an LSB system, the storage contents would be:

0000 0000	0000 0000	0001 0000	1011 1111
Byte 3	Byte 2	Byte 1	Byte 0

Thus, the difference between the two systems is basically on how to number the bytes. □

IBM, Motorola, and SUN are examples of the companies following MSB systems, while DEC and Intel are examples of those following the LSB system. Some of the newer systems, such as those from MIPS, allow either byte ordering to be used.

Byte order is an issue for a networking protocol if it uses multibyte data. Frame length and timer values are examples of multibyte data used in most protocols. The protocols, therefore, specify the order in which bytes of multibyte data should be sent. Some protocols use MSB order, while others use LSB order. DECnet Phase IV, for example, uses an LSB order. All IEEE 802 protocols, ISO protocols, and FDDI use the MSB order. In particular, FDDI SMT frames contain many 32-bit counters and timer values, which must be communicated using the most-significant byte first order.

Notice that the byte order of a protocol and that of the system on which it is implemented are independent. An MSB protocol can be implemented on an LSB system and vice versa. Of course, the protocol implementors have to be extra careful when the two orders are different because a multibyte protocol parameter may have to be sent using one system while all nonprotocol-related multibyte data have to be sent using the other system. To avoid this complexity, protocols designed by manufacturers generally follow the byte order used on their systems.

The byte order of a system is important for network interface (adapter) designers. Most direct memory access (DMA) devices use multibyte words to store and fetch memory contents. The adapter has to pack successive bytes into multibyte words. The choice of the packing order depends on the byte order of the system. An adapter designed to support both MSB and LSB systems should be able to pack either way.

Example 2.7 Consider the OSI end-system hello message. Different fields of this message in hexadecimal are:

Frame control	54	FDDI MAC frame
Destination address	09-00-2B-00-00-05	To all intermediate systems
Source address	08-00-2B-2B-06-96	
Destination LSAP	FE	OSI network layer
Source LSAP	FE	
LLC control	03	Unnumbered information
Information	82...	ISO 9542 end-system hello message

This frame corresponds to the following byte string:

54 09 00 2B 00 00 05 08 00 2B 2B 06 96 FE FE 03 82 ...

In an LSB system's memory the frame will be stored as:

54	—	—	—
00	2B	00	09
00	08	05	00
96	06	2B	2B
82	03	FE	FE

On the other hand, in an MSB system's memory, the frame will be stored as:

—	—	—	54
09	00	2B	00
00	05	08	00
2B	2B	06	96
FE	FE	03	82

For both types of systems, we have shown 4-byte words per line with the most-significant byte of the word on the left.

For transmission on FDDI, the source and destination addresses have to be bit reversed. The successive symbols as seen on an FDDI fiber would be:

54 90 00 D4 00 00 A0 10 00 D4 D4 60 69 FE FE 03 82 ...

These symbols are then encoded using 4b/5b and NRZI encoding. □

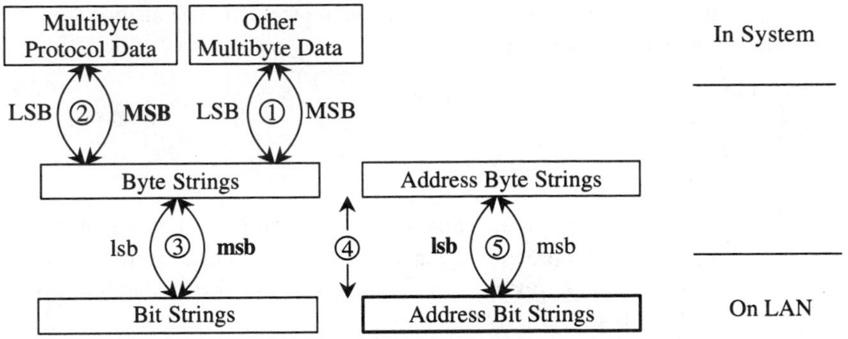

Figure 2.12 Bit and byte order issues.

Figure 2.12 presents a schematic view of the discussion on bit and byte orders. A total of five independent policies have to be followed:

1. The byte order of the system: MSB or LSB
2. The byte order of the protocol: MSB or LSB
3. The bit order of the link: msb or lsb
4. Source/destination address assignment: bit string or byte string
5. Source/destination address representation for humans: lsb or msb.

Among these, the first one depends on the system. For the other four, FDDI uses MSB, msb, bit string, and lsb, respectively. In Figure 2.12, the FDDI choices are shown in bold letters. Also, the box containing the address bit strings has been framed with a thick line to emphasize the fact that address assignments are bit strings.

Since each system implements many protocols and has many datalinks, numerous combinations of the preceding policies arise. No wonder this has been a confusing issue for the architects and implementors.

2.11 Stripping

The word *strip* means "to remove." In ring networks, the frames put on the ring have to be removed; otherwise they will keep going around the ring forever.

The simplest stripping alternative is that based on the source address. If a station recognizes the source address of a frame as its own, it strips the remainder of the frame. This is the method used by most stations on the FDDI ring. Unfortunately, this method cannot be used by transparent bridges that transmit frames belonging to several sources without any change in the frame contents.

For bridges, a number of *frame-content-independent stripping algorithms* have been developed. One method is to send a marker frame at the end of transmission and strip all incoming frames until the marker frame is received. A void frame can be used as a marker. Since it contains the bridge's source address, it can be easily identified by the bridge. This method works if there are no errors in the marker. It can be made more robust by transmitting more than one marker or by also counting the number of frames transmitted and stripped. In the latter scheme, the transmitter increments a counter for each frame transmitted and decrements it for each frame stripped. The stripping is stopped if any one of the following four conditions is met:

1. The marker frame is received.
2. The count is exhausted.
3. A token is received.
4. A MAC frame is received.

Only error-free frames stripped are counted. Thus, the first condition protects against errors in transmitted frames. The second condition protects against errors in the marker frame. The third condition protects against both types of errors happening simultaneously. The fourth condition protects against stations entering the ring before stripping is completed.

Regardless of the stripping algorithm, a fragment consisting of the starting delimiter, frame-control, destination address, source address, and some additional part of each frame may be left on the ring. Such fragments are harmless since they do not have any ending delimiter to qualify as a valid frame. They are removed when they reach a transmitting station. Also, a "gobbler" function in each station removes one or more symbols from the end of such fragments. This function is described in Section 3.3 on smoothing.

2.12 Creating the Token: Claim Token Process

When an FDDI network is initialized, or the token is lost, or a station is added or removed from the network, it is necessary to start a fresh token. The *claim token process* selects a station to create the token and determines the target token rotation time. This process is used whenever there is a change in ring configuration, or a fault is suspected, such as a lost token or multiple tokens.

To avoid having multiple tokens, it is necessary that only one station on the ring be allowed to create a new token. In the process, each station declares their desired target token rotation time (TTRT). The station with the shortest TTRT requirement is granted a *claim* to create the token. If several stations have the same shortest TTRT requirement, then the station with the longest address (48 bit or 16 bit) wins the claim. If these two rules do not result in a unique winner, the station with the numerically *highest* address wins the claim.

The claim winner is selected via a distributed bidding process. In centralized bidding, like that at an auction (see Figure 2.13), the participants send their bids to the auctioneer who selects the most desirable bid and lets everyone know. In the distributed bidding, all participants take the role of the auctioneer, that is, they examine the bids and let only the best bid succeed.

The distributed bidding is carried out as follows:

1. Every station on the ring starts announcing its bid. This is done via a special MAC frame called a **claim frame**. These frames have a frame control value of $1L00\ 0011_2$, where L is zero for a short address and one for a long address. The stations put their address in the destination address as well as the source address fields of the frame. The bid value of the TTRT (T_Bid) is included in the first four bytes of the information field of the frame. Actually, a negative (two's complement) of the time value is used in the information field of the claim frame. Since the procedure is easier to understand if we ignore this detail and assume that the bid is positive, the terms "higher" and "lower" as used here are opposite of those used in the MAC standard, which describes the process using negative values.

For a right to initialize the token: 8ms, 8ms, 8ms, ...
Do I hear any 7?

Figure 2.13 FDDI claim process is a distributed bidding process.

2. To transmit claim frames, a token is not required. Any station can send claim frames, whenever it wants to initialize the ring or suspects a fault. The frames are transmitted *continuously* until the process ends.
3. If a station receives a claim frame, it compares the bid with its own required target. If the received bid is lower, it stops bidding (or remains silent) and forwards (repeats) the received claim frames without any changes.
4. If the received bid is higher than that required by a station, the station enters the bidding process by blocking the incoming claim frames and generating its own claim frames with its bid value.
5. If the received bid is equal to that required by the station, the station compares the address length and address of the transmitting station with its own. If the received address length is longer, or the received address is higher, the claim frames are repeated; otherwise new claim frames are generated.
6. If a station receives its own claim frame, it's the winner! The frame has gone all around the ring, every station on the ring has examined the bid and agrees that this station has the claim to create the token. The winning station at this point takes actions as pointed out in the next section.
7. The process should normally end within an interval approximately equal to one round-trip delay around the ring (ring latency). However, if a station has been bidding for a long time (more than 165 ms) and has neither heard any lower bid nor received its own bid, there may be some fault in the ring. There are two possibilities. If the station had stopped bidding (since it had received a

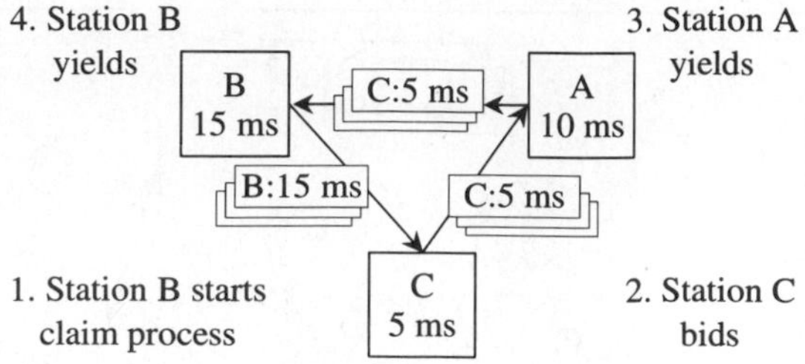

Figure 2.14 Claim process for a sample ring.

lower bid), it restarts the claim process. On the other hand, if the station is still bidding and has not received its bid, the ring is faulty and a fault location procedure called the *beacon process* described in Section 2.14 is begun.

The following example illustrates the claim process for a sample ring.

Example 2.8 Consider a three-station ring as shown in Figure 2.14. Stations A, B, and C have a required target of 10, 15, and 5 ms, respectively. Station B, suspecting a fault, starts the claim process by continuously sending claim frames with a bid of 15 ms.

Station C receives these frames. However, its required target of 5 ms is lower than that in the received claim frames. Therefore, it enters the bidding by generating claim frames with a bid of 5 ms.

Station A receives C's claim frames. A's required target of 10 ms is higher than those of C's and so it repeats C's claim frames.

Station B receives C's claim frames and notices that C's bid is lower. B yields by stopping its claims and repeating C's claim frames.

Station C receives its own claim frame. It realizes it's the winner. At this point, it proceeds to create the token. □

Notice that the claim process works even if several stations start sending claim frames simultaneously. New stations joining in the middle of the claim process may extend the process but do not result in an improper claim (wrong station winning the claim).

Any process that uses station addresses is affected by the presence of duplicate addresses (two or more stations having the same address). This is true of the claim process as well. For example, two or more stations may consider themselves to be the claim winner, resulting in multiple tokens or other misbehavior. The detection and resolution of duplicate addresses is discussed in Section 11.12.

The claim winner issues a nonrestricted token. On the first rotation, the token is not used by any station. The purpose of this rotation is to allow stations to align their timers. All stations simply clear their token rotation timers and set the lowest bid seen so far as the negotiated value of the TTRT. This value is stored in a register called T_Neg. The stations also maintain a *late count* (Late_ct) to keep track of the number of times in succession that the token has been received late. On the first rotation the stations set this count to one.

Since the late count is nonzero, only synchronous traffic can be transmitted on the second rotation. The late count gets reset on this rotation. Thus, asynchronous traffic can be transmitted on third and subsequent rotations.

Multiple Names of the Target: T_Req, T_Opr, T_Bid, T_Neg

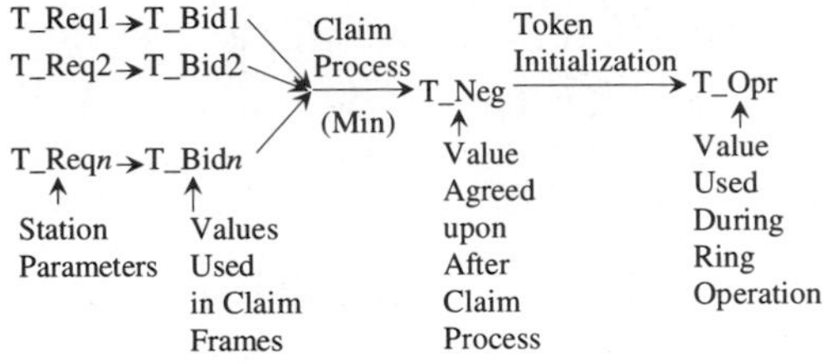

Figure 2.15 Relationship among various TTRT values.

In reading FDDI standard documents, you might encounter several variables that relate to the target token rotation time or TTRT, namely, T_Req, T_Opr, T_Bid, and T_Neg. The proper variable (and hence the register) to use depends on the state of the ring as follows:

T_Req The value *requested* by a station is called T_Req. Since this is a station parameter, different stations may have different T_Req values. Each station also maintains its minimum and maximum limits T_Min and T_Max. The final negotiated value must be between these limits for the station to be able to operate properly.

T_Bid The value *bid* by a station in its claim frame is called T_Bid. Since stations bid their T_Req, the T_Bid of each station is equal to its T_Req.

T_Neg The value *negotiated* using the claim process is called T_Neg. Notice that T_Neg is a ring-wide variable. The winning station's T_Bid becomes T_Neg for all stations.

T_Opr The *operational* value of the TTRT is called T_Opr. This is a pointer that points to the maximum value T_Max before ring initialization and to the negotiated value T_Neg after ring initialization. In other words, the value of T_Opr is T_Max before initialization and is T_Neg afterwards.

Figure 2.15 shows the relationship among the various incarnations of TTRT. Unless specified otherwise, a single symbol T is used for the target token rotation time. Since most discussion is about the ring after initialization, the symbol refers to T_Neg.

2.13 Monitoring the Ring: Valid Transmission Timer

Each station on the FDDI ring continuously monitors the proper operation of the ring. If an invalid condition, such as long-term noise, is sensed, the fault recovery process begins. This monitoring is done using a timer (alarm) mechanism called a *valid transmission timer* (TVX).

A valid frame or a nonrestricted token is defined as a valid transmission. Frame fragments, frames with an error, a restricted token, or even idle intervals should not continue for long before a valid frame or a nonrestricted token is received.

Normally on an idle ring, the token is seen every ring latency. Under load and no faults, the station should see valid frames approximately every 4500 bytes (maximum frame size) or so.

Imagine that each station has a built-in alarm clock, as shown in Figure 2.16. This clock is set to give an alarm TVX (2.5 ms) later. However, any time the station sees a token or a valid frame, it resets and restarts the alarm. Thus, if no token or valid frames are seen within the 2.5-ms interval, the alarm goes off, indicating a fault condition. Either all frames are getting affected by noise or the token has been lost. The station, therefore, starts the claim process to recreate the token.

Notice that TVX is not reset on a restricted token. The restricted dialog, if any, can continue as long as the token owner continues to transmit valid frames. However, if the owner of a restricted

Figure 2.16 Valid transmission timer (TVX).

token develops a fault or leaves the ring, the TVX alarm usually goes off at one or more stations and a new token is created.

The TVX is a station parameter and can be set by the network or station manager. Its value determines the interval during which faulty operation continues. The value should be set such that an error in one or two frames does not result in ring reinitialization. Therefore, TVX must be greater than the sum of ring latency and the time to transmit a maximum size frame. As shown later in Section 14.8, this lower bound is 2.497 ms. Therefore, the default value of TVX has been set at 2.5 ms.

The TVX mechanism has been borrowed from the older IEEE 802.5/token ring LANs. On FDDI, due to the presence of the late counter, TVX is not really required. The late counter will trigger initialization of the broken ring. However, that may take as long as two times the TTRT, which can be quite long. TVX can trigger initialization a lot sooner by timing not just tokens but frames as well.

2.14 Locating Faults: Beacon Process

The beacon process is used to locate a fault in a ring that is suspected of being broken. This process results in identifying the station that is directly downstream from the break.

The process begins with one or more stations sending a continuous stream of special MAC frames called *beacon frames*. The frames have a frame-control value of $1L00\ 0010_2$, where L is 1 if long addresses (48 bit) are used and it is 0 if short addresses are used. The destination address field is zero. (The use of directed beacon frames with nonzero destination address is described in Section 11.10.) The rules for the process are:

1. Whenever any station suspects a fault in the ring, it starts the beacon process by sending a continuous stream of beacon frames. Sending these frames is equivalent to the station announcing "I suspect that the ring is broken just before me." A token is not required to send these frames.
2. If a station receives beacon frames from another station, it stops *beaconing* (that is, it stops sending its own beacon frames) and repeats (forwards) the received beacon frames to the next station. Reception of a beacon implies that the ring is not broken just before this station (between this and its upstream neighbor).
3. If a station receives its own beacon frames, the ring is not broken (since the beacons have traveled around the ring). The station ends the beacon process and starts the claim process to recreate the token.

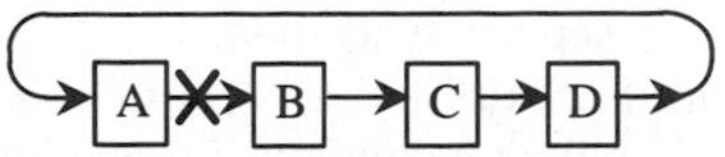

Figure 2.17 Beacon process.

4. If a station is *stuck beaconing* for a long time (10 seconds or so), that is, it does not hear either its own or anyone else's beacons while it is beaconing, the station concludes that the ring is broken just before it.

   The following example illustrates the beacon process.

Example 2.9 Consider the logical ring of four stations shown in Figure 2.17. Suppose station A malfunctions and the flow of the bits is affected. Several stations start beaconing. In particular, station B beacons. These beacons are received by station C, which stops beaconing and repeats B's beacons, which arrive at D. Station D stops beaconing and repeats B's beacons, which arrive at A. Station A stops beaconing.

Since B does not hear any beacons, it continues beaconing and, after 10 seconds, it concludes that the fault is either in the link or the station directly upstream from it. □

Beaconing is a MAC layer mechanism and generally detects failures internal to the stations. External failures such as broken cables are detected easily by the lower layers (PHY and PMD) by means of other mechanisms described in Sections 11.5 and 3.5.

Like the claim token process, the beacon process can be started simultaneously by several stations. Note also that the presence of duplicate addresses affects this process. Again, see Section 11.12 for detection and recovery from the duplicate address problem.

2.15 Comparison of IEEE 802.5 and FDDI MACs

Both the FDDI and IEEE 802.5 standards (used in 4- and 16-Mbps token rings) use a ring topology and a token access method. However, the two token access methods are quite different. The key differences are as follows:

1. *Token Holding Time*: Although both IEEE 802.5 and FDDI use a token access method, the two methods are quite different. In IEEE 802.5, a station can transmit for a preset token holding time any time it sees a token. Thus, the token rotation time can grow large. In the worst case:

   Maximum token rotation time = Number of stations on the ring × THT

   In FDDI, the token rotation time is guaranteed to be less than two times the target regardless of the number of stations on the ring. The timed token access allows longer transmissions to individual stations. Thus, larger amounts of data can be transmitted without letting the token go.
2. *Synchronous Traffic*: FDDI's timed token access has been designed specifically to support both throughput-sensitive (data) and delay-sensitive (real-time or voice) traffic. Delay-sensitive traffic uses synchronous transmissions. The token is guaranteed to arrive within two times the target. Thus a real-time station wanting to send frames every 20 ms simply declares a required target of 10 ms (and buffers for 10 ms of jitter).

IEEE 802.5 does not directly support synchronous traffic. Delay-sensitive traffic would generally be supported using a higher priority asynchronous class. However, that does not guarantee that the tight time requirements will be met unless the number of stations or the token holding time is limited.

3. *Restricted Asynchronous Traffic*: The IEEE 802.5 standard does not allow restricted asynchronous traffic. Thus, it is not possible for a station to ensure that successive tokens will be available to it as in FDDI. However, this is not a significant issue since restricted asynchronous mode, although available, is not known to be used by anyone. U.S. government procurement (GOSIP) guidelines specifically prohibit the use of the restricted token access.
4. *Immediate Transmission*: In the IEEE 802.5 standard, the stations are required to start frame transmission as soon as the token is received. This is because the token becomes the starting delimiter of the frame by changing a bit in the token. There are two problems associated with using such a mechanism at high speeds (of 100 Mbps):
   a. Full-duplex (bidirectional) data paths inside the stations are required. A station receiving the data may be suddenly called on to transmit the data. FDDI allows simplex (unidirectional) paths so that the same path can be used for reception as well as for transmission. The stations are allowed to transmit idle symbols for a limited time after capturing the token.
   b. Bit manipulation requires full-speed logic. This is not a problem at low speed, but can be expensive at high speed. For example, changing a bit would require 100-Mbps logic in FDDI. This is why FDDI requires only symbol (4-bit) or byte (8-bit) manipulation. Thus, most of the FDDI logic runs at 25 MHz or 12.5 MHz.
5. *Priority Scheme*: IEEE 802.5 allows eight priority levels, which are encoded in 3 bits in the frame. Each frame and token header has 3 bits that indicate its priority. Thus, to transmit a priority 4 message, a station must capture a token of priority 4 or lower. To ensure that the token is issued at the highest priority needed, each frame's header has three additional bits, which are used by stations on the ring to indicate the priority needed. The transmitting station looks at these bits as its frames arrive back. Further, if a station increases the priority of the token, it must remember this fact using a priority stack mechanism since this same station must decrease the priority of the token when there are no more higher priority messages.

   FDDI uses a load-level or TRT-based priority mechanism. This does not provide as strict a priority service as IEEE 802.5. For example, lower priority traffic at one station may be transmitted ahead of higher priority traffic at other stations. There are two reasons for this choice in FDDI. First, the token rotation is timed even without priority. Thus, priority using a token rotation time is a simple extension. Priority stacks are not required. Second, and more importantly, waiting for the frame before releasing the token introduces significant degradation in performance at higher speeds, as discussed next.
6. *Delayed Token Release*: In IEEE 802.5, after transmitting a frame, the stations wait for the frame to come back before releasing the token (see Figure 2.2). This is because the frame header contains information about the priority at which the token should be released. At low speeds or small rings, this does not cause any significant degradation in performance. For example, at 4 Mbps, a ring with a propagation delay of 1 ms can accommodate only 500 bytes in the ring. Thus, only 500 bytes worth of bandwidth is lost after transmission of a small frame due to delayed token release. At 100 Mbps, the frames are relatively short and the ring capacity is considerably large. For example, a 1-ms ring can accommodate 12,500 bytes and losing that much bandwidth after a transmission will lead to significant degradation. Incidentally, immediate token release has now been added to IEEE 802.5 also.

An important lesson to learn from the preceding list of differences is that the media access control is a function of the network speed. The mechanisms that work satisfactorily at a lower speed may not work well at higher speeds. This applies to FDDI's timed token access as well. As discussed in Section 16.4, the timed token access may not be appropriate at 1 Gbps.

2.16 Summary

The key points to remember about FDDI's media access control are summarized in Box 2.2.

Box 2.2 Summary of Media Access Control

1. Three classes of traffic are allowed on FDDI networks: synchronous, asynchronous, and restricted asynchronous traffic.
2. A timed token access method is used by the stations to share the medium. In this method, all stations measure the time interval since the token was last seen.
3. The asynchronous stations measure the token rotation time and strive to keep it below a prenegotiated target. The token holding time for asynchronous transmissions is limited to the difference between the target and the measured TRT.
4. The actual token rotation time can be as much as twice the target.
5. Priority is implemented using the token rotation time. If TRT is high, only high-priority messages can be transmitted.
6. Both 16-bit (short) and 48-bit (long) addresses are supported.
7. Three status indicators, E, A, and C, are used. If set, these indicate that an error was detected in the frame, the destination address was recognized by a station on the ring, and the frame was copied by a station on the ring, respectively.
8. The valid transmission timer (TVX) is used to monitor the signal on the ring and to detect faults.
9. The claim process is used to recreate the token and determine the target token rotation time using a distributed bidding procedure.
10. The beacon process is used to locate a hard fault in the ring.

2.17 Further Reading

Most of the issues discussed in this chapter are described in the FDDI MAC standard ANSI X3.139-1987 or ISO 9314-2:1989. Discussions of address formats and bit order are presented in the IEEE 802.1a standard.

The timed token access method was invented by Bob Grow and first presented in his 1982 paper. Torgerson (1989) discusses a few FDDI MAC design issues.

The bridge-stripping algorithm is patented by Yang, Ramakrishnan, Spinney, and Jain (1989) and is described in Yang and Ramakrishnan (1990) and in Yang, Spinney, and Towning (1991).

For a comparison of IEEE 802.5 and FDDI, see Iyer and Joshi (1985), Joshi (1986), and Green (1987a).

Table 2.2 and Figure 2.8 have been adapted from ANSI X3.139-1987.

2.18 Self-Test Exercises

Note: Some exercises have multiple correct answers. See Appendix D for answers.

2.1 How does FDDI support priority?

a. By making the token go fast when needed.
b. By slowing down the token when there are no high-priority messages.
c. By marking certain bits in tokens.
d. By marking certain bits in frames.
e. By allowing low-priority traffic only when the token is rotating quickly.

2.2 What is the main difference between the timed token access in FDDI and the token access method used in traditional token rings?

a. The FDDI token has a built-in timer.
b. The length of an FDDI token and hence its time is kept constant.
c. The difference between successive token rotation times is kept constant in FDDI.
d. The FDDI token rotation time has an upper bound regardless of the number of active stations.

2.3 Which of the following apply to the synchronous transmissions on FDDI?

a. They can be made even if the token is late.
b. They must be periodic.
c. They have no time limit.
d. They require more precise clock synchronization.
e. They require prior reservation.

2.4 What happens if a station's token holding timer expires in the middle of a long frame?

a. The transmission is aborted immediately.
b. The remaining frame is saved for transmission next time.
c. This and all other waiting frames are transmitted.
d. The speed of transmission is increased to ensure timely completion.
e. This frame is transmitted completely even though this delays the token beyond the target.

2.5 What is the meaning of *immediate token release* in FDDI?

a. The token is released immediately after its receipt.
b. The token is released as soon as all transmitted frames are received back at the transmitting station.
c. The token is released as soon as the last frame is transmitted.
d. The token is released as soon as the last frame is acknowledged.

2.6 What can always be said about a frame whose C indicator is set?

a. The frame was delivered to the intended application.
b. The frame was successfully received by the destination station.
c. The frame was received by the destination without an error.
d. All of the above.
e. None of the above.

2.7 What are common uses of void frames?

a. To void (invalidate) a previous successful transmission.
b. To interrupt the current transmitter.
c. To indicate that the token is corrupted.
d. Just to kill time when necessary.
e. To mark the beginning or end of a transmission sequence.

2.8 What is the primary purpose of implementor frames in FDDI?

a. To implement important station management (SMT) functions.
b. For communication among implementors.
c. For uses specific to a particular organization or networking architecture.
d. To help implementors debug their implementations.

2.9 How many 1-byte numbers have the same representation in little-endian and big-endian bit order (for example, 1101 1011)?

a. 1
b. 4
c. 16
d. 256
e. 1024

2.10 What bit order is used for transmitting data bytes in FDDI frames?

a. Least-significant bit first
b. Most-significant bit first
c. Depends on the bit order used by the source adapter
d. Depends on the bit order used by the destination adapter

2.11 What bit order is used for transmitting source/destination addresses in FDDI frames?

a. Least-significant bit first
b. Most-significant bit first
c. Depends on the bit order used by the source adapter
d. Depends on the bit order used by the destination adapter

2.12 Which of the following apply to all systems with big-endian byte order?

a. They transmit the most-significant bit first.
b. They transmit the least-significant bit first.
c. They transmit the most-significant byte first for all multibyte quantities.
d. None of the above.

2.13 What is the purpose of the claim process in FDDI?

a. To create a new token.
b. To reclaim a token after each rotation.
c. To reset the priority of a token.
d. To reclaim the space used by the token.

2.14 What can be said about a station that is stuck beaconing?

a. The station cannot stop its transmission.
b. The station is not receiving beacons from its upstream neighbor.
c. The station is not transmitting beacons to its downstream neighbor.
d. The station has failed the self-test.
e. The station's bypass is stuck.

2.15 What was the original purpose of allowing restricted tokens in FDDI?

a. To send confidential information.
b. To prevent misbehaving stations from using the token.
c. To allow long dialogs.

CHAPTER **3**

Medium Independent Physical Layer (PHY)

The ISO/OSI physical layer has been divided into two layers in FDDI. These are called PHY and PMD. PHY covers the media-independent part of the physical layer. This layer is medium independent in the sense that it applies to fiber, copper, and all other media that may be used in FDDI. In fact, this layer does not make use of any specific properties of the medium. On the other hand, PMD is medium dependent and there are a number of PMD standards—one for each medium, for example, multimode fiber PMD, single-mode fiber PMD, low-cost fiber PMD, twisted-pair copper PMD, and so on.

An FDDI network consists of several nodes interconnected via a number of point-to-point bidirectional links. The PHY layer deals with issues related to communications between two nodes on the opposite ends of a link. The key functions provided by the PHY layer are the following:

1. *Coding*: PHY specifies a coding scheme for transferring data symbols, control symbols, and line states between adjacent nodes. This coding scheme ensures that there are sufficient transitions in the transmitted signal. This helps in clock synchronization and framing.
2. *Elasticity Buffers*: PHY specifies the requirements for buffers used to alleviate clock rate differences among neighboring stations. Such buffers are called elasticity buffers.
3. *Smoother*: PHY ensures that there is sufficient interframe gap. The gap preceding a frame is called the *preamble*. PHY makes very small preambles larger by adding additional idle symbols and removes an equivalent number from long preambles. This process of smoothing the variance in preamble size is achieved by a smoother.
4. *Repeat Filter*: PHY provides a repeat path if there is no MAC associated with the PHY. The repeat filter ensures that the errors caused by line noise are not propagated.
5. *Line State Indication*: PHY specifies special control sequences for communicating the status of the link. This alleviates the need for separate status or control lines.

These five components are described in the next five sections of this chapter.

3.1 Coding

One of the first problems to solve in communications among two stations is that of how to communicate a bit stream. Figure 3.1 shows a sample bit stream of 1's and 0's. The simplest scheme is to code a zero as a low signal level and a one as a high signal level. Here the signal level could

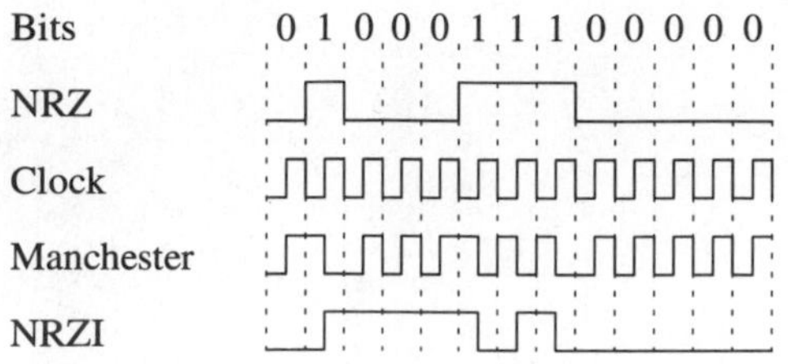

Figure 3.1 Various coding methods.

be electrical voltage or optical power level. This coding results in the signal waveform shown on the second line of Figure 3.1. This is a popular coding technique and is known as *nonreturn to zero* (*NRZ*). Using NRZ coding would cause several problems:

1. The pulse width is indeterminate. It is not possible to tell when a bit begins or ends. In other words, this coding lacks clocking information. NRZ can be used if the clock signal (which is shown in the third line of Figure 3.1) is transmitted on a separate line.
2. If many 1's occur in a row, the signal remains high. This confuses most receivers since they use the average signal level (baseline) as the threshold to distinguish a one from a zero. In coding theory, this change of the threshold level is known as *baseline wander*.
3. If many 0's occur in a row, no signal is received for a long time. This cannot be distinguished from a broken or faulty line. Thus, this coding does not provide *line state information*.
4. The coding does not provide any error protection. If a zero becomes a one or vice versa, the resulting signal is still valid.
5. The coding does not have any control signals. Control signals are useful to delimit frames. They should be such that they cannot occur in the data.

One solution to the problem of too many 1's in a row is to use *nonreturn to zero inverted* (*NRZI*) encoding in which a one is encoded as an inversion of the level. A transition of the signal from high to low or from low to high is interpreted as a one. A zero is encoded as no transition; the signal level after the clock remains the same as before. The signal using this coding is shown along the bottom line of Figure 3.1. The problem of too many 0's in a row is not solved by this encoding. Also, this encoding does not have clocking information or line state information.

One self-clocking alternative is to transmit an exclusive-OR of the NRZ coded data and the clock. This is the popular **Manchester** encoding that is used in IEEE 802.3/Ethernet, IEEE 802.5/token ring networks, and in several disk storage systems. This particular type of Manchester encoding is called *unipolar Manchester*. In this a zero is encoded as an upward transition, while a one is encoded as a downward transition. Both 0's and 1's result in a transition, thus the clock can easily be recovered. The signal is free from baseline wander. The main problem in using Manchester encoding at high speeds is that the number of pulses is twice the number of bits. A 100-Mbps data stream would produce a 200-Mbaud signal (see Sidebar on page 67). The ratio of the bit rate to the baud rate is called the *efficiency* of the coding scheme. Manchester encoding is only 50% efficient.

The problem of too many 0's in an NRZI stream is sometimes solved by stuffing (inserting) extra 1's whenever more than a certain number of 0's are encountered. These extra bits are then removed at the receiver. This bit stuffing technique results in more code bits than data bits. (The bits sent by the user of the coding device are called *data bits*, while the bits sent on the medium are

Table 3.1 4b/5b Code

Code Bits	Symbol	Assignment	Code Bits	Symbol	Assignment
Data Symbols:			**Control Symbols:**		
11110	0	0000	11000	J	First symbol of starting delimiter pair
01001	1	0001	10001	K	Second symbol of starting delimiter pair
10100	2	0010	00101	L	Embedded delimiter*
10101	3	0011	01101	T	Used to terminate the data stream
01010	4	0100	00111	R	Denoting logical zero (reset)
01011	5	0101	11001	S	Denoting logical one (set)
01110	6	0110	**Invalid Code Assignments:**		
01111	7	0111	00001	VH	The code patterns marked V or VH
10010	8	1000	00010	VH	shall not be transmitted because
10011	9	1001	00011	V	they violate consecutive code bit
10110	A	1010	00110	V	0's or duty cycle requirements.
10111	B	1011	01000	VH	Code marked VH shall however be
11010	C	1100	01100	V	interpreted as Halt when received.
11011	D	1101	10000	VH	
11100	E	1110			
11101	F	1111			
Line State Symbols:					
00000	Q	Quiet			
11111	I	Idle			
00100	H	Halt			

*Was a violation initially. Defined as a delimiter in PHY-2 (see Chapter 15).

called *code bits*.) The effective data rate varies depending on the data pattern. A better technique is to use an *m*b/*n*b code in which *m* data bits are coded as *n* code bits. The coding is specially selected to provide error protection and control symbols. There are a number of *m*b/*n*b codes such as 4b/5b, 4b/6b, 8b/10b, and so on.

In FDDI, a 4b/5b code is used along with NRZI encoding. The complete 4b/5b coding is shown in Table 3.1. The data stream is broken into 4-bit data symbols, which are labeled 0, 1, 2, . . . , F, respectively, as in the hexadecimal notation. Each symbol is represented as a group of 5 code bits. These code bits have been specially chosen such that data symbols have no more than one leading 0 and no more than two trailing 0's. Thus, in a stream of data symbols, there can never be any more than three 0's in a row. Limiting the number of 0's is important since the NRZI encoding has no transitions on 0's and too many 0's in a row are undesirable. The following example illustrates the 4b/5b with NRZI coding.

Example 3.1 Consider the transmission of 0000_2 (4 zero bits). These four data bits are grouped as a data symbol (zero), which is coded as a group of five code bits 11110_2. Assuming that the signal was at a low level (for instance, −5 V) before this symbol, the signal pattern generated by this symbol would be as shown in Figure 3.2(a). The first code bit (one) results in a transition to a

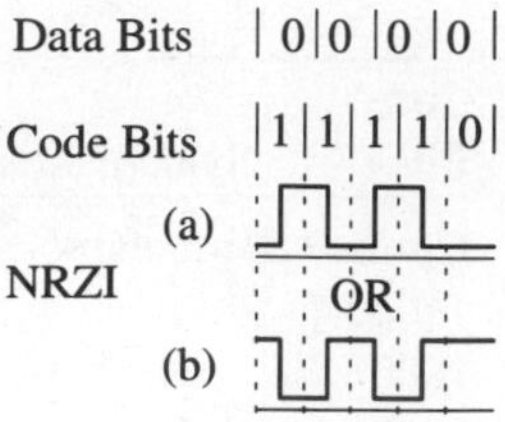

Figure 3.2 Transitions for data-symbol 0.

high level (+5 V), the second code bit (one) results in a transition to a low level, the third code bit (one) results in a transition to a high level, the fourth code bit (one) results in a transition to a low level, and finally the fifth code bit (zero) results in the absence of a transition and the signal remains at the low level.

Had the signal been at a high level before the transmission of the zero symbol, the signal shown in Figure 3.2(b) would result. □

In Figure 3.2(a), the signal is low (negative) for three pulse durations and high (positive) for two pulse durations. The average is $(-3+2)/(2\times 5)$ or -10%. This is called the *direct current* (dc) content of the signal. The dc content of the signal in Figure 3.2(b) is +10%. For all code groups used for data symbols in the 4b/5b coding, the maximum dc content is limited to 10%. The dc content is undesirable since charging and discharging of capacitors used in the couplers can limit the bandwidth of the circuits and cause baseline wander. Ideally, the dc content of the signal should be zero (over some reasonable interval), that is, the signal should be **dc balanced** as is the case with Manchester encoding.

Five code bits result in 2^5 or 32 code groups. Of these, 16 are used for data symbols. The remaining code groups are available for use as control symbols. The control symbols are labeled H, I, J, K, and so on. For decoding the data symbols, it is necessary to know the symbol boundary, that is, the bit at which the symbol begins. An error in the symbol boundary would cause all symbols to be incorrectly decoded. For example, a 0-1-F data symbol triplet would result in the code stream 11110-01001-11101 (Here, "-" denotes the symbol boundary). However, if the receiver misaligns the symbol boundary by one bit, it may be decoded as 1-11100-10011-1101. The receiver will interpret it as E-9-C or E-9-D.

The symbol pair J-K is encoded as "1100010001." The subpattern "100010001" cannot occur in a stream of data symbols. Thus, the J-K pair can be uniquely recognized regardless of the symbol boundary. That is why this is used as a starting delimiter in frames and tokens. Whenever a PHY detects the J-K pattern, it resets the symbol boundary. All subsequent bits are decoded using this new boundary.

The R-, S-, and T-symbols are also called reset, set, and terminator symbols. As their names imply, the T-symbol is used as the ending delimiter in frames and tokens, while R and S are used as frame status indicators. These symbols' waveforms are such that when used in pairs the resulting waveform is always dc balanced. Thus, TT, TR, TS, RR, RS, and SS are all dc balanced. This is why two T's are used as ending delimiters in tokens and why the number of symbols used in the ending delimiter and frame status indicators is always even.

Table 3.2 Comparison of Coding Techniques

Technique	Efficiency	DC Content	Run Length
NRZ	100%	50%	∞
NRZI	100%	50%	∞
Manchester	50%	0%	1
4b/5b+NRZI	80%	10%	3

The symbols I, H, and Q stand for idle, halt, and quiet, respectively. These symbols as well as their combinations are used as line state indicators. These symbols result in square waveforms of different periods. Line states can be recognized independent of the symbol boundary, provided the symbol (or the symbol combination) is repeated enough times.

The idle symbol is the most frequently occurring symbol since it is used to fill in the idle space between tokens and/or frames. This symbol is coded as 11111 and has five transitions. This pattern was chosen for I since it has the highest clock content (highest number of transitions).

The quiet symbol is encoded as 00000. Using NRZI encoding this results in no change in the signal level. A break in the fiber results in no light being received at the receiving end. This is automatically interpreted as a sequence of quiet symbols and the line is said to have entered a quiet state.

The halt symbol is encoded as 00100. A sequence of halt symbols results in a 25-MHz square waveform, which is interpreted as the halt line state. This and other line states are explained further in Section 3.5.

FDDI-II uses the I-L symbol pair as the starting delimiter for its packet channel (see Chapter 13). The L symbol is coded as 00101. Unlike J-K, the I-L pair can be recognized only on a symbol boundary.

All other code groups are called *violations* or V. They are never transmitted. If seen at the receiver, they indicate the occurrence of a noise event. Symbols marked "V or H" (violation or halt) are also never transmitted but on receipt they are interpreted as a halt. Notice that a sequence of any *one* of these symbols has the same waveform as that resulting from a sequence of halts.

Table 3.2 presents a comparison of the 4b/5b+NRZI combination coding used in FDDI with other well-known coding techniques. The criteria for comparison are coding efficiency, dc content, and run length.

The coding efficiency was defined earlier as the ratio of the data bit rate to the signal baud rate. For NRZ and NRZI, each bit results in at most one pulse, thus the coding efficiency is 100%. With Manchester encoding, the coding efficiency is 50%. With 4b/5b coding, the signal baud rate is 125 Mbaud and the efficiency is 80%. This is the principal reason for its selection.

The dc balance is defined as the deviation of the average from the center. With NRZ encoding, a sequence of 1's would result in the average becoming +1 (assuming low = -1, high = +1, center = 0). The dc balance is $1/[+1-(-1)]$ or 50%. NRZI encoding of a sequence of 0's would similarly give a dc balance of 50%. With Manchester encoding, the signal is dc balanced. This is, therefore, ideally suited for ac coupling. With 4b/5b encoding and NRZI, the dc balance is 10% as discussed earlier.

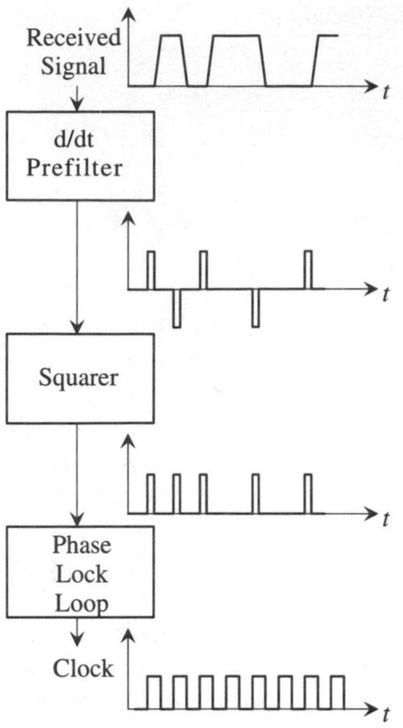

Figure 3.3 Block diagram of a clock recovery circuit.

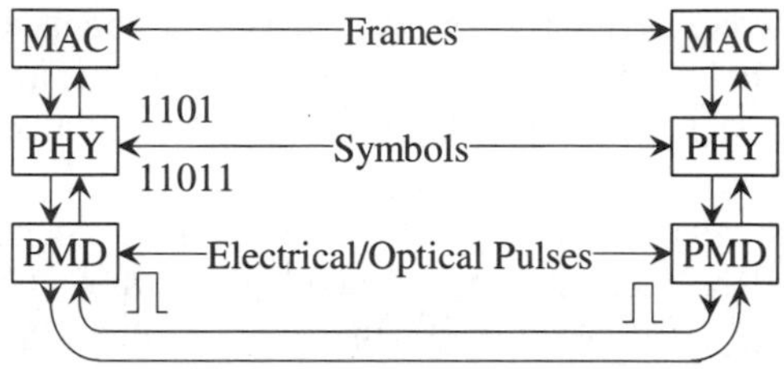

Figure 3.4 Communication between protocol layers of neighboring FDDI stations.

The run length is defined as the maximum number of code bit times between signal transitions. Using NRZ or NRZI, no transitions will be seen in a sequence of 0's. These, thus, have a maximum run length of ∞. Manchester encoding guarantees transition after every code bit. NRZI with 4b/5b as used in FDDI guarantees every third code bit since the number of 0's is limited to three in the data stream.

To summarize, Manchester encoding has the highest clocking information of the four schemes and is not susceptible to baseline wander. Its chief drawback is the low efficiency and the lack of control symbols. NRZI with 4b/5b trades off clocking information and dc balance for a higher efficiency and a larger number of control symbols.

The 4b/5b and NRZI encoding in FDDI allows easy recovery of the clock signal without requiring a separate line (or fiber) for it. Figure 3.3 shows a simplified block diagram of how the clock can be recovered in an FDDI receiver. There are three blocks: a prefilter, a squarer, and a narrowband filter. The prefilter consists of a differentiator or a high-pass filter. It generates a positive pulse when the signal switches from low to high, and a negative pulse on a high to low transition. No pulse is generated when the signal remains at the same level. A squaring circuit makes the stream of the pulses positive. Finally, a phase-locked loop (PLL) is used as a narrowband pass filter to regenerate the clock.

Now that you understand frames, symbols, and code bits, you may find it interesting to note that the three layers of the FDDI protocol use three different mechanisms for communication in the layer. As shown in Figure 3.4, two MACs communicate with each other using frames. Since frames contain

Bit, Baud, and Hertz

Rememberances of Things Past:
Frequency was measured in cycles,
Hertz referred to multiple pain,
Modem was a harvesting command,
for bringing in the grain.
Modelling was at fashion shows,
bauds were ladies of the night,
Prompting was helping actors,
contesting for resources, a fight.
— S. Greenfield in RFC 1300

The speed of the optical signal on FDDI fibers is 125 megabits per second, 125 megabaud, or 62.5 megahertz. What's the difference among bit, baud, and hertz?

A bit is simply a *bi*nary digi*t*. In a binary system, each digit can be either 0 or 1. There are many ways to code these bits before transmitting on the fiber. One possibility is to use a short pulse to indicate a 0 and a long pulse to encode a 1. The response time required of the encoding and decoding circuit depends on the duration of the shortest pulse used in the coding scheme. The inverse of this duration is called a baud. Hertz is the unit of frequency and indicates cycles per second. Depending on the waveform of the encoded signal, the cycle may consists of any number of (less than, equal to, or greater than 1) bits. So the frequency may be more than, equal to, or less than the bit rate.

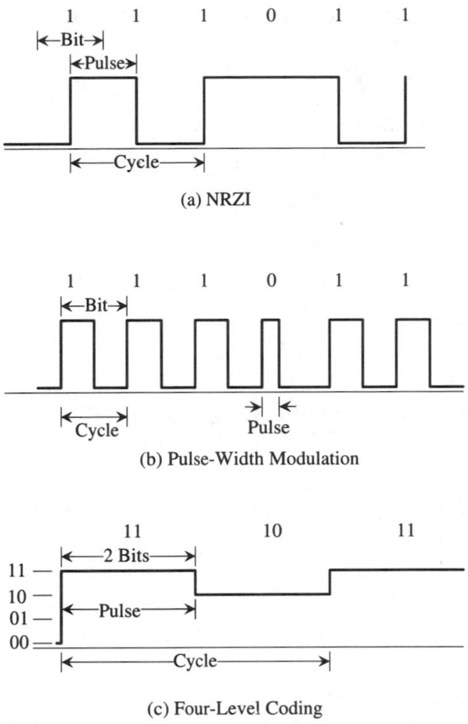

Figure 3.5 Three examples of coding illustrating the difference between bit rate, baud rate, and hertz.

Figure 3.5(a) shows a NRZI encoded signal on FDDI fiber. It has 125 megabits per second. The narrowest pulse in this signal is 8 ns wide, so the baud rate is 125 megabaud. The shortest cycle is 2 bits or 16 ns wide, so the maximum frequency is 62.5 megahertz.

Figure 3.5(b) shows a pulse-width-modulated signal with a bit duration of 8 ns. A zero is represented by a 2-ns pulse, and a one is represented by a 4-ns pulse. In this case, the bit rate is $1/8 \times 10^{-9}$ or 125 megabits per second; the baud rate is $1/2 \times 10^{9}$ or 500 megabaud; the cycle duration is 8 ns, so the frequency is 125 MHz.

Figure 3.5(c) shows four-level coding in which two successive bits are combined to determine the amplitude of the signal. In this case, if the bit rate is assumed to be 125 Mbps, the pulse width is 16 ns, so it has a baud rate of 62.5 Mbaud. At least two pulses are required to form a cycle. The cycle duration is 32 ns and the maximum signal frequency is 31.25 MHz.

source and destination addresses, any two MACs on the ring can communicate with each other. PHYs do not understand or use frames. They use specially coded symbols to communicate. Since there are no station addresses involved in the communication, only adjacent PHYs can communicate with each other. The physical layer medium dependent (PMD) component uses optical pulses on the fiber medium (or electrical pulses on copper medium). PMD does not deal with symbols.

3.2 Elasticity Buffer

In FDDI each station maintains its own clock. Crystal oscillators used for generating the clock provide a very high accuracy. Nonetheless, the clocks of the neighboring stations may have a slightly different frequency. For example, one station may send a million pulses during a period over which the receiving station may send one million and one pulses. Thus, the number of incoming and outgoing pulses is not always the same. If the incoming clock is faster than the local clock, more bits may be received than transmitted. Similarly, if the incoming clock is slower than the local clock, fewer bits may be received than transmitted.

To overcome a slight difference in clock speeds, a circular first-in-first-out (FIFO) buffer called the elasticity buffer is used as shown in Figure 3.6. The protection provided by the buffers is similar to that in routers connecting links of different speeds or that of water tanks with different input and output rates. Two independent pointers are maintained. The input pointer selects the buffer location to be written to and moves at the recovered clock rate. The output pointer selects the buffer location to be read from and moves at the local clock rate. During normal operation, the output pointer follows the input pointer and keeps a small distance. During the interpacket gap, the pointers are repositioned at the minimum distance. If more bits are received, the bits in the interframe gap (called the preamble) are deleted by recentering the FIFO at the end of the frame. If fewer bits are received, additional bits are transmitted after the end of the frame. The elasticity buffer thus changes the interframe gap.

The size of the elasticity buffer is determined by the maximum allowable clock difference. FDDI requires crystals with a frequency stability of 50 parts per million (**ppm**), and a maximum frame size of 4500 bytes or 45,000 code bits. The maximum difference between two clocks can be 100 ppm (or 10^{-4}). The maximum number of bits gained or lost during a frame is 45000×10^{-4} or 4.5 bits. Thus, the FIFO should allow an underflow of 4.5 bits and an overflow of 4.5 bits from its center. This results in a minimum theoretical FIFO size of 9 bits.

If the crystals do not meet the 50-ppm specification, it is possible for the clock difference to be more than 10^{-4}. In such cases, the elasticity buffer can underflow or overflow during a frame transmission and some bits may be added or deleted from the frame resulting in the so-called **elasticity buffer error**. To minimize such errors, most implementations use elasticity buffers larger than the specified minimum.

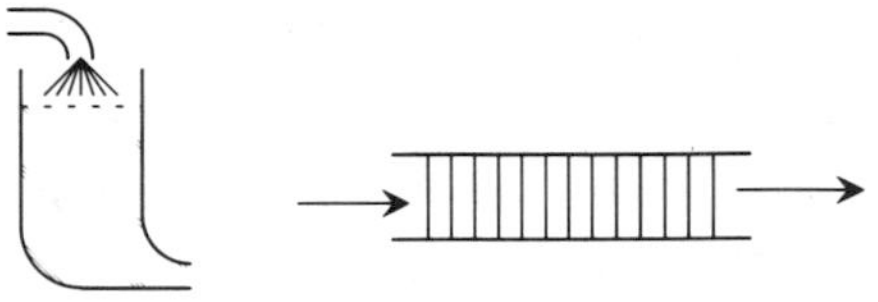

(a) (b)

Figure 3.6 Elasticity buffer.

Frames Versus Packets Versus Messages Versus PDU

More Rememberances of Things Past:
Windows were for looking out of,
in a Tandem, two could take a spin
Bridges were for crossing,
a frame was to keep pictures in.
— S. Greenfield in RFC 1300

Have you ever gotten confused about whether to call something a frame or a packet or a message? If you have, you are not alone. The networks were originally designed to transport messages that have some application level meaning such as routing messages are used by routers, disk control messages may be used to control remote disks, and so on. The messages can be very long. One way to transmit these messages is to break them into reasonably sized packets so that multiple sources can share a link. Therefore, the transport layer breaks messages into multiple, reasonably sized packets. The routing layer may further break these packets into segments and passes them down to the datalink layer, which places special symbols (called *framing delimiters*) to mark the beginning and end of the segments. The output of the datalink layer is called *frames*.

To reduce the confusion, the International Organization for Standardization (ISO) defined a new term called the *protocol data unit* (*PDU*). Each layer of the protocol at a station communicates with its counterpart at another station using PDUs defined for that layer. Thus, application layers communicate using application layer PDUs. Transport layers communicate using transport layer PDUs, and so on. The PDUs for the session layer and up are called messages. Those for the transport and routing layers are called packets. PDUs at the datalink layer and below are called frames.

The relationship among the terms "messages," "packets," and 'frames" is shown in Figure 3.7.

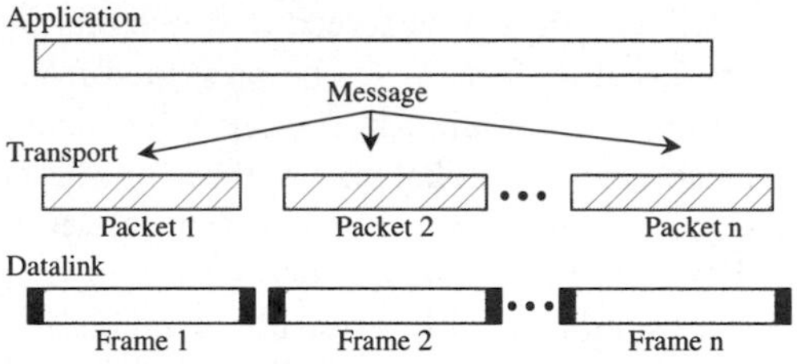

Figure 3.7 Relationship among messages, packets, and frames.

Note that the frames larger than 4500 bytes may cause an elasticity buffer error. To support larger frame sizes, either better quality crystals or larger elasticity buffers should be used.

It would appear that larger elasticity buffers would allow lower cost crystals to be used or longer frames to be transmitted. If this is so, why not make it really large? The main problem is that the elasticity buffers add to the station delay. The frame transmission does not begin until the elasticity buffer is half full. Thus, the frame is delayed at each station by an amount equal to half the size of the elasticity buffer. For example, a 10-bit elasticity buffer will add 5 code bit times or 40 ns to the station delay. A larger buffer will increase the station delay and hence the ring latency. A large ring latency adversely affects the ring's performance as shown in Section 22.5.

3.3 Smoother

The elasticity buffer function adds or deletes the bits from the interframe gap. This has no effect on the frames, provided there are enough bits in the gap. The FDDI standard requires that the stations transmit a preamble of 16 idle symbols, thereby ensuring that the interframe gap will be 80 code bits at the transmitter. However, it is possible that a series of station clocks is skewed such that their elasticity buffers chew away the whole gap between two frames as shown in Figure 3.8. The next station may then be forced to delete bits from the frames. To guard against this possibility, it is important that the preambles be prevented from getting too small. In other words, it is necessary to smooth out the variation in the preamble sizes. This is what is done by the smoother. Each station has a smoother that counts the number of idle symbols in the preamble. If the preamble is too short, it adds an extra symbol. Later, it can delete an idle symbol when it finds a preamble that is long. This is shown in Figure 3.9. The goal is to keep the minimum preamble size 14 symbols or longer. Thus the smoother adds extra idle symbols if it sees preambles shorter than 14 symbols. It keeps a count of added symbols and it refills its supply of idle symbols when it finds a longer preamble. Thus, longer preambles are shortened only if some symbols were added by that station to previous preambles.

A preamble gives a station breathing time between successive frame reception. During this time, it can reset its data path and state tables. The station may not have enough time to do this if a preamble is too short. For example, some stations may not be able to copy a frame if the preamble is shorter than 12 symbols. Some stations may not be able to recenter their elasticity buffer if the preamble is shorter than 4 symbols or they may not be able to even repeat a frame if the preamble is shorter than 2 symbols. It is therefore important that the preambles be prevented from becoming very short.

The decision to add the smoother to the PHY standard came after simulations of the elasticity buffer revealed that under some conditions, as many as 10% of the frames could be lost due to the interpacket gap becoming less than 12 symbols—the point at which a MAC may not be able to copy the frame. To solve the problem, a proposal was made in August 1987 to monitor and smooth the interframe gaps.

One way to understand the smoother's operation is to imagine that it borrows idle symbols from a bank to give them to short preambles. If it encounters a long preamble, it removes a few idle symbols and pays back its debt. Like most of us, the smoother has a credit limit. Thus, if it encounters a series of short preambles, it may exhaust the credit limit extended to it. In such cases it will not be able to elongate short preambles any more. The smoother is then said to be **fully extended**.

One more way for a smoother to reclaim idle symbols is the so-called *Gobbler* shown in Figure 3.10. This mechanism, which is optional, chews up the final symbols from partial frames

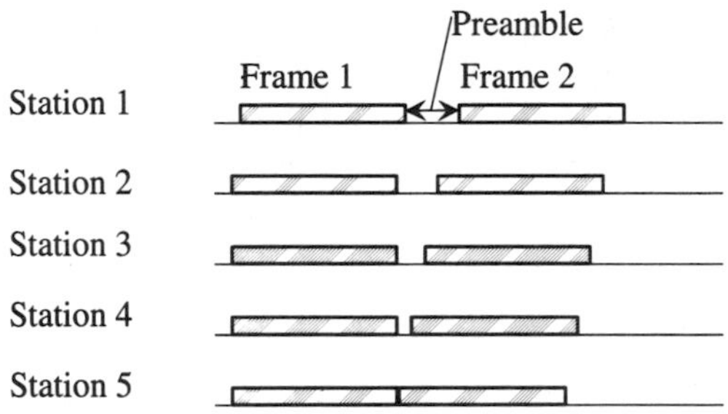

Figure 3.8 Removal of bits from the preamble may result in merging of two frames.

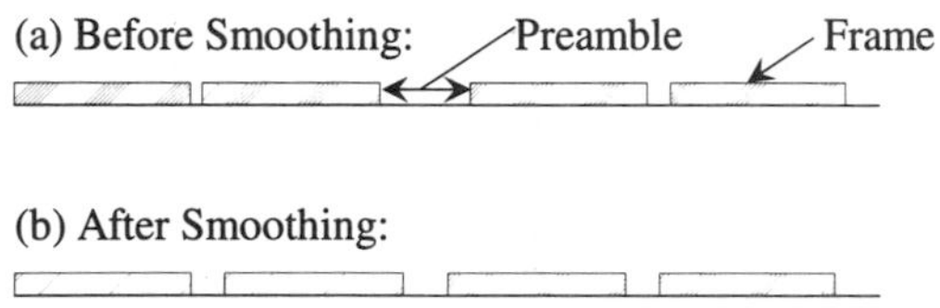

Figure 3.9 A smoother reduces the variation in the preamble sizes.

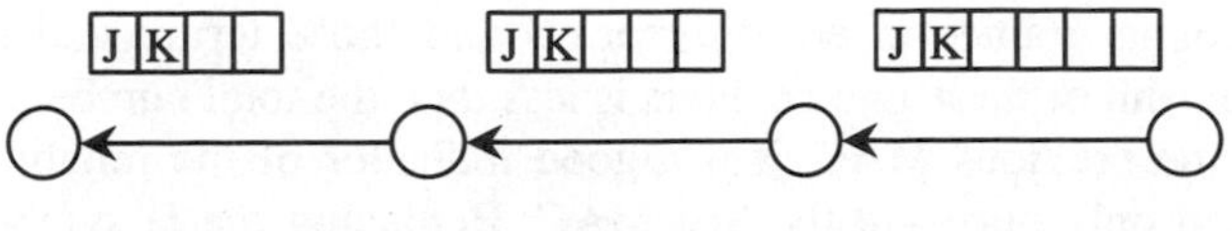

Figure 3.10 A fragment's size decreases slowly as it passes through the gobblers at various stations.

and replaces them with idles. Such partial frames are caused by stripping or by noise. Recall that a transmitter normally strips a frame by looking at the source address in the frame. Thus, some part of the frame before the source address may be left over on the ring. As these fragments pass through a smoother, the last symbol is replaced by an idle symbol and the fragment becomes one symbol shorter. In byte-wide implementations, two symbols may be replaced at each smoother. After passing through a sufficient number of stations, the fragments eventually disappear. The fragments also disappear when they meet a transmitting station.

3.4 Repeat Filter

The 4b/5b coding ensures that there are enough transitions in the signal to recover the remote clock from data. If noise affects a frame, the resulting bit pattern may not satisfy this requirement. The damaged symbols have to be replaced as soon as possible, which means at the next node. Generally, a MAC at the next node will replace all damaged symbols with idle symbols. However, if there is no MAC at a node, a repeat filter is used as part of the PHY to accomplish this function. If the noise results in a 4b/5b code violation (that is, it results in a V symbol) or control symbols such as I, K, H, or Q in the middle of a frame, the repeat filter replaces it and the subsequent three symbols with four H symbols as shown in Figure 3.11. The remainder of the frame is replaced with idle symbols.

Since a single H symbol has only one transition, four H symbols are used to minimize the possibility of second noise corruption resulting in good data, thereby either creating a valid frame with undetected error or causing the errors to be counted incorrectly. The MAC encountering these H symbols replaces them with idle symbols.

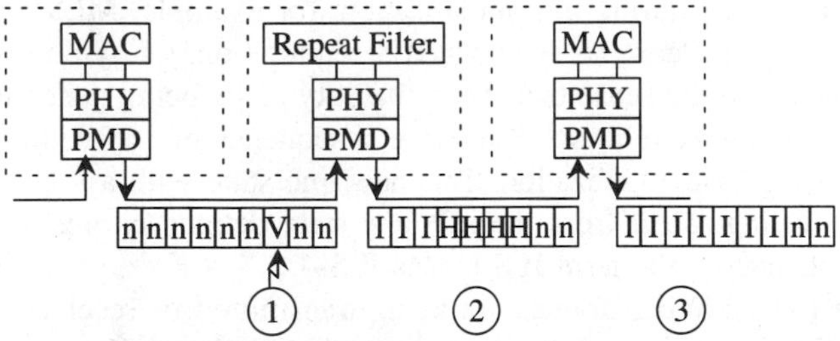

Figure 3.11 Repeat filter operation.

The MAC also counts frames in error (Error_ct) and those terminated prematurely by noise (Lost_ct). Although the sum of these two counters is less than the total number of errors that occurred on the set of links to the previous MAC, it is a good indicator of the reliability of the set. Notice that the error is counted only once—at the first MAC. Replacing the H symbols with idle symbols ensures that they are not counted in other stations.

The repeat filter is required only when there is no MAC at a port. This may happen, for example, at a concentrator or at the secondary path of a dual-attachment station with one MAC. Although a repeat filter is not required when there is a MAC, the presence of a repeat filter at a station with a MAC is allowed and does not affect the operation of the ring. In practice, a repeat filter is included in every PHY.

A repeat filter stops the replacement if it encounters a J symbol. This is to prevent overwriting of the next frame. In this case, the number of symbols replaced by H symbols may be less than four.

3.5 Line State Indication

In some computer interconnects, separate lines are used for control purposes such as link initialization and connection setup. In FDDI the line (fiber) used for data transmission is also used for all other control signals. This is possible since the 4b/5b encoding provides several control symbols, which can be used by two neighboring stations to exchange the information about the status of the connection between them. Repeated sequences of control symbols are used to indicate whether the line is in active use, down, being brought up, and so on. The following is the list of such line states:

1. *Quiet Line State* (*QLS*): A fiber that is either broken or simply not being used is indicated by no light being seen at the receiver end. According to 4b/5b coding, this is interpreted as a sequence of zero code bits (no transitions) or of Q symbols. Recall that a Q (quiet) symbol consists of five 0's. During the normal operation of the ring, if a sequence of 16 or more Q symbols is received on a link, the link is assumed to have entered the "quiet line state." Although power levels remaining either high or low will both be decoded as a sequence of Q symbols, normally no light is sent during QLS. This turns the signal detect off at the receiving end, which is similar to what would happen if a transmitter failure or a fiber break were to occur.
2. *Idle Line State* (*ILS*): When a continuous stream of idle symbols is received, the line is said to be in the "idle line state." This state is entered whenever a sequence of four or more consecutive I symbols is received and is exited on receipt of any symbol other than I. The frames are separated by a sequence of idle symbols. Thus, during interframe gaps the line enters the ILS. The idle stream is also used during link initialization.

   Other line states used during link initialization, for example, MLS and HLS (discussed in items 4 and 5), require at least 16 symbols. ILS requires only 4 symbols and is not as robust as the other line states in the sense that the probability of its being generated by noise is higher than that if 16 symbols were required. Therefore, a sequence of 16 idle (and not 4 idle) symbols is used for ILS during link initialization. This new line state with a longer sequence of idles is called **ILS-16** to distinguish it from the idle line state defined earlier, which is called **ILS-4**. Unless specified otherwise, the term ILS means ILS-4.
3. *Active Line State* (*ALS*): When frames are being transmitted or received on a link, the line is said to be active. The reception of the frame starting delimiter J-K causes the line to enter the "active line state." Since a frame can contain only R, S, T, and data symbols, the reception of

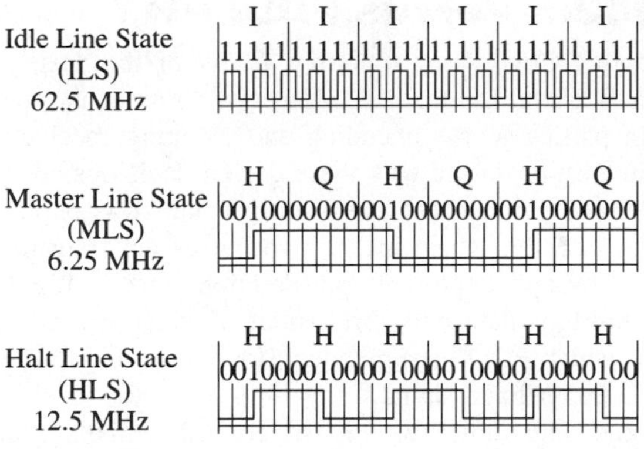

Figure 3.12 Line states.

any other symbols causes the receiver to assume that the link is no longer active and to exit the ALS. As discussed earlier, a sequence of four or more consecutive idle symbols causes the link to enter the idle line state. Some implementations exit ALS on receipt of a data symbol after an R-, S-, or T-symbol has been received or on receipt of an idle symbol. This is allowed by the standard.

4. *Master Line State* (*MLS*): During connection setup, two special signals are used for communication by neighboring stations. These are called the *master line state* (*MLS*) and *halt line state* (*HLS*). During link initialization, HLS is used to indicate 1 and MLS is used to indicate 0. MLS is indicated by sending a continuous stream of alternating halt and quiet symbols. At least eight or more H-Q symbol pairs should be received to enter this state. As shown in Figure 3.12, the H-Q pair consists of a 6.25-MHz square wave signal. If any symbol other than an H-Q pair is received, MLS is exited.
5. *Halt Line State* (*HLS*): As discussed earlier, this is one of the two line states (the other is MLS) used for signaling during connection setup. HLS is indicated by sending a continuous stream of H symbols. Sixteen or more consecutive H symbols must be received to enter this state. Again, as shown in Figure 3.12, this stream is a square wave with a frequency of 12.5 MHz.
6. *Line State Unknown* (*LSU*): The set of line states defined so far is mutually exclusive but not exhaustive. This means that at any particular instant a line can have only one state and that line conditions are possible that do not satisfy the criteria for any of the above defined line states. In this case, the condition is called *line state unknown* (*LSU*). Actually, LSU is entered on most state transitions. For example, 16 or more H symbols are required to change to the halt line state. However, when a sequence of 16 H symbols arrives at a node, the line enters LSU after receiving the first H, and exits LSU when the sixteenth H is received. It will stay in LSU for 15 symbols.
7. *Noise Line State* (*NLS*): When the received signal stays in the unknown line state (LSU) beyond a certain duration, the signal has probably been hit by noise and the line is said to have entered the "noise line state."

One line state, which has not been mentioned so far, is the cycle line state used in FDDI-II. It is explained later in Section 15.2.

3.6 IEEE 802.5 Versus FDDI PHY

IEEE 802.5 and FDDI both follow a ring topology. Many of the design concepts in FDDI were borrowed from the earlier IEEE 802.5 standard. However, some of the design decisions in the two standards are different. In particular, the encoding and clocking mechanisms of FDDI and IEEE 802.5 are opposite. It is interesting to see why these design decisions are different.

IEEE 802.5 uses differential Manchester encoding, which was explained in Section 3.1. This encoding has an efficiency of 50%, which means two pulses are transmitted for each data bit. At high speeds, efficiency becomes an important consideration since it affects the bandwidth required for the medium. For a 100-Mbps data rate, differential Manchester encoding would have resulted in a signal of 200 Mbaud, which FDDI designers considered too high. The 4b/5b encoding with an 80% efficiency results in a 125-Mbaud signal.

Also the IEEE 802.5 encoding allows for only two control symbols: J and K. The 4b/5b encoding allows many more control symbols such as H, I, J, K, L, Q, R, S, and T. These additional control symbols are helpful with frame delimiting and line state indications.

IEEE 802.5 uses a master station on the ring to provide the clock and elasticity buffer. This is centralized clocking. The size of the elasticity buffer at the master station depends on the total clock skew that is possible around the ring. This limits the number of stations that can be put in the ring since each station results in a slight clock skew. At high speed, the pulses are smaller and therefore the allowable number of stations using centralized clocking would have been very small. Therefore, FDDI uses distributed clocking with each station providing its own clock and elasticity buffer, thereby allowing a large number of stations on the ring. Also, there is no need for a master station, which may be considered undesirable by some proponents of networking.

3.7 Summary

The ISO physical layer has been divided into two layers in FDDI. These are called PHY and PMD. PHY covers the medium independent part of the ISO physical layer. At this layer, only two adjacent stations on the ring can communicate. They do so by means of symbols.

At a station the MAC layer provides a symbol stream to the PHY layer, which encodes it and passes it to PMD, which then transmits it in a media-dependent form. PHY is defined in a media-independent manner and so the same PHY rules are used for all types of media: multimode fiber, single-mode fiber, copper, or SONET.

The five key functions of PHY are to provide coding, an elasticity buffer, smoothing, a repeat filter, and line state detection.

For transferring information, the data stream is divided into groups of 4 bits, which are called data symbols. Each data symbol is then mapped into 5 code bits using a 4b/5b code. This code is self-clocking, so additional facilities to transmit clock information are not required. Also, the code is efficient and provides a rich set of additional symbols that can be used for control.

If the clocks at two stations run at slightly different rates, the number of bits received at a station may be different from those transmitted. This problem is solved by storing the received bit in a FIFO system called an elasticity buffer. The standard allows for a clock rate variability of $\pm 0.005\%$. This results in the maximum frame length of 4500 bytes. Longer frames may result in elasticity buffer overflow.

Due to the addition and deletion of bits by the elasticity buffer, the size of the frame preamble may vary as the frames traverse the ring. A sequence of bit deletions may result in the preamble becoming too short or even disappearing. This is avoided by using a smoother, which adds idle symbols to short preambles and takes them away from long preambles, thereby smoothing the variation in preamble sizes.

A noise on the line may cause unexpected symbols to appear in the signal, resulting in receiver malfunction. This is avoided by replacing all unexpected symbols by a predefined symbol. This function, called a repeat filter, helps localize the effect of line noise.

The 4b/5b code used in FDDI provides a number of control symbols that can be used to indicate the status of the link. For example, a continuous stream of Q, H, H-Q, and I symbols is used to indicate quiet, halt, master, and idle line states, respectively.

3.8 Further Reading

The FDDI PHY is specified in ANSI X3.148-1988 or ISO 9314-1:1989.

The 4b/5b encoding and the logic behind its design are best described in the patent by Hamstra and Moulton (1985).

For discussions of clock recovery, see Ju and Jabbour (1989) and Annamalai (1988).

Li (1988) presents simulation results comparing symbol-wide and byte-wide implementations of the smoother.

Figure 3.3 has been adapted from Ju and Jabbour (1989).

3.9 Self-Test Exercises

Note: Some exercises have multiple correct answers. See Appendix D for answers.

3.1 How many bits can a properly functioning elasticity buffer add or delete between two frames?

a. 0
b. 1
c. 4.5
d. 5
e. 9
f. 10
g. No limit

3.2 What is the maximum number of bits inside a frame that can be deleted by the elasticity buffer if the clocks are functioning properly?

a. 0
b. 1
c. 4.5
d. 5
e. 9
f. 10
g. No limit

3.3 Allowing frames longer than 4500 bytes would require the FDDI standard to:

a. Not use crystals
b. Require higher quality crystals
c. Require shorter elasticity buffers

3.4 The FDDI frames are limited to 4500 bytes because:

a. Most frames would not like to stand behind a longer frame.
b. Longer frames may cause elasticity buffer errors.
c. Longer frames are unreliable.
d. Longer frames take longer to transmit.
e. It is a good round number.
f. All of the above.

3.5 Which of the following applies to an elasticity buffer?

a. It protects two stations from each other.
b. It prevents two frames from accidentally running into each other.
c. It is made of an elastic material.
d. It uses crystals.
e. It is used to buffer (store) frames.
f. None of the above.

3.6 Crystals are used in FDDI stations:

a. To provide a local clock.
b. To synchronize clocks.
c. To predict future bits.
d. For good luck.

3.7 A smoother smooths out variations in:

a. Pulse width
b. Pulse height
c. Clock frequency
d. Interframe gaps
e. Frame sizes

3.8 A smoother must add extra symbols if the interframe gap is:

a. 16
b. 4
c. 13
d. None of the above

CHAPTER **4**

Fundamentals of Optical Communication

To understand the operation of FDDI optical components and to justify various design decisions, you need a basic knowledge of how light signals propagate in fibers and how various electro-optic devices operate. These fundamental concepts are explained in this chapter and are used later in Chapters 5, 6, and 7, where the discussion specific to FDDI standards is presented. The discussion in this chapter is general in the sense that reading it will help you understand any fiber optic LAN, including fiber optic versions of IEEE 802.3/Ethernet or IEEE 802.5/token ring networks. All discussion of products available to implement an FDDI network has been postponed to Chapters 19 and 21. In particular, the wiring products, such as cables and connectors, are discussed in Chapter 19, while interconnection products, such as adapters, concentrators, bridges, and routers, are described in Chapter 21.

4.1 Components of an Optical Link

Figure 4.1 shows the optical components required for one-way communication between two stations. The electrical signal in the form of a square waveform is fed to a **driver** circuit, which controls a **source** of light. The light signal travels over the **fiber** to a light sensor (called a **detector**) that converts the light signal back to an electrical waveform, which is then amplified. The driver-source combination is called a **transmitter** and the detector-amplifier unit is called a **receiver**. **Connectors** are used at both ends of the fiber to connect it to the transmitter and receiver. If a piece of fiber is not long enough, two pieces can be permanently **spliced** together. Unlike the connector, a splice cannot be easily disconnected but it provides a better connection. To establish a two-way connection, two fibers are used between each pair of stations. Each station is equipped with a transmitter as well as a receiver, which usually come in a single package called a **transceiver**.

Next we explain some fundamental concepts about light waves and discuss issues involved in the selection of fibers, transmitters, receivers, and connectors.

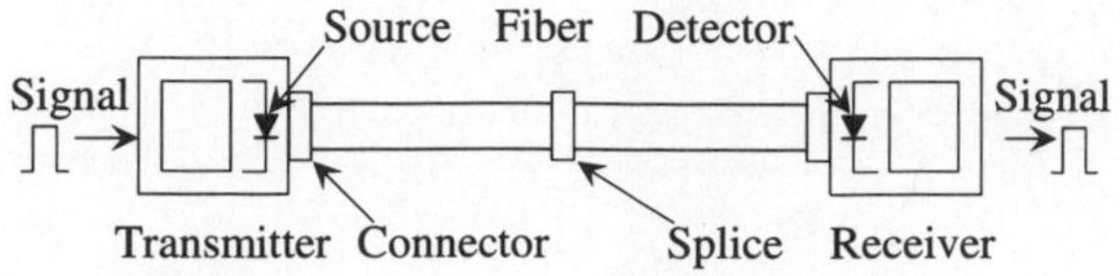

Figure 4.1 Optical components for communication between two neighboring stations.

4.2 Propagation of Light

Light consists of electromagnetic waves. These waves propagate in a manner similar to the waves you see when you throw a stone in a pond. The amplitude of the wave is a function of time as well as distance. Figure 4.2(a) shows the amplitude as a function of distance as seen at any particular instant in time. The distance between the peaks of successive waves is called the **wavelength**. Figure 4.2(b) shows the amplitude as a function of time at a particular point in space. The inverse of the interval between successive peaks at the same point is called the **frequency**. The product of the wavelength and the frequency is the speed with which the waves travel. When a wave moves from one type of medium to another, its frequency remains the same, but the wavelength and hence the speed changes. The wavelength depends on the medium. The values specified are those in the vacuum.

The preceding discussion about waves applies to all electromagnetic waves including those used for radio and television transmission and those used for x rays. Electrical current also consists of electromagnetic waves. A meter is officially defined (by the General Conference on Weights and Measures) as "the length of the path traveled by light in vacuum during a time interval of 1/299,792,458 of a second." Thus, by definition, light travels at a speed of 299,792,458 m/s, which is approximately 3×10^8 m/s or 300 m/μs.

Figure 4.3 shows a complete spectrum of electromagnetic waves. The wavelength is shown above the line and the corresponding frequency is shown below the line. In all cases, the product of wavelength and frequency is equal to 3×10^8 m/s. Normal house current has a frequency of 50 or 60 Hz. Radio waves have a frequency in the range of 200 kHz to 200 MHz. Television transmission uses waves with a frequency of 50 to 800 MHz. Satellite communication uses 4 to 9 GHz. Waves with frequencies higher than this are usually specified by their wavelength rather than frequency. The visible spectrum is from 380 to 770 nm (nanometers or 10^{-9}m). Different colors correspond to lights with different wavelengths. Red light has a wavelength of 700 nm and violet light 400 nm. The 50- to 400-nm wavelength range is known as the ultraviolet spectrum and the 700- to 100,000-nm

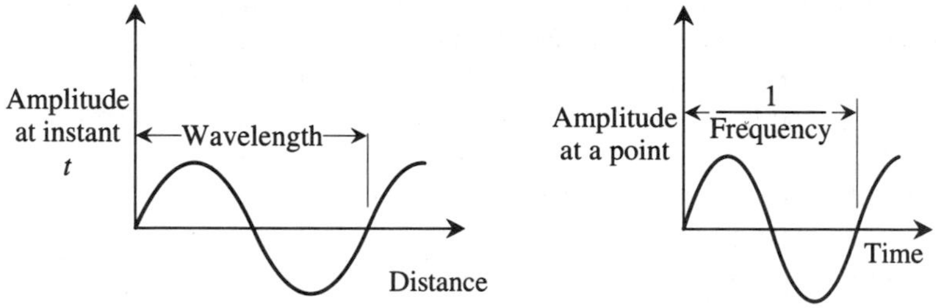

Figure 4.2 Wavelength and frequency.

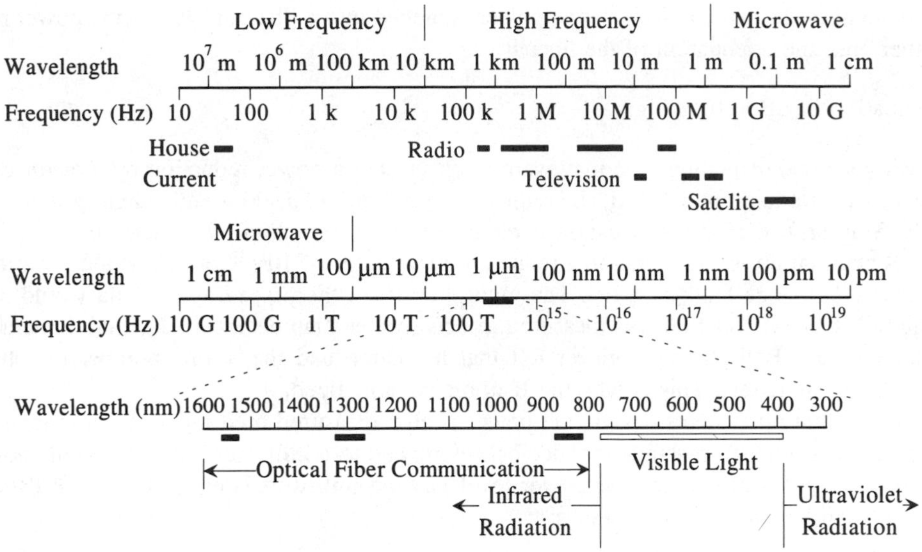

Figure 4.3 Electromagnetic spectrum.

range is known as the infrared spectrum. Most optical communication uses infrared light, which is invisible. Therefore, the fiber appears dark even when the light is traveling through it. Incidentally, do not try to look at it. Not only will the fiber appear dark, but afterward everything may appear dark since the light in the fiber could damage your eye, particularly if the fiber happens to be connected to a laser source.

The speed of light varies depending on the medium in which the light is traveling. In glass, the light travels at approximately 200 m/μs. The ratio of the light speed in the vacuum to that in the medium is called the **index of refraction** for that medium. Thus, the index of refraction of a glass in which light travels at a speed of 200 m/μs is 1.5. The index of refraction for the air is approximately 1, that is, light travels in air at almost the same speed as it does in the vacuum.

4.3 Attenuation

As light travels through a medium such as glass, its energy is absorbed or scattered by the medium and its intensity is reduced. After a certain distance, the light may become so feeble that it may not be sensed by any detector. This phenomenon is known as **attenuation** and relates the change in the pulse amplitude.

You are probably familiar with watts as the unit of power, which is how the power consumption of electrical devices is specified. The power levels used in optical communication are in the range of microwatts (μW).

The reduction in power is geometric. For example, after traveling 1 km in the fiber, the power of a 40-μW signal may reduce to half (20 μW). After another 1 km, it may become one-fourth (10 μW). It is much easier to do such calculations on a log scale (so that multiplication can be achieved by addition of log quantities). Therefore, communication engineers use a log scale to measure power and its attenuation. In general, if P_{in} is the power launched into a fiber and P_{out} is the power received at the other end, the attenuation of the fiber is:

$$\text{Attenuation in dB} = 10 \times \log_{10} \frac{P_{in}}{P_{out}}$$

To confirm your understanding, you may want to check that a power reduction by a factor of 100 is equivalent to an attenuation of 20 dB, and reduction by a factor of 1000 is equivalent to an attenuation of 30 dB. Similarly, a 10-dB attenuation is equivalent to a reduction by a factor of $10^{10/10}$ or 10, while 3-dB attenuation is equivalent to a reduction by a factor of $10^{3/10}$ or 2. The abbreviation "dB" stands for *decibel*—one-tenth of a bel. The multiplier 10 in the preceding formula would not have been required if the attenuation was measured in bels (rather than decibels). The unit is named after Alexander Graham Bell (Some engineer felt that his name had the wrong number of letters and shortened it by one letter). This is why the B in dB is capitalized.

In communication systems design, the power is also measured on a log scale. It is measured in dBm in place of watts; dBm stands for "decibel referenced to a *m*illiwatt." It simply tells how many decibels over a milliwatt a particular power level is. One milliwatt is equivalent to 0 dBm. Other power levels can be translated as follows:

$$\text{mW} = 10^{\text{dBm}/10} \quad \text{or} \quad \text{dBm} = 10 \times \log_{10} \text{mW}$$

Thus, 20 dBm is 100 mW, 46 dBm is 40 W, and -20 dBm is 10 μW.

The use of log scales makes it easier to design communication systems. For example, suppose a fiber has an attenuation of 2.5 dB/km. If a source with a launch power of -20 dBm and a detector requiring at least -31 dBm received power is used, the fiber loss cannot exceed 11 dB and so the fiber cannot be more than 4.4 km long. In practice, one would also need to allow the attenuation at the connectors and splices resulting in a shorter distance limit.

4.4 Modes

A fiber can be single mode or multimode. The definition of the term *mode* is rather complex. The easiest way to understand it is to consider modes as light rays that can propagate along the fiber or the paths that the light can take in the fiber. Strictly speaking, the geometric optics is insufficient to explain modes since the diameter of the medium and the wavelengths are of the same order of magnitude. But, unless you want to get into Maxwell's equations for electromagnetic fields, this is sufficient to provide an intuitive feel for all the issues we will encounter here. As shown in Figure 4.4, a single-mode fiber core is so thin (usually less than 10 μm) that only one ray—the one traveling along the axis—is propagated. All other rays are destroyed by their own reflections. A multimode fiber's core has a larger diameter (usually 50 to 100 μm). Several hundred modes (rays) can successfully enter and propagate along the fiber. A large number of modes reduces the bandwidth of the fiber as discussed in Section 4.6. First a formula for calculating the number of modes is given.

Figure 4.5 shows the cross section of a fiber. It consists of a core and a cladding, which have a slightly different index of refraction. The index of refraction of glass depends on the level of impurities in the silicon. By carefully controlling these impurities, any index close to 1.5 can be obtained. The cladding has a slightly lower index than the core. For example, the core may have an index of 1.48 while the cladding may have 1.46.

The figure also shows a ray of light entering the fiber at an angle θ to the axis of the fiber. If the angle θ is large, the ray enters the cladding (or is refracted into the cladding) and is lost forever.

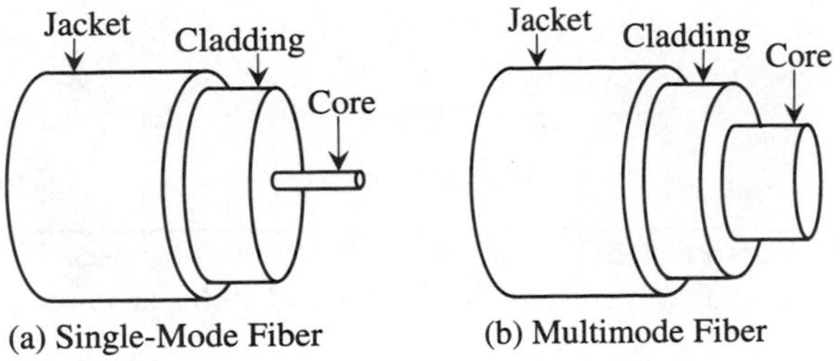

Figure 4.4 Single-mode and multimode fibers.

If the angle θ is small, the ray is reflected back into the core at the core-cladding surface and may be guided (or propagated) along the fiber. The maximum entrance angle θ_{max} over which the rays are not guided is given by

$$n \sin \theta_{max} = \sqrt{n_1^2 - n_2^2}$$

where n is the index of refraction of the air, n_1 is the index of refraction of the core, and n_2 is the index of refraction of the cladding. The quantity on the right-hand side of the preceding equation is also called the numerical aperture (**NA**):

$$\text{NA} = \sqrt{n_1^2 - n_2^2}$$

For example, a fiber with core and cladding indices of 1.48 and 1.46, respectively, has a numerical aperture of $\sqrt{1.48^2 - 1.46^2}$ or 0.24. The maximum entrance angle is $\sin^{-1} 0.24$ or 14°. All rays entering the fiber at an angle greater than 14 degrees will be lost into the cladding soon after entering the fiber.

The number of rays that enter the fiber at an angle less than the maximum entrance angle θ_{max} is enormous. However, most of these rays are reflected in such a manner that various reflections destroy each other due to their phases. Only a small finite number of rays have angles such that various reflections combine and continue to propagate. These constitute the modes of the fiber. Technically speaking, a **mode** is a pattern of electrical and magnetic fields, which is repeated every λ (wavelength) meters. Loosely speaking, the number of rays that enter and propagate along the fiber is called the number of modes. For a fiber with a fixed core index of n_1 and cladding index of n_2, the number of modes is approximately $V^2/2$ where V is the **normalized frequency** computed as

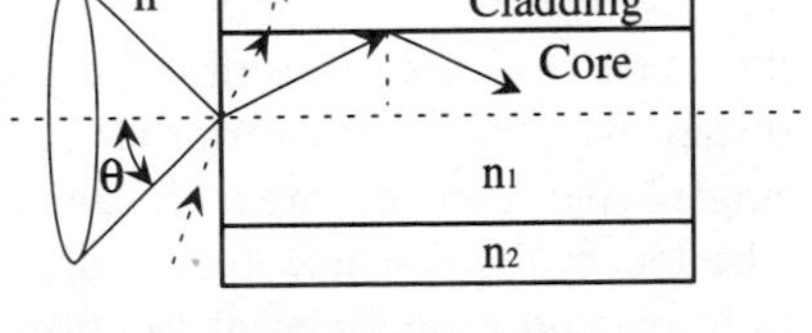

Figure 4.5 Cross section of a fiber.

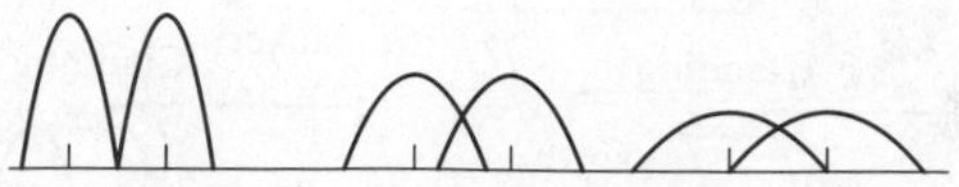

Figure 4.6 The increase in the width of pulses as they travel along the fiber is called dispersion.

follows:

$$V = \frac{2\pi a}{\lambda}\text{NA} \tag{4.1}$$

Here, a is the radius of the core and λ is the wavelength of the light. This formula is for step-index fibers. For graded-index fibers with parabolic index profiles (discussed in Section 4.7), the number of modes is $V^2/4$.

As an application of the preceding formula, consider a fiber with a core diameter of 62.5 μm and a source with a wavelength of 1300 nm. If the numerical aperture is 0.24, then the normalized frequency V is:

$$V = \frac{2 \times 3.14 \times (62.5 \times 10^{-6})/2}{1300 \times 10^{-9}} \times 0.24$$
$$= 36.61$$

and the number of modes is approximately $36.61^2/2$ or 669. If the fiber is graded-index, the number of modes is only about 334.

4.5 Dispersion

Due to attenuation, the amplitude of the light pulses becomes smaller as they travel through the fiber. In addition, the pulses also become wider as shown in Figure 4.6. This phenomenon of pulse-widening is known as **dispersion**. The width increases as the pulses travel farther, and after a certain distance two pulses may become so dispersed that they become indistinguishable. Thus, if the dispersion is high, the initial pulse separation (or width) should be high to be able to recognize the received pulses. This means that the number of pulses per second should be small, which in turn implies that the number of bits per second or the bandwidth should be small.

The two types of dispersion, modal dispersion or chromatic dispersion, are explained next.

4.6 Modal Dispersion

As discussed in Section 4.4, light modes traveling in a fiber correspond to different rays of lights. Different rays travel different distances. The ray traveling along the axis has to cover the least distance. Those traveling at an angle have to cover larger distances. The larger the angle at which the ray enters (and propagates), the longer the distance. Since all rays travel at the same speed, the different rays take different times to reach the other end of the fiber. For example, suppose we send an instantaneous pulse (impulse) of light into the fiber and it takes 100 ns for the axial rays to reach

Fiber Is Fattening

As shown in Figure 4.7, consider a magic fattening passageway, which makes people fatter and shorter. A tall and thin person entering the passageway comes out short and fat. The farther people travel in the passageway, the fatter and shorter they become. Different people would become indistinguishable if they become so short that they couldn't see each other. They would also find it impossible to exist if they became so fat that there were not enough space for them to stand next to each other without pinching their neighbors. Both of these phenomena would prevent a lot of people from traveling the passageway for a long distance.

A fiber is similar to this fattening passageway. If you send nice-crisp square pulses through a fiber, the pulses become shorter and wider as they travel. The decrease in the height is called attenuation and the increase in width is called dispersion. Both of these processes limit the distance over which a signal can be communicated over a fiber.

Figure 4.7 Fiber is like a fattening passageway. Travelers become fatter and shorter as they pass through the passageway.

the other end, while it takes 101 ns for the rays traveling at the maximum angle. At the receiving end, the light will be seen from $t = 100$ to $t = 101$. Thus the impulse has widened from a width of 0 to a width of 1 ns. Similarly, if we send a square pulse of, say, 4-ns duration, as shown in Figure 4.8, at the receiving end the light will be seen from $t = 100$ to $t = 105$. The pulse width increases from 4 to 5 ns. This increase in pulse width is called dispersion. This is just one of many reasons for the change in pulse width. In particular, this type of dispersion is called **modal dispersion** because it is caused by multiple modes.

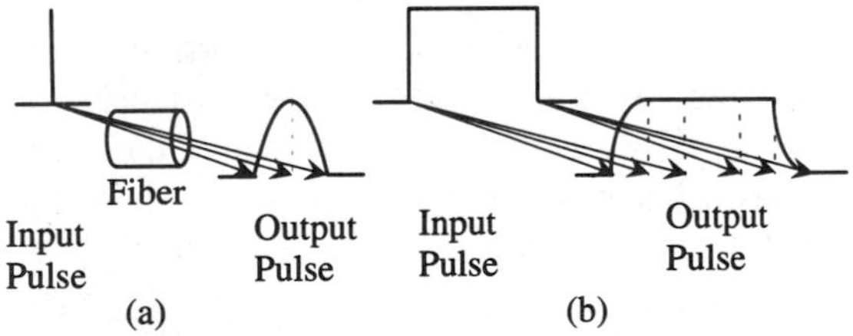

Figure 4.8 Pulse width increases due to different arrival times.

Figure 4.9 Modes of transportation.

Modes of light are analogous to modes of transportation. Figure 4.9 shows three modes of transportation—a truck, a plane, and a ship. Each of these modes travels at different speeds and also takes a different route. If cargo is divided and sent by multiple modes, the pieces of cargo will arrive at the destination at different times. This is modal dispersion. If pieces of different types of cargo cannot be easily distinguished, the rate at which successive types of cargo can be sent will be limited because we will have to ensure that the start of the second type of cargo arrives *only* after the end of the first type of cargo has arrived. Thus, modal dispersion limits the rate at which successive types of cargo can be dispatched. In other words, it limits the bandwidth.

Most communication components including the transmitter, fiber, and the receivers can be modeled as filters such that there is a frequency band that they allow to pass while blocking others. The width of this frequency band is called *bandwidth.* The modal dispersion limits the bandwidth of the fiber. The limit thus imposed is called *modal bandwidth.* The bandwidth decreases linearly with the length of the fiber. Therefore, the modal bandwidth is specified as a bandwidth-distance product. A fiber with a 500 MHz-km modal bandwidth will have a bandwidth of 500 MHz at 1 km or a bandwidth of 100 MHz at 5 km.

There are many ways to reduce or avoid modal dispersion. It is easy to see from Equation (4.1) that one way to reduce the number of modes is to reduce a—the radius of the fiber. The fundamental mode is always guided for all values of normalized frequency V and all wavelengths. The next order mode is guided only if V is larger than 2.405. For lower values of V, the fiber becomes a single-mode fiber. For example, for a fiber with core and cladding indices of 1.480 and 1.475, respectively, and a core diameter of 8 μm, using a wavelength of 1300 nm, we have:

$$V = 2.3487$$

Since V is less than 2.405, this fiber would allow only single-mode propagation at 1300 nm.

Notice from Equation (4.1) that V and hence the number of modes depends on the wavelength λ, thus a fiber may be single mode at one wavelength but multimode at a lower wavelength.

4.7 Graded-Index and Step-Index Fibers

The main reason for modal dispersion is that different rays arriving at the receiver have traveled different distances. Rays traveling along the axis travel the least distance while those traveling at an angle travel a larger distance. If we could somehow change the speed of rays such that those traveling a longer distance travel faster while those traveling a shorter distance travel slower, we could make all the rays arrive at the receiver at the same time and thereby eliminate (or reduce) the modal dispersion.

Recall that the speed of light in a medium depends on its index of refraction. A ray traveling in a medium with a lower index travels faster. Thus, if the index of the fiber core is varied such that the index decreases as we move radially away from the axis, it is possible to reduce modal dispersion.

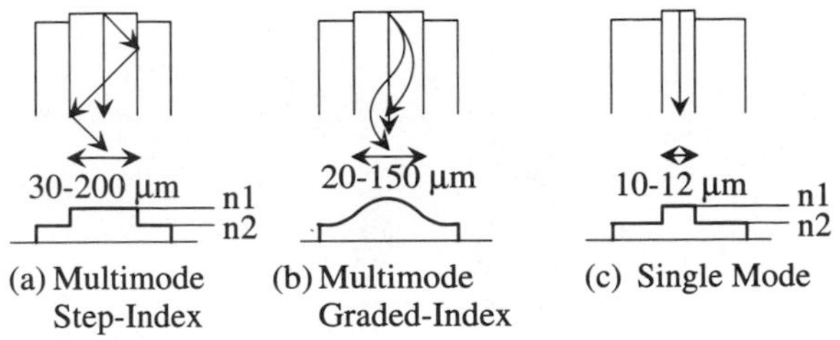

Figure 4.10 Index profiles for step-index and graded-index fibers.

Such a fiber is called a **graded-index** fiber and is shown in Figure 4.10(b). The core index decreases parabolically, and the change at the core-cladding boundary is rather smooth. Figure 4.10(a) shows a normal multimode fiber. Here, the index takes a step jump as we move from the core to the cladding. Such a fiber is therefore called **step-index** fiber.

If the core diameter is reduced, the number of modes in the fiber decreases and eventually the fiber becomes a single-mode fiber as shown in Figure 4.10(c). Thus, we have three types of fibers: multimode step-index, multimode graded-index, and single-mode step-index. Multimode step-index fibers are the easiest to manufacture. The core diameter is typically 30 to 200 μm. The thick core allows a large power to be easily launched into the fiber, thereby allowing the use of cheap LED sources (discussed in Section 4.9). However, modal dispersion limits the use of such a fiber to a bandwidth-distance product of 20 MHz-km, that is, 20 km at 1 MHz, or 10 km at 2 MHz, or 5 km at 4 MHz, etc.

A multimode graded-index fiber is slightly more difficult to manufacture than a step-index fiber. However, this fiber has the advantage of allowing a large power to be launched with cheap LED sources due to its thick core. Also the reduced modal dispersion allows it to be used up to a bandwidth-distance product of 1 GHz-km.

Because of its thin core, a single-mode step-index fiber is slightly more difficult to splice and connect than a multimode fiber. Due to its small cross-sectional area, the source must emit a highly focused beam of light, otherwise most of the light will be lost in space and only a small fraction will be propagated. For this reason most (surface-emitting) LEDs cannot be used effectively with a single-mode fiber. Either edge-emitting LEDs or laser sources, which are an order of magnitude more expensive, must be used. This type of fiber allows a high bandwidth-distance product of up to 1000 GHz-km. This limit is due to chromatic dispersion as discussed next.

4.8 Chromatic Dispersion

In single-mode fibers, although there is no modal dispersion, the light pulses are still widened due to chromatic dispersion.

In most optical fibers, the velocity of an optical pulse depends slightly on its wavelength. Since the sources emit a range of wavelengths, different wavelength components of a pulse may arrive at the receiver at different times and hence the pulse may become wider. This change in pulse width is called **chromatic dispersion**. The term *chromatic* implies the fact that the dispersion depends on the color (or wavelength) of light. The chromatic dispersion consists of three components: material dispersion, waveguide dispersion, and profile dispersion.

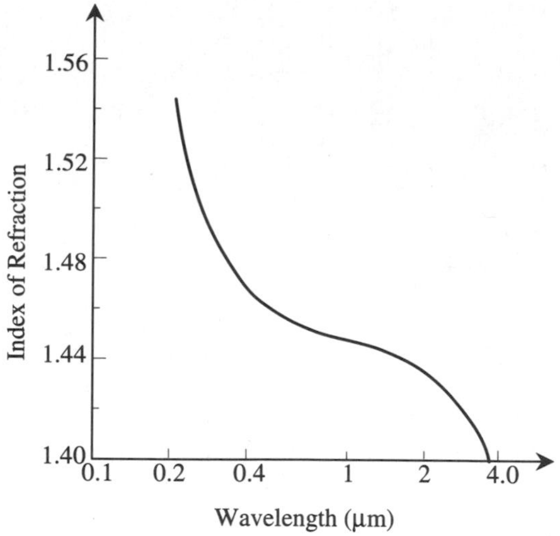

Figure 4.11 Refractive index as a function of wavelength.

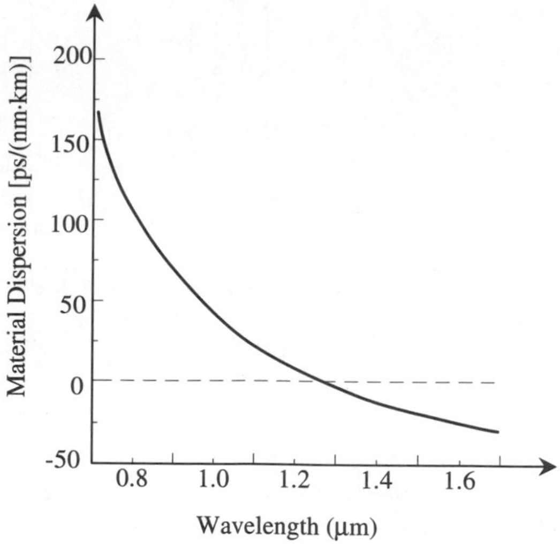

Figure 4.12 Material dispersion as a function of wavelength.

Material dispersion is caused by the fact that the refractive index of a material is a function of the wavelength (see Figures 4.11 and 4.12). This dispersion is proportional to the source bandwidth and is expressed as picoseconds per kilometer of fiber per nanometer of spectrum (ps/km/nm or ps/km-nm). For silica glasses, the material dispersion becomes very small near 1270 nm. It can even be negative and offset other dispersion mechanisms.

Waveguide dispersion is so called because it depends on the geometry of the waveguide (fiber). In step-index multimode fibers, both material and waveguide dispersions are smaller than the modal dispersion. In other fibers, waveguide dispersion becomes important particularly near the zero material dispersion region. In fibers, the light spot extends slightly into the cladding. A longer wavelength causes increased spot diameter. Thus, the effective index of refraction is somewhere between the index of the core and that of the cladding. A change in wavelength changes the spot diameter, which in turn changes the effective refractive index. The waveguide dispersion is also measured in ps/km-nm and is typically -2 ps/km-nm at 1300 nm. This shifts the zero dispersion point to a higher wavelength. In dispersion-shifted fibers, this phenomenon is utilized to move the zero dispersion point to the 1500-nm region. In these fibers, a much larger waveguide dispersion is created by segmenting the core of the fiber. Thus, a cancellation of the material dispersion can be accomplished at one or more wavelengths.

Profile dispersion is caused by the fact that the core and cladding materials are different. Therefore, the dependence of the group velocity on wavelength is different in the two materials. This dispersion is also measured in ps/km-nm. It becomes an important design parameter for graded-index multimode fibers, because the profile can be optimized for only one wavelength. The profile changes with wavelength and causes profile dispersion. In single-mode fibers, profile dispersion is treated as a part of the waveguide dispersion.

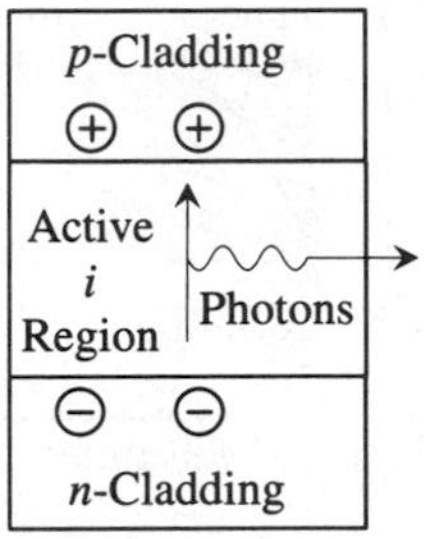

Figure 4.13 Cross section of a diode.

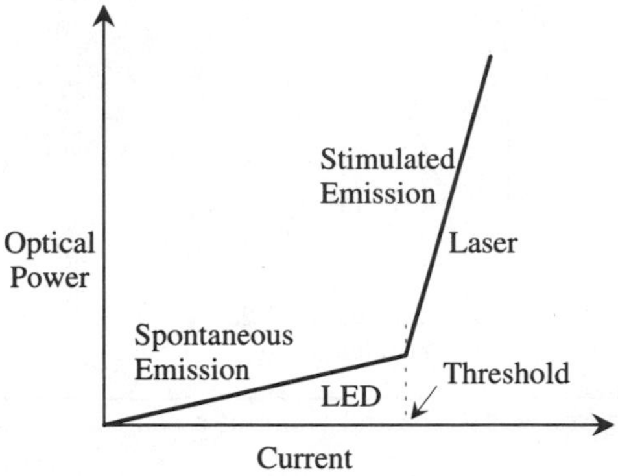

Figure 4.14 After a certain threshold, the optical power increases sharply due to stimulated emissions.

4.9 Light Sources: LED Versus Laser Diodes

The light source is the most important (and most expensive) component of the transmitter. It affects the transmitter's performance as well as cost by an order of magnitude. Two basic choices are available for sources: light-emitting diodes (LEDs) and laser diodes. The key characteristics of these types and when one is more appropriate than the other are the topics of this section.

Both LEDs and laser diodes operate on the same basic principle. As shown in Figure 4.13, in its simplest form, a diode consists of three layers of semiconductors called *p*-cladding, active region, and *n*-cladding. The *n*-cladding is rich in electrons (negatively charged) while the *p*-cladding is rich in holes (positively charged). When a current is applied to the diode, electrons and holes combine and the excess energy is emitted as photons (light quantums). As the injected current is increased, the amount of light emitted increases. At first the light increases slowly and the diode is said to be in a *spontaneous-emission regime*. After a certain threshold, the light output increases dramatically as shown in Figure 4.14. This is because the photons generated by electron-hole recombination stimulate even further recombination. The diode is, therefore, said to be in the *stimulated-emission regime*. LEDs operate in the spontaneous-emission regime, while laser diodes operate in the stimulated-emission regime.

The name laser (even though it's spelled with lowercase letters) is actually an acronym for *l*ight *a*mplifier using *s*timulated *e*mission of *r*adiation.

The performance and cost considerations in the selection of LEDs versus laser diodes are as follows:

1. *Power Output*: Larger power output is generally better since it allows transmission over a longer distance. LEDs typically generate tens of microwatts of power, which is sufficient for transmission over a few kilometers. Laser diodes generate a hundred times more power—typically in milliwatts—which allows transmission over several tens of kilometers.
2. *Spectral Width*: The light generated by a source typically has a range of wavelengths. Figure 4.15(a) shows the typical shape of the power versus wavelength curve for an LED. The

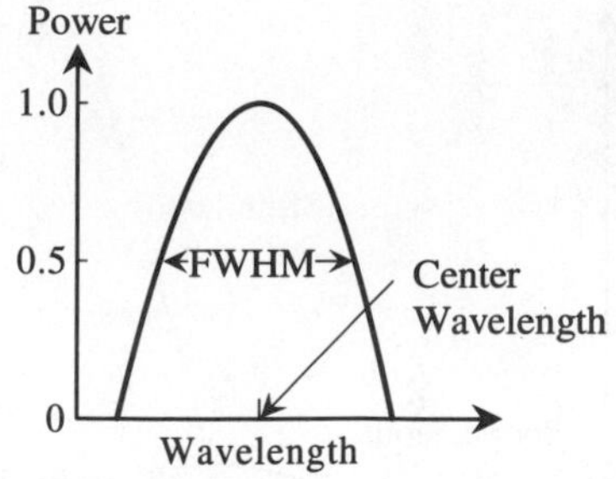

Figure 4.15 Spectral width of a source.

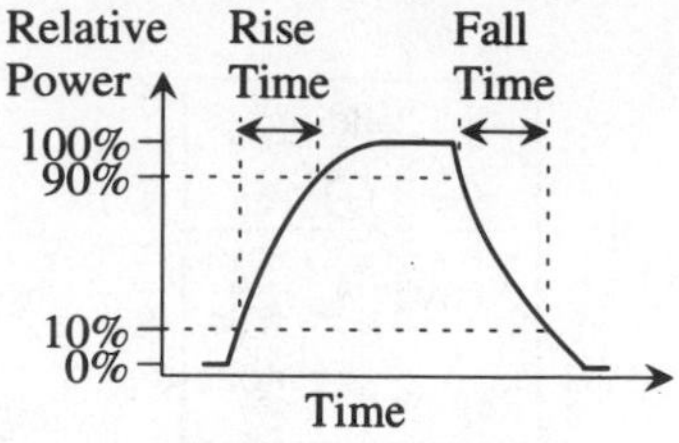

Figure 4.16 Rise and fall times.

difference in the wavelengths at which the power is one-half of (3 dB below) the peak power is called the spectral width of the source. The spectral width so measured is said to be the **full-width at half-maximum (FWHM)**. The average of the two wavelengths at which the power is one-half of the peak power is called the **center wavelength**. For a symmetrical spectrum, the peak power occurs at the center wavelength.

Surface-emitting LEDs typically have a spectral width of 100 to 200 nm. Light rays with different wavelengths travel at slightly different speeds and therefore cause chromatic dispersion (see Section 4.8). A smaller spectral width is therefore considered better. Edge-emitting LEDs have a spectral width of 50 to 100 nm, while laser diodes have a spectral width of only 2 to 5 nm. These types of sources are, therefore, used for higher bandwidth-distance applications.

3. *Rise/Fall Time*: To transmit optical pulses, the sources are continually turned on and off. Ideally, the state change should be instantaneous so that a perfect square wave is produced. In practice, the sources take time to reach the full-power level from the zero-power level. The time for the output power to rise from 10% of the peak to 90% of the peak is called the **rise time** (see Figure 4.16). For LEDs, the rise time is of the order of 3 to 20 ns, while for laser diodes it is in the 0.5- to 2-ns range. Thus, laser diodes are faster and can be used to produce narrower pulses for higher bandwidth applications.

The fiber dispersion as well as the source rise time affect the rate at which bits can be sent. In other words, they jointly determine the bandwidth of the channel. In fact, their effects can be traded off against each other. A lower rise time source combined with a more dispersive medium will give the same bandwidth as a higher rise time source with a less dispersive medium. The quantitative relationship between the rise time and bandwidth is explained later in Sections 4.12 and 20.7.

While the rise time measures the speed with which a source can turn on from an off state, the **fall time** measures the speed with which the source can turn off from the on state. It is the time for the output power to fall from 90% of the peak to 10% of the peak. Generally, rise and fall time values are similar but slightly different. The fall times for LEDs and laser diodes are in the same range as the rise times.

4. *Coupling Efficiency*: The fraction of the power generated by a source that can be launched into the fiber core is called the coupling efficiency. It depends on the connector used, the diameter of the fiber core, and on the spatial distribution of power emitted by the source. Much of the power that is emitted at a wide angle to the fiber core is lost, as shown in Figure 4.17(a). As

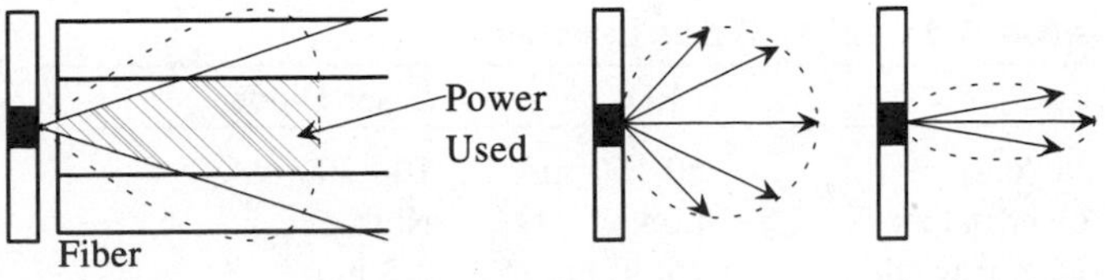

Figure 4.17 Amount of power transmitted into the fiber depends on the spatial distribution of power generated by the source.

shown in that figure, the power emitted from LEDs is generally less focused than that from laser diodes. Thus, laser diodes provide a higher coupling efficiency than LEDs.

5. *Failure Rate*: Because LEDs need simpler driving circuits and run at a lower power than laser diodes, LEDs are less prone to failure.
6. *Safety*: The power from laser diodes is not only high but also very focused. Such a concentration of energy can damage the retina of a human eye. Since the wavelength used in communication applications is in the invisible wavelength, it is not possible to tell by looking at a fiber whether it is lighted or not. Therefore, one should avoid looking directly at the fiber end.

   Government safety regulations, for example, those of the U.S. Food and Drug Administration (FDA), require access control to equipment that uses high-power laser transmitters. Only trained and certified personnel are permitted access. This has lead some manufacturers of communication equipment to use lower power laser sources, which are considered safe for general access although they limit the distance of communication. Laser safety is discussed further in Section 19.8.
7. *Fiber Type*: Single-mode fiber has a very narrow core and therefore it requires a highly focused laser diode. LEDs cannot be used with single-mode fibers for any useful distance. Multimode fibers can use either LEDs or laser diodes. However, cost considerations discussed next explain why LEDs and multimode fibers are the popular choice today for LAN applications.
8. *Cost*: Laser diodes are an order of magnitude more expensive than LEDs. The cost difference is mainly due to packaging, which includes drive circuits. The prices of laser diodes are decreasing as fast as the volume of their usage increases. The price difference between packaged LEDs and laser diodes is so great that all other factors become insignificant. Most people use LEDs unless distance is very long. In fact, this is also the reason for using multimode fibers because lower cost LEDs generally do not permit the use of single-mode fibers. Laser diodes with single-mode fibers are used for longer distances. The choice of the source dictates the choice of the fiber.

The LED versus laser diode discussion is summarized in Table 4.1. Laser diodes are better than LEDs in most performance considerations. They provide more power, narrower spectral width, a fast rise time, and better coupling efficiency than LEDs. The high cost is the key consideration against laser diodes in addition to lower reliability and safety. Today, LEDs and multimode fibers are a reasonable choice for short links. Laser diodes and single-mode fiber can be justified only for long distances or higher data rates. In the near future, the cost of laser diodes is expected to drop significantly and the reliability is expected to improve. At that point, we can then expect to be able to use single-mode fibers in all wiring.

Table 4.1 LEDs Versus Laser Diodes

Issue	LED	Laser Diode
Bias current	50-150 mA	100-500 mA
Power output	Low	High
Spectral width	25-40 nm	2-5 nm
Rise/fall time	3-20 ns	0.5-2 ns
Bit rate	Lower	Higher
Coupling efficiency	Medium	High
Fiber type	Multimode	Single-mode (generally)
Failure rate	Lower	Higher
Safety	Safe	Unsafe if high power
Cost	Low	High

4.10 Light Detectors: PIN Versus APD

At the receiving end, a photodiode is used to convert the light into electrical current. In optical communications, two types of detectors are used: PINs and APDs. The principle of operation of these photodiodes and a comparison of their characteristics are presented in this section.

The principle of operation of a detector is similar, although complementary, to that of a source. The PIN photodiode consists of a sandwich of a *p*-doped semiconductor and an *n*-doped semiconductor separated by an intrinsic (actually very lightly *n*-doped) region as shown in Figure 4.18. The name *PIN* stands for the types of doping of the three layers. The *p*-region has an excess of positively charged carriers (holes). The *n*-region has an excess of negatively charged carriers (electrons). In normal operation, a bias voltage is applied across the device so that the *i*-region is fully depleted of the carriers and the current flowing through the circuit is almost zero. When the light falls on the intrinsic region, the incident photons excite electrons in the semiconductor material. The electrons absorb the energy and move from the valence band to the conduction band. This process generates

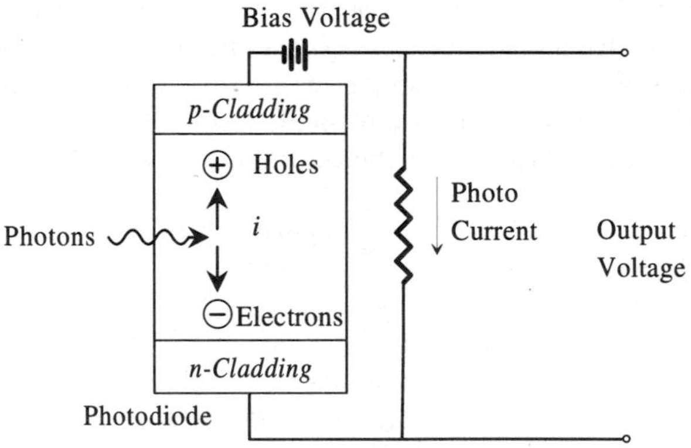

Figure 4.18 A PIN diode.

Table 4.2 Comparison of PIN Diodes and Avalanche Photodiodes

Characteristics	PIN	APD
1. Responsivity	0.5-0.7 μA/μW	30-80 μA/μW
2. Bias voltage	10 V	100+ V
3. Temperature sensitivity	Less	More
4. Availability	1300-nm PIN diodes easily available	Mostly 850 nm
5. Cost	Less	More

electron-hole pairs. These charge carriers are called **photocarriers**. As the carriers flow through the region some electron-hole pairs recombine and disappear. Those that remain reach the junction and give rise to a current flow in the external circuit. This current is called **photocurrent**.

The goodness of a photodiode is measured by the amount of current generated for a given power. It is called **responsivity** and is measured in microamperes per microwatt (μA/μW). A typical value is 0.45 μA/μW for a germanium PIN photodiode at 1300 nm.

Avalanche photodiodes (APDs) are similar to PIN diodes except that the photocarriers are passed through a region where a very high electric field is present. In this field, they gain enough energy to generate more electron-hole pairs by collision. The newly created carriers also gain energy, collide, and generate even more carriers. This phenomenon is known as the **avalanche effect**. It results in a very high current. Depending on the voltage, the avalanche effect may result in a current of 10 to 100 times the photocurrent. APDs, therefore, have a very high responsivity, for instance, 30 to 80 μA/μW.

Although avalanche photodiodes have better responsivity than PIN photodiodes, they present a number of problems. First, the bias voltage can be in the range of 100 V or more. Such high voltages not only present safety problems but also require bulkier power supplies. PIN photodiodes with bias voltages of 10 V are preferred by most electronic circuit designers. The avalanche photodiodes are more sensitive to room temperature than PIN photodiodes. Most avalanche photodiodes are made from silicon, which is suitable for 850-nm operation. For higher wavelengths, germanium and other materials are required but they have limited ionization rates and hence limited avalanche gains. Thus, avalanche photodiodes generally operate at 850 nm. For the 1300-nm window, avalanche photodiodes have limited availability and hence a higher cost, while PIN photodiodes are easily available at a much lower cost.

The PIN photodiode versus avalanche photodiode debate is summarized in Table 4.2. The conclusion is that PIN photodiodes are to be preferred except for their lower responsivity.

4.11 Connectors

Connectors are used to join a fiber with a source, detector, or another fiber. If a permanent bond between two fibers is desired, the fibers may be **spliced** together as described later in Section 19.6. If a demountable connection is required, a connector is used. The connectors consist of a receptacle (the female part) and a plug (the male part). The receptacle is attached to a transceiver and the plug is attached to both ends of a fiber cable. Incidentally, the FDDI standard connector is also called an FDDI media interface connector or **FDDI MIC**.

The key requirements for connector design are as follows:

1. *Low Loss*: A connector should provide low-loss coupling. While only one source and one detector are used per link, many connectors may be used in a link. Thus, connector loss reduces the loss budget for the fiber and hence the distance. The loss allowance per connector is generally 1 dB or less.
2. *Ease of Connection*: Untrained users should be able to connect and disconnect devices easily without damaging the connector or devices. In particular, it is important that the fiber connected to a transmitter be connected to a receiver at the other end and vice versa.
3. *Reliability of Connection*: A loose connection may vibrate and cause bit errors. The connector should have a very low bit error rate. This is particularly important for use in manufacturing plants where floor vibrations are common. The connection should be tight. Other environmental conditions such as humidity, temperature, and dust should also have a minimal effect on the connector operation.
4. *Simple*: Simplicity results in lower cost. It should be possible to connect any cable to any device with as few types of connectors as possible. It is desirable that all connectors have the same precise geometry.

The two major classes of connectors are simplex and duplex. A simplex connector connects only single fibers while a duplex connector allows for connection of both fibers of a link. Since all FDDI optical links consist of a transmitting and a receiving fiber, one duplex connector or two simplex connectors are required to make a two-way connection. Figure 4.19 shows a number of optical connectors. Of these, the first four are simplex; the last one is a duplex connector. The advantage

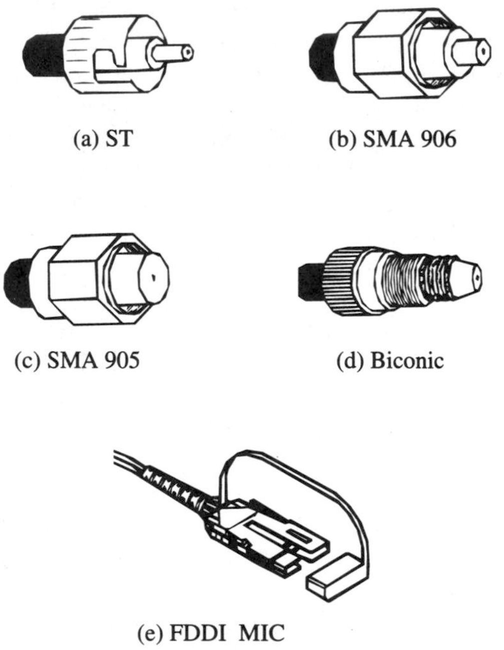

Figure 4.19 Optical fiber connectors.

of a duplex connector is that it can be keyed so that a transmitting fiber cannot be connected by mistake to another transmitting fiber. However, two simplex connectors are cheaper than one duplex connector. Therefore, many users prefer a pair of simplex connectors instead. These connectors are coded so that the transmitting and receiving fibers can be distinguished. The proponents of simplex connectors point out that for many applications, such as in wiring closets, only trained professionals have access to the connectors and once connected correctly the frequency of changes is very low. For such applications, the savings obtained by simplex connectors justify the slight risk of misconnection. For other applications, such as for wall outlets in offices, duplex connectors are required since the connections will be handled by untrained users.

4.12 Bandwidth

When designing communication systems, various components of the system, such as the transmitter, fiber, and receiver, can be modeled as filters that allow signals of certain frequencies to pass through while blocking others. The bandwidth of a component is simply the width of the frequency band that passes successfully through the component. The key problem with this definition is that the gain (or loss) versus frequency characteristics of most components is not rectangular and, therefore, it is difficult to decide which frequencies are *successfully* passing and which are not. The frequency response generally follows an inverse-U shape, which is close to a Gaussian curve. One can choose to define success as 70% of the maximum, 60% of the maximum, or 50% of the maximum. This leads to several different values of bandwidth for the same component. These different bandwidths and their relationships to bit rate are the topic of this section.

The Gaussian shape of the frequency response makes modeling the component easy. If a Gaussian-shaped pulse passes through such a component, it retains the Gaussian shape at the output. If an impulse (zero-width pulse) is injected through such a system, the output is Gaussian shaped. Although, the pulses used for communication are rectangular, Gaussian-shaped pulses are used in analysis because a Gaussian-shaped pulse (in the time domain) has a Gaussian-shaped frequency spectrum.

If a pulse has a Gaussian shape in the time domain, its optical power $p(t)$ at time t is given by:

$$p(t) = p(0)e^{-t^2/2\sigma^2} \tag{4.2}$$

The parameter σ determines the shape (breadth) of the curve. This is shown in Figure 4.20. The Fourier transform of this function (shown in Figure 4.21) is also Gaussian:

$$P(f) = P(0)e^{-2\pi^2 f^2 \sigma^2} \tag{4.3}$$

Based on these two functions, a number of characteristics for the signal and components can be defined:

- *rms Pulse Width*: The **root mean square (rms)** pulse width is simply 2σ:

  rms pulse width $= 2\sigma$

  For a Gaussian pulse, the power level at $t = \sigma$ is $1/\sqrt{e}$ or 0.606 times the peak value.
- *FWHM Pulse Width*: FWHM stands for full-width at half-maximum. The FWHM pulse width is the time interval between the instants at which power is just one-half of the maximum [$p(t)$ is $\frac{1}{2}p(0)$]. This value can be shown to be:

  FWHM pulse width $= 2\sqrt{2\ln 2}\sigma = 2.355\sigma$

  FWHM is sometimes called **full-duration at half-maximum (FDHM)**.

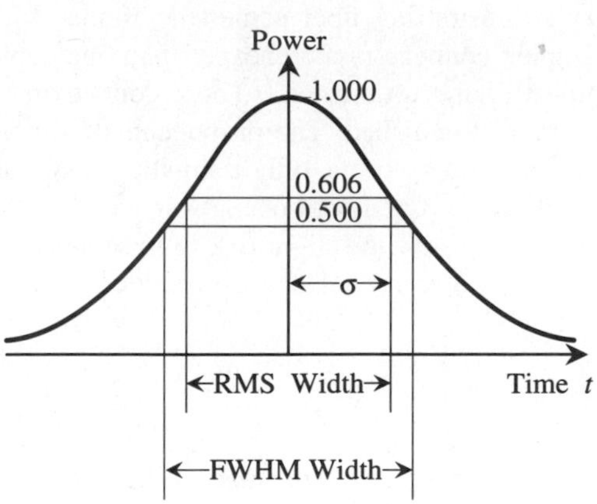

Figure 4.20 A Gaussian pulse in the time domain.

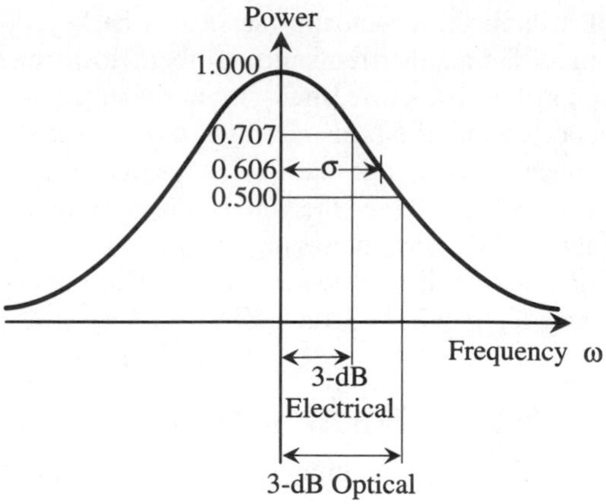

Figure 4.21 A Gaussian response in the frequency domain.

- *3-dB Optical Bandwidth*: This is the frequency at which the optical power is 3 dB below the maximum. Three decibels in log scale is equivalent to a power reduction by a factor of 2 in the linear scale. Thus, the power at the two points is just one-half of the maximum. With Equation (4.3), we can show that:

$$\text{3-dB optical bandwidth} = \frac{\sqrt{\ln 2}}{\sqrt{2}\pi\sigma} = \frac{0.187}{\sigma}$$

$$= \frac{2\ln 2}{\pi(\text{FWHM pulse width})} = \frac{0.441}{\text{FWHM pulse width}}$$

- *3-dB Electrical Bandwidth*: While analyzing a signal before the source or after the receiver, the signal bandwidth is measured by the frequency characteristics of the electrical power. At the receiver, the electrical current level of a signal is proportional to its optical power level. But the electrical power is proportional to the square of the current. The 3-dB electrical bandwidth is the frequency at which the electrical power is 3 dB below the maximum (that is, one-half of the maximum). At this point, the optical power is 1.5 dB below the maximum (that is, $1/\sqrt{2}$ of the maximum). Using Equation (4.3), the 3-dB electrical bandwidth can be shown to be:

$$\text{3-dB electrical bandwidth} = \frac{\sqrt{\ln 2}}{2\pi\sigma} = \frac{0.133}{\sigma}$$

$$= \frac{\sqrt{2}\ln 2}{\pi(\text{FWHM pulse width})} = \frac{0.312}{\text{FWHM pulse width}}$$

Notice that the 3-dB optical bandwidth can also be called the 6-dB electrical bandwidth.

$$\text{3-dB optical bandwidth} = 1.41 \times \text{3-dB electrical bandwidth}$$

- *rms Spectral Width*: Optical engineers prefer to use wavelengths instead of frequency when analyzing the power spectrum of a signal. As shown in Figure 4.22, the power spectrum can

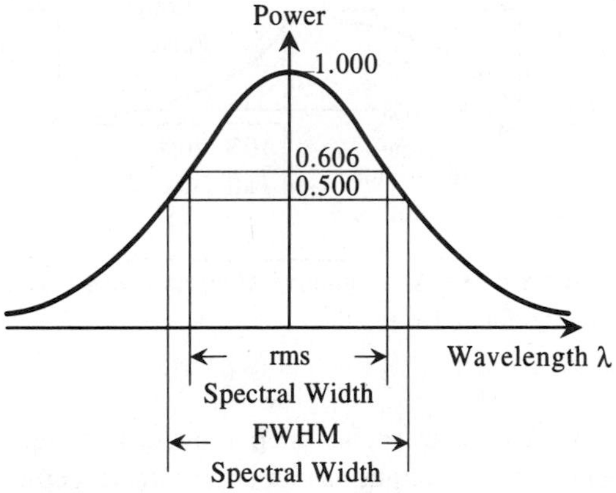

Figure 4.22 A Gaussian power spectrum.

also be approximated by a Gaussian function:

$$P(\lambda) = P(\lambda_c)e^{\{-[(\lambda-\lambda_c)^2]/2\sigma_\lambda^2\}}$$

Here, λ_c is the central wavelength. The parameter σ_λ determines the shape (breadth) of the spectrum. The rms spectral width of the source is given by $2\sigma_\lambda$.

- *FWHM Spectral Width*: The difference of the two wavelengths at which the power is one-half of the maximum is called the FWHM spectral width of the source. As shown in Figure 4.22, the FWHM spectral width is related to the rms spectral width as follows:

$$\begin{aligned}\text{FWHM spectral width} &= 2\sqrt{2\ln 2}\sigma_\lambda \\ &= 2.355\sigma_\lambda \\ &= 1.177 \times \text{rms spectral width}\end{aligned}$$

or, equivalently:

$$\text{rms spectral width} = 0.849 \times \text{FWHM spectral width}$$

If a source has a Gaussian spectral response, then its rms spectral width is 0.849 times the FWHM spectral width. Most LEDs and laser sources do not have a purely Gaussian spectral response and have rms widths of 0.850 to 0.950 times the FWHM spectral width. A multiplicative factor of 0.9 is used in practice.

- *Bit Rate*: The bit rate of a signal is measured in bits per second and is different from the bandwidth that is measured in hertz. Depending on the coding used, the system bandwidth required to carry a signal may be more than, equal to, or less than the bit rate. The minimum bandwidth needed to reproduce a signal faithfully is called the **Nyquist bandwidth**. With NRZI encoding, each cycle of the signal consists of two bit durations (see Figure 8.5). Therefore, the minimum required bandwidth is one-half of the bit rate.

$$\text{Nyquist bandwidth} = \frac{1}{2}\text{Bit rate for NRZI} \tag{4.4}$$

Given the FDDI code bit rate of 125 Mbps, the Nyquist bandwidth is 62.5 MHz.

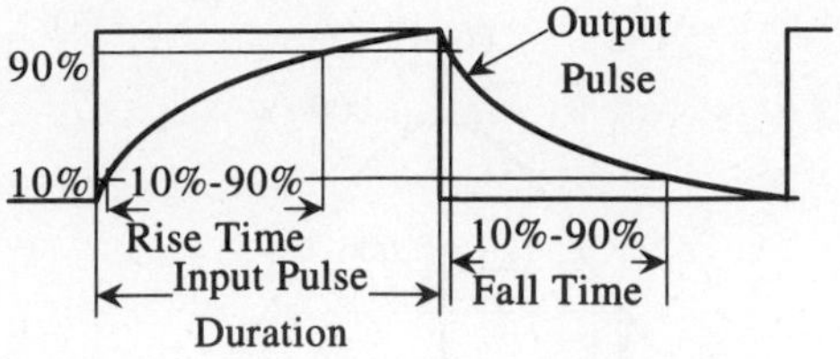

Figure 4.23 A cumulative Gaussian response to rectangular pulse input.

- *10% to 90% Rise Time*: If a square pulse (step function) is input into a component whose impulse response is Gaussian, the output has an approximate cumulative Gaussian [also called error function erf(t)] shape as shown in Figure 4.23. The time interval between the two instants at which power is 10% and 90% of the maximum is called 10%-90% rise time. Using Equation (4.2), the rise time can be shown to be:

$$\begin{aligned}\text{10\%-90\% rise time} &= \left[erf^{-1}(0.9) - erf^{-1}(0.1)\right]\sigma = [1.282 + 1.282]\sigma \\ &= 2.564\sigma \\ &= 1.089(\text{FWHM pulse width}) \\ &= \frac{0.340}{\text{3-dB electrical bandwidth}} \\ &= \frac{0.480}{\text{3-dB optical bandwidth}}\end{aligned}$$

If a link consists of n component in series, the frequency response of the link is simply the product of component frequency responses (Fourier transforms):

$$P_{\text{link}}(f) = P_1(f) \times P_2(f) \times \cdots \times P_n(f)$$

If component frequency responses are Gaussian, the link response is also Gaussian. If σ_i is the shape parameter for the ith component, the shape parameter σ for the link is given by:

$$\sigma_{\text{link}}^2 = \sigma_1^2 + \sigma_2^2 + \cdots + \sigma_n^2$$

The rise times are proportional to σ's. Therefore, if t_i is the rise time contribution of the ith component, the total rise time is given by:

$$t_{\text{link}}^2 = t_1^2 + t_2^2 + \cdots + t_n^2$$

The bandwidths are inversely proportional to σ's. Therefore, if B_i is the bandwidth of the ith component, the combined bandwidth is given by:

$$\frac{1}{B_{\text{link}}^2} = \frac{1}{B_1^2} + \frac{1}{B_2^2} + \cdots \frac{1}{B_n^2}$$

The following example illustrates an application of some of the preceding formulas to FDDI link design.

Example 4.1 Consider the problem of designing an optical link to transmit 125-Mbps NRZI encoded signal.

Since the link consists of a source, fiber, and a receiver, the link bandwidth is given by:

$$B_{\text{link}}^{-2} = B_{\text{source}}^{-2} + B_{\text{fiber}}^{-2} + B_{\text{receiver}}^{-2}$$

Using Equation (4.4), the Nyquist bandwidth is 62.5 MHz. Therefore,

$$B_{\text{link}} \geq 62.5 \text{ MHz}$$

One commonly used method to divide the bandwidth among different components is the so-called *matched filter concept*, which implies that the receiver bandwidth should match the bandwidth of the incoming signal. That is:

$$B_{\text{source}}^{-2} + B_{\text{fiber}}^{-2} = B_{\text{receiver}}^{-2} = \frac{1}{2} B_{\text{link}}^{-2}$$

or

$$\begin{aligned} B_{\text{receiver}} &\geq \sqrt{2} \times B_{\text{link}} \\ &\geq \sqrt{2} \times 62.5 \text{ MHz} \\ &\geq 88.39 \text{ MHz} \end{aligned}$$

The combined bandwidth of the source and the fiber should similarly be at least 88.39 MHz. The rise time of the signal at the input to the receiver is given by:

$$\begin{aligned} \text{Rise time at receiver input} &\leq \frac{0.480}{B_{\text{3-dB optical}}} \\ &\leq \frac{0.480}{88.39 \times 10^6} \\ &\leq 5.43 \text{ ns} \end{aligned}$$

If we arbitrarily allocate the bandwidth equally between the source and the fiber, we get:

$$\begin{aligned} B_{\text{source}} &\geq \sqrt{2} \times 88.39 \text{ MHz} \\ &\geq 125 \text{ MHz} \end{aligned}$$

The required rise time of the source is given by:

$$\begin{aligned} \text{Source rise time} &\leq \frac{0.480}{B_{\text{source}}} \\ &\leq \frac{0.480}{125 \times 10^6} \\ &\leq 3.84 \text{ ns} \end{aligned}$$

□

As you will see later in Section 5.4, the FDDI PMD standard limits the signal rise time to less than 3.5 ns at the source and less than 5 ns at the receiver. These limits were set based on analyses similar to that presented in Example 4.12.

A more detailed link bandwidth analysis procedure is presented in Section 20.7.

4.13 Summary

An optical link between two stations consists of a driver, source, connector, fiber, detector, and amplifier. The driver-source pair is called the transmitter and the detector-amplifier is called the receiver. For bidirectional communication, each station has a transmitter-receiver pair called a transceiver.

Light is an electromagnetic wave and travels at different speeds in different media. The ratio of speed to light in the vacuum to that in a medium is called the medium's index of refraction. As a light pulse travels through fiber, its amplitude decreases and its width increases. The decrease in amplitude is called attenuation while the increase in width is called dispersion.

Multimode fibers allow several rays (modes) of light to travel through the core. These modes travel different distances and cause modal dispersion. This can be reduced by varying the index of the core so that modes traveling shorter distances travel slower. This is the technique used in graded-index fibers. Another alternative is to use very thin cores resulting in single-mode fibers. These fibers have no modal dispersion but their bandwidth is limited by chromatic dispersion.

LED and laser diodes are the two choices for sources. Laser diodes are better than LEDs in performance but are very expensive. LEDs with multimode fiber provide the most economical configuration for distances of up to a few kilometers. For longer distances, laser diodes with single-mode fibers should be used.

PIN and APD diodes are the choices for receivers. APDs have higher responsivity but require high bias voltage and are also temperature sensitive. PIN diodes are, therefore, preferred.

Box 4.1 Summary of Optical Formulas

1. Parameters:
   n_1 = Index of refraction of the core
   n_2 = Index of refraction of the cladding
   a = Core radius
   λ = Wavelength
2. Speed of light = Wavelength × Frequency
3. Index of refraction $= \dfrac{\text{Speed of light in vacuum}}{\text{Speed in the medium}}$
4. Attenuation in dB $= 10 \times \log_{10} \dfrac{P_{\text{in}}}{P_{\text{out}}}$
5. mW $= 10^{\text{dBm}/10}$ or dBm $= 10 \times \log_{10}$ mW
6. Numerical aperture NA $= \sqrt{n_1^2 - n_2^2}$
7. Maximum entrance angle $\theta_{\max} = \sin^{-1}$ NA
8. Normalized frequency $V = \dfrac{2\pi a}{\lambda}$NA
9. Number of modes in step-index fiber $\approx \dfrac{V^2}{2}$
10. Number of modes in a graded-index fiber with a parabolic profile $\approx \dfrac{V^2}{4}$
11. FWHM pulse width = 2.355 rms pulse width
12. 3-dB optical bandwidth $= \dfrac{0.187}{\text{rms pulse width}}$
13. 3-dB electrical bandwidth $= \dfrac{0.133}{\text{rms pulse width}}$
14. 3-dB optical bandwidth = 1.41 × 3-dB electrical bandwidth
15. FWHM spectral width = 1.177 × rms spectral width, or rms spectral width = 0.849 × FWHM spectral width
16. 10%–90% Rise time $= \dfrac{0.340}{\text{3-dB electrical bandwidth}} = \dfrac{0.480}{\text{3-dB optical bandwidth}}$
17. For NRZI encoded signal:
    Nyquist bandwidth $= \dfrac{1}{2}$Bit rate for NRZI
18. Rise times combine in a squared manner:
    $t_{\text{link}}^2 = t_1^2 + t_2^2 + \cdots + t_n^2$
19. Bandwidths combine in an inverse squared manner:
    $\dfrac{1}{B_{\text{link}}^2} = \dfrac{1}{B_1^2} + \dfrac{1}{B_2^2} + \cdots + \dfrac{1}{B_n^2}$

Connectors can be simplex or duplex. Simplex connectors connect only one fiber. They are cheaper but can result in a misconnection if the receiving end of a fiber is inadvertently connected to a transmitter. Such connectors are used in applications where access is limited to trained professionals. Duplex connectors prevent such mistakes by correctly connecting the two fibers to the devices. However, they are expensive.

Box 4.1 summarizes the formulas presented in this chapter.

4.14 Further Reading

Almost any book on the subject of optical fiber communication should provide further discussion of all concepts presented in this chapter. For example, see Basch (1986), Keiser (1991), or Green (1992). Mahlke and Gössing (1987) and Sterling (1987) provide a nonmathematical treatment. Weik (1989) and Hentschel (1989) are suitable for quick reference because the entries are arranged in alphabetical order. Hoss (1990) explains various types of bandwidths.

Figures 4.11 and 4.12 are based on data presented in Keiser (1991).

4.15 Self-Test Exercises

Note: Some exercises have multiple correct answers. See Appendix D for answers.

4.1 A light with wavelength of 1.3 μm is sent through a fiber whose core has a refractive index of 1.5. What is the distance between successive peaks of the light waves in the fiber?

a. 0.87 μm
b. 1.3 μm
c. 1.95 μm

4.2 Who moves faster?

a. Photons in a fiber
b. Electrons in a copper cable

4.3 A fiber link has an attenuation of 20 dB. The source transmits a power of 10 μW. What is the power received at the receiver?

a. 1 μW
b. 0.5 μW
c. 0.1 μW
d. 200 μW

4.4 When a light source is turned off (no light), the output power level is:

a. 0 dBm
b. 1 dBm
c. $-\infty$ dBm
d. ∞ dBm

4.5 A 100/140-μm step-index fiber has a normalized frequency of 90. What is the approximate number of modes?

a. 90
b. 100
c. 140
d. 4050
e. 8100

4.6 There is no modal dispersion

a. If a single-mode fiber designed for use at 1.3 μm is used with 1.5-μm sources.
b. If a single-mode fiber designed for use at 1.5 μm is used with 1.3-μm sources.

4.7 The dispersion in a fiber is caused by:

a. Too much light coming from the source
b. Reflections caused by loose connectors
c. Microscopic breaks in the fiber
d. None of the above

4.8 A -10 dBm source in a link is replaced by a -20 dBm source. This will cause the current output (in amperes) at the detector to decrease by a factor of

a. 10
b. 2
c. $\sqrt{10}$
d. $\sqrt{2}$
e. 10^{10}
f. 100

CHAPTER 5

Optical Components: Physical Layer Medium Dependent

Architecture is a science of trade-off. You have to pick a design for the foreseeable future.—David Clark

In this chapter we describe the optical components used in FDDI. As we will see, most choices made for the FDDI standards were based on the cost, performance, and availability trade-offs. The designers of the FDDI standard foresaw the need for various kinds of fibers and other media, so the parts of the standard that deal with particular media have been segregated into several separate standards called *physical layer medium dependent* or **PMD**. The first PMD standard dealt only with multimode fiber. A single-mode fiber PMD (SMF-PMD) and a low-cost fiber PMD (LCF-PMD) have since been added. A twisted-pair copper PMD (TP-PMD) and a SONET physical layer mapping (SPM) are also being developed. Although the FDDI standard document dealing with multimode fibers is called PMD, we will refer to it as *multimode fiber PMD* (*MMF-PMD*) to use the term PMD to cover the entire set of PMDs. This chapter explains MMF-PMD; other PMDs are discussed in later chapters.

5.1 Overview of Multimode Fiber PMD

A brief overview of the design decisions related to MMF-PMD is presented first. The logic behind the choices and a detailed explanation of the concept forms the remainder of this chapter. These key design decisions are as follows:

1. *Optical Spectrum*: FDDI uses light with a wavelength of 1300 nm. Other possibilities that were considered but discarded were 850 or 1500 nm.
2. *Fiber Type*: As shown in Figure 5.1, a fiber consists of a thin core of glass covered with another layer of glass. The second layer is called the cladding, which is covered by a nontransparent buffer coating.

   A 62.5/125 multimode graded-index fiber is normally used in FDDI. The mode and index were defined earlier in Section 4.4. The two numbers specify the diameters of the core and the cladding in micrometers (μm). Thus, standard FDDI fiber has a core diameter of 62.5 μm and a cladding diameter of 125 μm. A few other sizes are also allowed. With multimode fibers the length of each link is limited to 2 km. For longer distances, single-mode fiber should be used.
3. *Sources*: As discussed in Section 4.9, there are two types of light sources: light-emitting diodes (LEDs) and laser diodes. LEDs are inexpensive but less powerful. Laser diodes are expensive

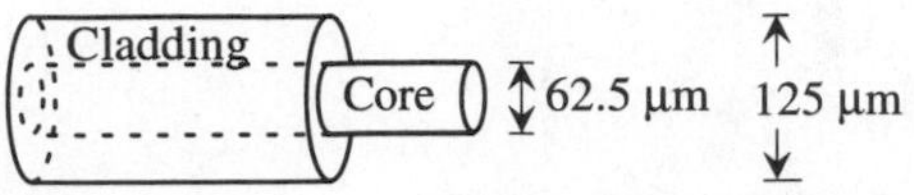

Figure 5.1 The fiber size is specified by the diameters of its core and cladding.

and more powerful. FDDI allows both types of sources. The choice of the source and fiber is intimately related to each other and to the distance. LEDs with multimode fibers are used for distances up to a few kilometers. Laser diodes with single-mode fibers are used for longer distances. LEDs cannot generally be used with a single-mode fiber. The cost of a laser transmitter can be as much as ten times that of an LED transmitter (hundreds of dollars versus tens of dollars). It is for this reason that multimode fiber is the fiber of choice instead of single-mode, even though the latter provides very high bandwidth for future use and is almost the same cost.

4. *Detectors*: The two types of detectors are PINs and APDs (avalanche photodiodes). PINs are inexpensive but less sensitive. APDs are more expensive and more sensitive. PINs are used in most applications. The use of APDs is generally limited to special situations and lab experiments.
5. *Connectors*: A duplex connector prevents the mistake of connecting two transmitters together. The FDDI standard recommends a duplex connector and specifies a precise geometry for the connector. However, many other designs including some simplex connectors are also popular.
6. *Optical Bypasses*: An optical bypass can be used to bypass a dual-attachment station. Whenever the station shuts down, the bypass allows the incoming light to go directly to the outgoing fiber without touching any electrical components at the station. A bypass is not used with single-attachment stations since they are always connected to a concentrator, which can bypass them electrically.

To summarize, FDDI uses 62.5/125 multimode graded-index fibers with 1300-nm LED sources, PIN photodiodes, and duplex connectors as the default. The reasons for these choices, an explanation of what these terms mean, and how these devices work form the remainder of this chapter.

5.2 Why a 1300-nm Window for FDDI?

FDDI uses 1300-nm window for sources and detectors. Other choices considered were 850 and 1500 nm. In this section, we explain why the particular choice was made.

Figure 5.2 shows a plot of attenuation as a function of the wavelength in a typical fiber. The attenuation results from scattering and absorption of light due to impurities in the glass. The figure shows two curves. The lower curve shows attenuation due to scattering alone. The scattering loss decreases with the fourth power of the wavelength. Thus, there is a considerable advantage to using as long a wavelength as possible. The upper curve shows total attenuation due to all causes. In particular, there is a marked peak at 1400 nm due to absorption caused by water impurities in the form of OH (oxygen-hydrogen) ions. At very long wavelengths, however, the photons interact with the thermal vibrations of the glass causing infrared absorption, which rises rapidly as the wavelength exceeds about 1500 nm. The range of wavelengths that can be used is thus bounded between 800 and 1550 nm. Below 800 nm, scattering loss increases rapidly. Above 1550 nm, infrafred absorption causes increasing attenuation.

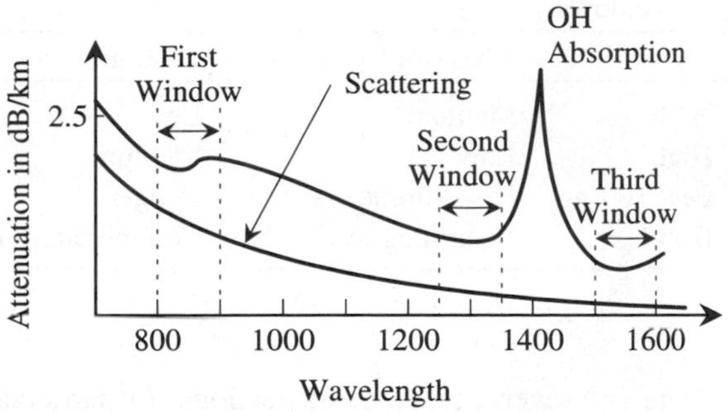

Figure 5.2 Attenuation of a typical fiber.

Notice that the upper curve has several local minima. If one were to choose a wavelength in a given range, it would better to be as close to the nearest minimum as possible. It is for this reason that three local minima are the wavelengths used for optical communication. Actually, one needs a range rather than a single wavelength for communication. This range is called a **window**. Initially, most optical communication devices used the 825- to 875-nm window. Second-generation devices used the second window covering the 1270- to 1380-nm range. Now third-generation devices using the third window with a 1475- to 1525-nm range are just appearing. A window is generally denoted by its **center wavelength**. Thus, the three windows are also called 850-, 1300-, and 1500-nm windows. FDDI uses a center wavelength of 1300 nm.

At the time FDDI was designed, 850-nm devices were easily available. They were used in fiber optic extensions of IEEE 802.5/token ring and IEEE 802.3/Ethernet networks. Due to their existing large volume usage, these devices were inexpensive compared to 1300-nm devices, which were not used in as high a volume. The 1500-nm devices were just emerging and were not commercially available. The prices were even higher. Price alone would have dictated the selection of 850 nm. However, the key problem with 850 nm is high attenuation (see Figure 5.2) and low chromatic bandwidth. This would have limited the transmission without regeneration to a few 100 m. That is, the distance between successive stations would have been limited to a maximum of a few 100 m. This was clearly unacceptable. The selection of a 1300-nm window extended this range to a few kilometers. Although 1500 nm would have extended this even further, the price of 1500-nm devices was too high.

Another advantage of the 1300-nm window is that the chromatic dispersion curve crosses the zero line in this window as shown in Figure 5.3. The concept of dispersion was explained earlier

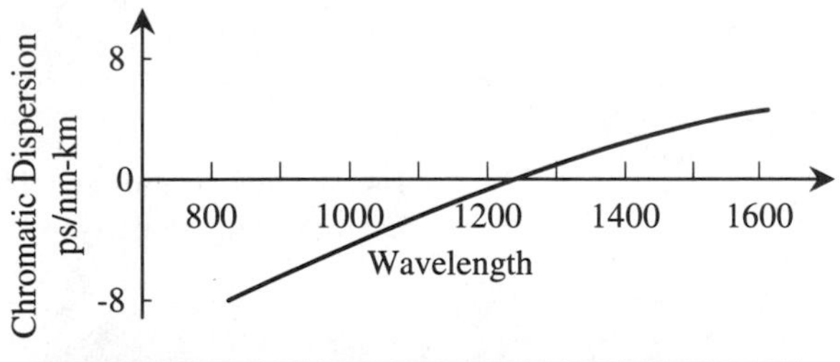

Figure 5.3 The dispersion curve crosses the zero line at around 1300 nm.

Table 5.1 Comparison of Windows

Criterion	850 nm	1300 nm	1500 nm
Attenuation	High	Medium	Low
Chromatic dispersion	High	Low	Medium
Distance at 125 Mbaud	Few 100 m	Few kilometers	Longer
Availability	Easy	Becoming available	Commercially not available at the time

in Sections 4.5 and 4.8. There are several types of dispersions. In particular, chromatic dispersion relates to the change in pulse width caused by differing speeds of different color (different wavelength) photons. Below 1300 nm, the chromatic dispersion is negative in the sense that the higher wavelength photons travel slower than lower wavelength and, therefore, the slope of the velocity versus wavelength curve is negative. Both positive and negative dispersions lead to widening of the pulse and are equally undesirable.

The comparison of the three windows is summarized in Table 5.1. The 1300-nm window was clearly the best choice given the distance requirements and the cost trade-off.

Actually the choice of window, fiber, sources, and detectors is related. In the case of MMF-PMD, first LEDs (instead of lasers) were chosen as the sources because of their cost and reliability. The choice of LEDs also dictated that multimode fibers be used instead of single-mode fibers. Given the wide spectral width of LEDs, the committee had to choose the 1300-nm window to achieve any realistic distances. The 800-nm window could not be used because of high chromatic dispersion.

Potential Bandwidth of Fiber

It was stated in Section 1.4 that the potential bandwidth of fiber is 25,000 GHz per window. This is a theoretical result not currently achievable. It is derived as follows.

The frequency f, velocity of light c, and the wavelength λ are related as follows:

$$\text{Frequency} = \frac{\text{Velocity}}{\text{Wavelength}}$$

or

$$f = \frac{c}{\lambda}$$

Differentiating it we get:

$$\Delta f = -\frac{c}{\lambda^2}\Delta\lambda$$

or

$$|\Delta f| = \frac{c}{\lambda^2}|\Delta\lambda|$$

Here, Δf is the available frequency band (bandwidth) when a wavelength band (spectral width) of $\Delta\lambda$ is used. If we use a 140-nm wavelength band around 1300 nm, the available bandwidth can be obtained by substituting $c = 3 \times 10^8$ m/s, $\lambda = 1300$ nm, and $\Delta\lambda = 140$ nm. We get:

$$\begin{aligned}\text{Potential bandwidth} &= \frac{3 \times 10^8}{(1300 \times 10^{-9})^2} \\ &\quad \times 140 \times 10^{-9} \\ &= 24.85 \times 10^{12} \\ &\approx 25 \text{ THz}\end{aligned}$$

Bandwidths at 850- and 1500-nm windows can be computed similarly.

5.3 FDDI Fiber Specifications

In this section, we present requirements for FDDI fibers as specified in the standard and explain the reasons behind these requirements.

1. *Multimode graded-index fiber is used normally.* As discussed in Section 4.4, there are three types of fibers: multimode step-index, multimode graded-index, and single-mode step index. A comparison of these three types of fiber was also presented there. Due to intermodal dispersion, the multimode step-index fibers have a limited bandwidth-distance capability and do not meet the requirement of FDDI. Single-mode fibers require laser sources, which are expensive. The connectors for single-mode fibers are also more expensive than those for multimode fibers. Therefore, multimode graded-index fibers are normally used. Single-mode fibers are used only for long-distance communications.
2. *The default fiber size is 62.5/125.* The two numbers specify the core and cladding diameters in micrometers (μm). Although the nominal cladding diameter is 125 μm, a variation of ± 3 μm in the cladding diameter is allowed. Thus, the cladding diameter can be anywhere from 122 to 128 μm.

   The core diameter of multimode fibers available in the market varies from 30 to 200 μm. A fiber with smaller core cross section allows less power to be launched from the source. However, a smaller core size results in smaller intermodal dispersion and hence a higher modal bandwidth. If modal bandwidth was the only consideration, a 30-μm fiber would have been chosen. On the other hand, if launch power was the only consideration, a 200-μm fiber would have been selected. The 62.5-μm size was chosen as a trade-off between these two conflicting requirements.

   Other fiber sizes such as 50/125, 85/125, and 100/140 are also allowed as discussed later in this section.
3. *Numerical aperture must be 0.275.* As explained in Section 4.4, the numerical aperture of a fiber determines the maximum entrance angle—the angle at which rays can enter the fiber and still propagate. A large numerical aperture allows more power to be launched or a cheaper (more diffused) source to be used. A numerical aperture of 0.275 allows a maximum entrance angle of approximately 16 degrees, which can be easily met by commercially available inexpensive LED sources. Incidentally, this aperture value applies only for 62.5/125 fiber. The values for other fiber sizes are specified later in this section.
4. *The total attenuation in the link must be 11 dB or less.* As explained later under receivers, any more attenuation may result in a received signal so feeble that the receiver may not be able to recognize it. The total attenuation includes that in the fiber, splices, connectors, and optical bypasses. A fiber may typically have an attenuation of 2 dB/km. Thus, a 2-km fiber without any splices may have an attenuation of 4 dB. The connectors have a loss of 1 dB at each end and splices typically have 0.5 dB. Since there is considerable variation in the quality of connections, splices, and fiber sections, allowance must be made for the variance. The loss analysis is explained in detail in Section 20.6.
5. *The modal bandwidth of the fiber must be 500 MHz-km at 1300 nm.* The modal bandwidth was explained earlier in Section 4.4.

   For FDDI, 125 mega code bits per second result in a signal with a fundamental frequency of 62.5 MHz. A 500-MHz-km fiber when combined with the bandwidth of the generally available transmitters and the receivers results in a system that is able to transmit a 62.5-MHz signal reliably over 2 km. Given the worst case transmitter response (rise/fall) times, a bandwidth-distance product of 500 MHz-km ensures that the pulse rise/fall time at the exit of the fiber or the *exit response time* shall be 5 μs or less—the maximum allowed at the receivers. This is explained further in Section 20.7. The requirement of 500 MHz-km can be easily met by a multimode graded-index fiber, which is the default fiber.

Most of the MMF-PMD design is based on the use of fibers with a 400-MHz-km modal bandwidth. It was found that 400-MHz-km fiber along with then existing transmitter and receiver characteristics was sufficient for the FDDI data rate. However, some manufacturers suggested that the cable plant should require twice as much bandwidth (800 MHz), which is absolutely needed to allow for future upgrades to higher speed (200-Mbps) networks. Others resisted the move arguing that it would increase the cost unnecessarily. After some discussions, 500 MHz-km was selected as a compromise.

6. *The fiber length between two stations must be less than 2 km.* This length ensures that the attenuation and dispersion of the signal will be within acceptable limits. A longer fiber may result in a very low power or (more likely) in a highly dispersed signal. In either case, the error rate would be higher than acceptable.

   Notice that 2 km is the distance between the transmitter and the receiver at the two ends of a fiber. Thus, for stations connected to a concentrator, the length of the cable connecting the concentrator and the station must be less than 2 km. In general, a fiber cable contains two or more fibers. It is the length of each fiber and not their sum, which is limited to 2 km. This is different from the 200-km limit on the ring circumference, where the sum of fiber lengths must be less than 200 km and so the total cable length (assuming a two fiber cable) is limited to 100 km.

7. *Chromatic dispersion slope.* In a multimode graded-index fiber, the modal dispersion is negligible. The bandwidth limitation is caused by chromatic dispersion (see Section 4.5). The chromatic dispersion of the fiber is a function of the wavelength (see Figure 5.4). The chromatic dispersion curve crosses the zero line in the 1300-nm window. (This was one of the reasons why a 1300-nm window was chosen instead of 1550 or 850 nm.) The wavelength at which the dispersion curve crosses the zero line is called the **zero-dispersion wavelength**. The total pulse-width increase depends on the pattern of the chromatic dispersion curve. For a small region around the

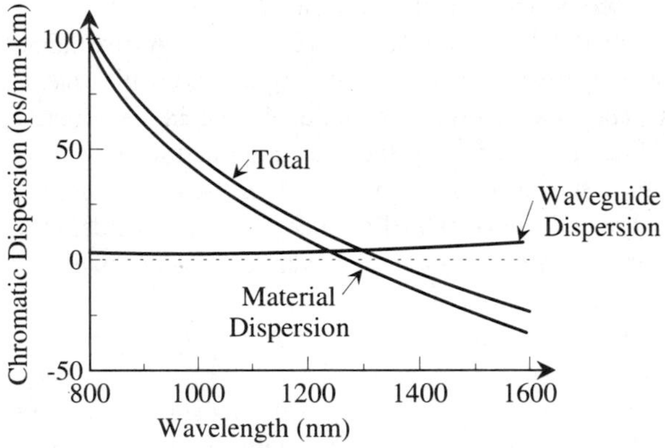

Figure 5.4 Dispersion as a function of wavelength.

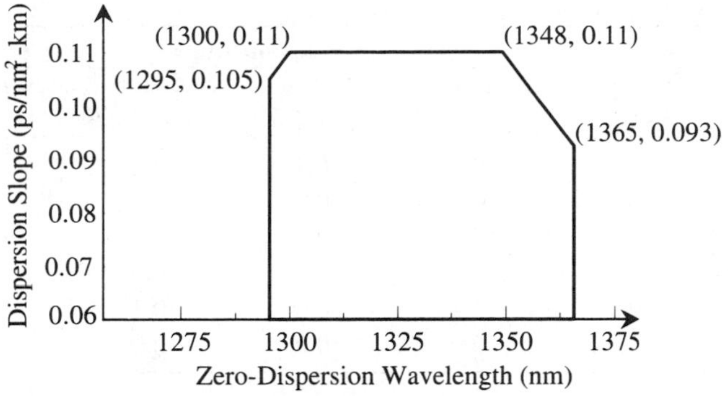

Figure 5.5 Specifications for the slope of the dispersion at the zero-dispersion wavelength.

zero-dispersion wavelength, the curve can be assumed to be a straight line with a given slope. Therefore, the standard specifies the slope of the dispersion curve at this point. The acceptable slope as a function of the zero-dispersion wavelength is shown in Figure 5.5. When the zero dispersion wavelength and the dispersion slope are in the shaded region, the modal bandwidth is sufficient for FDDI applications. This figure was produced by studying available 62.5/125 fiber specifications. The zero-dispersion wavelength and dispersion slope of fibers were plotted and a rectangular envelope was drawn that contained all points. The cutoffs on the two sides of the top part of the curves resulted from the observation that there were no fibers that had zero-dispersion wavelength and dispersion slope in those regions.

8. *Other fiber sizes.* Even before FDDI standardization, fiber was being used for data and voice communication. Fiber had already been installed in many buildings and across many countries. In particular, Japan had standardized building wiring using 50/125 fibers. The FDDI standard, therefore, allowed the use of these other types of fibers also. In particular, 50/125 fibers (with a numerical aperture of 0.20, 0.21, or 0.22), 85/125 fibers (with a numerical aperture of 0.26), and 100/140 fibers (with a numerical aperture of 0.29) are allowed.

   Although these fiber types have not been studied in detail, it is clear that the decreased/increased core cross section may allow less/more power to be launched at the source. Similarly, the sensitivity of the receiver may be less or more depending on the collecting optics. Thus, the loss budget available for the fiber may be less/more than 11 dB. Table 5.2 lists the extra loss at the transmitter and the receiver that must be allowed for different fiber sizes. For example, when

Table 5.2 Loss Budget for Different Fiber Sizes

Fiber Type	Adjustment at Transmitter	Adjustment at Receiver	Remaining Loss Budget for the Link
50/125 μm (NA = 0.20)	−5.0 dB	0.0 to 1.0 dB	6.0 to 7.0 dB
50/125 μm (NA = 0.21)	−4.5 dB	0.0 to 1.0 dB	6.5 to 7.5 dB
50/125 μm (NA = 0.22)	−4.0 dB	0.0 to 1.0 dB	7.0 to 8.0 dB
85/125 μm (NA = 0.26)	2.0 dB	0.0 to −2.6 dB	10.4 to 13.0 dB
100/140 μm (NA = 0.29)	2.0 dB	0.0 to −4.0 dB	9.0 to 13.0 dB

Table 5.3 Additional Loss (in dB) for Mixed Fiber Sizes

Receiving Fiber	**Transmitting Fiber**					
	50 μm NA = 0.20	50 μm NA = 0.21	50 μm NA = 0.22	62.5 μm NA = 0.275	80 μm NA = 0.26	100 μm NA = 0.29
50 μm (NA = 0.20)	0.0	0.2	0.4	2.2	3.8	5.7
50 μm (NA = 0.21)	0.0	0.0	0.2	1.9	3.5	5.3
50 μm (NA = 0.22)	0.0	0.0	0.0	1.6	3.2	4.9
62.5 μm (NA = 0.275)	0.0	0.0	0.0	0.0	1.0	2.3
80 μm (NA = 0.26)	0.0	0.0	0.0	0.1	0.0	0.8
100 μm (NA = 0.29)	0.0	0.0	0.0	0.0	0.0	0.0

using a 50/125 fiber with a numerical aperture of 0.20, a 5-dB additional loss at the source and a 0- to 1-dB loss at the receiver would leave only a 5- to 6-dB loss budget for the link. Depending on the quality of the fiber, connectors, and splices, the allowed distance may be less than 2 km in this case. To ensure that your link will provide acceptable signal quality, you should do both loss and bandwidth analyses, described in Sections 20.6 and 20.7.

9. *Intermixing different fibers*: In a single FDDI ring, different fiber sizes can be used between stations. For example, a concentrator connected to four stations might use 62.5/125 fiber for connection to two stations, while 50/125 fiber might be used for the other two. The adjustments in the link loss budget required for different fiber sizes were discussed earlier.

   It is also possible, although not desirable, to interconnect fibers of different sizes. For example, a 62.5/125 fiber cable attached to a concentrator may be connected to a 50/125 fiber cable attached to a station. Whenever the light passes from a fiber of larger core diameter (or larger aperture) to a fiber of smaller core diameter (or smaller aperture), there is some loss of power. This additional loss must be allowed in the link budget. Table 5.3 lists the additional loss (in dB) for various transmitting and receiving fiber combinations. For example, light suffers a loss of 0.1 dB when passing from a 62.5/125 fiber (with a numerical aperture of 0.275) to a 85/125 fiber (with a numerical aperture of 0.26). These values have been calculated theoretically. Actual loss may vary depending on the quality of the connection.

   Interconnection between fibers of different mode types is not allowed. Thus, *a single-mode fiber may not be connected to a multimode fiber*. The difference in core sizes of the two types is so large that there is hardly any budget left for the link after the adjustment at the connection.

5.4 Transmitters

The MMF-PMD standard specifies a number of requirements for sources used in FDDI transmitters. Since all FDDI devices are expected to satisfy these requirements, readers not interested in designing new equipment or those not interested in details can safely skip this section.

Requirements for transmitters for multimode fibers and single-mode fibers are specified separately. The receptacle component of the connector used to interface the source with the fiber is considered to be a part of the transmitter and is included in the following specification. This boundary of the transmitter (including the receptacle) is called the **active output interface** (**AOI**) in the standard. Here, we use the more common term *transmitter* for this interface. The transmitters to be used with multimode fibers should satisfy the following requirements:

1. *Center Wavelength*: FDDI uses the 1300-nm window. Sources with a center wavelength (see Section 4.9) in the range of 1270 to 1380 nm are allowed.
2. *Average Power*: Average power is defined as that measured by a power meter when the source is sending a stream of halt symbols. This stream results in the source being turned on for 40 ns and off for 40 ns or a 12.5-MHz square wave. The average power level (in watts) is halfway between the levels for high- and low-signal states:

   $$P_{\text{Avg}} = \frac{1}{2}\left(P_{\text{High}} + P_{\text{Low}}\right)$$

   The standard requires that the power output by the transmitter should be at least -20 dBm (10 μW) but no more than -14 dBm (40 μW). A lower power will result in an insufficient signal at the receiver. A higher power will result in excess current and cause the receiver to overload, resulting in signal distortion and data errors.
3. *Rise Time*: The pulse rise time was explained in Section 4.9. The PMD standard requires that the rise time be no more than 3.5 ns. This is based on an analysis similar to that presented in Example 4.1. A higher rise time will result in a pulse that may not be recognized at the receiver.

   The standard also specifies a minimum rise time of 0.6 ns. This was justified on the grounds that a very fast (or instantaneous) transition results in more energy being put in high-order harmonic frequencies. These frequencies are simply filtered off by the channel and therefore the energy is wasted and not really useful for data communication. This limit is no longer considered significant and the requirement has been removed in low-cost fiber PMD (see Chapter 7).
4. *Fall Time*: The fall time requirements are similar to those for rise time. Although the specified bounds for rise time and fall time are identical, a particular source may have a fall time that is different from its rise time, resulting in an unsymmetrical pulse.
5. *Spectral Width*: The combined bandwidth of the source and the fiber depends on a number of their characteristics. For the source, it includes rise/fall times, center wavelength (λ_c), and spectral width. For the fiber, it includes the intermodal bandwidth, zero-dispersion wavelength (λ_0), and dispersion slope (S). Figure 5.6 shows typical graphs of source spectral and fiber chromatic characteristics. Notice that the further apart the source center wavelength λ_c and fiber zero-dispersion wavelength λ_0 are, the larger the chromatic dispersion. This can be compensated by decreasing the source spectral width or fiber dispersion slope S. It can also be compensated by decreasing the source rise and fall times.

   Because of these considerations, the FDDI standard specifies the spectral width as a set of curves shown in Figure 5.7. These curves specify the spectral width as a function of the center wavelength and source rise/fall time. For example, a source with a center wavelength of 1300 nm and a rise/fall time of 3.0 ns is allowed to have a spectral width of about 150 nm. The maximum allowed spectral width is 200 nm. These curves are based on calculations such that a 2-km multimode fiber satisfying FDDI requirements for chromatic dispersion and modal bandwidth would result in a rise/fall time of less than 5 ns at the receiver.
6. *Jitter*: In most communication systems (including FDDI), the clock used to recover the received data is extracted from the bit stream. The recovered clock is used to sample the data. Nominally, the sampling must be done at the middle of the bit interval. Sampling close to the signal transition between bits causes errors. Thus, variations in the position of signal transitions are related to the bit error rate. These variations of the signal transition instants from their nominal positions are called **jitter**.

   There are three basic types of jitter: duty cycle distortion, data-dependent jitter, and random jitter. Duty cycle distortion (DCD) is caused by switching threshold variation and mismatched

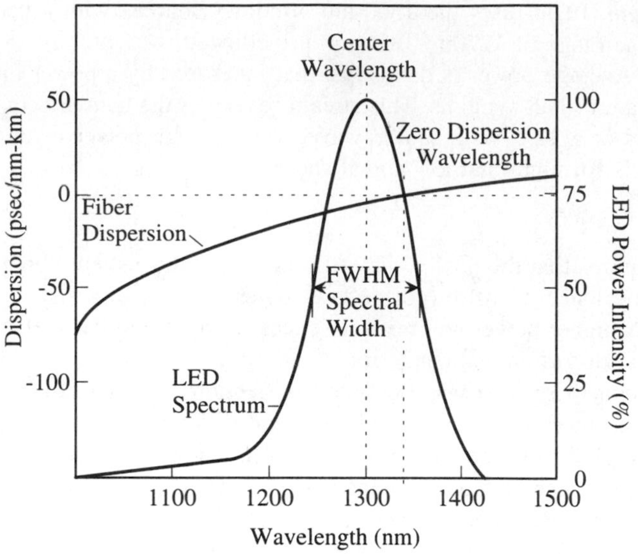

Figure 5.6 Source spectrum and fiber dispersion.

rise and fall times in driver circuits. The data-dependent jitter (DDJ) is caused by a bandwidth limitation in the transmission components and is also a function of the transmitted code bit stream. Random jitter (RJ) is caused primarily by thermal noise and is apparent at low optical powers. Further explanations of these three types of jitters and their specifications follow.

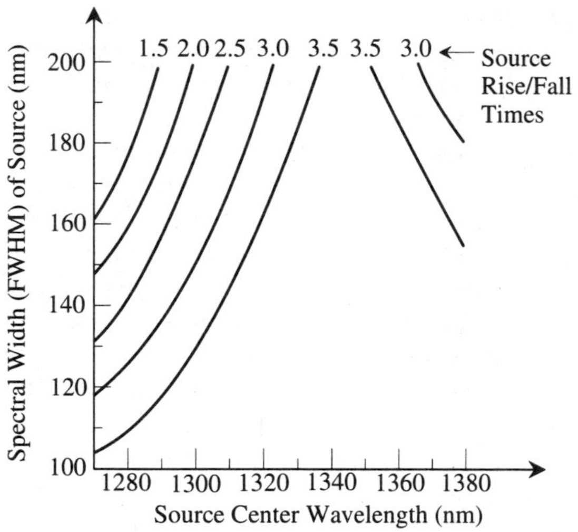

Figure 5.7 Maximum allowed spectral width as a function of the center wavelength and source rise/fall times.

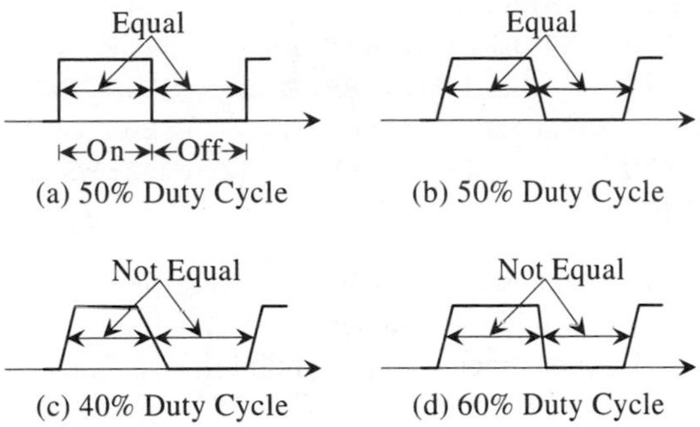

Figure 5.8 Duty cycle distortion.

a. *Duty Cycle Distortion*: The fraction of time the signal is on during a periodic wave is called its *duty factor*. Thus, for a signal with a duty factor of 50%, the pulse width (on time) is equal to the time gap (off time) between the pulses [see Figure 5.8(a)]. In practice, the signal transitions are not vertical. If the rise and fall times are equal, the pulse width (measured at 50% of the pulse height) remains equal to its nominal width as shown in Figure 5.8(b). However, if the rise and fall times are different, the effective pulse width is either decreased or increased as shown in Figures 5.8(c) and 5.8(d). This distortion in the pulse width (and hence in its duty factor) is called **duty cycle distortion**. It is measured by means of the following formula:

$$\text{DCD} = \frac{1}{2}(\text{Width of wider state} - \text{width of narrower state})$$

The FDDI standard requires that duty cycle distortion at the transmitter be less than 1 ns. This value has been chosen based on measured test results from a sample of optical sources. Passive optical components do not contribute to DCD and so the same number applies at the receiver. This is equivalent to requiring that the rise and fall times be within 2 ns of each other. DCD is measured using a stream of idle symbols (62.5-MHz square wave).

b. *Data-Dependent Jitter*: In electrical circuits the on and off states are represented by positive and negative voltages at the same level. For example, +5 V may represent the on state and −5 V may represent the off state. Under ideal conditions, the signal will average to zero, that is, there is no dc component. This is particularly desirable for ac coupling using capacitors. If the average is nonzero, that is, the signal lacks a **dc balance**, the threshold changes. This variation of threshold is called **base line wander**. It is undesirable, because if the threshold is too high, a high signal may be interpreted as low and vice versa—resulting in bit errors.

As discussed earlier in Section 3.1, some of the FDDI symbols have up to ±10% dc balance. Thus, depending on the data stream, the measured pulse width (at the average threshold) may be lower or higher than the nominal. This distortion of the pulse is called **data-dependent jitter**. The MMF-PMD standard requires that for any valid symbol sequence, data-dependent jitter must be less than 0.6 ns. This value is based on direct measurement of available sources. The standard also lists a particular data symbol sequence, which was constructed to provide a near worst case of base line wander. The sequence is:

```
IIIJK4D318BF8E39    5E69CA02424703BF    18193E596ECAD70D
7070702424224270    470274D318BF8E39    5E69CA02424703BF
18196E596ECE3951    4D2274D318BF8E39    5E69CATRSRST03BF
18196E596ECE3951    IJK274D318BF8E39    5E69CA02424703BF
18193E596ECAD70D    D07D27FD318BF8E3    95E69CA024242427
03BF18F9CE3ACEII
```

One problem with this sequence is that it has several control symbols; therefore, it cannot be used as an information field in a frame. The following modified version of the preceding sequence can be used to construct a valid maximum size frame:

```
18193E596ECAD70D    5E69CA02424703BF    18193E596ECAD70D
7070702424224270    470274D318BF8E39    5E69CA02424703BF
18196E596ECE3951    4D2274D318BF8E39    5E69CA02424703BF
18196E596ECE3951    18193E596ECAD70D    5E69CA02424703BF
18193E596ECAD70D    D07D27FD318BF8E3    95E69CA024242427
4D2274D318BF8E39
```

Alternatively, a frame with the information field consisting of all "7" symbols and correct CRC can be used as a test frame.

c. *Random Jitter*: Thermal noise in optical components may also result in a variation of time instants for signal transitions. This is called **random jitter**. It may be positive or negative and should average to zero. The standard requires that the random jitter be less than 0.76 ns. Random jitter is measured using a stream of idle symbols (62.5-MHz square wave). This stream is dc balanced and, therefore, the output has no data-dependent jitter.

For those proficient in statistics, a more detailed explanation of the random jitter requirement is as follows. Random noise is generally modeled to have a Gaussian (normal) distribution $N(0, \sigma)$—with a zero mean and standard deviation σ. The probability of an $N(0, \sigma)$ random variable exceeding $\pm 12.6\sigma$ is 2.5×10^{-10}. The standard requires that the standard deviation σ be less than 0.006 ns or equivalently 12.6σ be less than 0.76 ns.

Jitter in the recovered clock has three components: **static alignment error** (**SAE**), DDJ, and RJ. SAE is an offset of the decision time (clock) instant from the optical sampling position. When the clock coincides with the optimal sampling position, the bit error rate is minimum. The major causes of SAE are the initial misalignment error and differential delays between the data and clock paths induced by temperature fluctuation and aging.

The total jitter must not exceed the bit duration, which is 8 ns for FDDI. Various components of RJ add in a root-mean-square (rms) fashion. DDJ and DCD add linearly to RJ. The division of this jitter allowance at various points in the optical link is listed in Table 5.4 and shown in Figure 5.9. These allocations assume a combined SAE and DDJ value of 1.5 ns and a random jitter of 1.8 ns (peak-to-peak) for the clock. These clock jitter values depend on the implementation and are not specified in the standard. Using these values we get:

$$\begin{aligned}\text{Total jitter} &= \text{DCD}_{\text{PHY-in}} + \text{DDJ}_{\text{PHY-in}} + \text{SAE} + \text{DDJ}_{\text{Clock}} \\ &\quad + \left(\text{RJ}^2_{\text{PHY-in}} + \text{RJ}^2_{\text{Clock}}\right)^{1/2} \\ &= 1.4 + 2.2 + 1.5 + (2.27^2 + 1.8^2)^{1/2} \\ &= 8.0 \text{ ns}\end{aligned}$$

Table 5.4 FDDI Jitter Budget[a]

Interface	DCD	DDJ	RJ
PHY-out	0.4	0.0	0.32
PMD-out	1.0	0.6	0.76
PMD-in	1.0	1.2	0.76
PHY-in	1.4	2.2	2.27

[a] All values are in nanoseconds peak-to-peak.

Only the jitter components visible at the PMD interface (PMD-out and PMD-in) are the enforceable parts of the standard. Therefore, the standard does not specify the PHY-out and PHY-in values.

7. *Extinction Ratio*: Ideally it is desirable that there be no light coming out of a transmitter when the signal is low (or the injected current to the diode is zero). In practice, there is some light even during the low signal state. The ratio of the power output (measured in μW, not dBm) during the low state to that during the high state is called the **extinction ratio**. MMF-PMD requires that the extinction ratio be less than 10%.

$$\text{Extinction ratio} = \frac{P_{\text{Low}}}{P_{\text{High}}}$$

8. *Pulse Shape*: The optical signal produced by the transmitter is generally not very smooth. When viewed with high-precision equipment, the pulse may have an overshoot at the rising edge and an undershoot at the falling edge. The standard, therefore, specifies lower and upper bounds or

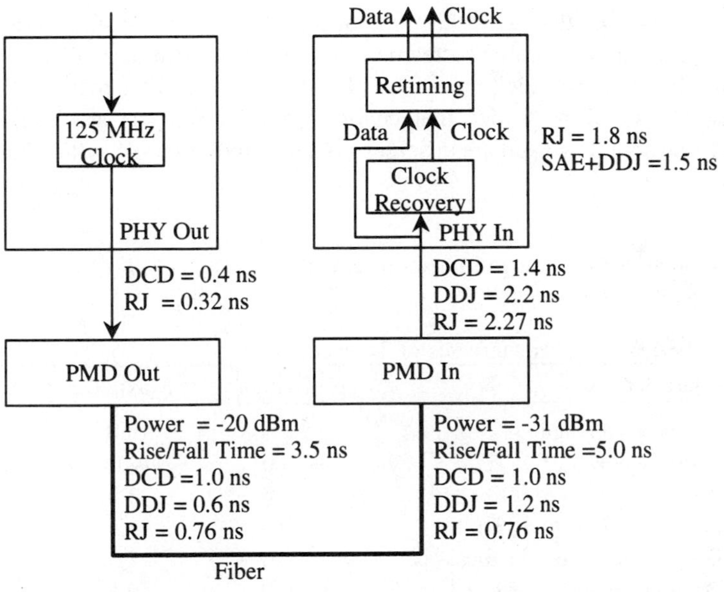

Figure 5.9 Allocation of jitter to the various components of an FDDI link.

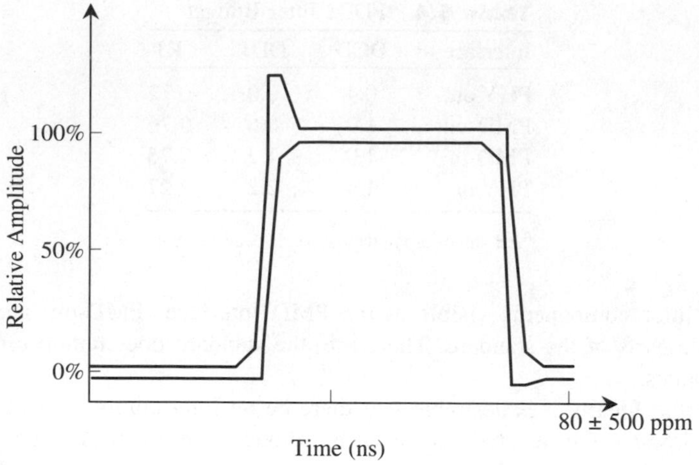

Figure 5.10 Pulse envelope.

a pulse envelope. The pulse must lie in the bound specified by this envelope. The envelope is shown in Figure 5.10. This sets bounds for pulse overshoot, undershoot, and slow tail response. The time width of the envelope was designed so that pulse shapes ranging from a straight line to an exponential would fit with the envelope as long as the rise/fall time requirements were met.

9. *Time to Enable/Disable a Transmitter*: It is possible to enable or disable an FDDI transmitter using station management commands. The standard requires that the transmitter follow those commands within 1 μs; that is, within 1 μs of the "Transmit Enable" command, the transmitter will start transmitting the specified stream. Similarly, the transmitter will stop transmitting within 1 μs of the "Transmit Disable" command. The power level after the disable command would drop to below −45 dBm. Notice that enable/disable commands are issued only during link initialization and shut down and are different from transmitter on/off, which happens continuously during link operation.

Table 5.5 summarizes the transmitter requirements.

Table 5.5 Characteristics of Transmitters

Characteristics	Minimum	Maximum	Units
Center wavelength	1270	1380	nm
Average power	−20.0	−14.0	dBm
Rise time (10% to 90%)	0.6	3.5	ns
Fall time (90% to 10%)	0.6	3.5	ns
Duty cycle distortion (peak–peak)	0.0	1.0	ns
Data-dependent jitter (peak–peak)	0.0	0.6	ns
Random-jitter (peak–peak)	0.0	0.76	ns
Extinction ratio	0.00	10.0	%

5.5 Receivers

FDDI receivers should satisfy a number of requirements specified in the standard. The receptacle component of the connector used to interface the receiver with the fiber is considered part of the receiver and is included in the following specification. This boundary of the receiver (including the receptacle) is called the **active input interface** (**AII**) in the standard. Here, we use the more common terms detectors and receivers. The receivers to be used with multimode fibers should satisfy the following requirements:

1. *Center Wavelength*: The receiver should be designed to detect wavelengths in the range of 1270 to 1380 nm. This is the same range specified for the sources.
2. *Average Power*: The receiver should be able to recognize reliably power levels as low as −31 dBm (0.8 μW) or lower. Also, it must be able to operate without overloading with an incident power as high as −14 dBm (40 μW) or higher. At lower power levels, the noise current becomes comparable to the signal current and the signal-to-noise ratio becomes large. At higher power levels, the current generated may be too large and a possibility of overload exists.

   Notice that the minimum power levels at the transmitter (−20 dBm) and at the receivers (−31 dBm) have been set so that the link can have a loss of up to 11 dB. The maximum power level (−14 dBm) is the same for both transmitters and receivers so that one can directly connect a transmitter with a receiver without any possibility of overload. This also allows testing a transceiver with a simple loopback connector.

   As in the case of transmitters, a stream of halt symbols is used to test receivers for average power. This stream results in a signal that has one transition per symbol and, therefore, consists of pulses that are 40-ns wide with a gap of 40 ns between them; that is, the power is on for 40 ns and off for 40 ns.
3. *Rise Time*: The receiver should be able to detect reliably a pulse with a rise time of 5 ns. The rise time is measured as the time for the power to rise from 10% to 90% of its peak value as shown earlier in Figure 4.16. Pulses with a larger rise time may not be recognized reliably by the receiver.

   Rise time contributions of different components, such as source and fiber, are combined using a square root of the sum of squares formula:

   $$t_{\text{total}} = \left(t_{\text{source}}^2 + t_{\text{fiber}}^2\right)^{1/2}$$

   The maximum rise time of the pulse at the receiver is 5 ns. This is allocated equally to the fiber and the source (3.5 ns each):

   $$t_{\text{total}} = \left(3.5^2 + 3.5^2\right)^{1/2} \approx 5$$

   Thus, the fiber is allowed to change the rise time by 3.5 ns. This puts a limit on the dispersion allowed in the fiber.
4. *Fall Time*: The fall time specifications are similar to those for the rise time, that is, a minimum of 0.6 ns and a maximum of 5 ns. The same considerations apply here except that the incident pulse may not be symmetrical. For example, the receiver should be able to recognize a pulse with a rise time of 3 ns and a fall time of 5 ns and vice versa.
5. *Duty Cycle Distortion*: As explained earlier in Section 5.4, the duty cycle distortion in a pulse is related to the on-off time measured at 50% of the peak power. A difference in the rise and fall times of a pulse leads to duty cycle distortion. The FDDI transmitters should have a duty cycle distortion of less than 1 ns and the receivers should be able to recognize pulses with this

Table 5.6 Characteristics of Receivers

Characteristics	Minimum	Maximum	Units
Center wavelength	1270	1380	nm
Average power	−31.0	−14.0	dBm
Rise time (10% to 90%)	0.6	5.0	ns
Fall time (90% to 10%)	0.6	5.0	ns
Duty cycle distortion (peak–peak)	0.0	1.0	ns
Data-dependent jitter (peak–peak)	0.0	1.2	ns
Random jitter (peak–peak)	0.0	0.76	ns

distortion. Notice that the dispersion in the fiber increases the rise and fall times equally and therefore does not contribute to the duty cycle distortion.

6. *Data-Dependent Jitter*: Again as explained in Section 5.4, the data-dependent jitter relates to the distortion in the pulse width caused by the dc balance in the data stream. A receiver should work reliably with a data-dependent jitter of up to 1.2 ns. This value is based on a 94-MHz transmitter and fiber bandwidth limitation.
7. *Random Jitter*: The receivers should be able to sustain a random jitter of up to 0.76 ns—the same amount allowed to transmitters. For a discussion of random jitter, see Section 5.4.

Table 5.6 summarizes the receiver requirements. The main requirement is that the receiver be able to operate at −31 dBm, which when compared with the minimum transmit power of −20 dBm results in a link loss budget of 11 dB, which in turn results in a limit of 2 km on the cable length between adjacent stations.

5.5.1 Signal Detect Timing

In addition to indicating the zero/one bits being received, the receiver also indicates whether any signal is being received at all. This latter indication is called **signal detect**. In normal operation, the signal detect remains asserted. When the link breaks, the link is taken off line. If insufficient power is received, the signal detect is deasserted. This gives an indication to the station management components that some remedial action is required. The standard puts a limit on the time required to assert/deassert signal detect and has a rather detailed specification of how these times should be measured. We prefer to give a simplified description, which should suffice for most readers.

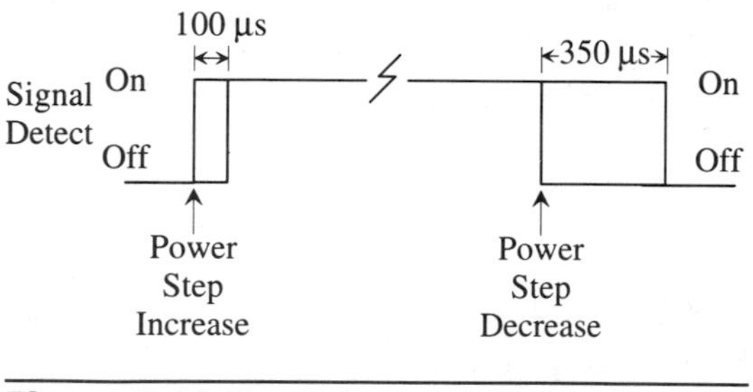

Figure 5.11 Signal detect timing requirements.

Table 5.7 Signal Detect Timing Requirements for Receivers

Requirement	Minimum	Maximum	Unit
Assert time		100.0	μs
Deassert time		350.0	μs
Assert power P_a	$P_d + 1.5$	-31	dBm
Deassert power P_d	$\max(-45, P_b)$		dBm
Hysteresis	1.5		dB

As the received power is decreased below −31 dBm, the receiver may still recognize the pulses although the bit error rate (BER) increases. If the power becomes so low that the bit error rate becomes 1% (0.01), the receiver should deassert signal detect. Let this power level be P_b, where b stands for BER.

The receiver is required to deassert signal detect whenever power *falls* below P_b and to assert signal detect whenever power *rises* above P_b+1.5 dBm. Notice that the levels for assertion and deassertion depend on the direction of change. The difference in the levels is 1.5 dBm and is called **hysteresis**. The hysteresis specification is designed to preclude an oscillation of the signal detect if the input optical signal level is close to the threshold of the receiver.

The standard also specifies fixed bounds for assertion and deassertion. The receiver should deassert whenever power falls below −45 dBm and should assert whenever power rises above −31 dBm. In other words, the deassertion level P_d is:

$$P_d = \max(P_b, -45 \text{ dBm})$$

and the assertion level P_a is:

$$P_a = \min(P_d + 1.5 \text{ dBm}, -31 \text{ dBm})$$

In the following description, we will need one more level, P_e, defined as follows:

$$P_e = \min(P_d + 4 \text{ dBm}, -31 \text{ dBm})$$

The signal detect should be asserted within 100 μs when power is increased from below P_d to above P_a in a step increase. This time is called **maximum signal acquisition time** or **AS_Max**.

After the signal detect is asserted, the bit error rate should be less than 1% as measured during the next 15 μs. This interval is called **maximum line state change time** or **LS_Max**. It is so named because during this interval, the station hardware determines the new state of the line. Incidentally, the default value of LS_Max has been changed to 25 μs in SMT draft version 7.2.

The signal detect should be deasserted within 350 μs when power is decreased from above P_e to below −45 dBm. This time is a receiver parameter called **maximum no signal acquisition time** or **ANS_Max**.

The signal detect timing requirements are summarized in Figure 5.11 and in Table 5.7.

5.6 Connectors

One of the considerations in the design of the FDDI standard was that untrained users should be able to connect and disconnect devices easily without damaging the connector or devices. In particular, it is important that the fiber connected to a transmitter be connected to a receiver at the other end and vice versa. Mixing the transmitter fiber with a receiver fiber may damage the devices.

The standard committee, therefore, chose a duplex design, in which both fibers are connected using one connector (as opposed to a simplex design, in which each fiber has its own connector). This decision was made in May 1984 and all connector companies were asked to propose designs. A connector manufacturer working group was formed to settle what is now known as the "Connector War." The group specified the following characteristics for the connector: have a snap lock, be polarized, be keyed, have a protective cover, be field installable, support both 125- and 140-μm fiber claddings, and be multisourced. The AMP design, which was based on their OPTIMATE simplex family, won the war in October 1985. The design was later improved by an ad hoc group of all connector manufacturers. In particular, the design and size of the ferrule was changed to provide more stability. The height of the receptacle was adjusted to enable mounting on a VME bus and PC-compatible printed circuit boards.

The FDDI connector has a key that prevents the plug from being inserted upside-down and thus a careless user cannot accidentally misconnect the devices. The key consists of a rectangular cavity on the plug with corresponding raised metal (or plastic) on the receptacle.

To ensure that any vendor's equipment can be connected to any fiber, it is necessary for a standard connector design to be used. (Imagine what would happen if all electric sockets used in your office were different.) The FDDI standard, therefore, specifies the receptacle geometry precisely. Any plug that is compatible with the specified geometry is allowed.

During standardization of the connectors, there was some debate about whether a metal piece should be placed between the two ferrules (see Figure 5.12). This piece provides additional strength to the connection. Opponents argued that it is not required since the transceiver packaging (on which the receptacle is attached) already provides the needed strength. Eventually, as is generally the case in the standardization process, both designs were accepted. The design without the strengthening member is used for receptacles on transceivers, while the design with the strengthening member is used on receptacles not attached to a device. Except for this member, the two designs are identical.

The standard does not specify any loss requirements for the connector. The connector loss is included in the link loss budget of 11 dB. A system using a high-loss connector will have little budget left for the fiber and hence may have to limit the distance between stations. Typically, a connector loss of 1 dB per connector is used in link loss budget calculations. Actual connector loss varies between 0.2 and 1 dB. Connectors that are close to the transmitter may exhibit higher losses than those farther away. This is because the connectors attenuate higher order modes more than lower order modes. After the first few connectors have stripped off the higher order modes, the attenuation decreases.

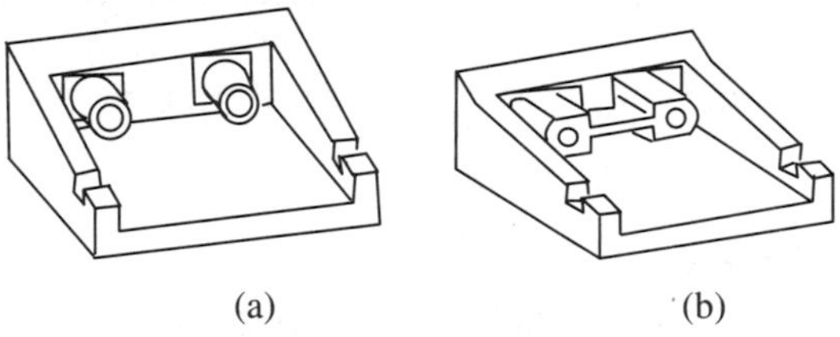

(a) (b)

Figure 5.12 The strengthening member between two ferrules is used in receptacles not mounted on devices.

5.7 Keying

The key on FDDI connectors not only protects untrained users from inserting it upside-down, it also protects them from interconnecting wrong devices. This is done by specifying a different size and position for the key for different types of ports. Recall from Section 1.9 that there are four types of ports: the port on a single-attachment station is called S; the port on the concentrator where a single-attachment station can be connected is called M; and the ports on dual-attachment stations are called A and B. The standard requires that the type of the port be labeled on the receptacle.

The relative size and location of the keys on thc receptacles for these four types of ports are shown in Figure 5.13(a). The hatched area shows the solid (so-called "metal") part of the receptacle. The cavities on the plugs are shown in Figure 5.13(b). Notice that the A-keyed plug inserts into an A-key receptacle only; an S-keyed plug, on the other hand, can be inserted into any (A-, B-, S-, or M-keyed) receptacle. The text on the right-hand side of Figure 5.13(b) lists the type of receptacle into which the plug can be inserted. The figure shows a total of six plug types. The plug type AM inserts into A or M receptacles. Similarly, the BM plug inserts into B or M receptacles. Such plugs allow for movement of a dual-attachment station from the trunk ring to a concentrator without changing the cable.

The keying helps prevent accidental miscabling. The following are examples of miscabling errors:

1. The dual-attachment station is reversed such that its A-port is connected to where its B-port should be and vice versa. This would cause the primary MAC to be connected to the secondary ring and vice versa.
2. The single-attachment station is connected on the trunk ring. This would cause a break in the trunk ring. Two such mistakes would result in a permanently wrapped ring.
3. The M-port of a concentrator is connected to the trunk ring. This would cause a break in the ring.

A cable with an M-keyed plug at one end and an S-keyed plug at the other end is called an M-to-S cable. This cable can be used to connect a single-attachment station to a concentrator. Similarly, A-to-B cables with A-keyed plugs at one end and B-keyed plugs at the other can be used to connect

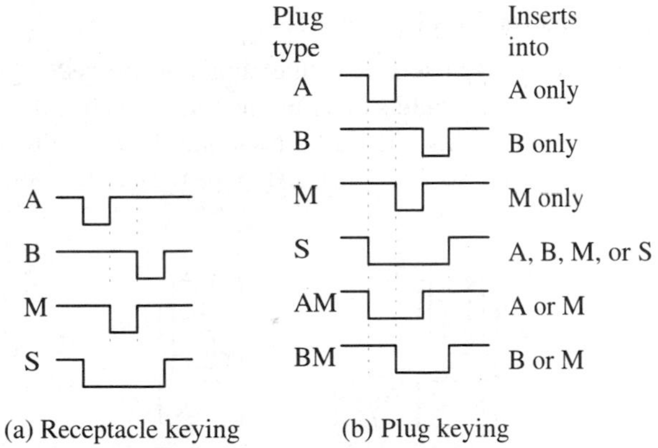

Figure 5.13 Keying on a multimode fiber connector.

dual-attachment stations and concentrators on the trunk ring. A cabling system using just these two types of cables prevents miscabling errors 1 and 2 and discourages miscabling errors 3. A dual-attachment station can still be connected to a concentrator if desired since the S end of the M-to-S cable will insert into the A or B receptacles.

A second type of cabling system would be to use M-to-S and AM-to-BM type cables. The AM-to-BM cable has an AM-keyed plug on one end and a BM-keyed plug on the other. This cable can be used to form the dual ring. The advantage of this cabling system is that a dual-attachment station can be connected to the M-port of a concentrator without replacing its cable. However, this also means that the system does not prevent miscabling error 3.

A third type of cabling system would be to use S-to-S cable for all connections. Recall that an S-plug inserts into all types of receptacle. The advantage of this system is that only one type of cable (or plug) is required in inventory. However, this system would not protect against any of the three miscabling errors.

Incidentally, all three cabling systems are allowed by the standard since keying of the plug is optional. However, keying of the receptacle is required. Also, the standard requires that all plugs and receptacles be labeled properly. That is, the letter "S," "A," "B," or "M" must appear on them.

At an interoperability test conducted by a leading FDDI chip manufacturer, miscabling was found to be the key problem in setting up a ring with equipment from different vendors. Since not all vendors use the duplex connectors, connecting a transmitting cable to another transmitter was one of the problems. The second problem was that of connecting an A-port to another A-port (miscabling error 1).

5.8 Optical Bypasses

A bypass allows a station to be taken off (bypassed from) the ring. In bypassed mode, the incoming optical signal is passed directly to the next station as shown in Figure 5.14. Since single-attachment stations are always connected to concentrators, they can be easily bypassed by the concentrator and there is no need to use optical bypasses. Bypasses can be used for dual-attachment stations on the trunk ring.

Notice that when bypassed, the station is left in a loopback mode such that the transmitter and receiver of one port is connected to the receiver and transmitter of the other port. The switching may be done mechanically (by rotating a prism) or optically.

The performance requirements for a bypass are:

1. *Low Loss*: When a station is bypassed, two fiber links are joined together. As shown in Figure 5.15, this new combined link should satisfy all the requirements of a single link. In particular, the total length of the combined link should be less than 2 km; the total attenuation of the link should be less than 11 dB; and so on. Since the bypass is a component of this new link, its

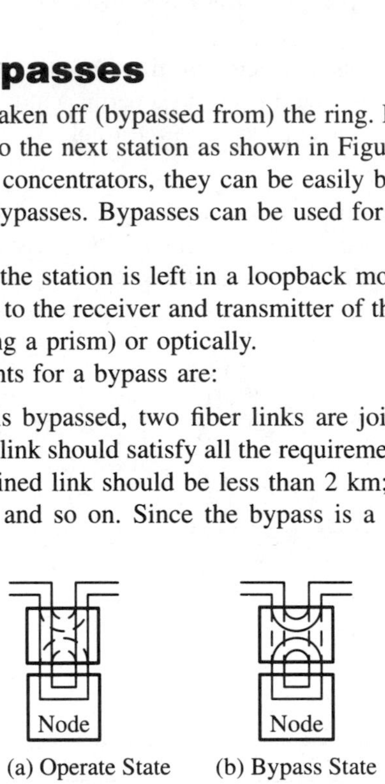

Figure 5.14 Two states of an optical bypass.

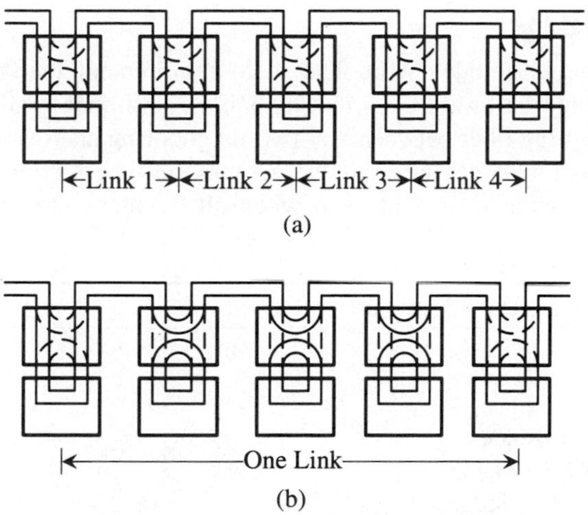

Figure 5.15 After a station bypass, the resulting link should meet the distance and attenuation requirements.

attenuation should be small to leave the budget for other components. The maximum allowed attenuation is 2.5 dB per bypass.

2. *High Channel Isolation*: Since light signals from both primary and secondary rings travel through the bypass, a possibility of crosstalk exists. It is desirable that light on one ring should have a minimal effect on the other ring. This is called **interchannel isolation**. The standard requires that the isolation be at least 40 dB.
3. *Fast Switching*: After a bypass is instructed to insert or deinsert a station, the action should be accomplished fast. The maximum switching time allowed is 25 ms. This is the amount of time that a station should wait after going into the bypass mode before the station can reconfigure. This time is denoted by the parameter **I_Max**.
4. *Least Interruption*: When a station is bypassed, the rings are interrupted briefly. This **media interruption time** should be as small as possible. The maximum allowed time is 15 ms. This time is denoted by the parameter **MI_Max**.

To summarize, optical bypasses may optionally be used on dual-attachment stations or concentrators. The combined link after bypass should satisfy all link requirements. This limits the number of neighboring stations that can be bypassed. Typically the number is two or three, which is very small compared to 500 stations allowed on a ring by the FDDI standard. Bypasses, if used, should satisfy the requirements listed in Table 5.8.

Table 5.8 Characteristics of Station Bypass Interface

Characteristics	Minimum	Maximum	Units
Total attenuation	0.0	2.5	dB
Interchannel isolation	40.0		dB
Switching time		25.0	ms
Media interruption time		15.0	ms

5.9 Summary

Box 5.1 summarizes the multimode PMD. The main requirement that most buyers of standard compliant equipment should be aware of is that 62.5/125 multimode graded-index fiber should be used and that the length of the fiber between any two neighboring stations (or concentrators) should be less than 2 km. If optical bypasses are used, the network designers should ensure that the distance requirement and link loss budget are met even when all bypasses are in the "station-deinserted" mode.

Box 5.1 Multimode Fiber PMD Summary

1. Window: 1300 nm
2. Fiber:
   a. Multimode graded-index.
   b. Default size: 62.5/125 μm.
   c. Other sizes: 50/125, 85/125, 100/140.
   d. Total link loss should be less than 11 dB.
3. Transmitter:
   a. LED sources are more economical than laser diodes. For multimode fibers, LED sources can be used.
   b. The average launch power must be between −20 and −14 dBm.
   c. The 10% to 90% rise/fall times should be between 0.6 and 3.5 ns.
   d. The center wavelength should be 1270 to 1380 nm.
4. Receiver: PIN photodiodes are more economical than APDs. For multimode fibers, PIN photodiodes can be used. The receivers should be able to recognize correctly an optical signal with the following properties:
   a. Average power of −31 to −14 dBm. (This leads to a maximum allowed link loss budget of 11 dB.)
   b. A 10% to 90% rise/fall time of 0.6 to 5 ns.
   c. A duty cycle distortion of 1 ns, data-dependent jitter of 1.2 ns, and random jitter of 0.76 ns.
5. Connectors: Duplex connectors with a specified receptacle geometry should be used. The receptacle and plugs have a key that designates it as A, B, M, or S type. Plugs can also be AM or BM type.
6. Optical Bypasses: Optical bypasses are not required (and are not defined) for single-attachment stations. They are optional for dual-attachment stations and concentrators. If used, the bypassed link should meet the distance and loss requirements. Other performance requirements of the bypass are:
   a. Attenuation should be less than 2.5 dB.
   b. Interchannel isolation should be at least 40 dB.
   c. The switching time should be less than 25 ms.
   d. The media interruption time should be less than 15 ms.

5.10 Further Reading

Multimode fiber PMD is specified in ANSI X3.166-1990 or ISO/IEC 9314-3:1990.

Burr (1986) describes the reasoning behind the major MMF-PMD selections such as window, transmitters, and receivers. For further discussion about the chromatic dispersion slope, see Refi

(1988) and Hanson and Hutchison (1987). Miller (1986), Ginzburg and Rieger (1988), and Hartmann, Chen, and Muoi (1986) give theoretical justification for Figure 5.7. Hutchison, Baldwin, and Thompson (1991) and Slawson (1987) discuss jitter budget for various components. Weber (1986) and Moore and Weber (1987) describe how the duplex connector for FDDI was designed and selected. Some history about the selection of transmit power levels can be found in Chown et al. (1988). Khan (1989) lists results of an interoperability testing among various FDDI chip manufacturers. Salwen (1984) argues that bypassing dual-attached stations is not a good idea since it severely limits the distance between stations.

Figures 5.7 and 5.12 and Tables 5.2, 5.3, 5.5, 5.6 and 5.7 have been adapted from ANSI X3.166-1990.

5.11 Self-Test Exercises

Note: Some exercises have multiple correct answers. See Appendix D for answers.

5.1 Why was a 1300-nm window chosen over 850 and 1500 nm for FDDI?

a. It provides the lowest attenuation.
b. It provides the lowest dispersion.
c. The devices are lowest cost.
d. All of the above.

5.2 Given the same other physical characteristics, why would you prefer a 62.5/125 fiber over 100/140 fiber?

a. 62.5/125 has a higher bandwidth.
b. 62.5/125 has a higher attenuation.
c. 62.5/125 allows more light to be launched.
d. 62.5/125 has a higher intermodal dispersion.

5.3 Why would you recommend the use of multimode fibers instead of single-mode fibers in FDDI?

a. Multimode fiber can be used for longer distances.
b. Multimode fiber is cheaper.
c. Transceivers for multimode fibers are cheaper.
d. Multimode fiber allows many more modes than a single-mode fiber.

5.4 Which of the following are valid FDDI configurations?

a. A 50/125 fiber is used between stations A and B while 62.5/125 fiber is used between stations B and C.
b. A 50/125 fiber is used to connect station A to a concentrator while 62.5/125 fiber is used to connect station C to the same concentrator.
c. A 50/125 fiber is used from station A to a patch-panel while 62.5/125 fiber is used from the patch-panel to station B. The two stations are connected via a patch cord.
d. A 50/125 fiber is used from station A to B while 62.5/125 is used from B to A.

CHAPTER 6

Single-Mode Fiber: SMF-PMD

Single-mode fiber allows longer distance communication than a multimode fiber. The distance (cable length) between two FDDI stations can be up to 40 to 60 km compared to 2 km for multimode fibers.

The characteristics of single-mode fibers and those of the transmitters, receivers, connectors, and bypasses for use with them are specified in a separate FDDI standard, the **Single-Mode Fiber Physical Layer Medium Dependent** (**SMF-PMD**) standard. This chapter explains the concepts and requirements specified in the SMF-PMD standard. The concept of modes and the differences between single-mode and multimode fibers were explained earlier in Section 4.4. Other concepts explained in Chapters 4 and 5 will be used extensively throughout this chapter. It is assumed that you have already read those chapters.

Since the initial PMD (Physical Layer Medium Dependent) standard described in Chapter 5 covers only multimode fibers, we will refer to it as the Multimode Fiber Physical Layer Medium Dependent (MMF-PMD) standard.

6.1 Differences from MMF-PMD

The increased distance for single-mode fibers is a result of the superior quality of the fibers, transmitters, and receivers used. A single-mode fiber has a lower loss (attenuation) than a multimode fiber. The laser sources used with single-mode fibers can launch more power than LED sources. The narrow spectral width of the sources (which reduces the chromatic dispersion) combined with the absence of modal dispersion results in a high bandwidth-distance product for single-mode fiber links. More sensitive receivers that can recognize lower power levels can be used with single-mode fiber.

Single-mode fibers are thinner than multimode fibers. The typical core diameter is 5 to 10 μm compared to 50 to 100 μm for multimode fibers. Although their manufacturing requires very precise equipment, single-mode fiber cables have become cheaper than multimode fiber cables because of their widespread use in telephone applications. All the fiber installed by telephone companies is single mode. In computer applications, multimode fiber is preferred because of the low cost of LED sources, which unfortunately cannot be used with single-mode fibers.

The key differences between single-mode and multimode PMD standard specifications are:

1. *Two Categories of Transceivers*: Laser sources used with single-mode fibers produce higher power than LED sources, resulting in a higher loss budget for cable plant. To allow for this high loss, more powerful transmitters and more sensitive receivers than those specified in the multimode PMD standard are required. The single-mode PMD standard, therefore, specifies two categories of transmitters and receivers. Category I devices operate at the same power levels as those specified in the multimode PMD standard. Category II devices are more powerful and more sensitive than Category I devices.
2. *Higher Loss Budget*: Category II transmitters output at least −4 dBm, while Category II receivers can recognize a signal with as little as −37 dBm of power. This would result in a cable plant loss allowance of 33 dB. However, optical reflections caused by the fiber and devices back toward the transmitters become an important consideration for laser sources. These reflections reduce the output power of the laser. This reduction in power is known as *transmission penalty*. Allowing 1 dB for transmission penalty leaves a loss budget of 32 dB for fiber (compared to 11 dB for multimode fibers). Using a fiber with an attenuation of 0.5 dB/km, this gives a limit of approximately 60 km between the stations (allowing a few decibels for connectors and splices).
3. *Need for Attenuators*: One problem with high-powered transmitters is that too much power may be received if the connecting fiber is short. This may result in an overabundance of electrons generated. The current may last for some time after the light is turned off. This causes signal distortion and data errors. To overcome this problem, special attenuators are required to reduce the received power in those configurations in which fiber attenuation is low.
4. *More Precise Connectors*: Since the cores of single-mode fibers are thinner than those of multimode fibers, the connectors are required to align them more precisely and closely. The single-mode connectors are, therefore, specified with tighter tolerances.
5. *Mixing Multimode and Single-Mode Fibers*: All fibers used in a single FDDI ring need not be of the same type. Thus, some stations may be connected by single-mode fibers, while other nodes in the same ring are connected by multimode fibers. This is shown in Figure 6.1(a). However, as shown in Figure 6.1(b), single-mode and multimode fibers cannot be used on one link between

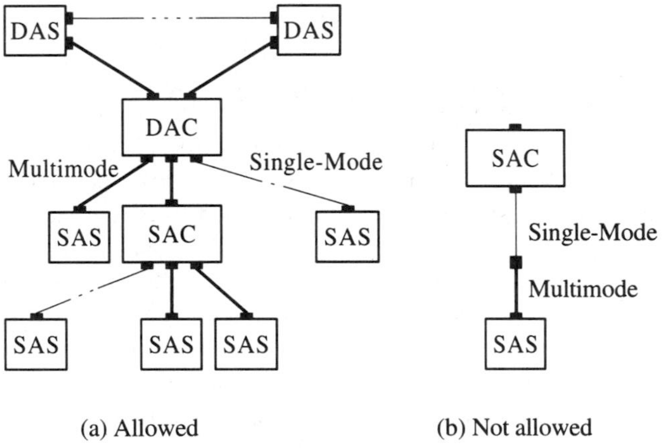

Figure 6.1 Using both single-mode and multimode fibers in the same ring.

two nodes. This is because most of the power coming from the large-diameter multimode fiber will not be able to enter the small-diameter single-mode fiber. The single-mode connectors use a different keying than the multimode connectors. The keying is designed specifically to prevent this possibility. A single-mode cable cannot be connected to a multimode device/fiber and vice versa. Also, the optical bypasses that would result in connecting fibers of different mode types are not allowed.

The specifications for single-mode fiber and devices are explained and described in the remainder of this chapter.

6.2 Single-Mode Fiber Specifications

In this section, we explain various requirements for single-mode fibers as specified in the FDDI SMF-PMD standard. Unless you have already done so, you may want to read Chapter 5 on multimode fibers. Most of the concepts explained in that chapter will be used here.

The single-mode fiber used in FDDI should satisfy the following requirements:

1. *Dimensions*: The structural imperfection in the fiber can cause losses due to scattering. These losses can become significant for low-loss fibers. It is, therefore, important to control structural imperfections such as variation in cladding diameter, core diameter, cladding circularity, and core-to-cladding concentricity. The SMF-PMD standard places limits on some of these imperfections.

   The nominal cladding diameter for single-mode fibers is the same as that for multimode fibers, that is, 125 μm. This results in the use of the same mechanical considerations for cable design. A variation of ± 2 μm in the cladding diameter is allowed. The noncircularity of cladding is measured by the diameters of the smallest circle that can circumscribe the cladding and the largest circle that can be inscribed within the cladding (both circles concentric), divided by the cladding diameter. A noncircularity of $\pm 2\%$ is allowed. The core and cladding must be concentric and the distance between their centers should not exceed 1 μm. The circularity and concentricity requirements are shown geometrically in Figure 6.2.
2. *Mode-Field Diameter:* Unlike multimode fibers, core diameter is not a meaningful parameter for single-mode fibers. This is because the signal extends well beyond the thin core of the single-mode fibers into the cladding. In other words, the field of the propagating mode extends into the cladding. The core diameter does not reflect the amount of power that is coupled in the fiber. The **mode field diameter (MFD)**, as the name implies, is the effective diameter of the field of the mode that is propagated. Assuming a Gaussian distribution of power, the mode-field diameter is measured as the diameter at which the electric and magnetic field strengths are reduced to $1/e$ of

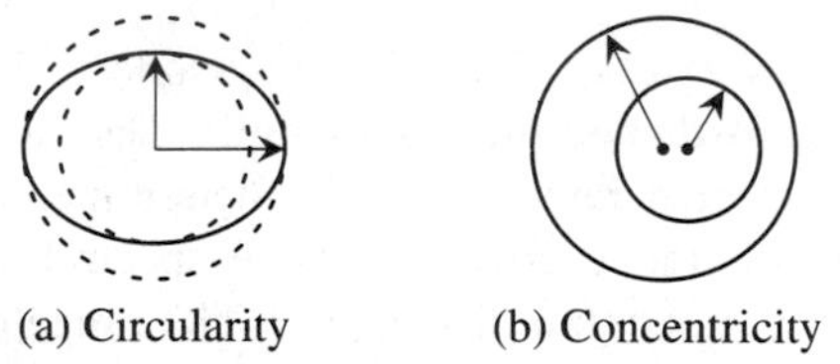

Figure 6.2 Circularity and concentricity of cladding.

their maximum values. At this diameter, the radiant power is reduced to $1/e^2$ of the maximum power since the power is proportional to the square of the electric or magnetic field strengths.

For FDDI, the mode-field diameter of the single-mode fiber should be 8.7 μm. A variation (standard error) of ± 0.5 μm is allowed.

3. *Cutoff Wavelength*: As explained in Section 4.4, the second- and higher order modes are guided only if the normalized frequency V is larger than 2.405. Recall that V is given by:

$$V = \frac{2\pi a}{\lambda} \text{NA}$$

Here, a is the radius of the core, λ is the wavelength of the light, and NA is the numerical aperture. The wavelength above which the second-order mode is not guided is called the **cutoff wavelength**. The following example illustrates the computation of cutoff wavelength.

Example 6.1 For a fiber with a core diameter of 8.5 μm and a numerical aperture of 0.113, the cutoff wavelength λ_c is calculated as follows:

$$V = \frac{\pi 2a\text{NA}}{\lambda}$$

If V is less than 2.405, only the fundamental mode is propagated. Hence,

$$2.405 = \frac{\pi 8.5 \times 0.113}{\lambda_c}$$

or

$$\lambda_c = \frac{\pi 8.5 \times 0.113}{2.405} = 1255 \text{ nm}$$

Notice that the number of modes depends on the wavelength. A single-mode fiber becomes multimoded at wavelengths lower than the cutoff wavelength λ_c. For FDDI fiber this wavelength is specified to be at most 1260 nm. If the source center wavelength is more than this, most of the power is concentrated in the fundamental mode. Higher order modes have negligible power. □

4. *Dispersion*: The photons entering the fiber at the same instant arrive at the other end at slightly different times. This results in pulse widening or dispersion as explained in Section 4.5. In single-mode fibers, the chromatic dispersion caused by the dependence of the velocity on the color (wavelength) of light is the chief cause of dispersion. The chromatic dispersion is defined as the slope of the velocity with respect to wavelength:

$$\text{Dispersion} = \frac{d(\text{Velocity})}{d\lambda}$$

The dispersion curve crosses zero in the 1300-nm window. The exact wavelength at which this happens is called the **zero-dispersion wavelength**. The slope S of the dispersion curve at this wavelength is an important parameter since it determines (to a first order) the difference in the velocity of wavelength range covered by the spectral width of the source. Since the dispersion curve is nonlinear, maximum dispersion in the range of wavelength is also specified. The zero-dispersion wavelength should be between 1300 to 1322 nm. The zero-dispersion slope should be less than or equal to 0.095 ps/nm^2-km. The maximum dispersion should be less than 3.5 ps/nm-km in the 1285- to 1330-nm range.

5. *Length*: Unlike the 2-km limit for multimode fibers, no length limit is specified for single-mode fibers. Instead, maximum attenuation and dispersion limits are specified. Depending on the quality of the fiber, transmitter, and receiver, the distance limit may vary. In particular, in some configurations the fiber length may be limited by dispersion and not by attenuation. This happens, for example, when a transmitter with a large spectral width is used with a very sensitive receiver. A Category I transmitter and Category II receiver pair may result in such a situation. In calculating the allowable length of the fiber, both attenuation and dispersion for the link should be computed and checked. This is explained further in Section 20.4.

   Note that the use of single-mode fiber increases only the interstation distance. The total length of the fiber on the two rings is still limited to 200 km. This limit is set to bound the signal propagation delay around the ring. A larger propagation delay results in lower efficiency as shown later in Chapter 22.
6. *Attenuation*: The allowable power loss on the link depends on the output power of the transmitter and the sensitivity of the receiver. In the case of single-mode fibers, the transmission penalties caused by optical reflections at fiber junctions become significant and should also be considered when determining the link budget (see item 2 in Section 6.1). In general, the allowed link loss budget is:

   Link loss budget = Minimum output power of the transmitter
   −Minimum input power allowed at the receiver
   −1 dB for transmission penalty

   If a Category II (more powerful) transmitter is used and there is not enough loss in the link, too much power may be received at the detector, causing overflow of current and saturation. The standard therefore also specifies a minimum link attenuation. Whenever the fiber attenuation is less than the minimum, an external attenuator should be used to meet the requirement. The minimum attenuation is given by:

   Minimum link loss = Maximum output power of the transmitter
   −Maximum input power allowed at the receiver

   Since there are two categories of transmitters and receivers, there are four possible combinations of transmitter-receiver pairs. These four pairs and the corresponding minimum and maximum link loss (or cable plant attenuation) for each are listed in Table 6.1. For example, when using a Category II transmitter and a Category II receiver, the maximum allowed link loss is 32 dB and the minimum is 15 dB. If the link loss is less than 15 dB, an attenuator should be used. The attenuator should always be placed just before the receiver.

Table 6.1 Cable Plant Attenuation

Category of		Attenuation	
Transmitter	Receiver	Minimum	Maximum
I	I	0 dB	10 dB
I	II	1 dB	16 dB
II	I	14 dB	26 dB
II	II	15 dB	32 dB

Table 6.2 Transmitters for Single-Mode Fibers

	Category I		Category II		
	Min	Max	Min	Max	Units
Central wavelength	1270.0	1340.0	1290.0	1330.0	nm
Spectral width (rms)	—	15.0	—	5.0	nm
Average power (using Halt symbols)	−20.0	−14.0	−4.0	0.0	dBm
Rise time (10% to 90%)	—	3.5	—	2.0	ns
Fall time (90% to 10%)	—	3.5	—	2.0	ns
Duty cycle distortion (peak–peak)	—	1.0	—	1.0	ns
Data-dependent jitter (peak–peak)	—	0.6	—	0.6	ns
Random jitter (peak–peak)	—	0.76	—	0.76	ns
Extinction ratio	—	10.0	—	10.0	%
Transmission penalty	—	1.0	—	1.0	dB

6.3 Transmitters

Two categories of transmitters are specified. The specifications for the transmitters include the receptacle part of the connector. This combination of the transmitter and the receptacle is called the **active output interface** (**AOI**) in the standard.

The specifications for the two categories of the transmitters are listed in Table 6.2. Most of the terms used in the table were explained earlier in Section 5.4. Transmission penalty was explained in item 2 of Section 6.1. Notice that the specifications for Category I transmitters are the same as those for multimode transmitters. Category II transmitters are more powerful than Category I and thus allow longer distances.

The pulse envelopes are also specified for the two categories of transmitters. The envelopes are very similar to those shown earlier in Figure 5.10 for multimode fibers. The differences are due to differences in LED and laser output pulse shapes. In particular, ringing (oscillations) during the first 5 ns following a transition is allowed to exceed the envelope as long as the ringing frequency exceeds 375 MHz and the 50% level of the ringing complies with the envelope.

Transmitters emitting the maximum power allowed for Category II allow distances up to approximately 60 km. However, they require special safety precautions to avoid occupational hazards. Because of these safety considerations, some manufacturers use lower-powered transceivers that limit the distance to approximately 40 km. Laser safety is discussed in detail in Section 19.8.

6.4 Receivers

Two categories of receivers are specified. The specifications for the receivers include the receptacle part of the connector. This combination of the receiver and the receptacle is called the **active input interface** (**AII**) in the standard.

The specifications for the two categories of the receivers are listed in Table 6.3. Most of the terms used in the table were explained earlier in Section 5.5. Notice that the specifications for the Category I receivers are the same as those for multimode PMD. Category II receivers are more sensitive than Category I and thus allow for longer distance fiber.

Table 6.3 Receivers for Single-Mode Fibers

	Category I		Category II		
	Min	Max	Min	Max	Units
Central wavelength	1270.0	1340.0	1290.0	1330.0	nm
Average power (using halt symbols)	−31.0	−14.0	−37.0	−15.0	dBm
Rise time (10% to 90%)	—	5.0	—	5.0	ns
Fall time (90% to 10%)	—	5.0	—	5.0	ns
Duty cycle distortion (peak–peak)	—	1.0	—	1.0	ns
Data-dependent jitter (peak–peak)	—	1.2	—	1.2	ns
Random jitter (peak–peak)	—	0.76	—	0.76	ns

The signal-detect timing requirements for SMF are similar to those shown in Figure 5.11 for MMF, except that the fixed thresholds of −31 and −45 dBm in Table 5.7 are replaced by P_{Min} and P_{Min} − 14 dB where P_{Min} is the minimum average power specified for the receiver.

6.5 Connectors

The media interface connector (MIC) for single-mode fiber is similar to that for multimode described earlier in Section 5.6. The three key differences are:

1. The tolerances are smaller. Single-mode fiber is thinner and more precise alignment is necessary.
2. The keying is different so that single-mode fiber cannot be connected to a transceiver designed for multimode fibers and vice versa.
3. The MIC is mandatory for a Category I transmitter-receiver pair. For the other three possible combinations of transmitter-receivers, the MIC interface is optional because Category II transceivers have to be handled only by trained professionals due to their high power levels; therefore the chances of errors are smaller.

The receptacles for single-mode fibers have two keys. One designates the type of the port: A, B, S, or M. The other designates the mode. As shown in Figure 6.3, this second key prevents a multimode fiber plug from being inserted in a single-mode device. The single-mode fiber plug,

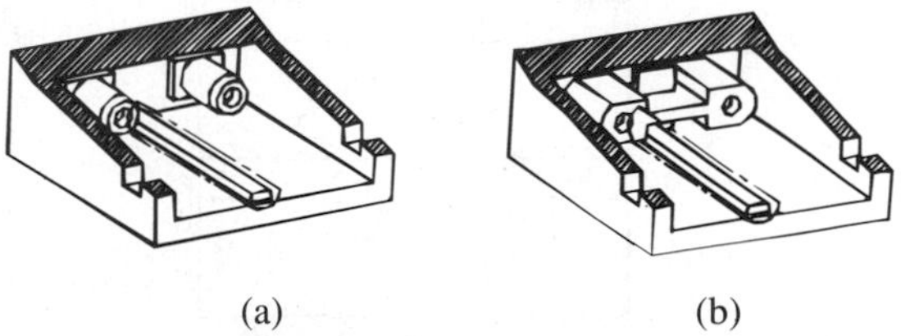

Figure 6.3 A single-mode receptacle.

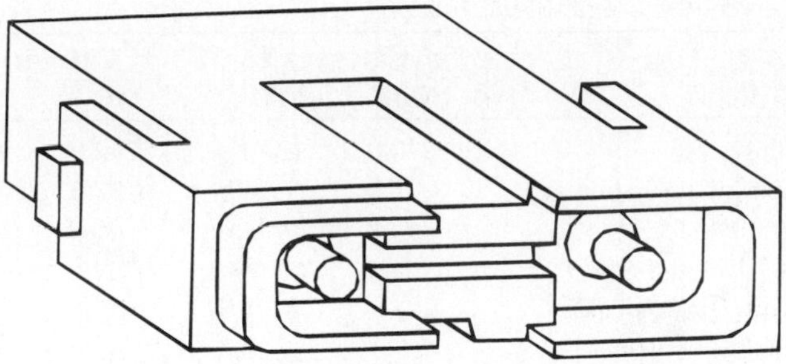

Figure 6.4 An SMF plug.

shown in Figure 6.4, has slots in the corresponding positions. Incidentally, the two receptacle designs shown in Figure 6.3 are for use with devices and fibers, respectively. The first design is used for receptacles on the transceiver. The second design is used for receptacles on fiber-to-fiber connections. The extra strengthening member provides stability to the connection.

The keys for the four ports are shown in Figure 6.5. The ports are labeled SA, SB, SM, or SS. The prefix "S" in the port type denotes single mode. The plugs as well as receptacles are also of four types. The SA plug inserts into SA receptacles only. Similarly, SB and SM plugs insert into SB and SM receptacles, respectively. The SS plug key is designed such that it can insert into all four types of receptacles.

Note that the keying for a receptacle is mandatory, while that for the plug is optional. In any case, the plugs should be labeled to indicate the type of port.

6.5.1 Cabling Systems

An SS-to-SM cable with an SS plug on one end and an SM plug on the other can be used to connect single-attachment stations to concentrators. Similarly, an SA-to-SB cable can be used to connect dual-attachment stations and concentrators to form the trunk ring. These two cable types are

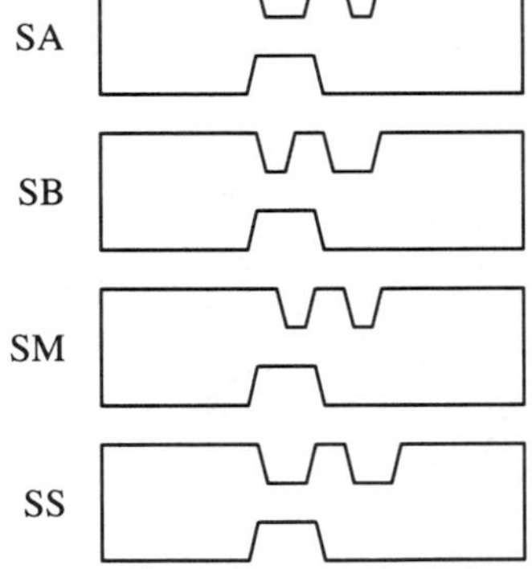

Figure 6.5 Keying for single-mode connectors.

sufficient to form any FDDI ring. A cabling system that uses these two types of cables prevents the following two types of cabling errors:

1. Reversal of dual-attachment stations (connecting the B-port where the A-port should be).
2. Connection of single-attachment stations in the trunk ring.

These errors were discussed earlier in Section 5.7.

It is also possible to form a complete FDDI ring with just SS-to-SS cables, that is, cables with SS-plugs on both ends. However, this is not a desirable cabling system, since it does not prevent any of the three cabling errors discussed earlier.

Because of the laser's sensitivity to back-reflections, it is important to ensure that the return loss of optical components such as connectors, splices, bypass switches, and attenuators is high. The return loss is measured by the fraction of incident optical power that is reflected back. The SMF-PMD standard requires that the optical return loss (ORL) for all optical components be at least 20 dB.

6.6 Optical Bypasses

An optical bypass allows a dual-attachment station to be disconnected from the trunk ring. As explained earlier in Section 5.8, in the bypass mode, the incoming signal is directly passed to the outgoing fiber.

The requirements for SMF bypasses are identical to those for MMF (listed in Table 5.8). The only additional requirement is that the optical return loss be at least 20 dB. A higher return loss means less power is reflected back to the source.

The use of an optical bypass is optional. The resulting combined link should satisfy all the link requirements. A bypass should not connect a single-mode fiber to a multimode fiber.

Optical bypass switches are not allowed on Category II and mixed Category I-II links. This is because the crosstalk from a high-powered bypassed transmitter is high enough to fool a downstream station into assuming that the transmitter is still active. The minimum crosstalk isolation expected is 40 dB while the maximum launch power is 0 dBm. Thus, the crosstalk generated by a bypassed transmitter could be -40 dBm, which is higher than signal deassert levels for both Category I and II receivers. The minimum deassert level is -45 dBm for Category I receivers and -52 dBm for Category II receivers.

6.7 Summary

Box 6.1 summarizes the single-mode fiber PMD. The main requirement that most buyers of standard compliant equipment should be aware of is that laser transmitters are required with single-mode fiber. These transmitters are an order of magnitude more expensive than LED transmitters, which work only with multimode fibers. The single-mode fiber standard specifies two categories of transceiver. Category II transceivers extend the distance between stations up to approximately 60 km. High-powered transmitters should be used only on long links. Using them on short links may overload the receiver unless an attenuator is used. The connectors for single-mode fibers are keyed so that they cannot be used on devices designed for multimode and vice versa.

Box 6.1 Single-Mode Fiber PMD Summary

1. Window: 1300 nm
2. Fiber:
   a. Single mode.
   b. Cladding diameter: 125 ± 2 μm.
   c. Mode-field diameter: 8.7 μm ± 0.5 μm.
   d. Allowable length is computed from total link loss and bandwidth analysis.
   e. Maximum allowed loss depends on the transmitter-receiver categories.
   f. One decibel should be allowed for reflections and dispersion penalties.
   g. The fiber bandwidth should be such that the 10% to 90% rise/fall time at fiber exit is limited to 5 ns.
3. Transmitter: Laser sources are required to meet the spectral width requirement.
   a. Two categories of transmitters are specified. The average power for Category I transmitters is −20 to −14 dBm. That for Category II transmitters is −4 to 0 dBm.
   b. The 10% to 90% rise/fall times should be less than 3.5 ns.
   c. The maximum rms spectral width is 15 nm for Category I and 5 nm for Category II.
   d. The maximum duty cycle distortion of 1 ns, data-dependent jitter of 1.2 ns, and random jitter of 0.76 ns.
4. Receiver: Two categories of receivers are specified. The average power for Category I is −31 to −14 dBm. That for Category II is −37 to −15 dBm.
5. Connectors: Duplex connectors with a specified receptacle geometry should be used. The receptacle and plugs have a port-type key and a single-mode key.
6. Optical Bypasses: Optical bypasses are neither required nor defined for single-attachment stations. They are optional for dual-attachment stations and concentrators. If used, the bypassed link should meet the distance and loss requirements. Other performance requirements of the bypass are:
   a. Attenuation should be less than 2.5 dB.
   b. Interchannel isolation should be at least 40 dB.
   c. The switching time should be less than 25 ms.
   d. The media interruption time should be less than 15 ms.
   e. The optical return loss should be more than 20 dB.
   f. Should not be used on Category II or mixed Category I-II links.

6.8 Further Reading

The requirements for FDDI single-mode fiber links are specified in the ANSI X3.184-199x or ISO/IEC CD 9314-4:199x.

See Sections 4.14 and 5.10 for further discussion of the concepts used in this chapter. For arguments in favor of using single-mode fibers (rather than multimode fibers) see Rocher (1988).

Figure 6.4 and Tables 6.2 and 6.3 have been adapted from ANSI X3.184-199x.

6.9 Self-Test Exercises

Note: Some exercises have multiple correct answers. See Appendix D for answers.

6.1 The cutoff wavelength for FDDI single-mode fibers is specified to be 1260 nm. What does this imply?

a. The fiber has a zero material dispersion at 1260 nm.
b. The fiber does not permit transmission of 1260-nm signals.
c. The fiber does not permit transmission of 850-nm signals.
d. The fiber does not permit transmission of 1300-nm signals.
e. The fiber permits multimode transmission at 850 nm.
f. The fiber permits multimode transmission at 1500 nm.

6.2 Why do single-mode links allow longer distances than multimode links in FDDI?

a. Laser transmitters used in single-mode links are more powerful.
b. Receivers used in single-mode links are more sensitive.
c. Single-mode fiber has a lower attenuation.
d. Single-mode fiber has a lower dispersion.
e. All of the above.

6.3 Which of the following can you connect directly?

a. Two stations with Category II transceivers
b. Two stations with Category I transceivers
c. One station with a Category I transceiver and another with a Category II transceiver

6.4 The maximum link length allowed by the single-mode fiber PMD is:

a. 2 km
b. 40 km
c. 60 km
d. not specified

6.5 Optical bypasses are allowed on

a. DASs with Category II transceivers
b. DASs with Category I transceivers
c. DASs with Category I transceivers but connected to another DAS with a Category II transceiver
d. DASs with Category II transceivers but connected to another DAS with a Category I transceiver

CHAPTER 7

Low-Cost Fiber (LCF-PMD)

After the initial FDDI specifications were completed in 1990, it was realized that one of the impediments to rapid deployment of FDDI was the high cost of optical components. To switch from the lower speed technology of IEEE 802.3/Ethernet or IEEE 802.5/token ring networks, it was necessary to rewire the building, install FDDI concentrators, install FDDI adapters in systems, install new software, and so on. Although the cost of all components was continuously decreasing, it was still high. Therefore, a standard effort was begun to find a low-cost alternative.

This effort has resulted in a new media-dependent physical layer standard called **Low-Cost Fiber PMD (LCF-PMD)**. Originally the committee intended to find a fiber that was cheaper than the 62.5/125 multimode fiber used in the standard FDDI. A number of alternatives such as plastic fiber and 200/230-μm fiber were considered but were quickly rejected when it was realized that the real expense was in the devices (transmitters and receivers) and not in the fiber. A search for lower powered devices then began. The resulting standard and its key design issues are described in this chapter.

LCF-PMD allows low-cost transmitter and receiver devices to be used on any FDDI link. These devices are cheaper because they have higher noise margins and are either lower powered or less sensitive than those specified in the original multimode fiber PMD (MMF-PMD). The specification has been designed for links up to 500 m long (compared to 2 km in MMF-PMD). This distance is sufficient for most intrabuilding applications.

Only the interbuilding links that are longer than 500 m need to pay the higher cost of MMF-PMD devices. Figure 7.1 shows a sample FDDI network connecting two buildings. Notice that any combination of LCF, MMF, SMF, SONET, and copper links can be intermixed in a single FDDI network as long as the distance limitations of each are carefully followed.

In this chapter, we make extensive use of concepts explained in Chapters 4 and 5. It is assumed that you have already read these chapters.

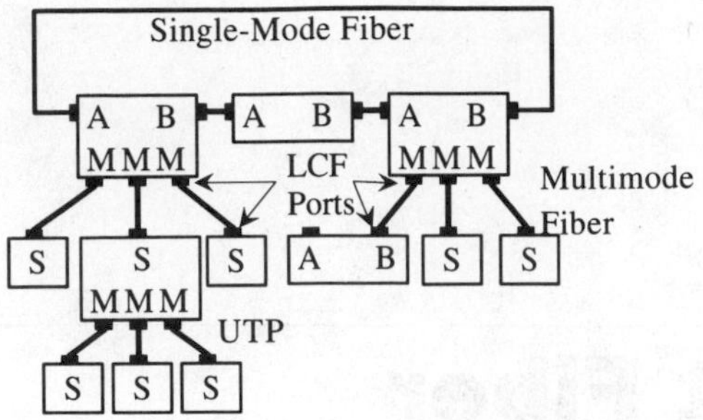

Figure 7.1 A sample FDDI network with multimode, single-mode, low-cost fiber, and copper links.

7.1 Key Design Decisions

Table 7.1 provides a comparison of the key design decisions for LCF and MMF PMDs, which are explained in the following:

1. *Wavelength:* LCF uses a 1300-nm wavelength, which is the same as in multimode and single-mode PMDs. Initially, an 850-nm wavelength was suggested because 850-nm devices are used in fiber optic Ethernet (IEEE 802.3 10BASE-F) and token ring (IEEE 802.5J) networks. They are sold in large volume and so are slightly cheaper than 1300-nm devices. However, using 850 nm would have introduced a problem of incompatibility because users would also have to remember (and label) the source wavelength and use the same wavelength device at the receiving end. This would have caused the receiving adapter to be replaced every time the transmitting adapter was replaced. With 1300 nm at both ends, the user need only worry about the distance. As long as the distance is less than 500 m, the two ends can use any combination of LCF and MMF devices. Also, the difference between the price of 850-nm and 1300-nm devices is decreasing fast as FDDI is coming into use.
2. *Fiber:* LCF specifies 62.5/125-μm graded-index multimode fiber—the same as that specified in MMF-PMD. Initially plastic fibers and 200/230-μm step-index fibers were considered. Plastic

Table 7.1 Low-Cost Fiber Versus Multimode Fiber PMD

Issue	MMF	LCF
Wavelength	1300 nm	1300 nm
Fiber	62.5/125 multimode	62.5/125 multimode
Transmit power	Max −20 dBm	Max −22 dBm
Receive power	Min −31 dBm	Min −29 dBm
Link length	2 km	500m
Connector	Duplex-FDDI	Duplex-SC or duplex-ST
Connector keying	Port & polarity	No port; polarity only
Optical bypass	Optional	Optional

fibers are inexpensive but they have a high attenuation. The use of plastic fibers would have severely limited the distance. Two-hundred micrometer fibers have a larger core, which allows for a larger amount of power to be coupled in the fiber. The connectors and splices for these fibers are also slightly cheaper since no active alignment is required. However, as discussed earlier in Section 4.5, the large diameter of the core implies more dispersion and therefore lower bandwidth. For 200-μm fiber, a bandwidth-distance product of 30 MHz-km was predicted while 80 MHz-km (800 MHz over 100 m) has been measured. Since the 200-μm fiber has an attenuation of 16 dB/km compared to 2 dB/km for 62.5/125-μm fiber, transmitters for 200-μm fiber would have been required to produce more power.

The main problem with 200/230-μm fibers is that intermixing them with 62.5/125 fibers on the same link causes a significant amount of power loss as shown in Figure 7.2. When it was realized that a 50% cost reduction goal could be achieved by simply changing the transmit and receive power levels by 2 dBm, all efforts to change the fiber came to a halt.

3. *Connector:* The duplex connector specified in MMF-PMD was designed specifically for FDDI. Due to its low-volume production, its cost is high. Significant savings can be obtained by using other simplex connectors. In fact, many FDDI installations use the simplex-ST connector. The LCF committee wanted to use a duplex connector to avoid misconnections resulting in two transmitters being connected to each other.

A duplex-SC connector, shown in Figure 7.3, was proposed. SC, which stands for subscriber connector, is a Japanese standard. It is an augmentation of the FC (fiber connector). The SC connector was developed in 1984 to provide a push-pull interface, which reduces the space required between the connectors (compared to the case in which the connector has to be rotated by fingers). As a result, a large number of connectors can be placed side by side. Considerable savings in packaging cost are obtained because it allows putting more ports on the given-size board in a concentrator.

SC has a connector loss of 0.3 dB and a return loss (reflection) of 43 dB. In the United States, ST (straight tip) connectors are more popular than SC or FC connectors. A number of companies have proposed the development of a duplex-ST connector with specifications matching those of the duplex-SC. After much heated debate, termed "Connector War II," duplex-SC was voted the main selection, with duplex-ST being the recommended alternative. Duplex-SC is described in the main part of the LCF-PMD standard while duplex-ST is described in an appendix. Fiber channel, which is a high-speed fiber optic link standard, also uses duplex-SC connectors.

Regardless of the ST/SC choice, the LCF standard does not require any port type (A, B, S, or M) keying on the connectors. A label on the connector shows the type of port and the users

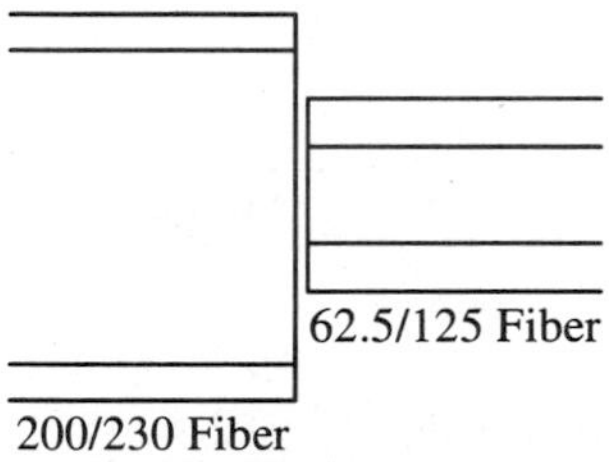

Figure 7.2 Connecting two different size fibers results in additional losses.

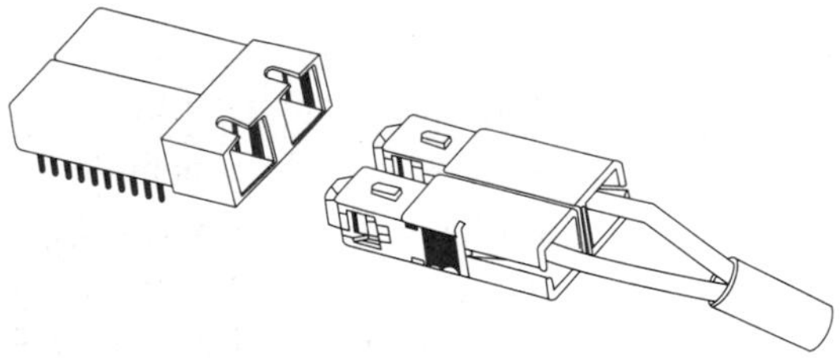

Figure 7.3 Duplex-SC connector.

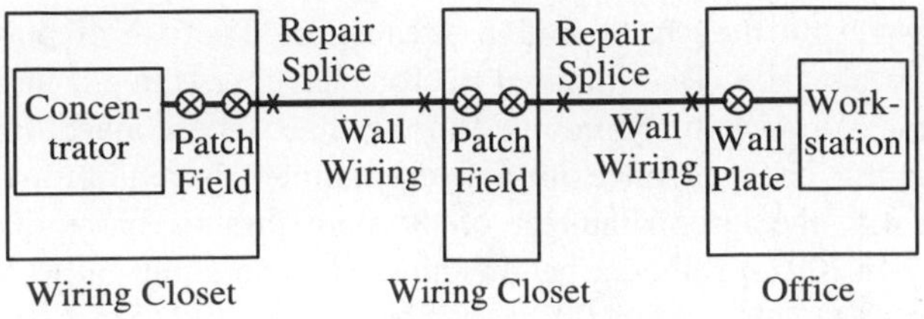

Figure 7.4 A typical concentrator to station link.

are expected to read the label and connect accordingly. The connectors do have a polarity keying such that it is possible to connect two fiber pairs only one way—two transmitting fibers cannot be connected to each other by mistake. The recommended labeling practices are described in Section 7.2.

4. *Transmitter/Receivers:* MMF-PMD requires a transmiting power of at least −20 dBm. The receiver is required to sense correctly a received power of −31 to −14 dBm, that is, a dynamic range of 17 dBm. Reducing the transmitted power and the dynamic range (even slightly) reduces the cost significantly. LCF-PMD reduces the required transmit power by 2 dBm and also the receiver dynamic range by 2 dBm. The transmitted power range is (−22, −14) dBm, while the received power range is (−29, −14) dBm. This means that the maximum loss allowed in the fiber is only 7 dB (= 29 − 22) instead of 11 dB. A typical concentrator to station link, as shown in Figure 7.4, has five connectors. Allowing for four repair splices, 7 dB is sufficient for a 500-m fiber as shown in Table 7.2.
5. *Chromatic Dispersion Parameters:* The 2-km length limit on multimode fiber links is primarily due to chromatic dispersion. Therefore, in MMF-PMD, chromatic dispersion parameters were very carefully specified including the slope of the dispersion curve (shown in Figure 5.5). The effect of dispersion on the bandwidth of the link is inversely proportional to the length of the link (see Section 19.8). For 500-m or shorter links, there is sufficient bandwidth to carry the FDDI signal and chromatic dispersion is not a problem. Dispersion parameters are, therefore, not specified for LCF links. Even the spectral width specification (shown in Figure 5.7) has been removed. This means that the sources do not have to be tested for spectral width. This results in lower cost transceivers.
6. *Jitter Budget:* MMF-PMD specifies a data-dependent jitter (DDJ) of 0.6 ns for the fiber. DDJ is caused by dispersion in the fiber. It is not a problem for short fiber lengths and, therefore, this jitter can be allocated to other components of the link. Three proposals were made. The first

Table 7.2 Loss Budget for LCF Links

Item	Minimum dB	Typical dB	Maximum dB
Connectors (5)	0.2 × 5 = 1.00	0.6 × 5 = 3.00	1.0 × 5 = 5.00
Fiber (500 m)	0.75 × 0.5 = 0.38	1.2 × 0.5 = 0.60	1.5 × 0.5 = 0.75
Repair splices (4)	0.1 × 4 = 0.40	0.2 × 4 = 0.80	0.2 × 4 = 0.80
Total	1.78	4.40	6.55

proposal was simply to tighten the bit error rate to 10^{-12} (instead of 2.5×10^{-10}). The second proposal was to increase the duty cycle distortion (DCD) allowance for the transmitter thus reducing its cost. The third proposal was to decrease the receiver sensitivity, thereby reducing the cost of the receiver. The cost savings in the transmitters/receivers were not found to be significant and, therefore, the first proposal was accepted. Jitter specifications are discussed further in Section 7.4.

7. *Rise/Fall Times:* Since LCF-PMD uses the same fiber as MMF-PMD but the link length has been decreased from 2 km to 500 m, the pulse broadening caused by fiber dispersion is less. The change then in pulse rise and fall times due to the fiber is not as much. The time thus saved has been allocated to transmitters and receivers to reduce their cost. Thus, LCF transmitters are allowed to have a rise/fall time of 4.0 ns compared to 3.5 ns for MMF transmitters. Thus, lower quality (hence, cheaper) transmitters can be used. Similarly, LCF receivers are required to receive pulses with a rise/fall time below 4.5 ns compared to 5 ns for MMF receivers. This again means less work (hence, lower cost) for the receivers.
8. *Optical Bypass:* Optical bypasses are optional for LCF links. The loss budget of 7 dB is too small to allow for two or more links (joined by the bypass) to be able to satisfy the loss requirement. Therefore, optical bypasses are not expected to be widely used with LCF links. If a bypass is used, the characteristics specified in the MMF-PMD standard apply.
9. *Signal Detect Time:* As explained earlier in Section 5.5, the receivers need to indicate whether any signal is being received on a link. This indication, called *signal-detect*, is on (asserted) during normal operation. It is turned off (deasserted) when the link is taken off line and insufficient power is received. The signal-detect timings for LCF receivers are same as those listed in Table 5.7 for MMF receivers except that the maximum value of assert power (level at which the signal is asserted) has been increased from −31 to −29 dBm.

Tables 7.3 and 7.4 present the requirements for the LCF transmitters and receivers, respectively. The corresponding values for MMF transmitters and receivers, if different, are also shown in these tables. Some characteristics have both minimum and maximum limits; these are specified by the interval notation (x, y), where x is the minimum and y is the maximum.

Table 7.3 Transmitter Characteristics

Characteristics	LCF-PMD	MMF-PMD
Center wavelength	(1270, 1380) nm	Same
Spectrum FWHM	Max 250 nm	*
Average power (Halt symbols)	(−22,−14) dBm	(−20, −14) dBm
Rise time (10% to 90%)	Max 4 ns	(0.6, 3.5) ns
Fall time (90% to 10%)	Max 4 ns	(0.6, 3.5) ns
Duty cycle distortion (peak-to-peak)	Max 1 ns	Same
Data-dependent jitter (peak-to-peak)	Max 0.6 ns	Same
Random jitter (peak-to-peak)	Max 0.76 ns	Same
Extinction ratio	Max 10%	Same

* Specified as a function of wavelength and transition times. See Figure 5.7.

Table 7.4 Receiver Specifications

Characteristics	LCF-PMD	MMF-PMD
Center wavelength	(1270, 1380) nm	Same
Average power (Halt symbols)	(−29, −14) dBm	(−31, −14) dBm
Rise time (10% to 90%)	Max 4.5 ns	(0.6, 5) ns
Fall time (90% to 10%)	Max 4.5 ns	(0.6, 5) ns
Duty cycle distortion (peak-to-peak)	Max 1 ns	Same
Data-dependent jitter (peak-to-peak)	Max 0.6 ns	Max 1.2 ns
Random jitter (peak-to-peak)	Max 0.76 ns	Same

7.2 Station and Connector Labeling

FDDI stations are labeled in a location close to or on the connector receptacles. The wall jacks are also similarly labeled. The FDDI cables connecting the FDDI equipment with the wall jack are also labeled. The LCF-PMD standard recommends (but does not require) a label format of FDDI-*xyz*, where *x* is the connector type, *y* is the PMD type, and *z* is the port type. The presence of the word "FDDI" identifies it as an FDDI device or cable. Possible port types are A, B, S, and M, with their usual meaning. Possible values for the type of connector and PMD are listed in Tables 7.5 and 7.6. The RJ-45 and DB-9 connectors are used for twisted-pair links as explained later in Section 8.5. The SONET links are covered in Chapter 9. An example of this type of labeling is FDDI-CLM, which refers to a duplex-SC connector (C) on a low-cost fiber interface (L) on one of the master ports (M) of a concentrator.

The standard recommends that the plug labels be visible before as well as after the connection. The type indicated on the wall jack must be maintained to indicate correctly the changes in the associated equipment, for example, a change from a dual ring to a concentrator structure would require a label change on the wall jack.

Table 7.5
FDDI Station Labeling (Connector Type)

Code	Meaning
M	MIC
C	Duplex-SC
T	Duplex-ST
J	RJ-45
D	DB-9

Table 7.6 FDDI Station Labeling (PMD Type)

Code	Meaning
P	Multimode fiber (MMF-PMD)
L	Low-cost fiber (LCF-PMD)
D	Data grade unshielded twisted pair (DTP)
S	Shielded twisted pair (STP)
U	Unshielded twisted pair (UTP)
1	Single-mode fiber (both receiver/transmitter of type 1)
2	Single-mode fiber (both receiver/transmitter of type 2)
3	Single-mode fiber (receiver type 1, transmitter type 2)
4	Single-mode fiber (receiver type 2, transmitter type 1)
H	SONET link (SPM)

7.3 Alternative Fiber Types

Like the MMF-PMD standard, the LCF standard specifies 62.5/125 multimode graded-index fiber as the recommended fiber type. Other fibers such as 50/125, 85/125, 100/140, and 200/230 fibers are also allowed. The first three of these were specified in MMF-PMD as well. The 200/230 fiber has been added in LCF. These fibers may launch excessive transmit power, which may exceed the dynamic range of the receiver.

The fiber core diameter affects the amount of power launched into the fiber. The transmitters are designed for launching a particular amount of power in a specific fiber type. If a larger diameter fiber is used, more power is launched. Similarly, the receiving optics is designed for a particular fiber type. If a larger diameter fiber is used, some power may be lost. The remaining loss budget for the link, therefore, depends on the fiber type used. Table 7.7 lists alternative fiber types, their numerical apertures, and the loss budgets remaining. All adjustments are relative to an implementation using 62.5-μm fiber, which has a loss budget of 7 dB.

Table 7.7 Loss Budgets for Alternative Fiber Types

Fiber Type	Transmitter	Receiver	Remaining
50/125 μm (NA = 0.20)	−5.0 dB	0.0 to 1.0 dB	2.0 to 3.0 dB
50/125 μm (NA = 0.21)	−4.5 dB	0.0 to 1.0 dB	2.5 to 3.5 dB
50/125 μm (NA = 0.22)	−4.0 dB	0.0 to 1.0 dB	3.0 to 4.0 dB
62.5/125 μm (NA = 0.275)	0.0 dB	0.0 dB	7.0 dB
85/125 μm (NA = 0.26)	−1.0 dB	0.0 to −2.6 dB	5.5 to 9.0 dB
100/140 μm (NA = 0.29)	2.0 dB	0.0 to −4.0 dB	5.0 to 9.0 dB
200/230 μm (NA = 0.40) step-index	2.0 dB	0.00 to −8.0 dB	1.0 to 9.0 dB
200/230 μm (NA = 0.40)	2.0 dB	0.00 to −8.0 dB	1.0 to 9.0 dB

Table 7.8 LCF Jitter Budget[a]

Interface	DCD	DDJ	RJ
PHY-out	0.4	0.0	0.320
PMD-out	1.0	0.6	0.760
PMD-in	1.0	0.6	0.760
PHY-in	1.4	1.6	3.002

[a]All values are in nanoseconds peak-to-peak.

7.4 Jitter Allocation

In Section 5.4, various types of jitters were explained and it was shown how various specified jitter values ensure that the total jitter does not exceed the bit duration, which is 8 ns for FDDI. For LCF links, the jitter allocations are slightly different than those shown in Table 5.4. The corresponding values for LCF are shown in Table 7.8. As in Section 5.4, these allocations also assume a combined static alignment error (SAE) and DDJ value of 1.5 ns and a random jitter (RJ) of 1.8 ns (peak-to-peak) for the clock. The clock jitter values depend on the implementation and are not specified in the standard. Using these values we get:

$$\begin{aligned}\text{Total jitter} &= \text{DCD}_{\text{PHY-in}} + \text{DDJ}_{\text{PHY-in}} + \text{SAE} + \text{DDJ}_{\text{Clock}} \\ &\quad + \left(\text{RJ}^2_{\text{PHY-in}} + \text{RJ}^2_{\text{Clock}}\right)^{1/2} \\ &= 1.4 + 1.6 + 1.5 + (3.002^2 + 1.8^2)^{1/2} \\ &= 8.0 \text{ ns}\end{aligned}$$

Only the jitter components visible at the PMD interface (PMD-out and PMD-in) are the enforceable parts of the standard. Therefore, the standard does not specify the PHY-out and PHY-in values.

The random jitter peak-to-peak values given are those at which the probability of the jitter exceeding the value is 10^{-12} (compared to 2.5×10^{-10} in the MMF standard). For this bit error rate, assuming a Gaussian distribution, the rms value or standard deviation of the random jitter is 1/14 of the peak-to-peak value.[1]

7.5 Summary

LCF-PMD allows cheaper fiber links, not by using cheaper fiber, but by using low-powered transceivers. The net link budget has been reduced from 11 to 7 dB. The reduced power allows such links to be used only if the link length is less than 500 m. Most intrabuilding links are within this distance range.

The cost of the connector has also been reduced by selecting duplex versions of popular simplex connectors. These connectors are required to only have polarity keying so that an untrained user cannot misconnect a transmitter to another transmitter. No port-type keying is required.

A further savings in the cost of transceivers is obtained by relaxing the rise and fall time requirements.

[1]The rms value of the random clock jitter is incorrectly specified in Table E.1 of LCF-PMD standard as 0.143 ns (this is equal to 1.8/12.6). The correct value is 1.8/14=0.129 ns.

7.6 Further Reading and Historical Notes

The work on low-cost fiber started in August 1990. At that time the ad hoc working group was named "FDDI Low Cost Fiber Optic Concentrator Link Working Group." A formal low-cost fiber standard committee was established in October 1990. Its initial goal was to design a PMD with at least 50% lower cost that would work over at least 100 m and would be compatible with the existing MMF-PMD such that links of either type can coexist in the same ring. All these goals have been met or exceeded.

The requirements for low-cost fiber links are specified in the draft standard ANSI X3.237 or ISO/IEC WD 9314-9.

See also Sections 4.14 and 5.10 for further discussion of the concepts used in this chapter.

Table 7.7 has been adapted from ASC X3T9.5/92-155.

7.7 Self-Test Exercises

Note: Some exercises have multiple correct answers. See Appendix D for answers.

7.1 Why are low-cost fiber links cheaper?

a. A lower quality fiber is used.
b. A cheaper but more efficient fiber is used.
c. The transceivers on the station are more powerful/sensitive.
d. The transceivers on the station are less powerful/sensitive.
e. The 850-nm transceivers are used.

7.2 What type of connectors are recommended in the FDDI low-cost fiber standard?

a. Two simplex connectors
b. Duplex-SC without port-type keying
c. Duplex-ST without polarity keying
d. Duplex FDDI MIC with polarity and port-type keying

CHAPTER 8

FDDI on Twisted-Pair Copper Cables

8.1 Overview

As soon as the initial FDDI products started appearing on the market, the realization was made that one impediment to FDDI acceptance was that it required users to rewire their buildings with fibers. Even if you only need to connect two nearby pieces of equipment on the same floor, you will need to install fibers. Rewiring a building is a major expense and is not easy to justify unless the technology is well proven or absolutely necessary.

Besides the wiring expense, the optical components used in FDDI equipment are also very expensive compared to the electronic components used in other existing LANs. This led several manufacturers to look into the possibility of providing 100-Mbps communication on existing copper wiring. It was found that 100-Mbps transmission using high-quality (shielded or coax) copper cables is feasible at a much lower cost than that of the fiber, particularly if the distance between nodes is limited to 100 m. The transceivers for copper wires are much cheaper than those for optical fibers.

The FDDI standard is currently being extended to run over copper cables. A description of various types of copper media and issues in their applications to FDDI is a topic of this chapter.

An FDDI ring can have a mixture of copper and fiber links. Therefore, short links used in office areas can use existing copper wiring installed for telephones or other LAN applications. This results in considerable cost savings and quicker migration from lower speed LANs to FDDI. Proprietary coaxial cable and shielded twisted-pair (STP) products, which support FDDI links of up to 100 m, are already available. More than 98% of the data cable running in offices is less than 100 m and 95% is less than 50 m. These can be easily upgraded to run at 100 Mbps. For those who may not be familiar with coaxial or twisted-pair cable, the next section gives an overview of various types of copper cables.

8.2 Types of Copper Cables

The copper cables used for data communication are of two major types: twisted-pair or coaxial. The relative advantages of these types and their subtypes are described in this section.

8.2.1 Twisted-Pair Cables

The simplest twisted-pair cable consists of two identical insulated metallic wires that are stranded (twisted) to reduce the inductive coupling between pairs and reduce the crosstalk. The twists in the wire create a coupling that cancels out opposing electromagnetic fields. The greater the number of times the wire twists around itself in a given distance (*twist ratio*), the tighter the coupling. When a wire is loosely twisted, there is less coupling and a greater chance of crosstalk leaking into adjacent wires.

A multipair cable consists of individually insulated pairs of conductors enclosed in a common protective sheath. Each wire pair is twisted together at varying rates to minimize and randomize the coupling of noise and crosstalk into other pairs. Depending on the application, a single cable may contain as many as 3000 pairs.

The placement of many pairs in such proximity has created some problems that were not so severe with open wire lines. The close proximity of the two conductors in the pair results in increased capacitance between the two wires, thus significantly increasing the attenuation (loss of signal). The twisting of the individual pairs within the cable sheath reduces the coupling between pairs but at the high frequencies used in data communication, the attenuation is higher and the problem of crosstalk between neighboring pairs also becomes worse. The interference can be minimized by using a metallic shield around the cable. Thus, there are two types of twisted-pair cables: **unshielded twisted-pair** (**UTP**) and **shielded twisted-pair** (**STP**).

Unshielded twisted-pair cables are normally used for telephone communication. They contain 22-24 gauge solid copper wires. IEEE 802.3 10BASE-T standard allows Ethernet protocols over UTP at 10 Mbps over a distance of 100 m. IBM Type 3 is a UTP. Generally voice and data cannot be run simultaneously within the same sheath. Also, UTP cables must remain at least 1 ft from fluorescent lamps and other high-voltage power devices.

Shielded twisted-pair cables have a metallic shield around the pair, which minimizes the effect of electromagnetic interference from external signals on the pair and reduces the radiated signals from the pair to an acceptable level. STP cables, therefore, have a higher bandwidth than UTP. The STP cable may have an overall shield along with internal shields for individual pairs.

STP cables are used in token rings. Now they can support the Ethernet protocol as well. IBM has specified several types of STP cables. Types 1, 2, 8, and 9 are used for data communication. Type 6 is used for patch cords.

8.2.2 Coaxial Cables

A coaxial cable consists of a single-wire conductor centered within a cylindrical outer conductor, which may be a solid or several layers of braided metal fabric. The two conductors are insulated from one another. The outer conductor is surrounded by a protective jacket. A coaxial cable has a very low loss at high frequencies and provides excellent isolation from external noise and crosstalk. Coaxial cables have a high bandwidth (400 to 10,000 MHz) that can be used to carry a large number of voice conversations, data channels, or television channels. Coaxial cable is commonly used for cable television. A single coaxial cable is used to transmit many channels using frequency-division multiplexing. Large-diameter, high-quality, rigid cable is used for the trunk lines. Smaller diameter, lower quality, more flexible cable is used for subscriber drops. A single coaxial cable can be used for bidirectional transmission by using separate amplifiers for each direction.

In local area network applications, a coaxial cable is used either in baseband or broadband. In the baseband mode, the digital signal is transmitted directly on the cable. In the broadband mode, the digital signal is first modulated onto a carrier and then transmitted using a radio-frequency modem. In the broadband mode, multiple carriers can be used. In the baseband mode, the data rate is equal to that of one LAN, for example, 10 Mbps for IEEE 802.3/Ethernet networks. In the broadband mode, the data rate is much higher. Coaxial cable for broadband applications has superior construction to minimize signal loss. It has multiple shielding to ensure signal integrity.

Coaxial cables became popular in data networking after their use in IEEE 802.3/Ethernet networks. One problem of using the coaxial cable was that it was too thick and difficult to bend around corners. A thinner and flexible version of the cable has therefore been developed. It has a diameter of only 0.18 in. compared to 0.4 in. for the original Ethernet coaxial cable.

Although proprietary FDDI adapters for coax cables are available, ASC X3T9.5 is not working on a coax based standard.

8.3 EIA Categories for UTP Cables

The performance of UTP cables varies considerably. To determine if a particular UTP cable has the capacity to carry a particular bit rate, UTP cables need to be classified by their performance. The Telecommunications Industry Association (TIA), which handles the telecommunication sector of the Electronic Industries Association (EIA), has developed a set of specifications for high-performance UTP cables. For brevity, we will refer to the EIA/TIA classification simply as EIA classification or EIA categories.

The EIA classification applies to cables consisting of four unshielded twisted pairs of 24 AWG insulated conductors enclosed by a thermoplastic jacket. Depending on their transmission performance, UTP cables are classified into five categories:

1. *Categories 1 and 2*: These are very low grade cables typically used for voice and low-speed data transmission. The cables of these categories are not suitable for LAN applications.
2. *Category 3*: The characteristics of these cables are specified for frequencies up to 16 MHz. These are typically used for voice and data transmission rates up to 10 Mbps. This is the cable used in 10BASE-T implementations of IEEE 802.3/Ethernet and in UTP implementations of 4-Mbps IEEE 802.5/token ring networks. This cable is also called **data-inside wire (DIW)** or **data in the walls (DIW)**.
3. *Category 4*: The characteristics of these cables are specified for frequencies up to 20 MHz. These are used for voice and data transmission rates up to 16 Mbps. This is the cable used in UTP implementations of 16-Mbps IEEE 802.5/token ring networks.
4. *Category 5*: The characteristics of these cables are specified up to 100 MHz. They are intended for voice and data transmission rates up to 100 Mbps. These cables are called **data-grade twisted-pair (DTP)**. However, not all DTP cables are of Category 5 since earlier even Category 4 cables were called DTP.

These categories have actually been adopted from the National Electrical Manufacturers Association (NEMA) classification of UTP cables. Categories 3, 4, and 5 correspond to NEMA "Standard 24 AWG," "Low loss 24 AWG," and "Low loss extended distance 24 AWG," respectively. The transmission characteristics requirements of these three categories are summarized in Table 8.1. The terms used in the table are as follows:

1. *Mutual Capacitance*: The capacitance of a pair results in the storage of an electrical charge. It limits the information bit rate that can be transmitted since the change of signal level (voltage)

Table 8.1 Transmission Characteristics of UTP Cables

Characteristics	Frequency	Category 3	Category 4	Category 5
Mutual capacitance (nF per 1000 ft)	1 kHz	20	17	17
Characteristic impedance	1 MHz+	100 Ω ± 15%	100 Ω ± 15%	100 Ω ± 15%
Maximum attenuation (dB per 1000 ft)	0.772 MHz	6.8	5.7	5.5
	1.0 MHz	7.8	6.5	6.3
	4.0 MHz	17	13	13
	8.0 MHz	26	19	18
	16.0 MHz	40	27	25
	20.0 MHz	—	31	28
	25.0 MHz	—	—	32
	31.25 MHz	—	—	36
	62.5 MHz	—	—	52
	100.0 MHz	—	—	67
NEXT Loss[a] (dB per 1000 ft)	0.772	43	58	64

[a] See text for NEXT loss at higher frequencies.

starts a charging/discharging process whose time depends on the capacitance. The capacitance is measured in farads. For UTP, it is specified in nanofarads per 1000 ft.

2. *Characteristic Impedance*: This is the impedance that a transmission line would present at its input terminals if it were infinitely long. A line will appear to be infinitely long if it is terminated in its characteristic impedance. If so terminated, there will be no reflections from the end of the line. For all three categories listed in Table 8.1, the characteristic impedance is 100 Ω ± 15% in the frequency range of 1 MHz up to the highest frequency applicable for that category.
3. *Attenuation*: The strength of the signal decreases as it propagates along a line. The signal loss is called attenuation and is measured in decibels per unit length.
4. *Near-End Crosstalk*: Crosstalk refers to the unwanted transfer of energy from one circuit (disturbing channel) to another circuit (disturbed channel). Depending on the direction of propagation, the crosstalk is defined as near-end or far-end. The crosstalk that is propagated in a disturbed channel in the direction opposite to the direction of propagation of the electric current in the disturbing channel is called near-end crosstalk or NEXT. The term "near-end" implies that the terminals of the disturbed channel (receiving circuit) and the energized terminal of the disturbing channel (transmitting circuit) are near each other. This is shown in Figure 8.1. The other type of crosstalk is far-end crosstalk (FEXT), in which the crosstalk is propagated in a disturbed channel in the same direction as the propagation of the signal in the disturbing channel. The terminals of the disturbed channel at which the crosstalk is present and the energized terminal of the disturbing channel are usually remote from each other.

   NEXT is measured by applying an input signal on one pair and measuring the crosstalk signal at the same (near) end of the other pair. At the far end, both pairs are terminated with a 100-Ω (characteristic impedance) resistance. The difference between the signal and the crosstalk level in decibels is the NEXT loss, which decreases as the signal frequency increases. The NEXT loss at 0.772 MHz is given in Table 8.1. At higher frequencies, the NEXT loss should be greater

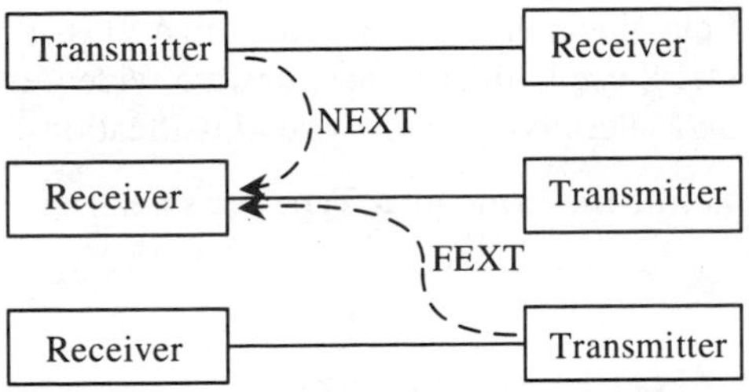

Figure 8.1 Near-end and far-end crosstalks.

than than the value given by the following formula:

$$\text{NEXT}(f) \geq \text{NEXT}(0.772) - 15\log(f/0.772)$$

Here, f is the frequency in megahertz in the range from 0.772 MHz to the highest referenced frequency. For twisted-pair lines, the NEXT loss is measured in decibels per 1000 ft.

8.4 IBM Classification for Cables

During discussions of copper cables, you will often hear a cable designated as Type 1, Type 2, and so on. These designations refer to IBM's classification of cables. IBM classifies cables as Type 1 through 9 depending on whether they are for data or telephone. Some types are available for multiple environments such as riser, outdoor, plenum, and so on, while others are limited to one environment. Cables certified for plenum use have low smoke producing properties and can be used in air plenums without the use of conduits. Such cables are used under suspended ceilings and under raised floors. The IBM classification includes STP, UTP, and fiber cables.

- *Type 1 Data Cables*: These consist of two twisted-pair number 22 AWG solid conductors. These are designed for data communications and are available for indoor (plenum and nonplenum), riser, and outdoor applications.
- *Type 2 Data and Telephone Cables*: These contain two twisted pairs of number 22 AWG solid conductors for data communication and four additional pairs of number 22 AWG solid conductors for telephones in one jacket. These are available for indoor (plenum and nonplenum) applications.
- *Type 3 Telephone Cables*: These consist of four unshielded twisted pairs of number 24 or 22 AWG solid conductors for telephone use. These are available in plenum and nonplenum versions.
- *Type 5 Fiber Optic Cables*: These contain two 100/140-μm multimode fibers for use indoors (nonplenum) and outdoors.
- *Type 6 Patch Cord Cables*: These include two twisted pairs of number 26 AWG stranded conductors. These cables are flexible for use as patch cables in wiring closets.
- *Type 7 Patch Cord Cables*: These contain one twisted pair of number 26 AWG stranded conductors. These are also used as patch cables.
- *Type 8 Undercarpet Cables*: These include two parallel pairs of number 26 AWG solid conductors for data communication. This can be used only under carpeting.
- *Type 9 Plenum Cables*: These contain two twisted pairs of number 26 AWG stranded or solid conductors for data communication. These are plenum cables and can be used in heating and cooling ducts without conduits.

Notice the use of Type (IBM classification) and Category (EIA classification). A Category 3 cable is not the same as a Type 3 cable. Since both classifications are widely used in the industry, confusion often arises by careless use and intermixing of the two classifications.

A Category 3 cable is not the same as a Type 3 cable.

8.5 TP-PMD Design Issues

FDDI twisted-pair PMD is still under development. Therefore, instead of describing what is in the standard, we concentrate on the major design issues that affect the design of the link. In this section, we briefly describe the issues. The issues are:

1. *Categories of Cables*: Sending a 125-Mbps signal over a coaxial cable (thin wire or thick wire) or STP is not as challenging as on **unshielded twisted-pair** (**UTP**) cable. Given the preponderance of UTP cabling to the desk top in most offices, it is clear that allowing FDDI on UTP, however difficult, will be a major win for FDDI. The first issue was whether we should have different coding methods for UTP and STP or one standard covering both. A decision has been made to have one standard for both. Which categories of UTP should it cover is the next issue. While it is easier to handle data-grade twisted pair (EIA Category 5), allowing Category 3 cable would introduce more complexity. It has been decided that the TP-PMD standard will not support Category 3 cables. A long-term TP-PMD working group has been formed to look at the issues surrounding Category 3 cables.
2. *Power Level*: The attenuation (loss) of a signal over copper wires increases at high frequency. To maintain a high signal-to-noise ratio, one must either increase the signal level (more power) or use special coding methods to produce lower frequency signals. Increased power results in increased interference and therefore special coding methods are required.
3. *Electromagnetic Interference*: The main problem caused by high-frequency signals over copper wires is the electromagnetic interference (EMI). After 4b/5b encoding, the FDDI signal has a bit rate of 125 Mbps. With NRZI encoding this results in a signal frequency of 62.5 MHz. At this frequency range, the copper wire acts as a broadcasting antenna. The electromagnetic radiations from the wire interfere with radio and television transmissions. The interference increases with the signal level. The Federal Communications Commission (FCC) in the United States places strict limits on such EMI. Similar regulations exist in other countries. This severely limits the power that the FDDI transmitters can use, which in turn means that the distance at which the signal becomes unintelligible is also limited.

   One solution to the EMI problem is to use shielded twisted-pair (STP). These wires have a special metallic shield surrounding the wires that prevents interference. Another solution is to use special coding techniques that result in a lower frequency signal. The advantage of this second approach is that the unshielded twisted-pair wires, which reach all desks, can be used for FDDI. As discussed in Section 8.6, the issue of coding has now been resolved and a three-level coding system called multilevel transmission 3 (MLT-3) has been selected. This reduces the signal frequency by a factor of 2.
4. *Scrambling*: Even though MLT-3 (and other) encoding schemes reduce the signal frequency, they are not sufficient to meet the FCC EMI requirements for UTP. One way to reduce interference is to scramble the signal so that the energy is not concentrated at one frequency. Instead, it is distributed uniformly over a range of frequencies.

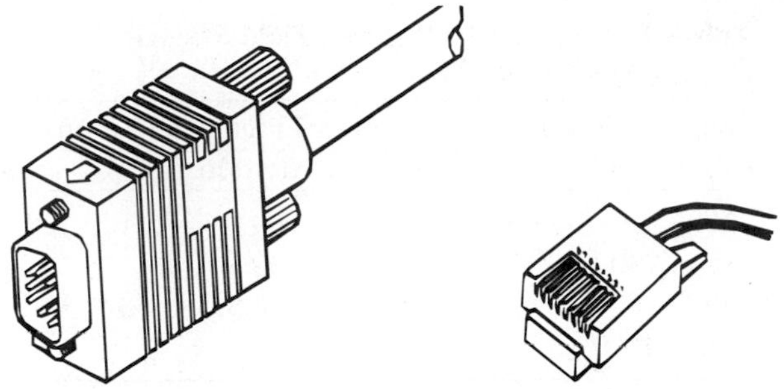

(a) DB-9 (STP) (b) RJ-45 (UTP)

Figure 8.2 Connectors for TP-PMD.

5. *Connectors*: Figure 8.2 shows the DP-9 and RJ-45 connectors proposed for STP and UTP use, respectively. Both are popular connectors. They are available at a very low price due to their widespread use in computer and communication industries.
6. *Equalization*: The cable's attenuation is an increasing function of frequency. An equalizer filter helps increase the channel bandwidth by flattening the frequency response characteristics. For example, an equalizer filter in the transmitter can be used to emphasize the high-frequency components of the signal. In the wire, these high-frequency components are attenuated more than the low-frequency components. The equalizer is designed so that a clean signal is delivered to the receiver. Alternatively, an equalizer filter in the receiver can be used to emphasize the high-frequency signal. However, the external high-frequency noise picked up on the wire will also be emphasized by the receiver equalizer. TP-PMD uses a receiver equalizer. With either approach, the equalizer is generally designed for an average length cable (unless an adaptive equalizer is used).

8.6 Coding

As discussed earlier, special coding techniques are required for copper links to reduce electromagnetic interference. In the United States, the FCC places strict requirements on the EMI generated by computing and communications equipment. All equipment for use in offices should meet FCC Class A requirements while that designed for use in homes should meet tighter FCC Class B requirements. These emission limits are specified in FCC CFR 47 Part 15 (1989). Similar laws or standards exist in other countries, for example, European Economic Council (EEC) directive 89/336, Standards Australia AS 3548-1988, British Standard 6527, German DIN VDE 0878 part 3, and Japan Voluntary Committee for Control of Interference (VCCI) level 0.

Tables 8.2 and 8.3 list composite radiated field strength limits generally used by manufacturers for worldwide products. The field strength is specified in *decibels referenced to microvolts per meter* [dB(μV/m)]. This is a logarithmic scale similar to dBm as explained in Section 4.3. Note that the field strength is measured at a distance of 10 m for Class A equipment, and at 3 and 10 m for Class B equipment.

Since the radiated field strength is measured only at 30 MHz and above, one way to meet these requirements is to reduce the signal to a frequency below 30 MHz. Twisted-pair Ethernet (IEEE

Table 8.2 Limits of Radiated Field Strength for Class A Equipment

Frequency Range (MHz)	Quasi-peak Limit in dB(μV/m) At 10 m
30 to 88	39.1
88 to 230	39.5
230 to 1000	46.5
Above 1000	49.5

802.3 10BASE-T) as well as 16-Mbps IEEE 802.5/token ring networks restrict their signal spectrum to below 30 MHz.

A well-known method to reduce the frequency spectrum is to increase the number of amplitude levels, that is, to use multilevel coding. To decrease the spectrum by a factor of n, generally a coding scheme with 2^n levels is used. Some special coding schemes need one less level, that is, $2^n - 1$ levels. For example, using these encodings, the spectrum can be halved ($n = 2$) by using three levels. Seven levels are required to decrease the spectrum by a factor of 3. Fifteen levels are required to decrease the spectrum by a factor of 4, and so on. As the number of levels increases, the reduced spectrum results in reduced EMI and NEXT. As a result, the signal can be transmitted longer distances. However, with many levels, the distance between voltage levels decreases, making the signal more susceptible to noise.

After considerable debate, the TP-PMD standards group has chosen a three-level coding called MLT-3. This is basically an extension of NRZI to three levels, so it is often called NRZI-3. The three levels are denoted by +1, 0, and −1. Like NRZI, a "zero" bit is coded as the absence of a transition and a "one" bit is coded as a transition. The successive transitions are all in the same direction (ascending or descending) except when the signal reaches a level of +1 of −1, at which point the direction is reversed. The complete transition diagram is shown in Figure 8.3. It consists of four states labeled +1, 0^+, 0^-, and −1. The labels indicate the level of the signal when the system is in that state. The input bits are represented by arcs. Thus, if the signal level is +1 and a zero is to be sent, the signal level remains +1 in the next bit period. On the other hand, if a one is to be sent, the signal level is changed to 0 (state 0^-). Another one in this state will cause the signal level to change to −1. Figure 8.4 shows a sample code-bit string and the corresponding MLT-3 signal.

Table 8.3 Limits of Radiated Field Strength for Class B Equipment

Frequency Range (MHz)	Quasi-peak Limit in dB(μV/m) At 3 m	At 10 m
30 to 88	40	30
88 to 216	43.5	30
216 to 230	46	30
230 to 1000	46	37
Above 1000	54	Not applicable

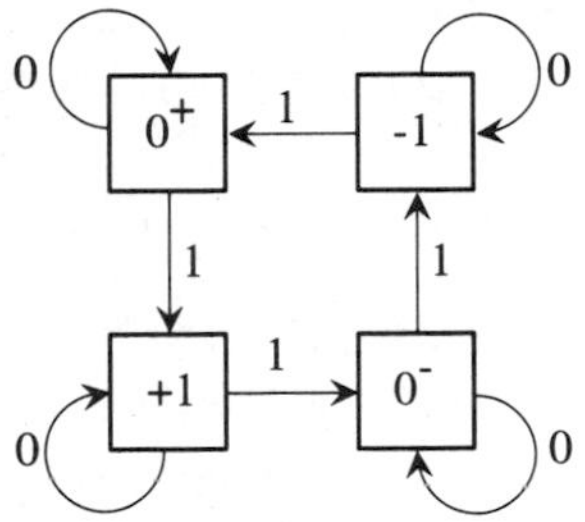

Figure 8.3 MLT-3 transition state diagram.

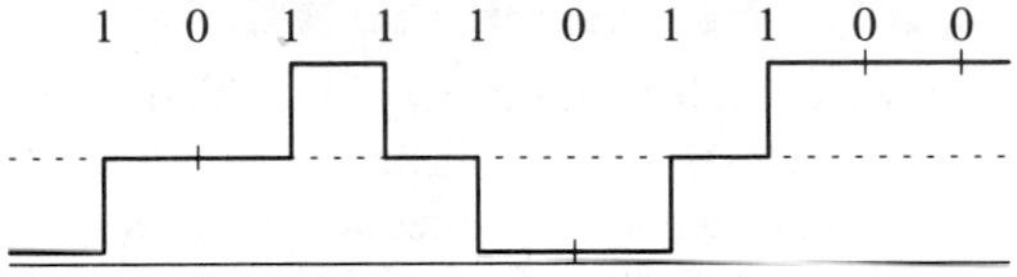

Figure 8.4 MLT-3 coding of a sample code-bit stream.

To understand the effect of multilevel encoding on the signal frequency, consider the NRZI and MLT-3 encodings of a stream of 1's. The signals for these two encodings are shown in Figure 8.5. Notice that with NRZI, each cycle of the signal consists of two bit times. Assuming an FDDI bit rate of 125 Mbps, the signal has a frequency of 62.5 MHz. With MLT-3, the cycle length is 4 bits and the signal frequency is 31.25 MHz.

8.7 Summary

The work on TP-PMD began in 1990. An ad hoc group to discuss the issues was authorized by X3T9.5 in June 1990. The project proposal to form a standards working group was approved by ANSI in October 1990.

Standardization of TP-PMD will reduce the cost of FDDI adapters considerably and help bring FDDI to the desk top. A single TP-PMD standard to cover both shielded and unshielded twisted-pair

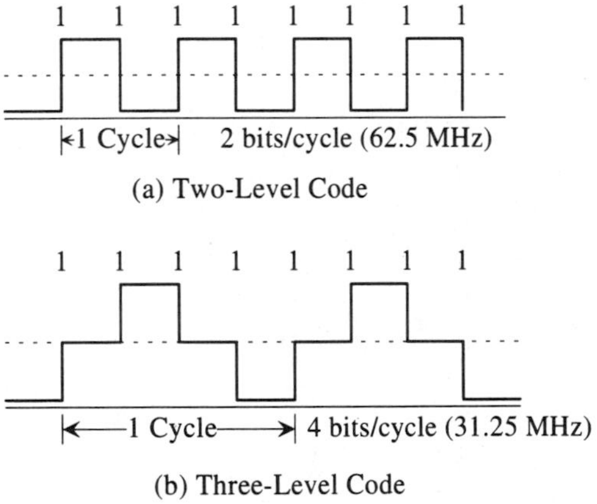

Figure 8.5 NRZI and MLT-3 coding of a stream of 1's.

cables is being designed. The key consideration in its design is the electromagnetic interference. The TP-PMD standards group has already selected the MLT-3 encoding with stream-cypher scrambling.

8.8 Further Reading

FDDI twisted-pair PMD is being specified in the working document ASC X3T9.5/93-022.

The UTP classification is presented in the EIA technical systems bulletin TSB-36 and connecting hardware requirements are specified in TSB-40. UTP cable's physical characteristics are covered by the ANSI/ICEA S-80-576 standard developed by the Insulated Cable Engineers Association (ICEA). STP cable requirements are covered in EIA Interim Standard EIA/IS-43. IBM classifications are described in IBM (1987).

Ginzburg, Mallard, and Newman (1990) discuss some of the problems of transmitting high-bandwidth signals over copper.

Table 8.2 is based on ASC X3T9.5/93-022.

8.9 Self-Test Exercises

Note: Some exercises have multiple correct answers. See Appendix D for answers.

8.1 Given a choice, which Category UTP would you use for FDDI?

a. Category 3
b. Category 4
c. Category 5

8.2 Transmitting FDDI signals on UTP requires special coding because:

a. The new coding prevents electromagnetic radiation at all frequencies.
b. The new coding lowers the power spectrum to below 30 MHz.
c. The new coding disperses the power spectrum over a wide frequency band and thus reduces the electromagnetic interference.

CHAPTER 9

FDDI on SONET

"SONET" stands for Synchronous Optical Network. It is a standard developed under ANSI and the Exchange Carriers Standards Association (ECSA) for digital optical transmission. If you want to lease a fiber optic line from your telephone company, you are likely to be offered a *SONET link* instead of a dark fiber link. A SONET link allows the telephone company to divide the enormous bandwidth of a dark fiber among many of its customers. Thus, a SONET link is much cheaper compared to a dark fiber link. In this chapter we explain what SONET is and how a SONET link is used for FDDI.

A SONET standard has also been adopted by the International Telegraph and Telephone Consultative Committee (CCITT). There are slight differences between the CCITT and ANSI versions. The CCITT version is called **Synchronous Digital Hierarchy** (**SDH**). We use the popular term SONET to refer to both specifications. The differences are pointed out wherever appropriate.

9.1 What Is SONET?

There are two ways to look at SONET—from a customer perspective or from a telephone company's perspective. To a customer, a SONET link appears like a dark fiber specially designed for digital transmission. In most places where you use a dark fiber for digital transmission, you can replace the fiber with a SONET link. For example, in an FDDI network, some fiber links can in reality be SONET links as shown in Figure 9.1. This is much cheaper than the expense involved in gaining right-of-way to install your own fiber. It is also much easier than negotiating with the owners of existing fiber facilities to lease dark fibers.

To a telephone company, SONET is a *network* of optical fibers over which their customers can send digital signals from one endpoint to another. Each fiber is shared by many customers; therefore, the company can offer a SONET connection much cheaper than a dark fiber connection. For example, a single SONET 2.488-Gbps fiber pair could carry up to 16 parallel FDDI links (since each FDDI link uses up a 155.52-Mbps SONET channel).

The two views of SONET are shown in Figure 9.2. For the customer, a SONET link is a physical link that has two ends. Since the physical characteristics of this link are slightly different from those of a dark fiber, the link needs a new media-dependent component of the physical layer (PMD). Higher layers of FDDI (or any other network) work on this new PMD just as they would work on a dark fiber. For a phone company, on the other hand, SONET is a network and not a link. This means that they have to ensure that the customer's signal follows the right path and is delivered reliably.

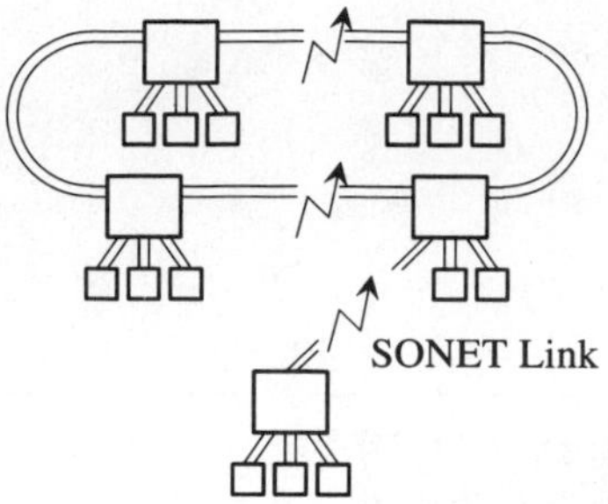

Figure 9.1 FDDI networks with SONET links.

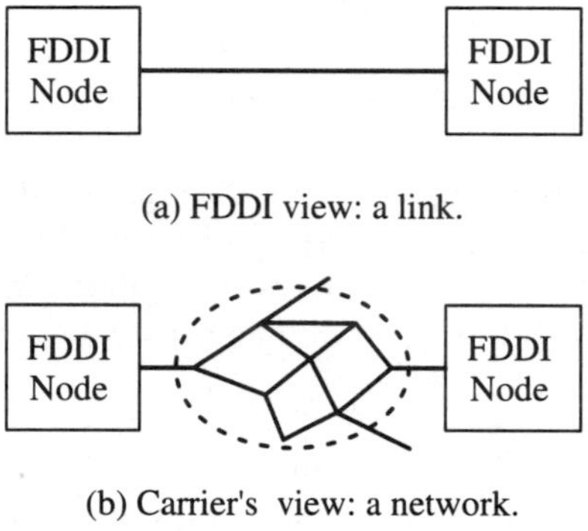

Figure 9.2 Two views of SONET.

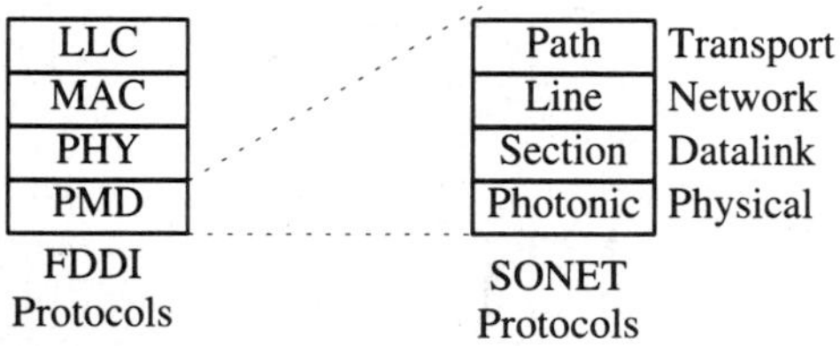

Figure 9.3 Protocol components of a SONET system.

They have to do all those functions that computer networking people do in their physical, datalink, network, and transport layers. Thus, what appears as a single layer (PMD) of networking protocol to an individual is actually four layers of protocols for the phone company. This correspondence between the protocol layers of FDDI and SONET systems is shown in Figure 9.3.

9.2 Protocol Layers of SONET

The four protocol layers of the synchronous optical network are as follows:

1. *Photonic Layer*: This is the physical layer. Like FDDI PMD, it specifies the characteristics of optical fibers, transmitters, and receivers that may be used and describes optical encoding of bits. The SONET optical interface (ANSI T1.106-1988) defines the spectral characteristics for 1310- and 1550-nm optics.
2. *Section Layer*: This layer deals with the transmission across a single fiber link and converts electronic signals to photonic ones. It also has some monitoring capabilities. The issues are similar to those of other point-to-point datalink layer protocols such as *High-Level Data Link Control* (*HDLC*) and *Link Access Procedure on the D Channel* (*LAPD*). This layer performs framing, scrambling, and error monitoring.
3. *Line Layer*: This layer deals with signaling between the multiplexer switches. It is responsible for frame synchronization, multiplexing of data onto SONET frames, maintenance, and switching. The multiplexer switches perform functions similar to those of a router. The services include line error monitoring, line maintenance, automatic protection switching, and installation or removal of a service. Automatic protection switching (APS) allows automatic switching to another circuit if the quality of the primary circuit drops below a set threshold.
4. *Path Layer*: This layer deals with the end-to-end signaling issues between the originating end-station (source) and the destination end-station. These issues are similar to those of the transport layer. This layer is responsible for mapping services, for example, DS3, FDDI, or BISDN, into the SONET payload format.

9.3 Physical Components

Figure 9.4 shows the physical components of a SONET system. A section represents a single run of optical cable between two optical transmitters/receivers. For short runs, the cable may run directly between two switches. For long runs, regenerating repeaters are used to receive and convert the optical

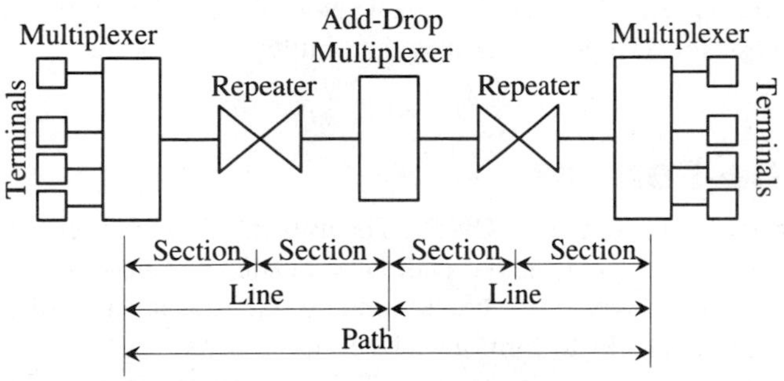

Figure 9.4 Physical components of a SONET system.

Table 9.1 SONET/SDH Signal Hierarchy

ANSI Designation	Optical Signal	CCITT Designation	Data Rate (Mbps)	Payload Rate (Mbps)
STS-1	OC-1		51.84	50.112
STS-3	OC-3	STM-1	155.52	150.336
STS-9	OC-9	STM-3	466.56	451.008
STS-12	OC-12	STM-4	622.08	601.344
STS-18	OC-18	STM-6	933.12	902.016
STS-24	OC-24	STM-8	1244.16	1202.688
STS-36	OC-36	STM-12	1866.24	1804.032
STS-48	OC-48	STM-16	2488.32	2405.376
STS-96	OC-96	STM-32	4976.64	4810.176
STS-192	OC-192	STM-64	9953.28	9620.928

signal to electrical form and then regenerate the optical signal. The issues of clock synchronization and timing are addressed at the section level. A line is a sequence of one or more sections between the multiplexers, switches, or endpoints. Channels may be added or dropped at the end of each line. Finally, a path corresponds to an end-to-end full-duplex circuit and connects two end terminals.

9.4 SONET Data Rates

A SONET system can run at a number of predesignated data rates. These rates are specified as STS-N rates in the ANSI standard. STS-N stands for **Synchronous Transport Signal level N**. The lowest rate STS-1 is 51.84 Mbps. Other rates of STS-N are simply N times this rate. For example, STS-3 is 155.52 Mbps and STS-12 is 622.08 Mbps. Table 9.1 lists the complete hierarchy. The corresponding rate at the optical level is called **Optical Carrier level N (OC-N)**. Since each bit results in one optical pulse in SONET (no 4b/5b type of coding is used), the OC-N rates are identical to STS-N rates.

For the CCITT/SDH standard, the data rates are designated STM-N (Synchronous Transport Module N). The lowest rate STM-1 is 155.52 Mbps. Other rates are simply multiples of STM-1.

In both cases, some bandwidth is used for network overhead. The data rate available to the user, called the **payload rate**, is also shown in Table 9.1. Note that, like data rate, the payload rates for STS-N are N times those for STS-1. This makes data multiplexing easier.

9.5 Frame Format

Figure 9.5 shows a protocol hierarchy for SONET. The user information is enclosed in a **synchronous payload envelope (SPE)**, which contains the path layer header for end-to-end communication. STS-N blocks are used at the line layer. Each block contains the line layer header. Finally, the section layer adds its headers to the blocks to form an STS frame.

A framing block (or a frame) is 125 μs long. The number of bits in the frame depends on the bit rate. At 155.520 Mbps (OC-3 rate), the frames are 2430 bytes long. At 622.080 Mbps (OC-12 rate), the frames are 9720 bytes long, and so on.

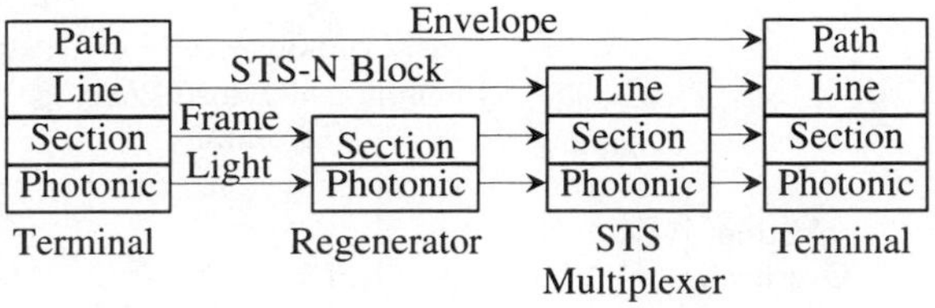

Figure 9.5 Protocol hierarchy of a SONET system.

It is best to view the frame format as a two-dimensional matrix (rather than a linear sequence of bytes as is done in data networking protocols) with several rows and columns. This is because in the circuit switching world, when *N* circuits are multiplexed, for instance, by byte interleaving, the resulting byte sequence can be represented either as a periodic sequence of *N* bytes or more simply as a matrix with *N* columns. This is shown in Figure 9.6. The matrix view allows us to see the successive bytes of each input circuit (along the column) as well as the successive bytes of the output circuit (along the row).

Figure 9.7 shows an STS-1 frame format. It consists of a 9-row and 90-column matrix. Each entry is 1 byte long. The transmission of bytes is row-wise. The 90 bytes of the first row are transmitted first. The 90 bytes of the second row are transmitted next and so on. The first three columns are used for section and line overheads.

Note the use of the term *overhead*. The corresponding term used in computer networking is *header*. For example, section and line overheads would be called section and line headers. However, the term *header* implies that these bytes are at the beginning of a frame, which is not the case here. As seen on the wire, the overhead bytes occur periodically and are distributed all over the frame.

After the first three columns of section and line overhead, the remaining 87 columns of the STS-1 frames are used for the payload (user information). The path layer encapsulates the user information in an SPE, which consists of 87 columns and 9 rows. One column of SPE is used for path overhead. The function of various overhead bytes is shown in Figure 9.8 and is described in Box 9.1. Notice that many of these bytes are for operation, administration, and maintenance (OA&M) of the system. This is necessary to locate and isolate faults quickly in a system designed with equipment from multiple vendors.

The A-bytes are used for framing. Each frame begins with F6-28_{16} (or 11110110-00101000_2). The B-bytes are for error detection using bit-interleaved parity 8 (**BIP8**). All the bytes of a frame are exclusive-OR'ed together and the result is placed in the B-byte of the next frame. This provides an

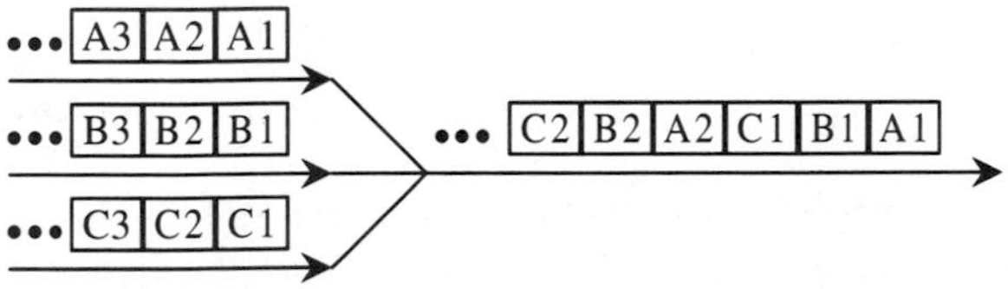

Figure 9.6 Byte multiplexing of circuits.

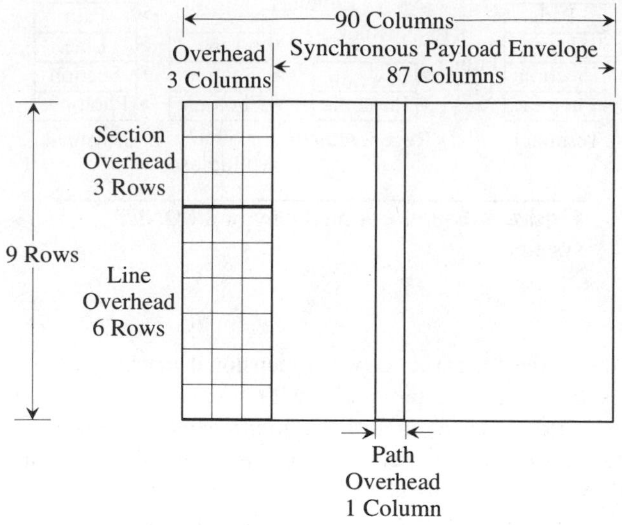

Figure 9.7 STS-1 frame format.

				Path Layer Overhead
Section Overhead	Framing A1	Framing A2	STS-1 ID C1	Trace J1
Section Overhead	BIP-8 B1	Orderwire E1	User F1	BIP-8 B3
Section Overhead	Data Com D1	Data Com D2	Data Com D3	Signal Label C2
Line Overhead	Pointer H1	Pointer H2	Pointer Action H3	Path Status G1
Line Overhead	BIP-8 B2	APS K1	APS K2	User Channel F2
Line Overhead	Data Com D4	Data Com D5	Data Com D6	Multiframe H4
Line Overhead	Data Com D7	Data Com D8	Data Com D9	Growth Z3
Line Overhead	Data Com D10	Data Com D11	Data Com D12	Growth Z4
Line Overhead	Growth Z1	Growth Z2	Orderwire E2	Growth Z5

Figure 9.8 Function of SONET overhead bytes.

Box 9.1 STS-1 Overhead Bytes

1. **Section Overhead**: Nine bytes.
   - A1, A2: Framing bytes = $F6\text{-}28_{16}$ ($11110110\text{-}00101000_2$).
   - C1: STS-1 ID identifies the STS-1 number (1 to N) for each STS-1 within an STS-N multiplex.
   - B1: Bit-interleaved parity byte 8 (**BIP8**) providing even parity over previous STS-N frame after scrambling.
   - E1: Section-level 64-kbps PCM voice channel for section maintenance.
   - F1: 64-kbps channel set aside for user purposes.
   - D1–D3: 192-kbps data communications channel for alarms, maintenance, control, and administration between sections.
2. **Line Overhead**: 18 bytes.
   - H1–H3: Pointer bytes used in frame alignment and frequency adjustment of payload data.
   - B2: Bit-interleaved parity for line-level error monitoring.
   - K1, K2: Two bytes allocated for signaling between line-level automatic protection switching equipment.
   - D4–D12: 576-kbps data communications channel for alarms, maintenance, control, monitoring, and administration at the line level.
   - Z1: Reserved for future use.
   - Z2: Count of blocks received in error.
   - E2: 64-kbps PCM voice channel for line maintenance.
3. **Path Overhead**: Nine bytes.
   - J1: 64-kbps channel used to send a 64-byte fixed-length string repetitively so a receiving terminal can continuously verify the integrity of a path; the contents of the message are user-programmable.
   - B3: Bit-interleaved parity at the path level.
   - C2: STS path signal label to designate equipped versus unequipped STS signals and, for equipped signals, the specific STS payload mapping that might be needed in receiving terminals to interpret the payloads.
   - G1: Status byte sent from path-terminating equipment back to path-originating equipment to convey status of terminating equipment and path error performance.
   - F2: 64-kbps channel for path user.
   - H4: Multiframe indicator for payloads needing frames that are longer than a single STS frame; multiframe indicators are used when packing lower rate channels into the SPE.
   - Z3–Z5: Reserved for future use.

even-parity protection for the 8-bit positions in each byte. BIP8 is used at both the section (B1) and line (B2) levels. The D-bytes are used for data communication channels to manage the network. D1 through D3 are used for section management and D4 through D12 are used for line management. The E-bytes are used for voice communications channels for maintenance people. The F-bytes are used for user communications channels for network management of customer-premises equipment. K-bytes are used for automatic protection and switching. H-bytes point to the start of the payload.

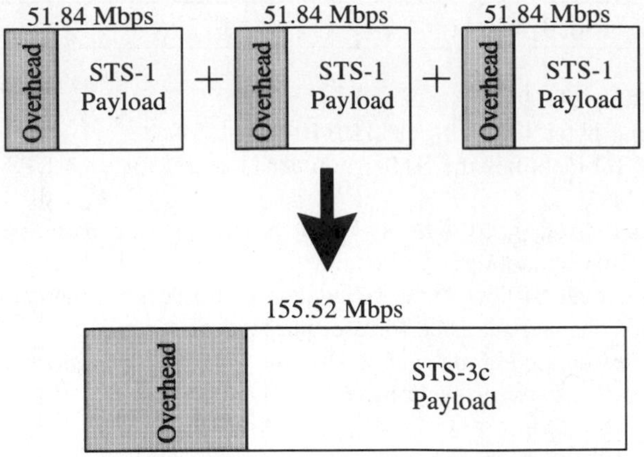

Figure 9.9 Concatenation of three STS-1 frames to form STS-3c.

This allows SPE to float in the SONET frame. The position of the first byte of SPE is indicated by H1,H2. The Z2-byte is used by the receiver to send back a count of blocks received in error (as detected by BIP8) on the incoming side of the line. Other Z-bytes are reserved for future use.

An STS-3 frame is obtained by byte interleaving three STS-1 frames. An STS-3c (STS-3 concatenated) is obtained by combining three STS-1 signals such that a single SPE, which is three times the SPE of a normal STS-1 signal, results as shown in Figure 9.9. This is used to carry user signals that have data rates larger than that allowed by an STS-1 payload. The format of an STS-3c frame, which is similar to the STM-1 frame in CCITT/SDH terminology, is shown in Figure 9.10. Each frame consists of 2430 bytes arranged in 9 rows of 270 bytes each. The first nine columns are used for section and line overheads. An additional column is used for path overhead.

Figure 9.11 shows the overhead bytes of the STS-3c frame. Since the overhead bytes are taken from those of the three STS-1 frames, most bytes are repeated three times. Considerable redundancy results and, therefore, many of the bytes are left unused. Only one column is used for the path overhead.

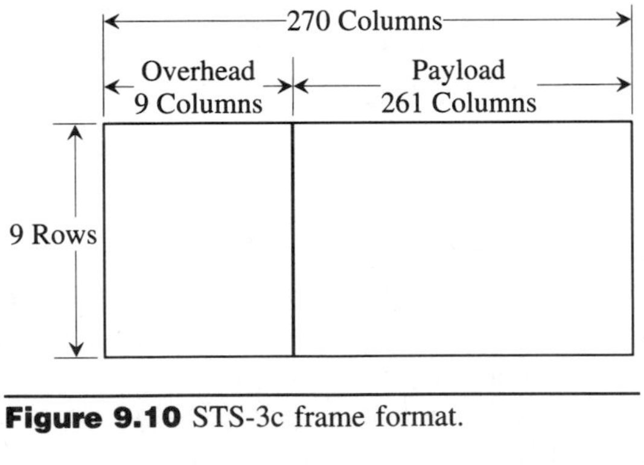

Figure 9.10 STS-3c frame format.

A1	A1	A1	A2	A2	A2	C1	C1	C1
B1			E1			F1		
D1			D2			D3		
H1	H1	H1	H2	H2	H2	H3	H3	H3
B2	B2	B2	K1			K2		
D4			D5			D6		
D7			D8			D9		
D10			D11			D12		
Z1	Z1	Z1	Z2	Z2	Z2	E2		

(a) Section and line overhead

J1
B3
C2
G1
F2
H4
Z3
Z4
Z5

(b) Path overhead

Figure 9.11 STS-3c overhead bytes.

Since the user payload envelopes may arrive at time instants different from the beginning of the frame, an SPE can start at any point in the frame payload. As shown in Figure 9.12, a pointer in the line overhead indicates the location at which SPE begins. This means that an SPE-1 can straddle two successive STS-1 frames. The floating position of the payload also helps in taking care of the clock rate differences. Recall from Section 3.2 that in FDDI, clock differences between successive stations can cause the interframe gap to increase or decrease. In the same manner, the position of the SPE may be adjusted by ± 1 byte at every multiplexer. The pointer indicating the SPE position is adjusted to reflect the new position. If the SPE is moved ahead by 1 byte, the last byte of the previous SPE is not lost. It is saved in the line overhead byte H3. If the SPE is delayed by 1 byte, the byte after H3 is left empty.

Figure 9.13 shows a block diagram of the SONET framing procedure. First the path overhead is added to the user-supplied payload and a path BIP8 parity is computed. This is saved for placement in position B3 of the next STS-1 SPE. Line overhead is then added. SPE is aligned in the SONET frame. A line BIP8 parity is computed and saved for placement in position B2 of the next SONET frame. Next, section overhead is added and if necessary multiple STS-1 frames are byte interleaved.

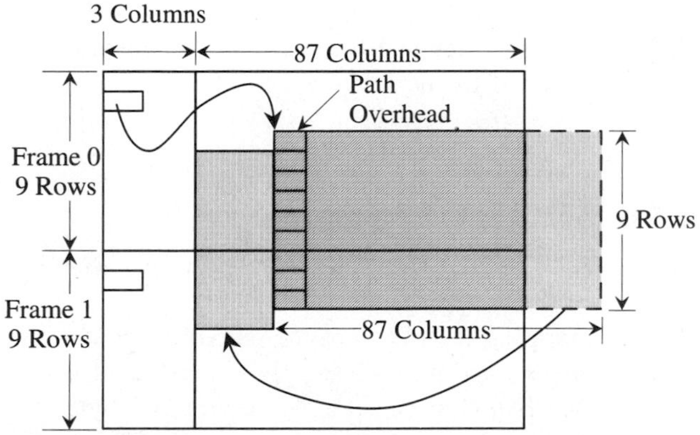

Figure 9.12 Location of SPE in STS-1 frame.

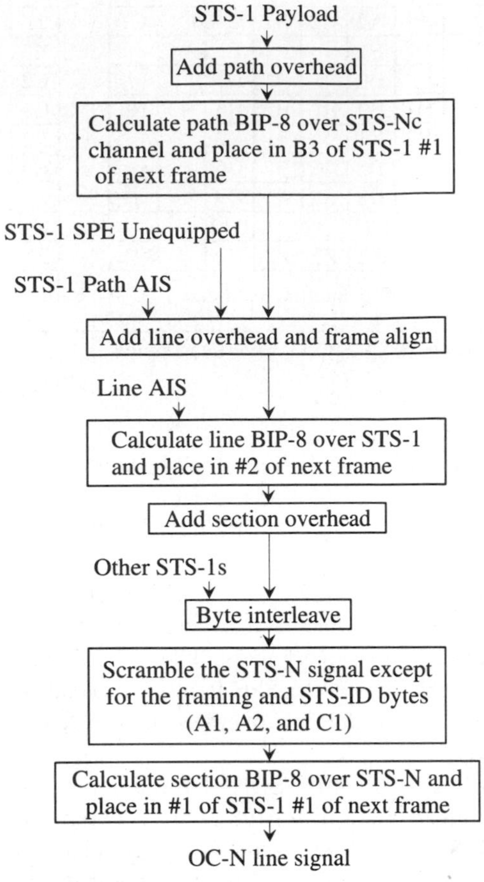

Figure 9.13 A block diagram of SONET framing procedure.

The resulting stream is scrambled. A section BIP8 parity is computed over the entire STS-N and saved for placement in position B1 of the next frame.

9.6 FDDI to SONET Mapping

In this section we describe how an FDDI bit stream is mapped to a SONET SPE and explain the issues involved in the design of this mapping.

SONET physical layer mapping (**SPM**) takes the output of the current FDDI physical layer, which is a 4b/5b encoded bit stream, and places it in appropriate bits of an STS-3c SPE. Recall that an STS-3c SPE consists of 2349 bytes (arranged as 9 rows of 261 bytes each). Of these, 9 bytes are used for path overhead. Since one SPE is transmitted every 125 μs, the available bandwidth is $(2340\times 8)/125$ or 149.76 Mbps. This is more than the 125 Mbps required for FDDI. Therefore,

(a) **SPE:** 9X261 bytes = Path overhead + 9 Rows of 20 cells (13 bytes per cell)

Path Overhead 1X9																				
	J	A	B	B	B	A	B	B	B	A	B	B	B	A	B	B	B	A	B	X
	J	A	B	B	B	A	B	B	B	A	B	B	B	A	B	B	B	A	B	Y
	J	A	B	B	B	A	B	B	B	A	B	B	B	A	B	B	B	A	B	X
	J	A	B	B	B	A	B	B	B	A	B	B	B	A	B	B	B	A	B	X
	J	A	B	B	B	A	B	B	B	A	B	B	B	A	B	B	B	A	B	Y
	J	A	B	B	B	A	B	B	B	A	B	B	B	A	B	B	B	A	B	X
	J	A	B	B	B	A	B	B	B	A	B	B	B	A	B	B	B	A	B	X
	J	A	B	B	B	A	B	B	B	A	B	B	B	A	B	B	B	A	B	Y
	J	A	B	B	B	A	B	B	B	A	B	B	B	A	B	B	B	A	B	X

(b) **Cell Types:**

J	=	O	I	I	I	R	I	I	I	R	I	I	I	I
A	=	C	I	I	I	I	I	I	I	I	I	I	I	I
B	=	R	I	I	I	R	I	I	I	R	I	I	I	I
X	=	S1	I	I	I	R	I	I	I	I	I	I	I	I
Y	=	S2	I	I	I	R	I	I	I	I	I	I	I	I

(c) **Byte Types:**

C = iiiiiic	I = iiiiiii	O = iiiiioo
R = rrrrrrr	S1 = iiiiiis	S2 = iiiiisr

(d) **Bit Types:**

i = Information bit r = Fixed stuff bit

c = Stuff control bit o = Overhead bit

s = Stuff opportunity bit (majority of row's 5 c's)

Figure 9.14 FDDI/SONET physical layer mapping.

as explained shortly, an opportunity rises to use the extra bandwidth (or bits) for network control purposes and for overcoming clock jitter.

The SONET mapping for FDDI has been adapted from that for the 139.264-Mbps DS4NA (DS4 North American) signal. Many of the techniques used for this mapping have been used for FDDI mapping as well. The FDDI mapping is shown in Figure 9.14(a). Leaving the first column of SPE for the path overhead, the remaining 260 columns of SPE have been arranged in 20 groups called **cells** of 13 columns each. The format of these cells is shown in Figure 9.14(b). Notice that they are all identical except for two or three bytes. The bit encoding of various bytes is shown in Figure 9.14(c) and bit types are indicated in Figure 9.14(d).

The stuff control bits marked c in Figure 9.14(c) are used to take care of clock rate differences. FDDI allows a clock jitter of 50 parts per million (ppm). SONET allows a clock jitter of 20 ppm. Thus, the difference in the clocks of an FDDI station and that of the SONET system could be as much as 70 ppm. At its nominal rate, FDDI produces 125 Mbps or 15,625 bits per 125 μs. Due to clock jitter, the number of actual bits transmitted may be slightly less or more.

Table 9.2 Information Bits per SPE

Cell Type	Number of Cells/SPE	*i*-bits per Cell	Total *i* bits
J	9	91	819
A	45	88	3,960
B	117	86	10,062
X	6	87	516
Y	3	86	258
Total	180		15,621

As shown in Table 9.2, each SPE contains 15,621 information bits. It also contains 9 stuff opportunity bits that can be used to carry additional information bits, if necessary. Thus, the total number of information bits per SPE is 15,621 to 15,630. This allows for a clock jitter in the range of −256 to +320 ppm. This comfortably exceeds the combined clock tolerances of SONET and FDDI at ±20 and ± 50 ppm, respectively.

The fact that a particular stuff opportunity bit is being used is indicated by the stuff control (c) bits. Five *c*-bits are used to indicate whether the stuff bit of that row is being used. If the stuff opportunity bit is not used to carry information, then all five *c*-bits are set to one and the *s*-bit is set to zero. Otherwise all five are set to zero. At the receiving station, a majority logic voting is used to determine if the stuff opportunity bit is being used. If three or more of the *c*-bits are zero, the *s*-bit of that row is processed as an information bit. The use of a majority vote protects the system against single- and double-bit errors in the *c*-bits and thus reduces the chances of unnecessary loss of synchronization caused by loss/introduction of a bit.

There are a total of 45 *c*-bits per SPE. At the exact nominal rates FDDI mapping uses four of the nine stuff opportunity bits.

The fixed stuff (*r*) bits are reserved unused bits, which are set to zero at the transmitting station and ignored at the receiving station. These unused bits are dispersed throughout the SPE in 42 columns of nine *R*-bytes each plus three extra reserved bits. This helps to ensure that a user cannot maliciously send data that results in no transitions, as discussed later under scrambling.

The overhead (*o*) bits are used for maintenance.

The FDDI mapping described in this section is also referred to as *Asynchronous Super-Rate Mapping* for transport of FDDI signals. The term **asynchronous** simply implies that there is no relationship between the clocks of the originating station (FDDI) and the SONET system. The term **super-rate** means that the user payload rate is more than that for STS-1 signal and, therefore, a concatenated STS-N framing is required.

A number of other networks have similar mapping for SONET. The STS path "signal label or payload identifier" (byte C2 in Figure 9.11) indicates which networking protocol mapping is being used by the payload. The four most-significant bits of this byte indicate the size of SPE (STS-1, STS-3, etc.) and the remaining four bits are used to identify the specific type of payload contained in the SPE. A value of 15_{16} (00010101_2) has been assigned as the unique identifier for carrying FDDI physical layer data in an STS-3c SPE. The labels for a few other mappings are listed in Table 9.3.

The STS path "multiframe indicator" (byte H4 in Figure 9.11) is unused by the FDDI mapping and is treated as a reserved byte, which is set to zero on transmission and ignored on reception.

Table 9.3 Some of the Assigned Codes for Path Signal Labels

Code (Hex)	Size	Identification
04	STS-1	Asynchronous mapping for DS3
12	STS-3c	Asynchronous mapping for 139.264 Mbps
13	STS-3c	Mapping for ATM (T1S1 BISDN)
14	STS-3c	Mapping for ATM (IEEE 802.6 MAN)
15	STS-3c	Asynchronous mapping for FDDI

9.7 Scrambling

SONET uses a simple NRZ encoding of bits. In this coding, a 1 is represented as high level (light on) and a 0 is represented as low level (light off). As discussed earlier in Section 3.1, one problem with this coding is that if too many 1's (or 0's) are transmitted, the signal remains at on (or off) for a long time, resulting in a loss of bit clocking information. To solve this problem, the SONET standard requires that all bytes in a SONET signal be scrambled by a frame synchronous scrambler sequence of length 127 generated by the polynomial $1 + x^6 + x^7$. Certain overhead bytes (A1, A2, and C1) are exempt from this requirement.

The scrambler consists of a sequence of seven shift registers as shown in Figure 9.15. At the beginning of a frame, a seed value of 1111111_2 is loaded in the register. As successive bits arrive, the contents of shift registers are shifted and the sixth and seventh registers' contents (this corresponds to terms x^6 and x^7, respectively) are exclusive-OR'ed and fed back to the first register (corresponding to the term 1 in the polynomial). The output of the final shift register is a pseudorandom binary pattern, which is exclusive-OR'ed to the incoming information bits.

The scrambling operation is equivalent to exclusive-ORing the bits with a repeated sequence of the following 127-bit pattern:

```
1111 1110-0000-0100-0001 1000-0101 0001-1110 0100-0101 1001-
1101 0100-1111 1010-0001 1100-0100 1001-1011 0101-1011 1101-
1000 1101-0010 1110-1110 0110-0101 010
```

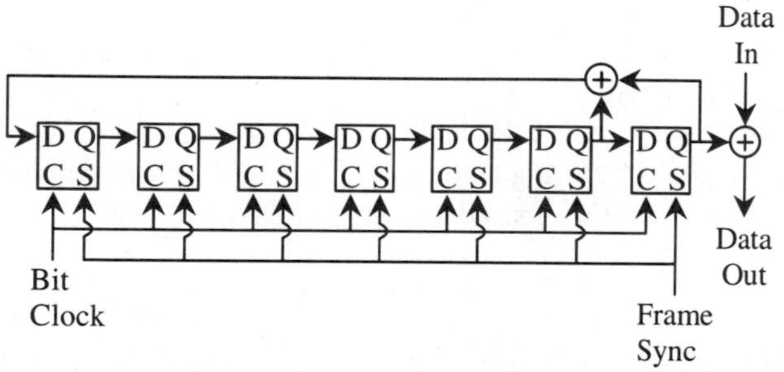

Figure 9.15 Shift-register implementation of a SONET scrambler.

Notice that this sequence appears highly random and does not contain long sequences of 1's or 0's. Therefore, this is expected to increase the frequency of transitions in the resulting stream. However, if the user data pattern is identical to any subset of this sequence, the resulting stream will have all 1's in the corresponding bit positions. Similarly, if the user data pattern is an exact complement of any subset of this sequence, the resulting stream will have all 0's in the corresponding bit positions.

One of the key issues in the design of the FDDI-to-SONET mapping was to ensure that the FDDI signal pattern does not result in long series of 1's or 0's after scrambling. Two steps have been taken for this purpose. First, several fixed stuff (*r*) bits are used throughout the SPE to break up the FDDI stream. As a result, FDDI data cannot affect more than 17 contiguous bytes. Even the 17-byte string has one bit that is a stuff control bit and, therefore, not under user control. Second, the scrambler sequence was analyzed to find the longest possible valid 4b/5b pattern that will match (or complement) a portion of the scrambler sequence. The longest possible match for random sequences of FDDI data or control symbols and the SONET scrambler sequence is the following subsequence of 58 bits (7.25 bytes):

```
10-0001 1100-0100 1001-1011 0101-1011 1101-1000 1101-0010 1110-1110 0110
```

This bit sequence is generated by sending FDDI symbol sequence J6H9TTFK2B6T. This is not a real case since FDDI users are not allowed to generate an arbitrary sequence of data or control symbols. But this represents the best that a malicious user with some special test equipment might be able to accomplish. Real users are only allowed to generate data symbols. FDDI interfaces generate the required control symbols using FDDI MAC and PHY rules. The longest match that a typical user might be able to generate was found to be the following sequence of 27 bits generated by sending 81AA0C:

```
0-0100 1001-1011 0101-1011 1101-10
```

The inverse of the SONET scrambler sequence is:

```
0000 0001-1111 1011-1110 0111-1010 1110-0001 1011-1010 0110-
0010 1011-0000 0101-1110 0011-1011 0110-0100 1010-0100 0010-
0111 0010-1101 0001-0001 1001-1010 101
```

The longest match for the inverse is the following 48-bit sequence generated by AT4Q7DEOBQ:

```
01 1001-1010 101-0000 0001-1111 1011-1110 0111-1010 1110-000
```

Again, FDDI users are not allowed to send this set of control and data symbols. For a valid FDDI data stream, the longest match occurs for the following 28-bit sequence generated by sending 27DE0B1:

```
0001-1111 1011-1110 0111-1010 1110
```

Thus, it is not possible for an FDDI user to cause serious errors in the SONET network by simply sending any particular data pattern.

The presence of long sequences of 1's and 0's was also an issue in ATM-to-SONET mapping. There the problem was resolved by using an additional scrambler (self-synchronizing scrambler with polynomial $1 + x^{43}$) before presenting the ATM cells to SONET.

9.8 Summary

SONET is an ANSI standard for transmission of digital optical signals. Outside of North America, SONET is known by its CCITT name of SDH (Synchronous Digital Hierarchy).

Instead of leasing a dark fiber line from the telephone company, it is easier to obtain a SONET link of STS-3 (155.52 Mbps) and use it as a link in an FDDI network. This is cheaper if the link has to cross an area where you do not have right-of-way.

A SONET link is actually a path through the telephone companies' fiber network. Therefore, it may cross through many multiplexers and demultiplexers. The SONET standard defines protocols for photonic, section, line, and path layers. A number of standard SONET data rates, all of which are multiples of 51.84 Mbps have been defined. For FDDI you need an STS-3c link, which has a data rate of 155.52 Mbps.

To use the SONET link, all you need to do is to replace the physical media-dependent (PMD) components by the SONET mapping components. Although, SONET links do not have a specified distance limitation, the total latency around the ring should not exceed 1.773 ms since that affects many timer parameters used in FDDI design.

The key issues in the design of an FDDI over SONET standard is that of scrambling. The scrambler issue has been analyzed and shown not to be a problem.

9.9 Further Reading and Historical Notes

The SONET standards effort began in ANSI in 1985. In 1984, MCI proposed an interconnecting fabric of multiple-carrier and manufacturer fiber optic transmission connections, known as *mid-span meets*, to the Interexchange Carrier Compatibility Forum (ICCF). In turn, ICCF requested the Exchange Carriers Standards Association (ECSA) to develop standards for an optical interface. In February 1985, Bellcore proposed to T1X1 the SONET concept, which went beyond the MCI request to allow the interconnection of all network elements with fiber terminations.

The goal of the SONET project was to allow different vendors' telecommunications systems to be interconnected with full maintenance and signal transparency. Prior to SONET, lightwave equipment was designed with proprietary signals and multiplexing formats such that the multiplexers on the two ends of the fiber had to be provided by a single vendor.

CCITT began in 1986 a parallel effort to provide international recommendations for a synchronous digital hierarchy. Changes have been made in both SONET and SDH to keep them consistent with each other. For example, the basic transmission rate of SONET was changed from 49.92 to 51.84 Mbps after a recommendation by CCITT. This required changing from a 13-row structure to a 9-row structure. An early version of SONET had specified a bit-interleaved frame structure, but the CCITT insisted that this be changed to a byte-interleaved frame structure. This "push-pull" process resulted in compatible SONET and SDH standards from T1X1 and CCITT in 1988. SONET standardization work is still going on in ANSI and CCITT. Much of this work is in the area of network management and synchronization.

The FDDI standards group began discussing the possibility of a SONET physical layer mapping standard in November 1989. The mapping has been stable since the summer of 1990. The SPM project had been placed on hold temporarily to allow resolution of a payload pointer jitter issue. A worst case bound for payload pointer activity over time needs to be established to allow designing an effective desynchronizer. The issue is being worked on in the SONET standard forums.

The first two SONET standards (ANSI-T1.106 and ANSI-T1.105) were released by ANSI in early 1988. These specify the optical parameters for interoffice connections and the basic rates and formats of the SONET signal. The optical parameters standard has since been superseded by CCITT Recommendation CCITT-G.957 and Bellcore TA-NWT-000253, issue 6. The second ANSI standard

(ANSI T1.105) has also been revised (ANSI T1.105-1991) and includes physical interfaces for optical signals at 51.84-, 155.52-, 622.08-, and 2488.32-Mbps rates (OC-1, OC-3, OC-12, and OC-48).

Bellamy (1991), Tosco (1990), and Stallings (1992) each has a chapter devoted to SONET. Davidson and Muller (1991) wrote a short book on SONET. A special issue of *IEEE Lightwave Telecommunications Systems* magazine (Ritchie 1991) was devoted to SONET and contains eight articles on various aspects of SONET.

FDDI SONET Mapping has been published as ANSI T1.105a-1991, which is a supplement to and is now included in the ANSI T1.105-1991 standard. It is also described in Rigsbee (1990a) and the analysis of the SONET scrambler for FDDI mapping is presented in Rigsbee (1990b).

Figures 9.4 and 9.5 have been adapted from Stallings (1993). Figures 9.8 and 9.13 have been adapted from ANSI T1.105-1991. Figure 9.9 has been adapted from Davidson and Muller (1991). Figures 9.12 and 9.15 have been adapted from Bellamy (1991).

9.10 Self-Test Exercises

Note: Some exercises have multiple correct answers. See Appendix D for answers.

9.1 What is SONET?

a. It is a CCITT standard for networking.
b. It is an ANSI standard for optical transmission.
c. It is the scientific optical network funded by the National Science Foundation.
d. It is a special type of fiber.

9.2 Which of the following links can you use for FDDI?

a. STS-1
b. STS-3c
c. STS-3
d. STM-4

9.3 What is the data rate of STM-1?

a. 51.84 Mbps
b. 100 Mbps
c. 125 Mbps
d. 155.52 Mbps
e. 622.08 Mbps

9.4 What is the maximum length limit for SONET links in FDDI?

a. 2 km
b. 60 km
c. 200 km
d. Limited by the total ring latency
e. No limit

CHAPTER **10**

Station Management (SMT)

10.1 Overview

Station management is a subset of network management. The function of network management is to allow initialization, control, and monitoring of all hardware and software components of a network. Architecturally, network management is concerned with all seven layers of the ISO/OSI reference model (see Figure 1.11). While defining each layer of the protocol stack, facilities required to manage that layer of the protocol should also be defined. These **layer management** facilities can be named after the specific layers for which they are responsible. Thus, we have application management, presentation management, session management, and so on. The management facilities that manage the three protocol layers of an FDDI station, namely, MAC, PHY, and PMD, are termed **station management** (**SMT**). In other words, station management is that subset of network management that allows initialization, control, and monitoring of hardware and software components related to FDDI protocol layers.

In particular, FDDI's station management allows initialization/control, monitoring, and fault isolation/recovery of MAC, PHY, and PMD components. Some examples of the facilities it provides are as follows:

1. *Initialization/Control*:
   a. *Connection Initialization*: SMT provides facilities for neighboring nodes to test the link and other components connecting them and to exchange information about themselves.
   b. *Topology Control*: During connection initialization, SMT enforces a set of topology rules that ensures that those connections that will result in an invalid ring topology will not be allowed.
   c. *Ring Initialization*: Facilities are provided for stations to form a ring and agree on a set of operational parameters such as target token rotation time.
   d. *Parameter Setting*: SMT allows station parameters, variables, and indicators to be set locally and, if permitted, remotely.
2. *Status Monitoring*:
   a. *Ring Maps*: Provides facilities for users to determine who is on the ring.
   b. *Traffic Monitoring*: Allows collection and exchange of information about valid and invalid frames observed by various stations. Facilities are provided for requesting and announcing various parameters, counters, events, and conditions.
   c. *Error Monitoring*: Provides facilities for on-going monitoring of various links. The error rate of links is continuously monitored to ensure that only good links stay on the ring.

Stations or People: Management Issues Are Similar

The easiest way to understand network management or station management is to think of it as a human manager managing a group of people, for example, your boss. The three key functions of a group manager are:

1. *Hiring*: To allow only good people to join the group. This requires interviewing them and hiring only if they are found satisfactory.
2. *Monitoring*: After the people are on board, they work as instructed. The manager keeps an eye on their work and issues periodic status reports.
3. *Firing*: Those whose performance is found unsatisfactory are terminated and replaced by good people.

Network management allows similar functions for network components. The functions are called initialization/control, monitoring, and fault isolation/recovery, respectively.

3. *Fault Isolation/Recovery*:
   a. *Fault Detection*: Many types of faults are automatically detected and reported.
   b. *Fault Isolation*: Location of broken cables, connectors, or stations can be pinpointed using SMT facilities.
   c. *Fault Recovery*: The ring can automatically reconfigure around faults and resume operation.

The key aspects of FDDI management facilities are that they are fully *distributed* and *automatic*. By fully distributed, we mean that no management station with special hardware is required to manage an FDDI network. The network can be managed equally well from *any* FDDI station. Also, fault detection, isolation, and recovery are automatic. No manual intervention is normally required.

Figure 10.1 shows a partitioning of SMT functions. The functions related to physical layer (PHY and PMD) management are called **connection management** (**CMT**). These functions, which relate to the management of physical connections between neighboring stations, deal either with issues internal to a station or with issues that require communication with a neighboring node (two-party issues). They do not require the use of a token or other MAC facilities and work solely based on specially designed signaling mechanisms. The functions relating to the management of the ring and MACs deal with *n*-party issues ($n \geq 2$) where n is the number of stations (not nodes) on the ring. A group of these functions, especially those relating to fault isolation/recovery, is called **ring management** (**RMT**). The remaining functions, generally relating to normal control and monitoring,

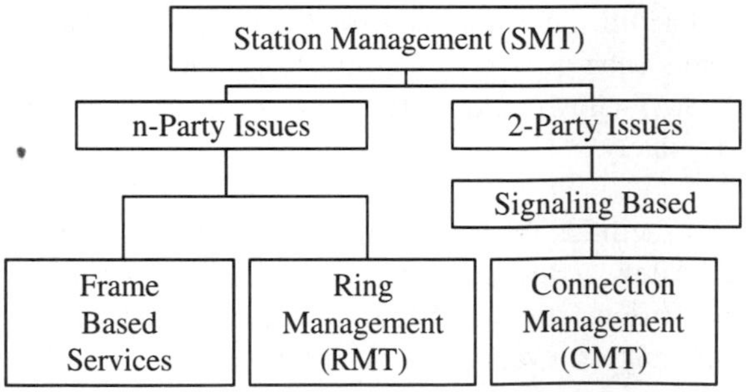

Figure 10.1 Components of station management.

Is SMT a Misnomer?

Strictly speaking, station management is a misnomer because SMT relates to management of not only stations but also concentrators. The correct name should be node management. Unfortunately, the fact that a concentrator may or may not be a station became clear to the SMT committee long after its formation. The term *node* was then introduced to include stations, concentrators, and other entities, such as repeaters. However, the name of the standard has not been changed.

Even the term *management* is used in SMT in a broader sense than that used normally in other protocols. Functions and facilities required for the normal operation of a protocol are generally considered a part of the protocol and not of the management. Management usually is an overhead that is helpful but not absolutely required, particularly if there are no problems. Many parts of CMT, for example, initialization of physical connections, are required for normal operation. Following this definition of management, the spanning tree algorithm used in bridges would be called bridge management.

are called **frame-based services**. In the remainder of this chapter we describe these SMT functions beginning with frame-based services in Section 10.2.

Following the ISO/OSI management model, SMT uses an object-oriented approach. Figure 10.2 depicts the SMT object model and the components of SMT. Four managed object classes are defined: SMT object, MAC objects, path objects, and port objects. While there is only one instance of an SMT object at each station, there may be multiple instances of MAC, path, or port objects at the station. The management of these objects is accomplished through notifications and operations. Notifications are unsolicited reports generated by a managed object. Operations are functions performed by a management agent on the object. For each object class, SMT defines the class behavior, attributes, notifications, and actions.

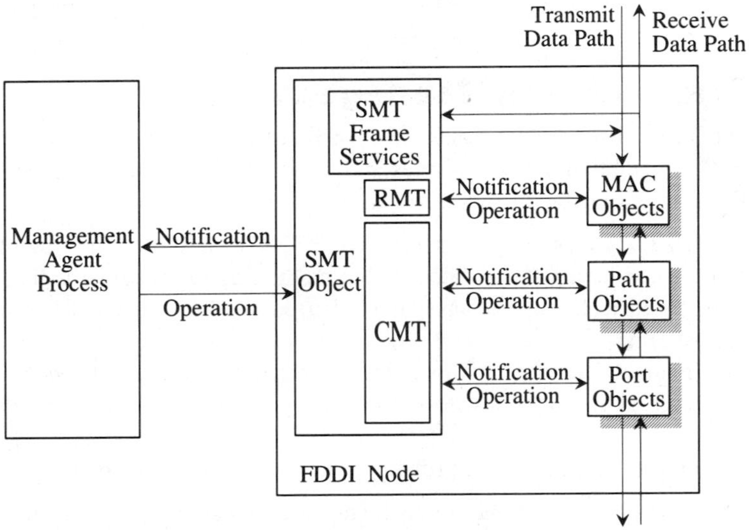

Figure 10.2 SMT management model.

A Classification of Management Issues

As shown in Figure 10.3, the issues relating to management of a group of people can be classified into two classes:

1. *One- or Two-Party Issues*: Those relating to individuals or between two individuals. These do not require explicit spoken languages. These can be distinguished by special signals, such as facial expressions and eye blinking, between the individuals.
2. *n-Party Issues*: These require group meetings and the use of spoken languages.

FDDI station management has been designed to follow this classification. CMT solves one- or two-party issues using signaling. RMT and frame-based services solve *n*-party issues using frames.

(a) Two-Party Issues: Signaling is sufficient

(b) *n*-Party Issues: Require message exchange

Figure 10.3 Two-party and multiparty management issues.

10.2 Frame-Based Management

SMT frame-based management services make use of special frames to initialize, monitor, and control the ring during normal operation. Special frames and protocols have been designed to facilitate the management of the ring. Examples of such services are:

1. Finding who is where. A map showing successive PHYs or MACs on the ring can be prepared.
2. Reporting and monitoring ring status. Each station on the ring sends out periodic status messages. Any station can listen to these messages. It is also possible to request a special status report from one or all stations.
3. Finding out parameter values used by a station and requesting a change if necessary.
4. Performing an external loopback test to ensure that a station can talk to another and receive replies.
5. Determining whether a station is on a primary or a secondary ring or both.

These services make use of special SMT frames that are sent using normal media access rules for asynchronous traffic, that is, on the capture of a usable token. Before describing these functions in detail, it is helpful to understand various types of SMT frames and their formats.

10.3 SMT Frame Format

SMT frames have a standard format, which helps stations understand SMT requests from other stations and respond accordingly. This format is described in this section. Various classes of frames are described in the next section.

All SMT frames follow the format of FDDI frames, which was described earlier in Section 2.3. In particular, they begin with a preamble, a starting delimiter, a frame-control field, a destination address, and a source address. They end with a CRC and frame status indicators. Figure 10.4 shows the format for an SMT frame. The key fields and their explanations are as follows:

1. *Frame Control*: SMT frames are distinguished by a special frame control. A frame control value of 41_{16} ($0100\text{-}0001_2$) indicates an SMT frame. In addition, the frame control value of $4F_{16}$ ($0100\text{-}1111_2$) is used to indicate **next station addressing** (**NSA**). This frame control indicates the frame is destined to the next station of a specified type on the ring. The type is indicated by the destination address field. If the destination address is the broadcast address FF-FF-FF-FF-FF-FF_{16}, the next station on the token path will receive the frame and set the frame status indicators. Other stations will ignore (receive and discard) the frame since the address-recognized indicator in the frame status field will indicate that some other station has already recognized the frame. If the destination address is a group (multicast) address, the first station on the token path who is a member of the group will receive the frame and set the frame status indicator. For example, 01-80-C2-00-00-00 is the *bridge group address*. An NSA frame with this destination address will be received by the first bridge on the token path.
2. *Destination Address*: This is the address of the station to whom the frame is being sent. Only long (48-bit) addresses in the IEEE standard format are allowed. Short (16-bit) addresses are not allowed. The destination address can be an individual, group, or broadcast address. Functional addresses (see Section 2.8) are not allowed.

   The group addresses that have been specifically assigned for use by SMT protocol are listed in Table 10.1. Both IEEE canonical representation and msb representation are shown. (See Section 2.9 for an explanation of these representations.) Notice that bytes are separated by a hyphen in the canonical representation and by colons in the msb representation.
3. *Source Address*: This is the address of the sending station. Only long addresses in IEEE standard format are allowed. The source address must be an individual address and not a group address. In particular, the use of an individual/group bit to indicate the presence of source-routing infor-

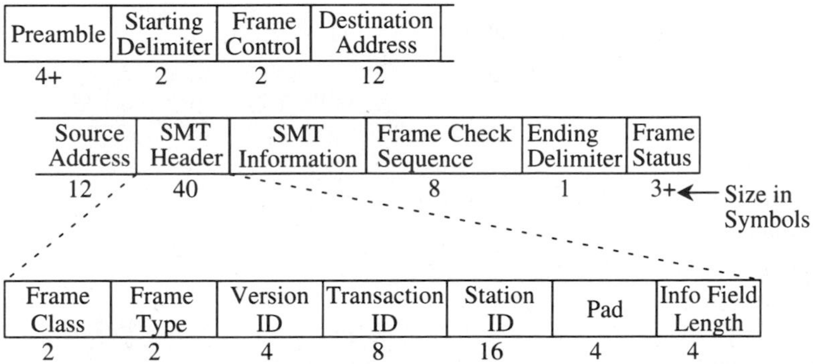

Figure 10.4 SMT frame format.

Table 10.1 SMT Defined Group Addresses

Name	Assigned Address in Hex	
	Canonical Representation	msb Representation
SMT directed beacon	01-80-C2-00-01-00	80:01:43:00:80:00
SMT status report frames	01-80-C2-00-01-10	80:01:43:00:80:08
SMT concentrator MACs[a]	01-80-C2-00-01-20	80:01:43:00:80:04
SMT synchronous bandwidth allocators	01-80-C2-00-01-30	80:01:43:00:80:0C
SMT monitors[b]	01-80-C2-00-01-40	80:01:43:00:80:02
SMT channel allocators[b]	01-80-C2-00-01-50	80:01:43:00:80:0A
SMT WBC allocators[b]	01-80-C2-00-01-60	80:01:43:00:80:06
SMT isochronous users[b]	01-80-C2-00-01-70	80:01:43:00:80:0E

[a]No protocol is defined for this address.
[b]Used only in FDDI-II networks.

mation is neither allowed nor required since SMT frames are valid only on the ring in which they originate. They are not forwarded by bridges.

4. *Frame Class*: This 1-byte field indicates the function of the SMT frame. Ten different classes have been specified. These classes are listed in Table 10.2 and are explained later in this chapter. The table also shows valid types for each class. The frame types are explained next.
5. *Frame Type*: The three types of SMT frames are request, response, and announcement. Response frames are sent to answer request frames. Announcements are unsolicited and are generally used by a station to provide information about itself.

   The response frames for all SMT classes have the restriction that their destination address must be an individual address (that of the requester) and their frame control must be 41_{16}. NSA frame control is not allowed on response frames. The response should normally be generated in 30 seconds or less. Sending requests to a broadcast address or a group address is allowed but it may result in a flood of responses (unless next station addressing is used).

Table 10.2 SMT Frame Class and Types

Class	Code in Hex	Allowed Types		
		Ann.	Req.	Resp.
Neighbor information frame (NIF)	01	√	√	√
Status information frame (SIF)				
Configuration SIF	02		√	√
Operation SIF	03		√	√
Echo frame (ECF)	04		√	√
Resource allocation frame (RAF)	05	√	√	√
Request denied frame (RDF)	06			√
Status report frame (SRF)	07	√		
Parameter management frame (PMF)				
Get PMF	08		√	√
Set PMF	09		√	√
Extended service frame (ESF)	FF	√	√	√

6. *Version ID*: This indicates the version number of the SMT standard that the frame is following. The presence of this field allows SMT to be extended. Stations implementing a new version of the standard may or may not understand frames from stations implementing old versions. A station may support a range of versions. Detailed rules to process frames of version below, in, or over the implemented range are specified in the SMT standard. In particular, if a station does not support a particular version number specified in an SMT request, it responds with a "request denied frame" including an indication that the SMT version indicated in the request is not supported by the receiving station.
7. *Transaction ID*: The transaction ID is used to match responses with their requests. Each request issued by a station has a transaction ID. The responding stations use the transaction ID of the request in their response frames. Successive transaction IDs should be unique and should not be reused within a short interval unless it is a retransmission of a previous request. However, these issues and the algorithm to generate these IDs are left to the implementors.
8. *Station ID*: This uniquely identifies the source station. Since a station can have more than one MAC, the source address in the frame is not sufficient to identify the source station. You cannot tell from the source address that the two MACs are part of the same station.

   This field is 8 bytes long. The first 2 bytes are arbitrarily selected by the station owner/manufacturer. The last 6 bytes must be an individual address in IEEE format. The address must be a universally administered address, that is, its U/L bit should be zero. Also, it must be an individual address, that is, its I/G bit must be zero.

   Although not required by the standard, most stations use the universal address of the MAC (or one of the MACs) in the station for the lower 6 bytes of the station ID.
9. *Pad*: This 2-byte field is reserved for future use. This must be transmitted as 0's.
10. *Information Field Length*: This field indicates the length of the information field in bytes. This value does not include the length of the SMT or MAC header of the frame. Its value can be between 0 and 4458 bytes. Actually, the information field is limited to 4332 bytes in all SMT frames except for echo frames. This along with an SMT header of 20 bytes results in a MAC information size of 4352 bytes. This limit was chosen for consistency with Internet RFC 1390 (Transmission of IP and ARP over FDDI Networks) based on a discussion at an Internet Engineering Task Force (IETF) meeting, where it was decided that the MAC information size should be large enough to allow 4-kB application level data. Allowing 256 bytes for headers of various layers resulted in a maximum MAC information size requirement of 4352 bytes.

    In echo frames a larger information size is allowed since the response may include the complete information field of the request along with other parameters. Notice that an information field of 4458 bytes will result in a MAC information field of 4478 bytes and hence the maximum size (4500 bytes) MAC frame.
11. *Information*: The information field is organized as a sequence of type-length-index-value (TLIV) encoded subfields as shown in Figure 10.5. Each subfield consists of a 2-byte parameter type,

Parameter Type	Parameter Length	Resource Index	Parameter Value	Parameter Type	Parameter Length	Resource Index	Parameter Value	•••
2	2	4	n1	2	2	4	n2	

Size in Bytes

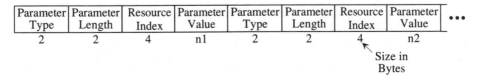

Figure 10.5 Information field of SMT frames.

a 2-byte parameter length, a 4-byte resource index, followed by the parameter value. Most parameters have been assigned a 2-byte parameter-type value. The type is specified as "*xx zz*," where *xx* indicates the object (10_{16} = SMT, 20_{16} = MAC, 30_{16} = Path, 40_{16} = Port), and *zz* indicates the attribute. Some SMT parameters do not map to any particular object. These have been assigned a parameter type of "00 *zz*". These are listed in Table 10.3. A complete list of other SMT parameters is presented later in Figure 12.4.

Table 10.3 SMT 00xx Encoded Parameter Types

Type Code in Hex	Parameter Name	Used in Class	Length in Hex
00 01	Upstream neighbor address (UNA)	NIF	00 08
00 02	Station descriptor	NIF, SIF	00 04
00 03	Station state	NIF, SIF	00 04
00 04	Message time stamp	SIF	00 08
00 05	Station policies	SIF	00 04
00 06	Path latency contribution per ring	SIF	00 08
00 07	MAC neighbors	SIF	00 10
00 08	Path descriptor	SIF	[a]
00 09	MAC status	SIF	00 28
00 0A	Port link error monitoring status	SIF	00 10
00 0B	MAC frame counters	SIF	00 0C
00 0C	MAC frame not copied count	SIF	00 08
00 0D	MAC priority values T_Pri's	SIF	00 20
00 0E	Port elasticity buffer status	SIF	00 08
00 0F	Manufacturer field	SIF	00 20
00 10	User field	SIF	00 20
00 11	Echo data	ECF	00 00 to 11 68
00 12	Reason code	RDF	00 04
00 13	First *n* bytes of a rejected frame	RDF	Variable
00 14	SMT supported versions	RDF, SIF	Variable
00 15	Resource type	RAF	00 04
00 16	SBA[b] command type (1 = Request, 2 = Report, 3 = Change)	RAF	00 04
00 17	SBA payload request (bytes per 125 μs)	RAF	00 04
00 18	SBA overhead request (bytes per 125 μs)	RAF	00 04
00 19	Address responsible for SBA	RAF	00 08
00 1A	SBA category	RAF	00 04
00 1B	Maximum T_Neg acceptable for synchronous service	RAF	00 04
00 1C	Minimum bytes per synchronous frame	RAF	00 04
00 1D	Total synchronous bandwidth available	RAF	00 04
00 21	Authorization data	PMF	Variable

[a] Length of path descriptor = 8 $\times$(Number of ports + Number of MACs)
[b] SBA = Synchronous bandwidth allocation

The parameter length gives the length of the parameter value in bytes. The resouce index identifies the particular instance of the object. For example, a station can have multiple MACs, which are distinguished by their resource-indices. This subfield is included only when referencing attributes associated with MAC, PATH, and PORT objects but omitted for parameters of type "00 *zz*" and for attributes of the SMT object since there is only one SMT per station.

For example, the parameter 00-12-00-04-00-00-00-01_{16} used in a request denied frame is interpreted as follows:

Parameter type: 00-12 ⇒ Reason Code
Parameter length: 00-04 ⇒ Four bytes
Parameter value: 00-00-00-01 ⇒ Frame class not supported

The key advantage of TLIV encoding is that the parameters do not have to be in any particular order. Also, new parameter values can be easily added.

12. *FCS and Frame Status*: Only SMT frames with good FCS and an E-indicator received as reset are received and acted on by the stations. For frames, using next station addressing, the A-indicator should be received as reset if the frame is to be acted on.

FDDI MAC frames and SMT frames follow a big-endian (or MSB) byte ordering for multibyte data, such as 32-bit timing parameters or counters. The byte-order and bit-order issues were discussed in Section 2.9.

10.4 SMT Frame Classes

The station management standard defines 10 special frames for SMT functions. The classes and types of these frames were listed earlier in Table 10.2. Each of these classes and their uses is explained in the next few sections.

10.5 Neighbor Information Frame

These frames are used by a MAC to determine or announce who its neighboring MACs are. Each MAC has two neighbors: upstream and downstream. Tokens and frames flow from an upstream neighbor through this MAC to the downstream neighbor. If each MAC knows and periodically announces its neighbors' addresses, a network manager can construct a map of the ring showing successive stations on the ring. Such **ring maps** are helpful in fault location. A map listing successive MACs on the token path is called a **logical ring map**. Similarly, a map listing successive PHYs on the token path is called a **physical ring map**, which incidentally requires the use of status information frames as discussed in Section 10.6.

All MACs on the ring normally broadcast information about themselves and their upstream neighbor's address approximately every 30 seconds by sending out a NIF request to the broadcast address with next station addressing (FC = NSA). The first station to receive this frame (with A-indicator reset) records the sending MAC's address as its upstream neighbor address (UNA) and sets the A-indicator on the frame. The station then responds with a NIF response frame telling the requester its (downstream neighbor) address.

If the NIF response frame sent to a station by its downstream neighbor has its A-indicator set, some other MAC also has the same address as the station. This can be used for duplicate address detection as explained further in Section 11.12.

By listening to periodic NIF requests, any station on the ring can collect information to prepare a ring map. This information can also be collected on demand by sending out a series of NIF requests—first to the upstream neighbor (UN), then to UN's UN and so on, or by sending one NIF request to the broadcast address and getting ready to receive the storm of resulting responses.

The information field of a NIF frame includes UNA and some information about the sending station, for example, whether it is a station or a concentrator, number of MACs, number and types of ports, state of these ports (wrapped or not), internal configuration of MACs and PHYs, and whether the station is a bridge to another network.

The address $00\text{-}00\text{-}F8\text{-}00\text{-}00\text{-}00_{16}$ has been specifically assigned by the IEEE to indicate an unknown address. This value (and not zero) is used in NIF if UNA is unknown. The all-zero address is reserved for a null address, which is used in the source address field by some implementations for a short time during fault recovery. If a station uses a null address, it is not allowed to provide any LLC services, which means it can be used only for recovery and not for normal user data transmission. If more than one station uses the null address, a duplicate address condition can occur and, therefore, the use of null addresses should be minimized.

The interpretation of a NIF depends on the frame-control field, destination address, and SMT frame type of the NIF. Table 10.4 lists valid NIF frames and their interpretation.

All FDDI MACs are required to transmit a NIF request every **T_Notify** interval, which can be set anywhere between 2 and 30 seconds. The default value is 30 seconds. To avoid the possibility of all MACs synchronizing and flooding the network at precisely the same instant, it is recommended that the actual interval be selected randomly, uniformly distributed over the range T_Notify$\pm$1 seconds. If no NIFs are received from the downstream neighbor or from the upstream neighbor for about 228 seconds (**T_NN_out**), a neighbor notification timeout is declared and the neighbor information maintained at the station is marked "unknown." The value of 228 seconds allows for the worst case possibility that every MAC on the ring is overloaded:

$$
\begin{aligned}
\text{T\_NN\_Out} &= \text{Maximum number of MACs} \times \text{Maximum TTRT} + 2 \times \text{T\_Notify} \\
&= 1000 \times 167.7 \times 10^{-3} + 2 \times 30 \\
&= 227.7
\end{aligned}
$$

To summarize, NIFs are used to determine and announce a MAC's upstream and downstream neighbors and for building ring maps. Each MAC on the ring is required to transmit a NIF request

Table 10.4 Meanings of NIF Frames

Frame Control	Destination Address	SMT Frame Type	Meaning
NSA	Broadcast	Announcement	Hi DN! I am still here.
SMT	Broadcast	Request	Hey World! What is your UNA?
NSA	Broadcast	Request	Hey DN! I am your UN. Please tell me who you are.
SMT	Group	Request	Hey group! What is your UNA?
NSA	Group	Request	Hey DN group member! I am your UN group member. Please tell me who you are.
SMT	Individual	Request	Hey, you! Who is your upstream neighbor?
SMT	Individual	Response	I am X and my upstream neighbor is Y.

DN = downstream neighbor, UN = upstream neighbor

periodically. This verifies that the MAC is connected to the ring. NIFs are also useful in duplicate address detection on an operational ring.

10.6 Status Information Frame

Status information frames (SIFs) are used to find detailed information about a station. For example, it is possible to find out the order in which various MACs and PHYs are connected inside a concentrator or how many frames were missed by a MAC due to a lack of buffers.

Two classes of SIFs are defined: configuration SIF and operation SIF. Configuration SIF requests and responses are used to find out information related to a station's configuration. Generally this information is relatively static because it does not change frequently. Operational SIF requests and responses are used to determine information about a station's operational counters, state variables, and timers. Much of this information is highly dynamic and varies frequently.

Unlike NIFs, there are no SIF announcements. An SIF configuration response is sent to answer an SIF configuration request. Examples of the information included in such a response are:

1. Type of station: station or concentrator
2. Number of MACs and their addresses
3. Number of ports; type (A, B, S, or M) and state of each port
4. Type of remote port to which each port is connected
5. SMT versions supported by the station
6. Whether the station is wrapped
7. Connection policies (topology rules) supported by the station (Station connection policies are explained in Section 11.2. For example, a station may not allow an A-to-A connection.)
8. Station delay in bytes; delay contributions to the latency of the primary and secondary rings are reported in bytes (1 byte = 80 ns)
9. Upstream and downstream neighbors' addresses
10. Internal arrangement of various MACs and ports in the station
11. Time stamp indicating the time of the configuration information

It should be obvious that any station on the ring can poll all stations on the ring by means of configuration SIF requests and can keep track of any changes in the ring configuration. In particular, physical and logical ring maps can be prepared using SIF configuration polling.

SIF operation requests and responses are used for performance monitoring and for fault location and isolation. Examples of information contained in operation SIF responses, which are sent to answer operation SIF requests, are:

1. MAC parameters: Various token rotation time parameters, such as T_Req, T_Neg (see Sidebar), T_Min, T_Max, valid transmission timer (TVX), and synchronous bandwidth allocation.
2. Token rotation time thresholds for various priorities (if supported): T_Pri0, T_Pri1, T_Pri2, T_Pri3, T_Pri4, T_Pri5, and T_Pri6. See Section 2.2 for details on how these thresholds are used.
3. Frame counters: Number of frames seen, number of frames in which errors were detected, and number of frames lost due to errors.
4. LEM status: A link error monitor (LEM) is used to keep track of the link error rate (LER) of a link (see Section 11.4). The current LER along with the LER thresholds for failing the LEM test and for taking the link out of the ring are included.
5. Number of frames that were not copied due to a lack of buffers.

6. Number of elasticity buffer overflows.
7. Manufacturer of the equipment. The manufacturer's organizationally unique identifier (**OUI**) assigned by the IEEE is used (see Section 2.8).
8. Set count: This indicates the number of times parameters at the station have been changed (set) by local or remote management commands. The use of set count is described in Section 10.11.

To summarize, SIFs are used for configuration, performance, and fault monitoring of the ring.

10.7 Echo Frame

Echo frames (ECFs) are used for SMT-to-SMT loopback testing. An ECF request frame allows a station to send any valid data up to a maximum of 4454 bytes to any other station on the ring. The receiving station responds with an ECF response frame containing the same data.

The receipt of a valid ECF response confirms that a station's port, MAC, and SMT are at least partly operational. We said *partly* because some data-dependent errors may not be detected. It is possible to confirm a data-sensitive failure by placing the suspect data in an ECF request frame.

The maximum data size of 4454 bytes results in a maximum size (4500 bytes) MAC frame. Recall that the maximum SMT information field size is 4458 bytes. Of these, 4 bytes are required for the parameter type and parameter length field, leaving 4454 bytes for the data.

10.8 Resource Allocation Frame

Resource allocation frames (RAFs) have been defined to request and grant network resources. At this time, the only identified network resource is synchronous bandwidth. Implementation of RAF frames is optional. All three classes—announcement, request, and response—are allowed. However, only request and responses are normally used. All stations on the network send their RAF requests for synchronous bandwidth allocation (SBA) to a central synchronous bandwidth manager who sends an RAF response granting/refusing the request. The **SBA command** parameter in the RAF frames indicates whether the request/response is for a new allocation, for reporting an existing allocation, or for changing allocation. The requests can be sent to the broadcast address, a group address, or to any individual address. The responses are always sent to answer requests and are therefore addressed to the individual station making the request. Table 10.5 lists the meaning of some common RAF exchanges. Note that the SBA command "report allocation" is used by the SBA manager to monitor the allocations periodically. If the manager determines that the synchronous bandwidth has been

Table 10.5 Meanings of RAF Frames

Frame Type	SBA Command	Source	Meaning
Request	Request	Other	Please give me a new SBA of X.
Response	Request	Manager	Congratulations, your request for an SBA of X has been granted.
Request	Report	Manager	What is your SBA?
Response	Report	Other	My SBA is X.
Request	Change	Manager	I am sorry but your SBA has to be reduced to X.
Response	Change	Other	That's OK.

Table 10.6 SMT Reason Codes

Code	Reason	Frame Class
00 00 00 01	Frame class not supported	RDF
00 00 00 02	Frame version not supported	RDF
00 00 00 03	Success	PMF
00 00 00 04	Bad set count	PMF
00 00 00 05	Illegal operation	PMF
00 00 00 06	No parameter	PMF
00 00 00 07	No more[a]	PMF
00 00 00 08	Out of range	RDF
00 00 00 09	Not authorized	PMF
00 00 00 0A	Length error	RDF, PMF
00 00 00 0B	Frame too long	PMF
00 00 00 0C	Illegal parameter[a]	PMF
00 00 00 0D	Synchronous bandwidth request denied	RAF

[a]Obsolete. Removed in SMT draft version 7.2.

overallocated, it can issue an SBA command "change allocation" to reduce the allocations of some or all stations. Synchronous bandwidth allocation is discussed further in Section 10.13.

10.9 Request Denied Frame

Request denied frames (RDFs) are used to indicate that a station is unable to respond to a request. This may be due to a variety of reasons, for example:

1. The request is formatted using an SMT version number that is not supported at the responding station.
2. The response would exceed the maximum SMT frame length.
3. The frame class is not supported by the responding station.

The reason for denial is included in the RDF response along with the range of supported SMT versions and a portion of the beginning of the rejected request frame to allow the requester to correlate the response to its request. Table 10.6 lists SMT reason codes.

10.10 Status Report Frame

Status report frames (SRFs) are used to announce the occurrence of certain events and abnormal conditions at the station. A network monitor listening to these announcements could alert the network manager to take corrective action if necessary.

Events, such as a neighbor change, a configuration change, or illegal connection attempt, are announced using SRFs. Any system status that lasts for some time is called a **condition**, for example, a high frame error rate, high link error rate, high elasticity buffer error rate, high frame loss rate, or duplicate address. The occurrence of such events and conditions is announced by sending an SRF announcement to a group address. The address 01-80-C2-00-01-10 has been specifically assigned for this purpose. A rate is said to be high when it exceeds a preset threshold. The condition remains asserted as long as the rate exceeds the threshold.

Normally, the stations check their status every 2 seconds. An SRF is sent if any new event or condition has occurred since the last SRF or if any previously reported condition has been deasserted. In the absence of new events or conditions, currently existing abnormal conditions are announced at geometrically increasing intervals leveling off at 32 seconds: 2, 4, 8, 16, 32, 32, 32, ... This **pacing algorithm** was chosen to minimize the SRF traffic due to old news while allowing quick notification of new news.

During normal operation, that is, during the absence of any abnormal events, conditions, or neighbor/configuration change, no SRF announcements are generated.

Note that the status report frames are sent not only when a condition becomes active (asserted) but also when it becomes deasserted, for example, when the frame error rate goes down from above a threshold to below the threshold.

10.11 Parameter Management Frame

Parameter management frames (PMFs) allow remote management of station parameters. Any station on FDDI can act as a management station and read or change any parameter at any station. Of course, a managed station may require authentication of the managing station.

There are two classes of PMF frames. "PMF get request frames" are used to read values of parameters and "PMF set request frames" are used to modify these values. Each request is confirmed (or denied) by a corresponding response frame.

Since more than one station may simultaneously want to change a parameter, a synchronization algorithm is required to avoid the possibility of inconsistent changes. This is done by maintaining a set count at each station. The set count is incremented each time any parameter at the station is changed locally or remotely.

If a managing station wants to change a parameter, it first reads this count, then sends the count back in the change request. The responding station changes the parameter as requested only if the set count in the change request is equal to that maintained locally. A different value indicates that some parameters have been changed and that the managing station's knowledge of this station's

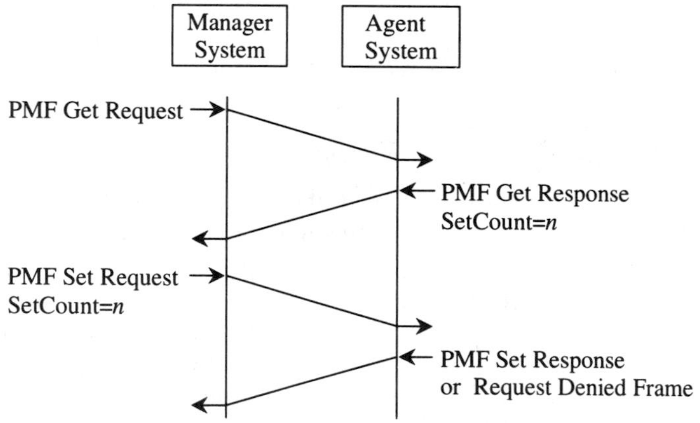

Figure 10.6 Sample message exchanges for parameter change.

parameters is out of date. Thus, as many as four messages may be required to modify a parameter as shown in Figure 10.6. However, since the set count is returned in all responses and in SIF frames, the PMF get request-response messages may not be used. Also, PMF get requests can be broadcast, thereby receiving multiple set counts with one request. All other PMF frames must be individually addressed.

A PMF request may be rejected for the various reasons listed earlier in Table 10.6. In such cases, the corresponding rejection criterion is specified in the response.

The standard allows the option of including authorization data in the PMF requests. However, the authorization algorithm is not specified. Implementors are allowed to choose their own algorithm.

Implementation of PMF get requests, PMF set requests, and PMF set response is optional. Only the PMF get response is mandatory. This ensures that all stations will respond to parameter reading requests.

Figure 10.7 shows how SMT parameters can be managed remotely with and without PMFs. In stations implementing PMFs, higher layers need not be involved in managing FDDI objects. In stations that do not implement PMFs, parameter management can be accomplished by means of a higher layer management protocol that is understood by both stations. PMFs were a topic of numerous hot debates in the standards committee. The proponents of the PMFs argued that it allows direct management of FDDI rings in a multivendor environment without the need for other protocols. The opponents argued that other protocols such as SNMP and OSI CMIP/CMIS are already in common use by vendors and there is no need to have one more protocol.

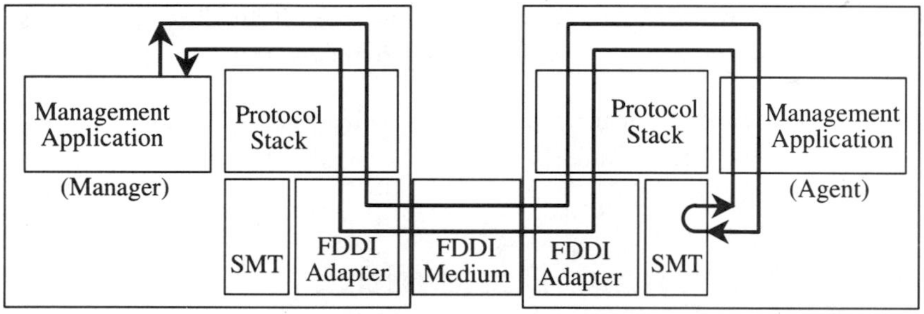

(a) Management without PMF frames.

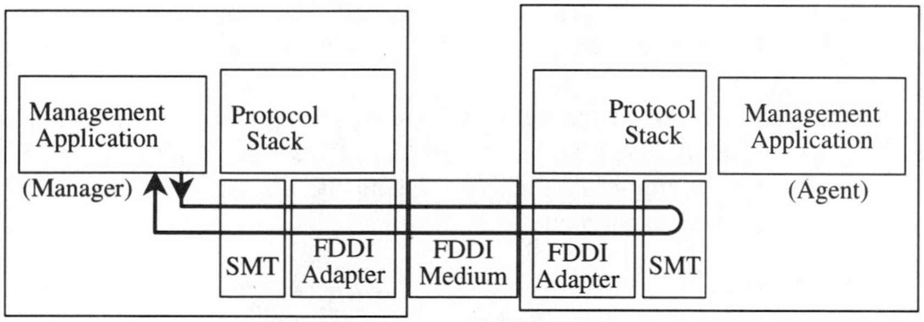

(b) Management with PMF frames.

Figure 10.7 Management of parameters with and without PMF frames.

Table 10.7 Summary of SMT Frame Classes

Frame Class	Purpose
Neighbor information frame (NIF)	To find/announce neighboring stations.
Status information frame (SIF)	
Configuration SIF	To find/report internal configuration of a station.
Operation SIF	To find/report station counters and parameters.
Echo frame (ECF)	Loopback test.
Resource allocation frame (RAF)	To request and grant network resources such as synchronous bandwidth.
Request denied frame (RDF)	To reject a request.
Status report frame (SRF)	To announce abnormal conditions and events.
Parameter management frame (PMF)	To manage stations remotely.
Get PMF	To read parameter values.
Set PMF	To change parameter values.
Extended service frame (ESF)	To provide new implementor-defined services.

10.12 Extended Service Frame

Extended service frames (ESFs) allow implementors to define new services. Any vendor can define a new frame and protocol. The vendor's protocol name appears as the first parameter in the information field. It is specified as a 48-bit universal (IEEE-assigned) address. Other vendors may choose to participate or not in these extended protocols. If a station receives an ESF and chooses to reject it, it can simply ignore it. All three types of ESFs, namely, request, response, and announcements, are possible.

This completes our discussion of the frame classes defined in SMT. Table 10.7 presents a brief summary of the function of various frame classes.

10.13 Synchronous Bandwidth Allocation

The SMT standard does not specify a precise algorithm for allocation of synchronous bandwidth. It only defines facilities (parameters and frames) that can be used to build a variety of allocation algorithms.

It is assumed that all stations on the network send their requests for synchronous bandwidth allocations (SBAs) to a central SBA manager by means of an RAF request frame. The manager in turn sends an RAF response frame granting or refusing the request. The requesting station can specify the following parameters in its request:

1. Data bytes per 125 μs
2. Overhead bytes per allocation
3. Maximum acceptable token rotation time
4. Minimum bytes per synchronous frame
5. Station address

Generally, synchronous traffic arrives at a constant bit rate. This rate is rounded *up* to an integral number of bytes per 125 μs. For example, a 1-Mbps stream is equivalent to:

$$\frac{1 \times 10^6 \times 125 \times 10^{-6}}{8} = 15.625 \text{ bytes per } 125\ \mu\text{s}$$

Rounding up gives 16 bytes per 125 μs.

While the arrival rate is constant, the departure rate is determined by the token rotation time. The average value of the token rotation time never exceeds the TTRT negotiated (T_Neg) at ring initialization. The number of data bytes per T_Neg determines the size of the information field in the synchronous MAC frame. For example, with a TTRT of 8 ms, a 1-Mbps stream would produce 1000 data bytes per T_Neg. With a TTRT of 4 ms, the same stream would produce only 500 data bytes per T_Neg.

So far we have computed only payload (data) bytes. To get total allocation, the overhead for frame transmission such as token capture, preamble, and frame header should also be known. This depends on the higher layer protocol being used by the station. For example, assuming a low value of 8 bytes for the headers of higher layers, 28 bytes for a MAC layer, and 11 bytes for token capture, the SBA overhead per frame is:

$$\begin{aligned} \text{SBA overhead} &= \text{Token capture} + \text{MAC frame overhead} + \text{Higher layer overhead} \\ &= 11 + 28 + 8 \\ &= 47 \end{aligned}$$

To compute the synchronous bandwidth used by the station, it should also declare the minimum number of data bytes (segment size) it will transmit and the maximum T_Neg that is acceptable to it. These parameters along with the station address help the SBA manager to determine if the request can be granted.

The standard does not specify a specific algorithm for the SBA manager to use. Any algorithm that uses these parameters can be used.

Notice that a central SBA manager is required for the ring. The SMT standard does not specify a particular election algorithm. Any suitable election algorithm can be used. Backup managers, if required, can also be elected.

Like any other management job, the responsibilities of the SBA manager include monitoring the proper use of the synchronous bandwidth and reducing or canceling allocations if necessary. All stations periodically send out NIF requests. These requests contain the station state. Bit 6 of the state indicates if the station provides synchronous service. The SBA manager can passively monitor these NIF requests and can make a list of all stations providing the synchronous service. Periodically, it should send RAF requests to these (or all) stations asking them to report their synchronous bandwidth allocations. By comparing these reports with its own database, the manager can detect errors in allocations. This may happen if a station shuts off without deallocation, if the T_Neg changes, or if a dual ring wraps and the synchronous allocations on the two rings exceed the available synchronous bandwidth.

The maximum available synchronous transmission time on a ring is:

$$\begin{aligned} \sum \text{Synchronous allocations} \leq\ & \text{TTRT} - \text{Ring latency} - \text{Maximum frame time} \\ & - \text{Token time} - \text{L\_Max} - 2 \times \text{Void frame time} \end{aligned}$$

If total synchronous allocations exceed this limit, some asynchronous stations may be starved, resulting in repeated claim-operating oscillations. Any time T_Neg or the ring state changes, the SBA manager should check that its understanding of allocations is correct and that they do not exceed the available capacity.

If the allocations exceed the capacity, the SBA manager can reduce or cancel allocations for all or some stations. The manager can do this by sending RAF request frames with an SBA command value of $00\text{-}00\text{-}00\text{-}03_{16}$ (change allocations) to the affected stations.

10.14 Summary

SMT provides facilities for management of MAC, PHY, and PMD components. The three key components of SMT are frame-based services, connection management (CMT), and ring management (RMT). Frame-based services are used for management during normal operation. MAC-level fault management issues are handled by RMT. CMT handles PHY-level and PMD-level management issues. In particular, it is responsible for initialization of connections between neighbors.

Frame-based services use special SMT frames for proper initialization, monitoring, and fault management of the ring. Frames have been defined for finding and announcing the station configuration, operating counters of the station, fault conditions, and abnormal events, obtaining information about neighboring stations, loopback tests, requesting synchronous bandwidth and other network resources, and for managing parameters of other stations. By means of these frames, one can detect duplicate addresses and prepare ring maps.

10.15 Further Reading and Historical Notes

Although the SMT project began in 1984, little real work was done until 1986 due to the heavy workload of the other FDDI standards. When the work began, the group found itself divided into two camps—one believed that SMT should provide a minimum functionality and should be completed as soon as possible and the other believed that SMT should provide a full set of functionality even if that avenue resulted in needing more time.

By early 1988, the second group had won and the SMT document began growing in size and in functionality, giving it the honor of being the thickest among the FDDI standard documents. A technical letter ballot was issued by Technical Committee X3T9 in the spring of 1990. A total of 564 comments, more than half of them technical in nature, were submitted. The process of resolving these comments continued into early 1992. By this time most participating companies had products waiting for SMT to finish and so started working with a high degree of cooperation. In April 1992, a second technical letter ballot on SMT was issued by Technical Committee X3T9. This letter ballot passed *unanimously*. In June 1992, SMT draft version 7.2, which incorporated comments received during the second ballot, was unanimously approved by roll call votes of both X3T9.5 and X3T9 for forwarding to Accredited Standards Committee (ASC) X3. The X3 public review ended January 1, 1993, with one editorial comment.

Much of the discussion in this chapter is from the FDDI SMT draft version 7.2 (ANSI dpANS X3.229-199x or ISO/IEC WD 9314-6:199x).

McClure (1987) presents an overview of SMT design philosophy. Figure 10.7 is based on McClure (1989), who argues in the favor of parameter management frames. Ocheltree and Montalvo (1989) explain RMT.

10.16 Self-Test Exercises

Note: Some exercises have multiple correct answers. See Appendix D for answers.

10.1 What is an SMT announcement?

a. A message sent by the network manager to announce an emergency such as the network shutdown
b. Unsolicited frames sent by stations for management
c. A group request to be answered by all stations on the ring
d. A message used to locate resources in the network

10.2 What is the purpose of neighbor information frames (NIFs)?

a. To determine the neighboring station
b. To determine if the neighboring station has changed
c. To announce the neighboring station's address
d. All of the above

10.3 Which SMT frames can be used to find a station's upstream neighbor address?

a. Neighbor information frame
b. Status information frame
c. Echo frame
d. Resource allocation frame
e. Parameter management frame

CHAPTER **11**

Connection and Ring Management (CMT and RMT)

In the previous chapter, the three components of FDDI station management (SMT) were introduced: frame-based services, connection management, and ring management. Frame-based services were described in that previous chapter. In this chapter we describe the remaining components.

11.1 Connection Management

The set of components implementing the media-independent part (PHY) and media-dependent part (PMD) of FDDI's physical layer is called the **port**. A port attaches a node to the medium. A single-attachment station has one port, a dual-attachment station has two ports, and a concentrator may have many ports. On one side the port allows the node to be connected to other nodes via the medium. On the other side, MAC(s) may be attached to some ports.

Connection management (**CMT**) deals with the management of a node's ports and their interconnections. CMT provides a wide variety of functions including control of the optional optical bypass switch, initialization of physical connections, support of connection policies (topology rules) by the withholding of unacceptable connections, testing of link quality before use (LCT), performance of loop tests with neighboring MACs, placement of available MACs inside a station, removal of no-owner frames (scrub), detection and location of faults (trace), testing of internal paths of a node, reconfiguration around faults according to the availability policies of the station (wrap/hold), and monitoring of link quality during use (LEM).

Testing of link quality before use (link confidence test) and monitoring of link quality during use (link error monitoring) are described in Sections 11.3 and 11.4, respectively.

The CMT functions are divided into three categories: managing the configuration of PHY and MAC elements within a node, managing the optical media interface, and managing the physical connection between a port and the port of the adjacent node. These three components of connection management are called *configuration management* (*CFM*), *entity coordination management* (*ECM*), and *physical connection management* (*PCM*), respectively. The relationships among the three areas of CMT and the FDDI protocol layers are shown in Figure 11.1.

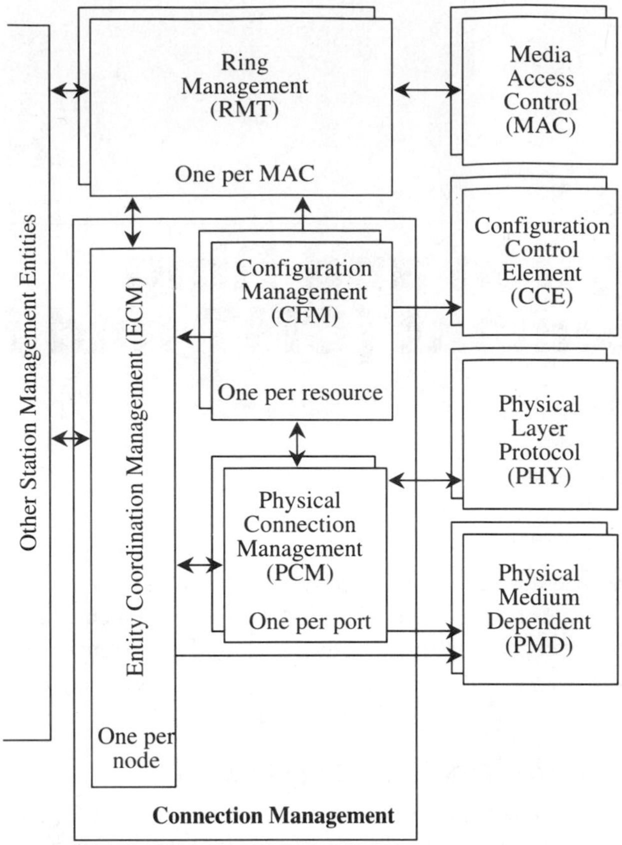

Figure 11.1 Relationship among the components of CMT.

11.1.1 Entity Coordination Management

ECM covers the management of the media interface. This includes coordinating the activities of all of the ports at the node. It also controls the optical bypass if present. There is one ECM per node, which manages PCMs at all ports (A, B, S, or M) of the node. ECM signals a PCM when its media becomes available/unavailable. This includes starting or stopping the physical connection management, coordinating the fault tracing, and also path testing within the node. Fault tracing is described in Section 11.5.

11.1.2 Physical Connection Management

PCM covers the management of the physical connection between a port being managed and another port in the adjacent node. There is one PCM per port. Thus, a concentrator may have many instances of PCMs. Each PCM provides all the necessary signaling to initialize a connection, to withhold a marginal connection, and to support maintenance. Functionally, PCM is divided into two parts: a

Table 11.1 Interpretation of PCM Signaled Bits

Bit Number	Meaning
0	Reserved. Must be zero. Future versions may use one.
1, 2	My port type: 00 ⇒ A, 01 ⇒ B, 10 ⇒ S, 11 ⇒ M
3	Port compatibility 0 ⇒ This connection is not allowed by my topology rules. 1 ⇒ This connection is allowed by my topology rules.
4, 5	LCT duration: 00 ⇒ Short, 01 ⇒ Medium, 10 ⇒ Long, 11 ⇒ Extended
6	MAC available for LCT 0 ⇒ I do not have a MAC for LCT. However, if you use a MAC, I will return frames. 1 ⇒ I will use MAC frames for LCT.
7	LCT result: 0 ⇒ Passed, 1 ⇒ Failed
8	MAC for local loop. 0 ⇒ I will not provide a MAC for local loop. 1 ⇒ I will provide a MAC for MAC local loop.
9	MAC on port output. 0 ⇒ I will not place a MAC on this port. 1 ⇒ I will place a MAC on this port.

LCT = Link confidence test

PCM state machine and PCM pseudocode. The **PCM state machine** contains all the state and timing information. **PCM pseudocode** specifies the bits that are to be sent by the PCM state machine and processes the bits received from the PCM at the other end of the link. Line state indications are used to signal each bit because line states have a high probability of being received correctly even on links with high error rates. Master line state (MLS)—a sequence of H and Q symbol pairs—is used to indicate a 0. Halt line state (HLS)—a sequence of H symbols—is used to indicate a 1. Table 11.1 lists the meaning of various bits exchanged during the connection initialization.

11.1.3 Configuration Management (CFM)

CFM manages the configuration of MACs and ports within a node. There is one instance of CFM per node. It follows instructions received from the PCM and connects and disconnects ports as instructed.

Configuration management uses paths to indicate interconnection of components. A **path** represents the segments of a logical ring that pass through a station. The portion of the primary ring passing through a station is called its **primary path**. The portion of the secondary ring that passes through a station is called its **secondary path**. A station may also have a **local path**, which represents segments that do not belong to either a primary or secondary ring.

The relationship of paths to rings is not always strictly true. For example, a station in a twisted ring (see Section 11.2) may call a segment a primary path thinking that it belongs to the primary ring, but the station's knowledge may be incorrect. Also, not all paths may be present in all stations. For example, some stations may not have a local path. Similarly, single-attachment stations may not have a secondary path.

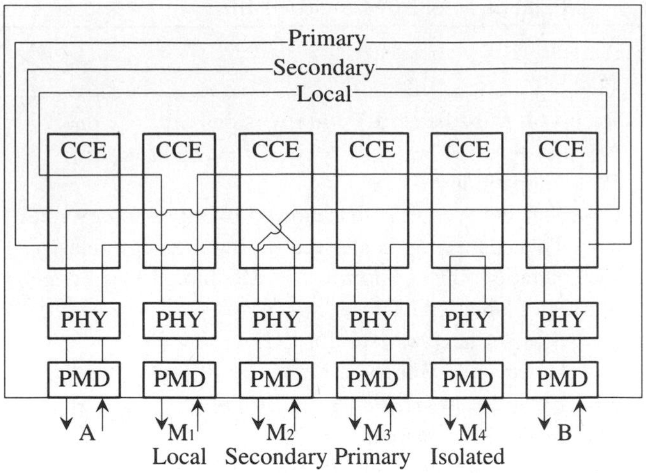

Figure 11.2 Primary, secondary, and local paths.

Figure 11.2 shows the three types of paths in a dual-attachment concentrator. Of the four M-ports on the concentrator, port M1 is connected to the local path, port M2 is connected to the secondary path, port M3 is connected to the primary path, while port M4 is isolated. The logic that implements these interconnections within a node is called the **configuration control element** (**CCE**).

Configuration control elements provide the flexibility of changing the configuration state of any port or MAC to any desired state. Depending on whether the port (or MAC) is connected to the primary, secondary, local, or no path, the port is said to be in a **primary**, **secondary**, **local**, or **isolated** state, respectively. Some ports are connected to both primary and secondary paths. For example, the A- and B-ports of the concentrator shown in Figure 11.2 are connected to both paths. In such cases, the port is said to be in a **thru** or **concatenated** state, depending on whether the primary and secondary paths remain separate or become joined inside the station.

Certain port (and MAC) states are illegal. For example, A-port in primary, B-port in secondary, M-port in concatenated or thru, S-port in thru, and MAC in concatenated or thru states are all illegal. Certain combinations of port states are also illegal. For example, in a dual-attachment station, an

Table 11.2 States of a Dual-Attachment Station

	A:Isolated	A:Local	A:Secondary	A:Primary	A:Concatenated	A:Thru
B:Isolated	Isolated	Local_a	Wrap_a	Illegal	C_wrap_a	Illegal
B:Local	Local_b	Local_ab	Wrap_a	Illegal	C_wrap_a	Illegal
B:Secondary	Illegal	Illegal	Illegal	Illegal	Illegal	Illegal
B:Primary	Wrap_b	Wrap_b	Wrap_ab	Illegal	Illegal	Illegal
B:Concatenated	C_wrap_b	C_wrap_b	Illegal	Illegal	Illegal	Illegal
B:Thru	Illegal	Illegal	Illegal	Illegal	Illegal	Thru

A-port in a secondary with a B-port in the concatenated state is illegal. Table 11.2 lists all possible states for a dual-attachment station. The meaning of these station states is listed in Table 11.3. In the concatenated station states (C_wrap_a or C_wrap_b), all resources on the primary path precede all resources on the secondary path with regard to the token flow. Some of the states for a dual-attachment station are shown in Figure 11.3. Although only two CCEs are shown in each diagram, other CCEs may be present to allow connecting MACs and other PHYs. This is indicated by dots in the diagrams. Similar diagrams can be constructed for other nodes, such as single-attachment stations, dual-attachment concentrators, and single-attachment concentrators.

The topology rules are described in the next section. Any change in configuration requires scrubbing the ring and removing all frames. The scrub function is described in Section 11.6.

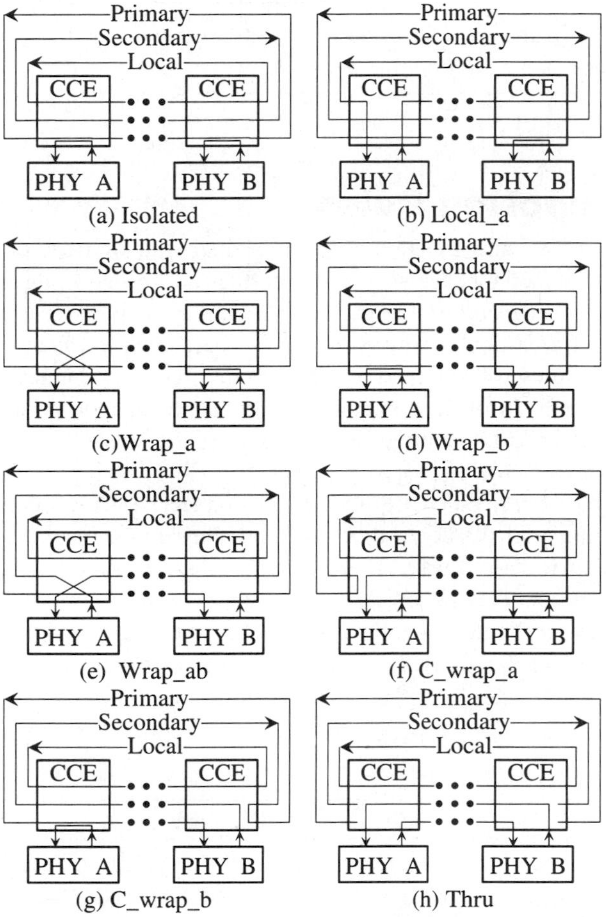

Figure 11.3 States of a dual-attachment station.

Table 11.3 Explanation of States of a Dual-Attachment Station

State	Meaning
Isolated	Both ports are not connected to any path.
Local_a	The A-port is in the local path and B is not in any path.
Local_b	The B-port is in the local path and A is not in any path.
Local_ab	Both A- and B-ports are in the local path.
Wrap_a	The A-port is connected to the secondary path and B is not in any path.
Wrap_b	The B-port is connected to the primary path and A is not in any path.
Wrap_ab	The B-port is connected to the primary path and A-port is connected to the secondary path. The two paths are not joined.
C_wrap_a	The primary and secondary paths are joined internal to the station and connected to the A-port.
C_wrap_b	The primary and secondary paths are joined internal to the station and connected to the B-port.
Thru	The primary path enters the A-port and exits from the B-port. The secondary path enters the B-port and exits from the A-port.

11.2 Connection Rules

The physical topology of a valid FDDI network is a dual ring of trees or its subset. The FDDI standard includes a number of mechanisms to ensure that an unsuspecting user does not bring the entire network down with an incorrect topology. In particular, all ports on the station are labeled as A, B, S, or M. A port of a particular type is allowed to be connected to ports of only certain other types. These connection rules are enforced by CMT so that if a user connects the wrong port types, CMT rejects the connection. In other words, cables connecting inappropriate ports are left unused. This makes an FDDI network autoconfiguring and protects the network from common mistakes of users who may not remember (or know) all the rules.

Table 11.4 lists which port pairs are allowed to connect. During connection initialization, a port asks the neighboring port about its type and uses the connection rules matrix of Table 11.4 to determine what action it should take. There are four possible actions: valid, invalid, undesired, and no-THRU. All valid connections are legal although some of them are undesirable. An invalid connection will result in an illegal network topology. Stations may treat the undesired connections as illegal or legal depending on the policy set by the network manager. In particular, the station

Table 11.4 Connection Rules

	Other Port			
This Port	A	B	S	M
A	Valid, Undesired	Valid	Valid, Undesired	Valid, Prevent THRU
B	Valid	Valid, Undesired	Valid, Undesired	Valid, Prevent THRU
S	Valid, Undesired	Valid, Undesired	Valid	Valid
M	Valid	Valid	Valid	Invalid, Undesired

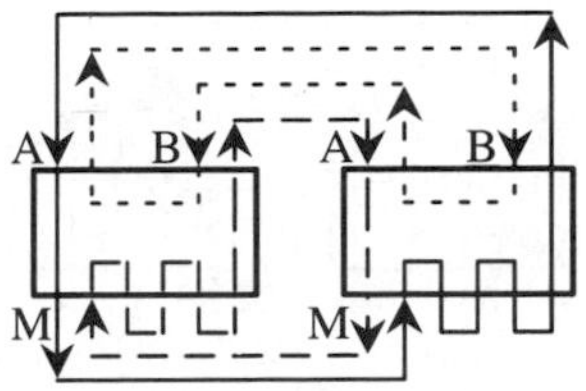

Figure 11.4 Connecting two M-ports would result in three rings.

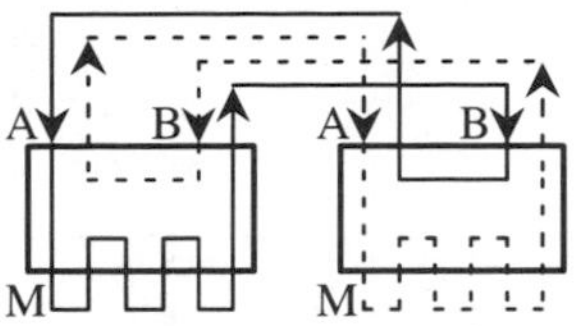

Figure 11.5 Connecting two A-ports would result in a confusion about which ring is primary.

management must be notified if such a connection is attempted. The station management may then alert the network manager by logging the attempt or any other action. The effect of such undesirable connections is explained later in this section. A "no-THRU" indicates a conditional acceptance denoted by the phrase "prevent THRU and Port B takes precedence." This is also explained later in this section.

Consider the correctly connected FDDI network shown in Figure 1.19. It consists of a dual-attachment station and two dual-attachment concentrators on the trunk ring. The concentrators provide connections to other nodes, resulting in tree topologies. Notice that all connections on the trunk ring consist of A-to-B (port A of one station connected to port B of another station) or B-to-A connections. Looking into the connection matrix of Table 11.4, we find that both these connections have a valid designation. The single-attachment stations are connected to concentrators using S-to-M (or M-to-S from the concentrator's point of view) connections. These are also valid connections. Thus, all connections in this network are valid and the network has a valid dual ring of trees topology.

To understand why M-to-M connections are illegal, consider the network shown in Figure 11.4, where one M-port of a dual-attachment concentrator has been inadvertently connected to the M-port of another dual-attachment concentrator. All other connections are valid connections. Notice that this results in three rings. Each ring is shown by a different line pattern. A single-attachment station on one ring cannot talk to any dual-attachment station on the other two rings. This topology is, therefore, invalid. A valid FDDI network has at most two rings. The station management is notified when such a connection is attempted. This in turn results in a notification to network manager(s) via status report announcements (see Section 10.10). Also, in some equipment, there may be an indicator light next to the port that turns red indicating an invalid connection.

The connection rules matrix indicates that A-to-A connections (similarly B-to-B connections) are undesirable. Figure 11.5 illustrates the problem caused by such connections. The resulting network has two rings. However, the left concentrator considers the solid ring as the primary ring since it enters on its A-port. The right concentrator considers the dashed ring as the primary ring. Thus, the information about which ring is primary and which ring is secondary is different (or twisted) in different stations. This configuration is called **twisted** ring. Some vendors treat this as unacceptable, while others treat it as acceptable on the grounds that accepting such a connection allows the network operation to continue. The standard chose a compromise position by declaring such connections undesirable but not illegal. If such a connection is attempted, SMT is notified, which alerts the network manager. The connection is rejected if both nodes' policies are to disallow such connections; otherwise the connection is accepted.

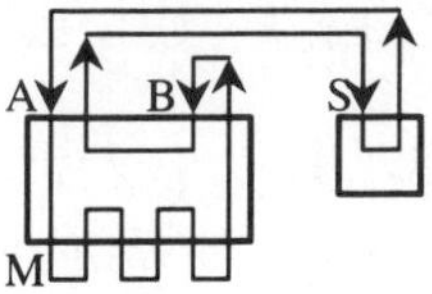

Figure 11.6 Connecting an A-port to an S-port would result in a permanently wrapped ring.

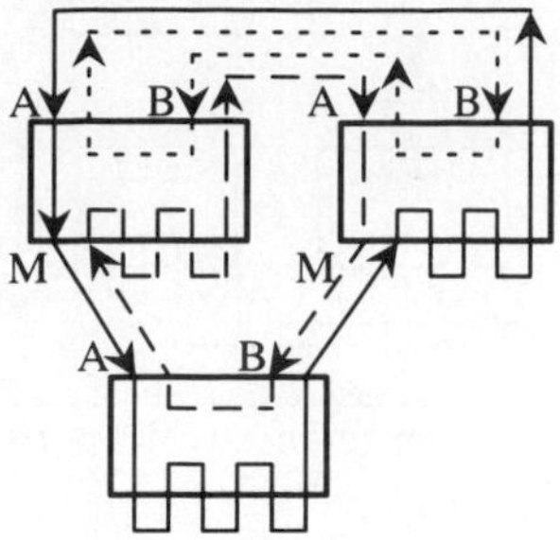

Figure 11.7 Connecting an A-port and a B-port to M-ports and allowing a thru flow of signal would result in three rings.

An example of an A-to-S connection, which is also undesirable, is shown in Figure 11.6. This results in a permanently wrapped ring, thereby making the trunk ring susceptible to single cable failures.

Figure 11.7 shows problems caused by having both A-to-M and B-to-M connections. Like an M-to-M connection, these connections result in an illegal network with three rings. One way to fix the problem is to divide the dual-attachment node (whose A and B ports are involved) as if it was one or two single-attachment nodes as shown in Figures 11.8(a) through 11.8(c). In all cases, a *through* flow of signal is prevented, which would have allowed a signal entering on the A-port to exit via the B-port and vice versa. This is denoted by the phrase "prevent THRU." Figure 11.8(a) shows a dual-attachment station with both ports enabled but no through flow of signals. Figure 11.8(b), similarly, shows a dual-attachment concentrator with both ports enabled without a through flow of signal. Figure 11.8(c) shows a dual-attachment concentrator with only one port enabled. Notice that in this case there is a choice for either the A- or B-port of the concentrator to be disabled. Initially the standards committee arbitrarily chose to prefer to use the B-port and disable the A-port in such cases. Although this preference was dropped in the final version of SMT, most implementations still follow it and disable the A-port. Note that when a node is split and both of its ports are enabled without a through flow of signal, it still remains *one* node since there is only one SMT object at the node.

For high availability, the A- and B-ports of a dual-attachment node can be physically connected to two different concentrators. Using the above rules, one of the ports is automatically disabled but is used if the path to the other port is lost. This is called dual-homing and is discussed in Section 20.3.

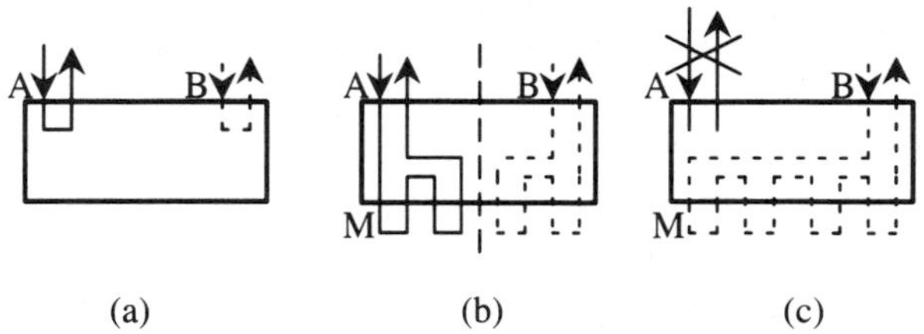

Figure 11.8 Valid alternatives if an A-to-M or B-to-M connection is accepted.

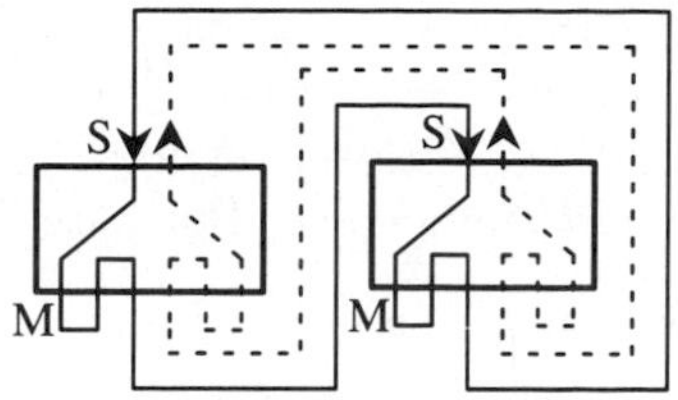

Figure 11.9 Master-slave problem.

Prevention of THRU, as explained earlier, also prevents a dual-attachment station from connecting to a tree on one port (using A-to-M or B-to-M) and the dual ring on the other (B-to-A or A-to-B).

The connection rule matrix helps prevent misconfigurations. Unfortunately, some misconfigurations are still possible. Figure 11.9 shows one such example of two single-attachment concentrators. Here all connections are M-to-S, which are all valid connections. Since all nodes have a single attachment, the network must be a tree (with one ring). However, the resulting network is not valid because there are two rings, resulting in confusion about which concentrator is the root of the tree. The left concentrator thinks it is a slave whose master is the concentrator on the right and vice versa. This invalid configuration, dubbed a **master-slave loop**, is possible in spite of the connection rules. However, hierarchical wiring practices considerably reduce the possibility of such loops. That is why, after a considerable debate, the SMT working group decided not to address this problem.

Table 11.5 summarizes the problems caused by various undesirable connections. Notice that connecting a single-attachment station to another single-attachment station results in a two-station

Table 11.5 Summary of Problems Caused by Miscabling

Connection	Problem
A to A	Twisted dual ring.
A to B	OK.
A to S	Permanently wrapped ring.
A to M	OK if THRU prevented.
B to A	OK.
B to B	Twisted dual ring.
B to S	Permanently wrapped ring.
B to M	OK if THRU prevented.
S to A	Permanently wrapped ring.
S to B	Permanently wrapped ring.
S to S	Two-station ring. OK.
S to M	OK.
M to A	OK.
M to B	OK.
M to S	OK.
M to M	More than two rings. Illegal.

FDDI ring without any concentrators. This is a *valid* configuration and can be used for a high-speed connection between two stations.

To conclude, connection rules in FDDI help in automatic configuration of an FDDI network. Those cables that connect improper ports are ignored. Thus, users' mistakes are largely detected by the connection management.

11.3 Link Confidence Test

All the links on an FDDI ring are automatically tested for reliability (low error rate) before being included in the ring. A link confidence test (LCT) is used to estimate the link error rate. The test consists of passing a symbol stream through the link and counting errors. Any link with an error rate higher than a certain threshold is not allowed to join the ring. On failure, the link confidence test is repeated, usually for a longer duration, until the link passes the test.

The confidence level of the estimated error rate depends on the length of the test. Since the required error rates are extremely low, the test duration for any realistic confidence level is rather long. For example, if no errors are observed during a 10-second test, we can be 99.9% sure that the link has an error rate better than 6.9×10^{-9}. There is still a 0.1% chance that a link of lower quality will pass this test. This means that if 1000 links on a ring use the test and pass it, one link may still have a higher error rate. Such a link will result in frequent token and frame losses even if all other links are of good quality.

Unfortunately, a long test also means a long delay in ring initialization. The standard, therefore, specifies four different durations for the test. A short test of 50-ms duration is used if there is no recent history of excessive link errors. If a link fails the short test, a medium test of 500-ms duration is used. If a link is taken off the ring due to a high error rate, it should pass a long test of 5-s duration. A really bad link may be tested for an extended duration of 50 seconds.

The method used to test the link depends on the manufacturer. One possibility is to transmit a stream of idle symbols, while the receiver counts the number of error events. This is done separately on the two fibers that make up the link. Another possibility is to transmit a stream of valid frames instead of idle symbols. Yet another possibility is to count frame check sequence (FCS) errors. This last possibility requires availability of a MAC.

During a T-seconds test, $T \times 125 \times 10^6$ code bits are transmitted. If N error events are detected during this interval, the **link error rate** (**LER**) is:

$$\text{LER} = \frac{N}{T \times 125 \times 10^6}$$

The actual LER is more than that calculated by the preceding formula because some errors are not detected. If the measured LER is greater than a cutoff value (default 10^{-7}), the link is declared to have failed the test.

Notice that it is the number of error events and not the number of bits in error that is counted. A single error event may cause an error in many bits or symbols. The **link error event detector** algorithm described next is used for this purpose.

The link error event detector algorithm is based on line states, which were described earlier in Section 3.5. Briefly, a link on which Idle symbols are being received is said to be in the idle line state or ILS. A link on which a frame is being received is said to be in the active line state or ALS. During normal usage or during a link confidence test, only idle symbols or frames are transmitted and, therefore, the link is expected to be only in these two states. An error will cause the line state to become unknown or **LSU** (line state unknown). This is shown in the simplified state diagram of

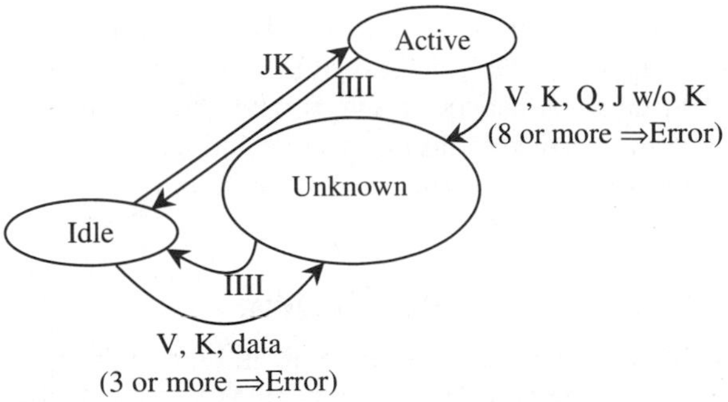

Figure 11.10 A simplified state diagram for link error detection.

Figure 11.10. Reception of four or more Idle symbols causes a link to enter ILS. Reception of the frame starting delimiter (a J-K symbol pair) during ILS causes the link to enter ALS. Reception of a violation (V), K (not preceded by J), or data symbol during ILS causes it to enter LSU. Reception of V, K, Q, or J (without K) during ALS causes the link to enter LSU.

A link error event is said to occur if the link transitions from ILS to LSU with the duration of LSU exceeding two symbol times (80 ns) or if the link transitions from ALS to LSU with the duration of LSU exceeding eight symbol times (320 ns). These duration limits have been designed to prevent double counting of some errors. Recall from Section 3.5 that LSU is entered on most state transitions since determining a line state requires several symbols. Short-duration transitions to LSU are therefore common and may or may not be caused by errors. A single noise in a frame will cause the repeat-filter to replace the affected symbol by four H symbols followed by idles. This will result in an ALS-LSU-ILS state transition sequence. Since at least four idles are required to enter ILS, the duration of LSU, in this case, is eight symbols. This is below the limit specified earlier. Therefore, this is not counted by LCT, but it will be counted by the MAC in Lost_ct.

The standard also allows the option of counting a few other transitions to LSU of shorter duration.

Notice that once the link enters LSU, the event count does not increase (in most implementations) until the link enters ILS or ALS again. Thus, a noise resulting in a burst of bit errors is generally counted as one event.

11.4 Link Error Monitoring

During normal use, all links on an FDDI ring are continuously monitored for errors. This service is called **link error monitoring (LEM)**. This is in addition to the link confidence test, which is used during ring initialization.

The algorithms used for counting errors and estimating error rates are the same as those used in the link confidence test described in Section 11.3. The SMT keeps track of the total number of errors and provides a long-term average link error rate.

If the link error rate exceeds an alarm threshold (default 10^{-8}), an alarm event is signaled to the SMT, which is conveyed to the network manager via status report frames. If the link further deteriorates and the link error rate exceeds a cutoff threshold (default 10^{-7}), the connection is flagged as faulty and taken off the ring.

Since errors are probabilistic, it is possible that a link passes LCT, joins the ring, fails LEM, and is taken off. This may happen repeatedly. A count is, therefore, also kept of the number of times a link has been removed by LEM. A network manager bothered by frequent ring initializations may inspect all such counts and may decide to take corrective action, such as removing or replacing the faulty components. The use of a longer LCT on successive initializations also reduces the possibility of such oscillations.

11.5 Fault Tracing (PC Trace)

Trace is an automatic fault location mechanism. It helps find the faulty component or determine the fault domain (set of components) between two successive MACs on the ring.

When a station (with a MAC) suspects that the fault is between it and its upstream MAC, it sends a special signal to the upstream MAC and all intermediate components. The meaning of this special signal is "Please test yourself." The receipt of this signal is acknowledged by the upstream MAC. Upon seeing this acknowledgment, all components including the initiating MAC go into a *path test*.

The key problem in this procedure is that the signal has to be sent *upstream*, which is the reverse of the normal frame transmission direction. It is possible to talk to the upstream station with some help from the concentrator (assuming for the moment that there is one). The physical connection management (PCM) entity in the concentrator port ensure that the trace signal is handled differently. It propagates the signal to the preceding port. In general, any port not connected to a MAC propagates the trace signal to the preceding port. When the signal reaches a MAC, it sends an acknowledgment signal back to the trace originator.

Figure 11.11 illustrates the trace operation using a concentrator with four stations attached to it. Normally the tokens and frames travel from station 1 to station 4 via stations 2 and 3. The ports in the concentrator are labeled C1 through C4, while those in the stations are labeled S1 through S4. Consider now the case of station 3 suspecting a problem between station 2 and itself. The ring management (RMT) in station 3 initiates a trace operation. Port S3 starts transmitting the special trace alert signal. Port C3 on the concentrator receiving this signal propagates it backward to port C2, which in turn propagates the trace signal to port S2 in station 2. Since port S2 is connected to a MAC, trace propagation stops. The ring management in station 2 acknowledges the trace. The acknowledgment travels backward from S2 to S3 via C2 and C3 using the normal token path. All components receiving this acknowledgment signal go into a path-test mode. After the test is complete, the faulty components will be isolated (in most cases) and the ring reinitialized.

A stream of alternating Halt and Quiet symbols (H-Q pairs) is used as the trace signal. This signal consists of a square waveform with a transition every 10 bits (6.25-MHz frequency). Whenever

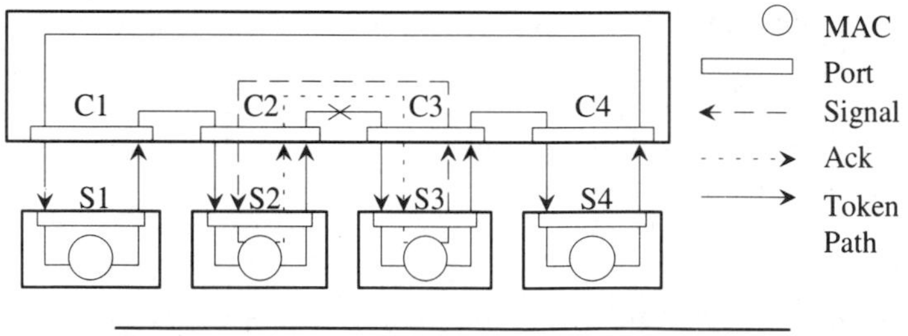

Figure 11.11 Trace.

this signal is received the line is said to be in the **master line state** (**MLS**). This and other line states were defined in Section 3.5. A stream of Quiet symbols is used to acknowledge the trace. This consists of turning off the transmitter. Whenever this happens the line is said to be in the **quiet line state** (**QLS**). The acknowledgment signal has been especially chosen such that it can propagate over broken paths. A broken transmitter, fiber, or receiver results in no light being received, which is interpreted as QLS.

The trace signal transmission is stopped as soon as the acknowledgment is received. It is also stopped if no acknowledgment is received within 7 seconds (default value of parameter **Trace_Max**). This timeout interval allows for the possibility of traversing 1000 ports. A delay of 12 ms (parameter **Trace_React**) per port is allowed for reacting to the trace in addition to the maximum ring propagation delay of 1.773 ms.

Note that each station in FDDI is expected to be able to test itself. In the SMT standard, this function is called **path test**. Although the standard does not define this test precisely, it is recommended that the test include testing of all data paths in the node, loopback testing of PHY components as close to the PMD as possible, checking of all MAC parameters, and verification that the node can correctly participate in beacon and claim processes.

The trace mechanism provides automatic fault location and isolation capabilities to FDDI networks. It pinpoints the faulty component, which can be removed with minimal interruption in operation.

11.6 Ring Scrubbing

Whenever a station leaves the ring, it is important that all frames sourced by that station be taken off the ring; otherwise the frames will continue to circulate around the ring since no other station will strip them. The bridges and routers on the ring will repeatedly forward the frames to other networks,

Your boss said you wanted to scrub your network.

Figure 11.12 Ring scrubbing consists of removing old frames from the ring.

creating multiple copies at the destination. If the frame happens to be a multicast or broadcast frame, many copies of the frame will be received by all stations on all bridged networks.

It is, therefore, important to ensure that the ring is free of all frames created by the MAC leaving the ring. This process of cleaning the ring of old frames is called **ring scrubbing** (see Figure 11.12). One way to accomplish this is to transmit Idle symbols (or claim frames) while discarding all input. Doing this for a time equal to the ring latency ensures that all old frames have been removed. Alternatively, a MAC may simply strip all of its frames before leaving. This method is allowed only when moving or removing MACs within a station.

If the scrubbing is done for a duration longer than the valid transmission time (TVX_value), the TVX timers in some stations on the ring will expire, causing them to initiate the claim process part of ring initialization. This is preferred by some vendors and is allowed by the standard. The claim process ensures that all stations have the same value of the target token rotation time.

In summary, the scrub function removes all orphan (no-owner) frames from the ring. This function is performed on all configuration changes and results in ring reinitialization.

11.7 Orphan Frame Removal: Ring Purging

The problems caused by no-owner frames were explained in the previous section. The no-owner frames created due to configuration changes are handled by the scrub function, but those created during normal operation may still cause the same problems. An error in the source address or faulty station hardware can result in a no-owner frame. Some vendors handle this problem by a ring purging mechanism, which is not part of the FDDI standard. In this mechanism, one station on the ring is elected as the ring purger using a distributed election algorithm. Whenever a token is received, the ring purger transmits two (or more) void frames and then releases the token but continues to strip incoming symbols and transmit Idles until the void frames are received back. This ensures that all frames transmitted during the previous token cycle have been removed from the ring and that no frame goes around the ring more than once. Notice that this is done on every token received and thus the purger behaves as if it is using the synchronous transmission mode. The time for two void frames should, therefore, be taken into account in determining the maximum available synchronous bandwidth for other purposes.

To ensure that the ring purger works correctly under frame loss and error conditions, the purger stops stripping when it receives either one of its error-free void frames, a token, or a ring initialization frame (claim or beacon). Note that the purger does not stop on void frames from other stations. They are stripped.

The load generated by the purger is inversely related to the ring load. If no one is transmitting, the token rotates fast and the purger uses up considerable bandwidth. As the load increases, the token frequency decreases and the extra load put by the purger becomes negligible. Also, the void frames are not copied by any station or forwarded by bridges.

Because this is not a standard mechanism, different purger election algorithms are used by different vendors, sometimes resulting in multiple purgers on the same ring.

The ring purging mechanism is a MAC-level mechanism and is, therefore, not covered by CMT. In fact, this mechanism is not a part of the SMT or MAC standards but uses mechanisms allowed by these standards. Note that this mechanism is not related to (and does not make any use of) purge frames described in Section 13.11.

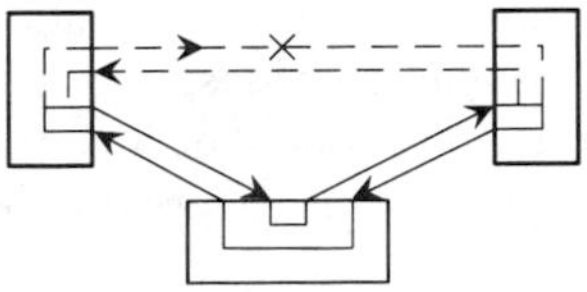

Figure 11.13 Wrapping removes both fibers of a broken cable.

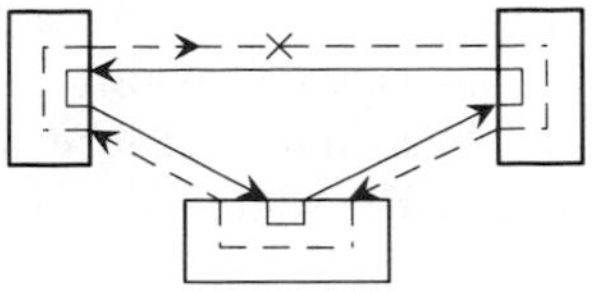

Figure 11.14 If primary and secondary fibers follow separate physical routes, continuing to use one ring (holding) is better.

11.8 Wrapping Avoidance: Global Hold

The two rings in FDDI provide redundancy such that after a fault the remaining fibers form a single ring and all stations can still communicate. There are several ways to form a single ring from the surviving fibers. The most common recovery policy, known as **wrapping**, is illustrated by the three-station dual ring in Figure 11.13. A break in the primary ring fiber between stations A and B causes stations A and B to wrap. All three stations can still communicate. In particular, notice that the secondary ring fiber between A and B is not used. In most cases, the chances of this fiber being broken when the primary fiber breaks are high. This assumes that the primary and secondary fibers between two stations are in the same cable.

In some circumstances, particularly if only one of the two fibers in a cable is broken, it is better not to wrap but to hold on to the surviving ring. This is shown in Figure 11.14. This **hold policy** has been found useful in naval applications where all primary fibers are installed on one side of the ship and all secondary fibers on the other side. When one primary fiber fails the likelihood that other primary fibers also fail is very high. The surviving ring does not make use of any fibers on the failed side. Figure 11.15 shows an example of two secondary fiber failures. In this case, wrapping results

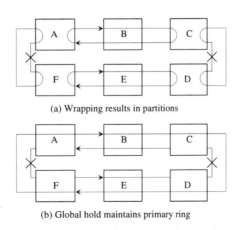

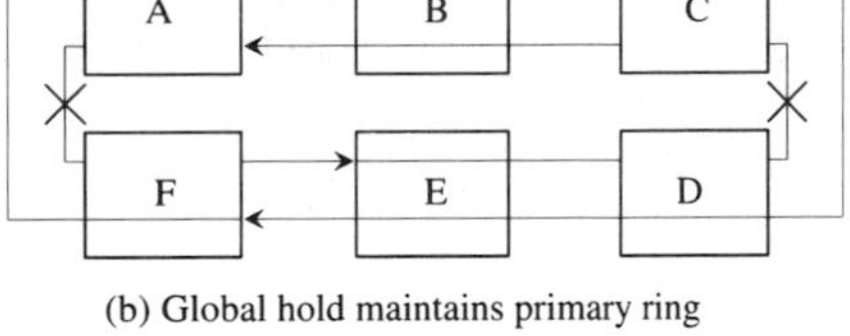

(a) Wrapping results in partitions

(b) Global hold maintains primary ring

Figure 11.15 With two or more faults, wrapping results in multiple partitions. With global hold, all stations can communicate when all faults are on the same ring.

in multiple partitions while with the global hold policy, all stations can still communicate with each other. The FDDI standard allows dual-MAC dual-attachment stations to choose this hold policy as an option. This option can be used when all stations on the network are dual-MAC dual-attached stations. Dual homing, discussed in Section 20.3, provides another alternative for higher availability.

11.9 Ring Management

The term **ring management (RMT)** is used in the SMT standard to refer to a subset of SMT that deals with MAC-level fault management issues. Specifically this includes fault announcement using directed beacons, starting the trace function, detecting and resolving duplicate addresses, and monitoring restricted tokens.

11.10 Fault Announcement: Directed Beacons

As explained earlier in Section 2.14, a beacon process is used to locate faults in a ring suspected of being broken. In the process, if a station finds itself in a *stuck beaconing* situation, it knows that there is a fault between its upstream station and itself. This knowledge is conveyed to network managers using directed beacons, whose meaning is "I am now sure that there is a fault between me and my upstream neighbor."

A directed beacon frame is similar to the beacon frame described in Section 2.14. The frame-control field is "1100 0010_2," which indicates that it is a beacon frame. The second bit is 1 because only long (48-bit) addresses are used. Unlike the MAC beacon frames, which have a destination address of zero, the directed beacon frames are addressed to SMT directed beacon group address 01-80-C2-00-01-00. Since they are directed to a particular group of stations and not to all stations, they are called *directed* beacons. A management station listening to this group address can notify the network manager if necessary. The network manager can take corrective action if the problem happens repeatedly. The information field of the directed beacon frames contains the upstream neighbor address (UNA) if known.

It should be obvious that no token is required to send directed beacons. Therefore, to ensure that they are not lost by stripping, or by other stations entering a claim process or beacon process, a continuous stream of such frames is sent for 370 ms (parameter **T_Direct**). After this interval, if the station is still stuck beaconing, the trace process, described in Section 11.5, is initiated to locate the fault through path tests.

11.11 Restricted Token Monitoring

The restricted token mode allows a station to continue transmitting on successive token rotations. This was supposed to be helpful in transmitting a large amount of data from disk drives without interruption. With the cost of memory going down, it is now possible to hold large amounts of data in the memory of disk controllers and the restricted token mode is no longer considered useful.

Also, only the stations that participate in the current restricted dialog can change the token from the restricted mode to the nonrestricted mode. If the stations malfunction and continue a restricted token dialog for a long time, other stations on the ring will be unfairly prevented from transmitting asynchronous traffic.

For these reasons, it is necessary that a restricted dialog continuing after a certain time be stopped. This time is controlled by a station parameter T_Rmode. Every station on the ring measures the time since it first saw a restricted token. If no nonrestricted token is received within T_Rmode, the claim process is started to reinitialize the token.

In the SMT standard, the default value of T_Rmode has been set to *zero*. With this value, no restricted dialogs are allowed and the token is reinitialized whenever a restricted token is seen.

11.12 Duplicate Address Detection

If two or more stations on the ring have the same address, the operation of those and all other stations on the ring is adversely affected. The detection and resolution of this duplicate address problem is the topic of this section.

To understand why duplicate addresses are a problem, first consider an operating ring with two stations A and B with the same address. Frames transmitted by station A will be stripped by station B and vice versa. The intended destination may or may not receive the frame. SMT requests sent to the address will be responded to by both stations, causing confusion.

If one station wins the claim process, the other station may think that it has also won the claim process. Both may start the token, which results in duplicate tokens.

It is also possible for the ring to fail to complete the claim process but pass the beacon process and continue this claim-beacon oscillation forever.

Another possibility is that claim frames of one station are received by the other making the second station think that it has won the claim process, thus prematurely terminating the process. This can result in a different type of oscillation with the ring not being useful.

To prevent duplicate addresses, it is recommended that only IEEE-assigned global addresses be used on FDDI. Locally administered addresses are more likely to cause duplicates.

Different algorithms are used for detection and resolution of duplicate addresses before, during, or after ring initialization.

After a successful ring initialization, a station can ensure that no other station on the ring has the same address by sending a NIF request to its downstream neighbor. If the resulting response is received with the A-indicator reset, no other station has the same address. If the A-indicator is set, there is at least one more station with the same address. If no response is received, the test is inconclusive and should be repeated. This is known as the **neighbor request/response (NRR)** test.

Another alternative duplicate address detection algorithm is for a station to send a frame to itself. If the frame is received with the A-indicator reset, there is no other station with the same address. If the frame is not received, then the frame was either lost or stripped by someone else with the same address. Thus nonreceipt indicates only a potential for a duplicate address but does not confirm its existence. The advantage of this test is that it does not require any other station's participation.

Therefore, in the absence of a duplicate address problem, the test can be completed in one round-trip delay. This is known as the **transmit-to-self (TS)** test.

The NRR test provides a positive indication when a station's source address is duplicated by an address in the destination address list of another station. In some cases, it is possible that a station has several addresses in its source address list and destination address list. The two lists need not be identical. In such cases, the NRR algorithm will not detect a duplicate address even if the source address lists of two stations have a common entry. Similarly, it may falsely indicate a duplicate address even if the source lists of two stations have no common entries.

The TS algorithm, on the other hand, does not provide a positive indication if a duplicate address exists. It is possible to combine the NRR and TS algorithms such that the positive aspects of the two are exploited. This is done by performing both NRR and TS tests in parallel independently. The combined test is stopped if either test gives a positive indication of presence or absence of the problem. The test is considered inconclusive if both tests are inconclusive or if the two tests give inconsistent results. If the combined test is inconclusive, both tests are repeated again.

During ring initialization, a duplicate address is suspected if a beacon or claim frame with the station's address as a source address is received at a time when it is not expected. For example, station A does not expect to receive its own beacons later than 1.773 ms (D_Max) after it stops beaconing. If it does, another station with the same address is beaconing. Similarly, a station does not expect to receive its own claims later than 1.773 ms after it stops claiming. If it does, a duplicate address is suspected. In practice, twice as much time (2×1.773 ms) is allowed before taking recovery action. A duplicate address is also suspected if a claim frame with a different information field (value of bid TTRT) but the same source address is received during claiming.

If a station detects that it has a duplicate address, it should strip the frames that it has already transmitted and change its address to an IEEE-assigned globally unique address. If the ring is operational, it can inform the network manager using status report frames (Section 10.10). Since the frames generated by a station with a duplicate address may not reach the management station, the downstream neighbor may report it via its NIF frames. The MAC in the station may be configured to lose the claim process or it may be removed from the ring.

To ensure that the other station with the same (duplicate) address also takes corrective action, it is informed of the problem by **jamming**. One method is to block the input and send beacon frames. The other station receiving these beacons (while it is not beaconing) will know that a duplicate exists. Another method is to not block the input but to send a beacon twice. The second beacon is started as soon as the first beacon stops (on receipt of the first stream of beacon frames). This is known as a **double beacon jam**.

11.13 Automatic Fault Detection and Recovery

One of the key design features of FDDI is that fault detection and recovery is distributed and automatic. Most fault conditions are automatically handled by station management and the ring operation continues. In this chapter, a number of fault detection, location, and recovery mechanisms have been described. Box 11.1 summarizes the symptoms that indicate faults. It also lists the fault detection, prevention, and recovery mechanisms. The following list shows how some of the common faults are detected, located, and isolated:

Box 11.1 FDDI Fault Symptoms, Detection, and Recovery Mechanisms

1. Physical Layer Symptoms:
   - No signal detect.
   - Persistent noise condition.
   - Incompatible connections.
   - Active line state not achieved after ring initialization.
   - Elasticity buffer underflow/overflow.
2. MAC Layer Symptoms:
   - A MAC is stuck beaconing.
   - The ring state oscillates between beacon and claim.
   - The ring state oscillates between operational/nonoperational.
   - No token is received.
   - More than one token is received.
   - A restricted token is seen circulating for a long time.
   - Data frames cannot be transmitted for a long time.
   - The frame corruption rate is high.
   - A no-owner frame is received repeatedly.
   - A station is unable to receive frames.
   - A station is unable to transmit frames.
   - Transmitted frames do not return.
3. Fault Detection Mechanisms: Recognize faults when they occur.
   - Path test.
   - Connection continuity test.
   - Compatible connection test (topology rules).
   - Link confidence test.
   - MAC loopback.
   - Link error monitor.
   - Duplicate address test.
   - Station notifications.
4. Fault Prevention Mechanisms: Prevent faults from occurring.
   - Scrubbing.
   - Stripping.
5. Fault Recovery Mechanisms:
   - Claim process.
   - Beacon processes: MAC beacon, directed beacon.
   - PC trace.

- *A short or open electrical path occurs within a station*. TVX expires. The claim fails. The station downstream from the fault is stuck beaconing. It uses direct beacons to announce the fault and starts a PC trace to locate the failed component. After the trace completes, the ring is reconfigured without the failed component.
- *A cable or connector breaks*. No light is received. The physical connection management (PCM) detects the problem and takes the link off the ring.
- *A connector becomes loose*. A high error rate results in a failure of the link error monitor (LEM). The network manager is notified. The failed link is reinitialized by PCM, which conducts a link confidence test (LCT). If the link fails the LCT, it is taken off the ring. The link remains off until it passes the LCT.
- *A user connects wrong ports with a cable*. Topology rules will not allow that cable to become part of the ring. If included in the ring, the error is reported to SMT.
- *Crystals in the stations become out-of-spec*. This results in faster or slower clocks causing elasticity buffer overflows and underflows. The counts are reported to the network manager via SMT frames.
- *A user enters a duplicate address on a station*. The duplicate address results in beacon/claim oscillations, beacon/claim/ring-op oscillations, or excessive frame loss. A duplicate address test during and after ring initialization isolates the offending station.
- *The token is lost*. No frames or tokens are seen. TVX at one or more station expires. The claim process is used to regenerate the token.

- *An extra token is created.* Frames generated by one token holder are stripped by the other token holder, resulting in a high frame loss rate. In some implementations, a MAC can detect a duplicated token when it receives a token while already holding one. In any case, the token is eventually stripped by a transmitting station.
- *A token becomes restricted.* No asynchronous traffic can be transmitted. Either TVX or the restricted token monitoring timer (T_Rmode) expires at one or more stations. The claim process is used to regenerate the token. Recall from Section 2.13 that a restricted token does not reset the TVX. However, it is reset if frames are transmitted using the restricted token.
- *A station stops stripping its frames.* The frames will be removed when they meet a transmitting station. A ring purger, if used, will remove the frames.
- *The source address of a frame becomes in error.* The frame will be removed when it meets a transmitting station. A ring purger, if used, will remove the no-owner frame.
- *A station is unable to receive frames although it can transmit.* No frames are received at this station and the TVX expires. The claim process fails because the station receives neither its own nor other stations' claim frames. The beacon process begins. The station is stuck beaconing, PC trace occurs, path test detects the failure by means of an internal loopback test, and the station removes itself from the ring.

11.14 Summary

Connection management provides facilities to initialize and monitor connections between neighboring nodes. It uses PHY-level signaling mechanisms to resolve two-party issues between neighbors that form a physical connection. It provides facilities to insert or remove a station, control the configuration inside a station, and test and monitor link quality. The topology rules enforced by CMT ensure that cables that will result in problem topologies will be left unused.

The ring management provides a facility for MAC-level fault management. It provides facilities for fault announcement, detecting duplicate addresses before and during ring initialization, and monitoring of restricted tokens.

11.15 Further Reading

FDDI CMT and RMT are parts of FDDI SMT standard (ANSI dpANS X3.229-199x or ISO/IEC WD 9314-6:199x).

Levenson (1988) and Kajos and Hunt (1989) describe the link error monitor.

Hutchison and Yang (1991) discuss the problem of duplicate addresses and propose the combined neighbor request/response and transmit-to-self test. Its implementation is described in Ciarfella, Benson, and Sawyer (1991).

Myles (1988) presents examples of invalid FDDI topologies. Paige and Howard (1990) describe the SAFENET-II network standard being developed for use in Navy computer networks.

The ring purging scheme is explained in Yang and Ramakrishnan (1991).

Ocheltree and Motalvo (1989) review ring management and discuss the stuck beacon problem and duplicate address test.

Box 11.1 has been adapted from Le (1989).

11.16 Self-Test Exercises

Note: Some exercises have multiple correct answers. See Appendix D for answers.

11.1 Why is connecting two master ports illegal?
a. A master port needs a slave port.
b. It results in three rings.
c. It results in a master-slave loop.

11.2 What is a twisted ring?
a. A ring of twisted-pair wire links
b. A dual ring in which two stations disagree about which is the primary ring
c. A single ring with wrong crossover resulting in an 8-shaped ring

11.3 If both A- and B-ports of a DAS are connected to M-ports of one (or more) concentrator, what would the DAS do automatically?
a. Accept both connections.
b. Prevent thru transfer of signals from the A-port to the B-port.
c. Reject connection on one of its ports.
d. Reject both connections and disconnect itself from the network.

11.4 When is the link confidence test run?
a. Every 30 seconds
b. At link startup
c. At link startup and shutdown
d. Continuously during use

11.5 When is the link error monitor run?
a. Every 30 seconds
b. At link startup
c. At link startup and shutdown
d. Continuously during use

11.6 If 10 successive bits of a frame are affected by noise, how many errors will be counted by the link error monitor?
a. 0 or 1
b. 1 or 2
c. 2 or 3
d. 9 or 10

11.7 When is an FDDI ring scrubbed?
a. Whenever a frame with errors is detected.
b. Whenever many frames with errors are detected.
c. Whenever a token is lost.
d. Whenever a station leaves the ring.
e. Whenever the connectors become dirty.

11.8 Duplicate address is the problem of
a. Two stations sending frames with the same source address
b. Two stations sending frames with the same destination address
c. One station sending frames with two different addresses
d. Two stations receiving frames of each other

CHAPTER **12**

Network Management: SNMP and FDDI MIB

The SMT standard provides facilities to manage stations in a single FDDI LAN. Since most real networks generally consist of many WAN links and LANs, SMT alone is not sufficient to manage a network. Additional protocols are required for managing higher layer protocols and for objects residing external to the FDDI. Two protocols commonly used for network management are the simple network management protocol (SNMP) defined in the TCP/IP protocol suite and the common management information protocol/services (CMIP/CMIS) defined in the ISO/OSI protocol suite. These are explained in the next few sections. SNMP is covered in more detail since it has become a *de facto* standard (see Sidebar on page 216) for management of multivendor networks. Most FDDI networks do contain equipment from multiple vendors and, therefore, use SNMP.

12.1 Simple Network Management Protocol (SNMP)

Back in 1987, the Internet Engineering Task Force (IETF), which is a group of researchers interested in developing protocols for the Internet (previously known as ARPAnet), was faced with the problem of managing a huge network consisting of equipment from almost every networking vendor on Earth—each having its own way of managing its equipment. In particular, the management of gateways was more important than the end systems, since the gateways are shared by many networks. This lead to the development of a *Simple Gateway Monitoring Protocol* (*SGMP*). This was later extended to manage all other equipment resulting in the so-called *Simple Network Management Protocol* (*SNMP*).

The main reason for the popularity of SNMP is that it is *simple*. While networking vendors, ISO, and CCITT were busy defining complex ways of managing every possible case, IETF decided to do something simple for the time being. IETF's goal was to adopt ISO/CCITT management standards whenever they became ready. Now that goal has been disbanded. SNMP has on caught on like a wildfire and it is now implemented by most networking vendors.

In SNMP terminology, the stations used for monitoring and control are called **network management stations** and the devices that they monitor are called **network elements**. Examples of network

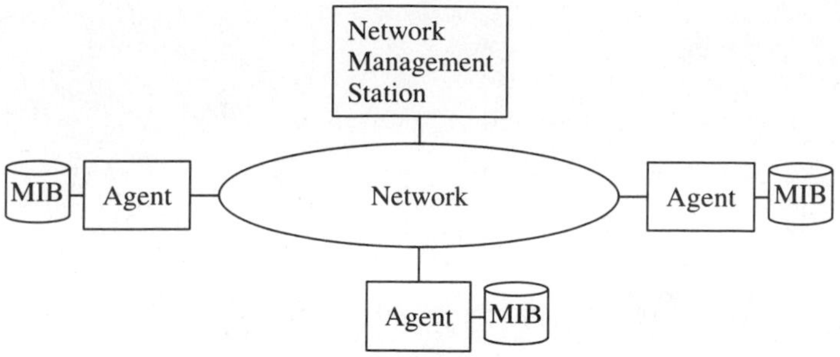

Figure 12.1 Network management entities.

elements are hosts, routers, terminal servers, and so on. Each management station has a *manager* entity that talks to *agents* in the network elements. This is shown in Figure 12.1. The protocol (messages) used for communication between the manager and the agent is defined by SNMP. The agents keep a database of management-related information. This database is called the **management information base** (**MIB**). Depending on the function of the network element, the information kept is different. For example, bridges have a different MIB than routers. The content and structure of these MIBs has been standardized by various IETF working groups. However, all these MIBs follow a fixed set of structuring and naming conventions, which are specified in a separate Internet standards document called **Structure of Management Information** (**SMI**).

SNMP models all management commands as reading or writing of parameters. For example, rather than implementing a reboot command, the desired action may be invoked by simply setting a parameter defined as "number of seconds until system reboot." This model reduces the types of messages considerably. SNMP has just five types of messages: GetRequest, GetResponse, SetRequest, GetNextRequest, and Trap.

To inspect the value of a parameter (or more generally the binding of an object), a GetRequest message is sent by the manager to the agent. The agent then responds with a GetResponse message. The request message contains a request-id, which is used to distinguish among outstanding requests. The request-id is returned in the corresponding response message. The manager can thus correlate

Types of Standards

There are three types of standards: *de jure*, *de facto*, and proprietary. *De jure standards* are those developed or adopted by a recognized standards body such as ISO, CCITT, or ANSI. FDDI is an example of a *de jure* standard. *De facto standards* develop because a particular product or set of rules become popular. The MS-DOS operating system and various personal computer related standards are examples of *de facto* standards. A proprietary standard is one developed by a particular manufacturer. DECnet, IPX/SPX, SNA, and XNS are examples of proprietary standards. Note that a standard may belong to more than one type. For example, IEEE 802 protocols are both *de facto* and *de jure* standards.

incoming responses with outgoing requests. The response also indicates whether the request was successful and if not, why not.

SetRequest messages are used to change parameters (objects). A GetNextRequest message is similar to the GetRequest message, but the object sought is one *lexicographically* following the object specified in the request. This is helpful in retrieving tables or retrieving an entire MIB subtree. The GetResponse messages are used to respond to all three types of requests: GetRequest, SetRequest, and GetNextRequest.

The Trap message is an unsolicited message sent by an agent to notify the manager of a significant event. This is similar to announcements used in SMT. Examples of events that may generate a trap include cold start (reinitialization such that the configuration may have changed), warm start (reinitialization without configuration changes), communication link going up or down, and so on. Traps are not acknowledged and may be lost.

12.1.1 Object Naming in SNMP

Since SNMP was intended to be replaced at a future date by an ISO management protocol, it was decided that the MIB specifications should follow the ISO conventions specified in Abstract Syntax Notation One (ASN.1). ASN.1, however, is too general. Therefore, only a small subset of it is used. For example, SGMP allowed only integer and octet string variables. Other ASN.1 types, such as Boolean, bitstring, and real, were not used. Similarly, only a subset of the basic encoding rules of ASN.1 is used. All SNMP encodings use the definite length form.

Naming an object such that there is no confusion is an interesting problem. In some countries, people have to write their father's name along with their own in all legal documents. This minimizes the chance of various John Smiths being confused from each other. But what if two fathers have the same name? ASN.1 solves this problem by requiring that you specify parent's name, grandparent's name, great-grandparent's name, and so on. This way all objects have a name that is globally unique (although very long).

FDDI MIB appears in three different places in the global tree used to assign names to managed objects. The tree is shown in Figure 12.2. As seen from the top level of the tree, the entire name space is managed by ISO, CCITT, or ISO and CCITT jointly. ISO has subdivided its name space among several organizations as indicated by its children in the tree. One such child is "org," which represents other "other international organizations." One of its children is the name space managed by the U.S. Department of Defense (dod).[1] The Department of Defense has given a node to the Internet community (internet). The Internet Activities Board (IAB) has subdivided its space among four nodes: for use with OSI directory (directory), management (mgmt), Internet experiments (experimental), and private. One child of mgmt is MIB, which itself has 11 children. The tenth child is transmission, which has a child labeled "fddi." This is the FDDI MIB as defined in Internet RFC 1285. Two other FDDI MIBs appear in the same figure. They are labelled as "fddiMIB" and "fddimib." These are discussed a bit later in this section.

There are six groups defined under "fddi": snmpFddiSMT, snmpFddiMAC, snmpFddiPATH, snmpFddiPORT, snmpFddiATTACHMENT, and snmpFddiChipSets. Under the "snmpFddiMAC"

[1] ASN.1 names are case-sensitive. The first letter of a module, type, local type, local value, or production reference must be an uppercase letter. The first letter of a value reference or an identifier must be a lowercase letter. The letters in a macro name are all uppercase.

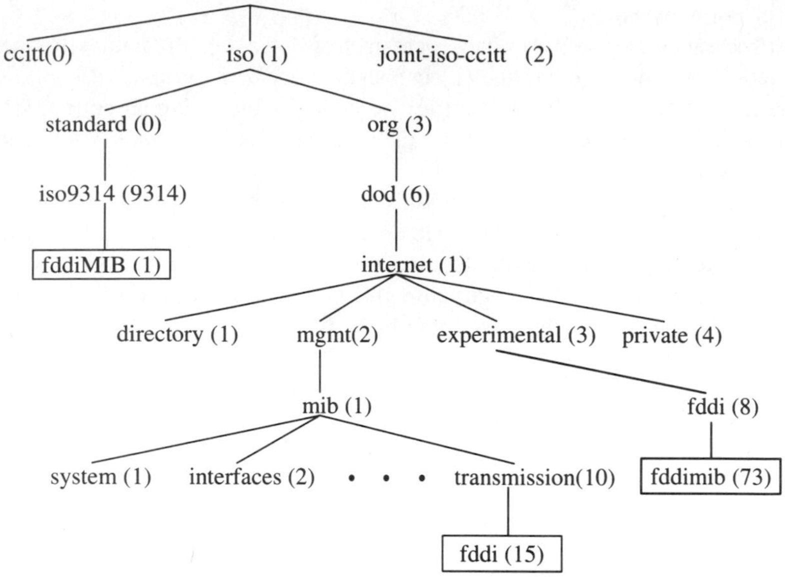

Figure 12.2 ISO's global naming hierarchy.

group, one object is snmpFddiMACNumber. This number indicates the total number of MACs in a station. To find out how many MACs there are in your workstation, the network manager might send a GetRequest to the agent in your workstation asking for the value of the object named:

(iso org dod internet mgmt mib fddi snmpFddiMAC snmpFddiMACNumber)

It is much easier for computers to use numbers rather than names. All children in the global naming tree of Figure 12.2 have been assigned unique numbers (indicated in the parentheses). Thus, the object named above is actually denoted as 1.3.6.1.2.1.10.15.2.1. The full name is specified in all SNMP messages. SNMP (and SMT) documents, however, specify only the parent's name since the rest of the hierarchy is clear from the context. For example, RFC 1285 defines the above object as follows:

snmpFddiMACNumber OBJECT-TYPE ::= { snmpFddiMAC 1 }

This simply means that snmpFddiMACNumber is the first child of snmpFddiMAC.

Each object in the MIB has an associated syntax, which defines its structure. ASN.1 defines a number of simple data types, such as integer, octet string, real, boolean, and so on. Octet string, incidentally, is an ordered list of zero or more bytes. ASN.1 also provides a number of *constructors* for building complex data types from these simple data types. An example of such a constructor is *sequence* defined as an ordered list of several object types. If all elements of a sequence are of the same type, that is, it is an array of some ASN.1 objects, it is called *sequence of.*

SNMP uses only a subset of types defined by ASN.1. Most FDDI parameters are integer, octet string, sequence, sequence of, or counter. A counter represents a non-negative integer, which increases monotonically until it reaches a maximum value; it then wraps around and starts increasing again from zero. The structure of management information (SMI) document specifies a maximum value of $2^{32} - 1$ for counters. An example of this type of object is the frame counter Frame_ct maintained by MACs in FDDI stations. In the FDDI MIB document, it is called snmpFddiMACFrameCts and is defined as follows:

```
snmpFddiMACFrameCts OBJECT-TYPE
SYNTAX Counter
ACCESS read-only
STATUS mandatory
DESCRIPTION ''Frame_Ct (refer to ANSI MAC 2.2.1).''
REFERENCE ''ANSI { fddiMAC 71 }''
::= { snmpFddiMACEntry 20 }
```

Notice that the numeric values assigned by the ANSI and IETF are different. The location of the name space used by ANSI for FDDI MIB is also shown in Figure 12.2. The ANSI name for the above parameter is fddiMACFrame-Ct and its numeric assignment is 1.0.9314.1.32.71 derived as follows:

iso		standard		iso9314		fddiMIB		fddiMAC		fddiMACFrame-Ct
1	.	0	.	9314	.	1	.	32	.	71

The IETF assignment for this parameter is 1.3.6.1.2.1.10.15.2.2.1.20 derived as follows:

iso		org		dod		internet
1	.	3	.	6	.	1
mgmt		mib		transmission		fddi
2	.	1	.	10	.	15
snmpFddiMAC		snmpFddiMACTable		snmpFddiMACEntry		fddiMACFrame-Ct
2	.	2	.	1	.	20

The numeric values and names are assigned arbitrarily by the name space administrators. Thus, the only way to find the numeric value for an object is to consult a published standard.

Among the new object types defined specifically for FDDI are FddiTime, FddiResourceld, FddiSMTStationIdType, and FddiMACLongAddressType. FddiTime is defined to be an integer that can take a value between 0 and $2^{31} - 1$. It specifies time in units of bytes (80 ns). It is used for conveying path latency and synchronous bandwidth values. FddiResourceld is defined to be a 16-bit integer that can take a value between 0 and $2^{16} - 1$. This data type is used to refer to an instance of a MAC, PORT, PATH, or ATTACHMENT Resource ID. Indexing begins at 1. Zero is used to indicate the absence of a resource. FddiSMTStationIdType is an OCTET STRING type defined to indicate 8-byte SMT station IDs. FddiMACLongAddressType is another OCTET STRING type defined to indicate 48-bit long MAC addresses.

A summary of FDDI MIB as defined in RFC 1285 is shown in Figure 12.3. In the figure, many long names have been shortened using a single italic letter to denote the common prefix part of the name. For example, using *s* to denote snmpFddiSMT, the name snmpFddiSMTStationAction has been shortened to *s*StationAction. Figure 12.4 shows the naming tree as defined in ANSI/SMT. Notice that the RFC 1285's FDDI MIB assignments are similar to but different from SMT's FDDI MIB assignments. One reason for this is that RFC 1285 is based on the SMT draft version 6.2 document. Since that version, the SMT document has been updated and SMT draft version 7.3 was finally approved as the standard. A new Internet RFC is being developed that defines an MIB close to that in SMT 7.3. The changes from SMT 6.2 to SMT 7.3 are so numerous that the new IETF MIB

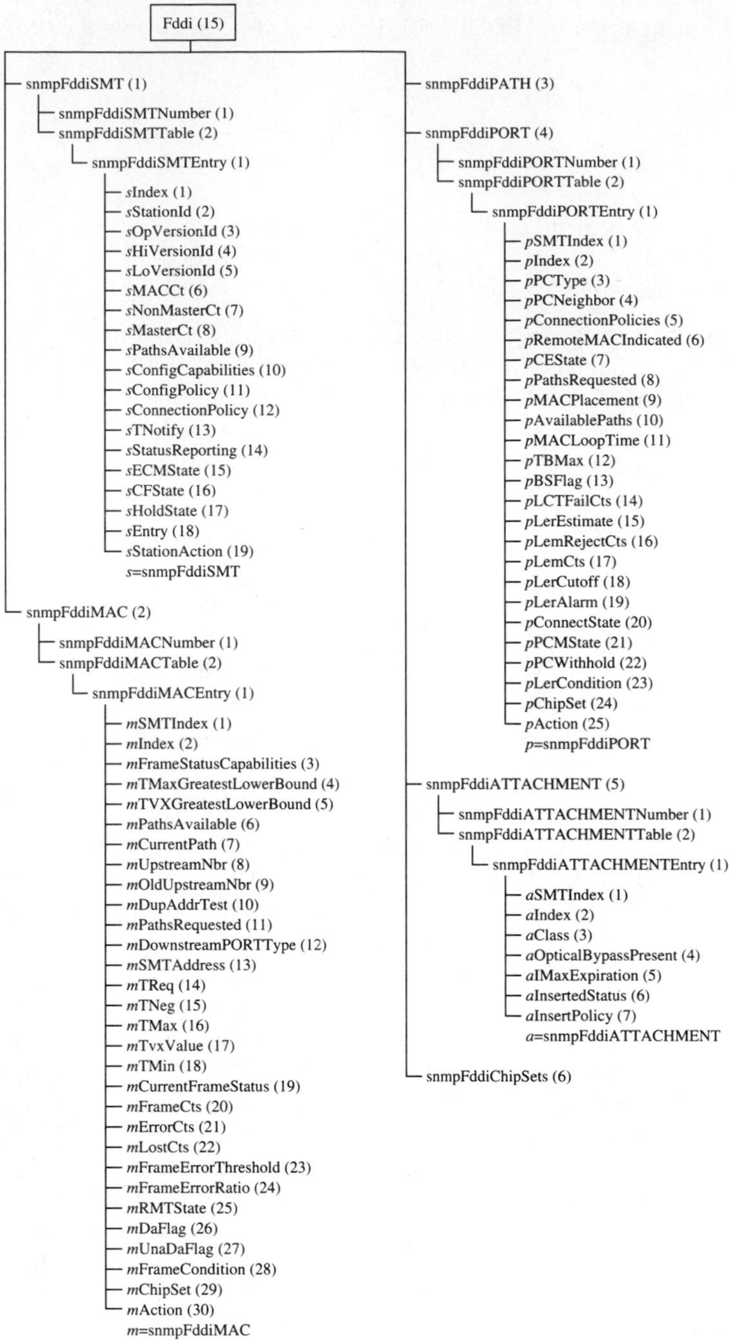

Figure 12.3 IETF's FDDI MIB assignments per RFC 1285.

Figure 12.4 ANSI's FDDI MIB assignments per SMT 7.3.

is located on a different branch of the global naming tree. This location is indicated as "fddimib" in Figure 12.3. When published, the updated RFC is expected to coexist with RFC 1285.

12.2 OSI Network Management Standards

Having mentioned SNMP, it is only appropriate to discuss what is being done in the ISO arena. The number of standards being developed by ISO on network management is large. Any attempt to explain all these would easily fill a book. In fact, several books have already been written on the topic. Here we provide only a brief description of some of the key standards.

An overview of ISO network management is provided in Management Framework (ISO/IEC 7498-4:1989) and Systems Management Overview (ISO/IEC 10040).

The protocols and services required to exchange management information are described in two standards called Common Management Information Protocol (CMIP) (ISO/IEC 9596-1:1991) and Common Management Information Service (CMIS) (ISO/IEC 9595:1991), respectively. CMIP is the application layer protocol and specifies the format of messages exchanged between the systems, while CMIS specifies the service interface to CMIP. As in SNMP, the management entity on one system acts as a manager, while a peer entity on the other system acts as an agent. CMIP exchanges include event notifications and information or action requests and responses. CMIS services include M-GET (read attribute), M-SET (write attribute), M-EVENT-REPORT (report an event), and M-ACTION (perform an action). Management objects and instances can be created and deleted by M-CREATE and M-DELETE, respectively.

The structure of the management information is described in three different standards. The Management of Information Model (MIM) (ISO/IEC 10165-1) uses an object-oriented model of management information. The information is divided into managed objects, their attributes, the management operations that can be performed on them, and the notifications that they can transmit. The Guideline for the Definition of Management Objects (GDMO) (ISO/IEC 10165-4) specifies notational tools, documentation structures, and templates for defining management information. The Definition of Management Information (DMI) (ISO/IEC 10165-2) defines often-used managed object classes, packets, attribute types, action types, parameter types, and notification types. Management Object Conformance Statements (MOCS) (ISO 10165-6) and Generic Management Information (GMI) (ISO 10165-5) are two new emerging standards.

ISO has partitioned system management activities into five Specific Management Functional Areas (SMFAs): configuration management, fault management, performance management, security management, and accounting management. Within each of these SMFAs, ISO is developing standards for System Management Functions (SMFs).

The Government Network Management Profile (GNMP) is the set of guidelines followed by U.S. government agencies when acquiring network management functions and services. GNMP builds on the Government Open Systems Interconnection Profile (GOSIP), which specifies the networking protocol stack. GOSIP includes services such as file transfer, message handling, and virtual terminal, but leaves the management protocols for GNMP. Version 1 GNMP specifies the use of ISO management protocols. Integrating SNMP is left as a work item for future versions of GNMP.

As mentioned earlier, SNMP was initially an interim management solution. Some expected it to be replaced eventually by OSI management protocols when they were ready. This was the reason for defining the management protocols and the management information separately. Although CMIP over TCP (CMOT) has been defined, it has been overrun by the SNMP epidemic. And now, with the emergence of SNMP Version 2, the chances of CMOT catching up with SNMP are remote.

12.3 Further Reading

ISO Standard 8824 describes the Abstract Syntax Notation One (ASN.1) for specifying data types in a machine-independent manner. ISO 8825 describes the transfer syntax for unambiguous representation of data values for transmission over the network. These standards have also been adopted by CCITT in the form of Recommendations X.205 and X.209, respectively. A good overview of ASN.1 can be found in Motteler and Sidhu (1992).

A number of Internet RFCs on SNMP are useful. For example, RFC 1155 defines the mechanism used for describing and naming objects. RFC 1156 describes MIB-I, the core set of management objects for the Internet suite. RFC 1157 explains the SNMP protocol used for network access to managed objects. RFC 1212 specifies an SNMP object description mechanism. RFC 1213 presents MIB-II, an evolution of MIB-I. RFC 1028 describes SGMP, the predecessor of SNMP. CMOT is described in RFC 1189. RFC 1052 explains IAB recommendations for evolving the network management protocols.

RFC 1285 and 1512 define FDDI MIBs. MIBs have also been defined for IEEE 802.4/token bus (RFC 1230), IEEE 802.5/token ring (RFC 1231), connectionless network service (RFC 1238), BGP (RFC 1284), IEEE 802.3/Ethernet (RFC 1269), bridges (RFC 1286), DECnet Phase IV (RFC 1289), frame relay DTEs (RFC 1315), character stream devices (RFC 1316), RS-232 devices (RFC 1317), and parallel printers (RFC 1318).

Comer (1990) has a chapter devoted to SNMP. For a more detailed description see Rose (1991). See also Case (1990), which includes an overview of SNMP. An overview of SNMP version 2 can be found in Case et al. (1992). Black (1992) covers both SNMP and OSI network management.

12.4 Self-Test Exercises

Note: Some exercises have multiple correct answers. See Appendix D for answers.

12.1 What is an SNMP network management station (NMS)?

a. A station with special hardware required to manage the network
b. Any station that contains software to manage the network
c. A station that is dedicated solely for network management
d. A station that is elected using a distributed voting algorithm

12.2 Which of the following apply to management information bases (MIBs)?:

a. They consist of information stored secretly by network managers.
b. It is the information stored by agents.
c. The agents decide the structure of MIB.
d. The managers decide the structure of MIB.

12.3 What can you say about the naming syntaxes used by SNMP and CMIP?

a. One uses ASN.1 while the other does not.
b. One uses full ASN.1 while the other uses only a subset.
c. There is no relationship between the two.

CHAPTER **13**

Extension for Telecommunications: FDDI-II

13.1 Overview

FDDI as described thus far supports asynchronous and synchronous traffic. Although the synchronous traffic is guaranteed a bounded delay, the delay can vary. For example, with a target token rotation time (TTRT) value of 165 ms on a ring with 10-μs latency, a station will get opportunities to transmit the synchronous traffic every 10 μs at zero load. Under heavy load, occasionally it may have to wait for 330 ms. This type of variation may not suit many constant bit rate (CBR) telecommunication applications that require a strict periodic access. For example, on an ISDN-B channel, which supports one 64-kbps voice conversation, 1 byte is received every 125 μs. Such circuit-switched traffic cannot be easily supported on FDDI. If an application needs guaranteed transmission of n bytes every T μs, or some integral multiples of T μs, the application is said to require **isochronous** service. The prefix *iso* means same or uniform; *chronous* means time. Thus, *isochronous* means same interval. In general, the term *isochronous* indicates that the time intervals between consecutive significant instants have either the same duration or durations that are integral multiples of the shortest duration.

FDDI-II provides support for isochronous service in addition to asynchronous and synchronous service provided by FDDI as shown in Figure 13.1. The original version of FDDI, sometimes called *FDDI Classic*, is denoted in the rest of this chapter as FDDI-I. Its protocol components are denoted as MAC-1, PHY-1, and SMT-1. The corresponding components of FDDI-II are called MAC-2, PHY-2, and SMT-2. There is no change to PMD and, therefore, notations PMD-1 and PMD-2 are not used.

Like FDDI-I, FDDI-II runs at 100 Mbps. FDDI-II nodes can run in FDDI-I or **basic** mode. If all nodes (stations as well as concentrators) on the ring are FDDI-II nodes, then the ring can switch to the **hybrid** mode in which isochronous service is provided in addition to basic mode services. However, if there is even one node on the ring that is not an FDDI-II node, the ring cannot switch to the hybrid mode and will keep running in the basic mode. In the basic mode on FDDI-II, synchronous, restricted asynchronous, and nonrestricted asynchronous traffic is transmitted in a manner identical to that on FDDI-I. Isochronous service is not available in the basic mode.

Most multimedia applications such as video conferencing, real-time video, and entertainment video can be supported on FDDI-I since the required time guarantee is a few tens of milliseconds. This can be easily guaranteed with synchronous service and a small TTRT. Since the TTRT cannot

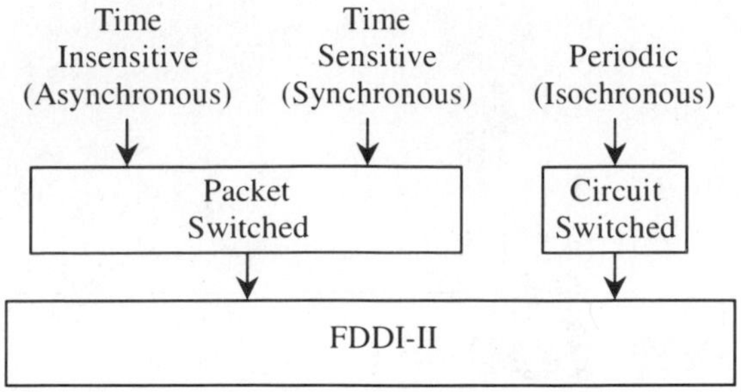

Figure 13.1 Services provided by FDDI-II.

be less than the ring latency, applications requiring time bounds less than twice the ring latency cannot be supported by FDDI-I. Similarly, applications requiring strict periodic access will require FDDI-II. The main problem facing FDDI-II users is that even if only one or two stations require isochronous service, hardware on all stations on the ring would have to be upgraded to FDDI-II.

In essence, FDDI-II provides circuit switching along with packet switching. Thus, any application that runs on a dedicated circuit can be switched over to FDDI-II in a shared mode provided the bandwidth requirements can be satisfied.

13.2 Cycles

To service periodic isochronous requests, FDDI-II uses a periodic transmission policy in which transmission opportunities are repeated every 125 μs. This interval has been chosen because it matches the basic system reference frequency clock used in most public telecommunications networks worldwide. (Little did the Bell Laboratories engineers, who happen to have selected an 8-kHz sampling rate for voice, know that they were establishing a new universal constant.) At this interval, a special frame called a **cycle** is generated. At 100 Mbps, 1562.5 bytes can be transmitted in 125 μs. Of these, 1560 bytes are used for the cycle and 2.5 bytes are used as the intercycle gap or cycle preamble. At any instant, the ring may contain several cycles as shown in Figure 13.2.

The bytes of the cycles are preallocated to various channels (for communication between two or more stations) on the ring. For example, a channel may have the right to use the 26th and 122nd bytes of every cycle. These bytes are *reserved* for the channel in the sense that if the stations owning

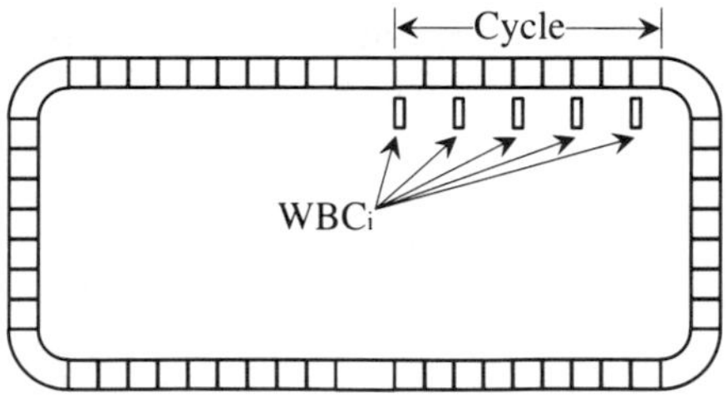

Figure 13.2 Cycles.

that channel do not use it, other stations cannot use it and the bytes will be left unused.

The 1560 bytes of the cycle are divided into 16 **wideband channels** (**WBC**s) of 96 bytes each. Each WBC provides a bandwidth of 96 bytes per 125 μs or 6.144 Mbps. This is sufficient to support one television broadcast, four high-quality stereo programs, or 96 telephone conversations.

Some of the 16 wideband channels may be allocated for packet mode transmissions and the others for isochronous mode transmissions. The allocation is made using station management protocols. For example, wideband channels 1, 5, and 7 may be used for packet mode transmissions or packet switching, and channels 2, 3, 4, 6, and 8 through 15 may be used for isochronous mode transmissions or circuit switching. It is possible to allocate all wideband channels for circuit switching alone or packet switching alone.

The 16 wideband channels use up 1536 bytes out of a total of 1560 bytes of the cycle. Of the remaining 24 bytes, 12 bytes are used for the cycle header and the remaining 12 bytes are permanently allocated for packet switching. These permanently allocated bytes are called **dedicated packet group** (**DPG**) and ensure that at least 0.768 Mbps of the bandwidth will be available for packet switching in case all wideband channels are allocated for circuit switching. Packet switching is required for ring monitoring and management (SMT) protocols. Additional bandwidth can be allocated for packet switching in increments of 6.144 Mbps by assigning additional wideband channels for packet switching. The maximum bandwidth of 99.072 Mbps is obtained by allocating all WBCs to the packet data channel.

13.3 FDDI-II Protocol Components

Figure 13.3 shows the protocol components of FDDI-II. This corresponds to Figure 1.11 presented earlier for FDDI-I. There are eight components:

1. *Physical Layer Medium Dependent* (*PMD*): This component deals with those parts of the standard that depend on the medium used for interconnection. For example, for fiber-based rings, this component specifies the characteristics of fibers, connectors, optical transmitters, and receivers.

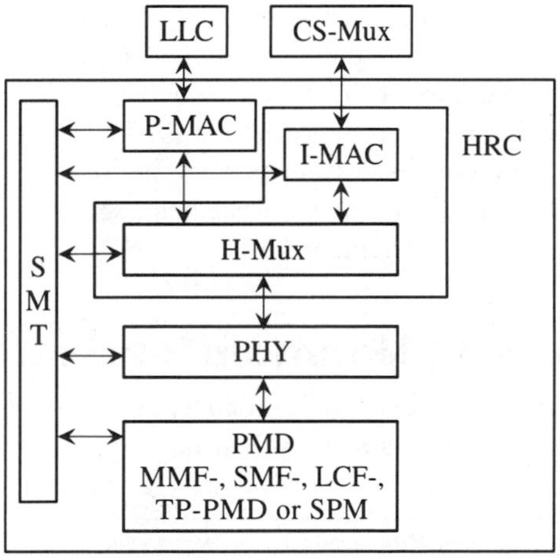

Figure 13.3 Protocol components of FDDI-II.

All PMD specifications for FDDI-I apply to FDDI-II without any changes. Thus, multimode fiber, single-mode fiber, SONET, and twisted-pair PMDs used for FDDI-I can be used for FDDI-II. In other words, conversion from FDDI-I to FDDI-II does not require any rewiring.

2. *Physical Layer Medium Independent* (*PHY*): This component deals with that part of the physical layer that does not depend on the medium. It specifies algorithms to overcome clock rate differences among the stations, to detect errors in the received bits, and to encode the information bits (data bits) into pulses (code bits) that are transmitted on the medium. PHY for FDDI-II is similar to that for FDDI-I. The new version of PHY, called PHY-2, incorporates the new services required for FDDI-II. It is described in Chapter 15.
3. *Hybrid Multiplexer (H-Mux)*: This combines (multiplexes) the packet-switched and circuit-switched traffic from the station for transmission on to the medium. It also separates out (demultiplexes) the traffic received from the medium into packet-switched and circuit-switched components. This is a new component not present in FDDI-I.
4. *Packet Media Access Control (P-MAC)*[1]: This component specifies the rules for sharing the channels allocated for packet switching. This is similar to MAC for FDDI-I. The new version of MAC, called MAC-2, incorporates facilities required for FDDI-II. It is described in Chapter 14.
5. *Isochronous Media Access Control (I-MAC)*: This component specifies the rules for sharing the bandwidth allocated for circuit switching. This is also a new component not present in FDDI-I. The specifications for H-MUX and I-MAC are combined into one standard document named **hybrid ring control** (**HRC**).
6. *Station Management* (*SMT*): This component specifies protocols and frame formats to automatically locate and isolate faults, reconfigure the network, and initialize it. Several extensions to SMT need to be made for FDDI-II. These extensions are briefly described in Section 13.13.
7. *Logical Link Control* (*LLC*): This component multiplexes/demultiplexes the packets received from numerous network layer protocols. It can also provide hop-by-hop flow control and error recovery procedures if needed. Both FDDI-I and FDDI-II use LLC specified by ISO 8802-2 standard. Therefore, there is no difference in the LLC components of the two versions of FDDI.
8. *Circuit-Switching Multiplexer* (*CS-MUX*): This component specifies methods for combining (multiplexing/demultiplexing) several circuits for transmission on a circuit-switched channel. A circuit allows bidirectional communication between two or more CS-MUX *service access points* (*SAPs*). Note that the communication is bidirectional and, therefore, a byte in the cycle allocated to a circuit may be reused by the destination station to transmit information back to the source. This allows the throughput of the circuit to be twice the bandwidth. Multipoint circuits allowing communications among more than two CS-MUX SAPs are also allowed.

   CS-MUX is also a new component not present in FDDI-I. It plays the role of LLC for circuit-switched traffic. Like LLC, no standard has been specified since this part of the datalink is technically not covered by the FDDI standards.

13.4 Monitor and Nonmonitor Stations

Like FDDI-I, an FDDI-II node can be a station or a concentrator (or both), and can have zero, one, or two peer attachments. Dual-attachment stations can have one or two P-MACs and zero, one, or

[1]The prefix "P-" has been dropped from the HRC standard. However, to avoid confusion with MAC components following the MAC-1 standard and also to keep symmetry with the name of I-MAC, we find it less confusing to call this component P-MAC.

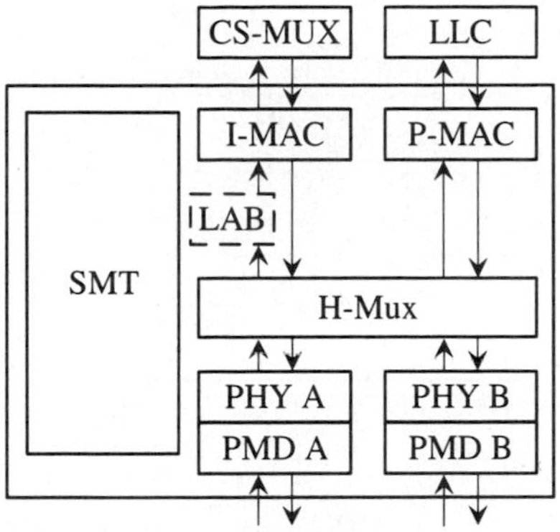

Figure 13.4 Components of an FDDI-II station.

two I-MACs. More importantly, FDDI-II stations are of two classes: monitor or nonmonitor. Monitor stations have the capability to generate and maintain cycles, while nonmonitor stations do not.

Each monitor station has a rank assigned to it in the range of 1 through 63. The monitor station with the highest rank is selected as the **cycle master**. If two monitor stations have the highest rank, the station with the highest MAC address becomes the cycle master. The cycle master initializes and maintains cycles. In particular, it ensures that there is an integer number of cycles on the ring. This is done by adding a **latency adjustment buffer (LAB)** in the signal path. The size of the buffer is adjusted continuously in a manner similar to that of the elasticity buffer. The size of the LAB is of the order of 125 μs (1562.5 bytes) or more. Nonmonitor stations do not have LAB. When the ring is running in the hybrid mode, all stations except the cycle master run in the **slave mode**. The cycle master provides special services and is said to be running in the **master mode**. Thus, an FDDI-II station can be in one of three modes: basic, slave, or master.

Although LAB is allowed to be active in any monitor station, it is generally active only in the cycle master station. The packet data stream is not subjected to the delay of the LAB in the cycle master. The bytes received on the packet data channel are allowed to proceed in the next available packet data byte on the outgoing stream.

Figure 13.4 shows the components of a dual-attachment, single-P-MAC, single-I-MAC FDDI-II station. H-MUX keeps a copy of the current programming template and uses it to demultiplex the incoming symbol stream (from PHY) into the packet mode stream and isochronous mode stream that are delivered to the P-MAC and I-MAC, respectively. On the outgoing side, it ensures that the symbols received from P-MAC are transmitted on the bytes reserved for packet switching and the symbols received from I-MAC are transmitted in the appropriate position in the proper wideband channel.

13.5 Cycle Format

The bytes of the wideband channels are interleaved. The zeroth bytes of channels 1 through 16 are transmitted first as a group. The bytes numbered 1 of the channels are then transmitted as another group, and so on. There are 96 such groups called **cyclic groups** identified as CG0 through CG95. Each cyclic group is 16 bytes long. Cyclic group CG*i* consists of *i*th bytes of wideband channels 1 through 16. The 96 cyclic groups are transmitted contiguously one after another except that the

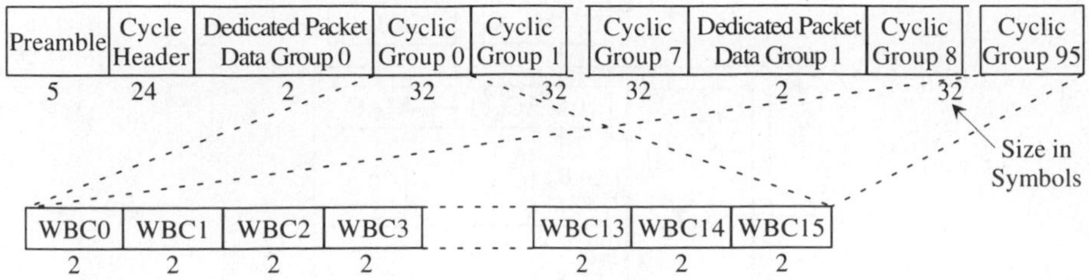

Figure 13.5 FDDI-II cycle format.

12 bytes of the dedicated packet group (DPG) are also interleaved. One byte of DPG precedes every eight cyclic groups. The complete cycle format is shown in Figure 13.5. There is a 2.5-byte (five symbols) preamble, and a 12-byte cycle header, followed by interleaved DPGs and CGs.

Figure 13.6 presents a matrix view of the cycle structure. Following a preamble and the cycle header, the cycle is organized as 96 rows of 16 bytes each. Rows 0, 8, 16, . . ., 80, and 88 (multiples of 8) are preceded by one DPG byte. The rows constitute the cyclic groups while the columns constitute the wideband channels. The order of transmission is row-wise. Bytes of row 0 are transmitted before those of row 1, and so on.

The format of the cycle header is shown in Figure 13.7. A J-K symbol pair is used as the starting delimiter. The next symbol, C1, is used for cycle synchronization control. It can take only two values, R or S, indicating whether cycle synchronization has been established. If C1 is R, cycle synchronization has not been established and the cycle can be interrupted by a new cycle. If C1 is S, the cycle cannot be interrupted by a new cycle.

The next symbol, C2, is used for sequence control. It can take two values, R or S. Their meaning is explained shortly. The cycles are sequentially numbered and the cycle sequence number is indicated

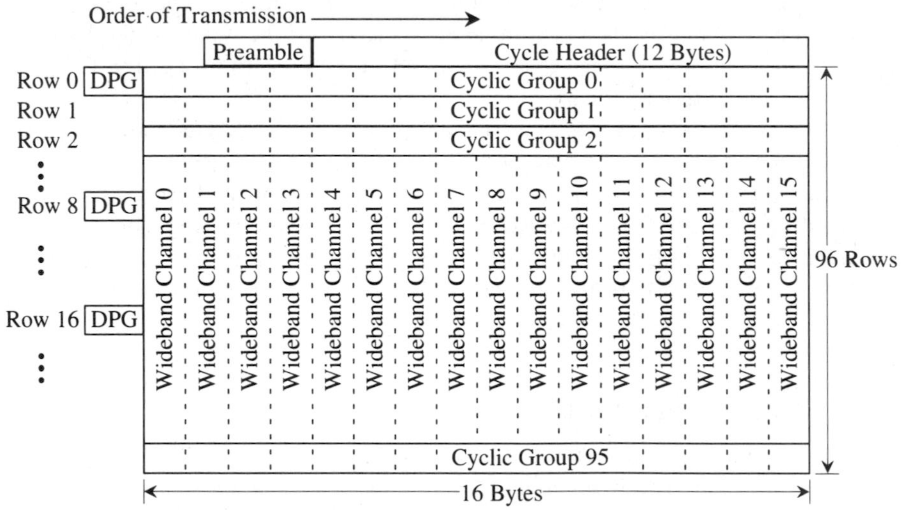

Figure 13.6 A matrix view of the cycle structure.

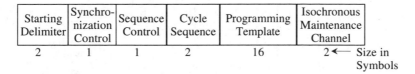

Starting Delimiter	Synchro-nization Control	Sequence Control	Cycle Sequence	Programming Template	Isochronous Maintenance Channel	
2	1	1	2	16	2	← Size in Symbols

Figure 13.7 Cycle header.

in the next two symbols labeled "CS." During cycle initialization or reinitialization, the CS field is used to indicate monitor rank.

Since the monitor ranks are between 0 and 63, the cycles are numbered from 64 through 255. After 255, the cycle sequence wraps back to 64 and repeats. Mathematically, the sequence number changes from n to $64 + [(n+1-64) \bmod 192]$.[2] When the cycle sequence field contains the monitor rank, the sequence control field is set to R. When the cycle sequence field contains the cycle number, the sequence control field is set to S. If any slave station detects an error in the sequence number, it sets the sequence control field to R. Table 13.1 lists the interpretation of various valid values of the cycle control C1, C2, and CS fields. All other combinations are considered invalid.

The next 16 symbols labeled P0 through P15 in the packet header give the current programming template for wideband channels 0 through 15, respectively. Each of these symbols can take three values, R, S, or T, indicating whether the corresponding channel is assigned for packet switching, circuit switching, or not assigned. Figure 13.8 shows an example of the programming template. As shown, channels 2, 5, 7, 8, and 15 are allocated for circuit switching; channels 0, 1, 4, 6, and 9 through 14 are allocated for packet switching; and channel 3 is unallocated.

The last two symbols in the packet header are for the **isochronous maintenance channel (IMC)**, which is dedicated to carrying isochronous traffic (generally voice) for maintenance purposes.

Notice that no cycle ending delimiter is required since a cycle is of fixed length. The cycle always ends 1559 bytes after the starting delimiter (J-K pair). In particular, the presence of a series of I symbols does not indicate a partial cycle. All control symbols except J-K, V, and Q may legitimately be present in a cycle.

Table 13.1 Interpretation of Cycle Control Fields

Synch Control C1	Sequence Control C2	Cycle Sequence n	Interpretation
R	R	$1 \leq n \leq 63$	Monitor contention
R	S	$64 \leq n \leq 255$	Hybrid mode initializing
S	S	$64 \leq n \leq 255$	Hybrid mode established and operating
S	R	$64 \leq n \leq 255$	Sequence number error detected

[2]HRC standard, Section 7.2.2.4, incorrectly specifies 64+(n mod 192) as the next sequence number.

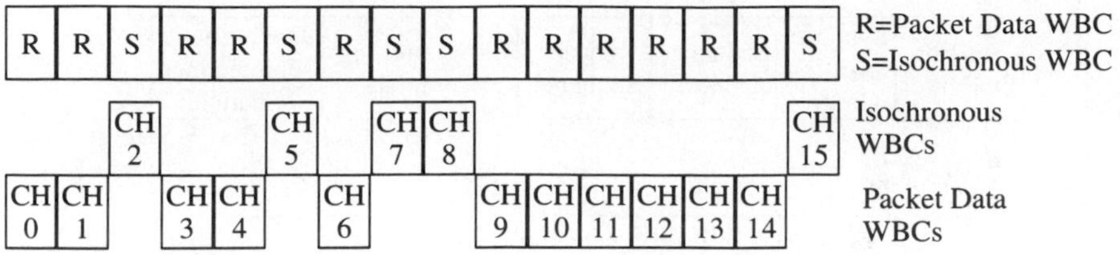

Figure 13.8 A sample programming template.

13.6 Packet Switching in the Hybrid Mode

In the basic mode, FDDI-II operation is identical to that in FDDI-I. Synchronous, restricted asynchronous, and nonrestricted asynchronous packet switching are provided using the timed token protocol in a manner similar to that in FDDI-I. It is interesting to see how these services are provided in the hybrid mode.

In the hybrid mode, the packet-switched symbol stream is intermixed with the circuit-switched stream. Therefore, the symbols belonging to the packet stream are not received contiguously. Depending on the assignment of the wideband channels, there may be time gaps between consecutive symbols of the packet-switched stream. The time to transmit a frame depends on the total bandwidth available for packet switching. For example, if eight WBCs are allocated for packet switching, the available bandwidth is $8 \times 6.144 + 0.768$ or 49.92 Mbps. Transmitting a 4500-byte frame would take 721 μs instead of 360 μs on FDDI-I. This affects the operation of the valid transmission timer (TVX). Either the TVX should be run intermittently (turned on only when the packet-switched stream is active) or its value should be scaled up/down to reflect the available bandwidth. The token rotation timer (TRT) and token holding timer (THT) are not affected and are run in real time.

Token and frame formats used in an FDDI-II packet-switched stream are similar to those in FDDI-I. The key difference is that the I-L symbol pair is used as the *in-cycle starting delimiter*. All frames and tokens start with this symbol pair instead of J-K. This is because J-K is used as the cycle starting delimiter and it cannot be transmitted in a cycle.

The physical layer of FDDI-II does not impose any limit on the frame size. Recall from Section 3.2 that the maximum packet size in FDDI-I was set to 4500 bytes based on the fact that differences in clock rates of successive stations would require stations to add or delete bits. This addition/deletion can be done only in the interframe gap. Therefore, the frame size was restricted to limit the size of the elasticity buffer required. In FDDI-II, the bits are added or deleted during the intercycle gap. A frame can span many cycles. The cycle length and not the frame length affects the number of bits accumulated in the elasticity buffer. Thus, there is no need to limit the frame size for this reason. This argument lead the FDDI-II committee to set the maximum frame size initially at 17,200 symbols. This limit was placed to achieve a reasonable probability of errors not detected by the CRC. Later the frame size was reduced to 9000 symbols to maintain compatibility between basic mode and hybrid mode packet switching.

13.7 Hybrid Mode Initialization

The first step of ring initialization in FDDI-II is the same as that in FDDI-I, namely, the claim process. This process (see Chapter 2) is used to initialize a token in the basic mode and to establish a target token rotation time (TTRT) for the ring.

A monitor station wishing to take the ring to the hybrid mode ensures that the sum of bandwidth allocated for synchronous packet traffic and the extra bandwidth required for hybrid operation does not exceed the allocatable synchronous bandwidth of the ring. The extra bandwidth required for hybrid operation includes the bandwidth for the cycle header and the sum of bandwidths for the isochronous wideband channels. The monitor station may also want to reserve additional synchronous bandwidth for programming template changes or mode switching.

A monitor contention procedure may be used to determine the highest ranking monitor that will initialize the hybrid mode. FDDI-II allows hybrid mode initialization with or without monitor contention. The initialization procedure without monitor contention is discussed first.

The monitor station, designated as the cycle master, captures the basic mode token and transmits a cycle with the synchronization control (C1) field set to R, the sequence control field (C2) set to S, and the cycle sequence field (CS) set to a valid sequence number. The monitor issues a new token in the packet data channel. If the ring is longer than 125 μs, the monitor continues to transmit additional cycles until a cycle returns. The latency adjustment buffer is used to ensure that an integral number of cycles is transmitted on the ring.

Other stations on the ring notice the cycle (J-K followed by RR, RS, SR, or SS) and enter the hybrid mode. Since the cycle sequence field is S, and the sequence number is greater than 63, the stations enter the slave mode and initialize their cycle sequence counter to this value.

The cycle master waits until it is sure that it is correctly receiving the cycles that it sent. It then sets the cycle control fields (C1) to S. This indicates that the ring has successfully entered the hybrid mode and the monitor takes on the responsibilities of cycle master.

If a monitor contention procedure is to be used to select the highest ranking monitor, all monitor stations on the ring start cycles with cycle control fields (C1 and C2) set to RR. The cycle sequence number field contains the rank of the monitor. Stations with lower ranks stop transmitting cycles and eventually the highest ranking monitor becomes the cycle master.

If there is any FDDI-I station on the ring, it does not recognize the cycles. The station considers the cycles (J-K not followed by data symbols) as invalid frames. Its valid transmission timer (TVX) expires, it starts a claim process, and the ring returns to the basic mode.

13.8 Transmission Channels

Different users of the isochronous facilities have different bandwidth requirements. For example, a single telephone conversation requires 64 kbps; a T1 connection requires 1.544 Mbps, and a CCITT G.703/G.732 channel requires 2.048 Mbps. FDDI-II meets all such user requirements by subdividing wideband channels into several **transmission channels** of varying bandwidth. Each transmission channel permits a dialog between I-MAC users (service access points) and occupies a preallocated time slot in the cycle. The time slot is always a set of contiguous bytes in a wideband channel. For example, the fifth and sixth bytes in WBC 13 may be allocated to a transmission channel. This channel will have 16 bits every 125 μs, which translates to a channel rate of 128 kbps.

The rate of a transmission channel can be any multiple of 64 kbps (1 byte/cycle) up to 6.144 Mbps. A station can submultiplex a transmission channel into lower rate channels if de-

Table 13.2 Popular Channel Sizes and Applications

Bits/Cycle	Channel Rate	Common Application
1	8 kbps	
2	16 kbps	ISDN D channel
4	32 kpbs	
8	64 kbps	ISDN B channel (one telephone conversation)
48	384 kbps	
192	1.536 Mbps	T1 with synch bit stripped (one high-quality stereo)
1 + 192	1.544 Mbps	T1 with synch bit
240	1.920 Mbps	
256	2.048 Mbps	CCITT G.703/G.732
768	6.144 Mbps	

sired. These lower rate channels are aligned so that it is easy to extract/substitute the desired bits. Thus, 32-kbps channels are set up on quartet (4 bits or nibble) boundaries; 16-kbps channels are set up on even bit boundaries; and 8-kbps channels are set up on bit boundaries.

Table 13.2 lists some of the popular channel sizes and their applications. A T1 circuit has a bandwidth of 1.544 Mbps, which consists of 193 bits per cycle. Of these, 1 bit is used for synchronization. On FDDI-II, this bit can be easily generated at the receiving node, and therefore it is not necessary to transmit this bit. A T1 circuit can therefore be supported with only 192 bits per cycle.

The channel rate of 6.144 Mbps allows efficient multiplexing of 2.048-Mbps CCITT G.703/G.732 lines and 144-kbps ISDN channels also. Three 2.048-Mbps lines can be multiplexed into a 6.144-Mbps WBC without further stripping or modification of synchronization or signaling information. Forty-eight 144-kbps ISDN basic rate (2B+D) access arrangements can be multiplexed into a WBC.

The bytes of a channel are received in the same sequence in which they are transmitted. Thus, the sequence integrity of data in a channel is maintained. It is also possible to maintain a sequence integrity across two or more channels. This is called **channel coherence**. Requiring coherence across channels allows the bandwidth of several channels to be combined for one application. In particular, the aggregate bandwidth of several wideband channels can be allocated for one application such as uncompressed TV. Note that coherence is a network interconnection issue. When a channel spanning multiple WBCs passes a bridge (or a switch) it will not necessarily maintain the sequence (coherence).

13.9 Circuits

Two users wishing to communicate using the isochronous facilities of FDDI-II need to establish a circuit between them and get a transmission channel allocated for their use. A **circuit** allows *bidirectional* communication between the users. Each user may write the bytes allocated for the channel after reading them. This allows for full-duplex communication resulting in a channel throughput that is twice the channel rate. Thus, a two-point circuit with a channel rate of 64 kbps can have an effective information transfer rate (throughput) of 128 kbps.

More than two users can also communicate using one circuit. For example, a multipoint circuit can be used for a conference call among several users. The participants decide who among them reads or writes the time slot allocated for their channel. Some participant may have only *receive access* while others may have *send access* or both to the circuit. For example, the slot might be written by one station but may be read by all others. This could be used to broadcast television signals. In another case, the slot might be read and written by one station, then read and written by another station, and so on. This could be used to support several simultaneous one-to-one phone conversations. This type of *spatial reuse*, although very difficult to implement in practice, allows the throughput of an *n*-point circuit to be as much as *n* times the channel rate.

Multicasts used in LANs allow one transmitter to communicate with many receivers. In this sense, they allow one-to-many conversations. The multipoint circuits are more general in that they allow many-to-many conversations.

13.10 Bandwidth Management

An FDDI-II network supports a variety of packet-switched and circuit-switched applications. Allocation of bandwidth among applications is controlled in a hierarchical manner as shown in Figure 13.9. The bandwidth management procedures have been divided into two categories. The first category is concerned with the allocation of bandwidth between the packet and isochronous channels. This is called **WBC management**. The second category is concerned with the allocation of isochronous bandwidth. This is called **transmission channel management**.

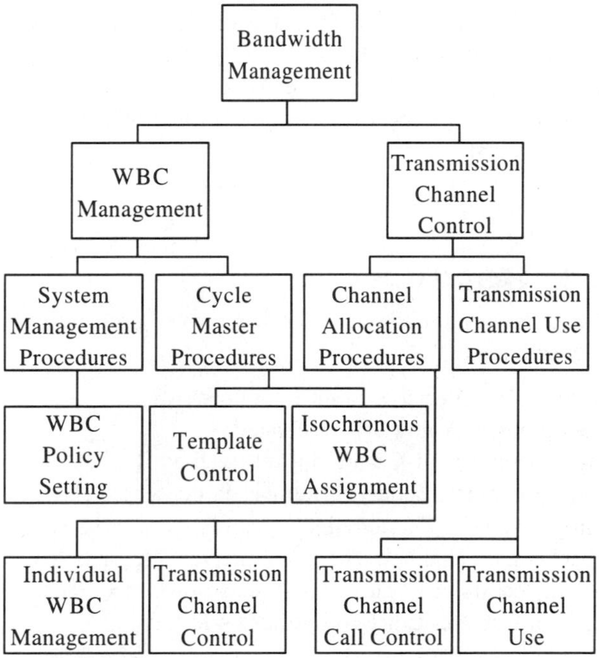

Figure 13.9 A hierarchical view of bandwidth management.

WBC management consists of two levels of hierarchy: the system management procedures and the cycle master procedures. The network manager may set a limit on the amount of bandwidth that must be always available for packet switching. This in effect sets a limit on the number of WBCs that can be allocated for circuit switching. Once the policy has been set, the cycle master is responsible for allocating WBCs for circuit switching as the need arises. All unused WBCs that are not likely to be reused soon are returned for packet switching. The cycle master indicates the allocation in the programming templates of each cycle.

The responsibility for individual WBC management is delegated to **channel allocators**. A number of channel allocators may exist concurrently. Each channel allocator manages a disjoint pool of WBCs. The pools are called *channel allocation domains*. Although the channel allocators are physically distributed to provide redundancy, logically they form one centralized server fuction. Any station wishing to start an isochronous dialog requests an allocation of a channel of the desired rate from a channel allocator.

The concept of channel allocator domain allows a WBC to be used as desired by the participating stations. The details are known only to the small set of stations privy to its use.

A channel allocator can request stations currently using an isochronous channel to move their connection onto a different channel in order to perform **WBC compaction**. This helps reduce unusable bandwidth due to fragmentation.

The time slot position of all open transmission channels at a station is maintained by the I-MAC at that station in a table called the **steering map**. The entries in this map specify the size of the channel, the WBC in which the channel is assigned, and the location of the channel within the WBC. Additional characteristics of the channels such as its access/security information may also be stored in the map.

Whenever a WBC is added or removed from the packet data channel, care must be taken to ensure that no packet data are lost. One way to ensure this is for the cycle master to capture the token on the packet data channel and release it in the next cycle with the modified programming template. Capturing the token allows the cycle master to strip all incoming packet data and thus ensure that no packet data are lost.

13.11 Error Recovery

Like FDDI-I, FDDI-II also has several automatic error recovery procedures for commonly occurring errors. Examples of such errors are:

1. Corrupted cycle starting delimiter: J-K is hit by a noise.
2. False cycle starting delimiter: A new J-K is created.
3. Error in cycle control symbols: C1-C2 are not received as R or S.
4. Error in cycle sequence number: Sequence number is not as expected.
5. Error in programming template: The template symbols are not R, S, or T.
6. Lost token in the packet data channel: The token arrives late or is lost.
7. Cycle clock too fast or too slow: Cycles do not arrive on time.
8. Failure to establish hybrid mode: Entry to hybrid mode fails.

FDDI-II stations maintain a number of parameters and timers to help recover from errors. One such timer is the **valid sequence timer** (**TVS**). Whenever a station changes the ring to the hybrid mode from the basic mode or vice versa, all existing cycles and frames on the ring must be removed. This is done using TVS. The timer is initialized to a value equal to the maximum latency for a cycle to go around the ring (parameter T_Hold) and all frames or cycles received are removed for this duration. Incidentally, this process of cleaning the stale frames or cycles from the ring is called **ring scrubbing**. TVS is also used for scrubbing stale cycle sequence numbers as described later in this section.

Another timer called the **new sequence timer** (**TNS**) is used to control latching of sequence numbers. Whenever a station detects an unexpected sequence number change or a new sequence number, it sets TNS to expire after the T_Hold interval. No new sequence numbers are accepted when this timer is active. During hybrid mode initialization, FDDI-II stations go through a number of state changes. TNS is used to ensure that the initialization proceeds normally. This is done by resetting TNS to expire after a certain timeout interval on all state changes except the final (master) state. If TNS expires and the state has not changed, an error is suspected and a recovery procedure is started.

These mechanisms are used for recovery from various types of errors as follows:

1. *Corrupted Cycle Starting Delimiter*: Each cycle begins with a starting delimiter of J-K. If this delimiter is corrupted by a transmission error, the cycle is not recognized by the next station on the path. When the cycle is not seen within six symbols of the preamble (parameter PA_max), a cycle error is signaled to the cycle control. Monitor stations have a Boolean parameter called a **sustain flag**. On a cycle error, a monitor station with the sustain flag set will begin to source a new cycle. This helps to maintain the hybrid mode synchronization even though all the data in the corrupted cycle are lost.
2. *False Starting Delimiter*: If a J-K pair is created by transmission error, it may falsely be taken to begin a new cycle. To avoid this possibility, a cycle-holding mode (cycle line state) has been introduced in PHY. In this mode, any J-K symbols seen during the cycle are reported as violations and the symbol boundary is not changed. However, the cycle-holding mode is cleared. The cycle-holding mode is resumed when the next valid cycle is seen.

   When not in the cycle-holding mode, all J-K pairs are reported as starting delimiters. Thus, if a second J-K pair is created during the same cycle, it can potentially start a new cycle. The probability of this happening is very small.
3. *Error in Cycle Control Symbols*: If control symbols C1 or C2 are affected by noise and are not received as R or S, they are reported as R symbols. Some combinations, for example, J-K-R-R, may cause the hybrid mode to be reinitialized. The interpretation of resulting C1-C2 combinations and subsequent actions was described earlier in Table 13.1.
4. *Error in Cycle Sequence Number*: The cycles are numbered sequentially from 64 to 255. Mathematically, after cycle number n, the next expected cycle number is $64 + [(n+1-64) \bmod 192]$. Each station computes the next cycle number and compares it with the sequence number in the received cycle. If they do not match, a cycle sequence error is reported, the C2 flag in the cycle is set to R, and the number received is latched in as n for future cycle number computation.

   If the sequence number field in one cycle is affected by noise, that cycle and the cycle following it will be reported to have incorrect sequence numbers. After that the operation will resume as normal. On the other hand, if the cycle master malfunctions and starts generating random sequence numbers, the cycle sequence error will continue for some time, causing TVS and TNS timers to expire. At this point, a monitor station will begin the monitor contention by transmitting cycles with C1-C2 fields set to RR and the CS field set to its rank. A new cycle master is elected and operation continues.

5. *Error in Programming Template*: The 16 symbols of the programming template indicate the service to which the WBCs have been assigned. An R symbol indicates packet service, while an S symbol indicates isochronous service. A T symbol is used to indicate that the channel is unassigned.

   An error in a programming template can cause the data for one service to be delivered to another service or be lost totally. FDDI-II rules for handling programming template symbols that are received as neither R nor S are as follows. If the channel was previously assigned to the packet service or if the channel was not assigned, the symbol is replaced by T; otherwise it is replaced by S. The goal of this set of rules is to avoid delivering spurious (extra) data to the packet channel where it can cause undetected errors.

   Considering the possibility that the channel assignment may have been changed for this cycle, this set of rules for handling programming template errors can lead to the nine possible cases as listed in Table 13.3. The resulting effect is also listed in the table. Notice that the extra data delivered to an isochronous channel do not cause any problem since no I-MAC will pick up that data. Losing isochronous data can also be detected since the I-MAC expecting data in that channel will realize the loss. Losing packet data can cause undetected errors. This may be considered serious in some applications since a single noise event can cause 96 bytes of the data to be lost without any indication.

6. *Late Token in the Packet Data Channel*: If the token is not received in time, there are two possibilities: either the token has been lost or some station held it longer than the rules allow. The second condition would occur if some station uses a larger value of TTRT than the others. In either case, if the stations were to use the claim process to reestablish the TTRT and recreate the token, the isochronous service would be interrupted. To avoid this interruption, FDDI-II uses a special procedure, the **purge process**, to reestablish quickly the TTRT and recreate the token without leaving the hybrid mode.

   The dictionary meaning of the term *purge* is to purify. During the purge process, the cycle master purifies the ring by stripping the incoming symbols and continuously transmitting a special

Table 13.3 Effect of Template Errors in FDDI-II

Previous Assignment	Possible New Assignment	New Symbol	Inter-pretation	Effect
Isochronous	Packet	S	Isochronous	96 bytes are lost from the packet channel.
	Isochronous	S	Isochronous	No error.
	None	S	Isochronous	Extra 96 bytes are delivered to the isochronous channel.
Packet	Packet	T	None	96 bytes are lost from the packet channel.
	Isochronous	T	None	96 bytes are lost from the isochronous channel.
	None	T	None	No error.
None	Packet	T	None	96 bytes are lost from the packet channel.
	Isochronous	T	None	96 bytes are lost from the isochronous channel.
	None	T	None	No error.

MAC frame called a **purge frame** in the packet channel. These frames contain the correct TTRT value and are interpreted by other stations on the ring as "Please reset your TTRT to the value specified in this frame." When the frames return to the cycle master, the ring has been purged and the cycle master issues a new token. At the end of the purge process, all stations have the same TTRT value. If the cause of the previous token loss was excessive noise somewhere on the ring, the token may be lost again soon. If this happens the stations return to the basic mode and enter the claim process.

The purge frame follows the MAC frame format specified in Section 2.3. The frame-control (FC) field is set to $1L00\text{-}r100_2$, where L indicates the length of the address field (0 = 16 bits, 1 = 48 bits) and r is reserved, which means that r is transmitted as zero but either value (zero or one) is accepted on receive. The source address contains the address of the transmitter (cycle master). The destination address also contains the same address. The information field contains only the TTRT value and its CRC.

7. *Cycle Clock Too Fast or Slow*: The cycle master uses a cycle clock to generate cycles every 125 μs. This clock may be derived from the bit clock or may be obtained from an external source. If the cycle clock runs too slow, the cycles may not be received in time. The slave stations treat this case in a manner similar to that of the corrupted cycle starting delimiter discussed earlier in this section. A monitor station with the sustain flag set will source a new cycle with cycle-control C1-C2 set to RR. However, if this happens repeatedly, the valid sequence timer (TVS) will expire and the monitor will start a monitor contention process to select a cycle master and reestablish synchronization.

   If the cycle clock runs too fast, the cycles will be received early. This case is treated in a manner similar to that of a false cycle starting delimiter. Again, repeated occurrence will cause TVS expiry and reinitialization.
8. *Failure to Establish the Hybrid Mode*: The FDDI-II stations time every stage of the hybrid mode initialization. If any process does not complete within a reasonable time-out period, the stations inform their SMT and return to the basic mode. The most likely cause is the presence of an FDDI-I station. Network management procedures may be used to determine the exact cause. After the source of the problem is removed, the initialization of the hybrid mode may be attempted again.

To summarize, most common errors and faults are easily detected and recovered by FDDI-II.

13.12 Hybrid Multiplexer (H-MUX)

The hybrid multiplexer is a new component of FDDI-II stations. It multiplexes and demultiplexes the packet-switched and circuit-switched traffic on the ring. In this section, we describe the the structure and operation of an H-MUX.

The H-MUX consists of four processes that share several common variables in the station but otherwise operate asynchronously. These processes are shown in Figure 13.10. Their functions are as follows:

1. *Cycle Acquisition Process*: This process monitors the incoming stream and identifies cycles and MAC frames. For cycles, it checks the cycle-control and sequence fields. The valid cycles are broken into a packet data channel and isochronous stream using the programming template. This process is present in all (monitor and nonmonitor) FDDI-II stations.

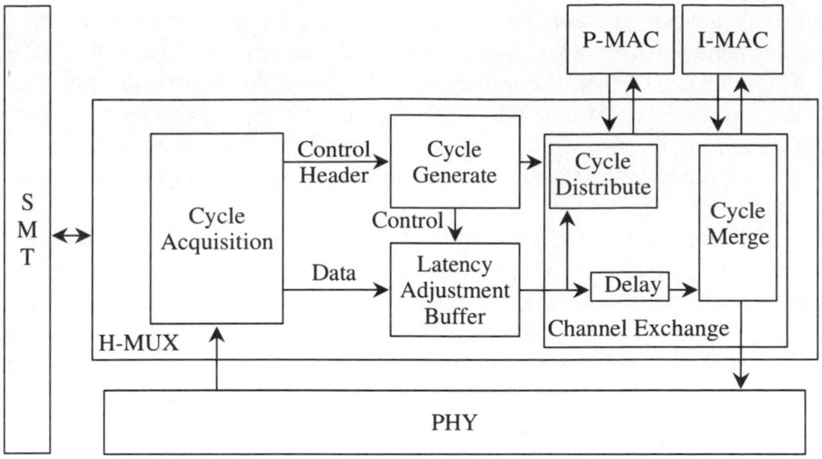

Figure 13.10 Components of a hybrid multiplexer.

2. *Cycle Generation Process*: This process, which is present only in monitor stations, determines the cycle header to be transmitted in the outgoing cycles. It generates the new cycle-control field, cycle sequence, and programming template. The new header is passed to the channel exchange process.

   The cycle generation process also generates the 8-kHz (125-μs) timing signal used for outgoing cycles. In the cycle master, this signal is based on a local clock or on an external timing reference source. In slave stations, the signal is obtained from the received cycles.
3. *Latency Adjustment Buffer* (*LAB*): This buffer ensures that the *isochronous* data take an integral multiple of 125 μs to travel around the ring. Although all monitor stations have a latency adjustment buffer and are allowed to engage them, only the cycle master normally engages it.

   The size of the latency adjustment buffer should be greater than one cycle (1562.5 bytes). This ensures that no overflow or underflow will occur as the ring latency changes due to PHY delay variation.

   Since the buffer introduces a delay in the path, the packet data are allowed to bypass LAB. The packet data are transmitted on the first available position on the outgoing cycle.

   Nonmonitor stations do not have LAB.
4. *Channel Exchange Process*: This is where the data originating at this station and that received from the ring are merged (multiplexed) and separated (demultiplexed). The packet data stream is passed to P-MAC, which returns the new symbols for this stream. The data corresponding to WBCs open at this station are passed to the I-MAC. These two functions are accomplished by means of a subprocess called **cycle distribute**. The cycle distribute process keeps a map of isochronous WBC slots available for this station.

   Another subprocess called **cycle merge** combines the remaining data with the data incoming from the P-MAC and I-MAC. Since the paths through the MACs introduce delay, a small delay is inserted in the path of the remaining data.

   The channel exchange process is present in all stations.

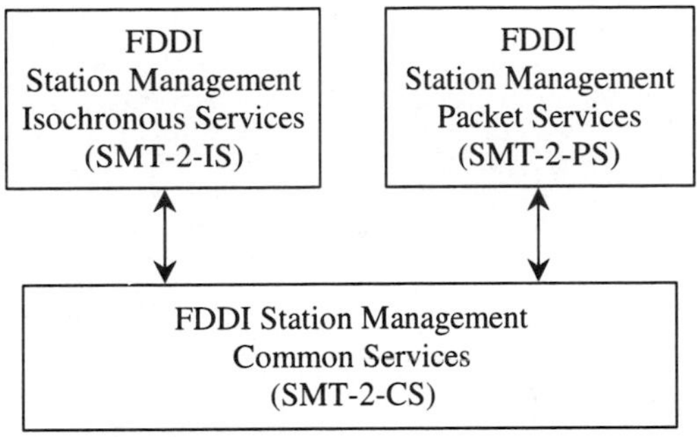

Figure 13.11 Component documents of SMT-2.

Notice that various components of the incoming cycle follow a different path in H-MUX and finally merge again. The control of which component goes where is divided into three different processes. The cycle acquisition process determines the location of the incoming data streams, the cycle generation process determines the location of the outgoing data streams, and the channel exchange process determines which symbols in the WBCs are used at this station.

13.13 Extensions to Station Management (SMT-2)

Introduction of FDDI-II has necessitated a change in MAC, PHY, and SMT standards. The changes in MAC and PHY have become stable and substantial enough to deserve separate chapters. Changes in SMT are still being discussed.

Since SMT was already the largest document among all FDDI standards and the added isochronous services would add to it considerably, SMT-2 has been organized into three separate documents:

1. *SMT Packet Services* (*SMT-2-IS*): This document describes facilities (including services, objects, attributes, and protocols) required to manage the isochronous media access controller (I-MAC).
2. *SMT Isochronous Services* (*SMT-2-PS*): This document describes facilities required to manage the packet media access controller (MAC).
3. *SMT Common Services* (*SMT-2-CS*): This document covers management facilities required to configure an FDDI topology and to produce a common channel that can be used by both packet and isochronous services.

Figure 13.11 shows the three parts of the SMT-2 and the relationship between them.

Figure 13.12 shows the SMT-2 management objects and the relationship among them. Note its similarity to Figure 10.2. The goal of the committee is to be as similar to SMT as possible.

13.14 Summary

FDDI-II is another version of FDDI. Both FDDI-I and FDDI-II run at 100 Mbps. FDDI-I supports asynchronous and synchronous traffic. Although the access time for synchronous traffic is bounded, it

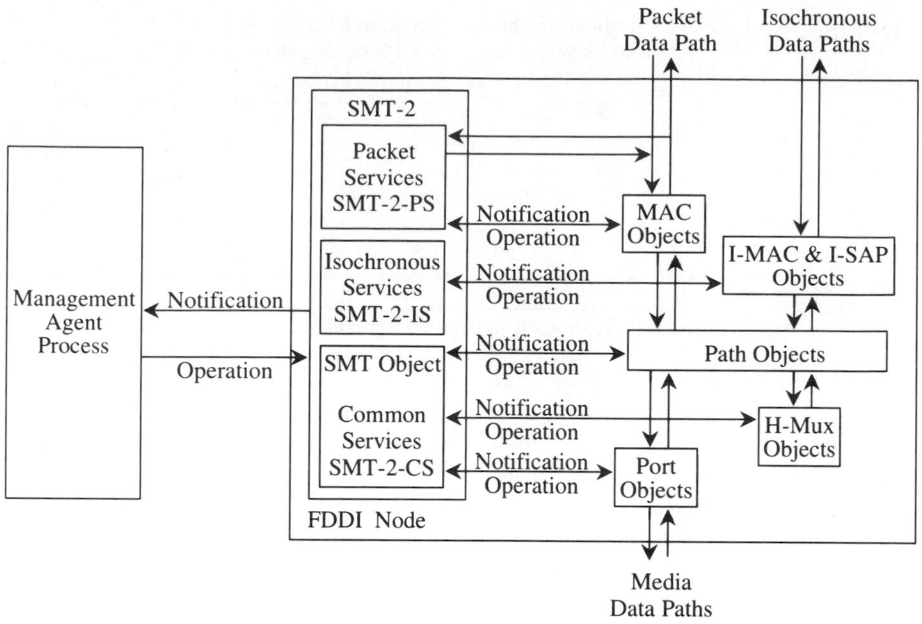

Figure 13.12 SMT-2 management model.

varies with the load on the network. Also, the access time cannot be less than the ring latency. FDDI-II provides all the services of FDDI-I, but adds support for constant bit rate, periodic, and circuit-switched traffic. This is called isochronous service, which means that the application is guaranteed to get n bits every T seconds or some multiple of T seconds.

FDDI-II has chosen a period of 125 μs for isochronous traffic. Thus, any applications requiring 8 kbps (1 bit per 125 μs) or any multiple of this can be easily supported. This matches well with telecommunication networks, which also use this interval. Note that SMT-2 will allocate a minimum of 64 kbps (1 byte per 125 μs) bandwidth to a station. The station can then submultiplex it if desired.

In FDDI-II, a cycle master station continuously generates cycles of 125 μs. The entire bandwidth is divided into 16 wideband channels of 6.144 Mbps each. Some channels are reserved for circuit-switching (isochronous) traffic, while others can be used for packet-switching (asynchronous and synchronous) traffic.

Stations using circuit switching have allocated positions in the cycle that are reserved for their use. Bytes allocated for one circuit cannot be shared or used by any other circuit.

FDDI-II stations run in two different modes: basic or hybrid. In basic mode, their operation is identical to that of FDDI-I stations and only packet-switched traffic is allowed on the ring. During the hybrid mode, a mixture of packet-switched and circuit-switched traffic is allowed.

Stations using packet switching share the bytes allocated for packet channels using the same timed token mechanism used in FDDI-I. However, the bytes do not arrive contiguously. Therefore, the physical layer (PHY) and media access control (MAC) components have to be specially designed for intermittent operation.

Requiring new MAC and PHY functionality implies that all nodes on the ring must have FDDI-II adapters (controllers) even if only one or two stations want to use isochronous traffic. If someone inserts a node with FDDI-I hardware on the ring, the ring will not enter the hybrid mode; it will operate only in the basic mode.

In terms of protocol components, FDDI-I stations have PMD, PHY, MAC, SMT, and LLC components. In addition to these FDDI-II stations have a hybrid ring controller, which multiplexes and demultiplexes packet-switched and circuit-switched streams to/from the bits received from the medium. FDDI-II stations requiring isochronous service also have one or more isochronous MACs (I-MACs) and a circuit-switching multiplexer (CS-MUX).

FDDI-II stations are of two classes: monitor and nonmonitor. Monitor stations have the special hardware required to become cycle masters and generate cycles. Nonmonitor stations are simpler and do not have this extra hardware. Each ring should have at least one monitor station. Each monitor station has a rank assigned to it. The station with the highest rank is selected as the cycle master.

The station management for new components introduced in FDDI-II is being developed.

Like FDDI-I, FDDI-II is also designed with automatic fault detection, isolation, and recovery mechanisms.

13.15 Further Reading and Historical Notes

The idea of cycles to allow isochronous traffic was proposed by Robert Grow to the FDDI Committee in September 1983. In his proposal, called "suspend/resume," he suggested that the isochronous traffic can be embedded in the normal packet stream using special control symbols to indicate the beginning and the end of isochronous data. This proposal was rejected by the FDDI committee. In January 1985, Gary Nelson made a proposal "FDDI Hybrid Ring Proposal" to the FDDI committee. This forms the basis of the current wideband channel approach.

The hybrid ring control is specified in ANSI X3.186-199x or ISO/IEC DIS 9314-5. SMT-2 is being specified in ASC X3T9.5/92-297, ASC X3T9.5/92-298, and ASC X3T9.5/92-299. See also Sections 14.10 and 15.12 for MAC-2 and PHY-2 documents.

Caves and Flatman (1986), Caves (1987), Boston (1988), Teener and Gvozdanovic (1989), Calvo and Teener (1990), and Ross (1991b) provide an overview of FDDI-II. Hills (1991) describes several issues in implementing an FDDI-II adapter.

13.16 Self-Test Exercises

Note: Some exercises have multiple correct answers. See Appendix D for answers.

13.1 What is the nominal data rate of FDDI-II?

a. 100 Mbps
b. 200 Mbps
c. 155.52 Mbps
d. 622.08 Mbps

13.2 Which of the following traffic can be supported only by FDDI-II (but not by FDDI)?

a. Audio
b. Video
c. Traffic requiring strict periodic access
d. All of the above

13.3 What needs to be changed to upgrade an existing FDDI network to FDDI-II?

a. Adapters in those stations that need FDDI-II service
b. Adapters in all stations
c. Those concentrators that are connected to FDDI-II stations
d. All concentrators
e. Wiring

13.4 What is the role of monitor stations in FDDI-II?

a. They serve as network management stations (NMS).
b. Like a concentrator, they provide connection to other stations.
c. They generate cycles.
d. They have the capability to generate cycles.

13.5 Which station is selected as cycle master in FDDI-II?

a. The station with the highest address
b. The station that wins the claim process
c. The monitor with the highest rank
d. The monitor that wins the claim process

13.6 What is the nominal bandwidth of each wideband channel in FDDI-II?

a. 1.544 Mbps
b. 4 Mbps
c. 6.144 Mbps
d. 10 Mbps
e. 16 Mbps
f. 51.480 Mbps

13.7 Which symbol pair is used as a frame starting delimiter during the hybrid mode in FDDI-II?

a. J-K
b. I-I
c. I-L
d. I-J

CHAPTER **14**

Enhanced Media Access Control: MAC-2

14.1 Overview

With the development of the FDDI-II standard, it became evident that the media access control (MAC) rules described in Chapter 2 needed to be updated. Therefore, a working group to produce a new version of the MAC standard called MAC-2 was formed. The MAC-2 standard includes several other changes that were agreed on since the publication of the MAC standard and for support of bridging.

In this chapter, several FDDI-II terms such as *cycle master*, *basic mode*, and *hybrid mode* are used. It is assumed that you have already read the chapter on FDDI-II. If you have not, please read at least the first few sections of Chapter 13 before proceeding further. Also, the notations MAC-1, PHY-1, FDDI-I are used to distinguish earlier versions of protocol components from later ones.

There are four key changes in MAC-2 compared to the MAC standard. First, new frames types and facilities have been defined to provide packet mode transmission for FDDI-II. The changes relate to the use of purge frames. All parameter values have been recomputed to allow for basic and hybrid modes of operation. Second, rules related to bridging of two or more networks have been incorporated. These relate to the setting of status indicators, stripping of frames, and handling of source-routing information. Third, a number of changes in MAC that were agreed on earlier by the standards committee have also been included. Among these changes are enhanced frame validity criteria, monitoring of restricted dialogs, and additional information in beacon frames. Finally, a few new counters that help in fault location and diagnostics have been added. Further details of these changes are the subject of this chapter.

14.2 FDDI-II Support

The main modification related to FDDI-II support is that of updating all parameters and descriptions to allow for the hybrid mode operation. The parameter value computation is discussed in detail in Section 14.8.

Another modification to support hybrid mode operation is the introduction of a new frame class called *purge frames*. As explained earlier in Section 13.11, the FDDI-II stations minimize interruptions to the isochronous service due to problems in the packet data channel. On a late or lost token, instead of using the claim process, the stations first attempt to use the purge process. The purge frames used in the process have a frame control of $1L00\text{-}r100_2$. Here, L is 1 or 0 depending on the length of the addresses used in the frame—1 for 48-bit addresses and 0 for 16-bit addresses. The fifth bit "r" is reserved for future standardization. It is transmitted as 0. However, since MAC-1 assigns a code with r = 1 for next station addressing (NSA) frames (FC = 0L00 1111), MAC-2 allows the bit to be transmitted as 1 in NSA frames in the basic mode (for backward compatibility). In the hybrid mode, backward compatibility is not an issue and the fifth bit must be zero (even in NSA frames). On receipt both 1 and 0 are accepted.

14.3 Bridge Support

Bridges allow multiple local area networks (LANs) to be interconnected to form an extended LAN. Although MAC-1 supports bridging, there was no explicit discussion of bridging issues in it. These issues were later discussed in a bridging working group and are now incorporated in MAC-2. MAC-2 addresses the following four bridging issues:

1. Which frames should be forwarded from the FDDI ring to other networks forming the extended LAN?
2. How should the bridges recognize and strip the frames that they forward on an FDDI ring?
3. How do source-routing bridges recognize and strip their frames?
4. Which frame status indicators do the bridges set on frames they copy from the ring for forwarding?

The bridge stripping issue was discussed in Section 2.11. The source address independent stripping method described in that section has now been included in MAC-2. The status indicator issue is discussed in Sections 14.3.1 and 14.4. The issue of which frames to forward is discussed next.

Consider a simple extended LAN consisting of two FDDI rings connected by a bridge. The bridge keeps track of the location of various stations and if it finds frames on ring 1 addressed to any station on ring 2, it copies the frame from ring 1 and transmits it on ring 2. However, just looking at the destination address is not sufficient to determine if the bridge should copy the frame. Several classes of frames, particularly those relating to the management and operation of the ring, must not cross the bridge. These classes include void frames, tokens, all SMT frames, and MAC frames (beacon, claim, purge). All of these classes are distinguished by the fact that the third and fourth bits in the frame control are 00. These bits are called *format bits*. The other three possibilities for the format bits are 01 (LLC frames), 10 (implementor-defined frames), and 11 (reserved). These other frames may be forwarded by the bridges depending on the destination address or source-routing fields. The frames with format bits of 00 are never forwarded by the bridges and should never have any source-routing field.

14.3.1 Source Routing

Bridges interconnecting two or more LANs have to determine on which LAN, if any, the frame should be forwarded. They can do so by observing the traffic on various LANs and keeping track of the source addresses in the frames. For example, if a bridge sees a frame from station A coming in

Preamble	Starting Delimiter	Frame Control	Destination Address	Source Address	
4+	2	2	12	12	← Size in Symbols

Routing Information	Info	Frame Check Sequence	Ending Delimiter	Frame Status
0-60		8	1	3+

Figure 14.1 Source-routing frame format.

from LAN L, all frames going to station A on other LANs can be forwarded on LAN L. This form of forwarding is called **transparent bridging**.

Another alternative is for the source of the frame to specify the complete route to the destination. It could indicate the sequence of bridges that should pick up and forward the frame. For example, if the route is A-B-C-D, the frame is destined to address D, via bridges A, B, and C. This form of bridging is called **source routing**.

The key philosophical difference between followers of source routing and transparent bridging is which component should be kept simple. Transparent bridging followers argue that the end-systems are numerous and should be kept simple, while the bridges can do all the extra work required to find paths. Source-routing followers argue that most end systems talk only to a few other end-systems and can easily remember or find paths to these and so the bridges should be kept simple.

Since the source of a frame is always an individual station, the individual/group bit in the source address field should always be zero. In this sense, this bit has no information. This realization lead to its use as a source-routing indicator. That is, if the individual/group bit in the source address field of a frame is 1, a routing-information field of length up to 30 bytes (60 symbols) follows the source address as shown in Figure 14.1. Stations not implementing source routing ignore the first bit of the source address and use the address as if the first (individual/group) bit was 0 and hence not confuse it as a group address. In other words, the first bit of the address is an individual/group or transparent/source-routing bit. In the destination address field, it indicates individual or group, while in the source address field, it indicates transparent or source-routing bridging. The source-routing information, if used, immediately follows the source address field. This convention was developed during the development of the IEEE 802.5/token rings and is now used on all IEEE 802 networks and on FDDI.

Up until 1991, most bridges on IEEE 802.5/token ring LANs were source-routing bridges, while those on IEEE 802.3/Ethernet LANs were transparent bridges. As a result, nodes on the two types of LANs could not communicate easily. This problem led to the invention of source-routing transparent or **SRT** bridges, which provide both source-routing and transparent bridging services. Figure 14.2 shows a schematic of such a bridge. The action taken by the SRT bridge depends on the value of the RII bit. In 1991, the IEEE 802.1d MAC bridge standard added the requirement that all bridges be either TB or SRT. That is, all bridges must provide the transparent service. SRT bridges additionally provide the source-routing service. This requirement ensures that all nodes on an extended LAN connected via bridges can communicate with each other. See Section 21.3 for further discussion on this topic.

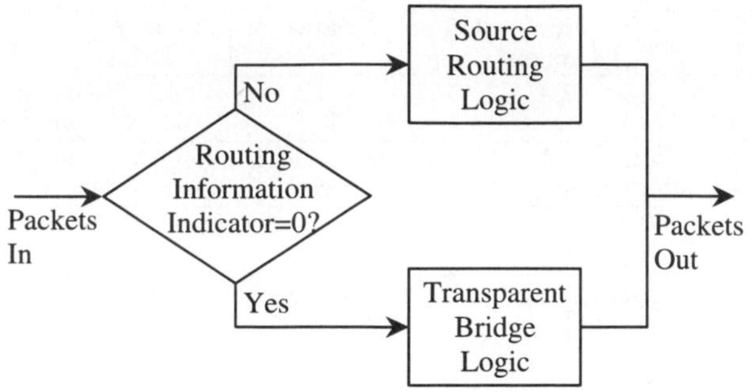

Figure 14.2 Schematic of an SRT bridge.

14.3.2 Stripped Fragment Length

Most stations remove (strip) their frames based on source addresses. A small fragment consisting of the starting delimiter, destination address, source address, and a few more bytes is left on the ring. Long fragments can turn into valid frames by noise. It is, therefore, desirable to keep these stripped frame fragments as small as possible. In the case of the source-routing bridges, the bridge may have to look at all 30 bytes of the routing information field before it can be sure if it transmitted the frame on the ring. The fragments may, therefore, be longer. MAC-2 standard sets a limit of six symbols after the source address on the stripped fragments. This limit was reached as a compromise between source-routing proponents, who wanted 30 bytes after the source address, and opponents, who wanted to keep it right at the source address. The six-symbol limit forces source-routing bridges also to use the source address independent stripping method.

14.4 Frame Status Indicators and Bridges

FDDI frames contain three or more frame status indicators. These are error-detected (E), address-recognized (A), and copied (C) indicators. The meaning and use of these frames was explained earlier in Section 2.4. Normally, destination stations set the A- and C-indicators to convey that they did recognize their address and that they copied the frame successfully. If the indicators are not set, the source may take some corrective action such as retransmission at a later time.

The meaning and use of these indicators in a bridged environment is not straightforward. There was considerable discussion between the transparent bridge and source-routing bridge camps. Transparent bridges typically copy all frames from the ring and later decide which frame to forward to other networks. The transparent bridge camp argued that the bridges should be allowed to copy and forward frames without setting the A-indicator; otherwise, a transparent bridge may have to set the A-indicator on almost all frames. The only other alternative for them is to use a fast address lookup algorithm using expensive content addressable memories (CAMs). Source-routing bridges can set the A-indicator more reliably since only the bridge that is on the route will pick up the frame. However, the indicator is based on the status at the time the source-route was set up.

How can a bridge set the indicators to the same values that the destination station would have set if it were on the same ring as the source? Consider the simple two-ring bridged extended LAN

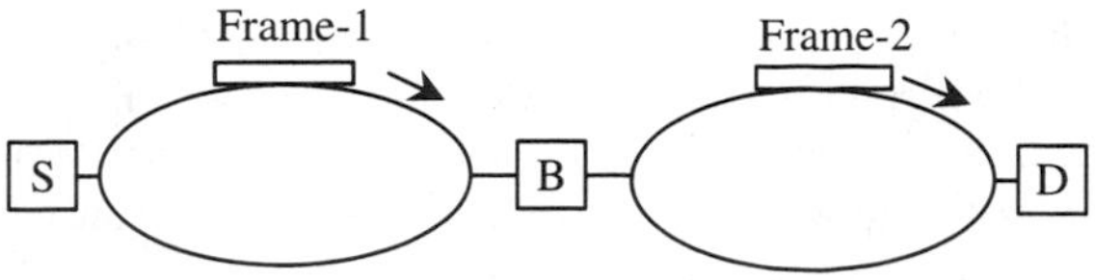

Figure 14.3 Two LANs connected via a bridge.

shown in Figure 14.3. Station S on ring 1 transmits a frame to station D on ring 2. The bridge copies the frame from ring 1 and forwards it on ring 2. Let us call these two incarnations of the same information frame-1 and frame-2. If D runs out of buffer, it will not set the C-indicator on frame-2. By the time the bridge learns about the problem, frame-1 has already left the bridge with the C-indicator set. The source would assume that the frame has been successfully delivered when in fact it has not been. Similarly, if the destination suddenly withdraws from the network, the A-indicator on frame-2 will be left reset. But the source would think that the destination is still on the network. The summary of this discussion is that frame status indicators on a bridged network indicate only one-hop status and not the end-to-end status of the frame delivery. To ensure end-to-end delivery, higher layer (such as LLC or transport layer) mechanisms are required. This leads one into a classic end-to-end versus hop-by-hop debate, which we do not wish to enter here.

As a result of this debate, the MAC-2 standard now specifies two different status setting policies. Source-routing bridges set the A- and C-indicators if they recognize the address and copy the frame for forwarding just as if its address had appeared in the DA field. Any bridge that implements this policy is called a **MAC status setting** (**MSS**) bridge. Transparent bridges repeat the A- and C-indicators as received. Bridges implementing this policy are called **MAC status repeating** (**MSR**) bridges.

If a transparent bridge implements a fast address lookup function (for example, using content addressable memory) so that it copies those and only those frames that it can forward, it can *optionally* set the C-indicator but not the A-indicator. If the transparent bridge does discard frames after copying them from the ring, the bridge cannot use this option; it simply repeats the indicators as received.

The "Set C but not A" option causes a problem if the destination station happens to be on the ring but not known to the bridge. If the frame reaches the bridge before the destination station, the bridge may copy the frame, set the C-indicator, and leave the A-indicator reset. Later, when the frame reaches the destination, it recognizes its own address and sets the A-indicator. However, if the station is unable to copy the frame, it should *clear* the C-indicator. This may be a problem for some implementations since stations do not normally reset indicators on frames originating at other stations. This ability of a station to clear the C-indicator is called **MAC status clearing** (**MSC**) capability and is optional.

14.5 SMT Group Addresses

Setting status indicators on multicast frames poses a problem for all stations similar to that faced by transparent bridges in recognizing destination addresses. Normally stations listen to numerous group addresses. Some stations use expensive content addressable memories (CAMs) to look up and recognize group addresses in real time before the end of the frame. Others copy all or some selected (by a hash) multicast frames and later drop those in which they are not interested. As a result, correctly setting the A- and C-status indicators on multicast frames is not always possible. In MAC-2, a station is not allowed to set the A-indicator on partially filtered multicast frames. It can set the indicater only on a precise match, that is, if it is sure that it listens to the group address specified. SMT frames cannot be partially filtered. All stations, therefore, implement SMT group address recognition in hardware. For this reason, some companies wanted the SMT group addresses to be bit-significant and have a format similar to functional addresses. This proposal was obviously unacceptable to others who wanted the group addresses to have a flat format. A compromise was reached by making SMT group addresses have a format in which just 4 bits need to be examined and used as an index into a 16-entry mask. All SMT group addresses have the following bit pattern:

1000 0000 0000 0001 0100 0011 0000 0000 1000 0000 0000 xxxx

The first 44 bits are fixed. Only the last four bits (xxxx) are different among various SMT group addresses. The stations keep a 16-bit mask. The bits corresponding to the addresses to be received are set while others are clear. If the first 44 bits of an address have the bit pattern shown here, the last 4 bits are used as an index into the mask. If the corresponding mask bit is set, the frame is received and the address-recognized indicator is set. Notice that the bit pattern shown corresponds to a hexadecimal canonical form of 01-80-C2-00-01-X0. A list of SMT group addresses is given in Table 10.1.

14.6 Other Corrections

MAC-2 incorporates several changes to provide more information about the status of the network than that obtainable with MAC-1. Such changes relate to the contents of beacon frames and a few new counters. These changes are described in this section.

1. *Beacon Frames*: Beacon frames are sent whenever a station suspects any malfunction in the network. In MAC-2, beacon frames have a 4-byte information field indicating the beacon type, receiver condition, last frame's frame-control field, and late count. Only one beacon type (00_{16}) indicating an unsuccessful claim has been assigned in MAC-2. Two other types, directed beacon (01_{16}) and jam beacon (02_{16}), are defined in the SMT standard. The second byte indicates whether the valid transmission timer (TVX) has expired and also the state of the MAC receiver at the time it started beaconing. The third byte contains the frame-control value from the last frame received. The fourth byte contains the count of number of times the token rotation time exceeded the maximum token rotation time (T_Max). These additional fields in the beacon frame help a network manager diagnose the cause of disruption.
2. *Frame Validity Criteria*: In the pre-1987 draft of the MAC standard, stations were allowed to restore a lost error indicator as R in the frames if the frame passed the cyclic redundancy check (CRC). This was shown to cause an increase in the undetected error rate (see Chapter 25) and, therefore, a footnote was added to the published MAC-1 standard indicating that the intermediate stations were not allowed to reset any frame status indicators. In MAC-2 this has been moved from the footnote to the main text of the frame validity criteria. The only exception is the MSC option (discussed in Section 14.4) in which stations are allowed to reset the C-indicator in frames addressed to them if they are unable to copy the frame.

When a received frame is found invalid, the MAC indicates this to the higher layers. The reason for invalidity is also indicated. The reasons include invalid frame check sequence, invalid length, E-indicator set or missing, and errors occurring after successful reception.

3. *Restricted Dialog*: The restricted asynchronous transmission mode in the MAC-1 standard allows stations to reserve the token for a long transmission. During this mode other asynchronous transmission is withheld. This provision causes a problem if the station starting the restricted mode malfunctions and does not finish the restricted conversation. To prevent this possibility, MAC-2 now allows any station to interrupt a restricted dialog if it exceeds beyond a threshold set by the network manager. The default value of this threshold is zero. Thus, unless specifically changed by the network manager, restricted dialogs are terminated after the first cycle of transmission. As soon as any station sees a restricted token, it starts a restricted dialog timer. If a nonrestricted token is not seen before this timer expires, the station reinitializes the ring using the claim process.

14.7 New Counters

FDDI stations maintain a number of counters that help determine the traffic and status of the ring. The counters required in MAC-1 were total number of frames received (Frame_ct), number of frames in which an error was detected at this station (Error_ct), number of frames that were lost due to an error at this station (Lost_ct), and the number of times a token was received late (Late_ct). These counters have already been discussed in Section 2.7. MAC-2 has the following additional counters:

- *Token Counter*: A count is kept of the number of times the token is received. This helps determine an average token rotation time (TRT):

$$\text{Average token rotation time} = \frac{\text{Time interval}}{\text{Token count}}$$

  Under no load, the token rotation time is equal to the ring latency D, while under full load, it is equal to the TTRT. Thus, the token counter (Token_ct) is helpful in determining the utilization of the ring. This is explained further in Section 24.2.
- *TVX Expired Counter*: The valid transmission timer (TVX) is used to detect loss of the token and very high frame error rate. The default value of TVX in MAC-2 is 2.5 ms in the basic mode and 3.6 ms in the hybrid mode. If no valid frames or tokens are seen during this interval, the timer expires and the ring is reinitialized. A count of TVX timer expiry events (TVX_Expired_ct) is kept at various stations. If too many ring initializations are seen during a short interval, the TVX expired count may help the network manager determine the cause of the problem. Note that a high expired count does not necessarily mean a mulfunctioning station. Given two stations with different TVX values, the station with the shorter TVX interval will generally time out more often than the other.
- *Frames Copied*: Each station keeps a count (Copied_ct) of the frames successfully copied from the ring. This count does not include the void frames or MAC frames (for example, claim frames). This count can be used to determine the receive frame rate at the station.
- *Frames Transmitted*: A count is kept of the frames transmitted by the station. This count includes only those frames (or service data units) whose transmission was requested by other protocol components such as SMT and LLC. It does not include the frames generated internally by

Table 14.1 MAC-2 Counters and Their Applications

Name	Meaning	Application
Late_ct	Late token arrival	Ring initialization
TVX_Expired_ct	TVX expiration	Fault determination
Token_ct	Token count	Determining ring utilization
Frame_ct	Frame count	Scaling Error_ct and Lost_ct
Error_ct	CRC errors detected	Fault prediction and location
Lost_ct	Frames lost due to errors	Fault prediction and location
Copied_ct	Frames copied	Throughput at the station
Transmit_ct	Frames transmitted	Throughput of the station
Not_Copied_ct	Frames not copied	Determining station receiver congestion

the MAC, such as the void frames, claim frames, purge frames, or beacon frames. This count (Transmit_ct) helps in determining the transmit frame rate of this station.

- *Frames Not Copied*: Sometimes a station is unable to copy a frame due to shortage of buffers. Often this happens if a long burst of frames is sent to the same destination. The stations keep a count of such frames. Again, the count (Not_Copied_ct) does not include the void frames, MAC frames, or frames generated by this station. This count is helpful in determining the congestion at the station.

Table 14.1 summarizes all the MAC-2 counters and their applications.

14.8 Relationships Among Timing Parameters

FDDI protocol and hardware is designed such that the number of stations, frame size, interstation distance, and total extent of the ring can be easily extended by suitably adjusting timers and parameters. Default timer and parameter values have been set so that most users can run their network without any changes. Nonetheless, it is helpful to know how these default values were set so that you can change these parameters if necessary. In this section, we explain a number of important parameters.[1]

- *Minimum Starting Delimiter Delay* (SD_Min): FDDI as well as other token ring protocols impose a lower bound on the delay introduced by a station. This ensures that the token transmission and reception conditions do not happen simultaneously at a station, otherwise the station will

[1] All limits and parameter values stated in this section are default values. These values have been used in the calculation of default values of other parameters and timers. If the manufacturers and the users conform to these limits, the network should operate satisfactorily without any need to change any parameter values. These are not absolute limits. If you exceed these limits, you have to recompute parameter values to ensure that the network will operate satisfactorily. Throughout the standard, the word *default* is used to express this intent. For example, the standard does not say that the maximum number of MACs is 1000. Instead, it says that the maximum number of MACs is M_Max, and the default value of M_Max is 1000. Notice that M_Max is a parameter. If you set it to 2000, you have to recompute all other parameters that depend on M_Max. While the standard allows this flexibility, in practice, you may run into problems (for example, reliability in this particular case). Therefore, unless you are ready to go through the whole standard redesign (which has been done), it is best to treat these maximum and minimum limits as absolute.

be confused and think that a duplicate token exists. Thus, the latency on a minimum size ring should be more than the token size, which in the case of FDDI is 5 bytes. This includes a four-symbol preamble. Theoretically, a minimum size ring consists of two nodes of which at least one has a MAC. (There is no reason for communication if there is only one node or if there is no MAC.) Therefore, FDDI PHY specifies a minimum delay of 2 bytes (160 ns) for a port without a MAC and 3 bytes (240 ns) for a port with a MAC. Since the station delay is measured as the time for a starting delimiter (J-K) to propagate through a station, it is called the *starting delimiter delay*. The arguments presented thus far would set the minimum starting delimiter delay at 240 ns. However, in the initial stages of FDDI PHY standard development, a preliminary design showed that it was possible to design a station with a latency of 592 ns. This was, therefore, chosen as the minimum starting delimiter delay (SD_Min).

SD_Min = 0.592 μs

- *Maximum Station Delay (SD_Max)*: The delay introduced by each station affects the total ring latency. Higher ring latency reduces the efficiency of the ring. Therefore, the station delay should be kept small. The specifications for station delay have changed several times in the past. Various possibilities are as follows:

1. The delay introduced by quantization and sampling error is added to SD_Min to give the maximum starting delimiter delay (SD_Max). At that time, the need for smoothers had not been realized. Since each code bit is 8 ns, 4 ns (one-half of the code bit) were allowed for clock sampling and timing error and another 4 ns were allowed for quantization errors giving a total of 600 ns for SD_Max.

$$\begin{aligned} \text{SD\_Max} &= \text{SD\_Min} \\ &\quad + \text{Sampling and timing error} \\ &\quad + \text{Quantizing error} \\ &= 592 + 4 + 4 = 600 \text{ ns} \end{aligned}$$

   This is the station delay value specified in the approved version of the MAC-1 standard. Initial values of ring latency and other parameters were based on this value.

2. When the elasticity buffer design was completed and smoothers were later added to PHY, it was realized that the delay through a station would increase due to them. The smoother can add a maximum of two symbols, thereby limiting the smoother's contribution to 80 ns. The combined elasticity buffer and smoother quantizing error is also limited to 10 code bits or 80 ns. The maximum starting delimiter delay, therefore, became 0.756 μs:

$$\begin{aligned} \text{SD\_Max} &= \text{SD\_Min} \\ &\quad + \text{Sampling and timing error} \\ &\quad + \text{Elasticity buffer} + \text{Quantizing error} \\ &\quad + \text{Smoother latency} \\ &= 592 + 4 + 80 + 80 = 756 \text{ ns} \end{aligned}$$

   This value is specified in the final approved version of the PHY-1 standard.

3. In 1990 the National Institute of Science and Technology (NIST) surveyed a number of FDDI vendors and found that the actual station delay in FDDI stations was of the order of 1 μs. This value was, therefore, used in the Government Open Systems Interconnection Profile (GOSIP) used for U.S. government procurements. This same value was later adopted in MAC-2 as

SD_Min. The new value of SD_Max, therefore, became 1.164 μs:

$$\begin{aligned} \text{SD\_Max} = {} & \text{SD\_Min} \\ & + \text{Sampling and timing error} \\ & + \text{Elasticity buffer} + \text{Quantizing error} \\ & + \text{Smoother latency} \\ = {} & 1000 + 4 + 80 + 80 = 1164 \text{ ns} \end{aligned}$$

4. In FDDI-II stations, the data have passed through the hybrid multiplexer, which can contribute as much as 6 bytes (480 ns) of delay. Thus, the FDDI-II station delay in basic mode is 1.164 + 0.480 or 1.644 μs.
5. During hybrid mode operation of FDDI-II stations, the data pass through two smoothers (see Section 15.8). The combined smoother delay is 3 bytes (240 ns). Therefore, the SD_Max is 1.804 μs:

$$\begin{aligned} \text{SD\_Max} = {} & \text{SD\_Min} \\ & + \text{Sampling and timing error} \\ & + \text{Elasticity buffer} + \text{Quantizing error} \\ & + \text{Smoother latency} \\ & + \text{HRC latency} \\ = {} & 1000 + 4 + 80 + 240 + 480 = 1804 \text{ ns} \end{aligned}$$

Notice that these values for FDDI-II stations do not include the delay introduced by the latency adjustment buffer (LAB). Each active LAB can contribute between 16 and 144 bytes of delay to the packet data channel and up to about 2 kB times of delay to the isochronous channel. The packet data channel is allowed to bypass the LAB. In the preceding computation a delay of 12 μs (144 bytes) has been included for the LAB bypass path.

Station delay affects ring latency, which in turn affects many operational and management parameters. Therefore, you may want to determine the actual station delay of the equipment that you buy and use it in the formulas presented in this section, particularly if you are constructing very large FDDI rings.

- *Maximum Number of Ports in a Ring (P_Max)*: The PHY and PMD components together constitute a port. The maximum number of ports in a ring is limited to 1000. This was actually a design goal based on the number of stations allowed on other LANs.

  Since each dual-attachment node has two ports, an FDDI ring cannot have more than 500 dual-attachment nodes. Although, a single-attachment station has only one port, it always uses up another port (on the concentrator). Thus, the ring cannot have more than 500 single-attachment nodes either. In general, it is not possible to put any more than 500 nodes on without exceeding the P_Max. Notice that the ports used to connect the concentrators to the dual ring or to other concentrators are also counted in P_Max. For example, the FDDI ring shown in Figure 14.4 has 12 ports.
- *Maximum Number of MACs (M_Max)*: The maximum number of MACs allowed in an FDDI ring is 1000 based on the same considerations as P_Max. However, because of reliability and availability considerations, it is recommended that the actual number of stations on a ring be kept much lower than this maximum limit. It is preferable to use smaller rings connected via bridges or routers. Since the number of ports is always either equal to or more than the number of MACs, the port limit is reached much before the MAC limit.

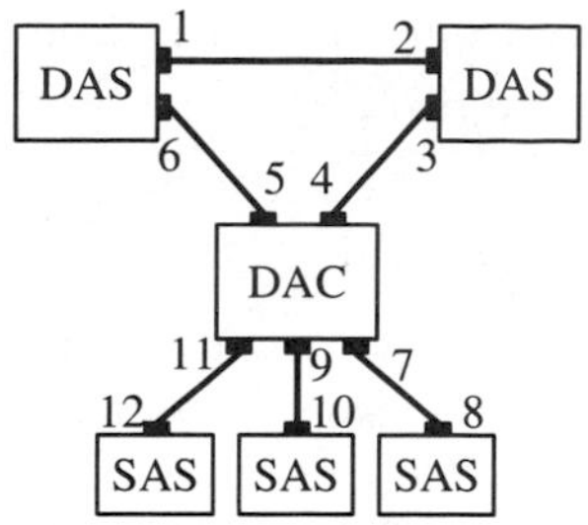

Figure 14.4 A sample FDDI network with 12 attachments.

- *Maximum Ring Latency (D_Max)*: The ring latency consists of the time taken by the bits to go around the ring. It depends on the fiber length and the station delays. The speed of light in the fiber depends on the index of refraction n. In most fibers, the light takes 5.085 μs/km. In MAC-1, the maximum ring latency is 1.617 ms. This value was computed using a station delay of 600 ns as follows:

$$\begin{aligned} \text{D\_Max} &= \text{P\_Max} \times \text{SD\_Max} \\ &\quad + \text{Maximum fiber length in km} \times \text{Light speed per km} \\ &= 1000 \times 0.600 + 200 \times 5.085\ \mu\text{s} \\ &= 1.617\ \text{ms} \end{aligned}$$

D_Max values corresponding to other possible station delay values discussed earlier can be similarly computed. The D_Max values corresponding to 0.756, 1.164, 1.644, and 1.804 μs for SD_Max are 1.773, 2.017, 2.661, and 2.833 ms, respectively. The last value is for hybrid mode operation of an FDDI-II ring.

Many of the FDDI parameters have been computed on the basis of the 1.773-ms ring latency. Although the ring latency has been increased several times since then, not all parameters have been updated. It is, therefore, safer to limit the number of stations on the ring so that the ring latency is below 1.773 ms. For example, if an FDDI-I ring has 50 km of fiber and each station has a latency of 1.7 μs, the number of attachments should be limited to $(1773 - 50 \times 5.085)/1.7$ or 893. This will limit the number of nodes to less than 446.

- *Various Frame Times*: The time to transmit a frame depends on the data rate (bits per second) and the frame size. In the basic mode, the data rate is 100 Mbps and the maximum frame size is limited to 9000 symbols due to elasticity buffer considerations (see Section 3.2). The 9000 symbols include 4 preamble symbols, but the source transmits 16 preamble symbols. Thus, a total of 9012 symbols is transmitted in a maximum size frame. The maximum frame time (F_Max) is:

$$\text{F\_Max} = \frac{\text{Frame + Preamble size in bits}}{\text{Data rate in bps}} = \frac{(9000 + 12) \times 4}{10 \times 10^6} = 360.48\ \mu\text{s}$$

In the hybrid mode, the frame time depends on the bandwidth allocated to the packet data channel. If all wideband channels are allocated for the isochronous traffic, the packet data rate is 0.768 Mbps. If all wideband channels are allocated to packet traffic, the packet data rate is

99.072 Mbps. The maximum frame time, therefore, varies between the following limits:

$$\frac{(9000+12)\times 4}{99.072\times 10^6} \geq \text{F\_Max} \leq \frac{(9000+12)\times 4}{0.768\times 10^6}$$

$$363.9\ \mu s \geq \text{F\_Max} \leq 46937.5\ \mu s$$

The time to transmit a token (Token_Time) is calculated in a manner similar to that for frames. The token consists of 16 symbols of preamble, 2 symbols for the starting delimiter, 2 symbols for frame control, and a 2-symbol ending delimiter giving a total of 22 symbols. In the basic mode, the token transmission time is 0.88 μs. In the hybrid mode, depending on the bandwidth allocated to the packet data channel, it may take 0.89 to 114.58 μs.

The time for claim frames (Claim_Fr), which are used only in the basic mode and are 64 symbols long including a 16-symbol preamble, is 2.56 μs.

The time for purge frames (Purge_Fr), which are used only in the hybrid mode and are 40 symbols long including a 4-symbol preamble, is 1.615 to 208.333 μs depending on the bandwidth allocated to the packet data channel.

Void frames (Void_Fr), which are used for some frame stripping and no-owner-frame removal algorithms, require 40 symbols plus a preamble. In the basic mode with a 16-symbol preamble, the time required is 2.24 μs. In the hybrid mode with a 4-symbol preamble, the time is between 2.26 and 291.67 μs depending on the packet data rate.

- *Maximum Transmitter Setup Latency (L_Max)*: After a station captures a usable token, it may take some time for it to set up its internal paths and start transmitting. During this setup time, the station transmits Idle symbols. This time, if very large, can reduce the bandwidth available for useful transmissions and is, therefore, limited to 3.5 μs. If a station needs more time, it can transmit a void frame. This will allow other stations to reset their valid transmission timer (TVX).

  Notice that L_Max puts a limit of 88 symbols on the preamble size preceding a frame at the transmitting station.

- *Minimum Safety Timing Allowance (S_Min)*: Normally, one should see a token or a frame every *D* interval where *D* is the ring latency. However, it is possible for a frame to be hit by a noise and not be recognized at a station. Therefore, to be on the safe side, some allowance must be made before concluding that the ring is not operating properly. This time is called the safety timing allowance. At a minimum, this should allow for a maximum size frame plus the maximum transmitter setup time. That is:

$$\text{S\_Min} = \text{F\_Max} + \text{L\_Max} = 360.48 + 3.5 = 363.98\ \mu s$$

- *Valid Transmission Timer Value (TVX_Value)*: The valid transmitter timer is used to recover from ring errors. If a station does not see a valid frame or a token within 2.5 ms, it starts the ring recovery. This value, called TVX_Value, is calculated as follows:

$$\begin{aligned}\text{TVX} &\geq \max(\text{D\_Max}, \text{F\_Max}) + \text{Token\_Time} + \text{F\_Max} + \text{S\_Min}\\ &\geq 1773 + 0.088 + 360.48 + 363.98\ \mu s\\ &\geq 2497.548\ \mu s\end{aligned}$$

The FDDI MAC-2 standard requires TVX to be at least 2.5 ms for FDDI-I stations and for FDDI-II stations in the basic mode. The limit is higher in the hybrid mode. The actual value can be computed using the preceding formula but it should not be less than 3.6 ms. If all wideband channels are allocated for isochronous traffic, only 0.768 Mbps is available for packet switching, then the TVX value (as computed using the preceding formula) can be shown to be 141 ms. Storing 3.6 ms using a byte-time (80-ns) counter requires 16 bits. It is convenient to use 2^{16} byte-times or 5.24288 ms as the default minimum hybrid mode TVX value.

- *Synchronous Allocations*: During the synchronous transmission mode, a station is allowed to transmit for a preallocated interval. If Synch_i is the synchronous allocation for the ith station, the token rotation time (TRT) may exceed the target by as much as $\sum_i \text{Synch}_i$. The synchronous allocation is controlled such that the TRT never exceeds two times the target (TTRT).

  To ensure that asynchronous stations are not starved and that at least one asynchronous station is able to transmit one maximum size frame during every rotation, the following relationship should hold:

  $$\text{D\_Max} + \text{F\_Max} + (2 \times \text{Void\_Fr}) + \text{Token\_Time} + \sum \text{Synch\_i} \leq \text{TTRT} \qquad (14.1)$$

  or:

  $$\sum_i \text{Synch}_i \leq \text{TTRT} - [\text{D\_Max} + \text{F\_Max} + (2 \times \text{Void\_Fr}) + \text{Token\_Time}]$$

  This formula assumes that two void frames are transmitted for the frame-content-independent frame stripping described in Section 2.11.

- *Minimum Token Rotation Time (T_Min)*: In addition to the desired target token rotation time (TTRT), each station also maintains two parameters: minimum TTRT (T_Min) and maximum TTRT (T_Max). The TTRT value bid by the station during the claim process is between these two limits.

  The standard requires that "the default value of T_Min shall not be greater than 4 ms." This is a confusing statement. This requirement, when stated mathematically, says:

  $$\text{T\_Min} \leq 4 \text{ ms}$$

  Now combine this with the requirement that TTRT should be more than T_Min:

  $$\text{TTRT} \geq \text{T\_Min}$$

  Both the requirements can be satisfied if TTRT is set above 4 ms. This is also desirable on the grounds that a lower value for TTRT may result in a rather low efficiency.

  Since the T_Min (and T_Max) value is not included in the claim frame, other stations are not aware of a station's T_Min requirement, and the negotiated value of TTRT can be less than a station's T_Min. Thus, this parameter has little effect, if any, on ring operation.

- *Maximum Token Rotation Time (T_Max)*: The original purpose of T_Max was to fix the number of bits required to implement the token rotation timer. A particular implementation at the time was using 22-bit timers; therefore, it was decided that the maximum TTRT should be in the range of 2^{22} symbol times, that is, 167.777216 ms, and a value of 165 ms was selected as the minimum default value of T_Max (that is, T_Max $\geq$ 165 ms). Later, when the committee required a value for maximum claim resolution time, this same value of 165 ms and the symbol T_Max was reused. This, in fact, has become its principal application. Whenever ring initialization is begun and stations enter the claim state, they set the token rotation timer alarm to go off after T_Max. If the alarm goes off (timer expires) before the token is seen, the claim process is assumed to have failed and further recovery measures are attempted.

  SMT draft version 7.2 specifies 200 $\geq$ T_Max $\geq$ 165. A new parameter T_Max_LB has been defined as the lower bound on T_Max. This new parameter also set an upper limit on TTRT. The default value of T_Max_LB is 165 ms.

In the hybrid mode, the minimum default value of T_Max is 670 ms. Although the derivation of this value involves use of the actual packet data rate, the value of 670 ms provides at least one attempt if the data rate is 0.768 Mbps. Many more attempts are allowed by this value if the date rate is higher.

- *Ring Initialization Time*: Whenever the ring configuration changes, the ring needs to be initialized. The initialization consists of two parts. First, the configuration change (station bypass, for example) must be detected. The time delay before reacting to the change is called the **reaction time** (T_React). Then, a claim process must be completed to reinitialize the token. The time spent in the second part is called the **recovery time** (T_Resp).

The reaction time includes the media interruption time (MI_Max) caused by station bypass, time for the TVX timer to expire (TVX_Value), signal acquisition time (A_Max), and time for the signal to go around the ring (D_Max).

T_React = MI_Max + D_Max + TVX_Value + A_Max

Table 14.2 Key Timing Parameters

			FDDI-I				FDDI-II	
							Hybrid Mode Packet Data Rate (Mbps)	
Parameter	Symbol	Unit	MAC-0*	MAC-1	MAC-2	Basic Mode	99.072	0.768
Minimum starting delimiter delay	SD_Min	ns	592	592	1000	1000	1000	1000
HRC latency		ns				480	480	480
Sampling and timing error		ns	4	4	4	4	4	4
Quantizing error + elasticity buffer		ns	4	80	80	80	80	80
Smoother latency		ns		80	80	80	240	240
LAB latency		μs					12	12
Maximum starting delimiter delay	SD_Max	μs	0.600	0.756	1.164	1.644	1.804	1.804
Maximum fiber length		km	200	200	200	200	200	200
Maximum number of ports	P_Max		1000	1000	1000	1000	1000	1000
Maximum number of MACs	M_Max		1000	1000	1000	1000	1000	1000
Maximum ring latency	D_Max	ms	1.617	1.773	2.181	2.661	2.833	2.833
Packet data bit rate		Mbps	100	100	100	100	99.072	0.768
Maximum frame size		Bytes	4500	4500	4500	4500	4500	4500
Maximum frame time	F_Max	μs	360.480	360.480	360.480	360.480	363.857	46937.500
Token time	Token_Time	μs	0.880	0.880	0.880	0.880	0.888	114.583
Claim frame time	Claim_Fr	μs	2.560	2.560	2.560	2.560		
Void frame time	Void_Fr	μs	2.240	2.240	2.240	2.240	1.776	229.167
Purge frame time	Purge_Fr	μs					1.615	208.333
Maximum startup delay	L_Max	μs	3.500	3.500	3.500	3.500	3.500	3.500
Minimum safety timing allowance	S_Min	μs	363.980	363.980	363.980	363.980	367.357	46941
Valid transmission timer	TVX	ms	2.500	2.500	2.906	3.386	3.600	140.931
TTRT − $\sum$ synchronous allocations		ms	1.983	2.139	2.547	3.027	3.201	50.343
Minimum TTRT	T_Min	ms	4	4	4	4	4	4
Maximum TTRT	T_Max	ms	165	165	165	165	670	670
Maximum media interruption time	MI_Max	ms	15	15	15	15	15	15
Maximum signal acquisition time	A_Max	ms	0.200	0.200	0.200	0.200	0.200	0.200
Reaction time	T_React	ms	19.317	19.473	20.287	21.247	21.633	158.964
Response time	T_Resp	ms	10.335	10.803	12.027	13.467	7.648	260.940
Ring initialization time	T_Init	ms	29.652	30.276	32.314	34.714	29.281	419.904
Number of initialization attempts			5	5	5	4	22	1

* ANSI MAC standard as printed in 1987 (ANSI X3.139 1987).

Using 15 ms for the maximum media interruption time, 1.773 ms for the maximum ring latency, 5.24288 ms for the TVX_Value, and 0.2 ms for the signal acquisition (0.1 ms for PHY and 0.1 ms for PMD), the maximum reaction time can be shown to be 23.2 ms.

The recovery time T_Resp includes the time for the claim process (in the basic mode) or the purge process (in the hybrid mode). It is computed as follows. In the basic mode:

$$\begin{aligned} \text{T\_Resp} &\leq (3 \times \text{D\_Max}) + (2 \times \text{M\_Max} \times \text{Claim\_Fr}) + \text{S\_Min} \\ &\leq (3 \times 2.661) + (2 \times 1000 \times 0.000256) + 0.00036396 \\ &\leq 13.5 \text{ ms} \end{aligned}$$

In the hybrid mode:

$$\begin{aligned} \text{T\_Resp} &\leq (2 \times \text{D\_Max}) + (\text{M\_Max} \times \text{Purge\_Fr}) + \text{S\_Min} \\ &\leq (2 \times 2.833) + [1000 \times (0.0001615 \text{ to } 0.208333)] + 0.00036396 \\ &\leq 7.648 \text{ to } 260.940 \text{ ms} \end{aligned}$$

The total ring initialization time (T_Init) is:

$$\begin{aligned} \text{T\_Init} &= \text{T\_React} + \text{T\_Resp} \\ &= 36.7 \text{ ms in basic mode} \\ &= 29.281 \text{ to } 419.904 \text{ ms in hybrid mode} \end{aligned}$$

It is possible for some other configuration change to occur during one ring initialization. The timeout interval (T_Max) of 165 ms allows at least four such reinitializations to happen, one after another in the basic mode, before declaring initialization failure.

Table 14.2 summarizes the parameter values.

14.9 Summary

Box 14.1 summarizes the enhancements incorporated in the MAC-2 standard.

Box 14.1 Summary of MAC-2 Enhancements

1. FDDI-II Support: Purge frames used to recover tokens without leaving the hybrid mode have been defined.
2. Bridge Support:
   a. Frames with format bits of 00 are not forwarded by the bridges. These include all SMT frames and MAC frames.
   b. Frames with format bits of 01 (LLC Frames), 10 (implementor defined frames), and 11 (reserved) may be forwarded.
   c. Mechanisms for frame-content independent stripping have been included. Bridges need these mechanisms. Other stations can also use them.
   d. Frames can have a source-routing information field, which allows source routing bridges to be used on FDDI.
   e. The stripped fragment length has been defined to be six symbols after the end of the source address. This implies that source-routing bridges cannot use the routing information field for stripping decisions. They must use frame-content independent stripping instead.

continued

Box 14.1 Summary of MAC-2 Enhancements (*Cont.*)

f. Two sets of rules for setting indicators have been defined. MAC status setting (MSS) bridges will set the A- and C-indicators on all frames that they copy for forwarding. MAC status repeating (MSR) bridges will not change the A- and C-indicators. A bridge can optionally set the C-indicator and leave A reset. Proper operation of this option requires stations to have a MAC status clearing (MSC) capability.

3. SMT group addresses have been defined such that the last 4 bits can be used as an index into a table. Expensive CAMs are not required for their recognition. A- and C-indicators must be set properly on all SMT group addresses.
4. Beacon frames contain information that helps network managers in diagnosing problems.
5. Frame validity criteria have been updated to reduce undetected error probability.
6. Restricted dialogs are now better specified. They are monitored and bounded.
7. Several new counters have been added to help network management and monitoring.
8. All MAC/PHY related parameter values have been updated to allow for the presence of HRC and for variable packet data rate of FDDI-II rings.

14.10 Further Reading and Historical Notes

The work on MAC-2 and PHY-2 was initiated in late 1988. The project proposal for MAC-2 was approved in November 1988 as Project 684-D. PHY-2 was approved in March 1990 as Project 761-D. Although the projects were described as replacements of the existing standards, the project number was inadvertently assigned as new coexisting standards. In 1990, the project proposals were revised to specify that the new standards will coexist with the old and that the current MAC and PHY standards will remain active standards. The revised project proposals were approved in March 1991.

MAC-2 is specified in ANSI X3.239.

Green (1989) provides a good tutorial on source routing and transparent bridging. Burr (1989) summarizes the issue of frame status indicators.

14.11 Self-Test Exercises

Note: Some exercises have multiple correct answers. See Appendix D for answers.

14.1 What is a source-routing bridge?

a. A bridge that provides routing information to sources
b. A bridge that forwards frames along a path specified by sources
c. A bridge that does both bridging and routing
d. A bridge that uses source addresses to route frames

14.2 Which flags are set by a MAC status setting (MSS) bridge on frames copied for forwarding?

a. A and C
b. A but not C
c. C but not A
d. E (neither A nor C)

14.3 What is the use of the token counter Token_ct?

a. It can be used to estimate ring throughput.
b. It can be used to estimate ring utilization.
c. It can be used to estimate load at various stations of the ring.
d. None of the above.

CHAPTER **15**

Enhanced Medium-Independent Physical Layer (PHY-2)

As discussed earlier in Chapter 3, the medium-independent physical layer (PHY) applies to all media types, including multimode fiber, single-mode fiber, and copper. FDDI-II stations require several changes in the PHY protocol. The revised specifications are called PHY-2. In this chapter, we describe only those parts of PHY-2 that differ from the initial version of PHY.

In this chapter, several FDDI-II terms such as *cycle master*, *basic mode*, and *hybrid mode* are used. It is assumed that you have already read the chapter on FDDI-II. If you have not please read at least the first few sections of Chapter 13 before proceeding further.

The key changes are:

1. A new symbol has been introduced to form starting delimiters for packets and tokens in the hybrid mode.
2. A new line state has been defined to indicate that the link is operating in the FDDI-II mode.
3. The station delay and ring latency specifications have been updated to reflect current implementations and to allow for additional buffering (latency adjustment buffer) in the cycle master stations of FDDI-II.
4. An error indication interface has been added.
5. The repeat filter has been modified to provide more reliable operation of the FDDI-II cycles.
6. Clock jitter specifications have been defined more precisely.
7. Two smoothers are used in the hybrid mode to reduce the cycle clock jitter.

The station delay and ring latency calculations were presented in Section 14.2. The details of the other issues follow. To avoid confusion, we use PHY-1 to denote the earlier version of PHY as discussed in Chapter 3.

15.1 New Symbol

FDDI-II uses a frame starting delimiter consisting of an I-L symbol pair during the hybrid mode. PHY-2, therefore, defines a new control symbol L in the 4b/5b encoding that uses a code bit pattern of 00101. Unlike the J-K symbol pair, I-L is recognized only on the current symbol boundary. Thus, the I-L pair does not change the symbol boundary as does the J-K pair.

The L symbol is not transmitted by PHY-1 or by PHY-2 in the basic mode. It is treated as an error if it is received during these states.

15.2 Cycle Line State

Stations with PHY-2 recognize cycles, which start with the starting delimiter J-K followed by R or S and may contain several control symbols. A MAC-1 station considers this an error since it would be expecting a frame-control field consisting of data symbols after J-K. When PHY-2 receives a cycle, it enters a **cycle line state** (**CLS**). During this state, control symbols I, L, R, S, and T are allowed in a cycle in addition to the data symbols. The cycle line state ends if any other symbol is received or if the cycle ends (after 125 μs). In particular, the receipt of a Q, H, or V symbol will end the cycle line state.

15.3 Error Indication

A new PHY service interface has been added that allows PHY-2 to indicate errors it detects. A frame or a cycle should not contain a V, J, or K. Thus, if any of these symbols is detected during the active line state (ALS) or CLS, PHY-2 will send an error indication to SMT. The J-K symbols are treated as an error only if they do not form a starting delimiter for another cycle or frame. The interframe gap should contain only Q, H, I, J, and K. Since Q or H symbols or a J-K symbol pair represent valid transitions to other line states, they are not considered an error. If any other symbols are received during the idle line state (including a J or a K, which does not form a J-K pair), PHY-2 indicates an error.

Recall from Section 11.4 that PHY-1 nodes use a link error monitor (LEM) to count errors. The count of the errors detected by PHY-2 as described here is slightly different from that counted by the LEM since the definitions of errors are different. For example, reception of several Halt symbols during a frame (an active line state to halt line state transition) is counted as an error by LEM but not by PHY-2. However, PHY-2 and LEM are compatible in the sense that the PHY-2 repeat filter works with LEM.

Elasticity buffer errors such as overflows or underflows are also reported to the SMT.

15.4 Repeat Filter

As explained earlier in Section 3.4, the repeat filter is used to replace errors with an "error noted" marker. If a MAC is present in the station, it will notice the error and handle it properly. If no MAC is present at a node, the repeat filter is required to prevent the errors from propagating. In PHY-1, the "error noted" marker was a sequence of four Halt symbols. The MAC converts these symbols into Idles. The problem with the H symbol is that it is too close to the R and S symbols. A single noise event can convert 00100 (H symbol) to 00111 (R symbol) or 11100 (S symbol). Therefore, the H symbol is not used in places where R or S can be a valid symbol. This applies to complete cycles in the hybrid mode and to frame status fields in the basic mode.

Since R and S are used in the cycle header, the errors are replaced by a sequence of four L symbols. The only problem with this choice is that it may inadvertently create I-L symbol pairs, which may be recognized as a frame starting delimiter in the packet data channel. Therefore, PHY-2 makes a special check for this possibility, and uses I instead of L if the symbol preceding an error is an I symbol.

In the basic mode, the H symbol is used unless the detected error is in the frame status field where T is used instead.

15.5 Clock Jitter

A man with one watch knows what time it is. A man with two watches is never sure.—Segal's Law

In FDDI-I, each node has its own bit clock. The bits are received based on the clock of the previous station while they are transmitted using the nodes' local bit clock.

FDDI-II nodes have to maintain two clocks: a bit clock and a cycle clock. This is shown in Figure 15.1. The bit clock is similar to that in FDDI-I. It runs at 125 MHz and has an accuracy of 50 parts per million (ppm). The difference between the clocks of different stations is taken care of by the elasticity buffers, which add or remove symbols from the preamble or intercycle gap. This changes the position of the cycles. Unless special precaution is taken, successive cycles may not remain exactly 125 μs apart. For isochronous operation it is important to ensure that the cycles be kept as close to 125 μs apart as possible. In other words, the cycle clock frequency must be as close to 8 kHz as possible. The cycle clock is used by the cycle master to generate successive cycles. The cycle clock may be internally generated or derived from an external source. Thus, it may or may not be independent of the bit clock.

In an isolated FDDI-II network, the cycle clock may be derived from the bit clock. The accuracy of the bit clock is 50 ppm, which is adequate for most applications. In an FDDI-II network with *plesiochronous* (nearly synchronous) connection(s) to the public network, circuit-switched data will be lost or repeated due to the slight difference in clock frequencies between the FDDI-II network and the public network. These events are known as **slips**. Each slip will result in loss of frame

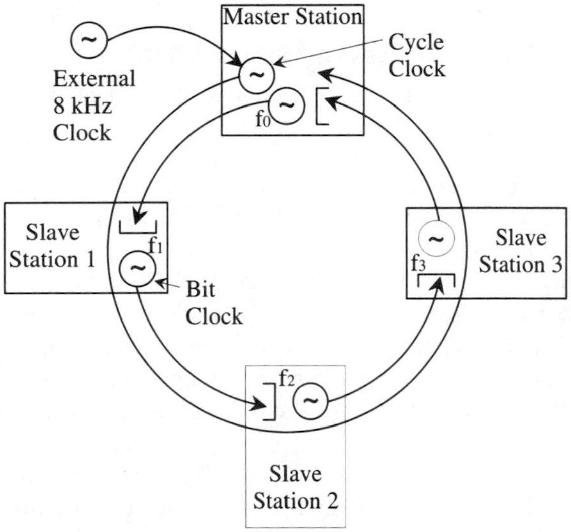

Figure 15.1 Bit clocks and the cycle clock used in FDDI-II.

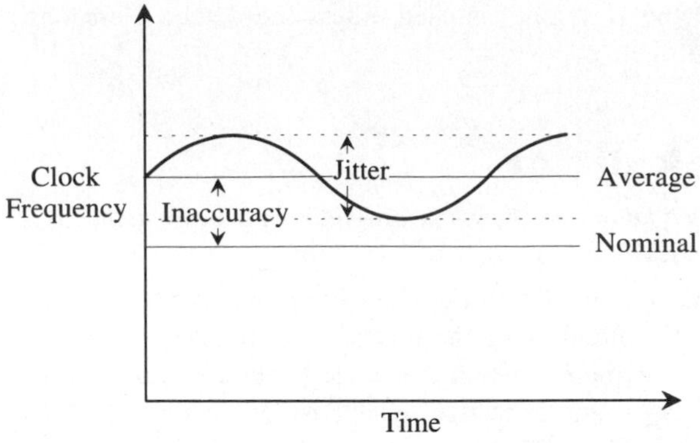

Figure 15.2 Clock accuracy and jitter.

synchronization unless a full-frame buffer is provided at the interface between the two networks. With the frame buffer, a full-frame slip will occur much less frequently, but the synchronization will be maintained.

The goodness of a clock is specified by two characteristics: accuracy and jitter. Accuracy of a clock is related to the difference between its long-term average frequency and the desired frequency. For example, if a station's bit clock runs at 125.05 MHz instead of the desired 125 MHz, the clock is inaccurate by 0.05 MHz. The jitter, on the other hand, relates to the fluctuations in the frequency (see Figure 15.2) as a function of time.

15.6 Bit Clock Characteristics

The PHY-2 standard includes a detailed specification of the code bit clock characteristics. These specifications and their explanations are as follows:

1. *The nominal code bit time should be 8 ns.* This is equivalent to saying that the nominal code bit frequency is 125 MHz. Since 5 code bits form a symbol, the nominal symbol time is 40 ns and the symbol frequency is 25 MHz.
2. *The code bit clock frequency accuracy should be 50 ppm.* The frequency can be off by ±0.005%. This implies a code bit frequency of 124.375 to 125.625 MHz. A difference in station clock frequencies can cause a difference in the number of bits received and transmitted. This difference is taken care of by the elasticity buffer function as explained in Section 3.2. Notice that the difference between the receiving clock and the transmitting clock can be as much as 125.625 to 124.375 MHz or 0.010%.
3. *The harmonic content should be less than −20 dB.* The harmonics refer to integral multiples of 125 MHz. A specification of −20 dB implies that the harmonic's amplitude should be less than 1% of the clock amplitude.
4. *The phase jitter should be less than* ±8 deg *above 20 kHz and less than* ±270 deg *below 20 kHz.* The phase jitter refers to the variation in the phase of the clock. Lower frequency jitter can

have higher peak-to-peak value. Incidentally, the phase jitter requirements below 20 kHz apply only in the hybrid mode.

15.7 Cycle Clock Characteristics

For isochronous service it is important that the cycle clock be closely aligned with the clocks of external sources, which expect to send information at fixed 125-μs intervals. The elasticity and smoothing functions cause the cycle interval to vary as the intercycle gap is increased or decreased. This has lead to two significant changes in PHY-2. First, the variation caused by the smoother has been restricted to just plus or minus one (± 1) symbol. Second, the jitter specifications on the bit clock have been specified precisely as discussed in Section 15.6. These characteristics can be used to calculate allowable jitter on the cycle clock as discussed next.

If the cycle clock is derived from an external source such as a public network, it is important to ensure that the combined jitter of the bit clock and the cycle clock is acceptable. In FDDI-II, the master station uses the external 8-kHz timing reference to generate cycles. The slave stations repeat the cycle and use the interval of received cycles as the 8-kHz timing signal for their isochronous applications. Depending on the bit clock frequency, the number of bits per cycle may vary at each station.

The number of bits per cycle n is given by:

$$\text{Number of bits per cycle } n = \frac{\text{Cycle duration}}{\text{Bit duration}} = \frac{T_C}{T_b}$$

or, taking a logarithm of both sides, we have:

$$\log n = \log T_C - \log T_b$$

Ideally, the cycle duration T_C is 125 μs, the bit duration T_b is 8 ns, and the number of bits per cycle n is 3125. Any variation in the cycle time T_C or bit time T_b would cause a variation in the number of bits per cycle and vice versa. Taking a differential of the preceding equation, it is easy to see that the variations are related as follows:

$$\frac{\delta n}{n} = \frac{\delta T_C}{T_C} - \frac{\delta T_b}{T_b}$$

Since the variations can be positive or negative, this relationship is usually expressed as follows:

$$\left|\frac{\delta n}{n}\right| = \left|\frac{\delta T_C}{T_C}\right| + \left|\frac{\delta T_b}{T_b}\right|$$

That is,

Allowed relative variation in bits/cycle = Allowed relative variation in cycle clock
+ Allowed relative variation in bit clock

In North America, the public network is normally synchronized to a Stratum 1 clock with accuracy better than $\pm 10^{-5}$ ppm. During network disturbances, the clock accuracy may degrade to ± 0.016 ppm (Stratum 2), ± 4.6 ppm (Stratum 3), or ± 32 ppm (Stratum 4). In networks outside of North America (for example, in Europe), the frequency accuracy may be as low as ± 50 ppm.

The smoothers may cause a variation of ± 5 bits per cycle. This is equivalent to a variation of 320 ppm. The maximum clock variation is equal to the sum of its accuracy and jitter. The variation of the two clocks should add up to 320 ppm. For the bit clock, the accuracy and jitter are 50 and 3.6 ppm, respectively. Using these data, the maximum allowed jitter for an external 8-kHz timing

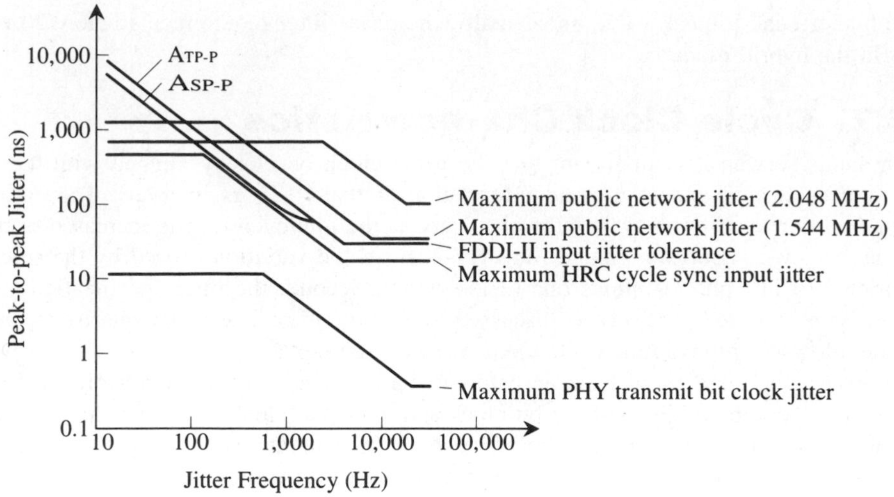

Figure 15.3 Cycle clock jitter.

reference with 32-ppm accuracy comes out to 234.4 ppm. This is calculated as follows:

Bit clock frequency accuracy	=	± 50 ppm
Bit clock jitter	=	± 3.6 ppm
Cycle clock frequency accuracy	=	± 32 ppm
Cycle clock jitter	=	± 234.4 ppm
Variation in bits/cycle (±5 bits per 3125 bits)	=	± 320 ppm

For countries where the public network clock accuracy is ±50 ppm, the maximum allowed jitter can be similarly computed to be ±216.4 ppm. This can be converted to a jitter amplitude specification.

The allowable cycle clock jitter tolerance for FDDI-II is shown in Figure 15.3. The figure shows peak-to-peak jitter as a function of the jitter frequency for the bit clock, symbol clock, cycle clock, public networks in North America, and public networks in Europe. The peak-to-peak jitter is specified in nanoseconds as well as in terms of **unit interval** (**UI**). The duration of the basic unit of information is called the unit interval. Thus, the UI for the FDDI bit clock is 8 ns (125 MHz). For the FDDI symbol clock, the UI is 40 ns. A complete derivation of the curves for FDDI cycle clock jitter is presented next. If you are not interested in details, you can safely skip the derivation.

Derivation 15.1 If the jitter is approximated as a sine wave (see Figure 15.4), the maximum jitter A_C in cycle duration T_C is given by:

$$A_C = A_S \sin(2\pi F_J T_C)$$

or

$$A_S = \frac{A_C}{\sin(2\pi F_J T_C)}$$

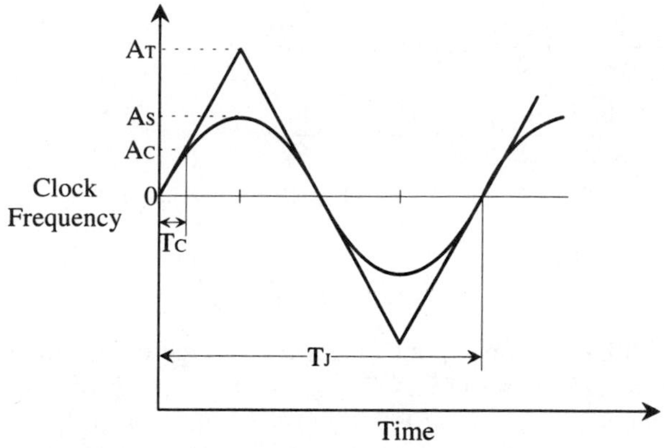

Figure 15.4 Relationship between maximum jitter and amplitude jitter.

Here, F_J is the frequency of the jitter and A_S is the amplitude of the jitter. The peak-to-peak jitter is twice the amplitude ($2A_S$). It is denoted by $A_{\text{SP-P}}$. The subscript SP-P indicates peak-to-peak using the sine wave approximation.

$$
\begin{aligned}
A_{\text{SP-P}} &= \frac{2A_C}{\sin(2\pi F_J T_C)} \\
&= \frac{2 \times 234.4}{\sin(2\pi F_J 125 \times 10^{-6})} \text{ ppm} \\
&= \frac{2 \times (234.4 \times 10^{-6}) \times (125 \times 10^{-6})}{\sin(2\pi F_J 125 \times 10^{-6})} \text{ sec} \\
&= \frac{58.6}{\sin(0.000785 F_J)} \text{ ns} \\
&\approx \frac{58.6}{0.000785 F_J} \text{ ns}
\end{aligned}
$$

or

$$A_{\text{SP-P}} \approx \frac{74640}{F_J} \text{ ns} \tag{15.1}$$

Another model that is often used for jitter is a triangular waveform. This is also shown in Figure 15.4. In this case, the peak-to-peak jitter $A_{\text{TP-P}}$ is given by:

$$
\begin{aligned}
A_{\text{TP-P}} &= 2A_T \\
&= 2 \times \frac{A_C}{T_C} \times \frac{T_J}{4} \\
&= 2 \times \frac{A_C}{T_C} \times \frac{1}{4F_J}
\end{aligned}
$$

$$= 2 \times \frac{234.4 \times 10^{-6}}{125 \times 10^{-6}} \times \frac{1}{4F_J} \text{ ppm}$$

$$= 2 \times \frac{234.4 \times 10^{-6} \times (125 \times 10^{-6})}{125 \times 10^{-6}} \times \frac{1}{4F_J} \text{ sec}$$

or

$$A_{\text{TP-P}} = \frac{117200}{F_J} \text{ ns} \qquad (15.2)$$

The two curves marked "FDDI-II input jitter tolerance" in Figure 15.3 for FDDI cycle clock jitter are drawn using Equations (15.1) and (15.2). These equations are used for jitter frequencies up to one-half of the cycle frequency ($F_J T_C \leq 0.5$). For higher frequencies, the peak-to-peak jitter is simply the product of cycle clock jitter and the cycle time, that is, $234.4 \times 10^{-6} \times 125 \times 10^{-6}$ seconds or 29.3 ns.

Notice from Figure 15.3 that the maximum input jitter for FDDI-II is less than the permitted jitter in public networks. A jitter filter is therefore required on the external clock input from the public telephone network in order to guarantee acceptable FDDI-II operation. The jitter filter's operation is similar to that of the elasticity buffer. The required amount of input buffering is equivalent to about 16 bytes at the 100-Mbps FDDI-II rate. □

15.8 Smoothers

Preamble smoothers were introduced in FDDI-I to avoid having very short interframe gaps, which may result in packet loss. A smoother reduces the variation of the interframe gap by elongating short preambles and shortening long preambles.

In FDDI-II, two smoothers are required: One to ensure that no preamble is too short and another to ensure that cycles arrive as close to their desired 125-μs period as possible. The first smoother,

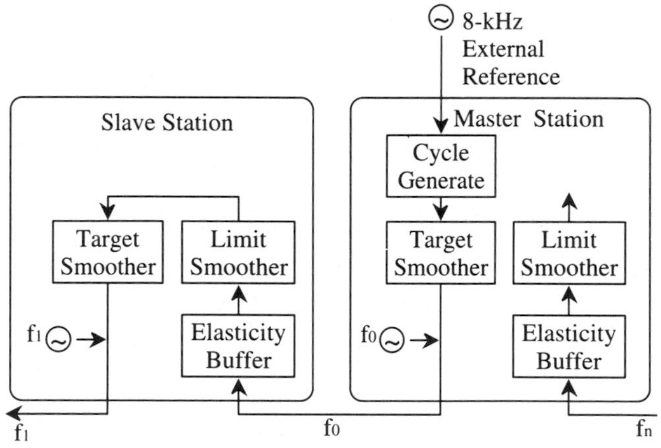

Figure 15.5 Smoothers in FDDI-II stations.

called a **limit smoother**, ensures that all preambles are between 4 and 6 symbols *limit*. The second smoother, called a **target smoother**, ensures that the cycles arrive as close to their *target* instants (125 μs apart) as possible. Figure 15.5 shows the relative locations of the two smoothers.

Without the target smoother, the cycles may have an average duration of 125 μs, but the variation (jitter) in the cycle clock may be too high. For example, consider a sequence of cycles each of 3120 symbols with preambles of size 4, 6, 4, 6, ... (alternating 4 and 6 symbols long). The average interval between cycles is 3125 symbols, but the cycle duration has a jitter of $\pm 1/3125$ or ± 320 ppm. While this is allowable, it is considered undesirable. As discussed in Section 15.10, a target smoother can eliminate this jitter by adjusting all cycle durations to 3125 symbols.

In FDDI-I or in basic mode on FDDI-II, only one of the two smoothers is required. It operates in a manner defined exactly as in Section 3.3. During hybrid mode operation on FDDI-II, both smoothers are required. The discussion in this chapter assumes the hybrid mode operation.

15.9 Limit Smoother

As explained in the last section, a limit smoother limits the variation in the preamble sizes. The nominal duration of an FDDI-II cycle including preamble is 3125 symbols. The goal of the limit smoother is to bring all cycle durations within limits of 3125 ± 1 symbols. It does this by borrowing symbols from the preamble of longer cycles and lending symbols to the preamble of shorter cycles. There is a limit to the total number of symbols it can borrow or lend. This limit is determined by the size of the smoother. The size cannot be too large since it contributes directly to the ring latency.

Figure 15.6 shows a sample limit smoother having a buffer of four symbols. The arriving symbols enter the buffer at the left. During preambles the exit point is adjusted to reduce or increase the size of the preambles. Depending on the position of the exit pointer, the smoother can be in five states: -2, -1, 0, +1, and +2. A state of -2 (exit pointer at the leftmost position) means that the smoother has an excess balance of two symbols. If it finds a short preamble it can increase its size by two symbols (by moving the exit pointer to the center). Similarly, a state of +1 means that the smoother has already lent one symbol to a previous preamble. It can lend at most one more symbol to a short preamble or preferably take back at least one symbol from a long preamble.

Table 15.1 shows a sample state transition diagram for the limit smoother just discussed. For any given cycle size at input and initial state of the smoother, the table entries indicate the size of the cycle at the output and the new state of the smoother. For example, if a cycle of 3126 symbols is

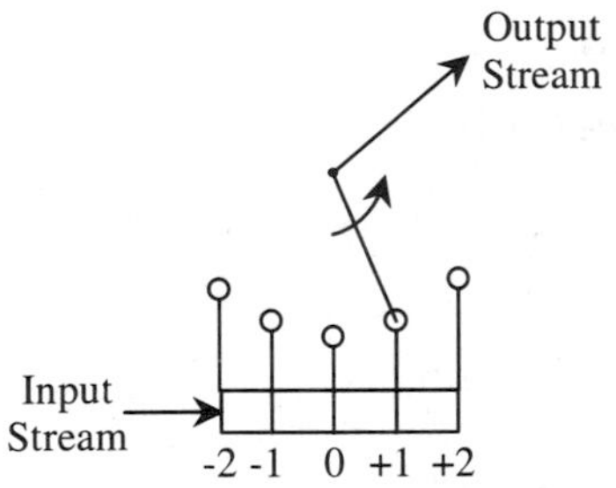

Figure 15.6 A limit smoother with a four-symbol buffer.

Table 15.1 A Sample State Transition Diagram for a Limit Smoother

Size at	Initial State				
Input	−2	−1	0	+1	+2
. . .					
3123	3125, 0	3124, 0	3124, +1	3124, +2	3123, +2
3124	3126, 0	3125, 0	3124, 0	3124, +1	3124, +2
3125	3126, −1	3126, 0	3125, 0	3124, 0	3124, +1
3126	3126, −2	3126, −1	3126, 0	3125, 0	3124, 0
3127	3127, −2	3126, −2	3126, −1	3126, 0	3125, 0
. . .					

received when the smoother is in state +1, the smoother reduces the cycle by 1 symbol and moves to state 0.

Notice that for all table entries the following holds true:

Input size − Initial state = Output size − Final state

The goal of the limit smoother is to keep the final state as close to zero as possible.

Figure 15.7 shows the cycle durations before and after limit smoothers in two successive stations. The bit clocks at the two stations are off from the nominal by +40 and −40 ppm, respectively. The

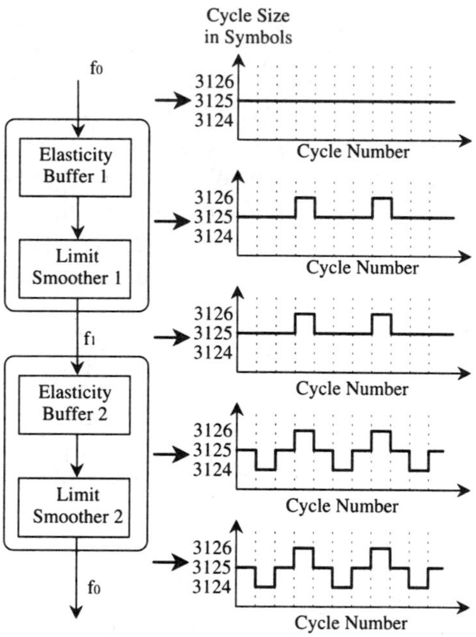

Figure 15.7 Cycle time as it passes through limit smoothers at two stations.

first station transmits $3125 \times (1 + 40 \times 10^{-6}) = 3225.125$ symbols in 125 μs. The second station transmits only $3125 \times (1 - 40 \times 10^{-6}) = 3124.875$ symbols in 125 μs. There is a discrepancy of 0.25 symbols per cycle. The elasticity buffer of the first station adds one symbol every fourth cycle, while the elasticity buffer of the second station takes away one symbol every fourth cycle. The cycles modified by the two stations may be different and so a stream of constant-duration cycles may be transformed by the two stations into a stream with cycle sizes varying between 3124 and 3126. The average cycle duration is 3125 symbols, but there is considerable jitter in the cycle clock. Since these cycles are within limits specified for the limit smoother, these cycle sequences will pass unchanged unless some additional mechanism is used to reduce the jitter. The target smoother, discussed next, is the mechanism selected by FDDI-II.

15.10 Target Smoother

As discussed in Sections 15.8 and 15.9, the limit smoother's job is to bring the preamble size within limits. However, even when all preambles are within limits, there may be considerable variation in the durations of successive cycles, causing jitter in the cycle clock. A target smoother attempts to minimize this jitter by adjusting all input cycles sizes to as close to 3125 symbols as possible. The mechanism used by the target smoother is similar to that of the limit smoother. It changes its own buffer length (data delay in the smoother) to adjust the size of the preamble.

Table 15.2 shows a sample state transition diagram for a target smoother. The smoother is assumed to have a length of two symbols and it can be in any one of three states: −1, 0, +1. These states are also known as contracted, center, and expanded, respectively. For any given cycle size at input and initial state of the smoother, the table entries indicate the size of the cycle at the output and the new state of the smoother. For example, if a cycle of 3126 symbols is received when the smoother is in state +1, it reduces the cycle by 1 symbol and moves to state 0.

As in the case of the limit smoother, the following holds true for all state transitions of the target smoother also:

Input size − Initial state = Output size − Final state

However, the goal of the target smoother is to keep the output size as close to 3125 symbols as possible. This is different from a limit smoother whose goal is to keep the final state as close to zero as possible.

Table 15.2 A Sample State Transition Diagram for a Target Smoother

Size at	Initial State		
Input	−1	0	+1
. . .			
3123	3125, +1	3124, +1	3123, +1
3124	3126, 0	3125, +1	3124, +1
3125	3125, −1	3125, 0	3125, +1
3126	3126, −1	3125, −1	3125, 0
3127	3127, −1	3126, −1	3125, −1
. . .			

15.11 Summary

PHY-2 is a revised version of PHY-1 and is intended to be completely interoperable with PHY-1. Most of the revisions have been made to accommodate FDDI-II stations. In particular, a new symbol L has been defined and an I-L symbol pair is used as the starting delimiter of packets and tokens within FDDI-II cycles. A new line state called the cycle line state has been defined. This state indicates that the line is operating in the hybrid mode. PHY-2 provides error indication whenever an invalid symbol is detected. The repeat filter has been changed to reduce the probability of generating false cycles.

Clock jitter specifications have been specified more explicitly and precisely than those in PHY-1. In particular, the problem of handling two separate clocks—a bit clock and a cycle clock — has been addressed. Efforts to minimize jitter on the cycle clock have resulted in requiring two smoothers during hybrid mode operation. The first smoother limits the preamble variations, while the second ensures that the cycles arrive as close to the target cycle time of 125 μs as possible.

15.12 Further Reading

PHY-2 is specified in ANSI dpANS X3.231-199x.

Ichihashi et al. (1991) provide an excellent discussion of jitter issues and smoother design. An updated version of the same paper appears in Ichihashi et al. (1992).

Yoneda and Kaji (1986) and Dodds and Hingston (1987) report the results of FDDI-II elasticity buffer simulations and explain the cycle clock jitter requirements.

Figure 15.1 is bases on Ichihashi et al. (1992). Figures 15.5 and 15.7 are based on Ichihashi et al. (1991). Figure 15.4 is based on ANSI X3.186-199x.

15.13 Self-Test Exercises

Note: Some exercises have multiple correct answers. See Appendix D for answers.

15.1 Which of the following symbol sequences will cause a PHY-2 to enter the cycle line state?:

a. J-K
b. J-K-R
c. J-K-S
d. I-J-K-L

15.2 What can you say about the goodness of an FDDI station clock that runs at 125.05 MHz as measured over a long interval?

a. The clock has a jitter of 0.05 MHz.
b. The clock has an inaccuracy of 0.05 MHz.
c. The clock has an jitter of ±0.025 MHz.
d. The clock has an inaccuracy of ±0.025 MHz.

CHAPTER **16**

FDDI Follow-On LAN

Both FDDI and FDDI-II run at 100 Mbps. To connect multiple FDDI networks, a higher speed backbone network is needed. The FDDI standards committee has realized this need and has started working on the design of the next generation of high-speed networks. The project is called **FDDI Follow-On LAN** (**FFOL**). FFOL will be designed to run with a data rate of around one **gigabit per second** (**Gbps**). It will serve initially as a backbone LAN and later as a primary workstation attachment LAN. As of 1993, the project was in its infancy and not much had been decided. All of the discussion in this chapter is preliminary and subject to rapid change.

Much of the discussion thus far in the FFOL working group has centered on surveying various options for coding and media access. Presentations on several high-speed network designs have been made. Some of these designs are presented in the last few sections of this chapter.

The key goal of FFOL is to serve as a backbone network for multiple FDDI and FDDI-II networks. This implies that it should provide at least the packet-switching and circuit-switching services provided by FDDI-II. Switched Multimegabit Data Service (SMDS), which provides connectionless variable-size packet networking, can also use FFOL. For a backbone network to be successful, it should be able to carry the traffic on a wide variety of networks. Other networks that run at speeds close to that of FDDI and that are expected to use FFOL are the Broadband Integrated Services Digital Networks (B-ISDN), which use the asynchronous transfer mode (ATM). ATM networks use small fixed-size cells. FFOL is expected to provide an ATM service that will allow the cells of one ATM network to be passed to another ATM network. This will allow IEEE 802.6 distributed-queue dual-bus (DQDB) networks to use FFOL as the backbone (see Figure 16.1). Easy connection to B-ISDN networks is one of the key goals of FFOL. The telecommunications industry networks and computer industry networks are merging slowly. The FFOL will be another link in this process.

The key issues in the design of a high-speed network are decisions about the bit rate, applications, physical encoding, the media access method, the frame stripping method, and topology. These issues are discussed in the next few sections.

16.1 Data Rate

Data rate is the key consideration in the design of a network. If the data rate selected is too high, the cost may become high, there may not be enough applications to make use of the available bandwidth, and the network design may not become successful. On the other hand, unless the data

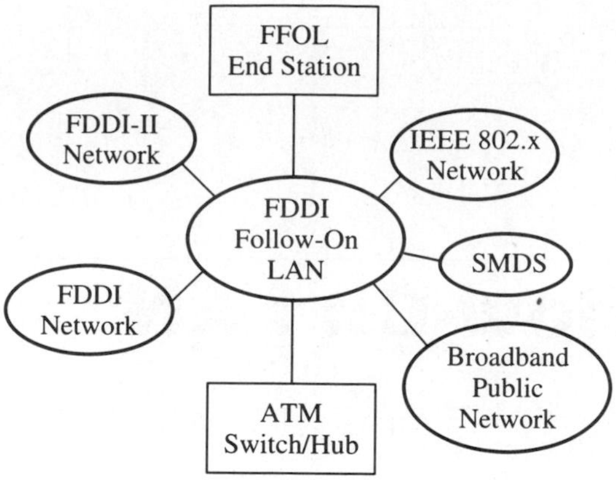

Figure 16.1 FDDI follow-on LAN as a backbone.

rate is significantly higher than that currently available there is not much incentive for users to change and adopt a new standard.

By the time FFOL is ready, multimode fibers are expected to be in common use because of FDDI. It is desirable that users be able to use the installed fiber in FFOL. It is well known from the FDDI design that these multimode fibers have the capacity to run 100 Mbps (125-Mbps signaling rate) up to 2 km. Their bandwidth-distance product is at least 250 Mbps-km. Therefore, they can also carry a signal of 1.25 Gbps up to 200 m or 2.5 Gbps up to 100 m. The latter (100 m) covers the length of the horizontal wiring supported by the ANSI/EIA/TIA 568 commercial building telecommunications wiring standard. Limiting FFOL to below 2.5 Gbps will allow much of the installed multimode fiber in the buildings to be switched from FDDI to FFOL.

To carry telecommunications network traffic, FFOL should support data rates that are compatible with SONET. As discussed in Chapter 9, CCITT has standardized a sequence of synchronous transport signal (STS) rates. An STS-N rate is $51.84 \times N$. Commonly used STS rates are STS-3 (155.52 Mbps), STS-12 (622.08 Mbps), STS-24 (1.24416 Gbps), and STS-48 (2.48832 Gbps). FFOL will be designed to exchange traffic efficiently at these rates from the public data networks. Incidentally, the STS rates mentioned here are the network rates. This includes network overhead. The rate available to users is called the **payload rate** and is slightly lower.

16.2 Applications

The next consideration in the network design is the type of applications that are expected to use the network. Their requirements determine the types of services offered by the network. The applications for FFOL include transfer of data, images, video, voice, audio (music), real-time interactive traffic, and video conferencing. Most applications of the past used only one of these various traffic types and are called **unimedia** applications. The trend is toward **multimedia** applications that require simultaneous transfer of multiples of these traffic types. Another similar term is **hypermedia**, which refers to a way of storing and accessing related pieces of information. Hypermedia applications are interactive and demand low latency in addition to high bandwidth.

Table 16.1 Application Requirements

Applications	Bandwidth	Number of Nodes	Response Time	Traffic Types
Scientific supercomputing	Large	Small	Low	Data, images
CAD/CAM	Medium	Medium	Medium	Data, images
Banking	Medium	Large	Medium	Voice, data, image
Insurance	Medium	Large	Medium	Voice, data, image
Medical diagnosis	High	Small	Medium	Voice, data, image
Education	Medium	Medium	Medium	Voice, data, image, audio, video
Real estate	Medium	Large	Medium	Data, image, video
Advertising	High	Large	High	Data, image, audio, video
Publishing	High	Large	High	Data, image, video
Travel agents	Medium	Large	High	Data, image, video
Hypermedia	High	Large	High	Voice, data, image, audio, video

One way to classify applications is to consider their bandwidth, responsiveness, and number of nodes requirements. Table 16.1 provides such a classification for some of the application areas.

Unlike the unimedia applications of the past, the network traffic of the future will be a mixture of various types. This means that the traffic will be heterogeneous, bursty, and more unpredictable. Guaranteeing throughput or delay for such traffic will require mechanisms for resource reservation and for using unreserved or unused bandwidth. Heterogeneity requires that the network be designed with service classes or at least priority mechanisms so that one class of traffic has a minimal effect on the other classes.

16.3 Media Access Modes

The term **media access modes** refers to the traffic switching modes supported by a network. FDDI supports three different modes of packet switching: synchronous, asynchronous, and restricted asynchronous. Depending on the delay and throughput requirements, an application can choose any one of these three media access modes. FDDI-II adds support for periodic (isochronous) traffic that normally requires circuit switching. FFOL is expected to support these modes. In addition, as shown in Figure 16.2, it is expected to support explicitly ATM switching as well. ATM switching is slightly

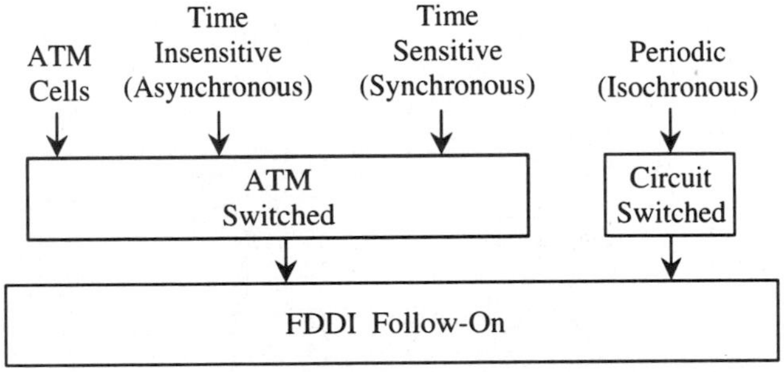

Figure 16.2 Services provided by the FFOL.

different from packet switching. All ATM cells are the same size, the switching instants are fixed, and a slotted network design is generally used. Packet traffic will be carried as ATM cells.

16.4 Media Access Method

The media access method refers to the rules for sharing the medium. Token, timed token, and slotted access are examples of the media access methods used in the IEEE 802.5 token ring, FDDI, and Cambridge ring, respectively. The token access method is not useful for long distances. Its deficiency can be easily seen by considering what happens at zero load or at very high loads. Even when nothing is being transmitted, a token must be captured. This may take as long as the round-trip delay around the network (ring latency). If the ring latency is D, the average access time at zero load is $D/2$. For networks covering large distances, this may be unacceptable. At high load, the maximum relative throughput (or efficiency) of the timed token access method, as derived in Chapter 22, is:

$$\text{Efficiency} = \frac{n(T-D)}{nT+D}$$

Here, T is the target token rotation time and n is the number of active stations. As shown in Figure 16.3, the efficiency decreases as the ring latency D increases. In the extreme case of $D = T$, the efficiency is zero. Access methods, whose efficiency is reduced with propagation delay, are also sensitive to the network bit rate. Their efficiency decreases as the bit rate increases. Since the geographic extent covered by a backbone FFOL network is expected to be large, FFOL is expected to select a media access method that is relatively insensitive to the propagation delay and network bit rate. Slotted access and register insertion rings are classical examples of such access methods.

For FDDI, the time to recover from faults also depends on the extent of the network. The beacon frames (see Chapter 2) used to locate the faults are sent around the ring. Thus, a very large ring will take longer to recover. FFOL will be designed so that the recovery is relatively insensitive to the extent of the network and the bit rate.

The FFOL MAC protocol is expected to continue to provide other facilities provided by the current MAC such as frame status flags, multicast addressing, broadcast addressing, and bridging. ATM cells and FDDI-II wideband channels may be bridged on to FFOL in addition to the IEEE 802 style frames.

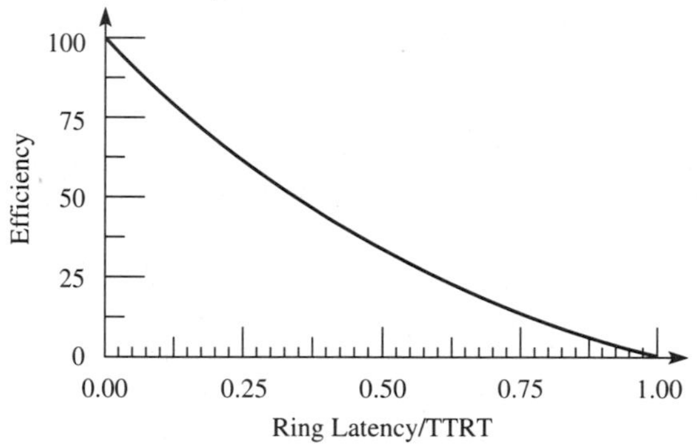

Figure 16.3 The efficiency of the timed token access method as a function of ring latency.

16.5 Physical Encoding

FDDI uses a 4b/5b encoding, which allows 4 data bits to be combined into one symbol. The electronic processing is done either on symbols or on symbol pairs. These are known as **symbol-wide** and **byte-wide** implementations, respectively. Assuming a symbol-wide implementation, the electronic circuits run at 25 Mbps for 100-Mbps FDDI. At 1 Gbps, using the same encoding, the electronic devices will have to run at 250 Mbps. Such devices are expensive. Using larger symbol sizes such as 8/10, 16/20, or 32/40 allows parallel processing using low-speed electronic circuits. A larger symbol size also allows more control symbols. These control symbols are useful for framing, fault recovery, and physical connection management.

The 4b/5b code is not balanced (see explanation in Chapter 3) in the sense that the signal has a 10% dc content. This causes a problem with base line wander. The problem is more pronounced at higher speeds. For this reason, it is expected that FFOL will consider only DC-free (balanced) codes. A balanced code increases the signal-to-noise ratio, thus allowing a greater loss budget.

A disadvantage of very large symbol sizes is that this limits the minimum parallelism. For example, with an 8/10 code, some implementations can be 10 bits wide, while others can be 20 bits wide or larger (if permissible). With a 16/20 code, all implementations will have to be at least 20 bits wide, requiring a large silicon area for their implementation.

16.6 Frame Stripping Method

In designing a ring LAN architecture, a decision has to be made about who should remove the frame. There are two alternatives: source or destination. In source stripping, the station transmitting the frame (source station) removes the frame. The advantage of source stripping is that the source can check the frame for errors and also receive several flags indicating successful reception of the frame. In destination stripping, the destination station strips the frame and releases the space for reuse.

Destination stripping allows **spatial reuse** such that the space on the media freed by the destination can be used by the destination or other succeeding nodes. As shown in Figure 16.4, several simultaneous transmissions can be in progress in networks implementing spatial reuse. Thus, the total network throughput can be as much as *N* times the link bandwidth, where *N* is the number of simultaneous transmissions.

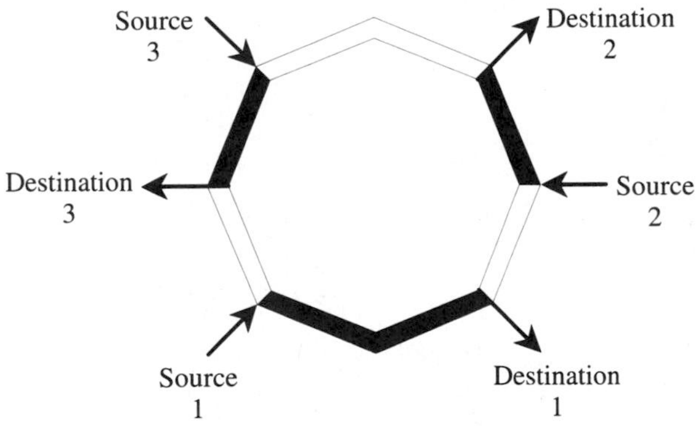

Figure 16.4 Spatial reuse allows several parallel transmissions.

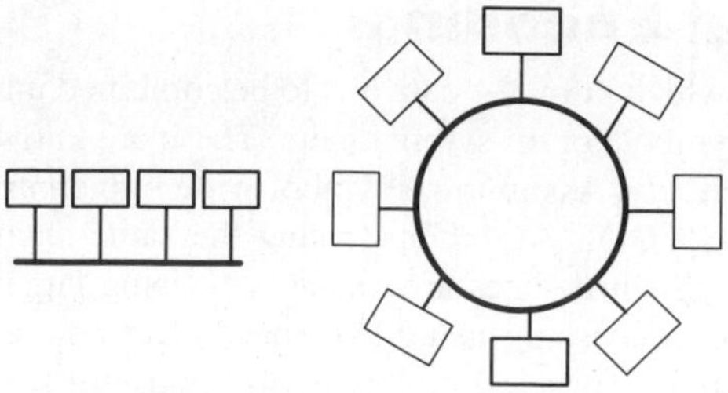

Figure 16.5 Shared-media distributed-switching approach.

Destination stripping is generally used in nontoken rings such as register insertion rings and slotted rings. In networks using simple token access methods, multiple simultaneous transmission is not possible since each transmitting station needs a token and there is only one token. Token networks, therefore, use source stripping.

Proposals have been made for FFOL to use destination stripping. This is because the extent of the network will be large and tying up the whole medium for one transmission is undesirable. Spatial-reuse increases network throughput and reduces message latencies.

16.7 Topology

FFOL will allow the dual ring of trees physical topology that is supported by FDDI. Additional topologies may be allowed. Since only one ring passes through a tree, there are two options. Either FFOL will be designed to allow operation over single rings, in which case the media access protocols requiring two rings will have to be modified for use on a single ring, or the tree portion can use a different protocol and be accessed via bridges.

Segments of public networks may be included in the FFOL networks. In current FDDI, only SONET links are allowed.

For logical topology, both rings and buses will be considered. Bus protocols do not have to address the frame stripping issue unless the spatial reuse is performed. Ring protocols provide advantages for distributed recovery mechanisms.

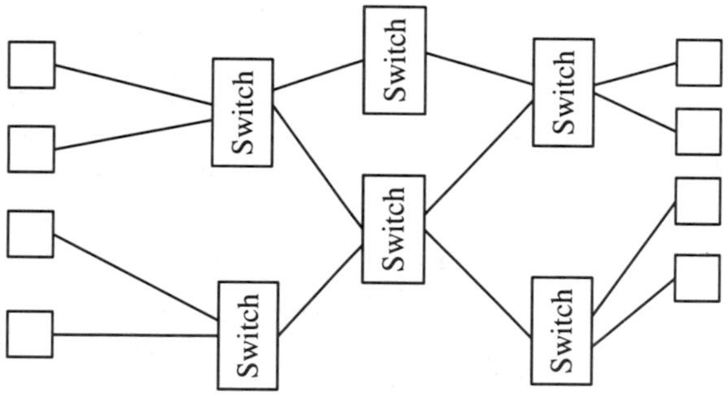

Figure 16.6 Shared-switch distributed-media approach.

All LANs are designed so that the responsibility for ensuring that the packet is delivered to the correct destination is shared by all nodes. In this case, as shown in Figure 16.5, the switching is distributed and the medium is shared. Another alternative, shown in Figure 16.6, is to distribute the medium and share switches. The advantage of this latter approach is that not all end-stations need to pay the cost of a high-speed connection. Their links can be upgraded to higher speeds only when necessary. The end-systems are simple and most of the design complexity is in the switches. Several parallel transmissions can occur at all times. Thus, the total throughput of the network is several times the bandwidth of any one link. For example, it is possible to get a total network throughput of several gigabits per second with all links having a bandwidth of only 100 Mbps. Notice that most of the telecommunication networks and wide-area computer networks use the switch-based approach. Even in high-speed LANs, there is a trend toward a switch-based mesh topology. It is not clear whether FFOL will consider a mesh topology.

16.8 FFOL Architecture

To develop a standard for FFOL, the work has been divided into six architectural components as shown in Figure 16.7. These components are PMD, PHY, SMT, SMUX, IMAC, and AMAC. Notice

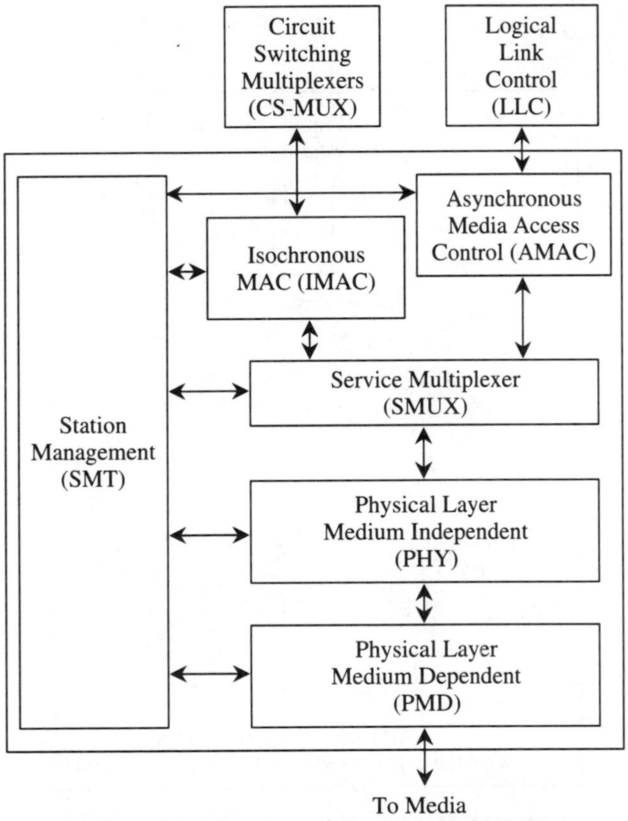

Figure 16.7 Architectural components of FFOL.

that these components are very similar to the protocol components of FDDI-II shown in Figure 13.3. The SMUX (service multiplexer) multiplexes and demultiplexes the isochronous and asynchronous streams. The two streams are handled by IMAC (isochronous media access control) and AMAC (asynchronous media access control). AMAC serves both frames and ATM cells. It has not yet been decided which mechanism will be used by AMAC. One possibility is to use an ATM/B-ISDN–based structure.

The initial rate may be limited to 600 Mpbs. With an 8b/10b coding, this will result in a 750-Mbaud signal. It is expected that low-cost 750-Mbaud laser diodes will be available by 1995. These diodes will be powerful enough to allow a range of 1 to 2 km over multimode fiber.

16.9 Summary

Box 16.1 summarizes the key features of FFOL. Of course, all of these features are preliminary and may change.

Much of the design of FFOL is based on what is required from future networks. Predicting the future is difficult (see Figure 16.8). Recently, FFOL activities have slowed down as the participants question the need for FFOL in view of the other competing gigabit standards such as the Fiber Channel, High-Performance Parallel Interface (HIPPI), and asynchronous transfer mode (ATM) based networks.

Figure 16.8 Predicting the future is difficult.

Box 16.1 Summary: FDDI Follow-On LAN

1. FFOL is designed to serve as a backbone for FDDI, FDDI-II, IEEE 802.3/Ethernet, IEEE 802.5/token ring, and other packet or ATM networks.
2. The data rates will be 155.52 Mbps, 622.08 Mbps, 1.24416 Gbps, and 2.48832 Gbps. These data rates have been selected to match SONET STS-3, STS-12, STS-24, and STS-48 rates. The initial target is 622.08 Mbps.
3. It will be suitable for a variety of applications including data, image, voice, and video.
4. In addition to the isochronous, synchronous, and asynchronous packet services, it will provide ATM cell transport services.
5. The goal is to use existing FDDI plant wherever possible.
6. The dual ring of trees topology and its subset will be supported.
7. Both single-mode and multimode fibers will be supported.
8. Shielded twisted-pair (STP) and data grade unshielded twisted-pair (Category 5 UTP) may be used at 155.52 Mbps.
9. Some segments (or links) of the FFOL network can be leased public network links, such as SDH/SONET links.

16.10 Further Reading and Historical Notes

Work on FFOL began in February 1990 and a requirement document had been agreed on by May 1990. An architectural structure was also agreed on and six project proposals covering this structure were submitted to the ASC X3 Standards Planning and Requirements Committee (SPARC) in October 1990. These projects were approved in January 1991. The project is expected to be complete by 1995.

FFOL requirements and design considerations are summarized in Ocheltree, Horvath, and Mityko (1991). Other design issues are covered in Fink and Ross (1992), Hamstra and Fink (1992), Mityko (1991), and Ross and Fink (1992). Grow (1990) provides a tutorial on FFOL. Table 16.1 is based on Horvath (1991).

16.11 Self-Test Exercises

Note: Some exercises have multiple correct answers. See Appendix D for answers.

16.1 Which of the following is expected to apply to FDDI follow-on LAN?:

a. It will act as a backbone to FDDI networks.
b. It will act as a backbone to FDDI-II networks.
c. It will act as a backbone to ATM networks.
d. It will support isochronous traffic.
e. It will run at 1.00 Gbps.

16.2 Why is destination stripping preferred sometimes over source stripping?

a. It is more secure than source stripping since frames do not go all around the ring.
b. It allows higher network throughput.
c. It guarantees that the destination receives the frame.
d. It simplifies multicasting.

CHAPTER **17**

Logical Link Control

FDDI standards cover one and one-half of the seven layers of the ISO/OSI reference model. PMD and PHY together cover the ISO/OSI physical layer. MAC covers one-half of the ISO/OSI datalink layer. The other half is called **logical link control** (**LLC**). FDDI uses the ISO 8802-2 LLC protocol. Chapter 18 discusses issues related to the use of TCP/IP and OSI protocols on FDDI. A knowledge of LLC helps in understanding these issues. This chapter, therefore, provides an overview of IEEE 802 and various types of LLC services defined in 802.

17.1 IEEE 802: Overview

Although FDDI is not a part of the IEEE 802 or ISO 8802 series of local area network (LAN) standards, it provides an equivalent MAC service. Several changes have been made to FDDI as well as IEEE 802 standards to make them compatible.

IEEE 802 is a family of standards for LANs and metropolitan area networks (MANs). The topics covered by the various members of the family are listed in Table 17.1 and the relationship among these members is shown in Figure 17.1. Of these, IEEE 802.1 and 802.2 specifications are applicable to all datalink protocols of IEEE 802 family and FDDI.

IEEE 802.1 provides an overview for the whole IEEE 802 family and consists of architecture and management issues common to all members of the family. It consists of a number of separate documents numbered 802.1a, 802.1b, and so on. IEEE 802.1a provides the overview and explains the structure of source and destination addresses used in IEEE 802 protocols. In particular, it addresses the issue of bit order. IEEE 802.1d specifies an architecture and protocol for the interconnection of IEEE 802 LANs using MAC bridges. IEEE 802.1i specifies modifications and additions to IEEE 802.1d to extend its scope to transparent bridging between FDDI and IEEE 802 networks.

17.2 IEEE 802.2: Logical Link Control (LLC)

Before the introduction of LANs, most datalinks were point to point. Datalink protocols were designed to allow reliable communication between two stations on the ends of the link. Most links at that time were point to point. The multipoint links were used as *time-shared* point-to-point links that used a

Table 17.1 IEEE 802 Family of Standards/Projects

Number	Topic
802.1	Overview, architecture, glossary, network management, and interworking
802.2	Logical link control
802.3	CSMA/CD access method and physical layer specifications
802.4	Token-passing bus access method and physical layer specifications
802.5	Token-passing ring access method and physical layer specifications
802.6	Metropolitan area network access method and physical layer specifications
802.7	Recommended practices for broadband LANs
802.8	Recommended practices for fiber optic LANs and MANs
802.9	Integrated services LAN interface
802.10	Interoperable LAN/MAN Security
802.11	Wireless access method and physical layer specification

polling mechanism. Because of the point-to-point nature of the link, the media access part of the datalink protocol was minimal.

With the introduction of LANs, media access became a more significant part of the datalink layer. The layer was, therefore, subdivided into two sublayers called **logical link control** (**LLC**) and **media access control** (**MAC**). Two stations talking to each other over an extended LAN (see Figure 17.2) are assumed to have a **logical link** between them, which may consist of one or more datalinks. Each datalink may use a different medium access method. While the media access control protocol covers issues related to each medium, the LLC protocol covers issues related to the transmission of information on successive hops of the extended LAN.

The **synchronous data link control** (**SDLC**) protocol used initially in SNA forms the basis of many datalink protocols including LLC. IBM submitted it to ISO for acceptance as an international standard. ISO modified it to become **high-level data link control** (**HDLC**). CCITT then adopted it as the datalink layer of the X.25 network interface standard, but modified it to become **link access procedure** (**LAP**). It was modified later to become **link access procedure balanced**

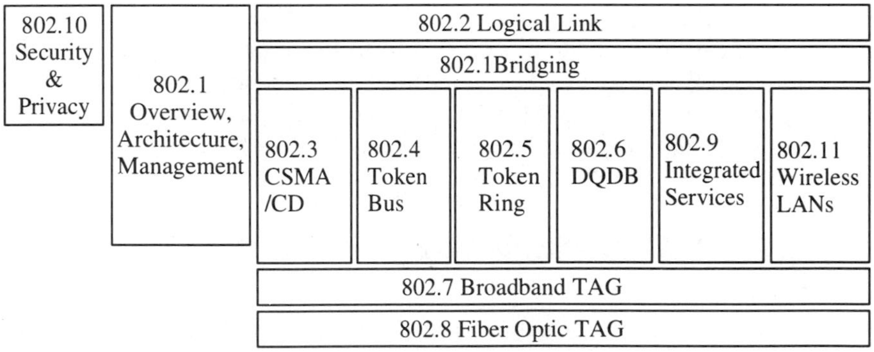

Figure 17.1 IEEE 802 standards family.

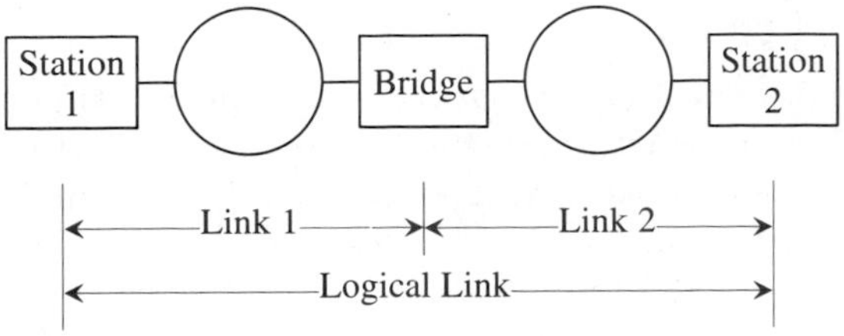

Figure 17.2 A logical link between two stations in an extended LAN.

(**LAPB**). IEEE took LAPB and modified it to develop LLC. While SDLC, HDLC, LAP, and LAPB are all connection-oriented protocols, LLC offers both connectionless and connection-oriented services.

Examples of services provided by various types of LLC are:

1. *Error Control*: The source can find out about missing protocol data units (PDUs) or PDUs affected by noise via acknowledgments received from the destination.
2. *Ordered Delivery*: PDUs can have sequence numbers that helps to ensure that the PDUs are delivered at the destination in the same order in which they are sent from the source.
3. *Flow Control*: The source can adjust the number or rate of PDUs sent to match the resources available at the destination.
4. *Congestion Control*: Source can adjust the number or rate of PDUs sent to match the resources available at intermediate stations (bridges), if any.
5. *Protocol Discrimination*: When there are several users of the datalink (network layer protocols), the PDU is delivered to the correct user using LLC level source and destination addresses.

Notice that these services are provided at the logical link level, that is, across an extended LAN. These hop-by-hop services have to be repeated at every hop to ensure reliable or ordered end-to-end delivery. Another alternative is to introduce these services only in the transport (end-to-end) layer. This choice initially leads to several different types of LLC protocols.

Theoretically, the LLC layer is shared by all media access protocols. In practice, this is not so. Followers of different networking religions have different beliefs about how resources should be managed and what services should be provided end to end and what should be done at every hop. Therefore, they designed two different types of LLC protocols called LLC Type 1 and LLC Type 2. LLC Type 1 offers an unacknowledged connectionless service, while Type 2 offers an acknowledged connection-oriented service. Most IEEE 802.3/Ethernet networks use LLC Type 1, while most IEEE 802.5/token ring networks use LLC Type 2. LLC Type 3 was later added to provide an acknowledged connectionless service (mostly for IEEE 802.4 users). LLC Type 4 is now under development. It offers stream-oriented high-speed data transfer. The various types of LLC are described in the next few sections.

Any LLC-type service can be used over FDDI. Most implementations use Type 1, which is compulsory. The LLC standard requires that stations implementing other types must also implement Type 1. This ensures that all stations on IEEE 802 LANs from different vendors can interoperate.

17.3 LLC Type 1

LLC Type 1 is a connectionless datagram service with a minimum complexity. The LLC layer provides only protocol discrimination for network layer protocols. That is, it simply ensures that the PDU is handed off to the right network layer protocol. Error control, flow control, congestion control, and ordered delivery are not handled by this LLC. This is a datagram service in that no connection-establishment or resource reservation is required before sending packets between two stations. Although this has been labeled "send and pray" by the opponents of Type 1, this service is appropriate if the error and flow controls are either not required or are implemented at the transport layer.

The format of an LLC PDU is shown in Figure 17.3. This format is used by LLC Types 1, 2, and 3. LLC Type 4 uses an extension of this format. An LLC PDU contains a destination address, a source address, and a control field followed by the information.

The address fields indicate the network layer protocol using the LLC services. Following the ISO/OSI terminology, the network layer accesses LLC using an LLC service access point (LSAP). The destination and source address fields of an LLC PDU are called destination service access points (Destination LSAP or DSAP) and source service access points (Source LSAP or SSAP), respectively. Each is 1 byte long.

A PDU can be addressed to multiple destinations using a *group DSAP*. The first bit of a DSAP indicates whether the address is an individual or a group SAP. The I/G bit is 0 for individual SAPs and 1 for group SAPs. SSAPs are always individual SAPs and, therefore, the first bit of an SSAP is used to indicate whether the PDU is an LLC command or a response. This bit is 0 in command PDUs and 1 in response PDUs. Like MAC addresses, LSAP values are also specified using a canonical (lsb) bit order. Figure 17.4 shows the bit order for DSAP and SSAP as seen on the wire. Notice that the least-significant bit in the figure is shown on the left, which is opposite of the convention used for writing binary numeric strings and confuses some people. Thus, a DSAP field of AA_{16} or 10101010_2 has 0 as its least-significant bit and is a group DSAP.

A DSAP value of FF (all 1's) indicates a broadcast address called the **global DSAP** address. PDUs addressed to this DSAP are delivered to all active DSAPs at the station.

The control field consists of 1 or 2 bytes.

Type 1 LLC uses only the so-called unnumbered format (U-Format) PDUs, which have a 1-byte control field. There are three types of PDUs: unnumbered information (UI), exchange identification (XID), and test.

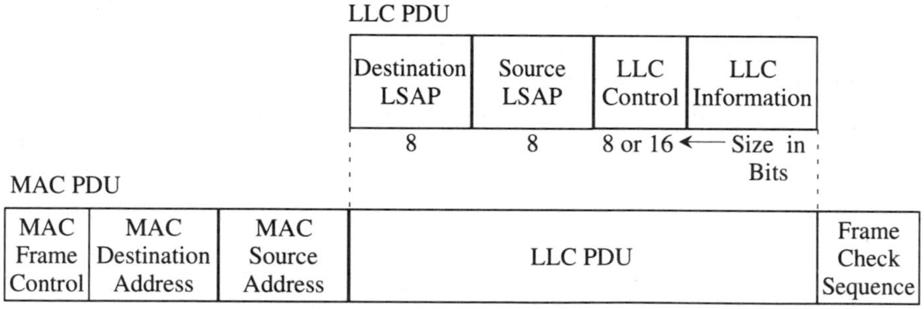

Figure 17.3 LLC PDU format and its position in a MAC PDU.

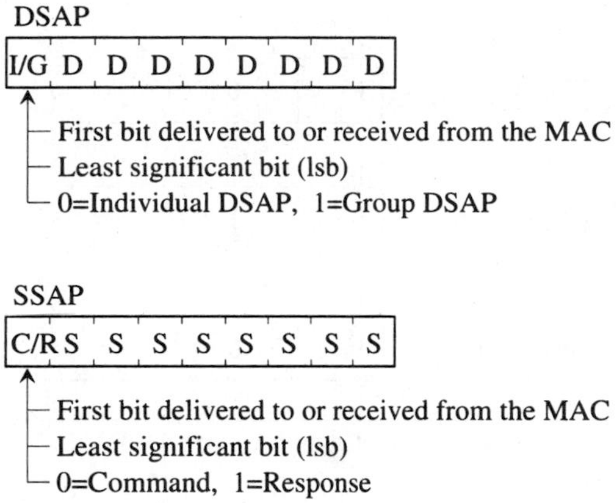

Figure 17.4 Bit order for DSAP and SSAP fields.

The UI PDUs are used to send information supplied by the network layer. The test command PDUs are used for testing continuity. They have a variable-length data field, which is echoed back in the test responses. The XID PDUs are used to determine the types of LLC services provided at the remote end.

The meaning of various bits in the control field of a U-Format PDU is shown in Figure 17.5. The first 2 bits in this format are always 1-1. The fifth bit is called the poll/final bit. The remaining 5 bits, called modifier function bits, are used to define various LLC PDU types. The bit patterns for the three types used in LLC Type 1 are shown in Figure 17.6.

The poll/final (P/F) bit is used in commands and responses as follows. In command PDUs, the P/F bit is called the P-bit. In response PDUs, it is called the F-bit. Following the receipt of a

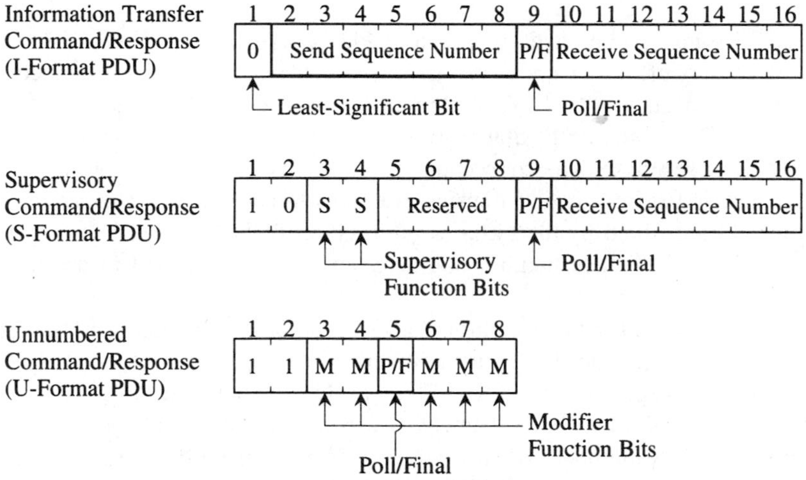

Figure 17.5 Control field of Type 1 PDUs.

	1	2	3	4	5	6	7	8
UI Command	1	1	0	0	P/F	0	0	0
XID Command	1	1	1	1	P/F	1	0	1
Test Command	1	1	0	0	P/F	1	1	1

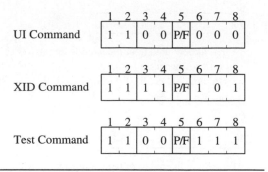

Figure 17.6 Bit patterns for Type 1 PDUs.

command PDU with the P-bit set to 1, the destination LLC sends a response PDU with the F-bit set to 1 as soon as possible. Only one PDU with a P-bit set to 1 can be outstanding in a given direction between any specific pair of LLCs. Before an LLC issues another PDU on the same link with the P-bit set to 1, the LLC should have received a response PDU with the F-bit set to 1. If no response PDU is received and the P-bit timer times-out, an error recovery procedure is started. An LLC can send response PDUs with the F-bit set to 0 at any time (without the need for a command PDU).

17.4 LLC Type 2

This LLC type provides a reliable connection-oriented service between two stations. Facilities are provided for setting up connections. Sequence numbers are used for ordered delivery. All PDUs are acknowledged by the destination. A window mechanism is used to provide flow control. The window is adjusted if PDUs are lost at intermediate points due to congestion. LLC Type 2 is considered appropriate if the error and flow controls are required and are not implemented at the transport layer.

An information transfer PDU and eight control PDUs, as listed in Table 17.2, are defined for this LLC type. If a network layer entity on station A wants to establish a connection to another network layer entity on station B, LLC at station A sends a *Set Asynchronous Balanced Mode Extended* (*SABME*) PDU to station B. Station B accepts the connection by sending an *Unnumbered Acknowledgment* (*UA*) response. The connection is now established and the network entities in the two stations can use it for information transfer in either direction. The information submitted by the network layer is transmitted by the LLCs as information PDUs. These PDUs use a modulo-128 sequence number. These sequence numbers are used for flow control and to determine whether a PDU has been lost.

A window scheme is used for flow control. An LLC authorizes the other LLC to set the window size at *k*. This means that the other LLC must never have more than *k* unacknowledged information PDUs. The window size is specified using XID PDUs as described earlier under Type 1 service. Correct in-sequence information PDUs are acknowledged using a *Receiver Ready* (*RR*) PDU containing the next expected sequence number. When a receiver detects an out-of-sequence PDU, it sends a *Reject* (*REJ*) specifying the sequence number at which the sender should begin retransmission.

If the sender does not receive an acknowledgment and times-out, it sends a supervisory command

Table 17.2 LLC Type 2 PDUs

PDU Name	Abbreviation	Command	Response
Information	I	√	√
Receive Ready	RR	√	√
Receive Not Ready	RNR	√	√
Reject	REJ	√	√
Set Asynchronous Balanced Mode Extended	SABME	√	
Disconnect	DISC	√	
Unnumbered Acknowledgment	UA		√
Disconnect Mode	DM		√
Frame Reject	FRMR		√

PDU (RR, RNR, or REJ, depending on the local state) with the poll bit (P-bit) set to 1. This forces the other station to send a response PDU with the final bit (F-bit) set to 1, which will contain the sequence number of the next expected information PDU. In either case, the sender then starts retransmission with the expected information PDU.

If a receiver is unable to process all of the incoming information PDUs, it can send a *Receiver Not Ready* (*RNR*) PDU. This requests that the transmission stop until a *Receiver Ready* (*RR*) or REJ PDU is received indicating that the busy status has been cleared.

If a connection request is to be rejected, a *Disconnected Mode* (*DM*) PDU is sent instead of an unnumbered acknowledgment PDU.

Any LLC can send a *Disconnect* (*DISC*) PDU to end a connection at any time. The other LLC then acknowledges the DISC PDU.

If a protocol error is detected, the station detecting the error sends a *Frame Reject* (*FRMR*) PDU containing a summary of the questionable parameters to the other station, which then logs the information and resets or more generally disconnects the connections.

17.5 LLC Type 3

This LLC type provides a simple "send one frame, receive one acknowledgment" service. It is suitable for applications that require acknowledgment of data but wish to avoid the complexity of a full connection-mode service. Type 3 service also allows one station to poll another for data. This service is used by the PROWAY-C Industrial Data Highway standards group because it is the simplest protocol allowing reliable transmission of data and it allows computers to poll measurement devices.

17.6 LLC Type 4

This new service is intended for applications that require stream-oriented, high-speed data transfers for point-to-point and multicast data transfers. It provides multiple concurrent connections between the same set of source/destination addresses. It supports full-duplex transfers and allows each direction of transfer to be closed separately. It allows the sender to control when acknowledgments (positive or negative) are returned. Window as well as rate based flow control mechanisms are provided. To reduce retransmissions, two error control schemes are provided: *go back n* and *selective retransmission*. This

LLC type has been designed for use over high-speed LANs and MANs. The term *stream-oriented* means that the data are treated as a sequence of bytes (rather than packets). For example, the destination can tell the source that it is missing only bytes numbered 2048 through 2304. It is specifically suitable for distributed processing applications in which the end systems are on the same extended LANs. In such cases reliable LLC operation provides reliable end-to-end communication at MAC speeds.

17.7 Summary

LLC can provide protocol discrimination, error control, sequencing, flow control, and congestion control. Several different types of LLC exist, with each providing a different level of service. Most FDDI implementations use LLC Type 1, which is an unacknowledged connectionless service. Other possibilities are connection-oriented (Type 2), acknowledged connectionless (Type 3), and high-speed transfer service (Type 4).

17.8 Further Reading

The original LLC standard is in ISO 8802-2. Type 3 operation is described in ISO/IEC 8802-2/AM2. Table 17.2 is based on Field (1986), which provides an excellent explanation and history of the three types of LLC operations. Type 4 operation is described in IEEE 802.2 working draft 91/6 being prepared under IEEE standards project P802.2g. LSAP assignments are listed in ISO/IEC TR 10178.

17.9 Self-Test Exercises

Note: Some exercises have multiple correct answers. See Appendix D for answers.

17.1 What is the primary function provided by the logical link control (LLC) sublayer?

a. Error control
b. Flow control
c. Congestion control
d. Ordered delivery
e. Protocol discrimination

17.2 What are the main differences between LLC Type 1 and LLC Type 2?

a. One is connectionless while the other is connection-oriented.
b. One provides flow control and the other does not.
c. One provides error control and the other does not.
d. One provides protocol discrimination and the other does not.

17.3 When does a network layer protocol use SNAP-SAPs?

a. When the networking layer protocol does not have built-in protocol discrimination
b. When the networking layer protocol does not have built-in flow control
c. When an ISO networking protocol is used
d. When a networking protocol not developed by ISO or its related organizations is used
e. When it wants to gather a snapshot of the network traffic

CHAPTER **18**

TCP/IP and OSI Protocols on FDDI

Would you need to change any higher layer protocols when you replace your current IEEE 802.3/Ethernet or IEEE 802.5/token ring network with an FDDI network? This question is the main topic of this chapter. The answer is yes; the introduction of FDDI has necessitated some changes in higher layer protocols. Although this question is primarily of interest to those who implement higher layer protocols, users of FDDI should be aware of these changes and ensure that the equipment they buy implements these changes. In particular, if your network contains equipment from different manufacturers, you need to ensure that these manufacturers all follow the same version of the Internet RFC or ISO/OSI protocol standard.

Layering was introduced in networking architectures so that the protocol on any layer can be changed without affecting other layers. For this reason all major networking architectures including ISO/OSI and the TCP/IP protocol suite have a layered architecture. Thus, in theory at least, when the datalink protocol is changed from IEEE 802.3/Ethernet or IEEE 802.5/token ring to FDDI, no changes should be required in higher layers. In practice, this has been found to be not quite true. Higher layer protocols were changed when Ethernet, IEEE 802.3, and IEEE 802.5 networks were introduced. The same applies to FDDI as discussed in detail in this chapter. All of these changes are in the network layer protocols.

18.1 TCP/IP over IEEE 802 LANs

As discussed earlier, LANs allow supporting of multiple hosts on one datalink. However, the hosts may be following a different set (stack) of higher layer protocols. For example, some stations on the LAN may be using an ISO/OSI stack, while others may be using a TCP/IP stack. This created a need for **protocol discrimination**, which ensures that packets originated from ISO/OSI protocols are delivered to ISO/OSI protocols (and not to TCP/IP protocols) at the destination and vice versa.

Ethernet LANs, which came into use before IEEE 802 standardization, provided protocol discrimination using a **protocol type** field. The Ethernet frame format used for IP packets is shown in Figure 18.1(a). The 2-byte protocol-type field allowed Ethernet datalink to deliver the packet to

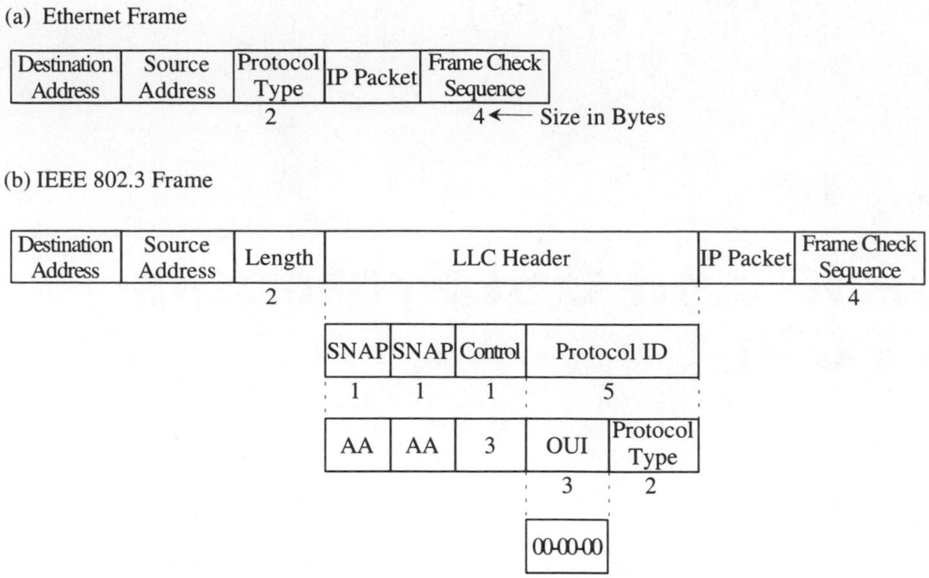

Figure 18.1 Formats of Ethernet and IEEE 802.3 frames with an IP packet.

the right network layer module. Each network layer protocol was assigned a unique protocol type number. Assignments for a few of the commonly used protocols are listed in Table 18.1.

Ethernet and IEEE 802.3 are often used synonymously. However, they are different. Ethernet refers to the protocol originally developed at Xerox and later updated by Xerox, Intel, and Digital. When Ethernet was standardized as IEEE 802.3, several changes were made to the frame format. One of the key changes was to remove the protocol-type field and to add the length field instead. Both

Table 18.1 A Sample of Ethernet Protocol Types

Decimal	Hexadecimal	Protocol Name
1536	0600	XEROX NS IDP
2048	0800	IP
2049	0801	X.75 Internet
2053	0805	X.25 Level 3
2054	0806	ARP
2560	0A00	Xerox IEEE 802.3 PUP
2561	0A01	PUP address translation
24583	6007	DEC local area VAX clusters, SCA
32824	8038	DEC LAN bridge
32923	809B	AppleTalk
32981	80D5	IBM SNA service on Ethernet

Ethernet and IEEE 802.3 restrict the minimum frame size to 64 bytes. Subtracting 16 bytes for the source address, destination address, and frame check sequence fields leaves 48 bytes for information in the minimum size frames. IEEE 802.3 allows higher layers to transmit pieces of information smaller than 48 bytes and pads them up to meet the minimum 64-byte frame size requirement. To determine where the information ends and padding begins, a length field is required in IEEE 802.3. Ethernet does not accept smaller pieces of information from higher layers and so does not need padding or the length field.

The format of an IEEE 802.3 frame carrying an IP packet is shown in Figure 18.1(b). Since a cable may carry frames of Ethernet as well as the IEEE 802.3 format, a station must be able to determine the format of the frame easily. This is done by ensuring that the Ethernet protocol types will always have a value higher than 1500. Since the information size in IEEE 802.3 and Ethernet frames cannot be more than 1500 bytes, the length field is always less than or equal to 1500. Thus, if the two bytes following the source address field are less than 1501, the frame is assumed to be in IEEE 802.3 format; otherwise it is assumed to be in Ethernet format.

In IEEE 802.3 frames, the length field is followed by the LLC header, which consists of a DSAP, an SSAP, and a control field. As discussed in Section 17.3, DSAP and SSAP are LLC-level source and destination addresses. They essentially indicate the network layer service used at the destination and source, respectively. All standard network layer protocols have been assigned a unique 1-byte **LLC service access point (LSAP)** value. These values are listed in Table 18.2. As seen from this table, the OSI network layer has an LSAP value of FE_{16}. An OSI packet traveling on IEEE 802.3 uses FE in DSAP and SSAP fields. The same applies to other IEEE 802 LANs.

LSAPs are only 1 byte long and thus are a scarce resource. LSAP values have been assigned only for standard network layer protocols. Proprietary network layer protocols, such as Digital's DNA or IBM's SNA, do not have unique LSAP assignments. Instead, they use an additional protocol layer called the **Subnetwork Access Protocol (SNAP)**, which has been assigned an LSAP value of AA_{16}. This value is known as **SNAP Service Access Point (SNAP-SAP)**. Whenever an unnumbered information (UI) frame has AA_{16} in the DSAP field and AA_{16} in the SSAP field, the 5 bytes following the control field are interpreted as a unique protocol identifier as shown in Figure 18.1(b). The first

Table 18.2 Assigned LSAP Values

LSAP	Assignment
00	Null address
02	IEEE 802.1b LLC management
42	ISO/IEC 10038 bridge spanning tree protocol
AA	IEEE 802 SNAP SAP
06	Internet protocol (IP)
0E	IEC 955 (PROWAY C) network management maintenance and initialization
8E	IEC 955 (PROWAY C) active station list maintenance
4E	ISO 9506 manufacturing message service
7E	ISO 8208 X.25 network layer protocol
FE	ISO/IEC TR 9577 OSI network layer
FF	ISO 8802-2 global DSAP address

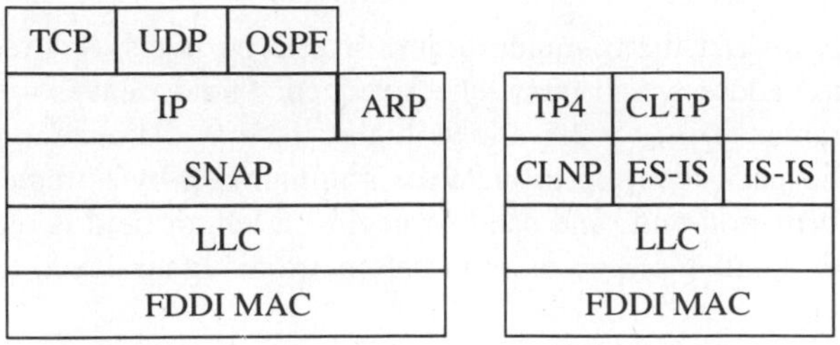

(a) TCP/IP Protocol Layering (b) OSI Protocol Layering

Figure 18.2 Protocol layers for TCP/IP and OSI protocols on FDDI.

3 bytes of the identifier indicate the organization owning the protocol and the remaining 2 bytes are a unique identifier assigned by the organization. The first 3 bytes are actually the **organizationally unique identifier** (**OUI**) assigned to the organization by the IEEE.

Although TCP/IP protocols have been assigned an LSAP value of 06_{16}, they do not use it because, unlike OSI protocols, the network layer of the TCP/IP stack does not have built-in protocol discrimination. It is said that when Internet folks asked ISO for an LSAP for IP, ISO gladly assigned 06 for it. However, later the Internet people realized that since they do not have the protocol discrimination, they needed another LSAP for ARP. At this point, ISO requested them to consider using the SNAP-SAP instead, which is what the TCP/IP protocols now use. For OUI, they use a value of 00-00-00, which incidentally belongs to Xerox Corporation. The 2-byte Ethernet protocol-type (EtherType) field follows the OUI. The complete IEEE 802.3 frame contents for an IP packet are shown in Figure 18.1(b). The LLC control field value of 3 indicates the frame contains **unnumbered information** (**UI**). This means that the frame is a datagram following LLC Type 1 and does not have any sequence number.

Unlike TCP/IP protocols, the OSI architecture expects protocol discrimination to take place within the layer in which the protocol is run rather than below it. Thus, LLC need not distinguish between various OSI network layer protocols. The OSI network layer does it itself. The first byte of the network layer header contains a **Network Layer Protocol Identifier** (**NLPID**). Since OSI protocols are self-discriminating, no SNAP header is necessary.

The protocol layering used with TCP/IP protocols and OSI protocols on FDDI is shown in Figure 18.2. The network layer protocols shown in the OSI stack are the Connectionless Network Protocol (CLNP) (ISO 8473), End System–Intermediate System Protocol (ES-IS) (ISO 9542), and Intermediate System–Intermediate System Protocol (IS-IS) (ISO 10589). Other OSI network protocols follow a similar layering. These OSI protocols are briefly described later in this chapter.

18.2 ARP over FDDI

In addition to the problem of protocol discrimination, the introduction of LANs also introduced the problem of finding datalink addresses of stations on the LANs. Each station on an IP network has an unique Internet address, which is used by the network layer to route the packets. Internet addresses are 32 bits long and consist of two parts—a network number followed by a local address. There are three formats or classes of Internet addresses. In Class a, the high-order bit is zero, the next 7 bits are

Frame Control	Destination Address	Source Address	AA	AA	3	00-00-00	EtherType
1	6	6	1	1	1	3	2

Hardware Type	Protocol Type	Hardware Address Length	Protocol Address Length	Operation Code	
2	2	1	1	2	← Size in Bytes

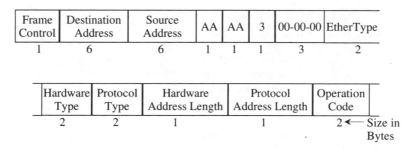

Figure 18.3 Format of an ARP packet.

the network, and the last 24 bits are the local address. In Class b, the 2 high-order bits are one-zero, the next 14 bits are the network, and the last 16 bits are the local address. In Class c, the 3 high-order bits are one-one-zero, the next 21 bits are the network, and the last 8 bits are the local address. The local address may be further subdivided into two parts of variable lengths—subnet number and host number. Each LAN in the network can be assigned a subnet number. Thus, the network number and the subnet number are sufficient to forward the packet to the final router, which is directly connected to the destination station. For stations connected to the router via point-to-point links, there is no subnet number, the host number consists of the complete local address and is sufficient for routing the packet to its destination. However, if the destination is on a LAN, the router (or source if it is also on the same LAN) should know the destination's hardware address (MAC address) to ensure that the destination will pick up the frame from the LAN. The **Address Resolution Protocol (ARP)** was designed to solve this problem of finding the MAC address corresponding to an Internet address.

The router maintains a translation table for this purpose. If the node is not found in the table, the router *broadcasts* an ARP request whose meaning is "Does any one know the datalink address corresponding to local address X?" The ARP can be responded to either by node X or by any other node on the network that knows about node X. The datalink address of node X is returned in the ARP response. The router then uses this address to forward the packet to X. The format of an ARP frame on an IEEE 802.3 network is shown in Figure 18.3. Notice that, as explained in Section 18.1, the ARP frame uses the SNAP-SAPs (AA), UI control, OUI of 00-00-00. The Ethernet protocol type value of 0806_{16} (2054_{10}) has been assigned for ARP. Other fields are hardware type (2 bytes), protocol type (0800_{16} or 2048_{10} for IP) that is being resolved (2 bytes), hardware address length (1 byte), protocol address length (1 byte), and an operation code (2 bytes). The hardware type of 1 indicates Ethernet, while a 6 indicates an IEEE 802 protocol. Table 18.3 lists these and other assignments. The hardware address refers to a MAC address. Its length is 6 bytes for all IEEE 802 protocols. The protocol address length gives the length of the address in the protocol being resolved. This value is 4 (bytes) for Internet addresses. The operation code of 1 indicates an ARP request, while 2 indicates an ARP response.

When FDDI rings were added to IP networks, the implementors did not foresee any need to change network and higher layer protocols since FDDI conforms to the IEEE 802 datalink standard. Presumably, the higher layer software written for IEEE 802.3 and 802.5 should continue to work over FDDI. This, as the implementors soon found out, was a myth. Stations from different vendors that used to talk happily over an IEEE 802 network could not talk over FDDI. An Internet engineering task force (IETF) group was formed to resolve all the issues related to the use of TCP/IP protocols over FDDI. ARP was one of the first protocols to be discussed by this group.

Table 18.3 Hardware Type Used in ARP Packets

Type	Protocol
1	Ethernet (10Mb)
2	Experimental Ethernet (3Mb)
3	Amateur radio AX.25
4	Proteon ProNET token ring
5	Chaos
6	IEEE 802 networks
7	ARCNET
8	Hyperchannel
9	Lanstar
10	Autonet short address
11	LocalTalk
12	LocalNet (IBM PCNet or SYTEK LocalNET)
13	Ultra link
14	SMDS
15	Frame relay
16	Asynchronous transfer mode (ATM)

The main issues related to the use of ARP over FDDI were the ARP hardware type for FDDI and the bit order for addresses in the data field. These are discussed next.

The hardware type value of 1 is used on Ethernet, while 6 is used on IEEE 802 networks. The issue was whether a new hardware type should be assigned for FDDI. Even before the issue was resolved some implementations of ARP on FDDI were already using either 1 or 6. Unfortunately, differing values between Ethernet and IEEE 802 networks cause interoperability problems in bridged environments. To avoid such problems, the IETF group resolved that FDDI stations shall send and receive a hardware type value of 1. This ensures that all IP stations on IEEE 802.3/Ethernet networks can communicate with all IP stations on FDDI networks.

The next and probably most confusing issue is that of the bit order. RFC 826, which describes ARP, says nothing about the bit order of data items. In most implementations, the data field is transmitted using the **native order** of the underlying LAN, that is, the least-significant bit (lsb) first for IEEE 802.3 and 802.4 LANs and most-significant bit (msb) first for IEEE 802.5 LANs. Station addresses on LAN interfaces are stored in a read-only memory (ROM). These ROMs are generally in native order. Thus, ROMs from 802.3 and FDDI interfaces from the same manufacturer have OUI bits reversed with respect to each other in the first 3 bytes of the address.

Although ARP was implemented on both IEEE 802.3 and 802.5 networks using their native order, the two types of networks were rarely bridged together. The problem of bit order was not an issue until FDDI came along as the backbone network supported by all camps. Little-endians and big-endians (see Sidebar in Chapter 2), who were foes for generations, were forced to be neighbors on FDDI. Which order should be used for addresses in the data field of FDDI frames? Big-endians, who belong to the IEEE 802.5/token ring camp, argued in favor of using the most-significant bit order. Little-endians, who belong to the IEEE 802.3/Ethernet camp, argued in favor of using the least-significant bit order. Although FDDI does use the msb for its data, the use of msb for addresses causes confusion for ARP exchanges between IEEE 802.3 and FDDI stations connected via a bridge.

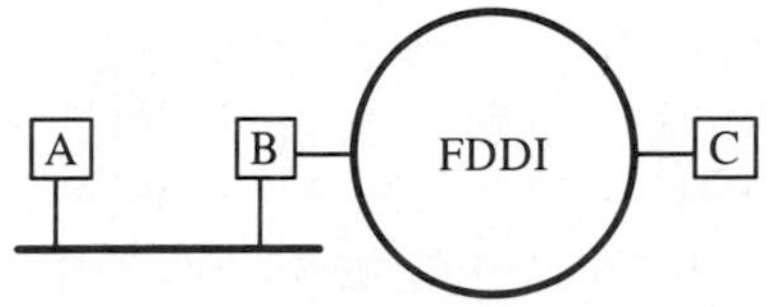

Figure 18.4 An extended LAN consisting of an IEEE 802.3/Ethernet and an FDDI network.

Figure 18.4 shows an extended LAN consisting of an IEEE 802.3/Ethernet and an FDDI LAN connected via a bridge. All stations on the extended LAN are part of the same IP network. When station A on the IEEE 802.3 LAN responds to an ARP request from station C on FDDI, the addresses in the data field of the ARP response will be misinterpreted by station C. The problem, of course, is that the bridge is supposed to be transparent to both stations A and C and they do not know that they are talking to a station on a different type of LAN. The bridge is the only one who knows that the frame is going from one type of network to another. But it is not supposed to read or interpret the network layer headers or data fields and cannot reverse them correctly.

The issue was finally resolved by the IETF working group by insisting that the addresses in the data field should be transmitted as a hexadecimal string in the canonical form regardless of the native order of the network. This was done due to a preponderance of existing Ethernet implementations. Later, IEEE 802 and FDDI committees also adopted this resolution.

The following example explains the bit order for an address at various points in the network.

Example 18.1 Consider the SMT synchronous bandwidth allocator address. In illustrative hexadecimal notation, this address is:

01-80-C2-00-01-30

In Example 2.4, we explained that in the address field of all IEEE 802 networks this address would appear as the following bit pattern (as seen on the wire):

10000000 – 00000001 – 01000011 – 00000000 – 10000000 – 00001100

FDDI does not transmit individual bits of the address. It uses 4b/5b coding to translate successive 4-bit symbols into 5-bit codes, which are transmitted on the fiber. Thus, the code bits seen on the fiber in the address field will be:

Symbols:	8	0	0	1	4	3	0	0	8	0	0	4
Code bits:	10010	11110	11110	01001	01010	10101	11110	11110	10010	11110	11110	11010

However, when this address is carried as data inside an FDDI frame, it is transmitted as if a hexadecimal string 0180C2000130 were being sent. The FDDI code bits corresponding to this hexadecimal string are:

Symbols:	0	1	8	0	C	2	0	0	0	1	3	0
Code bits:	11110	01001	10010	11110	11010	10100	11110	11110	11110	01001	10101	11110

Notice that these code bits are quite different. Incidentally, this address as seen on the wire in the data field of other IEEE 802 protocols will be

IEEE 802.3 or 802.4:

Hexadecimal	0 1	8 0	C 2	0 0	0 1	3 0
Binary	0000 0001	1000 0000	1100 0010	0000 0000	0000 0001	0011 0000
Wire	1000 0000	0000 0001	0100 0011	0000 0000	1000 0000	0000 1100

or IEEE 802.5:

Binary	0000 0001	1000 0000	1100 0010	0000 0000	0000 0001	0010 0000
Wire	0000 0001	1000 0000	1100 0010	0000 0000	0000 0001	0010 0000

□

Notice that the bit pattern on wire for the IEEE 802.5 (and FDDI) networks is different depending on whether the address is in the address field or the data field of the frame. For IEEE 802.3 and 802.4 LANs, the bit pattern for an address is the same in all fields.

The method described here for ARP is recommended for all other protocols in which MAC addresses are carried within a data field (RARP, BOOTP, SNMP, etc.).

18.3 Ethernet and IEEE 802.3 Frame Translation

One issue that has nothing to do with TCP/IP as such but is related to some of the topics discussed in the last two sections is that of translating Ethernet and IEEE 802.3 frames as they traverse through an FDDI.

As explained earlier, Ethernet and IEEE 802.3 are similar but different. They both use the carrier sense multiple access with collision detection (CSMA/CD) method to share the medium but use different frame formats. When you see an IEEE 802.3/Ethernet network, some stations on it may be speaking only Ethernet, others only IEEE 802.3, and some may be speaking both. IEEE 802.3 frames use LLC while Ethernet frames do not. FDDI stations understand only IEEE 802. Bridges connecting IEEE 802.3/Ethernet LANs to FDDI have to translate Ethernet frames to IEEE 802 format.

Figure 18.5 shows three different frames on the left and the corresponding FDDI translations on the right. Figure 18.5(a) shows an IEEE 802.3 frame with a DSAP/SSAP LLC header. FDDI translation of this is straightforward: The length field (and padding, if any) is removed, the frame-control (FC) field is added, the bit order of the addresses is reversed, and the CRC is recomputed. The LLC headers are not reversed. Figure 18.5(b) shows an IEEE 802.3 frame with a SNAP/SAP LLC header. Again, the length field is removed, the frame-control (FC) field is added, the bit order of the addresses is reversed, and the CRC is recomputed. Figure 18.5(c) shows an Ethernet frame. In this case, the bridge takes the data and protocol type fields from the frame, adds a SNAP/SAP LLC header with an OUI of 00-00-00, adds an FDDI header with a frame-control field, and recomputes the CRC. Note that in all three cases, the CRC has to be recomputed. If these frames exit FDDI on to another IEEE 802.3/Ethernet LAN, the exiting bridge converts the frame back to either IEEE 802.3 or Ethernet format by looking at the DSAP, SSAP, and OUI fields. If a SNAP format frame has zero in the OUI field, the frame is translated to an Ethernet format; otherwise it is translated to an IEEE 802.3 LLC format.

A SNAP/SAP format LLC frame with an OUI of 00-00-00 is known as RFC-1042 frame. The name is based on the Internet request for comment (RFC), which describes the rules. Notice that with the preceding rules, all IEEE 802.3 SNAP/SAP format frames sent with zero OUI (RFC-1042 frames) become Ethernet frames at the exit LAN. This is not a problem for TCP/IP hosts since RFC 1122 on host requirements specifies that all TCP/IP hosts on CSMA/CD LANs *must* be able to receive Ethernet format packets.

When the IEEE 802.1d committee discussed the preceding rules for IEEE 802.3/Ethernet frame translation, it discovered that unless the rules are changed, AppleTalk™ protocols, used in Macintosh™ personal computers, will stop working. AppleTalk has two different versions. AppleTalk I uses Ether-

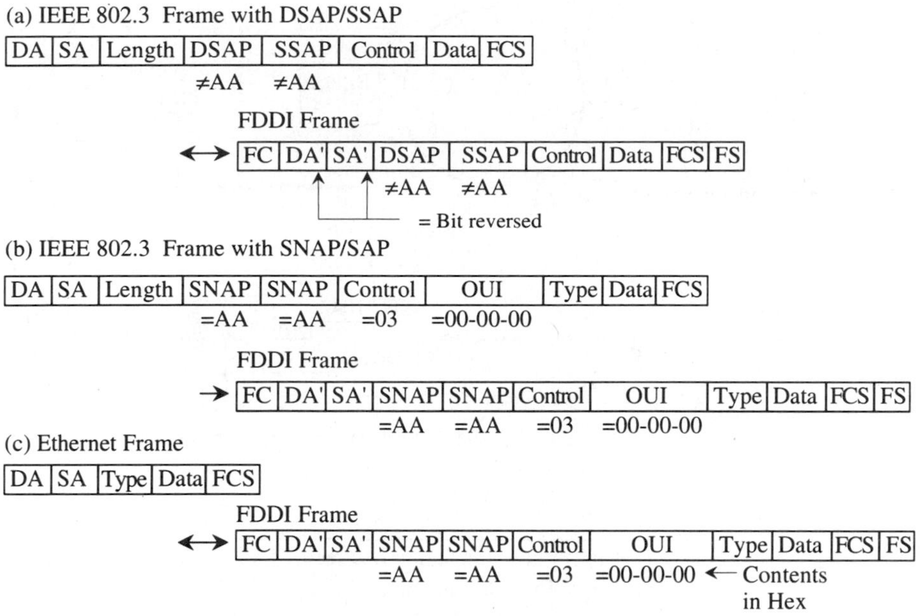

Figure 18.5 Ethernet, IEEE 802.3, and FDDI frame translations. See text and Figure 18.6 for further modifications.

net format frames while AppleTalk II uses *only* IEEE 802.3 format frames on CSMA/CD networks. This feature is used to prevent the hosts that are implementing the two versions from intermingling and confusing each other. However, the newer version uses an LLC SNAP/SAP format with an OUI of 00-00-00, which is same as that used for IP packets. Now consider what happens when two CSMA/CD networks, which used to be connected directly via a bridge, are connected via an FDDI backbone. This is shown in Figure 18.6(a). Host A on the left CSMA/CD network sends an IEEE 802.3 message to host D on the right CSMA/CD network. Host D receives an Ethernet format frame and cannot understand it. After some discussion, the problem was fixed by designing a *selective translation algorithm* that requires the bridges to look up the protocol ID value in a special table (called the *selective translation table*) and handle the frames differently if the value is found in the table. The table currently contains only one entry—AppleTalk Address Resolution Protocol ($80F3_{16}$). On entry to FDDI, the bridge classifies the frame as one of the following types:

1. Ethernet frame with protocol type in the table
2. Ethernet frame with protocol type not in the table
3. IEEE 802.3 frames.

Frames of the first category are transmitted on to FDDI with an OUI of 00-00-F8. Frames of the second category are transmitted with an OUI of 00-00-00. On exit from FDDI onto a CSMA/CD LAN, the bridge classifies the FDDI frames in the following categories:

1. Frames with OUI = 00-00-F8
2. Frames with OUI = 00-00-00 and protocol type in the table

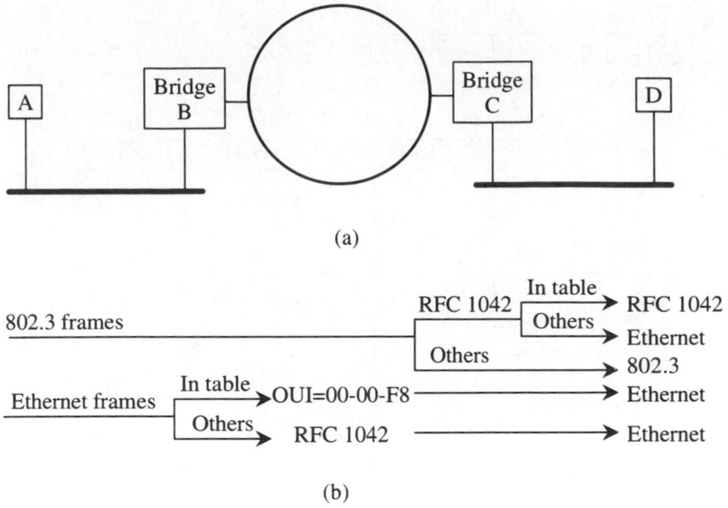

Figure 18.6 Frame translation between FDDI and IEEE 802.3/Ethernet networks.

3. Frames with OUI = 00-00-00 and protocol type not in the table
4. Frames with other OUIs.

Frames of the second and fourth categories are transmitted on the CSMA/CD LANs as IEEE 802.3 frames. Frames in the remaining two categories are converted to Ethernet format. Figure 18.6(b) shows how various types of frames get translated for traversing the FDDI backbone. All lookups in both directions are done using the same table. That is, each bridge contains only one table. It is a nonvolatile table in the sense that its contents are preserved across a power failure.

Note that the use of 00-00-F8 OUI allows a frame to maintain its type (Ethernet or IEEE 802.3) when it crosses an intervening FDDI (or other non-IEEE 802.3/Ethernet) LAN. It allows two bridges on such a LAN to use the LAN as if it were a tunnel (with no intermediate exits) and, hence, the protocol is called the *bridge tunnel encapsulation protocol*; the corresponding service is called *bridge tunnel service*; and the 00-00-F8 is called the *bridge tunnel OUI*. This OUI is not used in any other 802.3 frames.

SNAP/SAPs were assumed throughout the preceding discussion. IEEE 802.3 frames using other LSAPs or control fields are transmitted on FDDI without these lookup rules.

18.4 IP over FDDI

The ARP issues discussed in the previous section were only the beginning of issues raised by the introduction of FDDI. Several other issues have since been raised in IETF's IP Over FDDI Working Group meetings. Some issues have been resolved and others are still under study.

The most difficult issue is that of a dual ring. Much of this section is devoted to that problem. Before getting into that issue, let us discuss other simpler issues that have been resolved by the IETF. Most of these simple issues limit the options offered by the FDDI standard. The presence of many options introduces complexity because everyone is forced to implement every option. If some stations do not implement an option, interoperability becomes a problem. IETF, therefore, looked at several FDDI options and decided to ignore or limit them. These are as follows:

1. *Status Indicators*: FDDI frames contain address-recognized (A) and frame-copied (C) status indicators that can be used for flow control and retransmission. Thus, if a frame comes back with the A-indicator set but C reset, it indicates that the destination station is congested. The source could then wait and retransmit the frame. Such hop-by-hop retransmission strategies have been found to be less useful than end-to-end retransmission strategies. Also, setting of a C-indicator does not guarantee that the frame was successfully delivered to the host CPU. The frame can be dropped by an adapter if the host runs out of buffer. TCP/IP protocols, therefore, do not use the A and C status indicators. The use of these indicators for link level retransmission or ARP cache entry invalidation is left as a local implementation decision.
2. *Restricted Traffic*: FDDI offers a restricted asynchronous transmission mode for bulk data transfer. In this mode, the token is repeatedly used by a pair of stations. This mode can unfairly affect the response time of other traffic on the network and is, therefore, not recommended. TCP/IP protocols are not allowed to use this mode. Of course, the stations receive all frames addressed to them including those sent using the restricted mode.
3. *Synchronous Traffic*: The synchronous transmission mode allows a guaranteed access time and throughput. At this time, TCP/IP protocols do not use this mode for transmission. Again, all frames, whether synchronous or asynchronous, are received by stations.
4. *Maximum Frame Size*: FDDI allows a maximum frame size of 4500 bytes, which includes four preamble symbols, one ending delimiter, and three frame status indicators. The issue of what packet size should be used by TCP/IP application was discussed in IETF. A suggestion was made that the applications should limit the user data size to 4096 bytes (4 kB). Allowing 256 bytes for headers of all protocol layers would result in an FDDI frame size of 4352 bytes. Note that a 4352-byte frame can be segmented nicely into three Ethernet frames, while the largest FDDI frame (4472 bytes of information) requires three full Ethernet frames plus a small fourth frame. The latter is not efficient. Therefore, 4352 is the recommended maximum frame size in that all TCP/IP stations must not send larger frames and must be able to receive this size frame. The stations may choose to receive large frames also. Later the maximum frame size of 4352 was also adopted by the FDDI/SMT working group as the maximum SMT frame size.
5. *Padding*: IEEE 802.3/Ethernet networks require a minimum frame size of 64 bytes. Smaller frames are padded to bring their size to 64 bytes. There is no minimum frame size requirement on FDDI. In bridged environments, FDDI stations must be prepared to receive and ignore the trailing pad bytes.
6. *Address Length*: The FDDI MAC standard allows two different lengths for source and destination addresses in frames. The address can be either long (48-bit) or short (16-bit). Short addresses are used so rarely, if ever, that their presence introduces unnecessary complexity. IETF does not allow 16-bit addresses to be used in TCP/IP networks.
7. *IP Group Addresses*: IP supports a method for multicasting on an IP subnet. On an FDDI, the IP group address is mapped to an FDDI group address by placing the low-order 23 bits of the Internet address into the low-order 23 bits of the FDDI group address 01-00-5E-00-00-00. For example, the IP group address 224.255.0.2 (all numbers in decimal) is mapped to 01-00-5E-7F-00-02 (canonical order) or 80:00:7A:FE:00:40 (msb order).

   The broadcast Internet address (the address on that network with a local address of all binary 1's) is mapped to the broadcast FDDI address (of all binary 1's). For example, the address 36.255.255.255 is mapped to FF-FF-FF-FF-FF-FF.

The most difficult issue in running IP over FDDI is that of the dual ring. IP protocols assume that there is a single link connecting two stations in the same IP subnetwork. Thus, the issues of path splitting and load balancing could be left for the network and higher layers. Prior to the introduction of FDDI, all IP LANs offered a unique path from a given IP station to another IP station on the same LAN. Thus, a LAN was considered to be one IP subnetwork. The problem with a dual-ring FDDI occurs when there are a few dual-MAC stations and both rings are used simultaneously. Are the two rings two IP subnetworks? The answer is neither yes nor no. Either answer leads to technical difficulties.

If we treat the two rings of the dual-ring FDDI as one IP subnetwork, then we need to allow for the possibility of a single IP host having two MAC addresses. This is currently not allowed. For example, the dual-MAC station C of Figure 18.7 would respond with two ARP responses containing a MAC address C1 and C2. Other stations will have to try both MAC addresses since some will be able to reach C via C1 while others will be able to reach C via C2. The information about which address is on the primary and which is on secondary will have to be included in ARP responses. If this is done, it would give the benefit of load splitting on the two rings between two dual-MAC stations. However, stations on other LANs connected to FDDI via bridges would be highly confused by the two ARP responses.

IP broadcasts and multicasts do not work properly when single-MAC dual-attachment stations are placed on both rings. If a router forwards them on both rings, packets will be duplicated at some hosts and routers.

IP routing protocols always route toward the subnets (rather than the hosts) and expect that the last router will be able to reach the host in one hop. To achieve this on dual-ring FDDIs, all routers must have dual MACs.

If we treat the two rings of a dual-ring FDDI as two IP subnetworks, then there must be an IP router connecting the two subnetworks as shown in Figure 18.7. All subnetworks of an IP network are connected via routers. Any dual-MAC host could be used as a router. When the FDDI LAN wraps, the two subnets continue to behave as though they were on separate media (even though they are sharing the same cable). This implies that the traffic will be forwarded between the two subnets

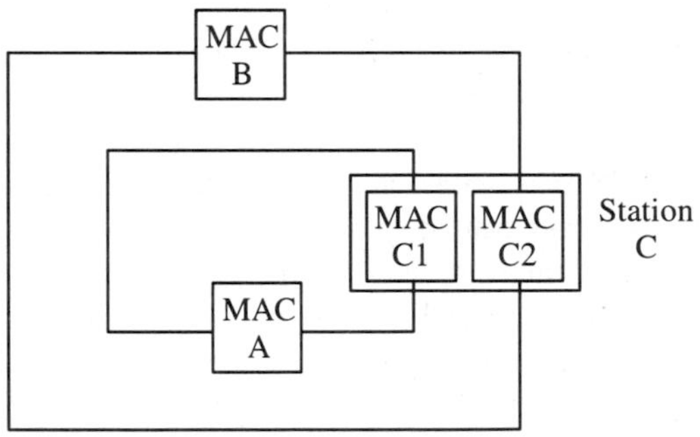

Figure 18.7 A dual-MAC station will respond with two ARP responses if both rings are treated as one subnet.

by the router. This helps MACs, which normally reside on different rings, avoid discovering that they are directly connected.

It is clear that using both rings of a dual ring creates problems for TCP/IP protocols. The IP Over FDDI Working Group of the Internet Engineering Task Force has disbanded and it seems unlikely that simultaneous use of both MACs in dual-MAC stations will be resolved in the near future.

18.5 RIP over FDDI

The routing information protocol (RIP) is one of the most common routing protocols in use in the Internet. The function of a routing protocol is to maintain the forwarding tables in the routers.

RIP implementations use IP single-subnet broadcasts for neighbor discovery and routing information distribution. RIP can work on the dual-subnet model provided FDDI stations implement the subnet broadcast reception correctly. This requires that a one-to-one mapping of subnet and interfaces be maintained and, during the wrap state, broadcasts meant for one subnet will be ignored if received on the other interface. This will prevent router interfaces on separate rings from discovering each other when the network wraps.

RIP has a problem working with the single-subnet model. When the ring wraps, the routers will find some MACs that will become unreachable when the ring unwraps. The RIP specifies a 180-second timeout interval for routing information. Global routing adjustments may take quite a bit longer and the traffic will be lost for an unacceptably long period.

18.6 OSI Network Layer Protocols

The OSI network layer protocols also needed to be modified when FDDI was introduced. The problems are somewhat similar to, although not as severe as, the case of TCP/IP protocols. We first describe the protocols and then discuss the effect of bit order and dual-MAC stations.

The OSI connectionless network protocol (CLNP) provides functionality roughly equivalent to that provided by IP. The users of the network service have addresses called **network service access points** (**NSAPs**). Typically, all NSAP addresses in a host are identical except for the last byte. The common part of the addresses is known as the **network entity title** (**NET**) and the last byte is called the **selector**. Each host has a single network address (NET) but can have several MAC addresses.

The End System–Intermediate System (ES-IS) protocol of the OSI protocol suite provides a functionality similar to ARP. However, the operation of the protocol is time-driven. ARP, on the other hand, is event-driven. An ARP request is sent only when a packet needs to be sent to a host with an unknown MAC address. If such an event does not occur for days, the MAC address will not be required or learned. End systems periodically multicast *hello messages* to an "all intermediate systems" group address. These messages contain the network layer address of the transmitter. The MAC address is taken from the source field of the frame. A host with multiple MACs transmits hellos on each of its MACs. Multiple MACs advertising the same network address do not cause any confusion. In fact, this feature can be used for load balancing traffic among various MACs attached to the same host.

The ES-IS hello messages also contain a holding time value, which indicates how long the information should be held before being discarded. If no new hellos are received from an end-system by the time the holding timer expires, the end-system is assumed to be unreachable. Generally the holding time value is twice the announcement interval.

The OSI routers use the Intermediate System–Intermediate System (IS-IS) protocol to detect each other and establish routes to each destination system. They periodically multicast *IS-IS hello messages* to other routers on the LAN. These messages also contain, among other things, a holding time value. If no hellos are received again within this time, the sending router is assumed to be down and its information is no longer used.

Various routers on the LAN elect a *designated IS*, which takes the responsibility of providing reachability information about end-systems on the LAN to other routers outside of the LAN. The designated IS is elected based on the *priority parameter* carried in the IS-IS hello messages. The IS with the highest priority wins.

When two ISs receive each other's hello messages, they form an *adjacency* or neighbor relationship and then report this adjacency to other ISs. This information is used to determine the paths between different hosts on the network.

18.7 Impact of FDDI

Introduction of FDDI has brought out issues related to bit order and support of multiple MACs. As discussed earlier, these have created some problems for TCP/IP protocols.

For OSI protocols, bit ordering is not as big a problem as for the TCP/IP suite. ES-IS does not encode MAC addresses in the data field of its hello messages. The MAC information is derived from the MAC header, which is always received in the native bit order and there is no ambiguity. ES-IS does carry MAC addresses in the redirect messages. The standard does not mention bit order. A defect report has been submitted to ISO and a correction will be made to state that the addresses in data fields should always be encoded in canonical bit order.

IS-IS encodes MAC addresses in certain messages but the standard initially did not mention bit order. A U.S. ballot comment was submitted later to make it clear that the addresses in data fields should be encoded as a hexadecimal string in canonical representation.

Wrapping and unwrapping of a dual-ring FDDI network has no direct impact on CLNP. The state of the ring affects reachability and routing but those functions are handled by the ES-IS and IS-IS protocols. Dual-MAC stations can take advantage of load-splitting across the two rings since a single host can have multiple MAC addresses.

Whenever a ring changes state (wraps or unwraps), the reachability information maintained by various hosts on the FDDI network becomes invalid and some of the traffic starts getting lost into a black hole. This continues until the information times-out. The timer-driver nature of the ES-IS and IS-IS protocols is, therefore, very helpful. The effect of ring state changes can be minimized by reducing the holding timers and the announcement periods. Since this increases the multicast hello traffic, the timers cannot be reduced arbitrarily. The need for rapid adaptation to topology changes has to be traded off against higher traffic when there are no changes. Nonetheless, the problem is solved simply by tuning the parameters. No protocol changes are required as was the case with TCP/IP protocols.

The impact of network state changes can also be minimized by proper configuration. The goal is to minimize the effect of the network state on the transit traffic. A secondary goal should be to maintain the stability of the designated IS. If the identity of the designated IS changes, all of the end-system adjacencies must be announced by the new designated IS, which requires significant network resources.

A simple rule of thumb to minimize the effect of the wrap state on transit traffic is to ensure that all ISs with external connectivity have only a single MAC. During the unwrapped state, these

MACs are on the primary. During the wrapped state, no new adjacencies are created among these MACs and, therefore, the transit traffic is not affected by the wrap state.

The stability of the designated IS can be maximized by choosing a dual-MAC IS to be the preferred candidate and configuring that IS to announce a higher priority value on both rings than any other IS. In this way, it will remain the designated IS on both rings, regardless of the wrap state of the network.

18.8 OSPF over FDDI

The Open Shortest Path First (OSPF) protocol has recently been introduced in the TCP/IP protocol suite as a candidate to replace RIP. We did not discuss it earlier because much of the IS-IS discussion applies to OSPF as well.

In OSPF, routers use a periodic multicast of hello messages to discover other routers. It is very similar to IS-IS. One major difference is that OSPF enforces the concept of IP subnets, while IS-IS ignores the concept of IP subnets when establishing adjacencies. In OSPF, the adjacencies are established only among routers on the same subnet. Multiple subnets can reside on the same physical cable without affecting the adjacencies. As a result, OSPF works well in the dual-subnet model, since the adjacencies between routers do not change when the network wraps and unwraps. In the single-subnet model, OSPF will behave similar to IS-IS and traffic will be lost on state changes. The effect can be minimized by reducing the holding timeout interval.

18.9 Summary

IEEE 802.3/Ethernet and IEEE 802.5/token ring network designers made several incompatible design decisions. These incompatibilities were known before the introduction of FDDI, but were not considered important. Use of FDDI as a backbone for these networks has brought to light the incompatibilities. In particular, the use of different bit orders in the two standards causes significant confusion when the addresses are exchanged between stations on different networks. The bit order issue has now been resolved successfully. This has required changes in both the TCP/IP and OSI suite of protocols as well as in the IEEE 802 standards.

Another major issue is that of dual-MAC dual-attachment stations. Before the introduction of FDDI, most LANs provided a unique path between stations. The dual-ring configuration of FDDI provides two paths. Wrapping of the ring can change these two paths into one and change reachability and connectivity of stations. This affects the operation of some networking protocols. In the TCP/IP suite of protocols, ARP, IP, and RIP are affected by this problem. The ISO/OSI protocols are less affected.

18.10 Further Reading

IEEE 802 CSMA/CD, token bus, token ring LANs are specified in ISO 8802-3, 8802-4, and 8802-5 standards, respectively. Selective translation and bridge tunneling is covered by IEEE 802.1H.

Much of the discussion in this chapter is from Katz (1990a and 1990b). RFC 1390, which supersedes RFCs 1188 and 1103, documents the method for use of IP and ARP on FDDI networks. This RFC builds on the material presented in RFC 1042, which describes the use of IP and ARP on IEEE 802 networks. Kochem, Hiscock, and Mayo (1991) discuss the issue of frame translation.

The Internet Protocol (IP), the Address Resolution Protocol (ARP), the Routing Information Protocol (RIP), and OSPF are described in RFC 791, RFC 826, RFC 1058, and RFC 1247, respectively. RFC 917 describes the address structure for subnets. See RFC 1329 for an idea on how IP and ARP can be used on FDDI networks with single-MAC and dual-MAC stations. The ARP hardware type assignments are listed in the Internet RFC 1340 entitled *Assigned Numbers*.

The use of OSI protocols over FDDI is not documented *per se*, but the use of OSI protocols over 802.2 is documented in ISO/IEC 8880-1, 8880-2 and 8880-3. The network layer discrimination process is described in ISO/IEC TR 9577. ISO CLNP, ES-IS, and IS-IS protocols are described in ISO 8473, ISO 9542, and ISO/IEC 10589, respectively.

Figures 18.2 and 18.7 have been adapted from Katz (1990a).

18.11 Self-Test Exercises

Note: Some exercises have multiple correct answers. See Appendix D for answers.

18.1 What is the purpose of the address resolution protocol (ARP)?

a. To convert IP addresses to MAC addresses
b. To convert MAC addresses to IP addresses
c. To resolve the duplicate address problem
d. To determine if the addresses in frames are from valid sources

18.2 What bit order should be used to carry MAC addresses in the data field of higher layer protocols?

a. Least-significant-bit first
b. Most-significant-bit first
c. Depends on the bit order used by the source system
d. Depends on the bit order used by the destination system

18.3 What are the differences between IEEE 802.3 and Ethernet?

a. There is no difference.
b. The frame formats are different.
c. The LLC sublayer can be used in one but not the other.
d. The routing layer can be used on one but not the other.

18.4 Which of the following apply when using IP over FDDI?:

a. Frame status indicators are used for error and flow control.
b. Restricted traffic is used for bulk data transmission.
c. Synchronous mode is used for real time traffic.
d. Maximum FDDI frame size of 4500 bytes is used.
e. Small frames are padded to bring their length up to 64 bytes.
f. Short (16-bit) addresses are used in small internets.
g. Multicast is not allowed.
h. Both rings are used simultaneously in a dual-ring configuration.
i. None of the above.

CHAPTER 19

Buying and Installing Fiber Cables

19.1 Overview

If you decide to use FDDI, you will have to design a plan for laying out fiber cables between the buildings and within buildings. You will have to analyze this plan to ensure that it meets all requirements. You will have to choose proper types of fiber cables for various sections of the cable plant. This includes choosing the proper types of connectors, splices, and other supplies. Finally, you should test the cable plant to ensure that there are no hidden breaks in the cable and that all parts meet the specifications.

The problem of designing a layout and analyzing it is addressed in Chapter 20. In this chapter, we explain various types of fiber cables and supplies and briefly discuss issues in the installation and selection of the fiber cables.

19.2 Selecting Fiber

The very first decision FDDI buyers have to make is about the fiber. Although most people will buy a fiber cable rather than a fiber, the characteristics of the fiber are the most important consideration in the selection of the cable. Therefore, in this section we review these characteristics. In Chapter 4, we explained a number of fiber characteristics and how they affect performance. It would be helpful if you read that chapter first. This section, which is meant for buyers, provides a less technical discussion of the choices. The key characteristics of the fiber are mode, size, bandwidth, and attenuation, which we discuss one by one.

19.2.1 Mode

A fiber can be single mode or multimode. Single-mode fibers have a smaller diameter core (8 to 10 μm) and better performance. Multimode fibers have a larger diameter core (50 to 100 μm) and lower performance than single-mode fibers. For FDDI, you can use either single-mode or multimode fibers as long as the manufacturer warrants that they meet the FDDI specifications. Both types of fibers cost approximately the same. Single-mode fibers are slightly cheaper because they are used extensively by the telecommunication industry.

Can You Use Multimode Fiber on Links Longer Than 2 km?

In some cases, the answer is yes! If the distance between two stations is slightly more than 2 km, for instance, 3 km, most people will tell you to use single-mode fiber. Actually, you may still be able to use multimode fiber and avoid the expense associated with the single-mode equipment. This is where knowing why the 2-km limit is specified in the FDDI standard helps. If you use a multimode fiber longer than 2 km, you may exceed the power loss and bandwidth requirements. Not all multimode fibers have the same performance. The 2-km limit was based on some worst case assumption about fiber characteristics. In particular, it assumed an attenuation of 2.5 dB/km. Multimode fibers with attenuation of 1 dB/km are easily available. Thus, if you use a better quality fiber and if you specifically analyze the link to ensure that you do meet the power loss and bandwidth requirements (see Sections 20.6 and 20.7), then you can safely use a multimode fiber. Longer multimode links are generally bandwidth-limited and so matching the center wavelength of the source to the zero-dispersion wavelength of the fiber and using a source with lower rise/fall times may be helpful as explained in Sections 4.9 and 20.7.

Another alternative is to introduce dummy nodes after every 2-km distance. These dummy nodes may be actual stations, concentrators, or repeaters. In this case, you should make sure that the total number of ports in the ring does not exceed the limit of 1000. If you have a large ring, it is better to partition it into several smaller rings and connect them via bridges or routers.

For FDDI, you will probably use a multimode fiber simply because the transmitters and receivers for such a fiber are considerably cheaper than those for a single-mode fiber. A single-mode fiber requires a laser source to enable large amounts of light to be launched into their tiny cores. These laser sources are an order of magnitude more expensive than the LED sources used with multimode fibers.

The multimode fibers are limited to a distance of 2 km or so between two nodes (see Sidebar above). For longer distances you need to use single-mode fibers and pay the higher cost of the single-mode equipment. Thus, the key determining factor is distance. Single-mode fibers can be used without repeaters for a distance of 40 km. Distances up to 60 km are also possible, but require the use of higher power transmitters and more sensitive receivers, which means that special laser safety guidelines should be followed as discussed in Section 19.8.

19.2.2 Size

The fiber size is specified by a pair of numbers that represents the diameter of the core and the cladding of the fiber. The light travels through the core while the cladding acts as a cylindrical mirror, constantly reflecting the light back into the core.

For multimode fibers, the FDDI standard specifies a size of 62.5/125, which means that the core diameter is 62.5 μm and the cladding diameter is 125 μm. If you have a choice, use this size. Other sizes such as 50/125, 85/125, and 100/140 can also be used but then you must perform the loss and bandwidth analyses (see Sections 20.6 and 20.7) and allow for additional losses if you mix different size fibers.

For single-mode fibers, although the core/cladding diameters are in the range of 10/125 μm, they are not meaningful. Any other size is equally good as long as the *mode field diameter* (see Section 6.2) is 8.7 ± 0.5 μm.

What About Plastic Fibers?

Plastic fibers are very inexpensive but they have a high attenuation (in the range of 200 dB/km). They have a large core diameter of 200 to 1000 μm. Also, they operate at wavelengths of 660 nm and not at the 850- or 1300-nm wavelengths used in LAN applications. Their use is limited to internal equipment links, industrial controls, and optical sensing. You cannot use plastic fibers for FDDI.

19.2.3 Bandwidth

Multimode fibers have a bandwidth of 200 to 500 MHz-km. For FDDI, the bandwidth must be at least 500 MHz-km. Over a distance of 2 km, this allows a bandwidth of approximately 250 MHz. This gives sufficient margin to transmit reliably an FDDI signal that has a maximum fundamental frequency of 62.5 MHz. If you use a fiber of lower bandwidth than 500 MHz-km, the internode distance may need to be reduced to less than 2 km to ensure a net bandwidth of 250 MHz. You should do the bandwidth analysis (see Section 20.7) to assure that the fiber can be used. Vendors usually specify bandwidth at both 850 and 1300 nm. Since FDDI uses only the 1300-nm wavelength, make sure that you use the 1300-nm bandwidth.

Bandwidth analysis is particularly important for long single-mode links. Although these fibers have a bandwidth of several GHz-km, the net bandwidth over a long span may become less than the required 250 MHz. In fact, the maximum distance that one can go using single-mode links is often limited by the bandwidth requirement and not by the loss requirement, which is discussed next.

19.2.4 Attenuation

Multimode fibers typically have an attenuation (power loss per unit length) of 1 to 4 dB/km. The total power loss in a link includes that in the fiber, connectors, and splices. The total loss should not exceed 11 dB. A good guideline is to use a fiber with attenuation better than 2.5 dB/km. This

Dual-Window Fiber

FDDI uses an 1300-nm wavelength. Older LAN standards such as fiber optic Ethernet and token rings use an 850-nm wavelength. The attenuation and bandwidth of the fiber depend on the wavelength. Some fibers may be suitable for use in the 850-nm window only, while others are suitable for use in the 1300-nm window. For example, 50/125 fibers are optimized for 850 nm. The 62.5/125 fiber is optimized for 1300 nm. The 100/140 fiber is designed for both 850- and 1300-nm operation but it is not optimized for either one.

Dual-window fibers can be used in either of the two windows. Using these fibers, you can start with a low-speed LAN and later upgrade to a higher speed without reinstalling the fiber.

The term *dual window* (or *double window*) refers to different windows for multimode and single-mode fibers. For multimode fibers, the term *dual window* generally means that the fiber is suitable for both 850- and 1300-nm windows. Thus, it can be used for fiber optic Ethernet, IBM channel extender, and FDDI applications. For single-mode fibers, it usually means that the fiber is suitable for 1300- and 1550-nm windows.

will allow sufficient margin for connectors and splices even after a 2-km span of the fiber. Loss analysis (see Section 20.6) should be done for each link to ensure that the total loss requirement is met. Again, vendors specify the attenuation for 850 and 1300 nm. The 1300-nm attenuation is the lower of the two and is the one to be used in the analysis.

Single-mode fibers have an attenuation of 0.2 to 1 dB/km. Depending on the power of the transmitter and the sensitivity of the receiver, you may have to limit the total loss to somewhere between 10 to 32 dB. This may determine the maximum distance you may go between two nodes.

19.3 Buying Fiber Cables

Fibers are very thin and fragile. Therefore, instead of fibers, one generally uses fiber cables, which contain one or more fibers along with other materials that provide the strength and durability to fibers. In selecting a fiber cable, you not only have to ensure that it has the right type of fibers but also that it is appropriate for the environment in which it will be used. These additional considerations are the topic of this section.

19.3.1 Type of Buffer

All fibers have a protective coating in addition to core and cladding. The coating helps preserve the inherent strength of the glass fiber. In some cases this strength is sufficient to allow the fiber to be used without additional protection. In most cases, however, additional protection is required. This is provided by applying additional layers of materials called **buffering.**

The two types of buffering are tight buffering and loose buffering. Tight buffering consists of a layer of harder plastic resulting in a diameter of 0.5 to 1 mm. Loose buffering consists of an oversized cavity to house the fiber. The loose buffering allows fiber to move freely and prevents cable strain and temperature expansion from affecting the fiber. The cavity is formed by a tube that may be filled with a moisture-resistant compound. The compound also provides a lubrication effect. The overall dimension of the tube is in the 1- to 3-mm range. The fiber in a loose buffer cable may be longer than the cable itself since it is slack in the tube. The two types of buffering are shown in Figure 19.1 and their characteristics are compared in Table 19.1. Tight-buffered cables are more suitable for indoor cabling, while loose-buffered cables are used for outdoor applications.

19.3.2 Structural Members

Structural members provide a core foundation to lay the buffered fiber strands in the cable. They also enhance the tensile stress resistance of the cable. These members may be made of steel, plastic,

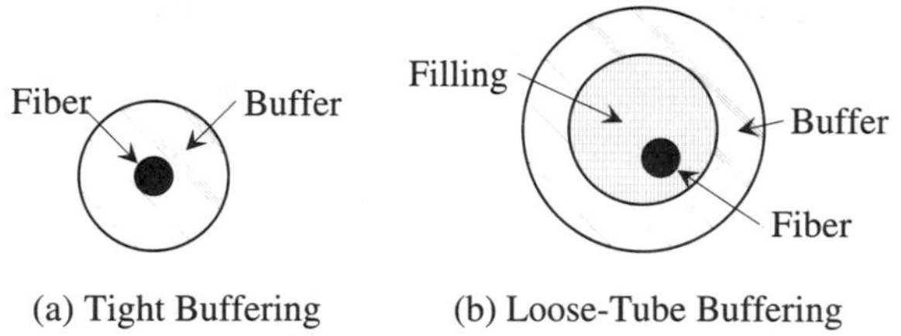

Figure 19.1 Loose-buffered and tight-buffered cables.

Table 19.1 Tight Buffer Versus Loose Buffer

Characteristics	Tight Buffer	Loose Buffer
Environment	Indoor	Outdoor
Bend radius	Smaller	Larger
Diameter	Smaller	Larger
Tensile strength	Lower	Higher
Crush resistance	Higher	Lower
Impact resistance	Higher	Lower
Temperature tolerance	Lower	Higher

fiberglass, or plastic-coated metal. Two common designs, called loose tube and slotted core, are shown in Figure 19.2. In the loose-tube design, loose-buffered fiber is stranded around a core. In the slotted-core design, tight-buffered fibers are laid in slots provided by the core.

A strength member consisting of steel, aramid yarns, or glass yarns may be used to enhance the load-bearing capacity of the cable. Moisture-resistant filling compounds may be used to fill the

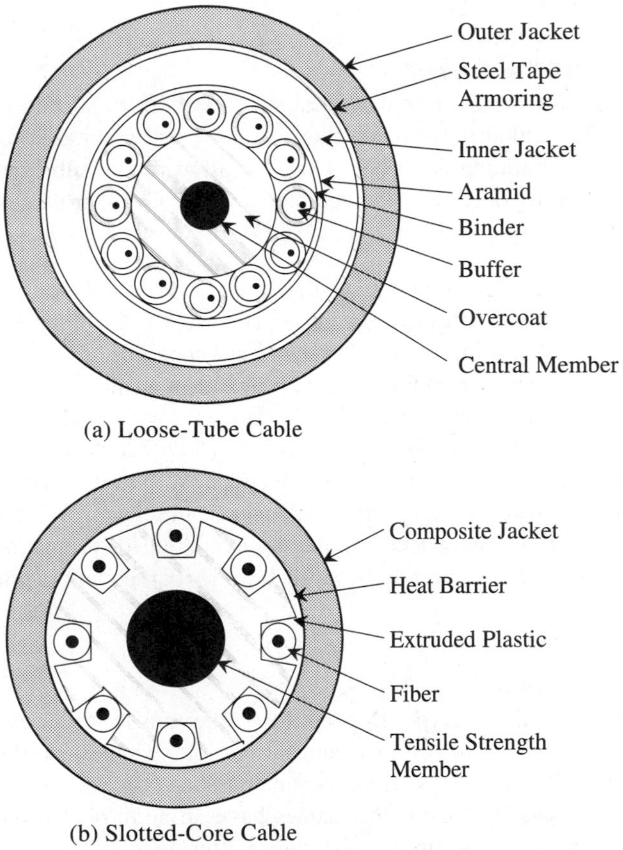

Figure 19.2 Loose-tube and slotted-core cables.

voids in the cable cross section. If a metallic armoring or strength member is used in the cable, it may be surrounded by a plastic coating or a flooding compound to prevent corrosion. Finally, the cables have a sheath covering it. Cables for indoor applications may be required to meet flammability requirements.

19.3.3 Flame Rating

In the United States, the National Electrical Code (NEC) specifies a number of flame ratings for optical fiber cables to be used within buildings. Similar codes exist in other countries. Underwriter's Laboratory (UL) has defined procedures to assure that the cable meets specific NEC requirements.

A cable may be certified for general use if it passes the UL 1581 vertical tray flame test. Such cables can be used for building wiring but not in risers or plenums unless installed in suitable conduits. A cable passing the UL 1666 test is certified for use as a riser cable in vertical passages connecting one floor to another. Cables passing the UL 910 Steiner tunnel test have low smoke producing properties and are suitable for use as plenum cables for installation in air plenums without the use of conduit. These are the cables that are used in suspended ceilings and under raised floors.

The NEC code is discussed in Section 19.7.

19.3.4 Outdoor Cables

Cables designated as outdoor cables have been designed specially to sustain the environmental and mechanical stresses of the outdoors. However, they are not usually suitable for indoor applications since they may not meet the building fire codes. The NEC allows loose-tube and slotted-core outdoor cables to extend into a building only up to the equipment room. Outdoor cables are available for the following applications:

1. *Direct Buried*: These are designed for direct burial in all types of soil. A loose-tube construction is used for stress protection and temperature control. The cable is gel filled for moisture prevention and is often rodent-proofed with an outer layer of steel tape armor.
2. *Buried Conduit*: These cables contain no metallic element. Thus, they can run next to power cables without inducing any voltage and there is no need for grounding such cables.
3. *Aerial*: This cable is strung on poles and is designed to withstand exposure to sun, wind, and ice-load conditions. Ultraviolet inhibitors are embedded in the outer jacket for protection from the sunlight. The loose-buffer design protects the fiber from tension and temperature cycles. All-dielectric (with no metallic components) cables are available for protection against lightning.
4. *Underwater*: With special moisture protection, such cables can be laid in ponds, rivers, or oceans.

19.3.5 Indoor Cables

Indoor cable is of the tight-buffered type. Depending on the tensile stress capacity of the cable it may be called light-duty cable or heavy-duty cable. Light-duty cables can be used if the pulling tension does not exceed 100 lb or 445 N. Here, N stands for newton, the metric unit for force. One newton is equivalent to 0.2248 lb. Heavy-duty cables have an additional layer of buffering around each fiber strand and, therefore, they can be used with pulling tension up to 250 lb (1112 N).

The indoor cables are available for the following applications:

Table 19.2 Cable Types

Type	Application	Structure
Outdoor		
Direct buried	Between buildings	Loose tube with armored dielectric strength member or slotted core
Buried in conduit	Runs in conduit buried in the ground	Loose tube with dielectric strength member or slotted core
Aerial	Strung on telephone or utility poles	Loose tube, all dielectric
Underwater	In lakes, streams, or river crossings	Loose tube with dielectric strength member or slotted core; may be armored
Indoor		
General-purpose	On a floor or in closets	Tight buffered
Plenum	In ceiling and environmental airspaces	Tight buffered
Riser	Between floors	Tight buffered with extra strength members; usually multifiber

1. *Plenum*: This cable meets the NEC requirements for fire protection and can pass through the areas that act as return systems for a building's heating, cooling, and ventilation systems. These areas are called **environmental airspace**.
2. *General Use*: These are nonplenum cables, which can be used in nonenvironmental airspace.
3. *Riser*: These cables are designed for use in vertical shafts between floors. Avoid using gel-filled cables in risers since the gel may move down leaving no protection in the upper part.
4. *Work Area*: These are two fiber cables used to connect a station to the wall outlet. Generally, preconnectorized (factory-terminated) cable assemblies are used.
5. *Patch Cables*: These are used in the telecommunication closets, cross-connects, interconnects, and distribution frames. Again, preconnectorized cable assemblies are used.
6. *Breakout Cable*: A breakout cable is essentially a bundle of several individual fiber optic cables in a single jacket. Each conductor has the strength and flexibility similar to that of single conductor cables. This *cable inside a cable* design allows easy installation of connectors on individual fibers. A breakout kit, required to install connectors on other multifiber cables, is not required with this type of cable. This reduces the field termination time.

   A breakout kit permits the installation of connectors on normal (nonbreakout style) multifiber loose-buffered cables. It effectively creates single-fiber cable with the proper strength for each fiber in the multifiber cable. Individual connectors can then be attached to each subcable. Tight-buffered cables do not require breakout kits.

Table 19.2 summarizes various types of cables and their characteristics.

19.3.6 Composite Cables

A composite cable contains several copper wires and fibers in a single cable. Various grades of copper wires (unshielded and shielded) along with fiber cables are packaged in a single cable. The copper cable can be used for voice communication and low-speed data communication. The fiber

The computer and fibers are guaranteed for fifty thousand miles or until they are obsolete... whichever comes first.

Figure 19.3 Technology is becoming obsolete fast.

can be left unused for future expansion. The fibers may also be of different types. For example, cables with 48 multimode fibers and 12 single-mode fibers in one cable are popular for campus backbone applications. Talking of future expansion, new technology and fibers are continually being developed, so you cannot plan for a very distant future and should expect the current technology to be obsolete within a decade or so (see Figure 19.3).

Table 19.3 presents typical values for fiber cable specifications. Incidentally, you can use the list of characteristics in the first column as the issues to consider when buying such cables.

19.4 Installing Fiber Cables

The installation of fiber cable is very similar to that of copper cables. The main difference is in the care required to meet the tensile and minimum bend radius specifications. Unlike copper, fiber should not be bent too much. This and other guidelines for cable installation are the topic of this section.

1. *Minimum Bend Radius*: The cable manufacturers specify a minimum bend radius for each cable. This is the radius to which a cable can be bent without damaging the cable or reducing its performance. It is 10 to 20 times the outside diameter of the cable. Typically it is 4 to 20 cm. Sometimes two different bend radius values may be specified: a lower value for installation and another larger value for long-term operation. During installation, you must ensure that the bend

Table 19.3 Typical Fiber Cable Specifications

Characteristics	Typical Range			Unit
Fiber size	10/125	to	100/140	μm
Number of fibers	2	to	144	
Attenuation at 850 nm	4	to	5	dB/km
Attenuation at 1300 nm	0.5	to	4	dB/km
Bandwidth at 850 nm	100	to	500	MHz-km
Bandwidth at 1300 nm	200	to	2000	MHz-km
Cable diameter	3	to	20	mm
Cable weight	6	to	70	kg/km
Operating temperature	−30	to	+80	degC
Tensile load	400	to	4300	N
Minimum bend radius	4	to	20	cm
Crush resistance	400	to	700	N/cm
Flame rating*	OFN, OFNR, OFNP			

*See Section 19.7 for an explanation of codes.

radius at all cable routing, support, and attachment points is never smaller than that specified by the manufacturer. Sharper bends may cause additional losses or may even damage the fiber. Sometimes the damage many not happen right away but cracks may develop over time. The cable should be slacked at sharp turns and immobilized at the point of the bend.

2. *Horizontal Runs*: Inside the buildings, fiber optic cable is usually laid in trays, raceways, conduit, or innerduct or suspended from the building beams. Suspended cable should be supported every 2 to 3 m using J-hooks or bar joists. Do not support unducted cable by pipes, suspended ceiling grid, or other wiring.

   Cable installed in conduits should be protected from the forces of other cables that can reside there. Conduits should not be filled more than 50% by cross-sectional area.

   The connectorized cable should not be pulled though a conduit containing other cables. If only one end of a cable is connectorized, pull the unconnectorized end. The same conduit should not be used for copper cables and fiber cables. If necessary, an innerduct should be used to separate the copper from the fiber cable. Tight pulls and sharp corners should be avoided to reduce the possibility of breaking the fiber.

3. *Vertical Runs*: Portable electric winches are used to pull cable up through vertical shafts. A pulling line is first lowered down through the floor openings. (It helps to attach a weight to the line.) The cable is then attached to the line and pulled up by the winch.

   If the cable is pulled through an innerduct or conduit, the cable can be lubricated to reduce the friction and hence the tension required to pull.

   Each cable has a tensile rating, which is the maximum pulling force that can be exerted on the cable. It is specified in pounds or newtons (and sometimes in kilograms). The pulling tension can be monitored using a tensiometer. When using pulling winches, a tensiometer should always be used.

   After the installation is complete, there should be no tensile forces on the cable. The only exception is the riser cable. The cable pulling tension at the highest point of a vertical run is

Rats Love Optical Fiber Cable

When FDDI cable was first installed at Nanyang Technological Institute, the ring did not come up in the initial trials (as generally happens). However, in this case, the problem was traced to the optical cable being broken at many places. Due to the attractive bright orange color of the FDDI cables, the rats at the institute could not resist and had taken several bites. The broken cables had to be replaced. First it was replaced with fiber of a different color. But that didn't stop the problem. Finally, they had to install PVC conduits to protect the fiber cables. This not only caused a delay but also added extra cost to the project—not to mention the problem of obtaining a huge consignment of PVC conduit at short notice.

equal to the cable weight. You should ensure that the maximum pulling tension specified for the cable is sufficient to withstand this weight.

The cable in the risers between the floors should be supported every 10 m (alternate floors) or less. When installing riser cable through vertical shafts, it is easier to drop the cable from the top floor to the lower levels than to pull the cable upward. After installation, use split mesh cable grips or cable ties to support the cable at designated intervals.

When installing a cable through a vertical conduit, first use a snake to run a fish line through the duct to serve as a leader for pulling in the wire rope or pulling tape (which is attached to the fiber cable). This will minimize the possibility of entanglement and bending.

4. *Horizontal to Vertical Transition*: Always provide a grip support at the point where the cable makes a transition from the vertical run to a horizontal run.
5. *Conduit Installation*: When a fiber cable has to run through a conduit, the cable should be installed in an innerduct, which is a semirigid plastic duct that helps guide the fiber cable through the duct and helps avoid exceeding the minimum bend radius. The innerduct prevents the fiber cable from getting twisted around or getting entangled with existing cables in the conduit. The diameter of the innerduct is 1 to 1.25 in. Innerducts can also be used in environmental airspaces. Spare (empty) innerducts can be installed in conduits for future cable installation. Innerducts are designed to handle one-time installation of cables. Pulling cables through an innerduct already containing cables is not recommended. The duct should be filled no more than 50% by area, which allows for a 0.7-in. maximum bundle diameter.
6. *Aerial Installation*: Although self-supporting steel-wired armored cables are available for aerial application, a better method is to lash the optical cable to a messenger wire made of steel. The messenger wire provides the support and can be installed with much less care than the self-supporting fiber cable. The optical cable is subsequently lashed to the messenger wire. Sometimes, the overhead ground wires (or even conductors) of existing power lines are used in place of the messenger wire. All-dielectric fiber optic cables can be attached to the ground wire using specially designed clipping machines.
7. *Crossover*: In connecting two devices, the transmitter of one device must be connected to the receiver of the other and vice versa. This requires a fiber optic crossover as shown in Figure 19.4. In a multiple-segment link, this crossover can occur at any point. Missing a crossover or having an extra crossover can cause equipment damage. This requires careful tracking of the fibers and their ends. Fiber manufacturers have developed color coding schemes to ensure correct crossovers.

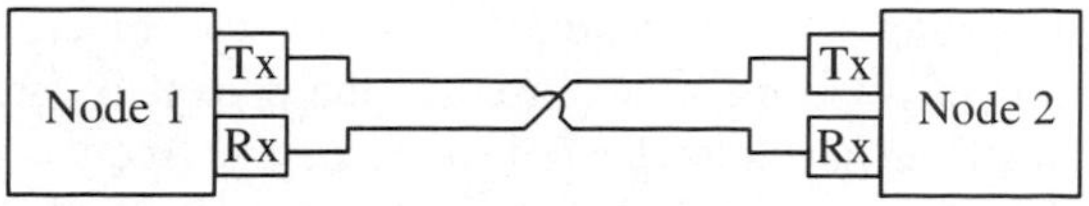

Figure 19.4 Crossover.

19.5 Buying Connectors

A connector is used to connect a fiber to transmitters and receivers. Connectors may also be used to connect two fibers. However, if a permanent connection is desired it is better to splice the fibers together. Splicing is discussed in Section 19.6. The fiber connectors align the fibers to the precision of a few micrometers. The FDDI standard specifies a duplex connector that connects both fibers of a link at the same time. This connector has a low insertion loss of 0.2 dB and is keyed to prevent accidental misconnection to the wrong equipment or fiber type. Unfortunately, this type of connector is expensive due to its specialized use. A number of simplex connectors that were in use before FDDI standardization are commonly used in FDDI applications because of cost and compatibility reasons. These simplex connectors connect only one fiber and, therefore, two connectors are required per link per end.

A number of popular fiber connectors were shown earlier in Figure 4.19. In the United States, commonly used connectors are FDDI MIC, ST, ST-II, SMA 905, SMA 906, and Biconic. In Japan, FC (JIS C 5970), D4, SC, and mini-BNC are popular. In Europe, DIN 47256/IEC, RADIALL, and STRATOS connectors are used. For each type, you must also specify the fiber type (single-mode or multimode) and the cladding diameter. Connectors designed for one diameter or type of fiber do not work on other diameters or types.

Since it is inconvenient to use many different types of connectors, you should continue to use the connector type already in use in your plant or country. The choice is also determined by the type of connector used on the FDDI equipment. You should ensure that the host adapters, concentrators, bridges, and routers that you intend to buy have the receptacles for the type of connectors you plan to use in your cabling plant.

If existing wiring and connectors are not a consideration, then the choice of the connector is based on cost, insertion loss, ease of connecting and disconnecting, and the time to install the connector. In general, an FDDI duplex connector is preferred but they are currently more expensive than other types.

The ST connector is slowly becoming the most popular simplex connector. It has a twist-lock type design with a very low loss, typically in the range of 0.5 to 1.0 dB. The keyed bayonet design prevents fiber rotation and allows quick connection and disconnection. ST-style connectors are available in ceramic ferrule or low-cost plastic. The ceramic connectors provide lower insertion losses, longer life, and greater operating temperature ranges.

Many versions of the ST connectors are available. In particular, ST-II represents an improved design that provides greater connector stability during rearrangements in crowded cabinets. These connectors are easier to mount and are fully compatible with all existing ST connectors. Another ST version called an ST physical contact (ST-PC) connector features a domed tip for maximum fiber contact, low insertion loss (0.3 dB), and a high return loss (low-power reflected-back).

To install a connector, the fiber is passed through a tiny close-fitting epoxy-filled hole within the barrel of the connector. Then the fiber end is ground and polished to a smooth finish flush with the end of the barrel. Finally, the cable jacket is secured to the connector by crimping. The entire process takes about 10 minutes. Most of this time is required for the epoxy to cure. ST connectors that do not require grinding and polishing have also been developed, thus reducing the termination time to about 3 minutes. These have a factory-polished fiber stub already bonded into the ferrule. The other end of the stub is precisely cleaved and placed into an alignment barrel. In the field, the fiber is cleaved, inserted into the alignment sleeve, and bonded with a ultraviolet light activated adhesive. The insertion loss is typically less than 0.5 dB.

The SMA connector was the first optical connector to be standardized and put into common use. It is less expensive than an ST connector but has a higher insertion loss, typically 1 to 3 dB. These connectors are available in two types. The SMA 905 has a straight front barrel containing the fiber and a threaded nut for mating. It is generally used for connecting fibers to equipment. The SMA 906 has a step-down front barrel and is generally used for fiber-to-fiber connections. SMA connectors are available in a variety of materials. Of these, stainless steel is the most widely used material because of its durability. SMA connectors are not commonly used these days because they can be overtightened and their insertion loss varies considerably.

If you do not have the time, skill, or the equipment necessary to install connectors, you can get preconnectorized cable assemblies. You have to specify the type of the connectors and the length of the cable. A short fiber optic cable with factory-fitted connectors on both ends is called a **jumper**. These are used to connect electronic equipment to patch panels.

The connectors on the two ends of a cable assembly do not have to be of the same type. For example, you can buy a cable with an FDDI duplex connector on one end and the ST connector on the other. You can also get a **pigtail**, which is the term used for fiber cable with connectors on only one end. The other end is meant for splicing to another cable in the field.

Couplers allow two connectorized fibers to be joined together. They consist of two receptacles bonded back-to-back permanently. **Adapters** allow connection of one type of connector to another type. For example, an FDDI-to-ST adapter allows connection of an ST-terminated cable to an FDDI duplex terminated cable.

All of the connectors, FDDI MIC, ST, SMA, Biconic, and so on, are available for multimode as well as single-mode fibers. A single-mode fiber requires more precise alignment. Therefore, a multimode connector cannot be used for single-mode fibers.

One of the key characteristics in selecting the single-mode connectors is the optical return loss caused by the reflections at the fiber junction. A domed tip and a good polish of the end result in better contact and a lower reflection. The optical return loss is typically 35 to 45 dB. (Higher loss is better since it means less reflection.)

The size of the connector is specified by its ferrule size and backshell size. The inside diameter of the ferrule should match the cladding diameter of the fiber. Thus, a ferrule with a nominal inside diameter of 128 μm can be used for 50/125 or 62.5/125 multimode fibers. This results in a tolerance of ± 3 μm, which is acceptable for multimode fibers. For single-mode fibers greater precision is required. A ferrule sized at 125, 126, or 127 μm may be required for a single-mode fiber with the cladding diameter of 125 μm. Note that a connector with a 128-μm ferrule cannot be used for 100/140 fiber.

The backshell is the part of the connector that secures the cable to the connector. The backshell size should therefore match the jacket diameter of the cable. Common jacket diameters are 2, 2.4, and 2.9 mm. Some connectors accept only one size of cable, others accept any size. Yet others can build the jacket up to a given size; for example, they can build up a 2- or 2.4-mm jacket to 2.9 mm.

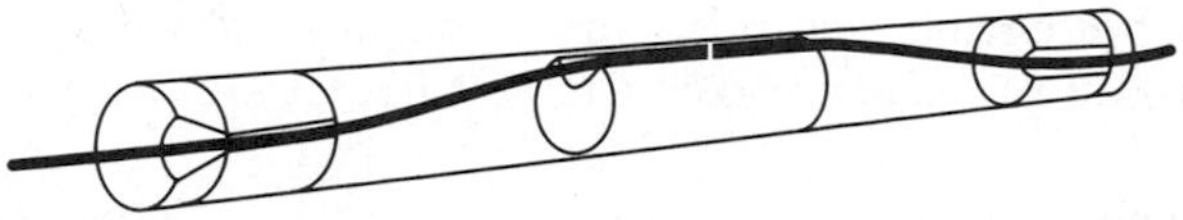

Figure 19.5 A mechanical splice.

19.6 Splicing Fiber Cables

If two fibers have to be connected permanently, splicing them is cheaper and results in a lower loss than does the use of connectors and couplers. The three common methods of splicing are butt splicing, mechanical splicing, and fusion splicing. A **butt splice** is basically an inexpensive coupler with two inexpensive plugs. The coupler aligns the plugs, which are connected to the fiber. This is the least expensive method to splice but it also has a high insertion loss (of the order of 3 dB). It is employed generally as a temporary repair.

A mechanical splice consists of a tube that accurately aligns two finished fiber ends to each other. A coupling medium applied to the finished fiber ends reduces the insertion loss to less than 1 dB. Such a splice is delicate and needs an outer housing for protection. Figure 19.5 shows a sample mechanical splice. After stripping the cable down to the buffer, the two fibers are cleaved and inserted into the splice. A ceramic V-groove precisely aligns the two fibers, an index matching gel fills the gap, and the fibers are held in place by two strain relief chocks. A special splicing tool is required to enlarge the opening and permit fiber insertion. Mechanical splices take approximately 30 seconds to complete and some can even be removed and reused.

Fusion splicing requires two fibers to be melted together. Special fusion splicers are required for this purpose. They can handle all fiber sizes from 8 to 140 μm and provide a very accurate splice with an insertion loss of less than 0.3 dB.

Both mechanical splices and fusion splices require additional outer housings for protection. All fibers of a cable can be put in one such housing.

19.7 National Electrical Code

The National Electrical Code (NEC) developed by the National Fire Protection Agency regulates the installation of electrical equipment and conductors within buildings. This code is widely adopted in the United States and other countries. The code is updated every three years. The first version was written in 1897! The current version is 1993. The 1993 NEC requires that the cables be listed according to their suitability for a given use. It applies to copper cables as well as fiber cables.

Class 1 wiring is used to control equipment whose failure to operate would introduce a direct fire or life hazard. Such wiring includes cables for fire alarms, nurse call systems, elevators, cranes, conveyers, or other moving equipment. This class does not generally apply to data communication equipment.

The copper cables used in computer networking are classified by NEC either as CL2 or CM.

- *CL2*: This is called the Class 2 copper wiring. It includes power-limited signaling circuitry whose failure would not introduce a direct fire or life hazard. Class 2 wiring includes low-power

heating, cooling control circuits, and voice transfer circuits and wiring used for computer data communication. Class 2 cables are marked CL2X, CL2, CL2R, and CL2P depending on their flame resistance.
CL2P Copper cable suitable for use in plenums.
CL2R Copper cable suitable for use in risers.
CL2 Copper cable suitable for general use (except plenums and risers).
CL2X Copper cable suitable for residential and restricted commercial use.

- *CM*: This class covers circuits used for telephones and/or data communications. Class CM cables can be used for CL2 applications but not vice versa. Class CM cables are further classified as CM, CMX, CMR, and CMP depending on their flame resistance.
  CMP Copper cable suitable for use in plenums.
  CMPR Copper cable suitable for use in risers.
  CM Copper cable suitable for general use (except plenums and risers).
  CMX Copper cable suitable for residential and restricted commercial use.

NEC also covers installation of fiber optic cables, which may be installed along with electrical cables. The fiber optic cables are divided into three types:

- *Nonconducting*: This class includes fiber optic cables containing no metallic members or electric conducting material. These cables are labeled OFN, OFNP, or OFNR, depending on their flame resistance.
  OFN Optical fiber cable without electrical conductors.
  OFNP Optical fiber cable without electrical conductors suitable for plenums.
  OFNR Optical fiber cable without electrical conductors suitable for risers.
- *Conducting*: These cables contain electric conducting material, such as metallic strength members or vapor barriers that do not carry current. Cables of this type are labeled OFC, OFCP, or OFCR depending on their fire resistance.
  OFC Optical fiber cable with electrical conductors.
  OFCP Optical fiber cable with electrical conductors suitable for plenums.
  OFCR Optical fiber cable with electrical conductors suitable for risers.
- *Hybrid*: These are composite cables that contain both fiber optic and current-carrying electrical conductors. These cables are classified according to the type of electrical conductors they contain.

These cable classes are further subdivided into four subclasses depending on their fire resistance. This subclass determines where the cable can be installed. Beginning with the least fire resistant subclass, these subclasses are as follows:

1. *Limited Use Cables*: These have the lowest fire resistance and are for use in single and multi-family dwellings only. Cables labeled CL2X or CMX are of this class. There are no fiber optic cables in this class.
2. *General Use Cables*: These cables can be installed in offices and rooms, but not behind or through walls or ceilings and not in heating or cooling ducts. Cables marked CL2, CM, OFC, or OFN are of this class.
3. *Riser Cables*: These cables can be used between floors or in vertical shafts. These cables are labeled CL2R, CMR, OFNR, or OFCR.
4. *Plenum Cables*: These cables have the highest flame resistance and can be used in plenums and ceiling. Such cables are labeled CL2P, CMP, OFNP, or OFCP.

Table 19.4 NEC Ratings for Various Types of Cables

IBM	Application		
Type	Plenum	Nonplenum	Riser
1	CL2P	CL2	CL2R
2	CMP	CM	
3	CMP	CM	
5	OFNP	OFN	OFNR
6		CL2	
9	CL2P		

In many buildings, cables are installed in the space above a suspended ceiling or below a raised floor. If these spaces are also used as the return for the building's heating, ventilation, and air conditioning systems, this space is considered environmental airspace and only plenum-rated cable can be used. If ducts are used for the air return above the ceiling, the area above the ceiling is considered nonenvironmental airspace.

The IBM classification for cables, which is used industry wide, was presented in Section 8.4. Table 19.4 shows the NEC ratings for various IBM types.

NEC allows a higher rated cable in a lower rated application. For example, plenum cables can be used in all four applications. Also, when a cable crosses from one fire-resistant rated zone to another (for example, for riser to ceiling), the cable penetration points must be fire-stopped. Prefabricated fire seals and caulking materials are available for this purpose.

Although NEC is only advisory, it is generally adopted by communities across the United States as part of their local building codes. Some communities may have local requirements that are different from NEC. Communities outside of the United States may have totally different requirements. If you have any questions about the requirements, you should consult your local building inspection authorities or building architects.

19.8 Laser Safety Considerations

If you are using or planning to buy single-mode fiber or equipment, you should be aware of the safety requirements for lasers. These requirements apply mainly for Category II laser transmitters. Light-emitting diodes used with multimode fibers and Category I transmitters used with single-mode fibers are both safe since their power output is low.

In the United States, laser safety is regulated by the Center for Devices and Radiological Health (CDRH), which is a subgroup of the Food and Drug Administration (FDA). The rules appear in U.S. Department of Health and Human Services (1985). In addition, two ANSI standards on laser safety (ANSI Z136.1 and ANSI Z136.2) have been adopted by many trade unions and manufacturers as guidelines. Compliance with CDRH standards is a legal requirement in the United States while compliance with ANSI standards is voluntary. Internationally, many countries have regulations based on the International Electrotechnical Commission (IEC) 825 standard.

Based on their ability to cause biological damage to the eye or skin during use, lasers are classified into four different safety classes: Classes 1, 2, 3, and 4. Classes 2 and 3 are further subdivided into subclasses—2a, 2b, 3a, and 3b. Classes 1 and 3b are the only classes that apply to fiber communication systems. Classes 2 and 3a apply only to lasers with visible radiation (400 to 700 nm). Class 4 is for infrared lasers and lasers with an output power exceeding 0.5 W. Class 1 systems are safe in that their power level is low enough to not cause any damage during normal operating conditions. Class 3b lasers can cause injury if viewed directly.

The exact procedure to classify a particular laser is quite complex because it takes several operating characteristics into account including power spectrum and type of beam (single-pulse or continuous). Also, the CDRH, ANSI, and IEC standards differ in their requirements. In general, the IEC standard has more restrictive power limits than the other two standards. ANSI classifies lasers into service groups (SGs). Thus, Classes 1, 2, 3a, 3b, and 4 are called SG1, SG2, SG3a, SG3b, and SG4 in ANSI terminology.

All FDDI optical transmitters are Class 1 except those emitting full power allowed for single-mode fiber Category II. Such high-powered Category II transmitters are Class 3b.

When Class 3b systems are used, employers are responsible for using safety control measures. This includes posting a label, such as "DANGER—DISCONNECTED OPTICAL CONNECTORS MAY EMIT INVISIBLE OPTICAL RADIATION. AVOID DIRECT EYE EXPOSURE TO THE BEAM." The labels should be located in plain view on the equipment in the vicinity of the connectors, for example, outlets, patch-panels, and patch cords. An area with a large number of connectors should have a warning sign with a similar message. Only authorized trained personnel should be permitted to install or service Class 3b systems. During splicing operations, optical sources should be turned off. Eye protection devices should be used if necessary. Personnel assigned to work routinely on energized Class 3b systems and whose job requires disconnecting optical connectors or splicing fibers on such systems should receive periodic eye examinations.

These safety considerations have lead some manufacturers to limit the output power of their SMF transmitters to −3 dBm. This makes them Class 1 equipment and does not require access controls. This category, called **safety enhanced Category II**, reduces the maximum achievable distance to approximately 40 km but makes the equipment safe.

19.9 Verifying Cable Installation

After the cable has been installed, you should verify that all connections are fault free and that all links meet the loss requirements.

One way to do this is to conduct a simple **power loss measurement**. It consists simply of launching some power from one end of the fiber and measuring the received power at the other end using an optical power meter. The difference between the launched and received power represents the total loss of the link.

The attenuation of a fiber is a function of the wavelength (see Figure 5.2). Therefore, the attenuation depends on the center wavelength of the source and its spectral pattern. A difference of 30 nm in wavelength can result in the measured attenuation being off by as much as 0.5 dB/km. This means that the power loss measurements should be done using a source whose characteristics are similar to those of the source to be used in actual operation.

Another method for installation verification is the use of an optical time-domain reflectometer as discussed next.

19.10 Optical Time-Domain Reflectometry

An **optical time-domain reflectometer (OTDR)** is a tool that can be used to locate faults and determine a fiber's length, attenuation, uniformity, and splice losses. Multimode dispersion can also be measured with some OTDRs.

An OTDR is connected to one end of the fiber. It launches short optical pulses in the fiber. The impurities in the fiber, splice points, and breakpoint reflect (backscatter) some of the light back toward the OTDR, which analyzes the reflected signal and produces a plot of power (in decibels) versus distance. A sample plot is shown in Figure 19.6. The plot always begins with a spike at the beginning of the fiber and ends with a spike at the end of the fiber. These spikes are due to reflections from the fiber ends. The connectors, splices, bends, and breaks show up as discontinuities in the plot. The horizontal axis indicates the location of these connectors, splices, and faults. The attenuation of the fiber can be determined from the slope of the smooth portion of the curve, while that of the connectors and splices can be measured approximately from the vertical size of the corresponding discontinuity.

Figure 19.7 shows a schematic diagram of an OTDR. A pulse generator drives a laser diode, which launches optical pulses of 10 mW or more in the fiber. The pulse widths range from nanoseconds to microseconds and are repeated at a rate of 1 to 20 kHz. The returning signal is separated from the launched signal by a directional coupler. An avalanche photodiode is used as a detector and its signal is analyzed by a computer. The signal is averaged for a period of time to improve the signal-to-noise ratio.

Since the signal falls with distance because of attenuation, there is a maximum distance above which the maximum signal-to-noise ratio is too small for proper measurement. An OTDR's range is

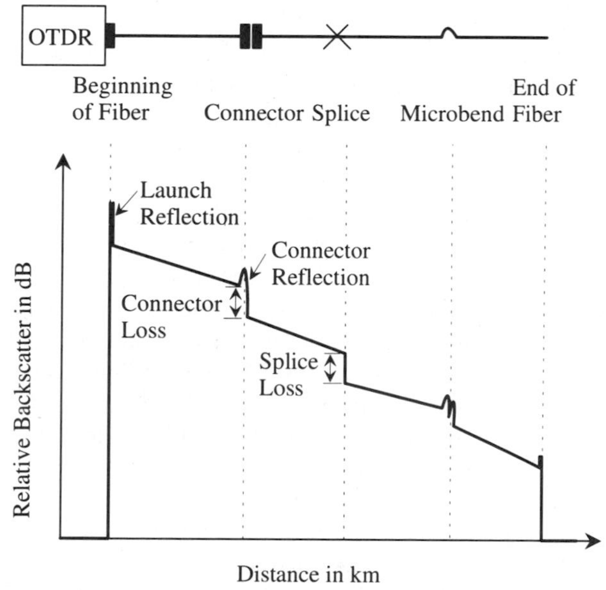

Figure 19.6 A sample OTDR output.

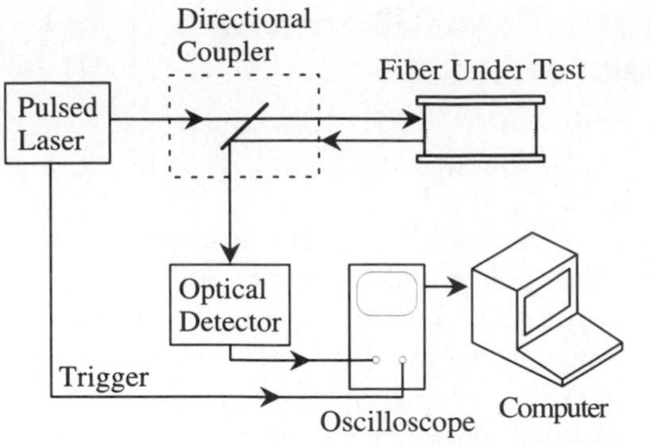

Figure 19.7 Schematic diagram of an OTDR.

usually stated in terms of maximum one-way loss for a particular function. Three different ranges may be specified: range of detecting a reflecting fault, range for a nonreflecting break (for example, a fiber end surrounded in oil), and the range for accurate measurement of splice losses. For example, an OTDR specification may require a 40-dB one-way range for reflecting end detection, 20 dB for the nonreflecting end detection, and 13 dB for a 0.2-dB resolution splice loss detection. Notice that only the first range uses reflections; the last two use backscattering, which depends on the scattering coefficient of the fiber. Thus, the ranges depend on the type of fiber as well as on the wavelength of light. The ranges for a 1300-nm wavelength are lower than those for 850 nm due to a smaller amount of backscattering. The difference between the ranges at these two wavelengths may be as much as 10 dB. The OTDR is actually a misnomer because it also measures backscatter, which is not a "reflectometry" measurement.

The range can be improved in several simple ways. The first method is to use wider pulses. A wider pulse produces more backscatter signal. Unfortunately, a wider pulse also reduces the length resolution. The length resolution is limited to half the pulse width. For example, a 1-μs pulse has a length of 200 m on the fiber and cannot distinguish two discontinuities that are less than 100 m apart.

Another method to increase the range is to increase the averaging time to improve the signal-to-noise ratio. With n samples averaged, the improvement is by a factor of $\sqrt{n}$. For example, if 2^{10} samples are averaged, the improvement is 17 dB. The time required to take this many samples depends on the pulse repetition rate. The maximum pulse repetition rate is limited to $v/(2L)$, where v is the velocity of the light in the fiber (200 m/μs) and L is the length of the fiber. For a 5-km fiber, this results in about a 20-kHz rate. A higher rate can be used for shorter fibers.

To calculate splice losses from the OTDR diagram, the vertical discontinuity at the splice must be divided by two to get one-way loss. This is because the signal is attenuated in the forward as well as in the reverse direction. The splice loss measured by an OTDR may sometimes be inaccurate. It can even be negative, indicating a power gain at the splice! This happens if the scattering coefficient of the far fiber is larger than that of the near one. Such inaccuracies can be overcome by taking OTDR measurements from both ends of the fiber and averaging the two measured splice losses.

OTDR can also be used for measuring dispersion in multimode fibers. For this, a narrow sub-nanosecond pulse is launched and the width of the reflection (or the pulse received at the other end) is measured. The impulse response of the fiber can be obtained from the ratio of Fourier transforms of the launched and the received pulses. That is,

$$h(f) = \frac{\mathrm{FT}[P_{\mathrm{out}}(t)]}{\mathrm{FT}[P_{\mathrm{in}}(t)]}$$

Here, $P_{\mathrm{out}}(t)$ is the output pulse shape, $P_{\mathrm{in}}(t)$ is the input pulse shape, FT[] denotes the Fourier transform operation, and $h(f)$ is the frequency response. The inverse transform of $h(f)$ gives the impulse response of the fiber. The frequency at which the power is 3 dB below the dc power is the frequency bandwidth (denoted by $f_{3\mathrm{dB}}$) of the fiber.

OTDR can be used with single-mode fibers also. However, a lower dopant level (higher purity of the glass) reduces the scattering. A lower number of modes also decreases the backscatter capture fraction. A smaller diameter core means less power is coupled in the fiber. These factors reduce the one-way dynamic range of an OTDR for single-mode fiber by 10 to 15 dB. Since fiber attenuation is also low, several tens of kilometers of fibers can still be viewed. The splice losses can also be measured. Measurements from the two ends may need to be averaged to avoid inaccuracies.

19.11 Summary

The key consideration in buying fiber cables is the environment in which they will be used. Different cables are available for installation in plenums, risers, office areas, patch-panels, buried conduits, direct buried, underwater, and on poles. You should make sure that the cable has the proper flame rating, tensile capacity, and weight.

A single cable can have several multimode and single-mode fibers along with copper conductors in it. You may want to leave some fibers and conductors for future expansion.

You should choose a cable with fibers that meet your mode, size, bandwidth, and attenuation requirements. Since interfaces with single-mode optics are rather expensive, most people use multimode 62.5/125 fiber. This is usually limited to a distance of 2 km. Single-mode fiber can be used for distances up to 40 to 60 km.

The FDDI standard specifies a duplex connector design. A pair of simplex connectors, such as ST connectors, can be used instead. This saves cost but introduces the risk of misconnections. Their use should, therefore, be limited to patch-panels accessed only by trained professionals.

After installation, you should measure the power loss in individual links to ensure that they meet the specifications. Optical time-domain reflectometry can be used to locate faults and to measure the losses.

19.12 Further Reading

Chapter 4 and the references cited there provide more information about fiber characteristics. In particular, Basch (1986) discusses cable characteristics.

The requirements for 62.5/125-μm fiber are specified in ANSI/EIA/TIA 492AAAA. The mechanical and environmental specifications for indoor fiber optic cable are specified in ANSI/ICEA S-83-596, while those for outdoor fiber optic cables are in Bellcore TR-TSY-000020.

NEC is specified in National Fire Protection Agency (1993a, 1993b).

The catalogs of fiber cable and accessories manufacturers are useful in determining the variety of cables, installation tools, and equipment available. Many such manufacturers are listed in Appendix F.

Figure 19.7 is based on Cherin (1983).

19.13 Self-Test Exercises

Note: Some exercises have multiple correct answers. See Appendix D for answers.

19.1 Fiber cables with loose buffering are used outdoors:

a. Because most of the interbuilding traffic consists of short frames that do not need big buffers
b. To increase the temperature tolerance
c. To prevent cable strain and to allow free movement

19.2 When would you use a plenum cable?

a. If strung on utility poles
b. In underwater applications
c. In ceilings and environmental airspaces
d. In airplanes

19.3 To connect two fibers permanently, splicing is preferable to using connectors because:

a. It is cheaper.
b. It has less loss.
c. It can be done using ordinary pliers.

19.4 The NEC rating of a fiber cable is stated as OFCR. This implies that:

a. The cable has copper wires.
b. The cable has no fibers.
c. The cable can be used in risers.
d. The cable can be used in environmental spaces.

19.5 Optical time-domain reflectometry is used:

a. To locate faults
b. To determine a fiber's length
c. To determine a fiber's attenuation
d. To determine connector losses
e. To check the time jitter of the clock

CHAPTER **20**

Cable Plant: Design and Analysis

If you want to connect a number of systems located in different buildings using FDDI, your first step should be to plan a layout structure for the cable between the buildings and for the cable inside the buildings. In the buildings, different considerations may apply in the office than in the computer rooms. Designing the proper layout for the cable plant is the first topic of this chapter.

After you have a preliminary layout design, you should analyze various links to ensure that they meet the FDDI specifications. The second half of this chapter is devoted to explaining this analysis. This step may not be necessary if you use FDDI-compliant fibers and equipment and keep all distances within the limits specified by the standard.

Cable layout is an important issue. Many vendors have developed guidelines for building and campus wiring. Most of these are extensions and adoptions of the EIA-568 commercial building wiring standard developed by the Electronic Industries Association (EIA). This standard is discussed in Section 20.2.

The problem of cabling a campus can be divided into three parts consisting of cabling between buildings, cabling inside the buildings, and cabling in the computer room. These three parts are covered next followed by a discussion of the EIA-568 standard that covers all three parts.

20.1 Campus Cable Layout

There are numerous ways to connect buildings of a campus. Figure 20.1 shows several alternatives such as a ring, a tree, a star, a bus, and a grid.

Choice of a particular geometric shape does not necessarily impose the same shape on the next level. For example, Figure 20.2 shows a star cabling layout realized by installing cables in bus-shaped pathways. Also, the choice of the layout does not have to match the logical topology required by the network. Figure 20.3 shows how a ring network or bus network can be obtained by a star layout.

Although the layout and the logical topology can be chosen independently, having the same layout and logical topology results in the least amount of fiber. Thus, a ring topology will require more fiber if a tree layout is used (compared to a ring layout). Similarly, a tree topology will require more fiber with a ring layout than with a tree layout.

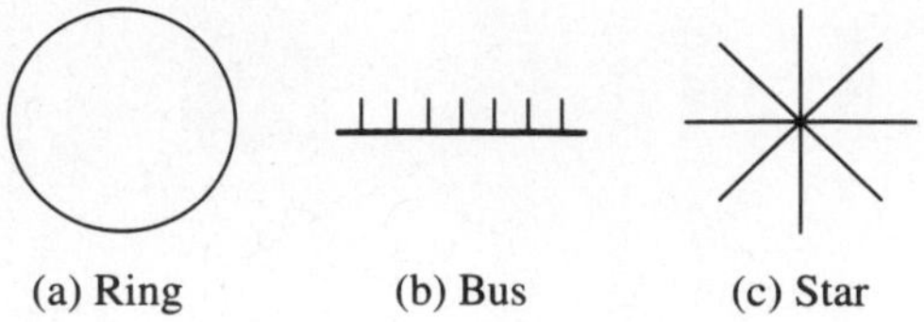

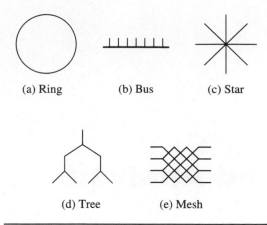

Figure 20.1 Possible ways to connect buildings in a campus.

Among the geometric shapes shown in Figure 20.1, the ring and tree (of which the star is a special case) are most commonly used. These alternatives are shown in Figures 20.4 and 20.5, which show a small campus of six buildings. Both layouts have their advantages and disadvantages. The advantage of the ring layout is that each building is connected via two trenches and if all cables in one trench are damaged, the communication can continue using cables in the other trench. With the star layout, each building is normally connected only by one trench and, therefore, if all the cables in the trench are damaged, the building will become unreachable until the cables are repaired. This may or may not be a big disadvantage considering that the chances of all cables in a trench being damaged are small compared to that of the active equipment (concentrator, bridge, stations) failures, which affect both layouts equally.

With more than one trench failure, a ring layout will partition the network, while the tree network may or may not continue with most buildings in one partition.

When a new building is added to the campus, a ring layout requires two new trenches to be dug, whereas a tree layout requires only one. This is shown via the dotted lines in Figures 20.4 and 20.5. Thus, the ring layout is slightly more expensive in terms of number of trenches.

With either layout, availability can be enhanced by providing additional connections between buildings using alternative approaches.

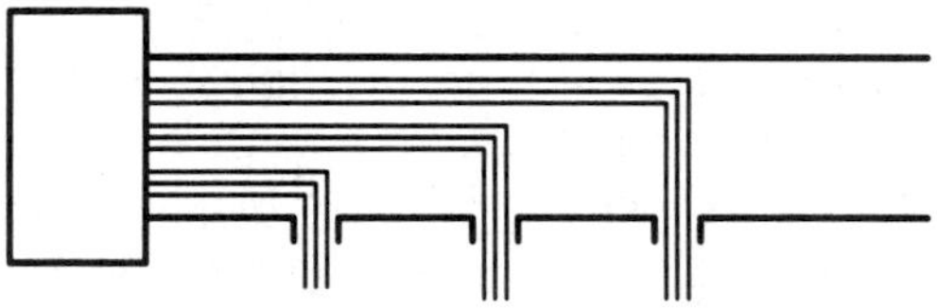

Figure 20.2 Star cabling layout using bus-shaped pathways.

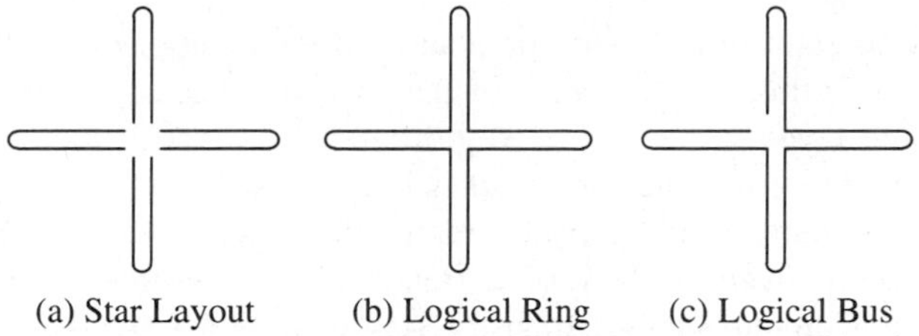

Figure 20.3 A logical ring or bus toplogy from a star layout.

The choice of layout may depend on several other factors such as the right-of-way between buildings and existing trenches and wiring. For example, you may or may not be able to cross a public road between the buildings.

Notice that the terms *logical topology, physical topology*, and *layout* are distinct. A logical topology shows individual fibers and light paths. A physical topology shows cables (with two fibers each) connecting different nodes of the network. A layout shows only conduits or trenches containing multiple cables. An FDDI network can have a logical topology of a single or a dual ring. In all cases, the FDDI standard limits the physical topology to a dual ring of trees or its subsets. The cable plant layout is covered by the EIA-568 commercial building wiring standard, which recommends a tree layout because it is easier to administer than a ring layout.

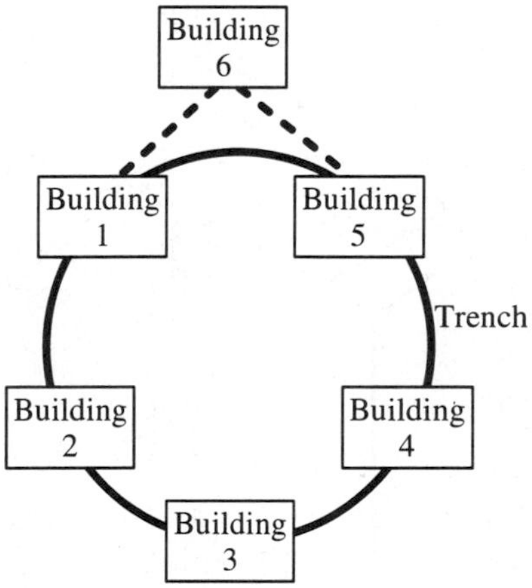

Figure 20.4 Ring cable layout for a campus.

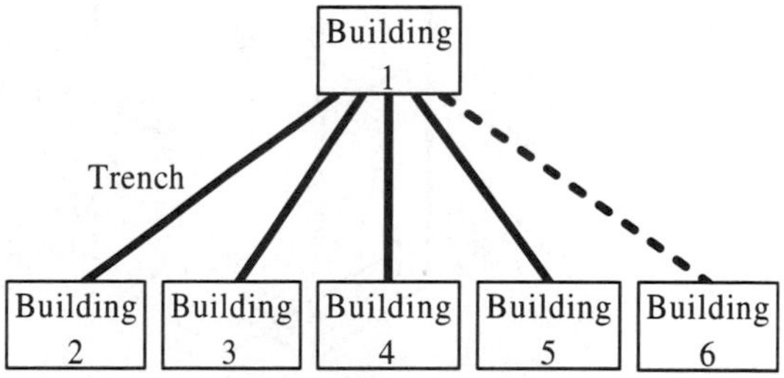

Figure 20.5 Star cable layout for a campus.

20.2 EIA-568 Commercial Building Wiring Standard

In laying out the cable to connect different floors and different stations on a floor, we again have a choice of a ring layout or a tree layout. Much of the previous discussion on campus wiring layout applies to building cable layout as well. The key difference is that inside the building, the layout can be changed much more easily since no trenches have to be dug.

Early in 1985, a large number of companies representing the telecommunications and computer industry expressed concern over the lack of a standard for building telecommunications wiring systems. The Computer Communications Industry Association (CCIA) asked the EIA to develop such a standard. In response, EIA has developed three related standards. The first standard, called ANSI/EIA/TIA 568, covers topology, distances, and media parameters for commercial enterprises. The second standard, ANSI/EIA/TIA 569, covers the design of the telecommunications closets and the equipment rooms. Finally, ANSI/EIA/TIA 570 covers topology, distances, and media parameters for residential and light commercial enterprises.

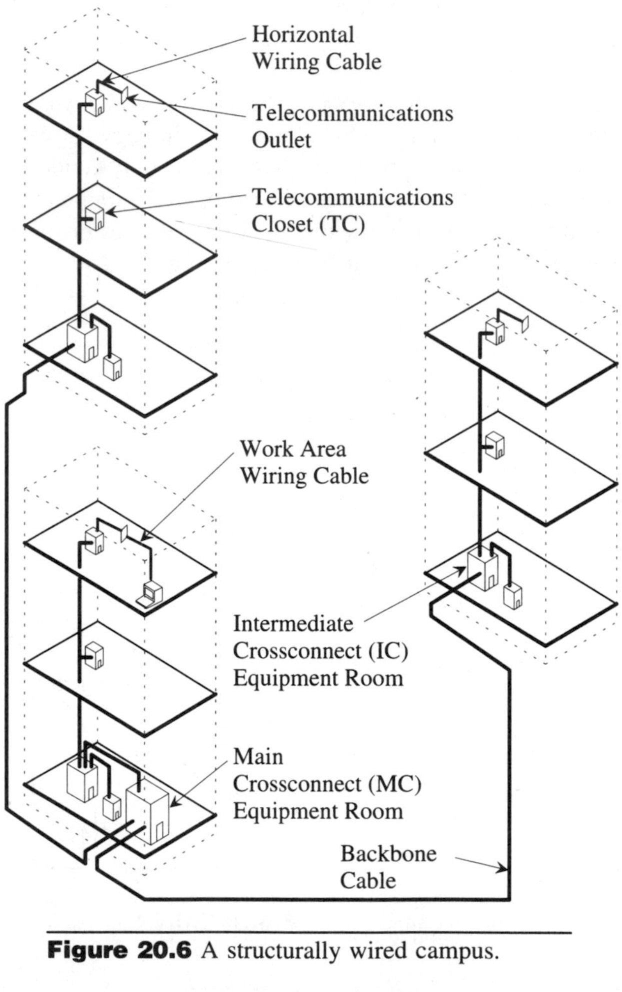

Figure 20.6 A structurally wired campus.

These standards have been developed by the Telecommunications Industry Association (TIA), which handles the telecommunication sector of EIA and conducts its standard activities through EIA. When EIA/TIA recommendations are ratified by the American National Standards Institute (ANSI), they become standard and are denoted by ANSI/EIA/TIA xxx. For brevity, we will refer to them simply as EIA-xxx standards.

The EIA-568 standard specifies minimum requirements for telecommunications wiring within a building and between buildings in a campus environment. It specifies recommended topologies, distances, media parameters, connectors, and their pin assignments. The standard is meant for commercial enterprises that are office oriented.

The EIA-568 standard recommends a hierarchical star layout as shown in Figure 20.6. Figure 20.7 shows an equivalent schematic. All neighboring offices on a floor are connected to a **telecommunication closet** (**TC**). There is one or more telecommunications closets on each floor. The TCs are then connected to an **intermediate cross-connect** (**IC**) equipment room in the building. Finally, all ICs in the campus are connected to a **main cross-connect** (**MC**) equipment room.

The complete wiring system is divided into three levels of hierarchy as shown in Figure 20.8. The **backbone subsystem** consists of main and intermediate cross-connects and the backbone cables interconnecting them. The **horizontal wiring subsystem** consists of the telecommunications closets, telecommunications outlets on office walls, and the horizontal wiring cables interconnecting the TCs and the outlets. A **work area subsystem** connects the station equipment to telecommunication outlets. The wiring between telecommunications closets is considered part of the backbone wiring.

Four types of cables are specified for the horizontal wiring system:

1. Four-pair 100-Ω unshielded twisted-pair (UTP) cables
2. Two-pair 150-Ω shielded twisted-pair (STP) cables
3. 50-Ω coaxial cables
4. 62.5/125-μm optical fiber cables.

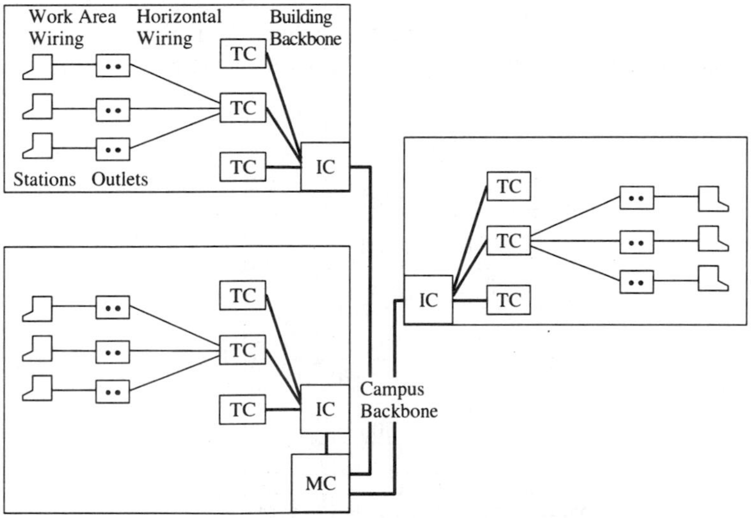

Figure 20.7 A schemetic of a hierarchical star layout recommended by the EIA-568 standard.

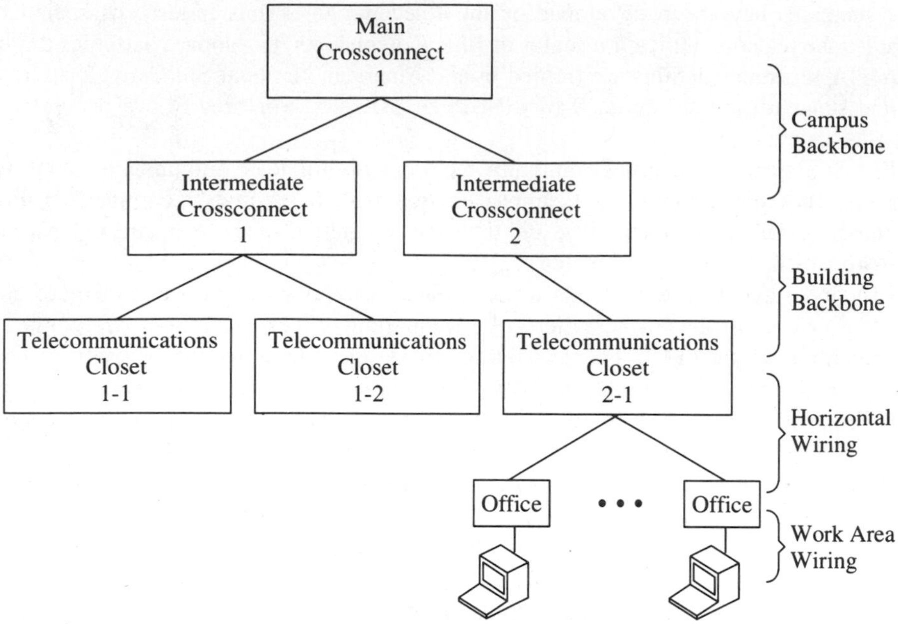

Figure 20.8 The three-level hierarchy recommended by the EIA-568 standard.

Hybrid cables consisting of more than one of these cables under a common sheath are also allowed. The EIA-568 standard limits the horizontal wiring to 90 m for all media types.

The standard specifies a star (actually a tree) topology for the backbone subsystem also. However, for the backbone subsystem, it accommodates nonstar configurations such as a ring or bus. The four media types specified for the horizontal wiring are also used in the backbone except that multipair

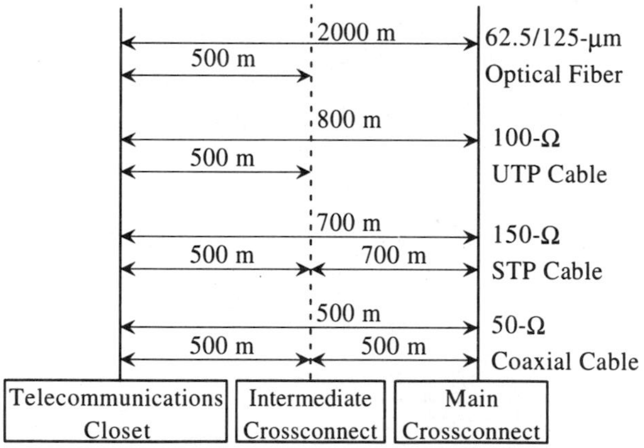

Figure 20.9 Backbone distance limits.

(instead of four-pair or two-pair) cables are allowed. The maximum backbone distance between the main cross-connect and the telecommunication closets depends on the media type, as shown in Figure 20.9.

The work area wiring consists primarily of the cable connecting the telecommunications outlet to the station (see Figure 20.10). Since this wiring is nonpermanent, the standard allows any wiring suitable for the application. In setting the maximum horizontal cable length, an allowance of 3 m of the same cable type as used in the horizontal wiring was made.

The EIA-568 standard also covers the characteristics of the cables and connectors that can be used. For cable characteristics, it essentially references other standards that cover these cables.

Telecommunications engineers use the term **cross-connect** to indicate passive interconnection. By passive, we mean that there is no electrically active component. Patch-panels are examples of passive components. Concentrators and bridges are examples of active components. If active equipment is present in an interconnection closet or room, then the facility is referred to as a **distribution frame**. Thus, the terms **main distribution frame** (**MDF**), **intermediate distribution frame** (**IDF**), and **horizontal distribution frame** (**HDF**) denote active interconnection facilities for the campus, building, and the floor, respectively.

Although the EIA-568 standard specifies a tree layout (of which the star is a special case), you still have the flexibility to construct a dual ring of trees using this wiring structure. This is shown

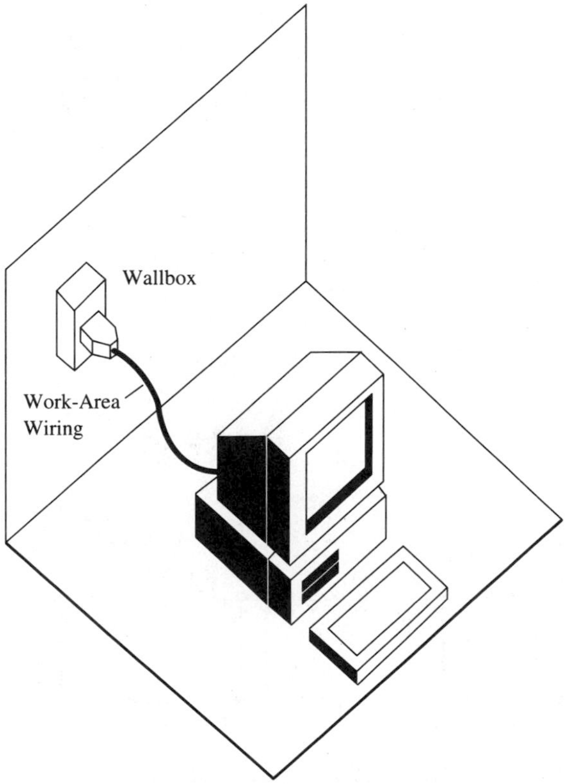

Figure 20.10 Work area wiring subsystem.

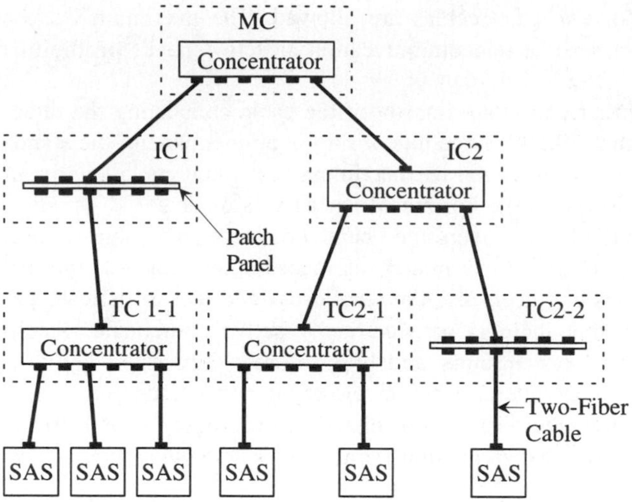

Figure 20.11 Tree topology using concentrators.

in Figures 20.11 and 20.12. Figure 20.11 shows how several stations can be connected in a tree topology using concentrators. Figure 20.12 shows a dual-ring topology of dual-attachment stations using the same layout. Again, the internode distance limitation may force the choice of one physical topology over the other.

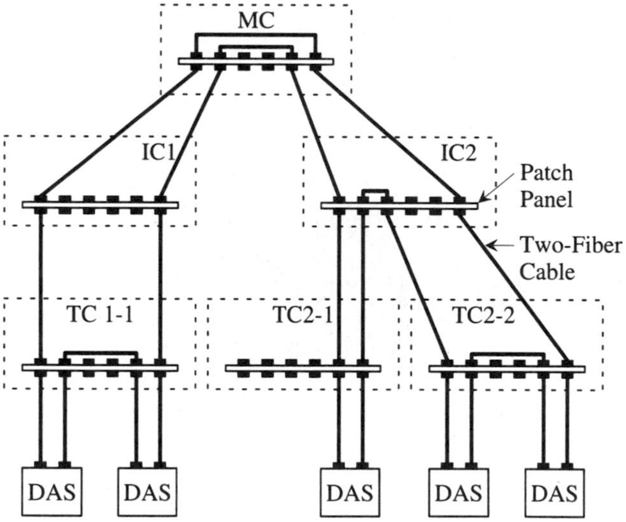

Figure 20.12 Dual-ring topology using structured wiring.

20.3 Dual Homing

Concentrators in an FDDI network provide a high degree of fault tolerance. Any number of stations attached to a single concentrator can break down, but the communications among the remaining stations continues. The concentrators are not protected in the sense that a fault in the concentrator may partition the ring such that the stations in the tree supported by the concentrator are unable to communicate with other stations in the network. A dual-homing configuration uses redundant concentrators such that on failure of one concentrator or its connections, another concentrator can take over the stations attached to the failed concentrator.

Dual homing allows the A- and B-ports of a dual-attachment node to be connected to different concentrators as shown in Figure 20.13. Only one of the two ports is used. The other port is in the standby mode. The standby connections are not part of the ring, but any of them can be quickly brought in if a problem occurs. This means that the PHY is not turned off in the standby mode. It does an extended link confidence test (see Section 11.3) with its neighbor and then restarts. If nothing changes they will do this forever. If one concentrator or the active connection fails, the stations switch over to the surviving concentrator or connection. This provides a very high level of fault tolerance. In some implementations of dual homing, both rings are available in all stations. In this case, if one ring fails, all stations switch over to the other ring. This is known as **dual-path** support.

Notice that dual homing is an optional part of the FDDI standard. Not all dual-attachment stations or concentrators support this function. Those nodes not supporing dual homing will simply turn off one of the ports. FDDI toppology rules (see Section 11.2) state that, given a choice of forming both A-M and B-M connections, a station should prefer to use B and not use A. Therefore, it is the A-port that generally goes in the standby mode.

Figure 20.14 shows a one-level concentrator tree configuration with dual homing. The standby connections are shown via dotted lines. This configuration continues to provide complete connectivity to all stations even if one concentrator or cable fails. On the second and subsequent failures, full connectivity may or may not remain depending on the locations of the failures. A dual ring, on the other hand, loses full connectivity on second and subseqent failures.

One side benefit of the dual-homing topology is that it reduces the size of the ring compared to a dual-ring topology. Therefore, it is especially useful with networks spanning large geographical areas. With the dual-ring topology each span has to be counted four times toward the maximum ring periphery of 200 km. If a wrap occurs, almost all fiber may be actively used. With a dual-homed tree

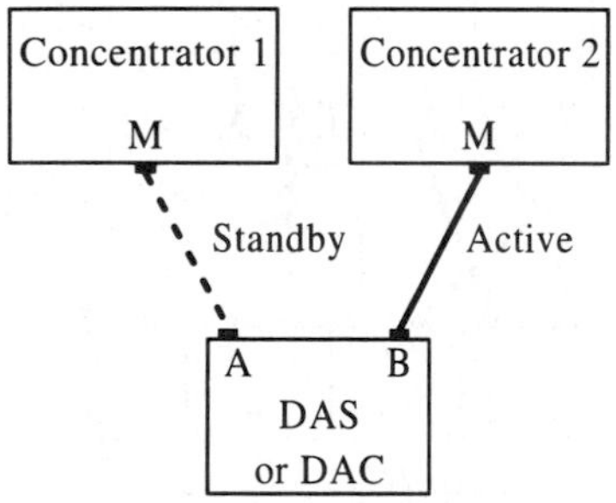

Figure 20.13 Dual homing.

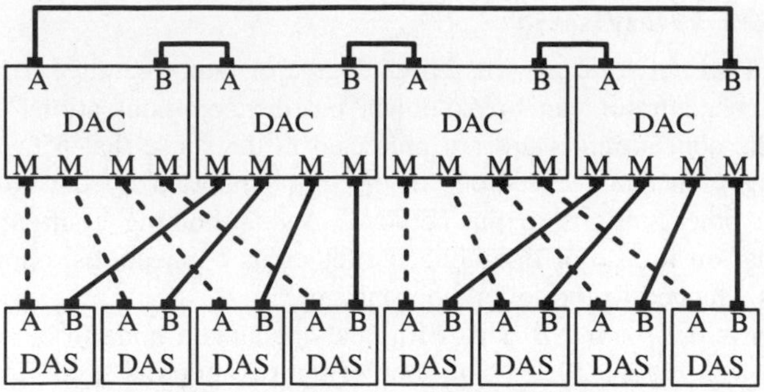

Figure 20.14 A dual-homing configuration.

topology, each span is counted only twice. Even if a failure occurs, only half of the fiber is actively used. This is used in Case Study 20.1.

Concentrators can also be dual homed. Figure 20.15 shows a bilevel concentrator tree with dual homing. There is no limit to the number of levels that can be dual homed. For example, in a trilevel tree topology, one can have all end-stations dual homed from concentrators in telecommunications closets (each floor) that are dual homed from concentrators in intermediate cross-connects (each building) that are dual homed from concentrators in the main cross-connect (campus).

Although dual homing increases the number of links (and associated equipment), it provides a better payoff in terms of survivability and availability of the network. Increasing the depth of the

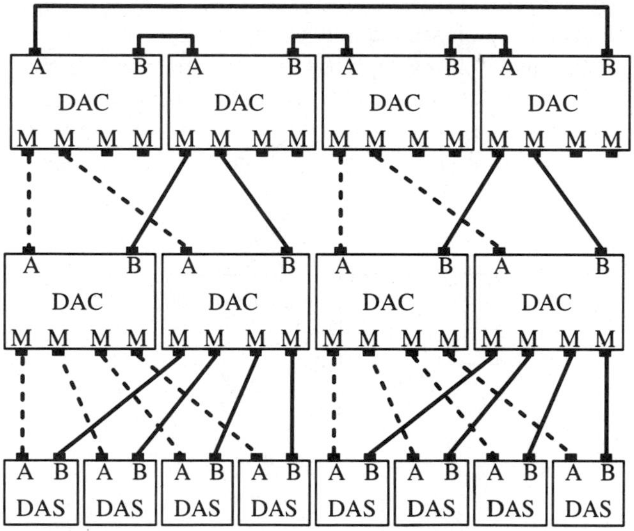

Figure 20.15 A bilevel dual-homing configuration.

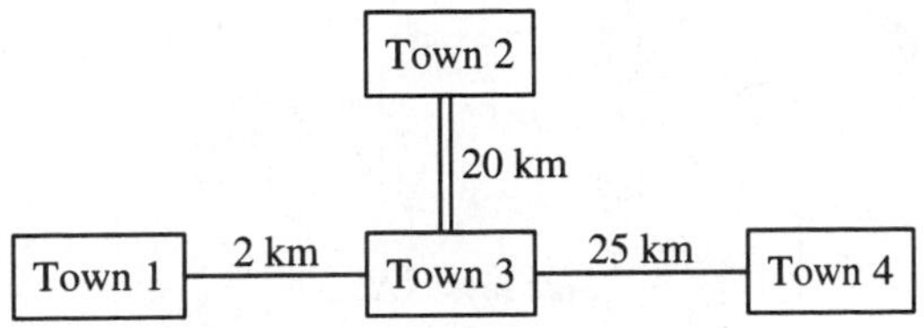

Figure 20.16 The cable layout for the insurance company.

tree normally increases the susceptibility of the network to faults. However, with dual homing, the susceptibility does not increase with depth.

The dual-homing configuration is sometimes called a dual-tree configuration since there are two (or more) roots. In a tree configuration, all children nodes are connected to one (and only one) parent. In a dual tree, all children nodes are connected to two parents.

Dual homing helps reduce the periphery of the ring. Therefore, if you find that the ring periphery exceeds the 200-km limit, changing the physical topology may also solve this problem. This is illustrated by the following case study.

Case Study 20.1 An insurance company had offices spread over four towns. Several years ago, the company installed private fiber for its telecommunications needs. Spare fibers were available but the layout was fixed as shown in Figure 20.16. The solid lines between the towns represent four or more fibers available between the towns. The cable lengths between the facilities are also shown. In this case, the problem is to decide the physical topology: a dual ring or a dual ring of trees.

The first alternative is to use a dual ring connecting the four sites. The shortest such arrangement is shown in Figure 20.17. This arrangement results in a total ring periphery of $4 \times (20 + 2 + 25)$ or 188 km. Although this is within the 200-km limit allowed by the FDDI standard, the company rejected it on the grounds that it was too close to the limit. Instead, the dual-homed dual ring of trees topology shown in Figure 20.18 was selected. Notice that the dual ring runs between two

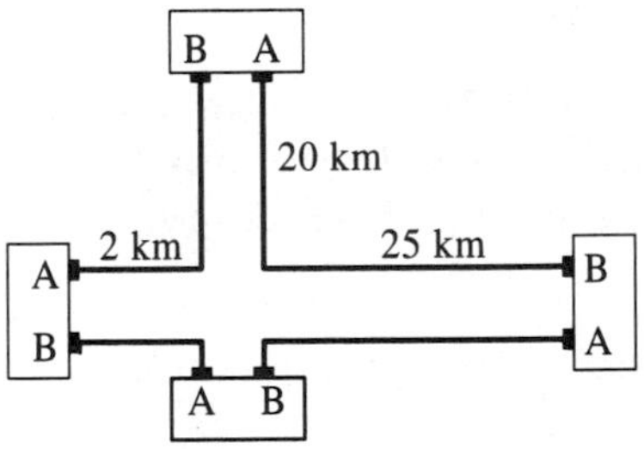

Figure 20.17 Dual-ring topology for the insurance company.

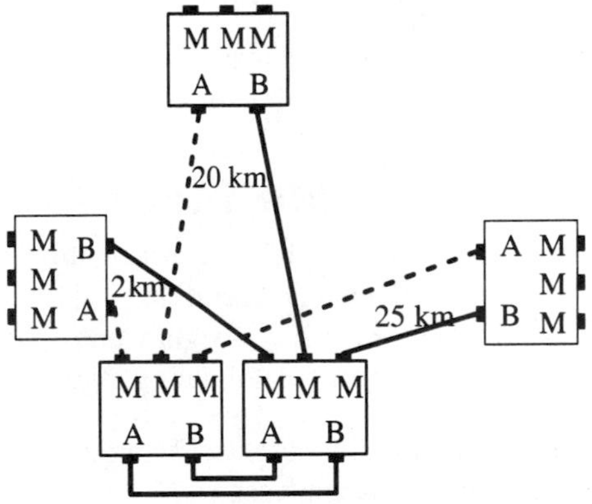

Figure 20.18 Dual-homed dual ring of trees topology for the insurance company.

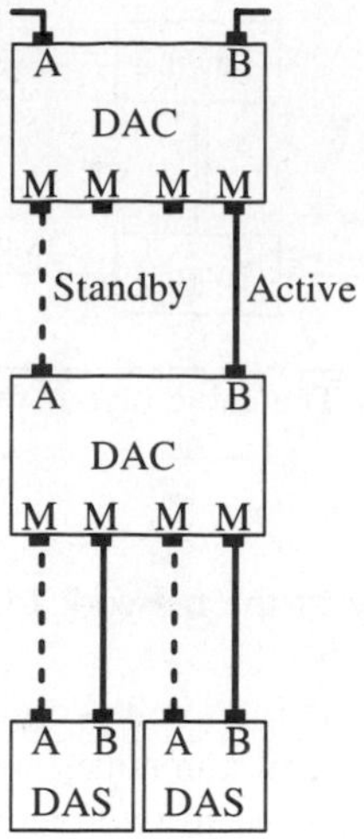

Figure 20.19 Alternate path topology.

concentrators in the same facility. With this alternative, only two of the four fibers are actively used at any instant and the other two remain in standby mode. The total ring periphery has been reduced to $2 \times (20+2+25)$ or 94 km while still providing complete protection against any single fiber failure.

Both configurations considered in this case have the problem of complete communication breakdown if the site in town 3 is destroyed. Given the existing layout with town 3 as the hub of the layout, this cannot be avoided. □

In some environments, cables pass through failure-prone (or hostile) surroundings and so protection against cable failures is desired but the equipment failures are not of concern. In such cases, the concentrators do not have to be duplicated. An *alternative path topology* shown in Figure 20.19 can be used. This topology is similar to dual homing in that the A-port link is in standby mode and becomes active only if the B-port link fails. Unlike dual homing, this topology does not protect against concentrator failures.

20.4 Cable Plant Analysis

In this section, we explain the procedure on how to ensure that the cabling between two stations will result in satisfactory operation. If the cable is too long, the received power may be too small or the received pulses may get significantly distorted, resulting in a high bit error rate. The assurance procedure consists of the following steps:

1. Trace each link's path and determine the fiber length and number of intermediate devices.
2. Conduct a loss analysis.
3. Conduct a bandwidth (or rise time) analysis.

These steps are explained further in the next three sections.

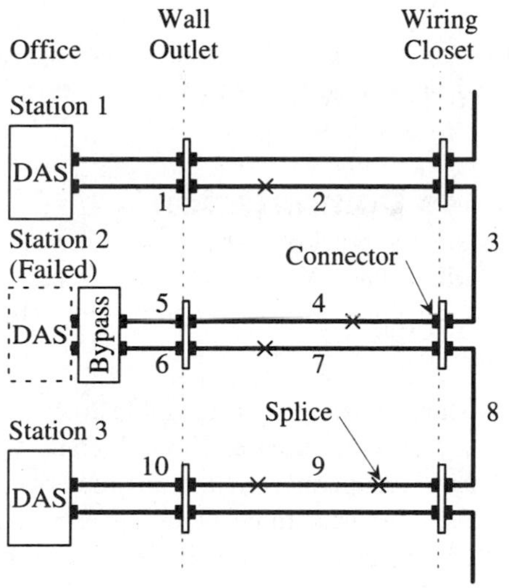

Figure 20.20 The sample configuration for path tracing.

20.5 Path Tracing

The connection between two stations (or a station and a concentrator) may go through several wiring closets, connectors, splices, and bypasses. The first step is to trace the path and count the number of fiber segments, connectors, splices, and bypasses in the path and to measure the length of each segment. The following example illustrates this step.

Example 20.1 Figure 20.20 shows three dual-attachment stations and the cabling between them.

Since station 2 has an optical bypass, the worst case scenario (and the correct scenario to analyze) occurs when station 2 is bypassed.

The path between station 1 and 3 is shown by a solid line. Its path is from station 1, wall outlet, wiring closet, wall outlet, station 2 bypass, wall outlet, wiring closet, wall outlet, station 2. There are 10 fiber segments (also counting the 2 fiber segments inside the closet). Each fiber segment has a connector at each end resulting in 11 connectors.

Assuming that the cables between wall outlets and wiring closets have one splice each (which is not usual), there are four splices in the path in addition to one optical bypass. The total combined length of all fiber lengths is, say, 440 m. □

20.6 Loss Analysis

The purpose of this analysis is to ensure that the total optical power loss between two nodes does not exceed the limits specified in the standard. The goal is to ensure a high probability of error-free transmission. The analysis can be done at two levels of statistical sophistication. At the simplest level, only the maximum values of component loss are used. For a more sophisticated analysis, the mean and standard deviation of the component loss are used to compute the 99-percentile of the link loss. Both analyses are described in this section. If after the first analysis, you find that there is not enough margin left for errors and omissions, you may want to do the more sophisticated analysis.

20.6.1 Simple Loss Computation

This first analysis is a simple arithmetic process. All you need is to know the maximum loss in each component and the number of components. You should make sure that you use the maximum loss specification (and not the average or typical) for each component. The following example illustrates the calculation.

Example 20.2 Figure 20.21 shows a sample wiring. Table 20.1 shows the steps in loss calculation for the link between the station and the concentrator. The link consists of 1-km fiber, six connectors, eight splices, and one bypass. These input parameters are obtained from the wiring diagram and listed as lines 1 through 4 of Table 20.1. The next three items are the maximum loss specifications for the fiber, connectors, splices, and bypasses. These are obtained from the manufacturer's specification sheets. The input/output power levels of the receiver and transmitter are similarly obtained from the manufacturer.

Subtracting the minimum input power required at the receiver from the minimum output power of the transmitter, we get the maximum allowed loss of 11 dB. Multiplying the number of splices and loss per splices gives a total splicing loss of 3.2 dB. The total loss for connectors and cable is similarly calculated. The total link loss is the sum of loss in the splices, connectors, and fiber. In this case, the total link loss is 10.4 dB. This leaves only a 0.6 dB margin for source aging, temperature variation, and the variation of individual components from the nominal specs. □

Generally a margin of less than 1 dB is considered risky. The link of the preceding example may, therefore, be considered unacceptable. One solution is to put a concentrator in the IDF, thereby breaking the link into two links.

In Example 20.2, we assumed that all fiber sections used the same fiber. If fibers with different numerical apertures or different sizes are used, additional loss should be allowed for the mismatch. Table 5.2 presented earlier in Chapter 5 lists the extra loss that must be allowed at the transmitter if fibers of size other than 62.5/125 are used. Table 5.3 lists the extra loss that must be allowed if fibers of different sizes are spliced or connected.

For single-mode links, a 1-dB allowance should be made for reflection and dispersion penalties. Thus, the allowable loss budget is minimum transmit power minus minimum power required at the receiver minus 1 dB ($P_T - P_R - 1$).

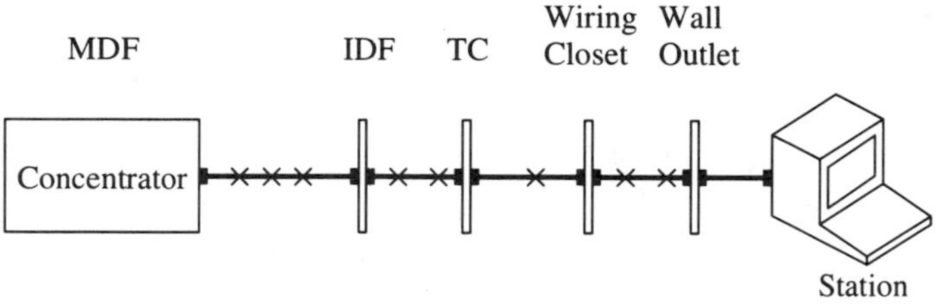

Figure 20.21 A sample link for loss computation.

Table 20.1 Link Loss Calculation

From the Wiring Diagram:	
1. Total length of the fiber	1 km
2. Total number of connectors	6
3. Total number of splices	8
4. Total number of bypasses	1
From the Component Specifications:	
5. Loss per kilometer of fiber	1.5 dB/km
6. Loss per connector	0.7 dB
7. Loss per splice	0.4 dB
8. Loss per bypass	1.5 dB
9. Minimum output power of the transmitter	−20 dBm
10. Minimum input power required for the receiver	−31 dBm
Calculations:	
11. Maximum allowed loss (subtract line 10 from 8)	11.0 dB
12. Total loss for cable (multiply lines 1 and 5)	1.5 dB
13. Total loss for connectors (multiply lines 2 and 6)	4.2 dB
14. Total loss for splices (multiply lines 3 and 7)	3.2 dB
15. Total loss for bypasses (multiply lines 4 and 8)	1.5 dB
16. Total loss (add lines 12, 13, 14, and 15)	10.4 dB
17. Remaining margin (subtract line 15 from line 11)	0.6 dB

20.6.2 99-Percentile Loss Computation

The analysis presented in Section 20.6.1 is satisfactory if there is not much variation among different pieces of various components. If there is considerable variance, an analysis using maximum component losses would be very conservative while one using average values may be too risky. In such cases, it is better to use the average and the standard deviation of the component loss and compute the 99-percentile loss value for the link. If 100 links using the same configuration are used, 99 of those links will have loss less than that indicated by this value. One link may have loss more than that indicated by this value. Thus, if you want to minimize your risk, you may want to compute the 99.9- or higher (e.g., 99.99-) percentile.

Those proficient in statistics know that the 99-percentile of a normally distributed random variable is given approximately by the mean plus 2.326 standard deviations. By testing several components, for example, several connectors, one can determine the mean and standard deviation of the loss in the component. These specifications can also be obtained from the manufacturers.

The mean loss of the link is simply the sum of mean losses in various components. The variance of loss in the link is also the sum of variance of losses in the components. Variance is defined as the square of the standard deviation. If the mean link loss is μ and the variance is σ^2, the 99-percentile link loss is $\mu + 2.326\sigma$. The following example illustrates this computation.

Example 20.3 Consider a link with 11 connectors, four splices, one bypass, and 4 km of single-mode fiber. The loss parameters for various components are shown in Table 20.2. The numbers for various components are also shown in the table. The total contribution of each component to the

Table 20.2 Parameters for Link Loss Analysis Example

	Component Loss			Total Loss	
	Mean	Std. Dev.	Quantity	Mean	Variance
Component	μ_i	σ_i	n_i	$n_i \times \mu_i$	$n_i \times \sigma_i^2$
Fiber (1 km)	0.40 dB	0.20 dB	4.00	$4 \times 0.40 = 1.6$	$4 \times 0.20^2 = 0.16$
Connectors	0.40 dB	0.20 dB	11	$11 \times 0.40 = 4.4$	$11 \times 0.20^2 = 0.44$
Splices	0.15 dB	0.15 dB	4	$4 \times 0.15 = 0.6$	$4 \times 0.15^2 = 0.09$
Bypasses	1.50 dB	0.50 dB	1	$1 \times 1.50 = 1.5$	$1 \times 0.50^2 = 0.25$
Link				8.1	0.94

link loss mean and variance is shown in the rightmost two columns of the table. The total link loss is obtained by separately adding these two columns.

In this case, the link loss has a mean of 8.1 dB and a variance of 0.94 dB^2. Taking a square root of the variance we get a standard deviation of 0.97 dB. The 99-percentile of the link loss is $8.1 + 2.326 \times 0.97$ or 10.36 dB.

Using Category I transmitters and receivers, the maximum allowed link loss budget is 10 dB. Therefore, this link is unsatisfactory. There are several ways to fix the problem in this case. For example, the number of splices can be reduced (by using unspliced fiber), the bypass can be removed, or a Category II receiver could be used. Use of a Category II transmitter may also fix the problem but it would result in the violation of the minimum loss requirements and an attenuator would have to be used to meet the minimum loss of 14 dB for a Category II transmitter and Category I receiver pair. The bypass would have to be removed if a Category I transceiver is used (see Section 6.6). □

In the preceding example we used a multiplier of 2.326 to obtain the 99-percentile loss. The corresponding multipliers for the 99.9- and 99.99-percentiles are 3.090 and 3.719, respectively.

20.6.3 Computing Allowable Link Span

The analysis procedure of Section 20.6.2 can also be used to determine the maximum length of the fiber that can be used if all other parameters are given.

Such analysis is often required for long-span single-mode links. Since the length of the link is not given, the number of splices is also not known. However, it can be computed from the length of the reels.

The number of splices n_s can be computed as follows from the length of the span l_f and the length of each reel l_r:

$$n_s = 1 + \left\lceil \frac{l_f}{l_R} \right\rceil$$

Here, $\lceil x \rceil$ denotes rounding up to the nearest integer. This number n_s includes two splices at the end of the span. Fiber cable usually comes in 2-km reels. Using this information, the maximum fiber length allowed for a given transmitter-receiver pair can be computed as shown by the following example.

Table 20.3 Link Span Computation Example

	Component Loss			Total Loss	
	Mean	Std. Dev.	Quantity	Mean	Variance
Component	μ_i	σ_i	n_i	$n_i \times \mu_i$	$n_i \times \sigma_i^2$
Fiber (1 km)	0.40 dB	0.07 dB	l_f	$l_f \times 0.40$	$l_f \times 0.07^2$
Connectors	0.40 dB	0.20 dB	4	4×0.40	4×0.20^2
Splices	0.15 dB	0.15 dB	$1 + \left\lceil \frac{l_f}{2} \right\rceil$	$\left(1 + \left\lceil \frac{l_f}{2} \right\rceil\right) \times 0.15$	$\left(1 + \left\lceil \frac{l_f}{2} \right\rceil\right) \times 0.15^2$
Bypasses	1.50 dB	1.50 dB	0	0	0
Link				$1.75 + 0.475 l_f$	$0.1825 + 0.0211 l_f$

Example 20.4 Consider the problem of determining the maximum link span allowed using Category II transmitter-receiver pair. In this case, the maximum allowed loss budget (after subtracting the reflection loss) is 32 dB.

Assuming that the fiber path goes through two wiring closets, there would be four connectors in the path. Using 2-km reels, the number of splices n_s is:

$$n_s = 1 + \left\lceil \frac{l_f}{2} \right\rceil$$

The analysis is shown in Table 20.3. The standard deviation of the link loss is:

$$\sigma_L \approx \sqrt{0.1825 + 0.0211 l_f}$$

The 99-percentile of the link loss is approximately:

$$1.75 + 0.475 l_f + 2.326\sqrt{0.1825 + 0.0211 l_f}$$

Equating this to 32 dB, we get $l_f = 54.95$ km as the maximum fiber length using a Category II transceiver. □

20.7 Bandwidth Analysis

The purpose of bandwidth analysis is to ensure that each link has the bandwidth capacity required to transmit the signal. The bandwidth capacity of the fiber is specified in MHz-km. If you are using a multimode fiber with at least a 500-MHz-km bandwidth, the link length is no more than 2 km, the receiver and the transmitter satisfy the FDDI specifications, your link will meet the bandwidth requirement, and you do not need to do this analysis. However, if any component in the link does not satisfy the FDDI specifications, you should do the bandwidth analysis presented here.

The behavior of fibers and sources is still not perfectly understood. Curve fitting by means of empirical data is often used to develop relationships among the parameters involved. Different measurement studies have been found to produce slightly different relationships. Many of the equations presented in this section were developed and refined while FDDI PMD was being designed. Therefore, the analysis should be considered approximate.

The formulas used in bandwidth analysis are summarized in Box 20.1. The logic behind these formulas is given next. Readers not interested in mathematical details can safely skip to the end of the following derivation.

Box 20.1 Bandwidth Analysis

1. **Output**:

B_{channel} = Combined bandwidth of the source and the fiber (MHz)

2. **Inputs**:

M = Modal bandwidth-distance product of the fiber (MHz-km)

L = Length of the fiber (km)

t_{source} = Transition (rise or fall) time of the source (ns)

Δ = RMS spectral width of the source (nm)
= 0.849 times the FWHM spectral width of the source (nm)

S = Slope of the fiber dispersion curve (ns/nm^2-km)

λ_c = Central wavelength of the source (nm)

λ_0 = Zero dispersion wavelength of the fiber (nm)

3. **Other Symbols**:

$B_{\text{3-dB optical}}$ = 3-dB optical bandwidth of the source (MHz)

B_{modal} = Modal bandwidth of the fiber (MHz)

$B_{\text{chromatic}}$ = Chromatic bandwidth of the fiber (MHz)

D_{eff} = Effective dispersion (ns/nm-km)

4. **Equations**:

$$D_{\text{eff}} = \frac{1}{4} S \left[(\lambda_c - 7) - \frac{\lambda_0^4}{(\Lambda_c - 7)^3} \right]$$

$$B_{\text{3-dB optical}} = \frac{480}{t_{\text{source}}}$$

$$B_{\text{modal}} = \frac{M}{L}$$

$$B_{\text{chromatic}} = \frac{375}{L\Delta\sqrt{D_{\text{eff}}^2 + [(S\Delta)^2/8]}}$$

$$B_{\text{channel}}^{-2} = B_{\text{3-dB optical}}^{-2} + B_{\text{modal}}^{-2} + B_{\text{chromatic}}^{-2}$$

Derivation 20.1 As discussed in Section 4.12, the bandwidths of a system consisting of source, fiber, and receiver can be combined using an inverse-square addition rule, that is:

$$B_{\text{system}}^{-2} = B_{\text{source}}^{-2} + B_{\text{fiber}}^{-2} + B_{\text{receiver}}^{-2}$$

The Nyquist theorem of communication states that the system bandwidth B_{system} must be at least one-half the baud rate to prevent errors. For FDDI, the code bit rate is 125 Mbps, the bit time is 8 ns, and the baud rate is 125 Mbaud. This means that the combined bandwidth of the source, fiber, and receiver must be at least 62.5 MHz. Practical systems require a somewhat greater bandwidth. Empirical measurements have shown that for an acceptable error performance, the combined bandwidth of the FDDI source and the fiber must be at least 95 MHz. Laboratory measurements show that the bit error rate of the link degrades significantly if the combined bandwidth of the fiber and source is lower than 95 MHz. If we call the combination of a source and a fiber a **channel**, the channel bandwidth is given by:

$$B_{\text{channel}}^{-2} = B_{\text{source}}^{-2} + B_{\text{fiber}}^{-2}$$

For an FDDI system to operate properly:

$$B_{\text{channel}} \geq 95 \text{ MHz}$$

The bandwidth of the source can be obtained from its transition times (rise and fall times), which are generally given in the source specifications. For an FDDI-compliant source, the transition time must be less than 3.5 ns. The optical rise-time of a source and its optical bandwidth are related as follows:

$$B_{\text{3-dB optical}} = \frac{480}{t_{\text{source}}}$$

Generally, the rise time and fall time are equal and either one can be used as the transition time t_{source}. If they are not equal, then the maximum of the two times should be used for the worst case analysis.

The bandwidth of the fiber depends on its dispersion, which consists of modal dispersion and chromatic dispersion. These individual components can be computed separately and combined using the squared addition rule:

$$B_{\text{fiber}}^{-2} = B_{\text{modal}}^{-2} + B_{\text{chromatic}}^{-2}$$

The modal bandwidth is a function of the fiber length:

$$B_{\text{modal}} = \frac{M}{L^q}$$

where M is the specified bandwidth-distance product of the fiber in MHz-km, L is the length in kilometers, and q is a constant that has been empirically shown to be between 0.5 and 1. For short fiber segments, q is close to 1. For very long fiber segments, q is close to 0.5. An average value of 0.7 was initially used in calculations. To be on the safe side (conservative), we will use a value of $q = 1$.

The chromatic bandwidth is inversely proportional to the length of the fiber and the spectral width of the source:

$$B_{\text{chromatic}} \propto \frac{1}{L|D_{\text{chromatic}}|\Delta} \tag{20.1}$$

where $D_{\text{chromatic}}$ is the chromatic dispersion in ps/km-nm, and Δ is the source spectral width in nm. The chromatic dispersion can be negative or positive. In either case, the absolute (positive) value is used in the calculation.

Equation (20.1) cannot be used in the 1300-nm window used in FDDI. In this window, the chromatic dispersion is close to zero and the second-order effects, which depend on the slope and shape of the dispersion curve, become more important. Based on empirical measurements, EIA has recommended fitting a three-term equation of the form:

$$\text{Pulse delay } \tau = A + B\lambda^2 + C\lambda^{-2} \tag{20.2}$$

Here, λ is the wavelength and A, B, and C are coefficients determined by curve fitting on measured data. Equation (20.2) is known as the *Sellmeier equation*. If λ_0 is the zero-dispersion wavelength for the fiber and S is the slope of the dispersion curve at λ_0, then Equation (20.2) results in the following formula for dispersion $D(\lambda)$:

$$D(\lambda) = \frac{\lambda S}{4}\left[1 - \left(\frac{\lambda_0}{\lambda}\right)^4\right]$$

Since a source produces light over a band of wavelength and not just one wavelength, what value of the wavelength λ should we use in the preceding formula? One choice is to use the center wavelength of the source. This gives:

$$D(\lambda_c) = \frac{S}{4}\left[\lambda_c - \frac{\lambda_0^4}{\lambda_c^3}\right]$$

This formula applies if the source has a perfectly symmetrical Gaussian spectrum. Measurements on several souces and fibers available in the market have shown the following to be a good approximation for the effective dispersion:

$$D_{\text{eff}} = \frac{1}{4} S \left[(\lambda_c - 7) - \frac{\lambda_0^4}{(\lambda_c - 7)^3} \right] \tag{20.3}$$

Here, λ_c is the central wavelength of the source (defined as the average of the FWHM wavelengths). It is reduced by 7 nm to account for the non-Gaussian shape of the low-wavelength side of the typical LED spectrum.

The chromatic bandwidth of the fiber is given approximately by:

$$B_{\text{chromatic}} = \frac{375}{L\Delta\sqrt{D_{\text{eff}}^2 + [(S\Delta)^2/8]}} \tag{20.4}$$

Here, Δ is the rms spectral width of the source and D_{eff} is the effective chromatic dispersion.

The combined bandwidth of the source and fiber is:

$$\begin{aligned} B_{\text{channel}}^{-2} &= B_{\text{source}}^{-2} + B_{\text{fiber}}^{-2} \\ &= B_{\text{source}}^{-2} + B_{\text{modal}}^{-2} + B_{\text{chromatic}}^{-2} \\ &= \left(\frac{480}{t_{\text{source}}}\right)^{-2} + \left(\frac{M}{L}\right)^{-2} + \left\{\frac{375}{L\Delta\sqrt{D_{\text{eff}}^2 + [(S\Delta)^2/8]}}\right\}^{-2} \end{aligned}$$

□

The following example illustrates the bandwidth analysis.

Example 20.5 Consider a multimode fiber link with a 2-km length using LED sources. Assume a source rise time of 3 ns, a central wavelength of 1290 nm, and the FWHM spectral width of 140 nm. The modal bandwidth of the fiber is 400 MHz-km, the zero-dispersion wavelength is 1340 nm, and the slope of the dispersion curve at this wavelength is 0.1 ps/nm^2-km.

In this case, the inputs are:

$M = 400$ MHz

$L = 2$ km

$t_{\text{source}} = 3$ ns

$\Delta = 0.849 \times 140 = 120$ nm

$S = 0.1 \times 10^{-3}$ ns/nm^2-km

$\lambda_c = 1290$ nm

$\lambda_0 = 1340$ nm

The optical bandwidth of the source is:

$$B_{\text{3-dB optical}} = \frac{480}{t_{\text{source}}} = \frac{480}{3} = 160 \text{ MHz}$$

The modal bandwidth of the fiber is:

$$B_{\text{modal}} = \frac{M}{L} = \frac{400}{2} = 200 \text{ MHz}$$

The effective dispersion D is:

$$D = \frac{1}{4}S\left[(\lambda_c - 7) - \frac{\lambda_0^4}{(\lambda_c - 7)^3}\right]$$

$$= 0.25 \times 0.1 \times 10^{-3}\left[(1290 - 7) - \frac{1340^4}{(1290 - 7)^3}\right]$$

$$= 0.25 \times 0.1 \times 10^{-3}(1283 - 1526.65)$$

$$= -0.00609 \text{ ns/nm-km}$$

The chromatic bandwidth of the LED-fiber combination is:

$$B_{\text{chromatic}} = \frac{375}{L\Delta\sqrt{D_{\text{eff}}^2 + [(S\Delta)^2/8]}}$$

$$= \frac{375}{2 \times 120 \times \sqrt{0.00609^2 + [(0.1 \times 10^{-3} \times 120)^2/8]}}$$

$$= \frac{375}{2 \times 120 \times \sqrt{0.00609^2 + 0.0000177}}$$

$$= 213.17 \text{ MHz}$$

The fiber bandwidth is:

$$B_{\text{fiber}} = \frac{1}{\sqrt{B_{\text{modal}}^{-2} + B_{\text{chromatic}}^{-2}}}$$

$$= \frac{1}{\sqrt{1/200^2 + 1/213.17^2}}$$

$$= 145.85 \text{ MHz}$$

The combined LED-fiber bandwidth is:

$$B_{\text{channel}} = \frac{1}{\sqrt{B_{\text{3-dB optical}}^{-2} + B_{\text{fiber}}^{-2}}}$$

$$= \frac{1}{\sqrt{1/160^2 + 1/145.85^2}}$$

$$= 107.79 \text{ MHz}$$

Since the combined bandwidth of 107.79 MHz is more than the required 95 MHz, the link does satisfy the bandwidth requirement. □

The curves shown in Figure 5.7 were calculated using a more exact version of the equations in Box 20.1. Also, since the results are supposed to be valid for all fibers, worst case assumptions were made about the fiber parameters. In particular, all curves on the left side assume a high zero-dispersion wavelength (λ_0 = 1365 nm and slope S = 0.093), while those on the right assume a low zero-dispersion wavelength (λ_0 = 1295 nm and slope S = 0.105). Both sets of curves assume a fiber bandwidth of 400 MHz.

The analysis presented here also applies to single-mode fiber. The spectral width of laser sources is very small (approximately 2 nm); the bandwidth of the single-mode fiber is several gigahertz. Therefore, single-mode links almost always pass the bandwidth analysis. For data transmission at FDDI rates, the distance is limited primarily by the attenuation.

One factor that is specific to the single-mode fibers is the so-called **mode partitioning noise** caused by random variations in the center wavelength of the laser diodes. For example, a laser diode may have a center wavelength of 1300 nm in one bit but may drift to 1305 nm in the next bit. When the signal passes through a dispersive medium (fiber), the wavelength variations cause a jitter (variation) in the signal transitions. Again, for most reasonable length links (even up to 100 km), mode partitioning noise is not significant at the FDDI data rate.

In the analysis so far, we have said nothing about the contribution of connectors and the splices to the bandwidth. They are not used in bandwidth analysis because they do not increase the transition time. In fact, the intermixing of modes at the connectors and splices can help reduce the modal dispersion slightly. Of course, this applies only to multimode fiber.

One advantage of understanding the bandwidth analysis is that it gives us an idea of what to do if a system does not meet the bandwidth requirement. This is particularly useful if you are trying to use links longer than those specified in the standard. The solution is to use a faster transmitter, a transmitter with a narrower spectral width, a lower dispersion fiber, or a faster receiver. As a rule of thumb, the changes in the source characteristics have more impact on the system bandwidth than those in the fiber. Thus, you will find that changing from 400-MHz fiber to 500-MHz fiber will increase the cost but do little in terms of improving the total system bandwidth compared to improvements in the source rise time and spectral width. Matching the source and fiber characteristics (for example, zero-dispersion wavelength λ_0 of the fiber and center wavelength λ_c of the source) helps improve the bandwidth.

20.8 Summary

The EIA-568 standard recommends a tree-structured hierarchical layout. Computing/terminal equipment in each office is connected to a wall outlet in the office. The wall outlets on each floor are connected to telecommunications closets on the floor. The telecommunications closets are, in turn, connected to an intermediate distribution facility on the main floor of the building. The intermediate distribution facilities of all buildings in a campus are connected to a main distribution facility in a central building.

The hierarchical layout of the cabling plant is easy to maintain and does not limit the physical or logical topology of the network. Both dual-ring and tree physical topologies can be obtained using this structure.

Dual-attachment stations and concentrators can be connected using a dual-ring or dual-homing topology. In the latter case, the station or concentrators are connected to two other concentrators but only one of the ports is active. The other is used in a standby mode. Dual-homing increases the fault tolerance of the network and increases its availability as well as survivability.

After designing a cable plant layout, each FDDI link should be analyzed to ensure that it meets the power loss and bandwidth specifications. The loss analysis ensures that that total loss between two nodes is less than that allowed by the transmitter-receiver pairs. This analysis must be done even if all links are within the 2-km length limit.

The bandwidth analysis ensures that the combined bandwidth of source, fiber, and receiver will exceed significantly that required to transmit a 125-Mbps FDDI code bit stream. This analysis is generally not required if the link length is below the 2-km limit.

20.9 Further Reading

Swastek, Vereeke, and Scherbarth (1989) and Stevens (1990) explain various campus and building layout issues. See McIntosh (1989) for a description of a sample color coding scheme to keep track of transmitting and receiving fibers. McClimans (1992) discusses horizontal and vertical distribution systems.

Ocheltree (1990) presents a quantitative analysis of various availability alternatives and concludes that dual homing substantially increases the survivability of the network.

Loss and bandwidth analysis are discussed in Keiser (1991) and in Kimball (1989). Hutchison, Baldwin, and Thompson (1991) describe the model presented in Section 20.7. The formula for D_{eff} presented there is incorrect. Equation (20.3) is correct. It is based on empirical analysis presented in Hutchison and Knudson (1986) and in Schicketanz and Jackman (1986). Hayes (1990) argues that multimode fiber links longer than 2 km are feasible.

Figure 20.12 has been adapted from Tiffany, Koning, and Kuenzel (1991). Figures 20.14 and 20.15 are based on Ocheltree (1990). Figure 20.19 is based on Hiles and Marlow (1992).

20.10 Self-Test Exercises

Note: Some exercises have multiple correct answers. See Appendix D for answers.

20.1 The EIA-568 standard recommends that the building wiring be structured as:

a. A star
b. A ring
c. A mesh
d. A bus
e. EIA-568 does not cover data communications wiring

20.2 What is the normal function of the intermediate cross-connects (ICs) in a campus with several buildings?

a. To connect floors of a building
b. To interconnect buildings
c. To provide temporary connections that are replaced eventually with main cross-connects

20.3 The wiring used to connect a workstation to the receptacle on the wall is called:

a. Work area wiring
b. Horizontal wiring
c. Intermediate cross-connect
d. Main cross-connect

20.4 What is the purpose of dual homing?

a. To get 200 Mbps throughput
b. To allow dual-attachment stations to be connected to a single concentrator
c. To improve availability
d. To allow two single attachment stations to be connected to one concentrator port

CHAPTER **21**

Buying FDDI Products: What to Look For

This chapter provides guidance about buying FDDI products. After reading this chapter you should be able to compare different products intelligently and understand features offered by various vendors.

Fiber optic cables were covered in Chapter 19. Copper cables were covered in Chapter 8. The products covered in this chapter are adapters, concentrators, bridges, routers, and performance monitors. It turns out that many of the considerations in buying adapters apply to all others products as well. Therefore, it is recommended that you read Section 21.1 even if you are considering buying concentrators, bridges, routers, or monitors.

21.1 FDDI Adapters

An adapter, also called a **controller** or a **network interface card** (**NIC**), allows your workstation or computer to be connected to the FDDI network. An adapter generally refers to the hardware board that is attached to the system bus. However, most adapters also require a software driver for networking applications. The driver may be sold with the adapter or it may be a part of the operating system. The key considerations in buying an FDDI adapter/driver combination are as follows:

1. *System Bus*: An adapter connects FDDI to the system bus. Thus, a large part of the adapter is devoted to handling the system bus. In buying an FDDI adapter, the first thing you should find out is the type of system bus for which the adapter has been designed. FDDI adapters are available for ISA/EISA (used in IBM PC and compatibles), TurboChannel (used in DEC RISC workstations), Sbus (used in Sun MicroSystem's Sparcstations), VME bus (used in industrial controllers), Micro Channel™ (used in IBM PS/2™ and IBM RS6000 systems), SCSI (used in many personal computers and workstations), NuBus™ (used in Apple Macintosh PCs), and XMI (used in high-end VAX™ systems). Adapters may also become available for Futurebus, which is an IEEE standard designed to be the next-generation replacement for VME bus. An adapter designed for one bus *cannot* be used for another. You should get an adapter designed for the bus to which you are going to attach it.

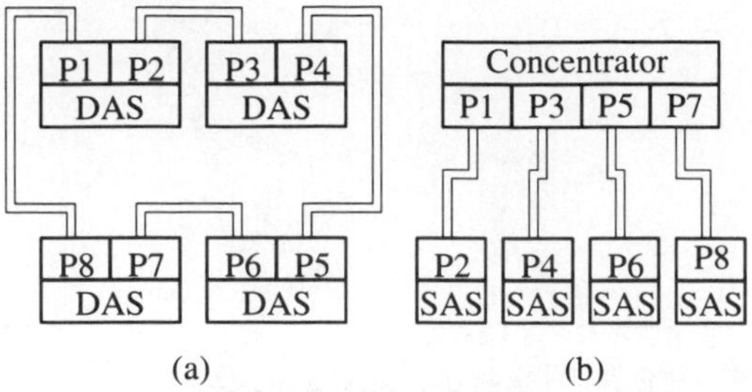

Figure 21.1 DAS versus SAS configurations.

2. *SAS or DAS*: An adapter may attach to only one or both rings of an FDDI, thereby making your computer a single-attachment station (SAS) or a dual-attachment station (DAS). A DAS can be connected directly to another DAS while a SAS *must* be connected to a concentrator. The only time a SAS does not need a concentrator is when it is connected to another SAS, thus forming a two-station ring. Any larger size network with SASs will require a concentrator. Having two attachments to a station requires twice as much optics. Since optic components are the most expensive parts of an adapter, a DAS is typically twice as expensive as a SAS. The cost savings of SASs are partially offset by the need to have a concentrator. Figure 21.1 shows two different ways of connecting four stations. In Figure 21.1(a), four DASs form a dual ring, while in Figure 21.1(b), four SASs are connected to a concentrator. Notice that in both cases the number of optical transceivers is eight (twice the number of stations). In essence, we have taken one transceiver from each of the four DASs and moved these to a separate box called a *concentrator*. Thus, the total cost of SAS and DAS configurations should be close.

   One advantage of the DAS configuration is that you have a dual ring. If any station, component, or fiber fails, the ring recovers by wrapping. This is true for the SAS configuration also except that the concentrator is a single point of failure. If a concentrator fails, the communication among its immediate descendants in the tree is lost. If any other component fails, communication among remaining components continues.

   One problem of the DAS configuration is that after the first failure, every component becomes critical. Failure of any subsequent component will cause the ring to partition. With the SAS configuration, any number of components can fail. As long as the concentrators are working, the surviving components can communicate. Since not all components are designed with the same reliability specifications, some components are more likely to fail than others. Generally, concentrators are designed much more conservatively (with a high mean time to failure) than adapters for stations.

   So far we have been using the term *failure*. Failures are supposed to be rare. What happens more often is a shutdown. If a DAS is shut down (powered off), the ring wraps. Further shutdowns will cause the ring to partition. One solution is to use an optical bypass with each DAS adapter. But that solution itself has its limitations as discussed in item 10 of this list.

   The use of dual attachments at every station requires bringing both rings to the work area. This increases the vulnerability of the rings. Each station is a part of the backbone and mistakes by a few users can disrupt the entire network. All equipment on the trunk ring needs to be carefully monitored and controlled (managed).

A better solution is to use DAS adapters only on nodes that remain powered up at all times. Bridges, concentrators, routers, and servers are examples of such nodes. These devices are generally kept in locked closets accessible only to networking personnel. Workstations that can be turned on/off by their users should use a SAS adapter and be connected via a concentrator. This is the recommended solution.

Although the choice of the physical layout and the logical topologies is orthogonal in the sense that both dual rings or trees can be supported using a ring or tree-structured wiring, generally, the use of the same physical structure as the logical topology requires less wiring. Thus, tree-structured wiring with a tree topology that uses concentrators and a small dual ring would provide both ease of wiring administration as well as the lowest cost.

The SAS versus DAS discussion is summarized in Table 21.1. The discussion so far assumed the use of DAS in the trunk ring without going through concentrators. As discussed in Section 20.3, DAS can also be *dual-homed* such that two ports are connected to two different concentrators. This increases the fault tolerance considerably and provides the best of both sides of the SAS-DAS argument. The dual homing of DASs is, therefore, highly recommended.

Another possibility is to use two (or more) SAS adapters in one system. This can give higher performance and fault tolerance than a DAS adapter, particularly if the adapter is the bottleneck and is unable to transmit or receive a full 100 Mbps. This is often the case in high-end systems with powerful CPUs.

3. *Number of MACs*: Each FDDI station should have at least one MAC. In most FDDI networks, only one of the two rings is used. One MAC is, therefore, sufficient. The second MAC in dual-attachment stations is optional. If you plan to use both rings simultaneously, you should

Table 21.1 SAS Versus DAS

Issue	SAS-Based Network	DAS-Based Network*
Total optical components	Same.	Same.
Total cost	Station cost lower. Concentrator cost extra.	Station cost higher (typically double). No concentrators required. Optical bypasses may be required.
Power	Can be turned on/off.	Should remain on.
Effect of shutdown	No effect. Interstation distances do not change.	Ring wraps or partitions. With optical bypass, interstation distances change.
Optical bypass	Not required.	May be used.
Concentrators	Required.	Not required.
Number of off stations	No limit.	Limited by link attenuation.
Effect of one station failing	No effect unless that node is a concentrator.	Ring wraps.
Effect of two or more stations failing	No effect unless one of the nodes is a concentrator.	Ring partitions.
Effect of concentrator failure	All nodes directly connected to the concentrator are disjointed.	Not applicable.
Physical layout	Ideal for tree-structured wiring.	Ideal for ring-structured wiring.

*Assumes DAS used in the trunk ring without concentrators or dual homing.

get a dual-MAC DAS rather than a single-MAC DAS adapter. Use of both rings simultaneously causes problems with some protocols as discussed in Section 18.4.

4. *Type of Medium*: FDDI supports various sizes of multimode fibers, single-mode fibers, and a variety of copper cables. The adapters come with a particular type of media. You should ensure that the media type of the adapter is available at the location of your computer. For example, a building may be wired such that fiber is used for backbone but the offices are wired with unshielded twisted-pair cable. If your computer is located in the office, you should get an adapter with unshielded twisted-pair FDDI interface.

   It is possible to use a *media converter* to convert from one type of interface to another. For example, an adapter with multimode optics can be connected to a single-mode fiber using a multimode to single-mode converter. This converter translates the optical signal into an electronic bit stream and regenerates the optical signal suitable for the outgoing media. Such converters are undesirable. The adapter-converter combination uses three times as much optics as required in a single-mode adapter. The optics is the most expensive component of the adapter and the use of extra optics unnecessarily increases the cost, increases the error rate (or equivalently decreases the maximum distance), and increases the chances of failure. If possible, try to get an adapter with the right media interface built into it. Some adapters have a modular structure such that you can replace the PMD module to suite your medium.

   The adapters for copper media are the least expensive but the copper links are limited to a length of 50 to 100 m depending on the quality of the cable. Low-cost multimode optics (called LCF) are next in terms of cost. Using lower powered transmitters and lower sensitivity receivers these LCFs support link lengths of up to 500 m. Regular multimode optics (often called ANSI optics, although LCF is also about to become an ANSI standard) allows up to 2 km. Single-mode optics, which is the most expensive of all, allows up to 40 to 60 km.

   If the distance limit of LCF optics is within your requirement, you can use the low-cost versions without sacrificing performance or reliability. LCF optics interoperates with the ANSI optics, so you can mix the two. That is, equipment with LCF optics can be connected to equipment with ANSI optics.

5. *Connector Type*: Each adapter comes with a connector for the copper wire or fiber cable. By convention, all equipment has the female half of the connector (or receptacle). The interconnecting cables have the male half (or plug). A number of fiber connector types, such as FDDI MIC, ST, SC, SMA, and Biconic, are available. These are described in Section 19.5. Although FDDI MIC is the standard, it is more expensive than simplex connectors used in other applications. You should ensure that the connector types used on your adapter ports are of the same type as those used on other equipment at your site. This helps minimize the various cables and connectors that have to be kept in stock as spares.

6. *Maximum Distance and Loss Budget*: Depending on the quality of cables, transmitters, and receivers, the maximum allowable link length varies. The FDDI standard specifies certain link length limits (such as 500 m for low-cost optics). These are based on the quality of commonly available components at the time of standardization. For single-mode optics, no distance limits are specified—only the loss budget is specified. You should check the adapter specification sheet to ensure that the transmitters and receivers on your adapter board have the power and sensitivity to meet the desired distance. This is particularly so for long-distance single-mode fiber links. Since the distance depends on the media also, the adapter spec sheet may contain only the loss budget (for example, 6 dB). Given the attenuation of the cable you should be able to compute the distance. This is explained in detail in Section 20.4.

7. *Driver Software*: As indicated earlier, adapter boards constitute only one-half of the components required to communicate using FDDI. The driver software that allows networking applications to interface with the adapter hardware is the other half. The software is written for a specific networking architecture on a specific operation system running on a specific processor. For example, if you get a driver for Novell NetWare™ on MS-DOS in x86 machines, you cannot use it for SCO UNIX™ on the same machine. Most vendors supply several drivers for each adapter board.
8. *Dual Homing*: Dual homing, which was explained in Section 20.3, allows the A- and B-ports of a dual-attachment node to be connected to different concentrators as shown in Figure 20.13. Only one of the two ports is used. In effect, the node is used as a single-attachment node. The other port is in standby mode. The standby connections are not part of the ring, but any of them can be quickly brought in if a problem occurs. This means that the PHY is not turned off in the standby mode.

   If one concentrator fails, the nodes switch to the surviving concentrators. Both rings are available in all stations. Thus, if one ring fails, all stations switch to the other ring.

   Dual homing is an optional part of the FDDI standard. Not all dual-attachment stations or concentrators support this function. Those nodes not supporting dual homing will simply turn off one of the ports.

   Dual homing provides a very high level of fault tolerance and is highly recommended for all dual-attachment adapters.
9. *Synchronous Frame Transmission Support*: Although the synchronous frame transmission is specified in FDDI standards, it is optional. Most first-generation FDDI products do not implement it. However, if your application requires a guaranteed bandwidth or bounded access delays, you should get an adapter that supports synchronous service.
10. *Optical Bypass*: An optical bypass, as discussed earlier in Section 5.8, can be used to bypass a dual-attachment station. Whenever the station shuts down, the bypass allows the incoming light to go directly to the outgoing fiber without touching any electrical components at the station. A bypass is not required with single-attachment stations since they are always connected to a concentrator, which can bypass them electrically.

    The main problem with optical bypasses is that several bypassed stations may result in a long link. The number of nodes that can be bypassed is limited. For example, with regular multimode optics, the total length of the combined link should be less than 2 km (or the net power loss of the combined link should be less than 11 dB). Since it is difficult to predict which stations will be powered down, ensuring these limits is difficult unless the entire dual ring is limited.
11. *Multicast Table Size*: Each station on LANs listens to one or two individual addresses and a number of multicast addresses. The adapter generally keeps a table of these addresses in a content addressable memory (CAM) to help it quickly decide which frames it should pick up from the network. If the size of this table is smaller than the number required, the adapter will pick up all multicast frames and filter them in software, or worse, pass them on to the host system for software filtering. This is undesirable because it slows down the system.

    The number of multicast addresses that a system needs to listen to depends on the applications running on that system. For example, a workstation may listen to fewer addresses than a server, a bridge, or a router. Also, more and more protocols are being designed using multicast addresses and, therefore, the size of CAMs required is increasing.

12. *Buffer Size*: Adapters use local memory to store the packets received and the packets to be transmitted. This local memory is called *buffer space*. Larger buffers usually improve the performance of the adapter. This is particularly true for FDDI since it allows bursty transmission. Once an adapter captures a token, it can transmit a substantial number of packets. The buffer size is, therefore, an important consideration in buying the FDDI adapters. A small receive buffer results in buffer overrun (packet loss), particularly if the time for the adapter to inform the host (interrupt latency) is significant.
13. *Manageability*: Manageability refers to the ability to observe and control the operation of the adapter. Most adapters can be managed locally from the computer to which they are attached. Network managers, who have to manage several such systems, find it more convenient to be able to manage all the systems remotely from their workstation. Remote management, if available, can be done *in-band* (using FDDI) or *out-of-band* (using extra wiring for management). For example, an RS232 link or an Ethernet link may be used for remote management of FDDI stations. In-band remote management is less expensive than out-of-band management. However, in some cases, out-of-band management may deliberately be used to restrict management access physically and to disallow other users on the FDDI to change station parameters.

    The FDDI station management (SMT) standard has been specifically designed to allow remote management. Unfortunately this standard has taken too long to be designed. Over the years, different vendors have implemented different versions of SMT, which may or may not interoperate. If you have equipment with different SMT versions, you should either find out from the vendor that they will interoperate or upgrade all of them to the same version.

    Another consideration is the higher layer protocol used for management. Many vendors have proprietary management protocols. In a multivendor environment, it is preferable to select a protocol that can be used with all equipment in your network. SNMP (simple network management protocol) is one such protocol. The adapter specifications will state whether the adapter supports SNMP. A node that can act as an *SNMP agent* can be monitored remotely using SNMP commands. A node that can act as an *SNMP manager* can be used as a network management station to send SNMP commands.

    SNMP is a management framework originally developed as a part of the TCP/IP suite of protocols. It is now widely used for all protocols. Each station keeps a database of management information, which can be manipulated remotely using SNMP commands. The components of this database, called management information bases (MIBs), have been standardized. A station may have to keep several MIBs corresponding to its roles in the network. For example, an FDDI router will have a MIB-II, an FDDI MIB, and others. These contain information related to the node's routing function, FDDI station functions, and so on. This is described in detail in Section 12.1.
14. *Upgradability*: Upgradability refers to the ease with which new versions of software, hardware, or firmware can be incorporated. The software and firmware upgrades should be *downline loadable*, which means that the network manager can upgrade the adapters remotely over the network. The feature may apply to software alone or both software and firmware. In terms of hardware, a modular design such that individual modules can be replaced without affecting other modules is to be preferred.
15. *Performance*: The performance of the adapter is specified by its throughput, delay, and CPU loading. Throughput indicates the maximum rate at which the data can be transmitted/received. Usually the throughput is specified both in packets per second (pps) as well as in megabits per second (Mbps). Both rates depend on the packet size. The pps rate drops and the bps rate

increases as the packet size increases. Thus, maximum pps indicates small packet throughput while the maximum bps indicates large packet throughput of the adapter.

Although you would expect an FDDI adapter to provide a full 100 Mbps, some adapters provide much less. The performance depends on the protocol layer at which it is measured. For example, the raw throughput of an adapter at the datalink layer may be 40 Mbps. But the throughput at the transport layer using the UDP protocol may be 30 Mbps, while that using TCP/IP may be only 15 Mbps.

In most cases the key limiting factor is the host and the driver software speed. This is particularly important to remember when comparing throughput at higher layers of the network. For example, if a manufacturer specifies a TCP/IP throughput of 50 Mbps, the throughput is as much a function of the processor used in the system as it is of the adapter. If the manufacturer used a 50-MIPS processor for their measurement, you will not be able to get the same throughput with your 15-MIPS processor. Thus, you should be careful when comparing throughputs specified by different manufacturers. The throughput number is meaningful if and only if the system hardware and software used in the measurement are close to your own system hardware and software.

Latency or packet delay is an important metric for applications using remote procedure calls (RPCs). The delay is measured by the time taken to transfer a packet from host memory to FDDI under no-load conditions. This indicates the minimum delay that each packet incurs. The actual delay under load will be more due to queueing. In specifying the delay, there is a choice of measuring the delay from first-bit-in or last-bit-in to first-bit-out or last-bit-out. The choice used and the packet size should be specified so that other possible combinations can be easily computed.

Delays on FDDI are not always lower than those on lower speed networks such as IEEE 802.3/Ethernet or IEEE 802.5/token ring. This is because FDDI covers longer distances and allows larger frames. Also the media access protocol is different. On an unloaded Ethernet network, a station can transmit a frame without any delay, while on an unloaded FDDI, the average delay is equal to half the ring latency. Thus, do not be alarmed if you find that the transfer delay or latency goes up as you switch to FDDI from lower speed networks.

The adapter designs are not symmetrical in terms of the receive and transmit paths. The transmit function is given lower priority than the receive function. This ensures that the frames that have already consumed network resources will not be lost. The receive throughput of an adapter may be more than the transmit throughput. In such cases, the two throughputs may be specified separately.

Also, some intelligent adapters implement higher level (transport level, for example) protocols, thereby saving the CPU considerable work. This, of course, increases the cost of the adapter. The load on the CPU is measured by its utilization when the adapter is running at its maximum throughput. Since the CPU loading depends on the speed of the CPU, you will have to scale it up or down using the speed of your CPU. The CPU speed is generally measured in MIPS (millions of instructions per second) or more reliably in SPECmarks using the benchmark suite designed by the Systems Performance Evaluation Cooperative (SPEC).

16. *Other Considerations*: Three obvious considerations not mentioned so far are the physical dimensions, power requirements, and the price. The card size of the adapter should match the space available in your system. You should determine that your system has sufficient spare power available. Replacing a power supply is an expensive proposition. In some cases, the use of more powerful supplies may not be possible.

Box 21.1 summarizes the preceding discussion in the form of a checklist that you may find useful for comparing different adapters.

Box 21.1 Buying Adapters: What to Ask

1. Manufacturer _______________ Model _______
2. System bus _______
3. Number of attachments: □SAS □DAS
4. Number of MACs: □One □Two
5. Media type _______ Connector type _______
   Maximum distance _______ Loss budget _______ dB
6. Driver software: Processor _______ Operating system _______ Network O/S _______
7. Dual homing: □Supported □Not supported □Not applicable
8. Synchronous transmission: □Supported □Not supported
9. Optical bypass: □Not available □Standard □Optional □Not applicable □External
10. Multicast table size _______ addresses
11. Buffer size _______ MBytes
12. Network management: □Remotely manageable: □In-band □Out-of-band
    SMT version _______
    Management protocol: □SNMP □Other _______ MIBs supported _______
13. Upgradability: □Downline-loadable software □Downline-loadable firmware
14. Performance:

Transmit throughput:	Peak	_______ pps	_______ bps
	Sustained	_______ pps	_______ bps
Receive throughput:	Peak	_______ pps	_______ bps
	Sustained	_______ pps	_______ bps

    Delay _______ μs
    CPU utilization at peak throughput _______%
    Protocol layer at which the performance was measured:
    □Datalink □UDP/IP □TCP/IP □Other
    System configuration used for performance measurement:
    CPU SPECmarks or MIPS _______
15. Physical dimensions: Card size _______
16. Power requirements _______
17. Price _______
18. Warranty period _______

21.2 Concentrators

A concentrator allows single-attachment stations to be attached to the FDDI ring as shown in Figure 21.2. When a station is turned on, the concentrator allows the station to become a part of the ring. Similarly, when a station is turned off, the station is removed from the ring and the remaining stations continue to operate in a ring. A network manager can instruct the concentrator to insert or remove specified stations into the ring. By means of multiple concentrators one can obtain any desired topology. A few sample topologies are shown in Figure 21.3.

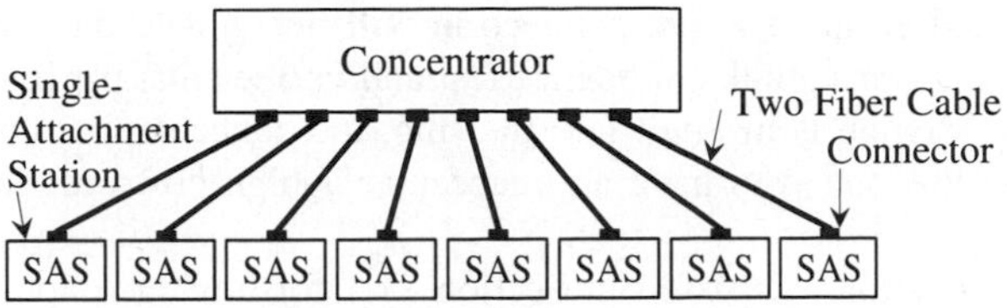

Figure 21.2 Concentrators.

Although a dual-attachment station can be connected directly to the dual ring without a concentrator, sometimes concentrators are still used for DASs for enhanced availability.

Although the key function provided by the concentrators is to replace a wiring closet or wiring hub, they provide several additional functions that improve the integrity of the network. When a station initiates a connection with the concentrator, the station and the concentrator exchange

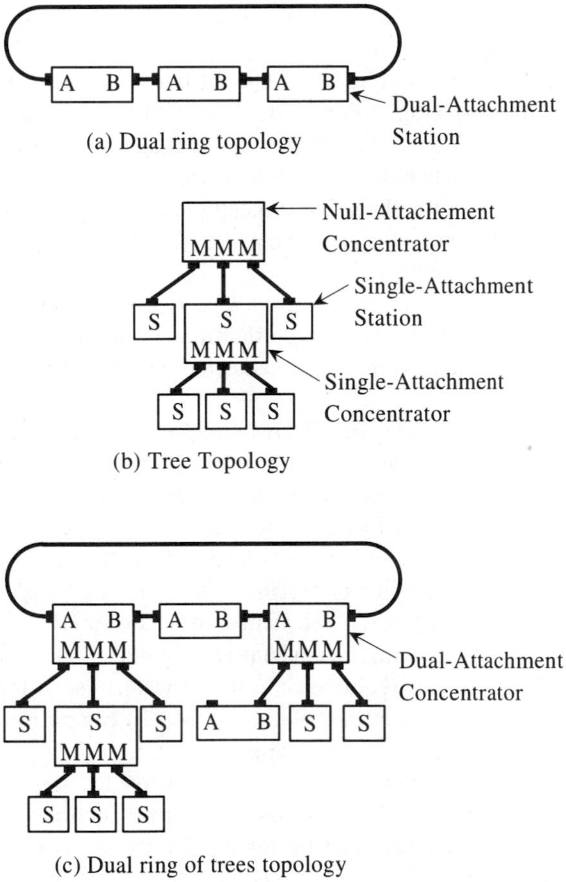

Figure 21.3 Sample topologies using concentrators.

topology information and ensure that the connection will not violate the topology rules for FDDI. The concentrator then performs a link confidence test and verifies that the link quality (bit error rate) is acceptable. After the station is inserted into the ring, the concentrators continuously monitor the link error quality. Any link found to have an unacceptably high error rate is disabled and removed from the ring.

Many of the considerations discussed in Section 21.1 for buying adapters apply to the concentrators as well. You should read that section before proceeding further. Here, the discussion is limited to newer issues as follows:

1. *Number of Peer Attachments*: A concentrator may be a single-attachment concentrator (SAC), a dual-attachment concentrator (DAC), or a null-attachment concentrator (NAC). An NAC can only be used as a root of a tree of nodes. Although it can have several nodes below it in the tree, it cannot have any nodes higher than it in the tree. A SAC has one S-port, which can be used to connect it to higher level concentrators. A SAC cannot be connected directly on the dual ring. A DAC has an A-port and a B-port to connect it to a dual ring. These ports can also be used to connect the concentrator to other concentrators higher up in the tree. Many vendors provide a modular configuration such that the customer can start a small network using a NAC and later add boards to upgrade it to a SAC or a DAC when the network grows.
2. *Number of M-Ports*: M stands for master. The M-ports are used to connect slave nodes to the concentrator. In a tree configuration nodes lower in the tree are said to be slaves to the nodes immediately above. The number of M-ports in a concentrator can be anywhere from 1 to 16 or higher. When the concentrator fails, the service to stations connected to it is disrupted and discontinued. Therefore, it is desirable to keep the number of stations connected to a single concentrator small. Depending on the cost, it may be worthwhile to have two 8-port concentrators rather than one 16-port concentrator.

   A SAC with just one M-port can be used as a repeater. Such repeaters are useful if you want to go farther than the 2-km limit using a multimode fiber or the 40- to 60-km limit using a single-mode fiber. The repeater essentially breaks one link into two, which can be broken further if necessary.
3. *Type of Ports*: Like all other nodes on FDDI, concentrator ports are designed for a particular type of cable. Ports with multimode fibers of different sizes (62.5/125, 50/100, etc.), single-mode fibers, low-cost fibers, shielded twisted-pair cables, unshielded twisted-pair cables, and coaxial cables are available. It is possible to mix different types of ports on a single concentrator. For example, a 12-port concentrator may have two 62.5/125 multimode fiber ports, two single-mode fiber ports, four shielded twisted-pair ports, and four unshielded twisted-pair ports. The type of wiring will dictate the choice of ports. See item 4 in Section 21.1 for further discussion.
4. *Number of MACs*: Strictly speaking, a concentrator is not a station and therefore it does not have to have a MAC. A MAC is required only if you want to send frame-based messages to it. A MAC-less concentrator (a concentrator without a MAC) can perform all of its physical layer functions such as connecting and disconnecting stations.

   A MAC allows a concentrator also to be a station on the same ring and thus any station on the ring can send messages to it. This allows authorized stations to manage the concentrator remotely. A MAC-less concentrator can be managed only by its local console switches or by using out-of-band signaling.

   For very small networks—those using just one concentrator with less than 10 closely located nodes—a MAC-less concentrator may be fine since the network manager can manage it by wandering around. For any reasonable size network, it is much more convenient and practical to have concentrators with MACs.

5. *Availability*: All concentrators run at the full FDDI speed of 100 Mbps. Therefore, speed is not an issue. The important considerations in selecting among different concentrators are mean time between failures (MTBF), mean time to repair (MTTR), startup time, and time to initialize a new connection. Most vendors will provide estimated MTBF if requested. MTBFs of 200,000 to 300,000 hours are common. An MTBF of 300,000 hours means one failure in 33 years. A large network with 100 concentrators will have a concentrator failure every 3000 hours (four months).

   Some concentrators have a self-monitoring capability such that if any component (for example, fans) fails, the network manager is notified. Others have redundant components, particularly power supply or CPU to avoid downtime upon a single failure.
6. *Connection Rules*: The FDDI SMT standard specifies a set of connection rules that is enforced automatically by the FDDI nodes. An invalid connection will be left unused by the nodes. This prevents a user from misconnecting equipment. This was discussed in detail in Section 11.2. Unfortunately, the standard allows manufacturers to choose from a number of possible options for some questionable connections. As a result, some connections that may be accepted by one manufacturer's equipment may be rejected by another manufacturer's equipment.

   A connection matrix is just one of numerous examples of options allowed by the FDDI standard that can lead to incompatibility among manufacturers. Manufacturers routinely stage compatibility tests with other manufacturers' equipment and the incompatibilities, which were routine in the initial versions of the products, are slowly disappearing. If you are planning to use equipment from different manufacturers, you may ask each one of them if its equipment has been tested for interoperability with others.
7. *Secondary Ring Attachment*: All dual-attachment concentrators have access to both rings of the FDDI. However, some DACs restrict attached stations such that they can be connected to the primary ring only, while others will allow a station to be connected to either one or both rings. These latter types of DACs are said to support a **dual path**. Connecting a station to a secondary ring is useful only if there is a token circulating on this ring. This increases the total FDDI throughput to 200 Mbps. The two rings are, in effect, two separate LANs, which need to have a bridge or a router to forward packets between them. Any failure will cause the two rings to wrap and form one LAN. This confuses some networking protocols—TCP/IP suite is a prime example. This TCP/IP problem is discussed in Section 18.4. Until the protocol problems are resolved, the only choice that users of these protocols have is to leave the secondary ring as a standby and connect all stations to the primary ring.
8. *Number of Internal Paths*: The standard allows concentrators to have additional local paths. As discussed in Section 11.1, these secondary and tertiary paths are optional. The secondary path may be used to connect a station to the secondary ring as discussed earlier. The tertiary path is used to test a station before insertion in the ring. Some concentrators have an additional MAC, which is used to form a local ring with a station. This additional MAC can be quickly moved from one port of the concentrator and is called a *roving MAC*. Among its uses are graceful insertion and MAC-level link error testing as discussed next.
9. *Graceful Insertion*: Graceful insertion refers to the capability of the concentrator to connect a station without interrupting the ring operation. Normally, when a station is inserted or removed from the FDDI network, the ring is reinitialized by conducting the scrubbing and claim token processes. Graceful insertion avoids this reinitialization by carefully timing the event so that no frames are lost or created.

For insertion, the station is first connected to a local ring formed by a local MAC and the tertiary data path in the concentrator. The target token rotation time and the token are established. The operation of the local ring is synchronized with that of the main ring and finally the two rings are merged. This synchronization mechanism is complex and may not always work. The worst case delay is, therefore, longer than normal insertion.

The time lost by ring reinitialization is so small that graceful insertion (dubbed "insert and pray") is worthwhile only in rare applications. The scrub process takes 5.3 ms and the claim token normally completes in less than four times the ring latency. Since the maximum ring latency is approximately 1.773 ms, the total time lost due to station insertion is only a few milliseconds. It has been shown that in a 500-station ring operating at 50% utilization with 100 insertions per

Box 21.2 Buying Concentrators: What to Ask

1. Manufacturer _______________ Model _______
2. Number of peer attachments: □NAC □SAC □DAC
3. Total number of M-ports: _______
4. Types of ports:

Media Type	Number of Ports	Media Size or Category	Connector Type	Maximum Distance	Loss Budget
Multimode	_______	_______	_______	_______	_______
Single mode	_______	_______	_______	_______	_______
STP	_______	_______	_______	_______	_______
UTP	_______	_______	_______	_______	_______
Coaxial	_______	_______	_______	_______	_______

5. Number of MACs _______
6. Dual homing: □Supported □Not supported □Not applicable
7. Optical bypass: □Not available □Standard □Optional □Not applicable □External
8. Network management: □Remotely manageable: □In-band □Out-of-band
   SMT version _______
   Management protocol: □SNMP □Other _______ MIBs supported _______
9. Upgradability: □Downline-loadable software □Downline-loadable firmware
10. Availability: MTBF _______ MTTR _______
    □Redundant CPU □Redundant power supply □Device fan monitoring
11. Connection rules: _______________________________________
12. Secondary ring attachment allowed (dual-path support): □Yes
13. Number of internal paths: □Dual □Triple
14. Graceful insertion: □Yes
15. MAC-level LCT: □Yes
16. Physical dimensions: Height _______ Width _______ Depth _______ Weight _______
17. Enclosure: □Desktop □Rack mount
18. Base price _______ Expansion cards _______ Fully loaded _______
19. Power requirements _______
20. Warranty period _______

day, only 0.00001% of the available bandwidth is wasted due to the insertion and removal of the stations during normal operation. Thus, the bandwidth savings are insignificant.

10. *MAC-Level Link Confidence Testing*: Before a station is inserted in the ring, all concentrators carry out a link confidence test (LCT) as discussed in Section 11.3. This ensures that the bit error rate of the link is acceptable. The test can be done using only PHY-level signaling. MACs are not required at either end. Concentrators with additional MACs can enhance the testing by using MAC frames and thereby discovering any data-dependent or MAC-related problem prior to the connection. Some of these problems may be discovered by self-tests (or path tests) that every station is supposed to perform itself.
11. *Manageability*: Concentrators are generally housed in remote wiring closets. It is preferable that they be remotely manageable using a multivendor management protocol such as SNMP (See item 13 in Section 21.1). Some vendors provide an RS232 port also to which you can connect a terminal for local management or a modem for remote diagnosis.
12. *Other Considerations*: You should ensure that the physical dimensions, such as height, width, depth, and weight, suit the space available in your installation. Concentrators are usually mounted in racks in closets. But desktop enclosures are also available. The price of the concentrators is usually stated in terms of modules. You start with a minimum configuration and add more ports by buying additional cards later.

Box 21.2 summarizes the preceding considerations in the form of a checklist that you can use to make a buying decision for concentrators.

21.3 Bridges

A bridge allows you to connect multiple LANs into an extended LAN. These multiple networks do not have to be of the same type. For example, you can form an extended LAN consisting of several FDDI LANs, IEEE 802.3/Ethernet LANs, IEEE 802.5/token ring LANs, and so on.

In its simplest form, a single bridge connects two LANs and forwards traffic between them. It filters out (discards) traffic between nodes on the same side of the bridge. All bridges in an extended LAN communicate with each other and ensure that the frames are correctly forwarded and do not keep looping.

Since bridges also act like any other stations on the LANs, many of the considerations in selecting adapters apply to bridges as well. It is assumed that you have read Section 21.1 on buying adapters.

The additional considerations in buying a bridge are as follows:

1. *Networks Bridged*: The first criterion in selecting a bridge is the type of networks that it bridges together. An FDDI bridge may connect an FDDI ring network with another FDDI, IEEE 802.3/Ethernet, or IEEE 802.5/token ring network. Two-port bridges connect just two networks. Multiport bridges connect more than two networks. For example, a single multiport bridge may connect two FDDI networks, three IEEE 802.3/Ethernet networks, and four IEEE 802.5/token ring networks. Frames will be picked up from all networks and forwarded if necessary to the proper network. This includes forwarding frames from one IEEE 802.3/Ethernet to another, from IEEE 802.3/Ethernet to FDDI, IEEE 802.3/Ethernet to IEEE 802.5/token ring, and vice versa.
2. *WAN Support*: A bridge that connects two adjacent LANs is said to be a **local bridge**. A **remote bridge** connects two LANs that may be several miles apart. Private or leased telephone links

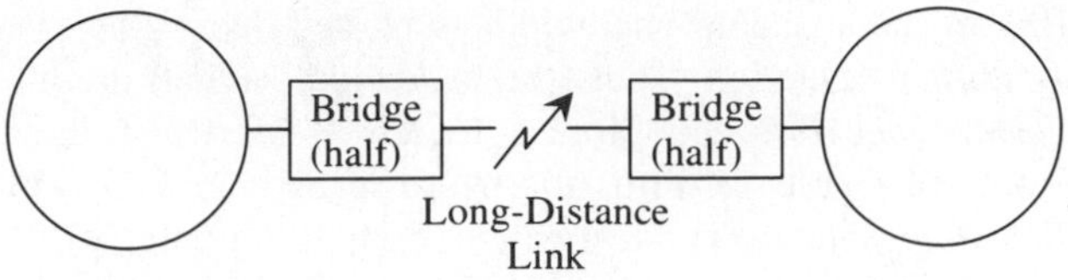

Figure 21.4 A remote bridge.

running at T1, T3, or higher speeds may be used to connect the two networks. As shown in Figure 21.4, a remote bridge comes in two halves, which communicate using a dial-up link (with modem), leased line, or wide area network (WAN) to provide a transparent connection between the LANs. For remote bridges, you should ensure that they conform to the IEEE 802.1G standard, which covers the operations of remote bridges.

3. *Number of Attachments*: FDDI bridges are available as single-attachment stations (SASs) or as dual-attachment stations (DASs). DAS bridges can be connected directly to the dual ring while the SAS bridges require a concentrator. If you already have a concentrator to connect other SAS stations to the FDDI ring, you can connect the SAS bridge to the same concentrator. However, if you do not have a concentrator port available, buying a DAS bridge may be cheaper than buying a concentrator and a SAS bridge. Of course, the second alternative, although more expensive, may provide an extra concentrator port for other stations and for future expansion. With a DAS bridge, you have the option of using a dual-homed configuration for high fault tolerance (see Section 20.3).
4. *Routing Method*: This refers to the method used by the bridges to decide where to route (forward) a frame. There are at least two alternatives: source routing or transparent bridging. As explained in Section 14.3, the first alternative requires the sources to include a complete route to the destination in the frame itself. With transparent forwarding, the sources send a frame as if they were sending it to another station on the same LAN. Transparent bridges know who is where and forward the frames appropriately.

   The IEEE 802.3/Ethernet camp (see Sidebar) chose a transparent bridging method in which

How FDDI Helped Join the Ethernet and Token Ring Camps

The concept of a bridge was invented in 1984 when IEEE 802.3 and 802.5 LAN standards were being developed. At that time the industry was religiously divided into two groups of manufacturers. One group supported the IEEE 802.3/Ethernet standard, while the other supported the IEEE 802.5/token ring standard. Although today most manufacturers make equipment for both types of standards, the division was highly religious for quite some time. The group supporting one standard did not care what was going on in the other standard and both chose alternatives without considering its impact on the other camp. The type of bridging (transparent or source routing), the format of group addresses (IEEE 802.1 or functional address), and the LLC type (1 or 2) are examples of such incompatible decisions. As long as these networks did not talk to each other, there was no problem. However, now that the two types of networks are being interconnected via FDDI, the problems of incompatibility are surfacing and steps are being taken to solve these problems.

all the bridges on an extended LAN form a spanning tree such that there is a unique path from one network to the other. All parallel paths are disabled by putting the bridges providing those paths in a standby state so that they do not forward any frames. The key advantage of spanning tree bridges is that the bridging is transparent. The end-stations do not need to know the location or route to the destination station. End-station logic is, therefore, simplified. The transparent bridges automatically learn the location of all stations by monitoring the source address of frames.

The IEEE 802.5/token ring camp rejected the transparent bridging idea and instead chose the source-routing bridging method. The key advantage of the source-routing method is that the bridge logic is simple. It does not need to know (or learn) paths to all destinations. In addition, multiple parallel paths can exist between two stations. Also, source routing allows a station to use multiple parallel paths to the same destination.

The FDDI standard has been adopted by both the IEEE 802.3/Ethernet and the IEEE 802.5/token ring camps. In fact, the camps have been disbanded and most manufacturers produce equipment for both types of networks. FDDI bridges are, therefore, either source routing or transparent. In an effort to provide complete connectivity, a new type of source-routing bridging method called SRT (source-routing-transparent) was adopted in 1991 by the IEEE 802.5 committee. In this method, transparent bridging is used as a common base for all bridges. The source-routing option is provided only as an additional feature. Thus, all stations can communicate using transparent bridging. Those stations that implement source routing can communicate using source-routing bridges also and take advantage of parallel paths. Although source-routing-only (without transparent routing) is being phased out, a few older implementations may provide only this service.

An FDDI bridge may implement transparent, source-routing, or SRT bridging. You should select a bridge that matches the method used by other bridges in your extended LAN. If your network has only transparent bridges, which would be the case if you had only IEEE 802.3/Ethernet LANs, a transparent FDDI bridge would be sufficient. SRT bridges are required to connect to IEEE 802.5/token ring networks.

5. *Address Learning*: To forward a frame, transparent and SRT bridges should know the location of the destination station. The bridges learn the location of nodes by monitoring the source addresses of frames. Thus, if a bridge sees a frame from station A on its port 2, it knows that A is either on the network connected to port 2, or on some other network further down in that direction. Therefore, whenever it sees frames addressed to station A on other ports, it forwards them to port 2.

   For complete control over traffic on their network, network managers often prefer to program manually the list of addresses that should be forwarded. They do not allow new stations on the network unless it is registered with the manager first.

6. *Address Filtering*: This feature allows you to override the bridge's decision to forward frames for some specified stations. For example, you can instruct the bridge to forward frames only for stations A and B but not for C. With this feature you can ensure that only certain authorized stations' traffic enters a certain part of the network. This feature is also helpful in preventing storms created by flooding of frames belonging to unknown addresses.

   Address filtering may be provided for source addresses, destination addresses, or both. Particular multicast addresses, including the broadcast address, can also be prevented from crossing the bridge. Source address filtering allows (or prevents) frames from a particular source to be forwarded by the bridges. Some bridges provide only destination address filtering since they do not look at the source address for forwarding decisions.

7. *Protocol Filtering*: This feature, which is similar to address filtering, allows you to indicate the protocol types that should or should not be forwarded by the bridge. Again, this is useful for security and for preventing broadcast storm.
8. *Rate Limiting*: One problem with address filtering and protocol filtering is that there is no connectivity for the specified addresses or protocols. Forwarding is a binary (yes or no) decision. Bridges with rate limiting generalize the filtering feature by allowing you to limit the maximum number of frames per second that will be forwarded and any excess traffic for those addresses and protocols will be discarded. This allows connectivity to continue while preventing storms.
9. *Protocol Translation Versus Encapsulation*: The frame formats on different LANs are different. Bridges interconnecting two different networks have two alternatives: encapsulation or translation (see Sidebar below). Bridges implementing the encapsulation method add an extra header to the message. Only stations who understand the encapsulation can interpret the entire message. Translating bridges, on the other hand, replace the old header with a new one so that all stations on the ring (including a bridge to another network) can interpret the message. The IEEE 802.1d bridging standard specifies only translating bridges. Encapsulating bridges do not comply with the IEEE 802.1d requirements. There is no standard for encapsulation. Most encapsulation schemes are proprietary and are understood only by the equipment specifically designed for it. In general, translating bridges are preferred and most manufacturers who initially used encapsulation are promising to provide translation in future upgrades.

   If many languages are spoken in a country, the translation problem can be a bit more complicated. This is the problem experienced in translating Ethernet and IEEE 802.3 protocols. The two protocols are very similar and yet different.

   Ethernet stations were designed before the IEEE 802.3 standard and, therefore, they do not use the IEEE 802.2 LLC header used by IEEE 802.3 stations. Ethernet frames also do not have frames length. Instead they have a protocol-type field that indicates the higher layer protocol of the frame.

   As explained in Section 18.3, a set of rules has been designed for bridges connecting IEEE 802.3/Ethernet LANs and FDDI to translate correctly the two types of frames. If a bridge does not

Handling Foreign Mail: Translate or Encapsulate?

Interpreting a frame header is like reading a language of a particular country. The problem of forwarding frames from one network to another is similar to that of a post office trying to deliver foreign packets with addresses written in a foreign language. As an example consider the problem of delivering a Japanese package in the United States. There are two solutions for the U.S. Postal Service. One possibility is to put the entire package in an envelope. The envelope contains the delivery instructions and the address in English. The original Japanese address and message are still inside the envelope. Once this is done at the port of entry, the packet can be easily forwarded inside the United States. At the destination, the addressee opens the envelope and takes action according to the original message in Japanese. (The addressee should know Japanese since he or she has been conducting business with Japan.) This is the encapsulation method.

The second possibility for the post office is to translate the entire message at the port of entry. Of course, there may be a footnote indicating that the original message was in Japanese. With this method, the destination addressee does not have to know Japanese but it can still conduct business there. This is the translation method.

do this correctly, the problem will probably be discovered by the manufacturer. As a customer, you should only be aware of this issue in case you experience some problems after installing a new bridge. You should ensure that the bridge handles the Ethernet and IEEE 802.3 format frames correctly.

10. *Specially Translated Protocols*: One problem with translation is that all protocols cannot be translated in a straightforward manner. Standard groups have identified a few such protocols and special handling mechanisms have been devised to handle these protocols. As discussed in Section 18.3, AppleTalk™ is one example of such protocols. In purchasing a bridge, you should ensure that all protocols used at your installation are correctly handled by the bridge.
11. *Address Bit Reordering*: If the bit orders used on the two LANs connected by a bridge are different, the bridge needs to reverse the source and destination addresses. This happens, for example, when a bridge connects an FDDI and an IEEE 802.3/Ethernet network. As explained in Section 2.9, FDDI uses a most-significant-bit first bit order while IEEE 802.3/Ethernet networks use the least-significant-bit first bit order. This issue has been quite confusing and some bridges were initially found to do it incorrectly. Actually most bridges, by the time they reach the market, do the address bit ordering correctly since without it they will not work. The issue has been added here simply for products under test or new products.
12. *IP Fragmentation*: Consider what happens if two FDDIs are interconnected via another network, for example, an IEEE 802.3/Ethernet network. This configuration, shown in Figure 21.5, is known as a *dumbbell configuration*. In this case, FDDI stations can generate 4500-byte frames. However, the maximum frame size on IEEE 802.3/Ethernet LANs is 1518 bytes. Some bridges will throw away such frames. Two FDDI stations can use this large frame loss to detect whether they are connected via an IEEE 802.3/Ethernet LAN. Thus, these bridges are not truly transparent. Other bridges attempt to keep the transparency by fragmenting and reassembling frames. Since this requires knowledge of the network layer headers, this is done only for some popular network layer protocols such as TCP/IP. A common application for this facility is to allow a server on FDDI to talk to IEEE 802.3/Ethernet clients.
13. *Padding*: Minimum frame sizes on different LANs are not compatible either. For example, IEEE 802.3/Ethernet networks require a minimum data frame length of 64 bytes. FDDI allows much shorter frames. This problem is solved by padding the short frames.
14. *Address Table Size*: Like any other station, the first function a bridge has to do is to look at the destination address of the frames to decide whether to pick them up. Normal stations have only a few addresses while the bridges have thousands of addresses that they pick up. Some bridges

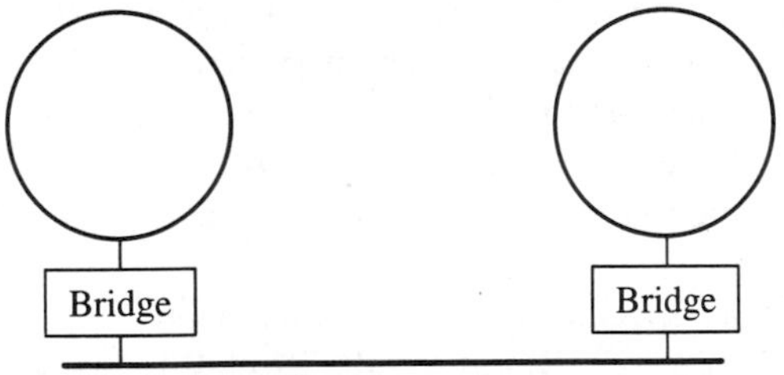

Figure 21.5 A dumbbell configuration consisting of two FDDIs interconnected via an IEEE 802.3/Ethernet network.

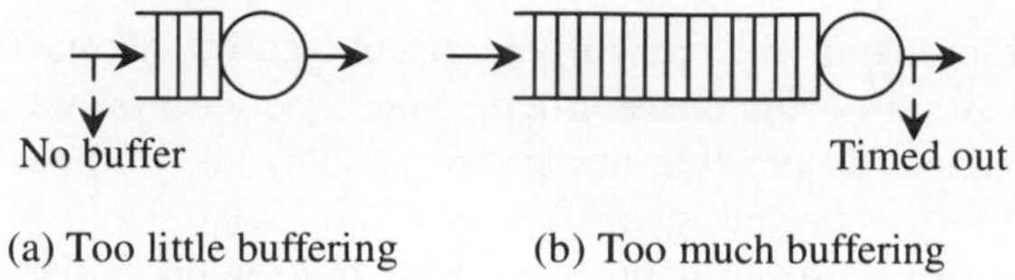

Figure 21.6 Too little or too much buffering are both undesirable.

keep this address list in a content addressable memory (CAM), which is fast but expensive, and so the address table size is limited. Others keep the addresses in regular speed memory. In either case, a small table size may result in excess traffic since addresses not in the table are flooded.

15. *Buffer Size*: The LANs connected by a bridge may operate at significantly different rates. For example, frames arriving at 100 Mbps from FDDI may have to be forwarded to a 16-Mbps token ring. The simplest way to handle this mismatch is to provide some buffering in the bridges. This allows short bursts of high-speed traffic to get through to a low-speed LAN without loss. While too little buffering causes loss, too much buffering (more than a few seconds worth) may cause unnecessary duplicates. This happens when the queues and the delay in the bridge (see Figure 21.6) become so large that the sources time-out and retransmit a second copy of the frame. The size of the buffer space is an important consideration. Too little or too large a buffer space in the bridges is undesirable.
16. *Performance*: The performance of a bridge is measured by its filtering rate, forwarding throughput, translation throughput, and forwarding delay. The filtering rate is the maximum rate at which the bridge can receive frames, examine their destination address (or route), and determine whether the frame should be forwarded or ignored. It is specified in packets per second.

    The forwarding throughput is the rate at which the bridge can forward the frames from one network to another. It is specified both in packets per second and bits per second. For small packets, packet per second throughput is limited, while for large frames the bits per second rating limits the throughput.

    Although the forwarding throughput of a bridge may be less than that of the networks it connects, the filtering rate should be equal to the sum of the maximum frame rate of all networks; otherwise many frames will be lost due to queue overflow in the bridge. For example, it is sufficient for a two-port FDDI-to-Ethernet bridge to forward only 14,880 pps. This is the maximum rate at which the smallest size frames can be received or transmitted on an Ethernet network. The maximum frame rate on FDDI is 403,226 pps for minimum size LLC frames (23-byte frame plus 16-symbol preamble). The maximum filtering rate for the two-port bridge should be 403,226 + 14,880 or 418,106 pps.

    If a bridge does not filter at the full rate, it may lose frames that are critical for correct operation, such as spanning tree and management frames, thereby making the whole extended LAN unstable.

    Translation throughput specifies the rate (again in pps and bps) at which frames can be translated between IEEE 802 and FDDI networks. Not all forwarded frames require translation. For example, frames forwarded from one LAN to another of the same type (FDDI to FDDI or Ethernet to Ethernet) do not require translation. Since translation requires a bit more work than straight forwarding, the translation throughput may be lower than the forwarding throughput.

Forwarding delay or latency refers to the time taken by a frame to cross the bridge. High latency is detrimental to protocols that are delay sensitive. Generally only the latency under no load is specified. The actual queueing delay under load can be several hundred times higher. Thus, a small difference in latency can mean a significant difference in performance as seen by the user. If a low latency is important for your application, you should also ensure that the latency in the end-systems (which is generally more than the bridge latency) is also low.

17. *Manageability*: Like concentrators, bridges are generally housed in wiring closets. It is preferable that they be remotely manageable using a multivendor management protocol such as SNMP. Some vendors provide an RS232 port also to which you can connect a terminal for local management. For further discussion on this topic, see item 13 in Section 21.1.
18. *Other Considerations*: You should ensure that the physical dimensions, such as height, width, depth, and weight, suit the space available in your installation. Bridges are usually mounted in racks in closets, but desktop enclosures are also available. The price of bridges is usually stated in terms of modules. You can start with a minimum two-port configuration and add more ports by buying additional cards later.

Box 21.3 summarizes the preceding discussion in the form of a checklist that you can use when buying a bridge.

Box 21.3 Buying Bridges: What to Ask

1. Manufacturer _______________ Model _______
2. Networks connected:

Network	Media Type	Connector Type	Number
FDDI	_______	_______	_______
IEEE 802.3/Ethernet	_______	_______	_______
IEEE 802.5/token ring	_______	_______	_______
Other _______	_______	_______	_______

3. WAN support? □No □T1 □T3 □V.35 □RS232 □IEEE 802.1G conformance
4. Number of attachments: □SAS □DAS
5. Number of MACs: □One □Two
6. Dual homing: □Supported □Not supported □Not applicable
7. Optical bypass: □Not available □Standard □Optional □Not applicable □External
8. Routing method: □Transparent □Source routing □SRT
9. Address learning: □Automatic □User programmable
10. Address filtering: □Source addresses □Destination address □Multicast addresses □Broadcast address □None
11. Protocol filtering: □No □User programmable
12. Protocol handling: □Translating □Encapsulating
13. Protocols specially translated _______
14. Address bit reordering: □Yes
15. IP fragmentation: □Yes
16. Padding: □Yes

continued

Box 21.3 Buying Bridges: What to Ask (*Cont.*)

17. Address table size: Individual _______ Multicast _______
18. Total buffer space for frames _______ MB
19. Network management: □Remotely manageable: □In-band □Out-of-band
    SMT version _______
    Management protocol: □SNMP □Other _______
    MIBs supported _______
20. Upgradability: □Downline-loadable software □Downline-loadable firmware
21. Availability: MTBF _______ MTTR _______
    □Redundant CPU □Redundant power supply □Device fan monitoring
22. Performance:

	Filtering Rate		Forwarding Throughput		Translation (To/From FDDI) Throughput	
Network	pps	bps	pps	bps	pps	bps
FDDI	_______	_______	_______	_______		
IEEE 802.3/Ethernet	_______	_______	_______	_______	_______	_______
IEEE 802.5/token ring	_______	_______	_______	_______	_______	_______
_______	_______	_______	_______	_______	_______	_______
_______	_______	_______	_______	_______	_______	_______

    Forwarding delay: _______ μs
23. Physical dimensions: Height _______ Width _______ Depth _______ Weight _______
24. Enclosure: □Desktop □Rack mount
25. Base price _______ Expansion cards _______ Fully loaded _______
26. Warrantee period _______

21.4 Routers

Like a bridge, a router also forwards packets from one network to another. Therefore, much of the discussion in Section 21.3 applies to routers as well. The key difference is that routers are network layer devices while bridges are datalink layer devices (see Figure 21.7). This leads to two key differences between them. First, routers can forward packets to networks that do not have any common datalink components. In particular, routers can forward packets to wide area networks while bridges cannot. (Remote bridges discussed in item 2 of Section 21.3 are an exception.) Second, routers are designed for one particular or a few network layer protocols and will not forward packets of other protocols. Bridges generally work on all network layer protocols. As an example, an OSI router will not be able to route TCP/IP packets and vice versa. A bridge can forward OSI, TCP/IP, SNA, DECnet™, and most other protocols as long as all datalinks on the path are compatible.

Which should you buy—a router or a bridge? This is a common question from buyers. It is also a highly debated topic among network architects and implementors. Proponents of both sides have been arguing for some time. Fortunately, the differences between the two are blurring away as bridges have started implementing many of the functions performed traditionally by routers. IP fragmentation and special protocol handling are examples of such functions. Also, many manufacturers have introduced

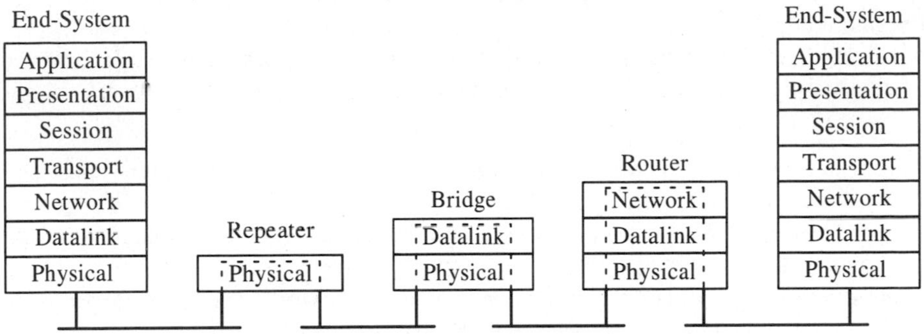

Figure 21.7 Repeaters, bridges, and routers.

combined **bridge+router** (**brouter**) boxes that provide both functions. Packets that use network layer protocols supported by the brouter are routed. Packets that use compatible datalink layers are bridged. The remaining packets are discarded.

The considerations in the selection of routers or brouters are the same as those in the selection of bridges. The key additional consideration is the set of protocols routed. You should ensure that the routing function will handle all (or most) of the network layer protocols used in your network. Routers that route as many as 14 different protocols are available. These protocols include TCP/IP, OSI, X.25, SNA, DECnet Phase IV, DECnet Phase V, AppleTalk, IPX/SPX, XNS, Apollo Domain, and so on. Some of these are protocol suites and contain many protocols and optional features. You should check that the router under consideration implements all protocols and features that you use. For example, users of TCP/IP protocol suite may want to check the router for the following network layer protocols: ARP (RFC 826), ICMP (RFC 792), BGP (RFC 1267), EGP (RFC 904), OSPF (RFC 1247, 1349), PPP (RFC 1331), and RIP (RFC 1058). In addition, they may want to check the IP routers for the implementation of the following features: IP and ARP over FDDI (RFC 1390), IP over 802 (RFC 1042), IP multicasting (RFC 1112), proxy ARP (RFC 1027), subnetting (RFC 950), and so on. Wide area network interfaces offered by the router are the next criterion. Examples of interfaces provided are T1, fractional T1, T3, fractional T3, SMDS, frame relay, ISDN, E1, V.11/24/35, 56 kbps, 9600 bps, X.21, and X.25.

21.5 Network Monitors

That which is monitored improves.—Source unknown

A network monitor allows observation of the events and traffic on the network. This is helpful in keeping track of what is happening on the network, who is consuming the resources, where the bottlenecks are occurring, and so on. Most FDDI product manufacturers also provide management facilities that allow you to look at the event counters at various stations. However, if you have a large network or if you are involved in the design of FDDI products, you may want to consider getting a network monitor. Strictly speaking, network monitoring and management tools are complementary. Monitoring tools allow you to find out what is happening on the network. Management tools allow you to control or alter the operation of the network. To manage properly, you need the information obtained by monitoring.

Network monitors can be used by performance analysts, network designers, and network managers. A few examples of types of problems that can be solved by using a network monitor are as follows:

- A network designer may use a monitor to find the frequently used frame types and activities on the network and optimize their performance.
- A network manager may use a monitor to measure resource utilizations and to find the performance bottleneck.
- A network manager may also use a monitor to tune the network. The network parameters (such as TTRT) can be adjusted to improve the performance.
- A network analyst may use a monitor to characterize the traffic. The results may be used for capacity planning and for creating benchmarks.

A number of FDDI monitors are available in the market. These are also called *protocol analyzers*. The following characteristics and features should be considered when buying a network monitor:

1. *Number of Taps*: A monitor may allow you to monitor one network, several networks, or several points in a single network. Some monitors allow the taps to be synchronized such that you can trigger monitoring action on one tap whenever a specified event happens on another tap. For example, using this facility, you could monitor the flow of a frame through a bridge connecting two networks.
2. *Networks Monitored*: Like other stations on the networks, you should ensure that the network monitor has the correct media and connector type for each of the networks to which it is going to be connected.
3. *Node Type*: There are three ways to connect a monitor to an FDDI network, as shown in Figure 21.8. The first method is simply to tap off a little optical (or electrical) power from any link using a splitter. This method, known as a **PMD tap**, is not visible to other stations and, therefore, does not introduce any additional communication activity on the network. It is particularly useful for monitoring a sequence of events between two nodes and debugging PHY-

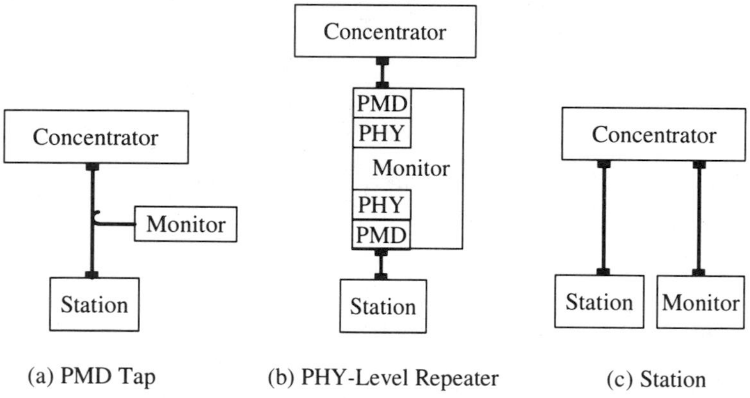

Figure 21.8 Three ways to connect an FDDI monitor.

level activities between them. The main limitation of this method is that it cannot introduce any signals or frames on the network.

The second method is to connect the monitor as a *PHY-level repeater*. In this case, the monitor acts as an FDDI concentrator without any MAC. It is involved in link initialization with neighboring nodes. This allows injection of PHY-level signals to debug the neighbor.

The third method is to connect the monitor as a regular FDDI station. Such monitors can inject frames into the network in addition to observing the traffic.

4. *Buffer Size*: The monitors store the observed information in memory. The size of this memory determines the monitoring duration and level of details that you can collect. A larger buffer size is better.
5. *Performance*: The performance of a monitor is measured by the rate at which it can observe and collect events. Generally, the monitors also add time stamps to these events. The accuracy and resolution of these stamps can affect those of the information derived from the monitored data. The resolution refers to the minimum time interval that can be differentiated. For example, it may be several nanoseconds or a few microseconds. The accuracy refers to the accuracy of the clock. If the clock drifts, the time stamps may become inaccurate.
6. *Facilities*: Monitors vary quite widely in terms of what they can and cannot do. The following are examples of some of the facilities provided by monitors.

   a. *Ring Utilization*: All network monitors provide a continuous display of network utilization. The utilization can be averaged over arbitrarily short intervals. Typically, an interval of 1 second is short enough to show the peaks that annoy users, but long enough to ignore the unimportant burstiness of the traffic. A monitor may also display tables of utilization for a variety of averaging intervals.

      If the load is too high, it is possible that some stations are not operating correctly. For example, a station may be sending out lots of useless frames or repeatedly trying a failed operation.

      FDDI monitors also show graphs of token rotation times. This gives an idea of the current delays in obtaining the token as well as the total load on the network.

   b. *Source-Destination Matrix*: It is possible to obtain a complete matrix that shows the number of frames being exchanged between each pair of stations on the ring. This matrix is helpful in reorganizing networks, in finding misbehaving stations, and in detecting broadcast storms.

      If the utilization stays high (for instance, above 60%) for significant periods, it is time to reorganize the network. One possibility is to split the network into two or more LANs connected via bridges or routers such that most of the traffic does not cross the division.

   c. *Frame Statistics*: You can obtain a continuous display of the network load in terms of packets per second and bits per second for all traffic or for a selected class of frames.

      Most monitors also allow you to *filter* the traffic, which means that you can instruct the monitor to look at only selected frames. Selection criteria can include specific values on fields such as frame control, destination addresses, source addresses, frame status indicators, or frame characteristics such as frame length and interframe gap, or frames with CRC errors. You can determine which protocols are producing most of the traffic.

      Most monitors will allow monitoring of valid frames. Some will also allow you to monitor frames with errors, fragments, or frames with a small preamble.

   d. *Trace Capture*: You can capture all or parts of selected frames for later analysis. The trace includes a time stamp for each frame. Such traces are helpful in debugging and in finding causes of network crashes or congestions. Traces are also useful in finding incorrectly configured hosts, incorrect protocol implementations, and sources of bad frames. For example, if a host is unable to boot over the network, a trace of frames to and from the host can show if it is successfully sending out the correct sequence of requests.

e. *Alarm*: The monitors can be programmed to send an alarm signal whenever a specified event happens or the thresholds on frame rates or counts are exceeded. The alarm signal could start a buzzer, dial a phone call, send electronic mail, or start detailed (PHY- or PMD-level) monitoring.

f. *Line State Capture*: This facility allows you to observe PHY line states. A sample is shown in Figure 21.9. Such displays are helpful in debugging and finding out why a particular station is not able to establish a connection. Line state capture requires monitoring the PHY-level signals between two stations. The monitor must be inserted between those two stations. Only those monitors that connect as PMD-level repeaters can provide this facility.

g. *Protocol Interpretation*: A frame trace usually shows the frame contents in hexadecimal. A better way is to interpret individual fields of the frame and show it. For example, a frame may be indicated to be a TCP/IP ack. This requires knowledge of the protocols. Some monitors have interpreters for a number of commonly used protocols and allow users to develop interpreters for others. A sample frame display is shown in Figure 21.10.

h. *Event Monitoring*: Network events such as claim processes, beacon processes, and ring initializations can be recorded. Depending on the frequency of occurrence of each event and its importance, you may get summary statistics or a time-stamped trace.

i. *Error Monitoring*: When the network appears to be sluggish, a monitor can provide the statistics on the error counters at various stations, number of fragments, void frames, and the

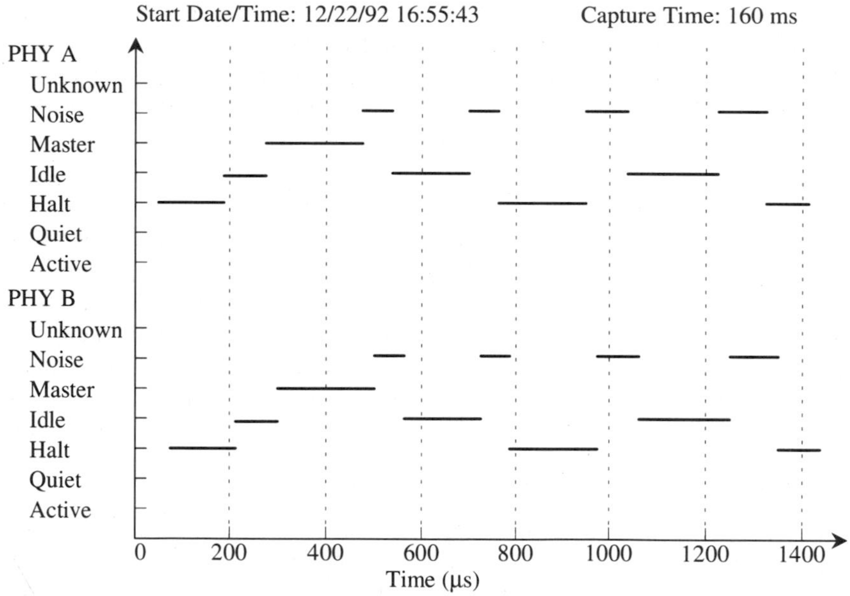

Figure 21.9 Example of a line state capture.

```
Time: 06:48:37 003 564 234
PHY: Interframe Gap: 130 Bits
     Frame Length: 61 Bytes
     MAC: Frame Type: LLC
          Priority: 1
          Service Class: Asynchronous
          Destination Address: FF-FF-FF-FF-FF-FF
          Source Address: 08-00-45-00-00-21
          Frame Status Flags: E=0, A=0, C=0
          LLC: Destination Service Access Point: AA
               Source Service Access Point: AA
               LLC Control: 03
               OUI: 00-00-00
               EtherType: IP
               IP: Protocol: 6
                   Checksum: 345A
                   Source Address: 2.3.0.2
                   Destination Address: 2.55.0.32
                   TCP: Source Port: 32
                        Destination Port: 2060
                        Sequence Number: 0
                        Acknowledgment Number: 0
                        Data Offset: 5
                        Window: 2048
                        Checksum: 8EA1
```

Figure 21.10 An example of protocol interpretation.

number of frames with the E-indicator set. The error statistics on various components of the network may be sorted to determine the unreliable parts of the network.

j. *Configuration Monitoring*: Configuration monitoring allows you to determine which stations are up. A monitor can determine this by promiscuous observation of station management announcements on FDDI or by polling various stations. A monitor can record network initializations and any configuration changes due to components joining or leaving the ring. A sample ring map prepared by a monitor is shown in Figure 21.11.

   Often, incremental configuration information is more useful than knowing the full configuration. Such information includes a list of nodes added or dropped from the network. Also useful is the list of nodes that are not on a list prepared by the network manager. This facility may be used, for example, on a network to identify unknown stations joining the network.

k. *Load Generation*: This feature allows you to generate test frames of specified characteristics at a specified rate. Strictly speaking, load generation is not a part of monitoring. Any node on the ring can be used as a load generator. However, since a load generation activity is often accompanied by monitoring, many monitors provide this facility. In addition to frames, they can produce any desired symbol sequence or line-state signal.

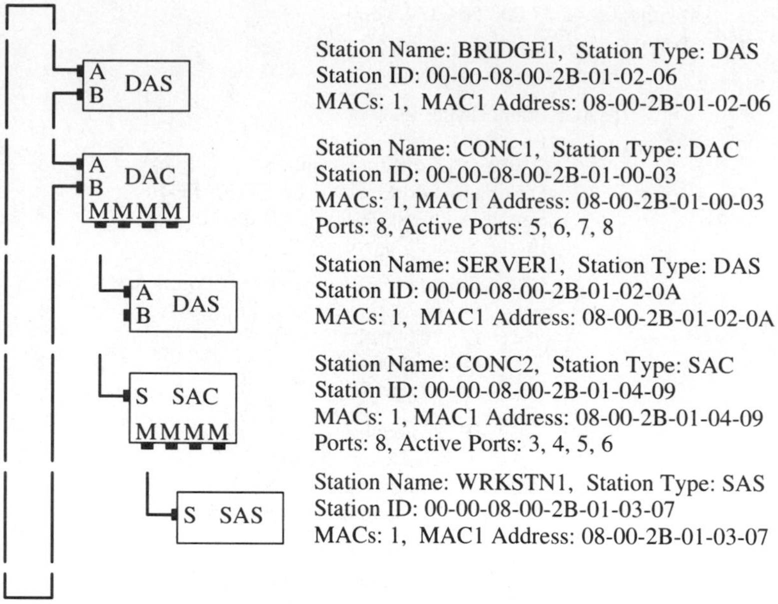

Figure 21.11 A sample ring map.

l. *Network Exercisers*: This is a special case of load generation. A frame generator can be used to test common FDDI problems by causing claim or beacon processes, creating duplicate addresses, violating interframe gaps, starting SMT trace processes, and so on.

m. *Error Injection*: Invalid frames can be deliberately injected in the network to see their impact on network operation and LEMs. Most host adapters have built-in protection that does not allow users to send such frames. Many network monitors, particularly those with a load generation facility, allow you to inject invalid frames, frames with any source or destination address or that violate any transmission rules. These features are useful in product debugging.

Box 21.4 presents the checklist that you can use in procuring monitors.

21.6 Summary

See Boxes 21.1, 21.2, 21.3, and 21.4 for issues that you should consider when buying and comparing different adapters, concentrators, bridges, and monitors, respectively.

21.7 Further Reading

Hutchison (1989), Hotard (1990), and Franzen (1991) describe several issues in the design and use of concentrators.

Mogul (1991) provides a good discussion of network monitoring.

Box 21.4 Buying Network Monitors: What to Ask

1. Manufacturer ________ Model ________
2. Number of taps ________
3. Networks monitored:

Network	Media Type	Connector Type	Number
FDDI	________	________	________
IEEE 802.3/Ethernet	________	________	________
IEEE 802.5/token ring	________	________	________
Other ________	________	________	________

4. Node type: □PMD repeater □PMD tap □MAC station
5. Number of attachments: □None □SAS □DAS
6. Number of MACs: □None □One □Two
7. Buffer size: Memory ________ MB Disk ________ MB
8. Facilities: □Ring utilization □Frame statistics □Alarm □Event monitoring □Configuration monitoring □Network exercisers □Source-destination matrix □Trace capture □Line state capture □Error monitoring □Load generation □Error injection
9. Protocol interpretation: Protocols ________________
10. Filtering/selection: □Frame control patterns □Destination address patterns □CRC (errors) □Interframe gap □Higher level protocol header patterns □Source address patterns □Length □Frame status flags □Fragments
11. Network management: □Remotely manageable: □In-band □Out-of-band
    SMT version ________
    Management protocol: □SNMP □Other ________
    MIBs supported ________
12. Upgradability: □Downline-loadable software □Downline-loadable firmware
13. Performance: Maximum reception rate: ________ pps ________ bps
    Time stamp resolution ________ Time stamp accuracy ________
14. Physical dimensions: Height ________ Width ________ Depth ________ Weight ________
15. Base price ________ Expansion cards ________ Fully loaded ________

21.8 Self-Test Exercises

Note: Some exercises have multiple correct answers. See Appendix D for answers.

21.1 Which of the following do you need to specify when buying an FDDI adapter?:

a. The bus used in your system
b. The operating system used in your system
c. The type of CPU in your system
d. The distance from the node to which it will be connected

21.2 Which of the following apply to dual-attachment adapters?:

a. They cannot be connected to concentrators.
b. They do not require concentrators.
c. They can be dual-homed.
d. They require optical bypass.

21.3 Which of the following apply to single-attachment adapters?:

a. They cannot be connected without concentrators.
b. They are less reliable than dual-attachment adapters.
c. They can be dual-homed.
d. They require optical bypass.
e. None of the above.

21.4 Which of the following metrics would you use to measure the performance of an adapter?:

a. The maximum throughput in bits per second
b. The maximum throughput in packets per second
c. CPU utilization when the adapter is idle
d. CPU utilization when the adapter is fully loaded

21.5 Graceful insertion means:

a. Inserting a slave station in a master port
b. Inserting a station without ring reinitialization
c. Praying while inserting a station in the ring

21.6 When is a MAC required in a concentrator?

a. If the concentrator has to be remotely managed inband.
b. If it is a dual-attachment concentrator.
c. Never.
d. Always.

21.7 When buying a bridge, which of the following are important considerations?:

a. Protocol translation versus encapsulation
b. Transport layer protocols used in your network
c. Routing method used by other bridges in your network
d. Routing method used by other routers in your network

21.8 Which of the following problems are normally handled by network monitors?:

a. Token creation
b. Traffic characterization
c. Parameter tuning to improve performance
d. Keeping track of network configuration changes

CHAPTER **22**

Performance Under Heavy Load

Performance is an important issue in the design, implementation, and operation of networks. Networks must be able to perform well even when the load is high (close to or even more than 100 Mbps). Of course, they must also perform well under normal loads. The network parameters that affect the performance in these two loading regions are different. Therefore, the discussion on performance has been divided into three parts. In the first part, covered in this chapter, performance under heavy load is considered. In the second part, covered in Chapter 23, the issues of performance under normal load are discussed. In the third part, covered in Chapter 24, the remaining performance issues such as analytical modeling, performance of FDDI-II, and adapter performance design issues are considered.

22.1 Performance Parameters

As shown in Figure 22.1, the performance of any system depends on the workload as well as the system parameters. Parameters can be either fixed or user settable. Fixed parameters are those that the network manager has no control over (after the network has been installed). These parameters vary from one ring to the next. Examples of fixed parameters are cable length and number of stations. The study of performance with respect to these parameters is important because if it is found that performance is sensitive to these, a different guideline may be used for each set of fixed parameters. The settable parameters, which can be set by the network manager or the individual station manager, include various timer values. Most of these timers affect the reliability of the ring and the time to detect malfunction. The key parameters that affect performance are the target token rotation time (TTRT) and the synchronous time allocations.

The workload also has a significant impact on system performance. One set of parameters may be preferable for one workload but not for another. The key parameters for the workload are the number of *active* stations and the load per station. At any instant in time, only those stations that are either transmitting or waiting to transmit on the ring are said to be active. There may be a large number of stations on the ring, but only a few of these are generally active at any given time. Active stations include the currently transmitting station (if any) along with those that have frames to transmit and are waiting for access, that is, for a usable token to arrive.

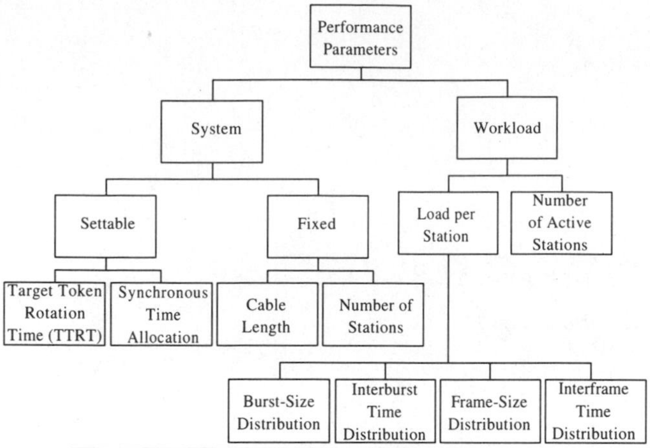

Figure 22.1 Performance parameters.

Throughput, Load, and Utilization

Performance analysts use the terms *throughput*, *load*, and *utilization* somewhat interchangeably. Strictly speaking, they are different.

The throughput measures the good output of the system. Throughput of an FDDI ring can be measured by counting the number of good (error-free) frames delivered to correct destinations. Multicast frames are counted just once. The throughput can be expressed in packets per second (pps) or bits per second (bps). In either case, fragments, frames with error, and time spent in setting up a path are not counted as completed work. Whether to count the preamble (2 bytes) and void frames as part of the throughput is a matter of definition. That is, whenever the throughput is stated, it should indicate whether or not these are included.

The load measures the input to the system. In lossless systems at loads below capacity, the throughput is equal to the load. This applies to FDDI as well. If the load on the ring is 40 Mbps, the throughput is also 40 Mbps. This, of course, does not hold if the load is high. For example, if there are three stations on the ring, each with a 100-Mbps load, the total arrival rate is 300 Mbps and the throughput is obviously much less.

Utilization measures the level of resource usage. It indicates the fraction (or percentage) of time a resource is used (or is busy). The utilization is a dimensionless quantity. In a system with multiple resources, the utilization of different resources may be different. If a system has frame losses or errors, some time is wasted in handling these abnormal conditions. This increases resource utilization but does not increase the throughput.

Figure 22.2 shows the relationship between the three quantities.

If no frames are lost or contaminated with errors, and all token capture time is used for data transmission, the ring utilization is equal to the throughput (measured relative to the capacity). The throughput, in turn, is equal to the load if the ring is operating below saturation. Thus, a 50-Mbps load results in a 50-Mbps throughput and a 50% token utilization under these conditions.

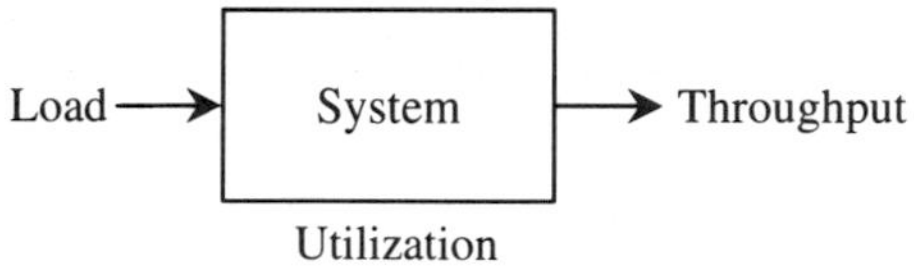

Figure 22.2 Relationship among load, utilization, and throughput.

In most of this chapter, the performance has been studied for asynchronous traffic only. The presence of synchronous traffic further restricts the choice of TTRT. This is discussed in Section 22.9.

22.2 Performance Metrics

The quality of service provided by a system is measured by its productivity and responsiveness. For FDDI, productivity is measured by its throughput, and responsiveness is measured by the response time and access delay. The time can be measured in a number of ways. To understand important time metrics, consider Figure 22.3, which shows the sequence of events that occurs when transmitting a frame on an FDDI network. The events are sequentially numbered as shown in the figure. The various events and their corresponding times are as follows:

- t_1 The frame arrives at a station for transmission.
- t_2 The frame arrives at the head of the queue containing frames to be transmitted. This is also the instant at which transmission of the previous frame begins.
- t_3 The transmission of the previous frame finishes. The next frame is now eligible for transmission.
- t_4 The station obtains rights to transmit the new frame. If the token holding timer (THT) permits, this can happen immediately after the transmission of the previous frame; otherwise, the station may have to wait until the next usable token arrives.
- t_5 The first bit of the frame arrives at the destination, which begins receiving the frame.
- t_6 The first bit of the frame arrives back at the source station, which begins to strip (remove) it.
- t_7 The last bit of the frame is transmitted.
- t_8 The last bit of the frame is received at the destination.
- t_9 The last bit of the frame is stripped at the source.

Note that the events may not always happen in this order. In particular, it is possible for a transmission to end before reception or stripping begins.

A number of *responsiveness* metrics have been considered in the literature. Some of the familiar ones are:

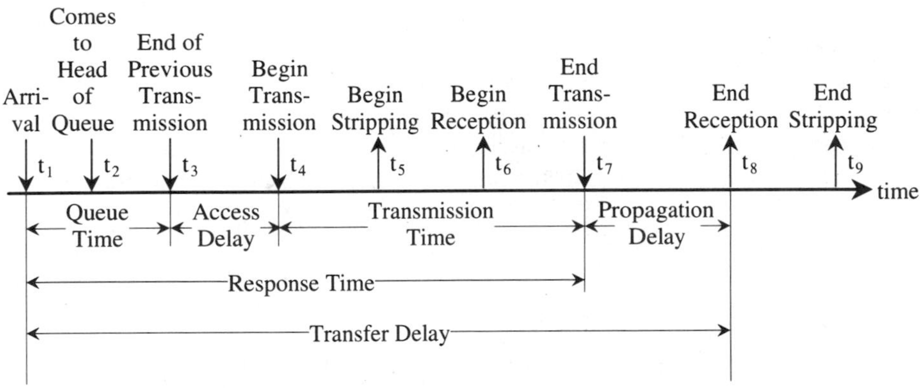

Figure 22.3 Sequence of events in a frame transmission on FDDI.

1. *Queueing Time*: The time between the arrival of the frame and the end of the previous transmission: $t_3 - t_1$.
2. *Access Delay*: The time between the end of the previous transmission and the beginning of a new transmission: $t_4 - t_3$.
3. *Transmission Time*: The time between the transmission of the first bit and the last bit: $t_7 - t_4$. This time is determined entirely by the frame size.
4. *Propagation Delay*: The time required for a bit to travel from the source to the destination station. Measuring it for the last bit, this time is $t_8 - t_7$. This is determined by the location of the source and the destination stations on the ring.
5. *Response Time*: The time between the arrival of the frame at the transmit queue and the completion of its transmission: $t_7 - t_1$.
6. *Transfer Delay*: The time between the arrival of the frame and the reception of its last bit at the destination: $t_8 - t_1$.

Of these metrics, access delay and response time are the key ones. Given response time and access delay, the queueing time can easily be computed. The transmission time and propagation time can be computed from the frame size and the station location, and they are not affected by the network parameters.

Notice that the response time, as defined here, is measured from the "first-bit-in" to the "last-bit-out." Since this includes queueing delay, it is a meaningful metric only if the ring is not saturated. At loads near or above capacity, the response time reaches infinity and does not offer any information. With these loads, the access delay, which is defined as the amount of time needed to obtain a usable token (the "want-token" to "get-token" interval) is more meaningful. Also, note that all performance metrics here are at the media access control (MAC) layer. Higher layer protocols may cause the response time seen by the user to be more than that presented here.

The productivity metric that the network manager may be concerned with is the total throughput of the ring in megabits per second. Thus, the key metric is not the throughput under low load but the maximum obtainable throughput under high load. This latter quantity is also called the *usable bandwidth* of the network. The ratio of the usable bandwidth to nominal bandwidth (100 Mbps for FDDI) is defined as the *efficiency*. Thus, if for a given set of network and workload parameters, the usable bandwidth on FDDI is never more than 90 Mbps, the efficiency is 90% for that set of parameters.

Another metric that is of interest for a shared resource, such as FDDI, is the **fairness** with which the resource is allocated. Fairness is particularly important under heavy load. The FDDI protocols have been shown to be mostly fair provided the priority levels are not implemented. Given a heavy load under single-priority operation, the asynchronous bandwidth is equally allocated to all active stations. Fairness is discussed further in Section 23.5 and multiple-priority operation is covered in Section 23.6. In the remainder of this chapter, single-priority operation is assumed.

22.3 A Simple Model

Maximum access delay and efficiency can be easily computed using the simple model presented in this section. All you need to know is the ring latency and the TTRT. The ring latency is defined as the time taken by the bits to go around the ring. This can be easily computed for a given ring configuration as shown later in Example 22.1.

The model assumes that the ring is operating under heavy load and that there are n active stations and that each one has enough frames to keep the FDDI fully loaded.

For an FDDI network with a ring latency of D and a TTRT value of T, the efficiency and maximum access delay are:

$$\text{Efficiency} = \frac{n(T-D)}{nT+D} \tag{22.1}$$

$$\text{Maximum access delay} = (n-1)T + 2D \tag{22.2}$$

Equations (22.1) and (22.2) constitute the model. Its derivation is simple and is given next. Readers not interested in mathematical details can safely skip the derivation.

Derivation 22.1 Consider a ring with three active stations, as shown in Figure 22.4. (The general case of n active stations is considered later.) The figure shows the space-time diagram of various events on the ring. The space is shown horizontally and the time is shown vertically. The token is shown by a thick horizontal line. The transmission of frames is indicated by a thick line along the time axis.

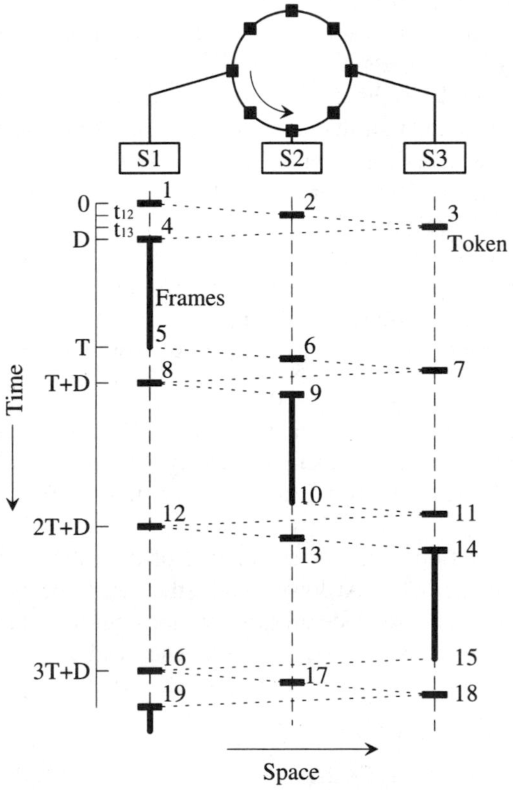

Figure 22.4 Space-time diagram of events with three active stations on an FDDI network. The numbers refer to the event numbers in the text.

Assume that all stations are idle until $t = D$, when the three active stations suddenly get a large (infinite) burst of frames to transmit. The sequence of events is as follows.

1. $t = 0$: Station S_1 receives the token and resets its token rotation timer. Since it has nothing to transmit, the token proceeds to the next station.
2. $t = t_{12}$: Station S_2 receives the token and resets its token rotation timer. Here t_{12} is the signal propagation delay from stations S_1 to S_2.
3. $t = t_{13}$: Station S_3 receives the token and resets its token rotation timer. Here t_{13} is the signal propagation delay from stations S_1 to S_3.
4. $t = D$: Station S_1 receives the token. Since it now has an infinite supply of frames to transmit, it captures the token and determines that the *token rotation time* (*TRT*)—time elapsed since the last time it received the token—is D, and so it can hold the token for the TTRT − TRT = $T - D$ interval.
5. $t = T$: The THT at station S_1 expires, and S_1 releases the token.
6. $t = T + t_{12}$: Station S_2 receives the token. It last received the token at $t = t_{12}$. The time elapsed since then (and hence its TRT) is T. The station finds that the token is unusable at this time and lets it go.
7. $t = T + t_{13}$: Station S_3 receives the token. It last received the token at $t = t_{13}$ and so its TRT is also T. It finds the token unusable and lets it go.
8. $t = T + D$: Station S_1 receives the token. It last received the token at $t = D$ and so its TRT is T.[1] It finds the token unusable and lets it go.
9. $t = T+D+t_{12}$: Station S_2 receives the token. Since TRT is only D, it sets the THT to the remaining time, namely, $T-D$. It transmits for that interval and releases the token at $t = T+D+t_{12}+(T-D)$.

11. $t = 2T + t_{13}$: Station S_3 receives the token. Since TRT is T, it lets the token go.
12. $t = 2T + D$: Station S_1 receives the token. Since TRT is T, it lets the token go.
13. $t = 2T + D + t_{12}$: Station S_2 receives the token. Since TRT is T, it lets the token go.
14. $t = 2T + D + t_{13}$: Station S_3 receives the token. Since TRT is only D, it transmits for $T - D$ and releases the token at $t = 2T + D + t_{13} + (T - D)$. The token passes through stations S_1, S_2, and S_3, all of which find it unusable (events 14, 15, and 16).

19. $t = 3T + 2D$: Station S_1 captures the token, and the cycle of events repeats starting with event 4.

This sequence illustrates that the system goes through a cycle of events and that the cycle time is $3T+D$. During each cycle, the three stations transmit for $T-D$ intervals each for a total transmission time of $3(T - D)$. The number of bits transmitted during this time is $3(T - D) \times 10^8$ bits and the throughput is $3(T - D) \times 10^8/(3T + D)$ bps. The efficiency (ratio of throughput to the bandwidth) is $3(T - D)/(3T + D)$.

During the cycle, each station waits for an interval of $2T + 2D$ after releasing the token. This interval is the maximum access delay. At lower loads, the access delay will be lower. Notice that the access protocol is fair in this case since all three stations get their turn in each cycle.

Thus, for a ring with three active stations, the efficiency and access delay are:

$$\text{Efficiency} = \frac{3(T - D)}{3T + D}$$

$$\text{Maximum access delay} = (3 - 1)T + 2D$$

---

[1]Notice that the TRT is measured from the instant the token arrives at a station's receiver, that is, event 4 for Station S_1 in this case, and not from the instant it leaves a station's transmitter (event 5).

This analysis can be generalized to n active stations. Replacing 3 by n, Equations (22.1) and (22.2) result. This completes the derivation of the formulas. □

The following example illustrates how to use Equations (22.1) and (22.2) to compute the maximum access delay and the efficiency for any given FDDI ring configuration.

Example 22.1 Consider a ring with 16 stations and a total fiber length of 20 km. Using a two-fiber cable, this would correspond to a cable length of 10 km.

Light waves travel along the fiber at a speed of 5.085 μs/km. The station delay, the delay between receiving a bit and repeating it on the transmitter side, is of the order of 1 μs per station. The ring latency, therefore, can be computed as follows:

$$\text{Ring latency } D = (20 \text{ km}) \times (5.085\ \mu\text{s/km}) + (16 \text{ stations}) \times (1\ \mu\text{s/station})$$
$$= 0.12 \text{ ms}$$

Assuming a TTRT of 5 ms and that all 16 stations are active, the efficiency and maximum access delay are:

$$\text{Efficiency} = \frac{16(5-0.12)}{16 \times 5 + 0.12} = 97.5\%$$

$$\text{Maximum access delay} = (16-1) \times 5 + 2 \times 0.12$$
$$= 75.24 \text{ ms}$$

Thus, on this ring the maximum possible throughput is 97.5 Mbps. If the load is more than this for any substantial length of time, the queues will build up, the response time will become very long, and the stations may start dropping the frames. The maximum access delay is 75.24 ms, that is, it is possible for asynchronous stations to take as long as 75.24 ms to get a usable token. □

The key advantage of the model is its simplicity. Yet, it allows us to see immediately the effect of various parameters on the performance. With only one active station the efficiency is:

$$\text{Efficiency with one active station} = \frac{T-D}{T+D} \tag{22.3}$$

As the number of active stations increases, the efficiency increases. With a very large number of stations ($n = \infty$), the efficiency is:

$$\text{Maximum efficiency} = 1 - \frac{D}{T} \tag{22.4}$$

This formula is easy to remember and can be used for back-of-the-envelope calculations of FDDI performance. For example, if the TTRT is five times the ring latency, the maximum efficiency, computed using the formula, is 80%.

Equation (22.1) also indicates that the maximum access delay with one active station ($n = 1$) is $2D$. That is, a single active station may have to wait as long as two times the ring latency between successive transmission opportunities. This is because every alternate token it receives would be unusable.

The fact that FDDI does behave as indicated in Figure 22.4 has been verified experimentally. In these experiments, the *asynchronous overrun* (explained in Section 2.1), which was ignored in Figure 22.4, was found to cause the durations of the transmission intervals to be off by plus or minus

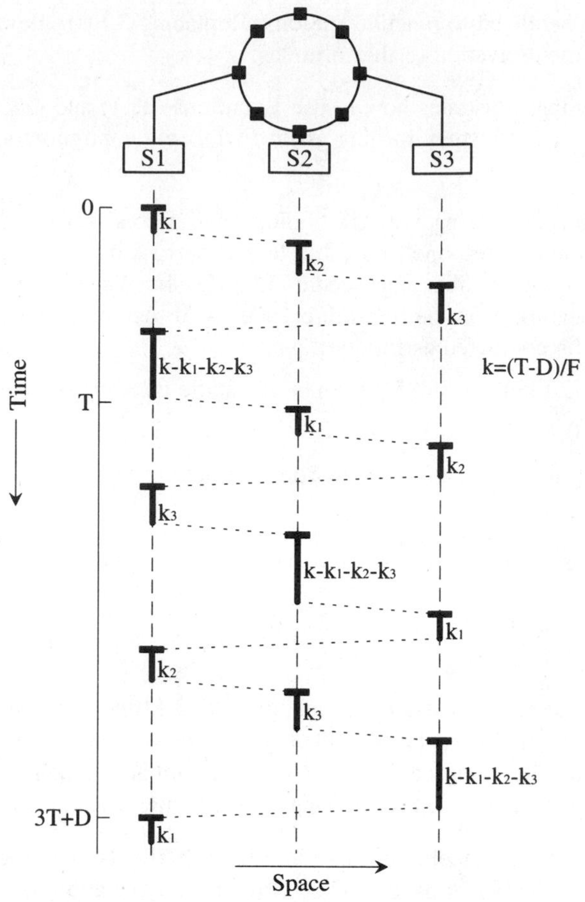

Figure 22.5 Another possible transmission sequence.

one frame. Let F denote the frame time, which was fixed in these experiments. If $k = \lceil \frac{T-D}{F} \rceil$, then a station was seen to transmit $k-1$, k, or $k+1$ frames in a transmission opportunity resulting in transmission durations of $(k-1)F$, kF, or $(k+1)F$. These experiments also showed another possible variation of the space-time diagram, which is shown in Figure 22.5. In this case, the stations transmit k_1, k_2, and k_3 frames (in place of k frames) during first token rotation, then all future transmissions are broken into four parts consisting of k_2, k_3, $k-k_1-k_2-k_3$, and k_1. In any case, total transmission per cycle averages out to $\lceil n(T-D)/F \rceil$ frames and the formula for efficiency still holds. Notice that Figure 22.4 is a special case of Figure 22.5 with $k_1 = k_2 = k_3 = 0$.

22.4 Guidelines for Setting TTRT

The FDDI standard specifies a number of rules that must be followed for setting TTRT. These rules are:

1. A synchronous station may not see the token for $2 \times T$. Therefore, *synchronous stations requiring a guaranteed access delay should request a TTRT value of one-half the required service interval.* For example, a voice station wanting to see a token every 20 ms or less should ask for a TTRT of 10 ms.

   Even though the token may be delayed on one rotation, it makes up on the next rotation and the average token rotation time never exceeds the TTRT significantly. Thus, synchronous stations requiring a guaranteed bandwidth (a guaranteed average access delay) should request a TTRT value equal to the desired average.
2. *TTRT should allow at least one maximum size frame along with the synchronous time allocation, if any.* That is:

$$\begin{aligned}\text{TTRT} \geq\ & \text{Ring latency} + \text{Token time}\\ & + \text{Max frame time}\\ & + \text{Synchronous allocation}\\ & + 2 \times \text{Void frame time}\end{aligned} \tag{22.5}$$

   The maximum size frame on FDDI is 4500 bytes (0.360 ms). The maximum ring latency is 1.773 ms. (See Section 14.8 for other possible values.) The token time (11 bytes including 8 bytes of preamble) is 0.00088 ms. This rule, therefore, prohibits setting the TTRT at less than 2.13 ms plus the synchronous allocation. Violating this rule, for example, by overallocating the synchronous bandwidth, results in unfairness and starvation.

   Synchronous allocation is often expressed as a fraction of the TTRT. Thus, if the synchronous allocation is αT, a fraction α of the bandwidth is said to have been allocated for synchronous operation. For example, if 50 Mbps is allocated for the synchronous class, then $\alpha = 0.5$. Using α, Equation (22.6) can be written as follows:

$$\text{TTRT} \geq \frac{\text{Ring latency} + \text{Token time} + \text{Maximum frame time} + 2 \times \text{Void frame time}}{1 - \text{Fraction of bandwidth allocated to synchronous class}}$$

   or, using symbols:

$$T \geq \frac{D + \text{Token\_Time} + \text{F\_Max} + 2 \times \text{Void\_Fr}}{1 - \alpha} \tag{22.6}$$

3. *No station should request a TTRT of less than T_Min*, which is a station parameter. The default maximum value of T_Min is 4 ms. Assuming that there is at least one station with T_Min = 4 ms, the TTRT on a ring should not be less than 4 ms.
4. *No station should request a TTRT of more than T_Max*, which is another station parameter. The default minimum value of T_Max is 165 ms. Assuming that there is at least one station with T_Max = 165 ms, the TTRT on a ring cannot be more than this value. (In practice, many stations will use a value of $2^{22} \times 40$ ns = 167.77216 ms, which can be conveniently derived from the symbol clock using a 22-bit counter.)

In addition to these rules, the TTRT values should be chosen to allow high-performance operation of the ring. These performance considerations are discussed next.

22.5 Effect of TTRT on Performance

Figure 22.6 shows a plot of efficiency as a function of TTRT. The plot was obtained using Equation (22.1). Three different configurations called "typical," "big," and "largest" are shown.

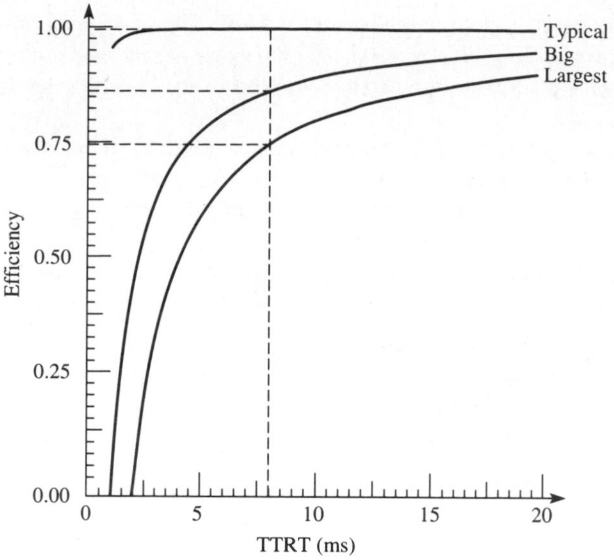

Figure 22.6 Efficiency as a function of the TTRT.

The typical configuration consists of 20 single-attachment stations (SASs) on a 4-km fiber ring. The numbers used are based on an intuitive feeling of what a typical ring would look like and are not based on any survey of actual installations. Twenty offices located on a 50- by 50-m floor would require a 2-km cable or a 4-km fiber.

The big configuration consists of 100 SASs on a 200-km fiber. As will be discussed in Chapter 25, putting too many stations on a single ring increases the probability of bit errors. The big configuration is assumed to represent a reasonably large ring with acceptable reliability.

The largest configuration consists of 500 dual-attachment stations (DASs) in a ring that is assumed to have wrapped. A DAS can have one or two media access controllers (**MAC**s). In the largest configuration, each DAS is assumed to have two MACs. Thus, the LAN consists of 1000 MACs in a single logical ring. This is the largest number of MACs allowed on an FDDI. Exceeding this number would require recomputation of all default parameters specified in the standard.

Figure 22.6 shows that for all configurations the efficiency increases as the TTRT increases. As TTRT values get close to the ring latency, the efficiency is very low, but it increases as the TTRT increases. This is one reason why the minimum allowed TTRT on FDDI (T_Min) is 4 ms. This may lead some to the conclusion that the TTRT should be chosen to be as large as possible. However, notice also that the gain in efficiency by increasing the TTRT (that is, the slope of the efficiency curve) decreases as the TTRT increases. The "knee" of the curve depends on the ring configuration. For larger configurations, the knee occurs at larger TTRT values. Even for the largest configuration, the knee occurs in the 6- to 10-ms range. For the typical configuration, the TTRT has very little effect on efficiency as long as the TTRT is in the allowed range of 4 to 165 ms.

Figure 22.7, obtained using Equation (22.2), shows the maximum access delay as a function of the TTRT for the three configurations. To show the complete range of possibilities, a semilog graph was used. The vertical scale is logarithmic, while the horizontal scale is linear. The figure shows that

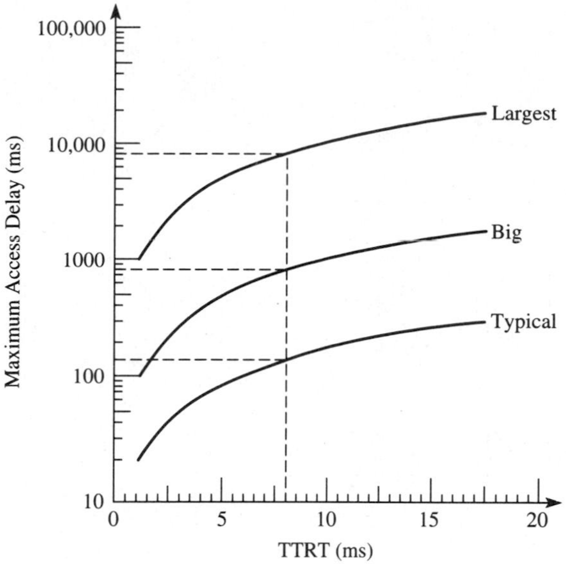

Figure 22.7 Access delay as a function of the TTRT.

increasing TTRT increases the maximum access delay for all three configurations. On the largest ring, use of a TTRT of 165 ms would cause a maximum access delay as long as 165 seconds. This means that in a worst case situation a station on such a ring may have to wait a few minutes to get a usable token. For most applications, this would be considered unacceptable, therefore, a smaller number of stations or a smaller TTRT is preferable.

The summary of the results presented so far is that if the FDDI load is below saturation, TTRT has little effect. At saturation, a larger value of TTRT gives larger usable bandwidth, but it also results in larger access delays. Selection of TTRT requires a trade-off between these two requirements. To allow for this trade-off, two performance metrics are listed in Table 22.1 for the three configurations.

Table 22.1 Maximum Access Delay and Efficiency as a Function of TTRT

	Max. Access Time (in seconds)			Percent Efficiency		
TTRT ms	Typical 20 SAS 4 km	Big 100 SAS 200 km	Largest 500 DAS 200 km	Typical 20 SAS 4 km	Big 100 SAS 200 km	Largest 500 DAS 200 km
4	0.08	0.40	4.00	98.94	71.87	49.55
8	0.15	0.79	8.00	99.47	85.92	74.77
12	0.23	1.19	11.99	99.65	90.61	83.18
16	0.30	1.59	15.99	99.74	92.95	87.38
20	0.38	1.98	19.98	99.79	94.36	89.91
165	3.14	16.34	164.84	99.97	99.32	98.78

Welcome aboard. This place is equipped with the latest fiber communications technology. We expect to have access delays of no more than 3 minutes.

Figure 22.8 Large TTRT on large rings may be unacceptable for some applications.

A number of TTRT values in the allowed range of 4 to 165 ms are shown. It can be seen that a very small value such as 4 ms is undesirable because it gives poor efficiency (60%) on the largest ring. A very large value such as 165 ms is also undesirable because it causes long access delays that may be unacceptable for many applications (see Figure 22.8). The 8-ms value is the most desirable one because it gives 80% or more efficiency on all configurations and results in a less than 1-second maximum access delay on big rings.

A value of 8 ms is, therefore, the recommended default TTRT.

22.6 Other Problems with Large TTRT Values

There are a few additional reasons for preferring 8-ms TTRT over a large TTRT (such as 165 ms). First, with a large TTRT a station may receive a large number of frames back to back. To be able to operate in such environments, adapters should be designed with large receive buffers. Although the memory is not considered an expensive part of computers, its cost is still a significant part of low-cost components such as adapters. Also, the board space for this additional memory is significant, as are the bus holding times required for such large back-to-back transfers. Many higher layer protocols are not able to handle such large bursts. For example, standard TCP/IP windows cannot even use 8-ms worth of data (100 kB) at 100 Mbps.

Second, a very large TTRT results essentially in an exhaustive service discipline, which has several known drawbacks. For example, exhaustive service is unfair. Frames coming to a higher load station's transmit queue have a higher chance of finding the token there in the same transmission opportunity, while frames arriving at a low-load station's transmit queue may have to wait. Thus, the response time depends on the load—lower for higher load stations and higher for lower load stations.

Third, the exhaustive service makes the response time of a station depend on its location with respect to that of high-load stations. The station immediately downstream from a high-load station may get better service than the one immediately upstream (see Section 23.6).

22.7 Effect of Ring Configuration

Three configuration parameters affect performance: extent, total number of stations, and number of active stations.

The total length of the fiber is called the *extent* of the ring. The maximum allowed extent on FDDI is 200 km. Figures 22.9 and 22.10 show the efficiency and maximum access delay as a function of the extent using a TTRT value of 8 ms. A star-shaped ring with all stations at a fixed radius from the wiring closet is assumed. The total cable length, shown along the horizontal axis, is

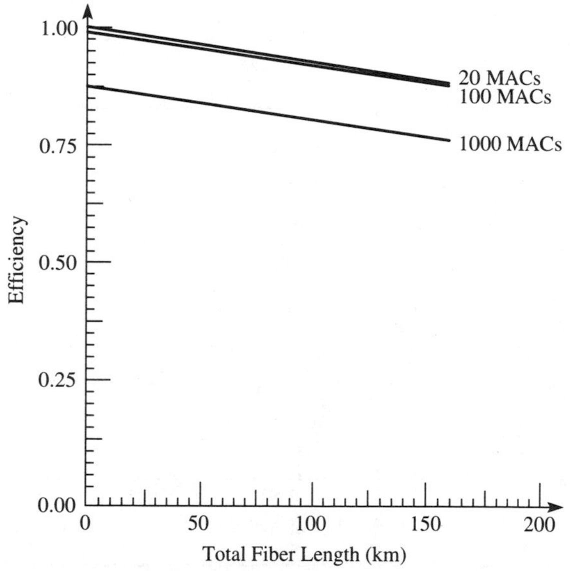

Figure 22.9 Efficiency as a function of the extent of the ring.

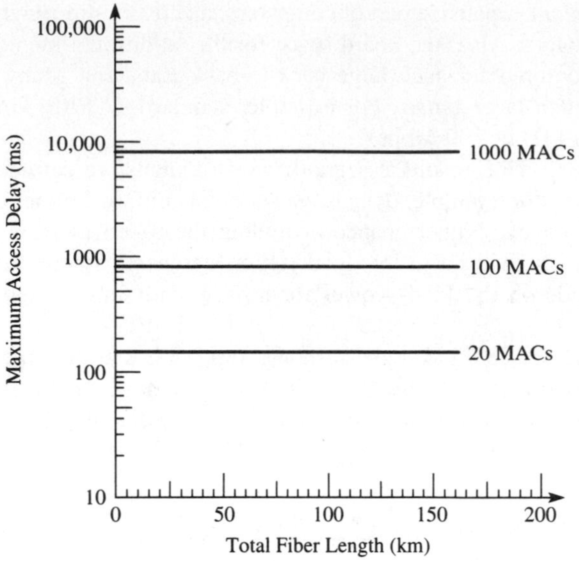

Figure 22.10 Access delay as a function of extent.

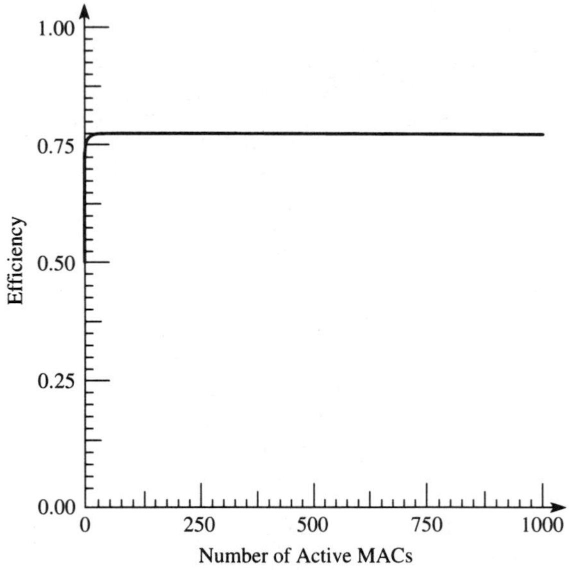

Figure 22.11 Efficiency as a function of the number of active stations.

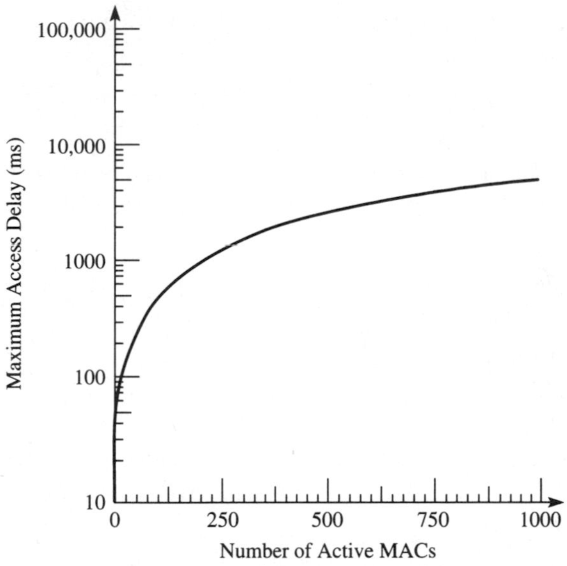

Figure 22.12 Access delay as a function of the number of active stations.

calculated as 2 × Radius × Number of stations. From the figures, it can be seen that larger rings have a slightly lower efficiency and longer access delay. (The increase in access delay is not visible due to the logarithm scale on the vertical axis.) In all cases, the performance (with TTRT = 8 ms) is acceptable.

The total number of stations includes active as well as inactive stations. In general, increasing the number of stations increases the ring latency due to an increase in fiber length and an increase in the sum of station delays. Thus, the effect is similar to that of the extent. That is, a larger number of stations on one ring results in a lower efficiency and longer access delay. Another problem with a larger number of stations on a ring is the increased bit error rate. Once again, it is preferable not to construct very large rings.

As the number of active stations (or MACs) increases, the total load on the ring increases. Figures 22.11 and 22.12 show the ring performance as a function of the active number of MACs on the ring. A maximum size ring with a TTRT value of 8 ms is used. The figures show that a larger number of active MACs on a ring results in a better efficiency but a longer access delay. Therefore, if low delay is desired, active stations should be segregated on separate rings.

22.8 Effect of Frame Size

Note that frame size does not appear in the simple models of efficiency and access delays because frame size has little impact on FDDI performance. In this analysis, no *asynchronous overflow* is assumed, that is, the transmission stops instantly as the THT expires. Actually, the stations are allowed to finish the transmission of the last frame. The extra time used by a station after THT expiry is called *asynchronous overflow*. Assuming all frames are of fixed size, let F denote the frame transmission time. On every transmission opportunity an active station can transmit as many as k frames:

$$k = \left\lceil \frac{T-D}{F} \right\rceil$$

Here, $\lceil\ \rceil$ is used to denote rounding up to the next integer value. The transmission time is kF, which is slightly more than $T - D$. With asynchronous overflow, the modified efficiency and access delay formulas become:

$$\text{Efficiency} = \frac{nkF}{n(kF+D)+D}$$

$$\text{Access delay} = (n-1)(kF+D)+2D$$

Notice that substituting $kF = T - D$ in these equations results in the same formulas as in Equations (22.1) and (22.2).

Figures 22.13 and 22.14 show the efficiency and access delay as function of frame size. Frame size has only a slight effect on these metrics. In practice, larger frame sizes also have the following effects:

1. The probability of error in a larger frame is larger.
2. Since the size of protocol headers and trailers is fixed, larger frames result in less protocol overhead.
3. The time to process a frame increases only slightly with the size of the frame. A larger frame size results in fewer frames and, hence, in less processing at the host.

Overall, you should use as large a frame size as the higher layer protocols and the undetected error considerations allow.

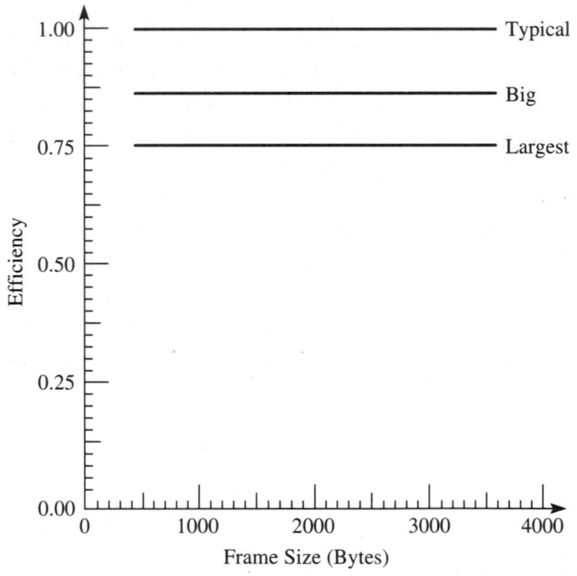

Figure 22.13 Efficiency as a function of frame size.

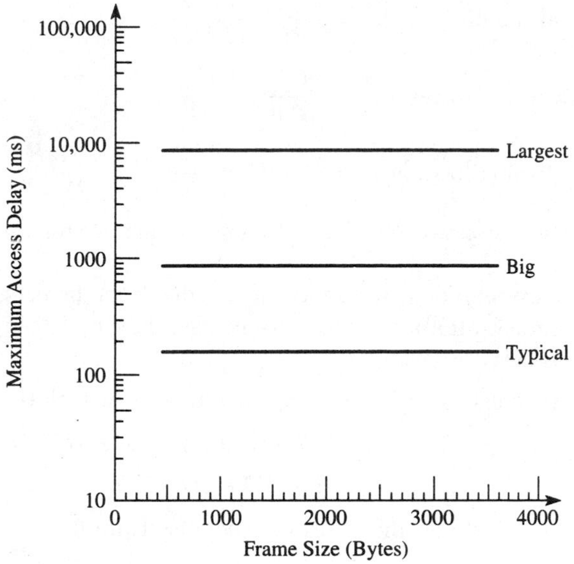

Figure 22.14 Access delay as a function of frame size.

22.9 Effect of Synchronous Traffic

So far it was assumed that all traffic on the ring was asynchronous. If synchronous traffic is present, the token rotation times become longer.

Assume that the *i*th station has a synchronous allocation of $\alpha_i T$ and that the total synchronous allocation is αT. Here:

$$\alpha = \sum \alpha_i$$

Since total synchronous allocation cannot exceed the TTRT, $\alpha < 1$. If we assume that the stations use their synchronous allocation on every token rotation regardless of the actual token rotation time, then the transmission sequence will be very similar to that presented in Figure 22.5 except that αT time will be used by synchronous transmission on every token rotation. The lengths of asynchronous transmissions will be $T - D - \alpha T$. The transmission pattern will repeat after every $n+1$ token rotations. Each repetition cycle (of $n + 1$ token rotations) will consist of the following:

$$\begin{aligned}
\text{Total asynchronous transmission time} &= n(T - \alpha T - D) \\
\text{Synchronous transmission/rotation} &= \alpha T \\
\text{Total number of token rotations/cycle} &= n + 1 \\
\text{Total synchronous transmission time} &= (n + 1)\alpha T \\
\text{Total time lost in token rotations} &= (n + 1)D \\
\text{Total length of cycle} &= n(T - \alpha T - D) + (n + 1)\alpha T + (n + 1)D \\
&= nT + \alpha T + D
\end{aligned}$$

$$\text{Asynchronous utilization } U_a = \frac{n(T - \alpha T - D)}{nT + \alpha T + D}$$

$$\text{Synchronous utilization } U_s = \frac{(n + 1)\alpha T}{nT + \alpha T + D}$$

$$\text{Total utilization } U = U_a + U_s = \frac{n(T - D) + \alpha T}{nT + \alpha T + D}$$

Notice that if there is no synchronous traffic ($\alpha = 0$), this formula for total utilization reduces to that derived earlier.

From the formula for asynchronous utilization, notice that from the perspective of asynchronous traffic, the effect of synchronous traffic is simply to increase the ring latency from D to $D + \alpha T$.

The maximum access delay is given by:

$$\begin{aligned}\text{Max access delay for asynchronous traffic} &= \text{Total cycle time} - \text{Asynchronous transmission time}\\ &= (nT + \alpha T + D) - (T - \alpha T - D)\\ &= (n - 1)T + 2D + 2\alpha T\end{aligned}$$

The following example illustrates the effect of synchronous traffic.

Example 22.2 Consider the 16-station 25-km ring considered earlier. The ring latency was computed to be 0.12 ms. With a TTRT of 5 ms and a synchronous allocation of 2.5 ms ($\alpha T = 2.5$ ms), the efficiencies are as follows:

$$\begin{aligned}\text{Max asynchronous utilization } U_a &= \frac{n(T - \alpha T - D)}{nT + \alpha T + D}\\ &= \frac{16(5 - 2.5 - 0.12)}{16 \times 5 + 2.5 + 0.12} = 46.09\%\end{aligned}$$

$$\begin{aligned}\text{Max synchronous utilization } U_s &= \frac{(n + 1)\alpha T}{nT + \alpha T + D}\\ &= \frac{(16 + 1) \times 2.5}{16 \times 5 + 2.5 + 0.12} = 51.44\%\end{aligned}$$

$$\text{Max total utilization } U = U_a + U_s = 46.09 + 51.44 = 97.53\%$$

The maximum utilization in the asynchronous-only case considered earlier was 97.5%. Notice that there is little change in efficiency with the presence of synchronous traffic. This is true for most cases since αT is small compared to nT. □

22.10 Effect of Asymmetric Loading

The simple model for efficiency and access delay [Equations (22.1) and (22.2)] assumes symmetric loading, that is, all stations have identical loads. If the load is different either in frame size or frame rate, the model does not apply. In this section, we address the case of asymmetric loading.

As a first step assume that there is no synchronous traffic. In this case, the efficiency under asymmetric loading is given by:

$$\text{Efficiency} = \frac{T - D}{T + r_{\max} D} \tag{22.7}$$

Here, r_{max} is the fraction of loading caused by the highest loading station. Derivation of this equation is as follows.

Derivation 22.2 Suppose the total throughput (or utilization) is U, of which the ith station's share is $U_i = r_i U$. Here,

$$\sum_i r_i = 1$$

The average token rotation time C (see Section 23.2) is:

$$C = \frac{D}{1-U}$$

If the average transmission time per rotation for the ith station is T_i, then

$$T_i + C \le T$$

During each rotation, the total traffic transmitted at the ith station is $U_i C$. For the system to be stable, the traffic that arrived during each token rotation must equal that transmitted. Therefore:

$$U_i C + C \le T$$

or

$$r_i U \frac{D}{1-U} + \frac{D}{1-U} \le T$$

or

$$U \le \frac{T-D}{T+r_i D} \quad \text{for all } i$$

or

$$U = \frac{T-D}{T+r_{max} D}$$

Here, r_{max} is the maximum value of r_i. □

Equation (22.7) gives the efficiency for asymmetric loading. In the symmetric case, $r_i = r_{max} = 1/n$, and the efficiency formula reduces to that presented earlier in Equation (22.1). If only one of the n stations is active, $r_{max} = 1$, the efficiency formula becomes identical to Equation (22.3) for a single station ring.

The following example illustrates the use of the preceding model.

Example 22.3 Consider the ring of Example 22.3. It has 16 stations, a ring latency of 0.12 ms, and a TTRT of 5 ms. Suppose one of the 16 stations transmits 50% of the load while the other 15 share the remaining 50%. In this case,

$$r_i = \begin{cases} 0.5, & i = 1 \\ \dfrac{0.5}{15}, & i = 2, 3, \ldots, 16 \end{cases}$$

The maximum share r_{max} is:

$$r_{max} = \max_i (r_i) = r_1 = 0.5$$

The efficiency is:

$$\begin{aligned}\text{Efficiency} &= \frac{T-D}{T+r_{max}D}\\ &= \frac{5-0.12}{5+0.5\times 0.12}\\ &= \frac{4.88}{5.06}\\ &= 0.9644\end{aligned}$$

The ring efficiency is 96.44%, which is what you would get from the simple model if only two stations on the ring were active. □

Now consider the case of both synchronous traffic and asymmetric loading. In this case, the delay term D is replaced by $D+\alpha T$, where αT is the total synchronous allocation. Assuming that the synchronous allocations are also in the same proportions as the asynchronous loading (that is, $\alpha_i = r_i\alpha$), the synchronous utilization and total utilizations are given by:

$$U = U_a + U_s = \frac{(1/r_{max})(T-D)+\alpha T}{(1/r_{max})T+D+\alpha T}$$

The right side of this equation gives the desired efficiency. The following example illustrates this case.

Example 22.4 Consider again the 16-station ring of Example 22.9. In this case, the synchronous allocation is 2.5 ms. Other parameters are $D = 0.12$ ms and $T = 5$ ms. Assuming that one of the 16 stations transmits 50% of the load, we have $r_{max} = 0.5$.

The maximum asynchronous utilization is:

$$\begin{aligned}U_a &= \frac{(1/r_{max})(T-D-\alpha T)}{(1/r_{max})T+D+\alpha T}\\ &= \frac{(1/0.5)(5-0.12-2.5)}{(1/0.5)\times 5+0.12+2.5} = 37.72\%\end{aligned}$$

The maximum synchronous utilization is:

$$\begin{aligned}U_s &= \frac{[1+(1/r_{max})]\,\alpha T}{(1/r_{max})T+D+\alpha T}\\ &= \frac{[1+(1/0.5)]\times 2.5}{(1/0.5)\times 5+0.12+2.5} = 39.62\%\end{aligned}$$

The total utilization is:

$$U = U_a + U_s = 37.72 + 39.62 = 77.34\%$$

Again, as in Example 22.3, the ring behaves as if there are only two stations on the ring. □

One problem with asymmetric loading is that of fairness, which is discussed in Section 23.5.

22.11 Summary

The target token rotation time is the key network parameter that network managers can use to optimize the performance of their FDDI ring network. Other parameters that affect the performance are extent (length of cable), total number of stations, number of active stations, and frame size.

The response time is not significantly affected by the TTRT value unless the load is near saturation. Under very heavy load, response time is not a suitable metric. Instead, maximum access delay, the time between wanting to transmit and receiving a token, is more meaningful.

A larger value of TTRT improves the efficiency, but it also increases the maximum access delay. A good trade-off is provided by setting TTRT at 8 ms. Since this value provides good performance for all ranges of configurations, it is recommended that *the default value of TTRT be set at 8 ms.*

22.12 Further Reading

Much of the discussion in this chapter is from Jain (1990b). Figure 20.1 has been adapted from the *Digital Technical Journal* version of the paper. See also Jain (1991) for a general discussion on performance metrics and modeling techniques. Equation (22.4) is presented in Ulm (1982). Similar results have been derived in Dykeman and Bux (1987, 1988).

The properties of token rotation time are derived in Sevcik and Johnson (1987) and in Johnson (1987).

LaMaire (1991a) presents the formulas for efficiency in the presence of synchronous traffic and asymmetric loading.

22.13 Self-Test Exercises

Note: Some exercises have multiple correct answers. See Appendix D for answers.

22.1 What is the maximum possible throughput on an FDDI ring with a latency of 1 ms using a target token rotation time of 10 ms?

a. 90 Mbps
b. 10 Mbps
c. 100 Mbps
d. 50 Mbps

22.2 What is the maximum token access delay on a ring with 10 stations, a ring latency of 1 ms, and a target token rotation time of 10 ms?

a. 1 ms
b. 10 ms
c. 20 ms
d. 92 ms

CHAPTER **23**

Performance Under Normal Load

Under normal operating conditions, the total load on FDDI is generally much below saturation. Under these conditions, the throughput is equal to the offered load. The throughput, therefore, is not an interesting metric. The response time is the key metric in this region of operation.

The response time, which was defined in Section 22.2, includes queueing delay. It depends primarily on the time to service one packet and the load level. For FDDI, the time to service a packet and hence the response time are related to the token rotation time (TRT). If TRT is low, the response time is low and vice versa. In this chapter we begin with a formula for the TRT and then point out various known results about the response time.

23.1 Computing Token Rotation Time

The time between successive arrivals of the token at a station is called the token rotation time. In FDDI, TRT is bounded. It can never exceed twice the target token rotation time (TTRT), as was explained in Chapter 22.

Average TRT can be measured by simply counting the number of tokens seen at a station. For example, if you monitor activities at a station for 1000 μs and see the token 100 times during this interval, the average TRT is 10 μs.

The TRT (and hence its average) is related to the load on the ring. If the load is high, the token is seen less often and the TRT is high. Similarly, if the load is low, the token rotation time is low. In fact, there is a very simple relationship between average TRT C and ring utilization U:

$$\text{Average TRT} = \frac{\text{Ring latency}}{1 - \text{Utilization}} \tag{23.1}$$

$$C = \frac{D}{1 - U}$$

Here, D is the ring latency. The utilization U is defined as the fraction of time used for data transmission. Since a station must capture the token for data transmission, the ring utilization is equal to the fraction of time the token is busy (that is, captured by stations). When the token is not busy, it is idle and simply circulates around the ring.

Equation (23.1) is very useful. It applies not only to FDDI but to other token rings as well. Its derivation is rather simple and is given next.

Derivation 23.1 Utilization of any resource is simply the fraction of time the resource is busy:

$$\text{Utilization} = \frac{\text{Busy time}}{\text{Total time}}$$

For FDDI and other token rings the key resource is the token. The token becomes busy when it is captured by a station. The busy time is equal to the time spent inside various stations. Thus, the idle time (total time $-$ busy time) is equal to the time the token has spent in simply going around the ring. Every time a station sees a token, the token has spent one "ring latency" worth of idle time. Thus, if the ring latency is D and a station sees a token m times in τ seconds, then:

$$\text{Total time} = \tau$$

$$\text{Idle time} = mD$$

$$\text{Busy time} = \text{Total time} - \text{Idle time} = \tau - mD$$

$$\begin{aligned} \text{Utilization } U(\tau) &= \frac{\text{Busy time}}{\text{Total time}} \\ &= \frac{\tau - mD}{\tau} \\ &= 1 - \frac{D}{\tau/m} \\ &= 1 - \frac{\text{Ring latency}}{\text{Average TRT}} \end{aligned}$$

or

$$\text{Average TRT} = \frac{\text{Ring latency}}{1 - \text{Utilization}}$$

□

Notice that the token busy time does not include the normal path latency inside a station that the token would incur if the token were not "captured" by the station. However, it does include the time that the station may take to set up its transfer path (L_Max) even though only idles are transmitted. Also note that every token is counted regardless of whether it is usable, unusable, late, restricted, or unrestricted.

The following example illustrates the use of Equation (23.1).

Example 23.1 A ring network with a round-trip latency of 1 μs was monitored for 100 seconds. During this interval, the token was seen 10 million times. What is the ring utilization?

$$\begin{aligned} \text{Average TRT} &= \frac{\text{Total time}}{\text{Number of token rotations}} \\ &= \frac{100}{10 \times 10^6} \\ &= 10\ \mu\text{s} \end{aligned}$$

$$\text{Utilization} = 1 - \frac{\text{Ring latency}}{\text{Average TRT}}$$
$$= 1 - \frac{1}{10}$$
$$= 0.90$$

Thus, the ring utilization during the observation interval was 90%. □

23.2 Seven Known Properties of the Token Rotation Time

The token rotation time on the ring has a number of known properties as follows:

1. *The token rotation time on FDDI cannot exceed twice the TTRT.* As discussed in Chapter 22, this well-known property is a result of the token holding rule. A station with asynchronous traffic is required to leave the token alone (and not use it) if the token rotation time is more than T, where T is the TTRT. The token holding time is also limited to ensure that no new asynchronous transmissions will begin if the rotation time is about to exceed T. However, due to asynchronous overflow and synchronous bandwidth allocation, the total time at some stations can be more than T. But the synchronous allocation is limited such that the token rotation time is always less than $2T$.
2. *The total time for n consecutive rotations cannot exceed* $(n+1)T$. This means that the total time for two successive rotations cannot exceed $3T$, that for three successive rotations cannot exceed $4T$, and so on. Substituting $n = 1$, you see that the time for any one rotation can be as much as $2T$.
3. *A negative correlation exists between successive token rotation times.* A long cycle is always followed by a short cycle. This follows from the limit on n cycle times. The time for two token rotations cannot exceed $3T$. Thus, you cannot have two rotations each $2T$ long. The negative correlation means that token rotation times are not independent. Unfortunately, this point is ignored in many analyses.
4. *At loads below saturation, TTRT does not affect TRT.* This follows directly from Equation (23.1). Notice that the expression does not involve the TTRT. For a wide range of loads, the average TRT is within an order of magnitude of the ring latency and much less than the TTRT.
5. *The average token rotation time is always less than TTRT*:

   $$\text{Average TRT} \leq \text{TTRT}$$

   This follows easily from the second property. Suppose the time for the ith rotation is c_i, then:

   $$\text{Average TRT} = \lim_{n\to\infty} \frac{1}{n}\sum_{i=1}^{n} c_i$$
   $$\leq \lim_{n\to\infty} \frac{1}{n}(n+1)T \qquad (23.2)$$
   $$\leq T$$

   The equality in Equation (23.3) holds only when the ring is fully loaded. At lower loads, the average TRT is related to the utilization of the ring as given by Equation (23.1). Combining

Equations (23.1) and (23.3), we get:

$$\text{Average TRT} = \min\left(T, \frac{D}{1-U}\right)$$

6. *The coefficient of variation of TRT follows a bell-shaped curve such that it is small at low loads and at high loads but large at medium loads.* Coefficient of variation is a statistical term indicating variability of a quantity. It is defined as the ratio of standard deviation to the mean value of a variable. If a variable has the same value and does not change at all, the coefficient of variation is zero. Higher coefficient values indicate higher variability. At low loads, the TRT is mostly equal to the ring latency and the coefficient of variation is close to 0. At high loads, the token rotations alternate between idle and full load. TRT is either equal to the ring latency or TTRT each with 0.5 probability. This results in a coefficient of variation of $(T-D)/(T+D)$ or approximately 1 since TTRT is much greater than the ring latency. Figure 23.1 shows a sample plot of the coefficient of variation of TRT as a function of load for various values of TTRT. The ring latency in this case was 250 μs.
7. *Extreme variations in loading level may cause corresponding variations in TRT.* In one experiment, with two nodes running at 10% and 90% load, the TRT was observed to be bimodal. On some rotations, the TRT was equal to ring latency and on others it was equal to the TTRT. These two values are several orders of magnitude apart. Packets arriving at the less busy station during long rotations generally timed out but the retransmissions generally made it. The round-trip delay estimation algorithm, which used round-trip times for successful packets only, kept the estimate close to the ring latency. This caused those packets that had to wait for the long rotation to time out.

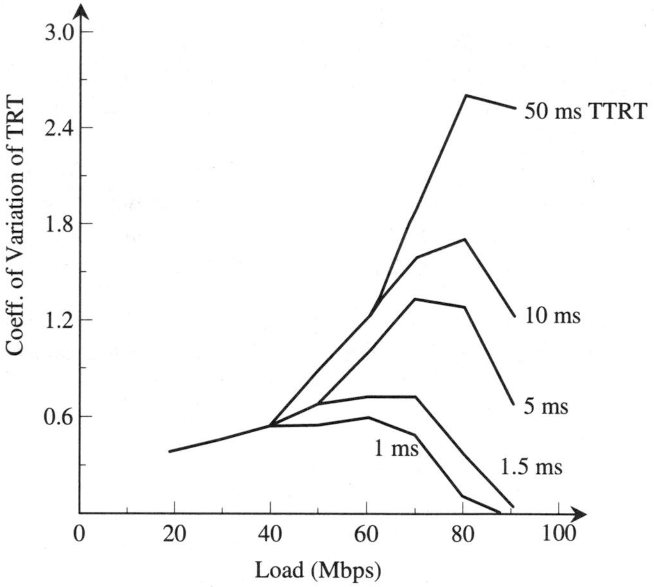

Figure 23.1 Coefficient of variation of token rotation time as a function of load.

Box 23.1 Seven Known Properties of FDDI Token Rotation Time

1. The token rotation time on FDDI cannot exceed twice the TTRT.
2. The total time for n consecutive rotations cannot exceed $(n + 1)T$.
3. There is a negative correlation between successive token rotation times.
4. At loads below saturation, TTRT does not affect TRT.
5. The average token rotation time is always less than TTRT.
6. The coefficient of variation of TRT follows a bell-shaped curve such that it is small at low loads and at high loads but large at medium loads.
7. Extreme variations in loading level may cause corresponding variations in TRT.

Box 23.1 summarizes these properties of token rotation times. These are very helpful in answering common concerns about FDDI performance. In particular, the average access delay at loads below saturation is equal to half the token rotation time. For synchronous traffic, the maximum access delay (at least at loads below saturation) is equal to the token rotation time and so it is comparable to the ring latency.

23.3 Response Time

Response time is much more difficult to compute than token rotation time because the shape of the response time curve depends on many parameters, such as the mean, variance, and distribution of interarrival time; mean, variance, and distribution of frame size; mean, variance, and distribution of burst size; and so on. The number of parameters that affect response time is large and, therefore, simulation modeling is generally used for this purpose.

The results presented in this section are based on our own simulation study and on other published studies. In our simulations, a workload based on an actual measurement of traffic in an industrial environment was used. The chief application at this site was *warehouse inventory control* (*WIC*). Hence, the workload is called the *WIC workload.* Measurements on networks have shown that when a station wants to transmit, it generally transmits not one frame, but a burst of frames. This was found to be true in WIC workloads as well. Therefore, a *bursty Poisson* arrival pattern is used in the simulation model. The interburst time used was 1 ms and each burst consisted of five frames. The frames had only two sizes: 65% of the frames were small (100 bytes) and 35% were large (512 bytes). A simple calculation shows that this workload constitutes a total load of 1.23 Mbps. Forty stations, each executing this load, would load an FDDI to 50% utilization. Higher load levels can be obtained either by reducing the interburst time or by increasing the number of stations. The measured interburst time was approximately 8 ms. It was scaled down to represent more powerful processors and to get meaningful results while keeping the number of stations in the simulation small.

The workload and system parameters used in the simulation runs are listed in Table 23.1. While studying the effect of a particular parameter, the parameter was varied in the range specified under the minimum and maximum columns; all other parameters were kept at the values specified under the default column. Notice that the workload uses bursty arrivals since each I/O to the network results in a burst of frames. The size of the burst depends on the size of the I/O.

Table 23.1 Simulation Parameters

Parameter	Default	Min	Max
Total number of stations	20	20	100
Number of active stations	20	1	20
Number of rings	1		
Radius of the ring in meters	100	100	1000
Target token rotation time (μs)	8000	8000	167,000
Distribution* of interburst time	2		
Mean interburst time	3000	1000	6000
Distribution* of burst size	0		
Constant burst size	5	1	5
Distribution* of frame size	6		
First mode of frame size	100	100	4500†
First mode probability of frame size	0.65		
Second mode of frame size	512		
Frame error probability	0		
Buffer-unavailable probability	0		

*0 = Constant, 1 = Uniform, 2 = Exponential, 3 = Log normal, 4 = Erlang, 5 = Geometric, 6 = Bimodal
†While varying frame size, all frames were assumed to be equal size.

23.4 Properties of FDDI Response Time

Based on the results of our simulation studies and on those of other published studies, the following general statements can be made about the response time on FDDI:

1. *At loads below saturation, TTRT does not affect the average response time.* At such loads, the token rotation time depends only on the ring utilization and ring latency. The TTRT does not affect the operation of the ring unless the burst sizes are large. Figure 23.2 shows the response time as a function of TTRT at three different load levels: 28%, 58%, and 90%. Two of the three curves are horizontal straight lines, indicating that TTRT has no effect on the response times at these loads. It is only at a heavy load that the TTRT makes a difference. In fact, it is only near the usable bandwidth that TTRT has any effect on the response time. Thus, TTRT affects only the maximum throughput and the maximum access delay but not the average response time.
2. *At loads below saturation, TTRT does not affect the average queue length.* This is a direct result of the previous observation. The queue length and response time for all systems without loss are directly related as follows:

   Average queue length = Average response time × Average arrival rate

   This is the well-known queueing theory result called **Little's law**.
3. *The coefficient of variation of response time is small.* The variation of response time depends on the variation of frame sizes, arrival pattern, and load. As the load increases, the variation increases. For the WIC workload, even at a load as high as 70%, the coefficient of variation was found to be less than one.

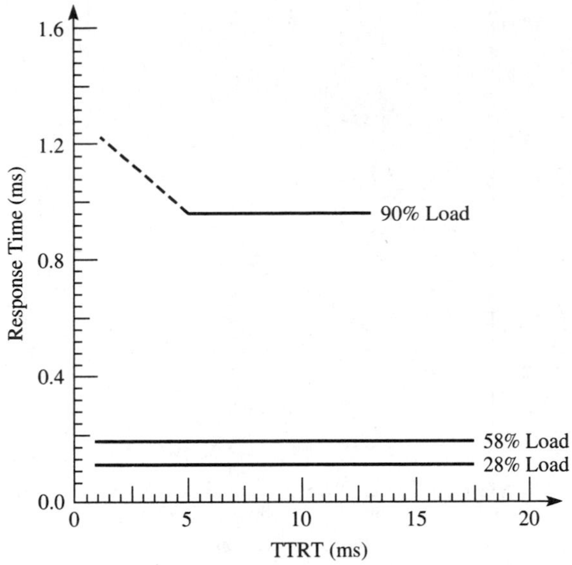

Figure 23.2 Response time as a function of the TTRT.

4. *Most packets get service on the first token rotation.* Normally stations exhaust their queue before running into the time limit imposed by the TTRT. Figure 23.3 shows the percentage of packets that received exhaustive service on a 250-μs ring. Notice that with load almost up to 50% of the maximum allowed throughput for any given TTRT, the service is exhaustive.

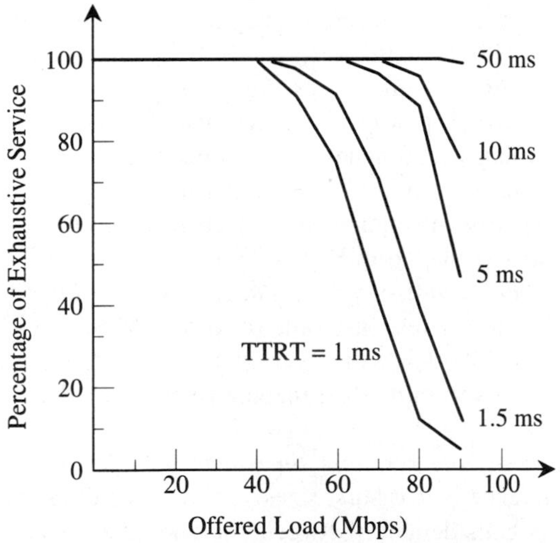

Figure 23.3 Percentage of packets that receive exhaustive service.

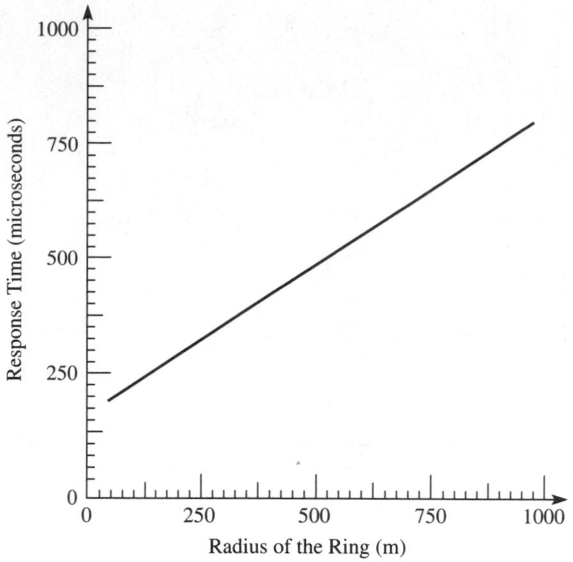

Figure 23.4 Response time as a function of ring latency.

5. *As the ring latency increases, the response time increases proportionately.* This is shown in Figure 23.4. A star-shaped ring is assumed and the radius of the star is plotted along the x axis. A station delay of 1 μs is assumed. The ring has 100 stations and therefore the total latency of the ring is $100(1 + 2 \times 0.005r)$ μs, where r is the radius in meters and the speed of light is 0.005 μs/m. Only 8 of the 100 stations are active, resulting in a total load of 28%.

   Equation (23.1) shows that as the ring latency increases, the average TRT increases proportionately. An increase in TRT increases the average response time as well.
6. *The variation of the response time decreases slightly as the ring size increases.* The decrease is primarily due to the fact that response time is dominated mostly by the ring latency and as the latency increases the varying part (queueing delay) becomes even less dominant.
7. *As the burst size increases, the response time increases.* The burst size increases the load and thus increases the average token rotation time. It also increases the wait for the last frame of the burst. The net effect is as shown in Figure 23.5.
8. *The response time is within an order of magnitude of the ring latency.* The load in Figure 23.5 varies from 14% to 70% but the response time remains between 48 to 273 μs. The ring latency in this case is 40 μs. At 70% load, the average token rotation time is seven times the ring latency. Most frames are served in the first token arrival unless the frames are large or TTRT is too small.
9. *As the frame size increases, the response time increases.* The effect is similar to that of the burst size. The key difference is that burst sizes vary by a small factor (between 1 and 5), while the frame sizes can vary considerably (between 100 and 4500 bytes). At large frame sizes, the frame transmission time dominates the response time, as shown in Figure 23.6. Notice that the response time is now several orders of magnitude greater than the ring latency.

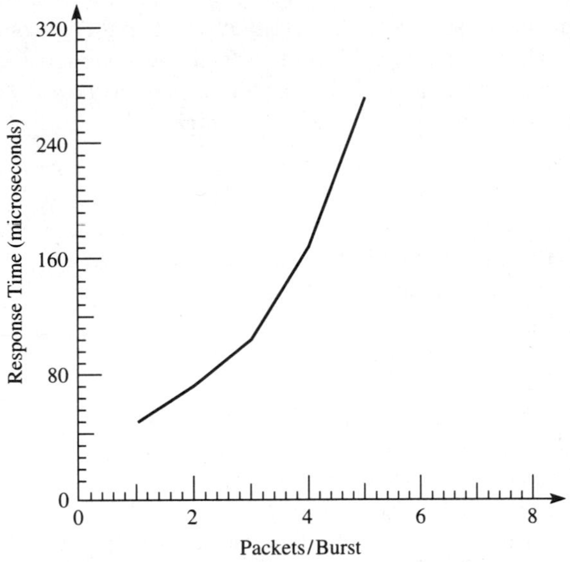

Figure 23.5 Response time as a function of burst size.

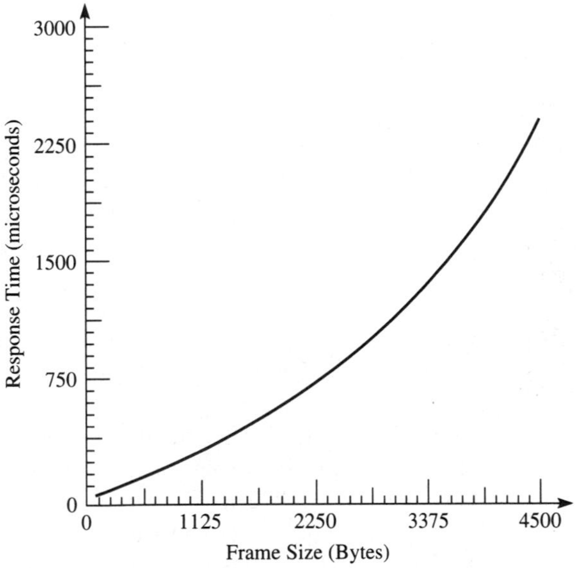

Figure 23.6 Response time as a function of frame size.

10. *The response time with only one active station may be more than that with two or more stations.* This result may seem counterintuitive at first. However, when there is only one station, the token can service only one burst per rotation. With more than one station, the token can service several bursts per rotation. Thus, the response time per frame may go down. This effect is particularly noticeable if the load is low and the ring latency is high.

Box 23.2 summarizes these properties of response time. The key parameter that affects performance during normal operation is the ring latency D. The effect of ring latency can be minimized by organizing a campus network into several smaller rings interconnected via bridges. Since most of the traffic is local, this traffic enjoys low response time and high efficiency. Only the nonlocal traffic that crosses bridges suffers an increased latency.

Box 23.2 Properties of FDDI Response Time

1. At loads below saturation, TTRT does not affect the average response time.
2. At loads below saturation, TTRT does not affect the average queue length.
3. The coefficient of variation of response time is small.
4. Most packets get service on the first token rotation.
5. As the ring latency increases, the response time increases proportionately.
6. The variation of the response time decreases slightly as the ring size increases.
7. The response time is within an order of magnitude of the ring latency.
8. As the burst size increases, the response time increases.
9. As the frame size increases, the response time increases.
10. The response time with only one active station may be more than that with two or more stations.

23.5 Fairness

FDDI has been shown to be fair in most cases. That is, two stations having similar traffic have similar response times. In particular, if there is only one priority level and all stations have identical arrival patterns and the synchronous bandwidth has been properly allocated, the protocol is fair. If any one of these three conditions is violated, it is possible for some stations to get better service than others. Multiple-priority operation is discussed next in Section 23.6, where we show that, among the stations operating at the same priority, those immediately downstream from a higher priority station get better service than others. In this section, the discussion is limited to single-priority operation. Examples of unfairness under asymmetric traffic and overallocation of synchronous bandwidth are presented.

Equation (22.5) sets a lower limit on the TTRT. This equation ensures that even if all stations use their allocated synchronous transmission time, the token rotation time will be less than two times the target. If the synchronous bandwidth is overallocated so that TTRT is below the limit set by Equation (22.5), it is possible for some stations to be starved and not receive a usable token, while other stations on the network keep getting serviced. This is illustrated by the following example.

Example 23.2 Figure 23.7 shows three stations on a ring. Stations 1 and 3 transmit asynchronous traffic, while station 2 transmits synchronous traffic and has an allocation of 4.5 ms. The ring latency is 1.5 ms, the TTRT is 5 ms.

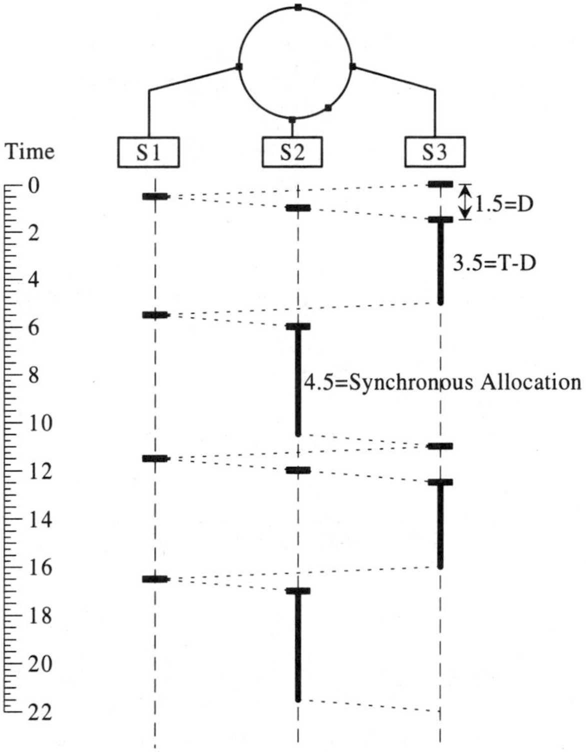

Figure 23.7 Unfairness caused by overallocation of synchronous bandwidth.

Notice that the TTRT violates the rule of Equation (22.5). Figure 23.7 shows a timing diagram in which station 2 transmits its full allocation on alternate tokens. Both stations 1 and 3 have frames always waiting for transmission, but only station 3 gets to transmit on rotations not used by station 2. Station 1 is starved and never gets a chance to transmit since all unused time is used up by station 3, which is ahead of it in the token rotation path. □

Overallocation of synchronous bandwidth can also result in the token rotation time being more than two times TTRT. This causes the late counter (Late_ct) to become more than one, which starts the claim process. Unless the synchronous bandwidth allocation or the TTRT is changed, the ring may keep getting frequently reinitialized.

In Section 24.1, we explain that FDDI's timed token service generally results in an exhaustive service in the sense that most stations are able to transmit all their frames in the first token capture. At heavy loads, however, stations may have to release the token without exhausting their transmit queues. All exhaustive service systems have a known unfairness property under asymmetric loading. Frames at heavily loaded stations are expected to get quicker service than those at lightly loaded stations. This is because the frames arriving at the heavily loaded station have a better chance of finding the token at the station than those arriving at the lightly loaded station. Also, the lightly loaded stations just downstream from highly loaded stations get poorer service than other stations of the

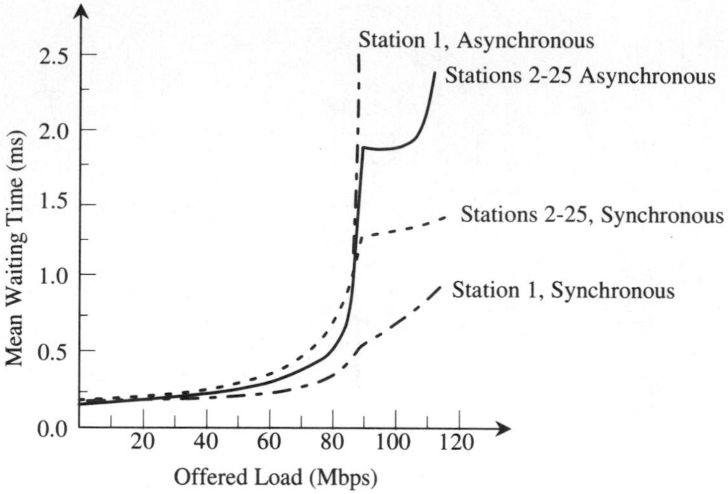

Figure 23.8 Average waiting time for ring with asymmetric load.

same load. Figure 23.8 shows the average waiting times for a 25-station ring with both synchronous and asynchronous traffic. Station 1 is a high-load station. All other stations have identical loads. Notice that station 1 has a shorter delay than the other stations. Figure 23.9 shows the delay for stations 2 and 25 along with the composite average for stations 2 through 25. Station 25, which is immediately upstream from station 1, experiences shorter delays.

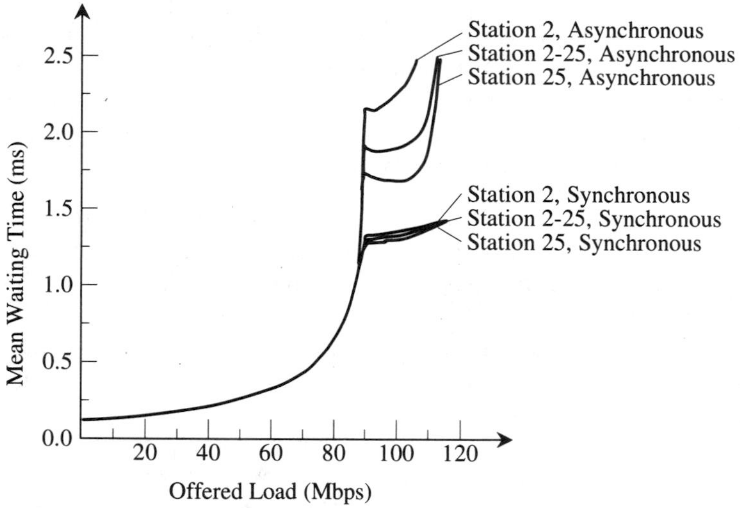

Figure 23.9 Unfairness caused by asymmetric load.

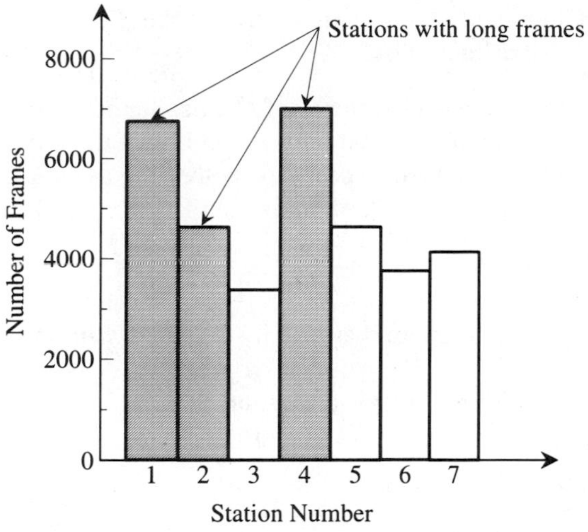

Figure 23.10 Unfairness caused by different frame sizes.

A high TTRT value results in FDDI operation closer to exhaustive service. A lower TTRT value results in better fairness.

Unfairness has been seen even if different stations have the same load but different frame sizes. Figure 23.10 shows the number of frames transmitted in a seven-station ring. Stations 1, 2, and 4 transmit frames that are 10% longer than other stations. It was expected that all stations would have the same throughput and that stations 1, 2, and 4 would transmit a lower number of frames than the other stations. The simulation showed the opposite. Stations with smaller frames were seen to transmit a smaller number of frames. There was no synchronous traffic in this case.

23.6 Multiple-Priority Operation

FDDI allows multiple-priority operation using multiple token rotation time thresholds as explained in Section 2.2. The mechanism itself works for any number of priority levels. However, the number of priorities is limited to eight mainly because the SMT database allows only seven priority thresholds in addition to the TTRT. The frame-control field has three bits for specifying the priority level of a frame, but those bits are not used by any protocol entity. In particular, the priority does not have to be maintained when the frames cross a bridge to another LAN.

The FDDI SMT standard allows for the specification of seven priority thresholds: T_Pri0 and T_Pri1 through T_Pri6. These can be called priority levels 0 through 6. Priority 0 is the lowest priority, while priority 7 is the highest priority. No threshold is required for the highest priority since it uses TTRT as the threshold. The procedure for setting these priority thresholds correctly is discussed next.

Equation (23.1) shows that with a ring utilization U, the average token rotation time is $D/(1-U)$. If T_Pri for a particular priority is set at a value greater than $D/(1-U)$, the throughput for that priority will drop to *almost* zero at this utilization. (It may not be totally zero since some token rotation times may be smaller than the average, allowing some lower priority frames to get through.)

Given desired *load* thresholds for various priorities, the T_Pri's can be easily set using this observation. Example 23.3 illustrates this.

Example 23.3 Consider a ring with a latency of 150 μs. Suppose four priorities are required such that priority 0 (lowest priority) traffic should not use the ring if the utilization is more than 92.5%. Similarly, priorities 1 and 2 are required to cease using the ring at 95% and 97.5%, respectively.

The average token rotation time at 92.5% utilization is:

$$C = \frac{D}{1-U} = \frac{0.150}{1-0.925} = 2 \text{ ms}$$

Thus, setting T_Pri0 at 2 ms will ensure that priority 0 frames will not generally be transmitted at this utilization.

The average token rotation time at 95% utilization is:

$$C = \frac{D}{1-U} = \frac{0.150}{1-0.95} = 3 \text{ ms}$$

Thus, T_Pri1 should be set at 3 ms.

Similarly, T_Pri2 can be computed. Its value is 6 ms. □

Figure 23.11 shows a throughput versus load curve for the system of Example 23.3. Throughputs for individual priorities as well as for the total system are shown. All four priorities are assumed to have an equal offered load, which is increased slowly from 0 to 100 Mbps (for a total of 0 to 400 Mbps). Priority 0 is limited when the total throughput is close to 92.5 Mbps. Priority 1 is limited when the total throughput is 95 Mbps, and so on.

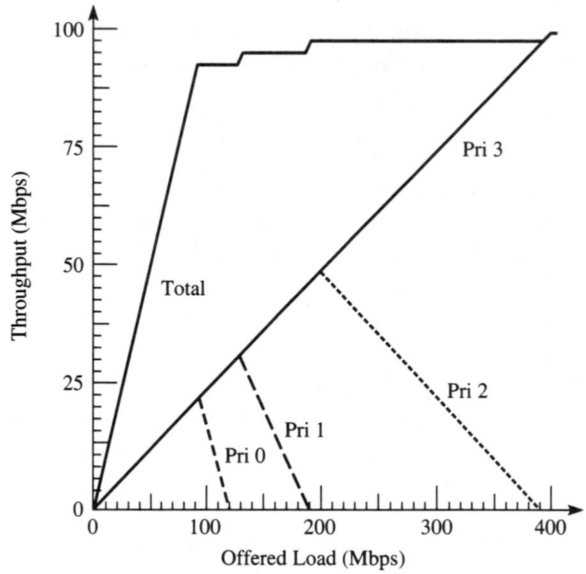

Figure 23.11 Throughput as a function of offerred load.

23.7 Thirteen Known Properties of the FDDI Priority Mechanism

The FDDI priority mechanism is quite different from the priority mechanism used in other systems. The following is a list of known facts about FDDI priorities:

1. *The priority in FDDI has only a local significance.* This means that if there are two frames of different priorities at a station, the higher priority frame will be transmitted first. However, if the two frames are at different stations, the lower priority frame may be transmitted before the higher priority frame depending on the locations of the stations.
2. *The priority thresholds T_Pri's do not depend on the TTRT.* Thus, if in Example 23.6, the TTRT is increased from 9 to 160 ms, T_Pri0 through T_Pri2 still remain at 2, 3, and 6 ms.
3. *The priority thresholds T_Pri's depend on the ring latency.* For example, suppose you want to have two priorities such that lower priority traffic is blocked if the load is more than 50%. In this case, you should set T_Pri0 at two times the ring latency.
4. *The priority thresholds should be recomputed after every reconfiguration.* Since ring latency may be different after each reconfiguration, T_Pri's cannot be set ahead of time. The ring latency must be measured periodically and T_Pri's set accordingly.
5. *To avoid starvation the low-priority threshold T_Pri0 should be kept above a certain minimum.* This minimum is given by Equation (22.6). That is,

$$\text{T\_Pri0} \geq \frac{D + \text{Token\_Time} + F\_Max + 2 \times \text{Void\_Fr}}{1 - \alpha}$$

   Here, α is the fraction of bandwidth that has been allocated for synchronous transmissions.
6. *A wide separation of priority thresholds is not sufficient.* One common mistake in setting T_Pri's is to set them arbitrarily. For example, on a ring with TTRT of 100 ms, one may choose to have four priorities with T_Pri0 through T_Pri2 at 25, 50, and 75 ms, respectively. This is justified on the grounds that T_Pri's are widely separated. Now suppose that it is a small ring with a ring latency of 100 μs. In this case, the lowest priority traffic will continue using the ring all the way up to a load of 99.6%! The four priorities will hardly ever see any difference in service.
7. *Setting a low-load threshold for the lower priority also limits the maximum throughput that can be achieved if there is no higher priority traffic.* For example, if in a two-priority system T_Pri0 is set to cut off priority 0 traffic at 50% load, then the low-priority traffic will not be able to use the ring beyond 50% load, even if there is no higher priority traffic.
8. *The priority threshold for one priority determines the average delay for the next higher priority after cutoff.* That is, T_Pri$n$ determines the average delay for the $(n + 1)$th priority traffic after the nth priority is cut off. As the load is increased, the nth priority is cut off when the average token rotation time is T_Pri$n$. At this point, the remaining priorities continue to receive service and experience an average delay of approximately T_Pri$n$/2 (half the average token rotation time). This is shown in Figure 23.12 for the four-priority system of Example 23.3. Notice that the delays following the limiting of priorities 0, 1, and 2 are 1.0, 1.3, and 2.6 ms, respectively.
9. *At loads below the limiting values, all priorities get the same delay.* There is no delay prioritization. This can be seen from Figure 23.12. This is especially true if the variance of the token rotation time is small. This happens on large rings, that is, on rings where the ring latency is large compared to the frame size. In this case, the number of frames transmitted on each token rotation is large and, consequently, the variance in TRT is small. Figure 23.13 shows the

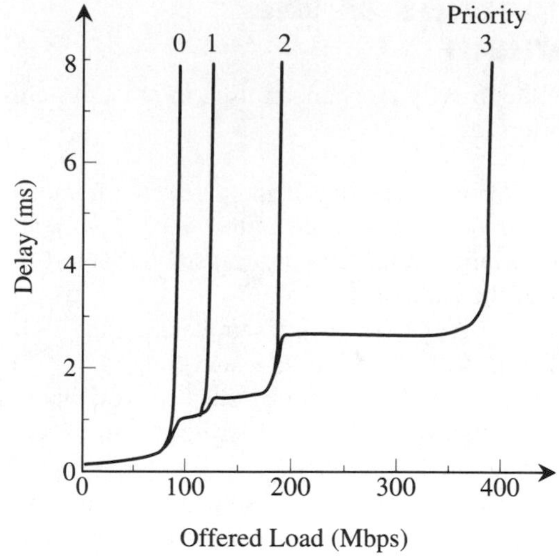

Figure 23.12 Average delay as a function of load for various priorities.

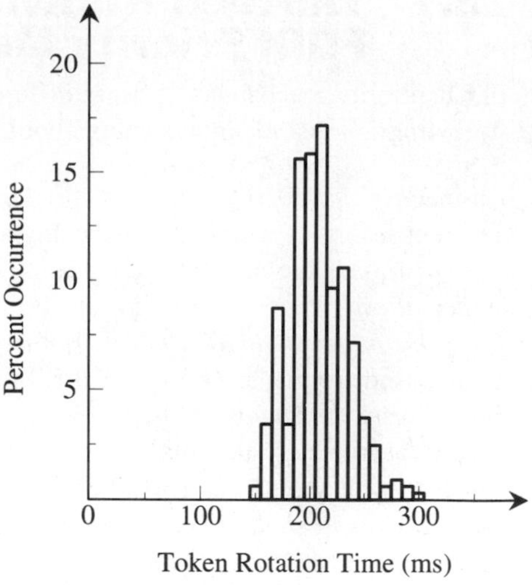

Figure 23.13 Histogram of token rotation times at 50 Mbps.

histogram of token rotation time at 50 Mbps throughput for the system of Example 23.3 with an average frame size of 11 μs.

10. *Delay prioritization is observed only on small rings, that is, on rings with latency comparable to or smaller than frame size*. In this case, the number of frames transmitted per rotation is small and the variance in TRT is large even at low to medium throughput. On such rings, all priorities get service on rotations with small TRT. On rotations with large TRT, only higher priorities get

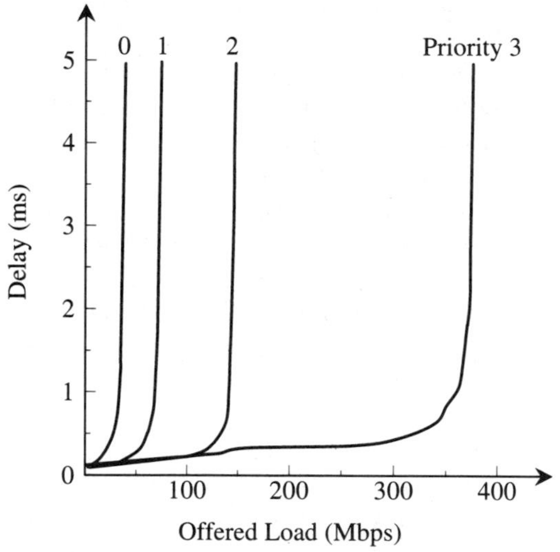

Figure 23.14 Delay prioritization.

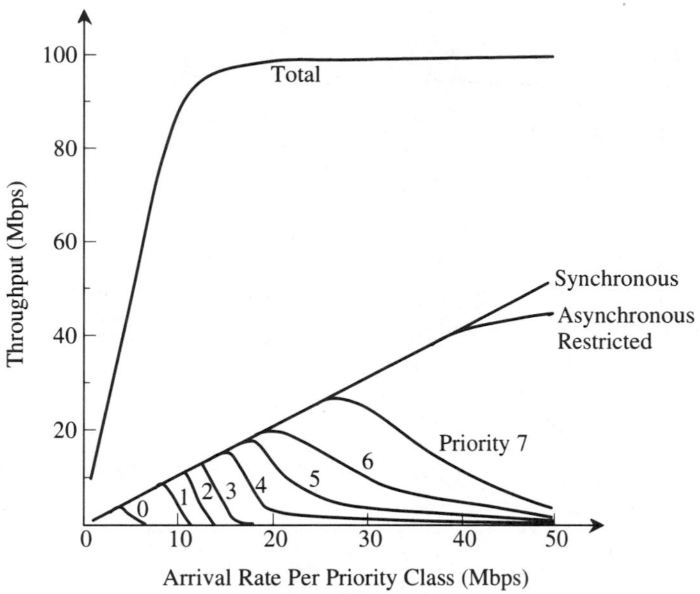

Figure 23.15 Station throughput versus load curve for an eight-priority system.

service. Thus, the average delay for higher priorities is lower. This is shown in Figure 23.14 for a ring with a ring latency of 15 μs, packet length of 1000 bytes, and T_Pri0 through T_Pri3 of 200, 250, 450, and 2000 μs, respectively. At 75 Mbps throughput, the average TRT is 60 μs. However, the variance is large.

11. *Lower priority traffic may continue to be transmitted even when higher priority traffic is being constrained.* Figure 23.15 shows throughput versus load curve for an eight-priority system with the T_Pri's set at 1.5, 6.2, 14, 25, 39, 56.2, 76.5, and 100 ms. The ring latency is 1.0236 ms. This curve was obtained from a simulation. Notice that in this case at high load, some priority 6 frames continue to be transmitted even though priority 7 queues become saturated and are limited.
12. *The total throughput for a priority level depends on the number of stations transmitting at that priority.* Figure 23.16 shows the throughput versus load curve for a system similar to that of Figure 23.15 except that there are now four priority 6 stations while there is only one station transmitting at other priorities. When all stations continuously have frames to transmit, the throughput per station for priority 6 is less than that for priority 7 but the total throughput for priority 6 is more than that for priority 7. In general, the number of stations transmitting frames of a given class affects the total throughput for that class.
13. *All stations operating at the same priority do not always receive the same throughput.* Figure 23.17 shows the average delay for a 10-km ring with 10 stations. One of these stations transmits at priority 7 while the other nine transmit at priority 6. The arrival rates at all priority 6 stations are equal. As the load at the priority 7 station is increased, the throughput of priority 6 stations decreases and the delays become large. However, not all priority 6 stations receive

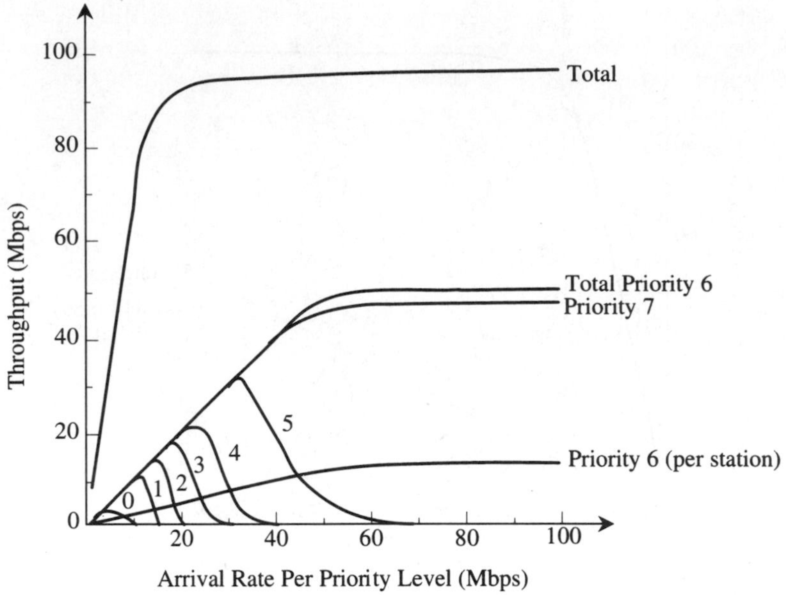

Figure 23.16 Throughput versus load curve for a network with four priority 6 stations.

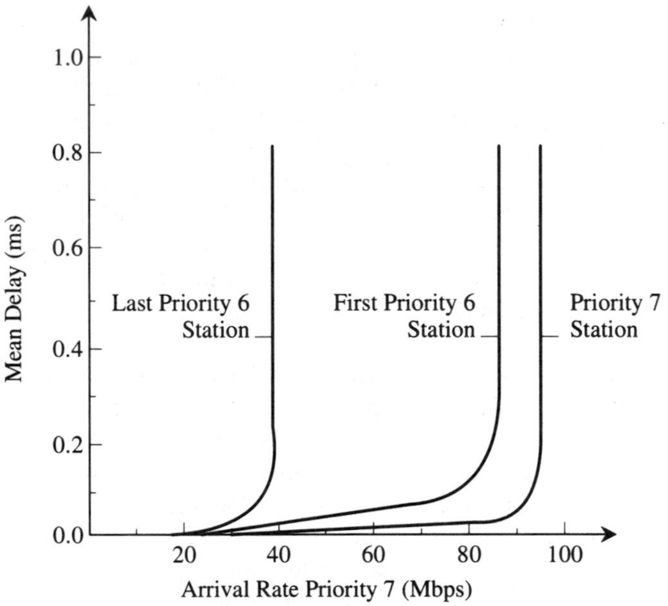

Figure 23.17 Unfairness caused by station location. Stations downstream from high-priority stations get better service.

the same service. The first priority 6 station downstream from the priority 7 station continues to receive usable tokens while others become blocked. In this sense, the service is location sensitive. Given a choice, you should connect your station immediately downstream from your boss's (higher priority) station.

Box 23.3 summarizes this discussion. Again the key point to remember is that the ring latency is the key to setting priority thresholds. Since the ring latency is much much smaller than TTRT, the priority thresholds should be close to ring latency and not TTRT.

Box 23.3 Thirteen Known Properties of the FDDI Priority Mechanism

1. The priority in FDDI has only a local significance.
2. The priority thresholds do not depend on the TTRT.
3. The priority thresholds depend on the ring latency.
4. The priority thresholds should be recomputed after every reconfiguration.
5. To avoid starvation, the low-priority threshold T_Pri0 should be kept above a certain minimum.
6. A wide separation of priority thresholds T_Pri's is not sufficient.
7. Setting a low-load threshold for the lower priority also limits the maximum throughput that can be achieved if there is no higher priority traffic.
8. The priority threshold for one priority determines the average delay for the next higher priority after cutoff.
9. At loads below the limiting values, all priorities get the same delay.
10. Delay prioritization is observed only on small rings, that is, on rings with latency comparable to or smaller than frame size.
11. Lower priority traffic may continue to be transmitted even when higher priority traffic is being constrained.
12. The total throughput for a priority level depends on the number of stations transmitting at that priority.
13. All stations operating at the same priority do not always receive the same throughput.

23.8 How Many Priority Levels?

Although FDDI allows eight priority levels, a very small number such as two priorities are sufficient for most applications. Higher levels of granularity introduce unnecessary complexity.

Having a priority is not very useful if the resource is easy to get even without the priority. In FDDI, the queue lengths of packets waiting for transmission remain small even at high loads. In Chapter 24, in Example 24.2, we show that the average queue length for a 20-station ring at 60% load is approximately 0.296. Thus, a station receives three tokens for each frame transmitted. This happens even at loads as high as 95%. Most frames find the queue empty when they arrive. Having a priority when you are the only one in the queue is not much of an advantage!

Priorities are useful only if a resource is a bottleneck. At this time in the life cycle of FDDI, the software implementations of higher layer protocols are more likely to be the bottleneck. The time to travel FDDI links is expected to be a small part of the total time along the path from the source to the destination. Thus, priority at FDDI may not be helpful. If priorities are implemented, they should be assigned as soon as the frame is generated in the application layer.

For priorities to be effective the following four conditions must occur simultaneously:

1. High load
2. Short packets
3. Nonexhaustive service
4. Small number of stations on the network.

These conditions become obvious from Equation (24.4) in Chapter 24 for average queue length. The equation shows that in the absence of any one of these conditions the queue length is small. It is easy to see why this is so even without the formula. The first condition is obvious. If the load is low, there are no queues and everyone gets the same service. The second condition ensures that there are many frames contending for the resource. With larger frames, the queue lengths for the same load are smaller and there is little contention. The third condition is required since all frames get transmitted if the service is exhaustive and the difference between the delays of various frames is minuscule compared to the token rotation times. For FDDI this condition occurs only at very high loads. Finally, if the number of stations is large, the total number of waiting frames is divided among many stations and the average queue length per station becomes small.

23.9 Summary

The token rotation time is a good indicator of load on the network. The average TRT is related to the ring latency and utilization as follows:

$$\text{Average TRT} = \frac{\text{Ring latency}}{1 - \text{Utilization}}$$

This formula can be used to monitor ring utilization.

Boxes 23.1 and 23.2 summarize the behavior of TRT and the response time. These boxes show that the key parameter that affects performance at high load is TTRT. However, at low load, TTRT has little effect and ring latency becomes the key parameter. Increasing the ring latency increases the token rotation time, response time, transfer time, and station queues at any given level of load. It also decreases efficiency at high load. It is, therefore, best to organize a campus network as several small FDDI rings interconnected via bridges.

FDDI provides a fair service to all stations particularly if there is only one priority level, all stations have similar loads, and the synchronous bandwidth is properly allocated. If any one of these three conditions is not satisfied, it may be possible for some stations to get better service than others.

The FDDI priority mechanism is very different from that on other networks. Its key properties are summarized in Box 23.3. The number of priorities should be as small as possible. The priority thresholds depend on the ring latency (and not on TTRT). Therefore, a fixed threshold will not work for all configurations. The threshold should be recomputed and set after each ring configuration.

23.10 Further Reading

The example of unfairness due to unequal frame sizes is from Johnson (1988). Figures 23.8 and 23.9 are from LaMaire (1991b). Figures 23.1 and 23.3 are based on the data from Martini and Meuser (1990).

Karvelas and Leon-Garcia (1987) compare the performance of the FDDI ring with that of a multiple-priority cycle ring for voice and data traffic. They show an example of unfairness caused by the FDDI protocol if the synchronous bandwidth is overcommitted. Variation of response time is studied in Welzel (1989, 1990).

Dykeman and Bux (1987, 1988) have studied the behavior of the FDDI priority scheme in detail. An algorithm to compute the throughput versus load curve for multiple-priority operation is given in Dykeman and Bux (1988). Data for Figures 23.15, 23.16, and 23.17 came from these papers.

Watson and Ward (1991, 1994) present excellent studies of the FDDI priority mechanism. Figures 23.12, 23.13, and 23.14 are based on their data. Peden and Weaver (1988a, 1988b) discuss the conditions under which having priorities in FDDI is useful. See Schill and Zieher (1987), Goyal and Dias (1987), and Grow (1989) for discussion of FDDI priority.

23.11 Self-Test Exercises

Note: Some exercises have multiple correct answers. See Appendix D for answers.

23.1 What is the average token rotation time at 50% utilization on a ring with a ring latency of 1 ms and target token rotation time of 8 ms?

a. 0.5 ms
b. 1 ms
c. 2 ms
d. 8 ms

23.2 On a ring with latency of 1 ms, the token was seen at a station 1000 times during a 5-second interval. What is the utilization of the ring?

a. 20%
b. 80%
c. Insufficient information

23.3 What is the maximum duration for five successive token rotations on a ring with a TTRT of 10 ms?

a. 50 ms
b. 60 ms
c. 100 ms

23.4 The average utilization on an FDDI ring is 10%. Which of the following is likely to decrease the response time by a factor of 2?:

a. Decreasing the ring latency by a factor of 2
b. Decreasing the target token rotation time by a factor of 2
c. Increasing the target token rotation time by a factor of 2

23.5 The T_Pri0 and TTRT for an FDDI ring with a latency of 1 ms are set at 50 ms and 100 ms, respectively. At approximately what load would the priority 0 traffic be prevented from using the ring?

a. 2%
b. 50%
c. 98%

CHAPTER **24**

Analytical Models, FDDI-II, and Adapter Performance Issues

The previous two chapters on FDDI performance covered the operation under heavy load and normal load. In this chapter, we discuss analytical models for response time and currently known results about FDDI-II performance, and we also describe the issues involved in the design of FDDI adapters.

Analytical models are helpful in predicting the response time for a given network load. You can use a simple spreadsheet program to study the effect of varying different parameters on the performance.

The issue of monitoring ring utilization may be of interest to network managers. This is discussed in Section 24.2.

FDDI-II performance is similar to that of FDDI. A comparison of FDDI-II with its main competitor, the IEEE 802.6 distributed-queue dual-bus (DQDB) protocol, is presented in Section 24.3.

Although FDDI adapter performance issues would be of interest to adapter designers, even buyers and users will find it interesting to know which features of the design improve performance and why.

24.1 Analytical Models

One problem in developing an exact analytical model of FDDI is that most analytical modeling methods assume memoryless operation of the system. This assumption does not apply to FDDI since successive token rotation times (TRTs) are correlated. If the token takes a long time to complete a cycle, the next cycle will be short.

The approximate models described in this section are modifications of those used for cyclic servers with exhaustive service. Queueing theory results are used. Readers not interested in mathematical details can safely skip and go to the summary in Box 24.1 and read Example 24.1, which illustrates the method.

In FDDI, frames wait in transmit queues at stations until they are served by the arrival of a usable token. Such a queueing system is called a **cyclic queue** since the server (token) goes from one queue to the next in a circular manner as shown in Figure 24.1. Such cyclic queues have been

Box 24.1 Approximate Analytical Model for FDDI

1. Inputs:
   a. Ring Configuration Parameters:
      n = Number of stations on the ring
      T = Target token rotation time in seconds
      D = Ring latency in seconds
      B = Ring bandwidth in code bits/second = 125×10^6 bps
   b. Traffic Characteristics:
      F = Average frame size in code bits
      I = Average interarrival time for frames
      σ_F = Standard deviation of frame size
2. Output Symbols:
   λ = Arrival rate in frames per μs = $1/I$
   U = Traffic intensity = ring utilization
   $\bar{h}$ = Frame transmission time
   $\ddot{h}$ = Second moment of frame transmission time
   R = Average response time
   σ_w = Standard deviation of propagation delay between stations
3. Exhaustive Service:

$$\lambda = \frac{1}{I}$$

$$\bar{h} = F/B$$

$$\ddot{h} = \frac{F^2 + \sigma_F^2}{B^2}$$

$$U = \lambda\bar{h}$$

$$R_{\text{exhaustive}} = \bar{h} + \frac{\lambda\ddot{h}}{2(1-U)} + \frac{D(1-U/n)}{2(1-U)}$$

4. FDDI Model I:

$$R_{\text{FDDI}} = \bar{h} + \frac{\lambda\ddot{h}}{2(1-U)} + \frac{1-\frac{U}{n}-\frac{D}{T}}{1-U-\frac{D}{T}}$$

5. FDDI Model II:

$$U_{\max} = \frac{n(T-D)}{nT+D}$$

$$R_{\text{FDDI}} = \frac{1-U}{1-U/U_{\max}} R_{\text{exhaustive}}$$

6. Transfer Delay:

$$E[\text{Transfer delay}] = R_{\text{FDDI}} + \frac{D}{2}$$

7. Average queue length at stations:

$$Q_i = \frac{U}{n\bar{h}} R_{\text{FDDI}}$$

   The frame being transmitted, if any, is included in the queue length.
8. Assumptions:
   a. The frame arrivals follow a Poisson process. That is, the interarrival times are exponentially distributed. (Bursty arrivals do not satisfy this assumption.)
   b. Traffic at all stations has the same statistical pattern.
   c. All interstation distances are the same. If the distances are not equal, an additional $n\sigma_w^2/(2D)$ delay should be added to the response time. Here σ_w^2 is the variance of the interstation delay. Generally this term is small and can be safely ignored.

extensively studied in the queueing literature. It is possible to compute the waiting time for the frames to receive service under certain simplifying assumptions. One such assumption relates to the duration of service. One possibility is that the server services all frames of a queue and then moves to the next queue. This is called **exhaustive service**. Another possibility is that the server services a maximum of k frames from each queue before moving to the next queue. Other frames wait for the next cycle. This is called **limited-k service**. This type of model is applicable to IEEE 802.5/token ring networks since the amount of time each station can transmit is fixed.

Strictly speaking, FDDI's timed token service is neither exhaustive nor limited. But in practice it is close to an exhaustive service unless the load is high or the TTRT is low. In most cases, the stations are able to transmit all their frames on the first token arrival. Therefore, the models for exhaustive service can be used to determine approximately the waiting time for frames.

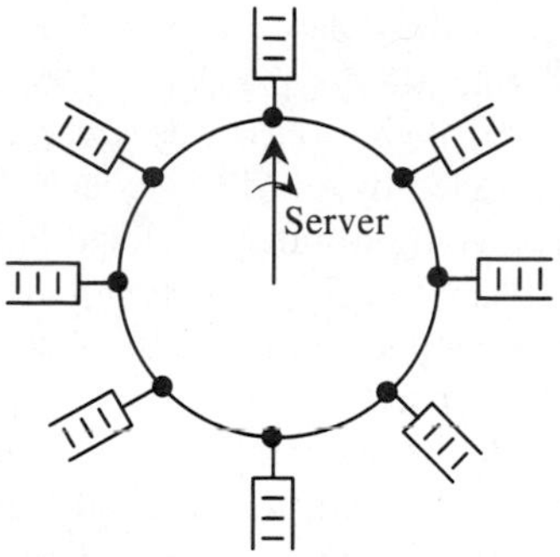

Figure 24.1 A cyclic queueing system.

For a cyclic server with exhaustive service, if all stations have similar loads (symmetric traffic pattern), the average response time $R_{\text{exhaustive}}$ is given by:

$$R_{\text{exhaustive}} = \bar{h} + \frac{\lambda\ddot{h}}{2(1-U)} + \frac{\ddot{w}}{2\bar{w}} + \frac{(n-1)\bar{w}}{2(1-U)} \tag{24.1}$$

where

n = Number of active stations
$\bar{w}$ = Mean walk time = Time for the token to travel from one station to next
$\ddot{w}$ = Second moment of the walk time
D = Ring latency = $n\bar{w}$
λ = Ring throughput in frames per unit of time
$\bar{h}$ = Mean frame transmission time
$\ddot{h}$ = Second moment of frame transmission time
U = Traffic intensity = $\frac{\text{Total load in bps}}{\text{Bandwidth in bps}} = \lambda\bar{h}$

The frame transmission time $\bar{h}$ can be calculated by dividing the frame length F (in code bits) by the media bandwidth B in code bits per second (125×10^6 bps):

$$\bar{h} = \frac{F}{B}$$

If x is a random variable, then the expected value of x^2 or $E[x^2]$ is called its *second moment*. For frame transmission time, the second moment is given by

$$\ddot{h} = \bar{h}^2 + \text{Variance of frame transmission time}$$

If all frames are of the same size, the variance of the frame transmission time is zero and

$$\ddot{h} = \bar{h}^2$$

If the walk times between stations are constant and are equal to D/n, Equation (24.1) simplifies to:

$$R_{\text{exhaustive}} = \bar{h} + \frac{\lambda\ddot{h}}{2(1-U)} + \frac{D}{2n} + \frac{n-1}{2n(1-U)}D \tag{24.2}$$

$$= \bar{h} + \frac{\lambda\ddot{h}}{2(1-U)} + \frac{1-U/n}{2(1-U)}D \tag{24.3}$$

The first term in Equation (24.2) gives the delay that would be incurred if there was no load (and hence no queueing) and the token was always present at the station. The second term gives the queueing delay that would be incurred if the token was always present at the station. This would happen in a ring with one station modeled by an M/G/1 queue. The third and fourth terms give the additional delay caused by the token going to other stations. In particular, the third term gives the time to complete the current walk (if any) to the next station and the fourth term covers time spent in all token rotations required before coming to service the frame.

This result assumes that the interarrival times of successive frames at stations follow a **Poisson process**, which essentially means that the interarrival times are exponentially distributed. Bursty arrivals do not satisfy this assumption. Second, traffic at all stations is assumed to have the same statistical pattern. Finally, all interstation distances are assumed to be the same. If the distances are not equal, an additional $n\sigma_w^2/(2D)$ delay should be added to the response time. Here σ_w^2 is the variance of the interstation delay. Generally this term is small and can be safely ignored.

The exhaustive service gives a lower response time than limited-k service.

$$R_{\text{exhaustive}} \leq R_{\text{limited}}$$

This is because the server's walk time to go around the queues is an overhead that affects the response time. All limitations cause the server to make more rounds for the same total amount of work. Walk times for these additional rounds increase the response time.

In FDDI, the service is not exhaustive, particularly at heavy loads. In such cases, the token may have to make several cycles to empty all queues. If the service were exhaustive, the token would make just one round. Thus, the response time on FDDI is more than that predicted by Equation (24.2).

Two different ways have been suggested to obtain a closer approximation for FDDI. The first method requires adjusting the effect of ring latency. Section 22.3 showed that with n stations having a continuous supply of data, the token makes $n + 1$ cycles before returning to a station and the load is

$$U(n) = \frac{n(T - D)}{nT + D}$$

These $n + 1$ rotations take $nT + D$ time, of which only $n(T - D)$ is used and $(n + 1)D$ is lost. In other words, the service overhead is $(n + 1)D$. If the service were exhaustive, the same amount of work would have been done in just one cycle with an overhead of D. The increased overhead in FDDI results in increased response time. Substituting $(n_{\text{eff}} + 1)D$ in place of D in Equation (24.2) gives a good estimate of FDDI response time. Here, n_{eff} is the effective number of active stations computed as follows:

$$U = \frac{n_{\text{eff}}(T - D)}{n_{\text{eff}}T + D}$$

or

$$n_{\text{eff}} = \frac{DU}{T(1 - U) - D}$$

Substituting $(n_{\text{eff}} + 1)D$ in place of D in the fourth term of Equation (24.2), we get:

$$R_{\text{FDDI}} = \bar{h} + \frac{\lambda \ddot{h}}{2(1-U)} + \frac{D}{2n} + \frac{n-1}{2n(1-U)}(n_{\text{eff}}+1)D$$

$$= \bar{h} + \frac{\lambda \ddot{h}}{2(1-U)} + \frac{1-\frac{U}{n}-\frac{D}{T}}{1-U-\frac{D}{T}}$$

This is Model I. Note that if TTRT is infinite ($D/T \to 0$), the formula becomes identical to that for the exhaustive service. This is not surprising since with very large TTRT all stations get exhaustive service.

Another alternative is to scale the exhaustive service response time by a factor:

$$R_{\text{FDDI}} = \frac{1-U}{1-U/U_{\max}} R_{\text{exhaustive}}$$

This is Model II. Here, $U_{\max}$ is the maximum possible utilization (or efficiency, in this case) for the given ring latency and TTRT. From Section 22.3 we know that:

$$U_{\max} = \frac{n(T-D)}{nT+D}$$

Notice that at low load ($U \approx 0$), the response time for FDDI is the same as that given by the exhaustive service time, and at saturation ($U \geq U_{\max}$) the FDDI response time approaches infinity.

The two models presented in this section are summarized in Box 24.1 and are illustrated by Example 24.1.

Example 24.1 Consider a 30-km FDDI ring with 20 stations. The station delays are 1 μs per station. The frame sizes were observed to follow a bimodal distribution with 80% at 128 bytes and 20% at 1500 bytes. Find the average response time at 60% load.

Since the speed of light is 5 μs/km, the ring latency is:

$$D = 30 \text{ km} \times 5 \ \mu\text{s/km} + 20 \text{ stations} \times 1 \ \mu\text{s/station} = 170 \ \mu\text{s}$$

The transmission time for small frames is:

$$h_{\text{small}} = \frac{128 \times 10}{125 \times 10^6} = 10.24 \ \mu\text{s}$$

For large frames:

$$h_{\text{large}} = \frac{1500 \times 10}{125 \times 10^6} = 120 \ \mu\text{s}$$

The mean frame transmission time is:

$$\bar{h} = 0.8 \times 10.24 + 0.2 \times 120 = 32.192 \ \mu\text{s}$$

The second moment of frame transmission time is:

$$\ddot{h} = 0.8 \times 10.24^2 + 0.2 \times 120^2 = 2963.89 \ \mu\text{s}^2$$

The frame arrival rate is:

$$\lambda = \frac{U}{\bar{h}} = \frac{0.6}{32.192} = 0.0186 \ \text{frames}/\mu\text{s}$$

The response time for exhaustive service is:

$$\begin{aligned} R_{\text{exhaustive}} &= \bar{h} + \frac{\lambda \ddot{h}}{2(1-U)} + \frac{D(1-U/n)}{2(1-U)} \\ &= 32.192 + \frac{0.0186 \times 2963.89}{2(1-0.6)} + \frac{170(1-0.6/20)}{2(1-0.6)} \\ &= 32.19 + 69.05 + 206.13 \\ &= 307.37\ \mu\text{s} \end{aligned}$$

The response time for FDDI using Model I is:

$$\begin{aligned} R_{\text{FDDI}} &= \bar{h} + \frac{\lambda \ddot{h}}{2(1-U)} \frac{1 - \frac{U}{n} - \frac{D}{T}}{1 - U - \frac{D}{T}} \\ &= 32.192 + \frac{0.0186 \times 2963.89}{2(1-0.6)} \frac{1 - \frac{0.6}{20} - \frac{170}{8000}}{1 - 0.6 - \frac{170}{8000}} \\ &= 32.19 + 69.05 + 212.92 \\ &= 314.16\ \mu\text{s} \end{aligned}$$

With Model II, the maximum utilization is:

$$U_{\max} = \frac{20(8000 - 170)}{20 \times 8000 + 170} = 0.9777$$

The FDDI response time is:

$$\begin{aligned} R_{\text{FDDI}} &= \frac{1-U}{1-U/U_{\max}} R_{\text{exhaustive}} \\ &= \frac{1-0.6}{1-0.6/0.9777} 307.37 \\ &= 1.0354 \times 307.37 \\ &= 318.25\ \mu\text{s} \end{aligned}$$

Rounding off the results of the two models to two digits, the FDDI response time is seen to be approximately 310 to 320 μs. □

A comparison of these approximations to simulation results indicates that the computed response times are close to those obtained by simulation by a factor of 2. That is, the predicted response times may be as much as twice or half that obtained by simulation. The exhaustive service and the two approximations give results close to each other and simulations for utilizations up to 80% of the maximum.

Neither method is recommended for use at very high loads. It is fruitless to try to predict response time near saturation since in that region a slight deviation from the assumptions (for example, Poisson arrival or frame size distribution) will cause a significant change in the response time. Thus, in that region it is better to use access delay as discussed earlier in Section 22.2.

The main use of these analytical models is for getting an idea of the range of response times and for predicting the effect of various system and workload parameters.

The formulas given so far are for response time. Transfer delay, which is defined as the time between arrival of the last bit of the frame at the source and the reception of the last bit at the destination, is related to the response time as follows (see Figure 22.3):

Transfer delay = Response time + Propagation delay between source and destination

Since response time and propagation delay are independent random variables, the average transfer delay is given by:

$$E[\text{Transfer delay}] = E[\text{Response time}] + E[\text{Propagation delay}]$$

If the traffic is uniformly distributed among all source-destination pairs, the average propagation delay is equal to half the ring latency. Therefore,

$$E[\text{Transfer delay}] = R + \frac{D}{2}$$

Given throughput and response time for any system, the average queue length can be calculated using the so-called Little's law [see Jain (1991) for details]:

Average queue length = Average throughput $\times$ Average response time

Using Q_i to denote the average queue length at the ith station, we have:

$$Q_i = \lambda_i R_i$$

For symmetric traffic ($R_i = R_{\text{FDDI}}$ for all i):

$$Q_i = \frac{\lambda}{n} R_{\text{FDDI}} = \frac{U}{n\bar{h}} R_{\text{FDDI}} \qquad (24.4)$$

The queue length, by definition, includes the frame that is being transmitted in addition to those waiting for transmission.

Example 24.2 For the system of Example 24.1, the average queue length at 60% utilization is:

$$\begin{aligned} Q_i &= \frac{U}{n\bar{h}} R_{\text{FDDI}} \\ &= \frac{0.6}{20 \times 32.192} 318.25 \\ &= 0.296 \end{aligned}$$

The average queue length of 0.296 means that the queues are generally empty. The frames are serviced in the same rotation in which they arrive. □

24.2 Utilization Monitoring

Network managers like to monitor the operation of the ring. They are interested in finding out the load level on their network. As explained earlier (see Sidebar on Throughput, Load, and Utilization in Chapter 22), load is measured by the input to the system. Generally, it cannot be measured easily. Most monitoring tools, therefore, give token utilization instead, which is easy to measure and is a good indicator of load if the system is not saturated.

Token utilization over any specified interval can be computed using Equation (23.1). All you need is to count tokens. Many FDDI MAC chips maintain a token count. By sampling this count at the beginning and end of the monitoring interval, you can compute the average token rotation time and the token utilization.

Notice that this procedure for computing token utilization is valid only if the ring latency is constant. Every time the ring latency changes, due to the change in the ring configuration, the token count and the total time should be zeroed.

Long-term token utilization across several ring reconfigurations can be measured by keeping a cumulative "busy time" and "total time" in a management station. On a configuration change (or at other suitable interval), the cumulative times are updated as follows:

$$\begin{aligned}
\tau &= \text{Duration of the last monitoring interval}\\
m &= \text{Increase in token count during } \tau\\
D &= \text{Ring latency during } \tau\\
\text{Cumulative total time} &= \text{Cumulative total time} + \tau\\
\text{Cumulative idle time} &= \text{Cumulative idle time} + mD\\
\text{Cumulative busy time} &= \text{Cumulative busy time} + (\tau - mD)\\
\text{Cumulative utilization} &= \frac{\text{Cumulative busy time}}{\text{Cumulative total time}}
\end{aligned}$$

The following example illustrates this.

Example 24.3 A ring network was monitored from 10:00 A.M. to 11:00 A.M. During this interval, the ring configuration change was detected at 10:10, 10:30, and 10:45. The token counter at a management station was initialized at 10:00 A.M. and at each configuration change. The token counter values just before the configuration change and at 11:00 A.M. were 54, 30, 36, and 57 million, respectively. The ring latency during the four subintervals was measured to be 10, 30, 20, and 15 μs, respectively. What is the utilization of the ring during this hour?

The computation is shown in Table 24.1. For each of the four intervals, the idle time is computed as the product of the token count and the ring latency. The busy time is then obtained by subtracting the busy time from the total time. The utilization is the ratio of the busy time to total time. The overall utilization is obtained from the sums of the busy times and total times. The ring utilization during the hour was 16.25%. □

24.3 FDDI-II Performance

Very little has been published on the performance of FDDI-II. The performance of asynchronous traffic is expected to be similar to that for FDDI except that the available bandwidth has to be reduced by the amount reserved for isochronous traffic. Thus, if 2 of the 16 wideband

Table 24.1 Computation of Long-Term Utilization

Interval	Total Time s	Token Rotations	Ring Latency μs	Idle Time s	Busy Time s	Utilization
10:00–10:10	600	54,000,000	10	540	60	0.1000
10:10–10:30	1,200	30,000,000	30	900	300	0.2500
10:30–10:45	900	36,000,000	20	720	180	0.2000
10:45–11:00	900	57,000,000	15	855	45	0.0500
Total	3,600			3,015	585	0.1625

channels (WBCs) are allocated for isochronous traffic, the bandwidth available for packet switching is 86.784 Mbps (14 WBCs of 6.144 Mbps each plus a dedicated packet switching bandwidth of 0.768 Mbps). The formulas for calculating ring utilizations should use 86.784 Mbps in place of 100 Mbps.

The exact location of isochronous channels in the cycle has a slight effect on the response times seen by the packet channel. The results should therefore be considered approximate.

The key competition to FDDI-II is the IEEE 802.6/DQDB protocol. DQDB uses slots, some of which are reserved and others can be captured on demand using certain rules. Due to the availability of slots on demand, *the delays seen on IEEE 802.6 are lower than those on FDDI-II at low load.* However, *at high load the FDDI-II protocol has been shown to provide shorter delays than IEEE 802.6.* Figure 24.2 shows a sample transfer time versus load graph for the two schemes. Notice that a logarithmic scale is used for the transfer time and that at heavy load the delays on FDDI-II are several orders of magnitude smaller than those on IEEE 802.6. The point at which the two delay curves cross over depends on many factors such as the ring latency, frame size distribution, arrival patterns, etc.

FDDI-II is also fair in that all stations with the same load get the same throughput. IEEE 802.6 is known to have a fairness problem in that the station throughput depends on the station location. A probabilistic slot capture scheme has been designed to partially overcome this problem.

Schodl and Tangemann (1990) compare the performance of ATM traffic on FDDI-I synchronous mode, FDDI-II isochronous mode, and DQDB. The ATM traffic consisting of 69-byte frames (ATM cells encapsulated in FDDI frames) was sent to and from an ATM gateway at 25 Mbps each way. The remaining bandwidth was used by normal data traffic, which consisted of 1-kB frames. Figure 24.3 shows the average transfer times for the ATM cells. Six different curves are shown: two for FDDI-I synchronous class with TTRT at 5 and 10 ms, two for FDDI-II with 5 and 9 WBCs allocated for the ATM traffic, and two for DQDB with and without priority. DQDB with priority offered the lowest transfer times but the FDDI-II performance was very close. FDDI-I synchronous service transfer

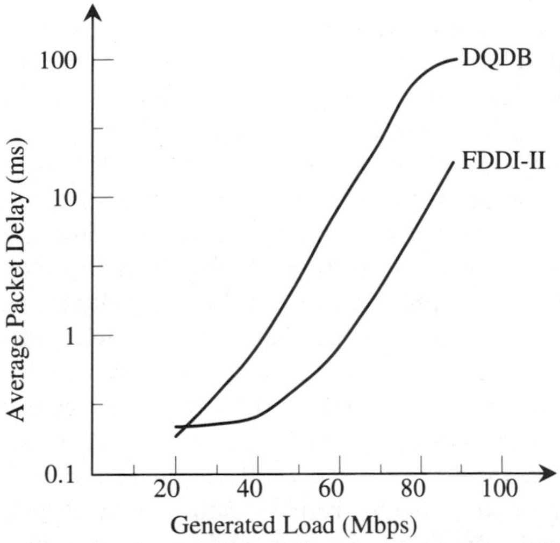

Figure 24.2 Transfer time as a function of load.

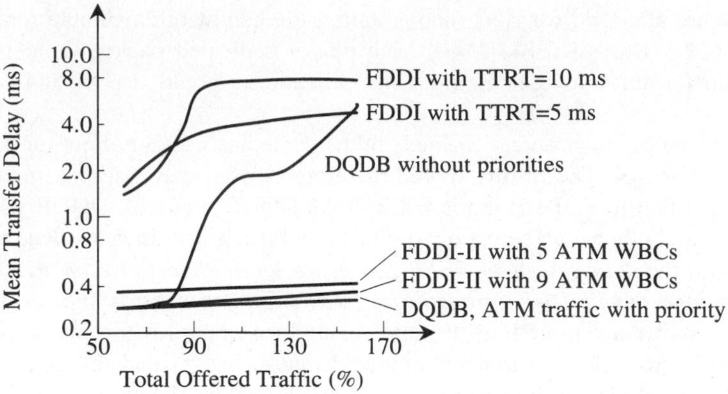

Figure 24.3 Transfer time for ATM cells on FDDI, FDDI-II, and DQDB.

times become close to TTRT as the total load approaches saturation. DQDB without priority works satisfactorily at low loads, but the transfer times increase substantially as the load increases.

24.4 Adapter Performance Issues

An adapter or host controller refers to the hardware board used to connect a computer system to external devices or networks. As explained in Section 21.1, the adapter is used in conjunction with a software component, which runs on the main processor (CPU) of the computer system and is called the *driver*.

Several design decisions affect the performance of the adapter. The goal of the design is to maximize the performance under a given cost constraint. Some decisions, as discussed later in this section, improve performance in one respect but degrade it in another. Many of the design issues discussed in this section apply to any high-speed adapter and are not limited to FDDI or networking.

The minimum frame size on FDDI is 28 bytes (assuming these are LLC frames). At 100 Mbps, these frames take only 2.24 μs to transmit. To keep up with the FDDI, the adapter should be able to process 450,000 minimum size frames per second. This is a challenging task.

The performance seen by the FDDI user depends on that of the processor, adapter, and the FDDI networking protocol. Higher layer network protocols are generally implemented in software and are executed by the processor. Driver software is used to communicate with the adapter board. Figure 24.4 shows several levels at which performance is generally measured. To transmit the data, the user application makes an I/O call to the operating system, which generally transfers the data from user memory into its kernel (operating system) memory. The kernel memory is typically organized as a chain of fixed-size buffers (called **mbufs** in UNIX). A packet may occupy one or more of these buffers. Higher layer networking protocols, such as TCP, IP, or UDP, are implemented in the software. They make a call to the device driver, which communicates with the adapter hardware and ensures that the data are transferred from the kernel memory to the adapter memory from which they are transmitted to the network. The received packets follow the opposite path from adapter memory to kernel memory and then to the user memory.

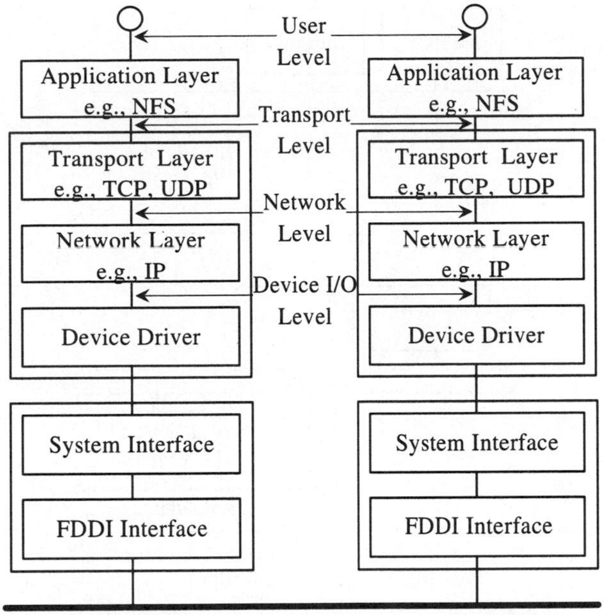

Figure 24.4 Levels at which performance is specified.

The key adapter design issues follow:

1. *System Bus or I/O Bus*: There are two ways to connect an adapter to the system. It can be put on the system bus as shown in Figure 24.5(a) or it it may be connected via a separate I/O bus (for example, a SCSI bus) as shown in Figure 24.5(b). In the second case, a separate I/O controller is required to access the memory. Thus, there is an added latency on the read transactions performed to access memory locations that are not local to the I/O bus. The I/O bus design is usually cheaper since the same adapter can be used for a variety of systems and the product development cost can be amortized over a larger volume. For example, SCSI adapters are used for disks on most personal computers and workstations.
2. *Intelligent or Dumb Adapter*: As shown in Figure 24.4, all higher layer protocols are implemented in the software. This approach, called the **dumb adapter** approach, uses the main processor's time and may affect the performance of other applications during network transfers. An alternative is to implement all of the protocols in the adapter. This may reduce the load on the host processor. In most cases, the copying of data from kernel space to user space still requires the intervention of the host processor. The protocol processing at the host is replaced by protocol bookkeeping, which may have the same cost. Also, the capacity of the processor required on the adapter may turn out to be too high. Therefore, this approach is rarely used.
3. *Memory Mapping*: One reason the processor is the bottleneck is that the data have to be copied effectively as they pass from one layer of the protocol to the next. The socket layer copies data from the user space into the operating system's kernel space. The IP layer checksums the data. The driver start routines copy the data to the adapter. Better space mapping schemes that avoid copying by remapping the address space can reduce CPU loading significantly.

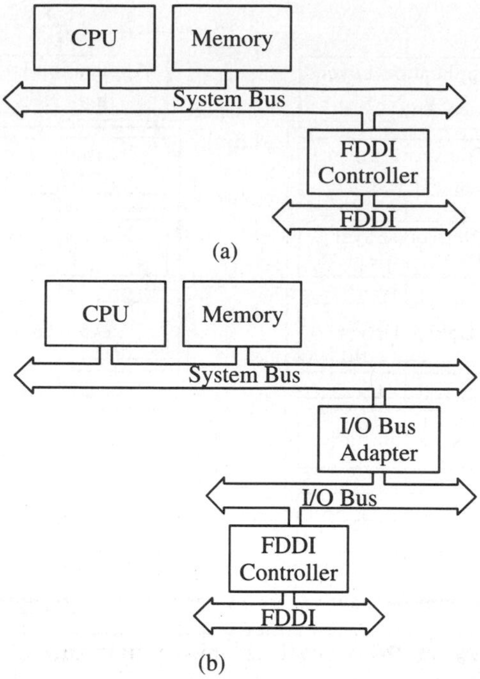

Figure 24.5 Two ways to connect an adapter to the system.

4. *DMA*: In low-cost adapter designs, the CPU is responsible for transferring all data from its host memory to adapter memory. This design, called **programmed I/O,** places a substantive load on the CPU since the CPU is interrupted numerous times during the transfer of each packet. A better design is to use **direct memory access (DMA)** circuitry on the adapter, which takes care of the data movement and interrupts processors only on completion of the transfer. Such DMA designs reduce the CPU load considerably. In one study, DMA implementation reduced the CPU time by a factor of 15!

   DMA has two side effects. First, DMA uses system bus bandwidth and the memory cycles. The host CPU has to wait for each memory cycle that the DMA engine *steals* from it. Thus, the CPU may not function at its full speed during DMA transfers. Second, since the CPU cycle time is smaller than the memory cycle time, high-speed memory caches are used to reduce access to the main memory. If the memory locations written over by the DMA engines are accessed by the CPU, they may contain stale data and should, therefore, be marked invalid. This invalidation slows the CPU. An alternative is to send all DMA data through the cache. That also is not very effective because the network data either are not used repeatedly or are too large to fit in the cache. Thus, the cost-performance effectiveness of the DMA depends heavily on the speed and architecture of the CPU and the memory.
5. *Scatter-Gather*: Each packet to be transmitted may be scattered over several kernel buffers. Simple DMA engines interrupt the CPU after transferring each kernel buffer. This means that the driver has to copy the data to a large contiguous kernel buffer. More expensive designs have

a scatter-gather capability, which means that the DMA engine can follow the buffer chain and interrupt the CPU only after the complete packet has been transferred.

6. *Video RAM*: The problem of simultaneous access to the memory by the processor and I/O also happens in video displays. One solution is to use a special two-port memory, which is accessible via the video controller as well as by the processor. Such two-port memory is called **video RAM**. This same approach can be used in high-speed network communications. However, the cost of video RAM is currently too high to justify its use in low-cost adapters. Also, it does not eliminate the major bottleneck—copy to/from user buffers.
7. *Interrupt Batching*: The network traffic is bursty and several frames are usually received back-to-back. Instead of posting a separate interrupt for each arrival, a performance optimization is to post the interrupt for the first arrival but service all frames that may be available. The number of packets processed in a batch should, however, be limited to avoid excessive delays and timeouts for other lower priority interrupts.
8. *Receive Versus Transmit*: The driver and the adapter have to share their resources between the outgoing and incoming traffic. It would appear that the receive traffic should be given higher priority otherwise it would be lost. The transmit traffic can normally wait. However, if the receive traffic is given a higher priority for an unlimited time, the transmit traffic may not get any service during overloads. Such **transmit starvation** leads to timeouts at other nodes and may result in unnecessary retransmission of messages. It is, therefore, important to ensure that allocation of resources is guaranteed for both receive and transmit. Also, the total internal bandwidth of the adapter must be more than the maximum possible receive rate.
9. *Receive Livelocks*: If the time to service a packet is longer than the interpacket arrival time, which is often the case on high-speed networks such as FDDI, the adapter processor might spend all of its time in posting interrupts but not completing any processing. There is a lot of action but no progress. For example, suppose that the next arrival is serviced as soon as the the datalink layer processing for a packet is completed. The packet cannot be delivered to the user until higher layer protocol headers have been processed. Many back-to-back arrivals will result in the adapter busily receiving packets but not delivering any to the user, resulting in loss of packets. This is called **livelock** since it stays only as long as the traffic is active (alive). This is the opposite of a **deadlock**, which continues even if there is no activity in the network. The solution is to stop servicing arrivals after a certain backlog.
10. *Receive Latency*: For remote procedure call (RPC) applications, the packets must be delivered to the user in a minimum amount of time. The adapter processor should be designed to have adequate capacity so that the queues do not become very long under normal loads. Scheduling policies on the host also affect the latency. The use of priorities and interrupts, which normally help reduce the latency, can cause excessive latency during overload. If strict priority is used, the first packet of a burst may not be delivered until the higher priority components of processing are completed for all packets of the burst. Longer bursts may result in longer latency.
11. *Address Filtering*: One of the first tasks an adapter has to perform is to decide whether to keep a frame seen on the ring. It looks at the destination address field and checks if it matches any address in its list. This filtering should be performed as close to the ring as possible. Some adapters may pick up all frames and let the processor decide which frames it wants to keep. Such implementations will not be able to receive back-to-back frames for long.
12. *SMT Frame Handling*: SMT frames can be processed by the adapter's processor or by the host processor. Processing them in the the adapter has the advantage that the station can be on the ring even when the host operating system is not functioning, for example, during diskless booting.

Box 24.2 Adapter Design Issues

1. Adapters that attach directly to the system bus provide lower delays than those that go on the I/O bus.
2. Intelligent adapters implement several layers of protocols and may reduce the load on the host processor.
3. Memory remapping schemes that avoid copying can reduce CPU loading significantly.
4. Adapters with DMA I/O put less load on the CPU than those with programmed I/O.
5. Scatter-gather ability allows an adapter to follow a buffer chain without the assistance from the CPU.
6. Video RAM reduces memory contention but it is very expensive.
7. Batching several interrupts can save some CPU time.
8. Both receive and transmit traffic should have guaranteed allocation of resources to avoid the transmit starvation.
9. Livelocks should be avoided by limiting the amount of backlog.
10. Scheduling policies should be carefully optimized to minimize latency.
11. Address filtering should be performed as close to the ring as possible.
12. The adapter should be able to process most of the SMT frames without interrupting the host.

Also, if there is a noisy link or the ring topology is changing rapidly, the host CPU is not bothered by the rapid state transitions of the ring.

Box 24.2 summarizes the issues just discussed.

There are a few other issues that affect the performance of FDDI systems, although these are not really adapter design issues. Three such issues are as follows:

1. *Flow Control Parameters*: Network flow control parameters such as maximum window size and request buffer size have been found to affect significantly the performance of TCP/IP-based applications. In TCP, window size is negotiated between the source and the destination. Both propose a maximum size and the smaller of the two is selected. Changing the window size from 16 to 64 kB improved the throughput by 17% in one configuration.
2. *Request Buffer Size*: This determines the amount of information passed to the transport layer in each request. A certain number of CPU cycles are used by each request. Thus, small buffer sizes result in CPU saturation at lower throughput. The throughput increases as buffer size is increased up to 4 kB—the maximum that will fit in one FDDI frame. Any larger size requires segmentation and the throughput decreases. For example, in one case, changing the buffer size from 4 to 5 kB resulted in 30% throughput degradation.
3. *Checksum*: Optional services such as checksum could be turned off if not required. For example, UDP provides the option of per packet checksum. This guarantees the integrity of data sent over many links and gateways. But if both the source and the destination are on the same FDDI LAN, the datalink layer's CRC provides acceptable integrity and the UDP checksum can be turned off. This can increase the throughput by 5% to 20%. However, this may cause problems if the source and destination *appear* to be on the same LAN but, in fact, they happen to be on different LANs connected transparently via bridges.

This discussion highlights ways to improve the performance of systems on FDDI. To the end user it appears as if the FDDI adapter has been improved.

24.5 Summary

FDDI can be modeled as a cyclic queueing system. Its service discipline is close to (but different from) the exhaustive service. Based on this observation, response time on FDDI can be computed analytically provided a correction is made for the difference from exhaustive service. Two different analytical models that use this approach were presented. These are summarized in Box 24.1. Transfer delay and average queue lengths can also be computed. The models give acceptable results only at loads below 80% of the maximum possible utilization.

Token counts, which are maintained in most FDDI stations, can be used to monitor ring utilization.

Performance of packet data traffic in FDDI-II is similar to that of FDDI-I except that the available bandwidth has to be changed from 100 Mbps to that available to packet data channels. When compared to the IEEE 802.6/DQDB protocol, FDDI-II provides lower delays and fairer service at high load. DQDB's delay is lower only at low loads.

Design issues that affect the performance of an adapter are summarized in Box 24.2.

24.6 Further Reading

The first analytical model is a modification of that presented in Karvelas and Leon-Garcia (1988). It was modified by LaMaire and Spiegel (1990). They present a comparison of several analytical models. The second analytical model is from Yue and Brooks (1990). See also Brooks and Yue (1989) and LaMaire (1991b).

Bux and Truong (1983) present models for cyclic-service queueing systems and discuss the problems with exhaustive service discipline.

For a general survey of cyclic queueing models, see Takagi (1988), Bux (1989), and Watson (1984). In particular, Takagi presents formulas for asymmetric systems in which loads at different stations are unequal.

Variations of the cyclic polling models with exhaustive service have been used by several researchers, for example, see Sachs, Kan, and Silvester (1985).

Figure 24.2 comparing the performance of FDDI-II to that of IEEE 802.6 networks is based on the data from Martini and Meuser (1990). See also Huber, Sauer, and Schödl (1988) and Davids and Meuser (1991) for FDDI-II performance.

Figure 24.3 is based on the data from Schödl and Tangemann (1990).

Figure 24.5 is from Kalkunte (1991). Ramakrishnan (1993) provides an excellent discussion of adapter design issues. Rege (1991) presents a sample adapter design.

Pang (1989) and Pang and Tobagi (1988, 1989a, 1989b) have studied several generalizations of FDDI's timed token protocol and discuss conditions under which the generalized methods are stable.

DQDB is specified in the ANSI/IEEE 802.6 standard.

24.7 Self-Test Exercises

Note: Some exercises have multiple correct answers. See Appendix D for answers.

24.1 Given two adapters with similar designs except that one connects to the system bus (for example, EISA) and the other connects to the I/O bus (for example, SCSI), which is expected to provide better performance?

a. I/O bus adapter
b. System bus adapter

24.2 When is an adapter said to be in a receive livelock?

a. When no usable token is received from the ring.
b. When no traffic is being received from the ring.
c. When excessive traffic is being received by the adapter but not delivered to the host.
d. When the receive paths are locked due to all resources being used by the transmit paths.

CHAPTER **25**

Error Analysis

One advantage of optical fibers is that the signal is not affected by electromagnetic interference. Nonetheless errors can occur as a result of other causes such as thermal noise (random electron motion) in optical fibers and devices. These noise events can cause the receiver to misjudge the optical signal level, that is, "on" (or high) may be interpreted as "off" (or low) and vice versa. Such errors, in turn, may result in loss of a frame or token or in undetected errors in the frame. These effects are analyzed in this chapter. In particular, the frame error rate, token loss rate, and undetected error rate are computed. Several characteristics of the 32-bit frame check sequence (FCS) polynomial, which is also used in IEEE 802 LAN protocols, are discussed. The probability of undetected errors due to creation of false starting delimiters, false ending delimiters, or merging of two frames is analyzed.

25.1 Taxonomy, Notation, and Assumptions

As discussed in Chapter 3, the optical signals on the FDDI fibers use NRZI encoded pulses, where a polarity transition represents a logical "1" (one). The absence of a polarity transition denotes a logical "0" (zero). These logical 1's and 0's are called *code bits*. Five consecutive code bits are grouped to form a *symbol*. Each symbol thus consists of five code bits. The term *code cell* is used to denote the time interval of one code bit. The receiving logic detects the changes in optical signal levels from one cell to the next.

In this chapter, the term *link* is used to denote all optical components from the transmit function of one PHY entity to the receive function of the adjacent PHY entity. The link error rate includes errors in the fiber, connectors, optical receiver, and optical transmitter.

A nonbursty model for noise events is assumed such that each event affects signal reception during only one code cell duration. This results into two code bit errors and one to four data bit errors.

The following symbols are used in the analysis:

L = Number of links in the ring
l = Number of links between the source and destination of a frame
p = Noise event probability per link (link BER)

F = Frame size in code bits
B = Link bandwidth in code bits/second = 1.25×10^8 for FDDI
D = Ring latency
$P(x)$ = Probability of event x
$MT(x)$ = Mean time between events x

The FDDI standard specifies the following default maximum values for the ring parameters. The maximum number of links on the ring is 1000 ($L \leq 1000$). The maximum frame size is 9000 symbols ($F \leq 45,000$ code bits). The size includes four idle symbols in the preamble and six control symbols in the *starting delimiter* (*SD*), *ending delimiter* (*ED*), and *frame status* (*FS*) fields. The remaining symbols are data symbols. The maximum ring latency is 1.773 ms. The maximum allowed *fiber link* bit error rate is 2.5×10^{-10}. This is the probability of noise events per link and should not be confused with code bit or data bit error probability, which would be a multiple of this.

The analysis presented here is based on the following assumptions:

1. *Noise events are independent.* That is, occurrence of one noise event does not change the probability of occurrence of the next noise event. This simplifies the analysis considerably. This is a valid assumption if the noise is mostly due to thermal causes, which are independent in nature.
2. *Noise events are nonbursty.* That is, each event affects signal reception during only one code cell. As shown later, this results in bursty errors in the data bits. Each noise event may result in a data error burst as long as four data bits.
3. *The link can be modeled as a binary symmetric channel (BSC).* This means that the probability of a "high" level being interpreted as "low" on receipt is the same as that of a "low" signal being interpreted as "high."
4. *Noise events do not add or delete code bits.* Only misinterpretation of signal levels is modeled. Addition or deletion of code bits is not modeled.
5. *The noise event probability p is small.* Most expressions presented here include only the lowest order term in p. Higher order terms make a negligible contribution if p is small. This is not true if p is close to 1. In general, it is assumed that $pLF \ll 1$, i.e., $p \ll 1/(45,000)(1000)$, or 10^{-9}.
6. *All data bit patterns are equally likely.* In particular, this implies that all 16 data symbols (0–F) are equally likely in every data symbol position where data symbols are allowed.
7. *Data bit errors in MAC layer electronic components are not modeled.* Only the errors caused by misinterpretation of the optical signal level are considered. Electronic components, e.g., buses, memories, FCS logic, etc., can cause errors in individual data bits. Such errors are not modeled.
8. *Loss of data or code bits due to clock missynchronization is not modeled.* It is also possible to add extra bits in the received stream due to clock missynchronization. In the analysis, it is assumed that the number of bits received is the same as that transmitted.
9. *Only fiber links are considered.* In particular, twisted-pair copper links use MLT-3 coding, which is not modeled here.

25.2 What Error Rate Is Acceptable?

The maximum acceptable detected and undetected error rates vary not only among applications and environments but also with time. As LAN technology matures, the minimum required reliability and data integrity are also increasing. Any specified numerical value of maximum acceptable error rates is bound to become outdated and even at the time of specifications it may not be applicable to some applications and environments. Nonetheless, it is important to set certain well-specified goals to help select the design or configuration alternatives available at the time. This helps during the design phase in ruling out many alternatives that will not meet the goals. Also, it helps in setting configuration limits by ruling out the configurations that will not meet the requirements.

Many transport protocols today are designed to allow a certain percentage of packet loss due to congestion and errors. An end-to-end (over many hops) frame loss rate of 1% is generally considered acceptable. A major part of this loss is allocated to congestion. Thus, a fiber optic datalink with more than, say, 0.1% frame loss due to error alone may be considered unacceptable. For unreliable media, such as radio links, one may either allocate a larger share to error loss, or design higher level protocols to be able to sustain a higher loss rate.

As the speed of links increases, the acceptable error (or loss) rate decreases. This is because most human beings perceive the quality of a link by the time between successive packet losses. For the same percent rate, the packet losses happen more often in higher speed networks. Thus, the acceptable error rate on FDDI is less than that on older lower speed LANs.

While the detected errors are harmful in that they require retransmissions resulting in inefficient use of resources, undetected errors have no bounds on the damage that they may cause. The damage caused by undetected errors in financial transactions or in defense applications is unimaginable. One may, therefore, like to limit the number of undetected errors per year to less than, say, 1/1000; that is, no more than one undetected error per 1000 years. For a manufacturer, this implies that if the manufacturer sells several thousand FDDI networks, it will result in several undetected error cases per year, with each case having a certain probability of resulting in a liability suit. For a user, such as a defense installation, this implies that if the messages generally pass through, say, 100 LANs, the overall mean time between undetected errors will be about 10 years.

The error analysis by nature tends to be pessimistic. This is because the designers want to ensure an "upper bound" on errors. This is unlike traditional performance analysis (throughput or delay analysis) in which "average" performance of an "average workload" on an "average configuration" is more meaningful. For error analysis, one would like to ensure that the error rates on all valid workloads (frame sizes and arrival rates) and on all valid configurations (number of links, length of links, etc.) do not exceed a maximum acceptable error rate. We, therefore, use the default maximum configurations (e.g., 1000 links, 4500-byte frames) as examples in this chapter. Applications in which the resulting error rates are unacceptable may further restrict allowable configurations or workloads. Note that the analysis presented here is not a worst case analysis. For example, it is assumed that all data symbols are equally likely. For a worst case scenario, one could design frames consisting solely of symbols that are more likely to result in undetected errors.

In the remainder of this chapter, the term *large FDDI rings* is used to denote this default maximum configuration with large size frames being continuously transmitted on the ring.

25.3 Effect of One Noise Event

Before computing the probabilities of detected and undetected errors in frames, it is helpful to study the impact of a single noise event on a symbol in detail.

Consider the example of the symbol 0. It consists of four data bits 0000. By means of the 4b/5b coding, it is encoded into the five code bits 11110, which in turn result in the transition sequence shown in Figure 25.1. A noise in the optical signal may cause the receiver to misjudge the signal level during the fourth code cell, for instance, and so the received code bit pattern is 11101, which

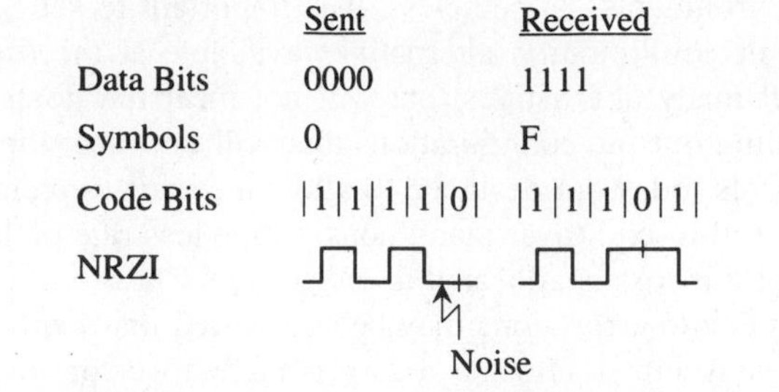

Figure 25.1 A single noise event can cause up to four data-bit errors.

is interpreted as symbol F, or data bits 1111. This is an example of a single noise event resulting in four data bit errors.

The key observation from the preceding example is that *one noise event results in two code bit errors*. This is true for all cases. If the noise affects the transition between two symbols, it affects the last (fifth) code bit of the first symbol, as well as the first code bit of the second symbol.

Table 25.1 lists the effects of noise on data symbols. Six possibilities are listed for each of the 16 data symbols. The first and the last column, labeled code bits 1 and 5, respectively, correspond to intersymbol errors, while the middle four columns are for intrasymbol errors. For example, the entry in the row labeled 3 and the column marked 4,5 is interpreted as follows. If the data symbol 3 (0011) is affected by noise so that its fourth and fifth code bit positions are affected, the resulting symbol is A (1010).

Table 25.1 Effect of Noise on a Data Symbol

			Resulting Symbols Bit Positions Changed					
Original Symbol	Data Bits	Code Bits	1	1,2	2,3	3,4	4,5	5
0	0000	11110	6	V	8	J	F	I
1	0001	01001	S	K	V	7	4	VH
2	0010	10100	H	V	J	8	B	3
3	0011	10101	V	T	S	9	A	2
4	0100	01010	C	8	V	V	1	5
5	0101	01011	D	9	R	T	VH	4
6	0110	01110	0	A	VH	VH	T	7
7	0111	01111	I	B	V	1	V	6
8	1000	10010	VH	4	0	2	K	9
9	1001	10011	V	5	I	3	VH	8
A	1010	10110	V	6	C	VH	3	B
B	1011	10111	R	7	D	K	2	A
C	1100	11010	4	VH	A	E	S	D
D	1101	11011	5	V	B	F	J	C
E	1110	11100	V	H	VH	C	I	F
F	1111	11101	T	V	K	D	0	E

From Table 25.1, it possible to compute the percentage of data symbol errors that results in other data symbols, control symbols, and violations. These percentages are listed in Table 25.2. The percentages for intrasymbol errors and intersymbol errors are given separately. The middle column, labeled "count," is simply the count of the resulting symbols in Table 25.1. For example, J occurs three times in the middle four columns (corresponding to the intrasymbol errors) of Table 25.1. Assuming that each of the 16 data symbols is equally frequent and that each of the five code cells is equally likely to be affected, this corresponds to 3/(16)(5) = 3.75%.

To study intersymbol errors, one needs to analyze all (16)(16) = 256 data symbol pairs. The results of this analysis constitute the bottom half of Table 25.2.

In FDDI, many errors will be detected because the resulting code bit pattern may translate to a *violation* symbol. The MAC layer keeps a count of format errors due to such *symbol violations*. Frames with symbol violations are discarded.

Some of the other errors will be detected if the resulting code bit pattern translates to a *control symbol*, which makes the frame an invalid frame, for example, a data frame ending with an R symbol rather than a T. Such errors, called *framing violations*, are also counted by the MAC layer as format errors.

Using Table 25.2, the probabilities of symbol violations and framing violations can be bounded as follows:

1. 33.91% of the data errors results in I, V, or H symbols, which will cause the MAC layer to terminate the frame prematurely and replace the remaining part of the frame with Idle symbols. This is called *symbol violation*.

Table 25.2 Percentage of Data Symbol Errors

Resulting Symbol	Count	Percent
Intrasymbol errors:		
Data	32	40.00%
J	3	3.75%
K	4	5.00%
R	1	1.25%
S	2	2.50%
T	3	3.75%
H,I,V,VH	19	23.75%
Subtotal	64	80%
Intersymbol errors:		
Data-data	84	6.56%
Data-T	14	1.09%
Data-R	14	1.09%
Data-S	14	1.09%
At least one H,I,V,VH	130	10.16%
Subtotal	256	20%
Total		100.00%

Table 25.3 Data Error Patterns

	Error Pattern					
	Bit Positions Changed					
Symbol	1	1,2	2,3	3,4	4,5	5
0	0110	—	1000	—	1111	—
1	—	—	—	0110	0101	—
2	—	—	—	1010	1001	0001
3	—	—	—	1010	1001	0001
4	1000	1100	—	—	0101	0001
5	1000	1100	—	—	—	0001
6	0110	1100	—	—	—	0001
7	—	1100	—	0110	—	0001
8	—	1100	1000	1010	—	0001
9	—	1100	—	1010	—	0001
A	—	1100	0110	—	1001	0001
B	—	1100	0110	—	1001	0001
C	1000	—	0110	0010	—	0001
D	1000	—	0110	0010	—	0001
E	—	—	—	0010	—	0001
F	—	—	—	0010	1111	0001

— ⇒ The resulting symbol is a nondata symbol.

2. 46.56% of the data errors results in other data symbols and will not be detected by framing violations or symbol violations.
3. The remaining 19.53% of data errors results in control symbols that *may or may not* be detected by framing violations.

For those errors that result in new data symbols, it is interesting to analyze the data bit error patterns. The results of this analysis are presented in Table 25.3. For each of the 16 data symbols, six possibilities are presented. A dash (—) is used to indicate the cases in which the resulting symbol is a nondata symbol. Notice that even though a single noise event can affect up to two symbols, it never affects more than four data bits.

Notice from Table 25.3 that not all error patterns are equally likely. By counting the number of times an error pattern appears in this table, one can compute the frequency of various error patterns. This is shown in Table 25.4. Again, intrasymbol and intersymbol errors have to be considered separately. For example, of the 256 possible data symbol pairs, 28 will result in a data bit error pattern of 0001-0110, thereby accounting for 28/(256)(5) = 2.19% of all data symbol errors. Notice that the sum of all data error pattern percentages is 46.56%, which is consistent with that in Table 25.2.

25.4 Frame Error Rate

A frame error results if the noise event affects any of the *F* code cells in the frame. Also, a noise in the code cell immediately preceding the starting delimiter will affect the first code bit of the frame.

Table 25.4 Frequency of Data Error Patterns

Error Pattern	Count	Percent
0010	4	5.00%
0101	2	2.50%
0110	6	7.50%
1000	2	2.50%
1001	4	5.00%
1010	4	5.00%
1100	8	10.00%
1111	2	2.50%
0001-0110	28	2.19%
0001-1000	56	4.38%
Total		46.56%

Given that each code cell has a probability p of being hit with noise, it is easy to compute the probability of no errors in any of the $F+1$ code cells on any of the L links.

$$\text{P(No error in } F+1 \text{ code cells on any of the } L \text{ links)} = (1-p)^{L(F+1)}$$

$$\text{P(Frame error)} = 1-(1-p)^{L(F+1)} \approx pLF \quad \text{for} \quad pLF \ll 1$$

The mean time between frame errors (sometimes referred to as error-free seconds) can be computed if the mean time between frame arrivals is known. This time would be smallest on a fully utilized ring:

$$\text{Frames per second on a fully utilized link} \approx \frac{B}{F}$$

$$\text{Frames with error per second} = \frac{B}{F}[1-(1-p)^{L(F+1)}]$$

$$\text{MT(Frame errors)} = \frac{1}{(B/F)[1-(1-p)^{L(F+1)}]} \approx \frac{1}{BpL}$$

On large rings with large frames, the frame error probability comes out to 1.13% and the mean time between frame errors is 32 ms. If this error probability is considered too high to be acceptable, the solution is to further restrict allowable values of L, F, or p; that is, decrease the number of links allowed on a ring, or decrease the maximum frame size allowed on the ring, or allow only higher quality components on the ring.

25.5 Token Loss Rate

As described earlier, the FDDI token consists of six symbols, i.e., 30 code cells. An error in any code cell or the code cell immediately preceding will cause the next station not to recognize the token, resulting in a *token lost* event, which will eventually require the ring to be reinitialized with a new token. The probability of this event occurring during one pass around the ring can be computed in a manner similar to that for frame error rate with a frame size of $F = 30$ code bits.

$$\text{P(Token loss per token rotation)} = 1 - (1 - p)^{31L} \approx 31pL$$

On large rings the probability of token loss is 7.75×10^{-6}. On an idle ring, the token is continuously rotating around the ring. The mean time between token loss under such conditions can be computed as follows:

$$\text{MT(Token loss on an idle ring)} = \frac{\text{Ring latency}}{\text{P(Token loss per rotation)}} = \frac{D}{31pL}$$

For a large ring the ring latency is 1.773 ms, which yields a mean time between token loss of 3.82 minutes. This is not the worst case time. For a given link BER, the time will be larger on busy rings and smaller on idle rings of smaller cable length. Since the ring latency is generally proportional to the number of links ($D \propto L$), the only way to increase this time (if unacceptable) is to allow only better quality links (with lower BER).

Note that there are two types of tokens: restricted and nonrestricted. These two types have been designed to differ from each other in only one *code bit* position. Since a single noise event in the optical components always results in two code bit errors, one event cannot change a nonrestricted token into a restricted token and vice versa.

25.6 FCS Polynomial

As explained earlier in Section 2.6, FDDI uses the following polynomial for the frame check sequence:

$$g(x) = x^{32} + x^{26} + x^{23} + x^{22} + x^{16} + x^{12} + x^{11} + x^{10} + x^{8} + x^{7} + x^{5} + x^{4} + x^{2} + x + 1$$

This polynomial is also used in IEEE 802 LAN standards and in AUTODIN-II networks. One way to check if a frame has the correct FCS would be as follows. Sequentially number the data bits in the frame as 0, 1, 2, 3, ..., starting with the data bit before the ending delimiter and working backward until the first data bit after the starting delimiter. Let the ith data bit be b_i, $b_i \in \{0, 1\}$. The frame can then be represented by the polynomial:

$$f(x) = \sum_i b_i x^i$$

If the remainder $\text{Mod}[f(x), g(x)]$ is zero, the frame is said to have the correct FCS. This statement is a simplification. The FCS procedure specified in the MAC standard requires complementing the first 32 bits and the last 32 bits of the frame and shifting the result by 32 bits before the division operation. This is equivalent to the following condition:

$$\text{Mod}\left[x^n I(x) + x^{32}\{f(x) + I(x)\}, g(x)\right] = 0$$

Here, n is the number of data bits in the frame including FCS and $I(x) = \sum_{i=0}^{31} x^i$. The addition of $I(x)$ in the preceding equation is equivalent to complementing the first 32 data bits and the last 32 data bits of the frame before the division operation.

This FCS polynomial has the following properties:

1. It is a linear code. Linear codes have the important property that the "sum" of two code words is also a code word. For FDDI and IEEE 802 protocols, this implies that if you take any two valid frames and do the following:

   a. right-align the frames,
   b. complement the first and the last 32 bits of each frame,
   c. take a bit-wise exclusive-OR of their data bits, and
   d. complement the first and the last 32 bits of the result,

   then the resulting data bit sequence would form a frame with a valid FCS.
2. Adding a multiple of the divisor (FCS polynomial) to the dividend (frame polynomial) does not affect the remainder. The minimum degree polynomials, which are multiples of the FCS polynomial for various Hamming weights, are listed in Table 25.5. The Hamming weight of a polynomial is defined as the number of nonzero terms in the polynomial. For example, the $1 + x^{41678} + x^{91639}$ is a multiple of the FCS polynomial and has a Hamming weight of three. All other polynomials of lower degrees have higher weights. Such polynomials are important because if you add this polynomial to any frame (this corresponds to complementing the 0th, 41678th, and 91639th data bits of the frame), the resulting FCS would still come out correctly. Thus, for frames with lengths greater than or equal to 91,640 data bits (11,455 bytes), the minimum Hamming distance between two valid frames is three and the FCS can detect only two and one data bit errors. Fortunately, this does not apply to FDDI or IEEE 802 since they do not allow such long frames.
3. For frames size between 3007 data bits and 91,639 data bits, the minimum Hamming distance is four and the FCS detects all three, two, or one data bit errors. This implies that for maximum size FDDI frames ($\approx$9000 symbols or 36,000 data bits), the FCS will not detect some four data bit errors. Examples of four data bit errors that will not be detected can be constructed by complementing the data bits i, $i + 2215$, $i + 2866$, and $i + 3006$ in any valid frame. This is true for all values of i.

   Similarly, statements can be made about other frame sizes by looking at the degree of polynomials in Table 25.5. The maximum frame size for various minimum Hamming distances

Table 25.5 Multiples of FCS Polynomial

Hamming Weight	Minimum Degree Polynomial
3	$1 + x^{41678} + x^{91639}$
4	$1 + x^{2215} + x^{2866} + x^{3006}$
5	$1 + x^{89} + x^{117} + x^{155} + x^{300}$
6	$1 + x^{79} + x^{85} + x^{123} + x^{186} + x^{203}$
7	$1 + x^{45} + x^{53} + x^{74} + x^{80} + x^{120} + x^{123}$
8	$1 + x^{5} + x^{13} + x^{16} + x^{36} + x^{41} + x^{88} + x^{89}$
9	$1 + x^{2} + x^{3} + x^{18} + x^{19} + x^{32} + x^{37} + x^{57} + x^{66}$
10	$1 + x^{3} + x^{7} + x^{25} + x^{27} + x^{30} + x^{33} + x^{36} + x^{38} + x^{53}$
11	$1 + x^{5} + x^{7} + x^{16} + x^{31} + x^{32} + x^{35} + x^{37} + x^{41} + x^{43} + x^{44}$
12	$1 + x^{3} + x^{5} + x^{7} + x^{8} + x^{13} + x^{18} + x^{21} + x^{24} + x^{26} + x^{30} + x^{42}$
13	$1 + x + x^{6} + x^{15} + x^{18} + x^{20} + x^{23} + x^{29} + x^{33} + x^{35} + x^{37} + x^{40} + x^{42}$

Table 25.6 Hamming Distance of FCS Polynomial

Hamming Weight	Max Frame Size: Data Bits	Max Frame Size: Bytes
3	91,639	11,454
4	3,006	375
5	300	37
6	203	25
7	123	15
8	89	11
9	66	8
10	53	6
11	44	5
12	42	5
13	42	5

are listed in Table 25.6. Notice from this table that if the frame length is restricted to less than 375 bytes, the minimum Hamming distance is five.

4. There are 2^d possible data bit patterns, which are d data bits long. Of these, only 2^{d-32} patterns have a valid FCS. This is because given any data bit pattern of $d - 32$ you can compute its FCS and append it to make a valid d data bit pattern. Thus, the probability of any randomly constructed d data bit pattern having a valid FCS is $2^{d-32}/2^d$ or 2^{-32} or 2.33×10^{-10}.
5. If several data bits are in error in a frame, the group of data bits beginning from the first data bit in error up to the last data bit in error is called an *error burst*. The burst size b includes the first and the last data bits (which are in error) and all intermediate data bits (which may or may not be in error). The FCS polynomial detects *all* error bursts of size 32 or less. Thus, if several noise events affect a frame such that the resulting error burst is less than 32 data bits, the FCS will detect it. The fraction of error bursts larger than 33 data bits that are not detected is 2^{-32}. For bursts of exactly 33 data bits, this fraction is 2^{-31}.

   This property implies that all single-noise events will be detected by the FCS since the event would produce a burst of, at most, four data bits.

These statements do not say anything about two noise events that affect symbols far apart. One may suspect that some two noise events will not be detected by the FCS. Fortunately, this is not so. As discussed in the previous section, there are only 10 possible error patterns. An exhaustive search using a computer program has shown that the FCS polynomial detects all possible two noise events. Some combinations of three noise events are not detected. For example, if you sequentially number the symbol positions of an FDDI frame as 0, 1, 2, ..., starting from the last symbol position of the FCS field and proceeding backward toward the FC field, and introduce error patterns 1010, 1111, and 0010 in positions i, $i+625$, and $i+3605$, respectively, the resulting frame will still have a valid FCS for all values of i. A complete list of other possible three noise events that will not be detected is shown in Table 25.7. The search included the possibility that a symbol may be affected by more than one noise event. Also listed in the table are the corresponding probabilities. For example, to

Table 25.7 Complete List of Three Noise Events Not Detected by the FDDI FCS

Noise 1		Noise 2		Noise 3		Probability
Symbol Position	Error Pattern	Symbol Position	Error Pattern	Symbol Position	Error Pattern	for Large Rings
i	1010	$i+625$	1111	$i+3605$	0010	3.29×10^{-25}
i	1000	$i+1366$	1001	$i+6398$	0010	1.58×10^{-25}
i	1001	$i+1630$	1001	$i+5509$	1000	2.12×10^{-25}
i	1111	$i+1835$	1001	$i+8404$	0101	1.79×10^{-26}
i	0010	$i+1947$	1111	$i+3096$	1000	1.80×10^{-25}
i	1100	$i+2239$	00010110	$i+3289$	0110	9.14×10^{-25}
i	0101	$i+3881$	00011000	$i+5609$	0110	2.71×10^{-25}
i	1100	$i+3882$	0010	$i+5609$	1000	4.13×10^{-25}
i	00011000	$i+4209$	1111	$i+8972$	00010110	3.98×10^{-28}
i	1001	$i+6092$	0110	$i+6340$	0101	2.43×10^{-25}
					Total	2.74×10^{-24}

compute the probability corresponding to the first line of the table, observe that only 5% of the data errors results in error pattern 1010, 2.5% of data errors results in the error pattern 1111, and 5% of the data errors results in the pattern 0010. A frame has $(F-50)/5$ data symbols, therefore, $0 \le i < [(F-50/5)-3605]$. The symbol error probability is $5p$. Assuming that there are $L/2$ links on an average between the source and destination, the required probability is:

$$\begin{aligned}
&\text{P(Positions } i, i+625, i+3605 \text{ are affected by error patterns 1010, 1111, and 0010,}\\
&\quad\text{respectively)} = \sum_{\forall i}(0.05\times 5p)(0.025\times 5p)(0.05\times 5p)(0.5L)\\
&\quad = \sum_{\forall i}(7.8125\times10^{-3})p^3(0.5L)\\
&\quad = \left(\frac{F-50}{5} - 3605\right)(7.8125\times10^{-3})p^3(0.5L)\\
&\quad = \left(\frac{F-50}{5} - 3605\right)(3.91\times10^{-3})p^3L
\end{aligned}$$

The total probability of undetected errors is obtained by summing for all possible patterns listed in the table. For the largest size frames this probability is 2.74×10^{-24}. For other frame sizes the probability is approximately $(3.89\times10^{-3})p^3LF$.

The fraction of undetected four noise events is 2^{-32}. Hence, the probability of undetected errors due to four noise events can be computed as follows:

$$\begin{aligned}
\text{P(Four noise events not causing symbol or FCS violations)} &= \binom{F-50}{4}(0.4656p)^4(1-p)^{(F-50-4)}(L/2)(2^{-32})\\
&\approx \frac{[0.4656p(F-50)]^4(L/2)(2^{-32})}{24}\\
&\approx (2.28\times10^{-13})p^4F^4L\\
&\approx (2.28\times10^{-13})p^4F^4L
\end{aligned}$$

Table 25.8 Maximum Frame Size Versus Detected Noise Events on FDDI

# of Noise Events	Maximum Frame Size Symbols			
	Data	Nondata	Total	Bytes
3	3096	10	3106	1553
4	434	10	444	222
5	30	10	40	20

On large rings with large frames, the probability of undetected errors due to four noise events is 3.64×10^{-30}. Probabilities for larger number of noise events can be calculated similarly.

The relationship between maximum frame size and the maximum number of noise events per frame allowed on FDDI is shown in Table 25.8. Notice from the table that if the frame size is limited to 3106 symbols (3096 data symbols, four Idle symbols in the preamble, and six control symbols for the delimiters and status indicators), the FCS will detect all three noise events. For frames shorter than 444 symbols, the FCS will detect all four noise events. The corresponding number for five noise events is 40 symbols.

25.7 Merging Frames

The concentrators and dual-attachment stations can internally reconfigure their data paths to allow MACs to be added or removed from the ring. If a station is allowed to go on/off the ring improperly, frames or parts of frames on the fiber connecting the station to/from the concentrator may be lost. It is possible to lose parts of two frames such that the resulting data bit pattern is a valid frame as shown in Figure 25.2. Since the FCS is 32 data bits long, the probability that any data bit pattern has a valid FCS is 2^{-32} or 2.33×10^{-10} or one in 4.34×10^{9}. In other words, one in every 4.34 billion merged frames will have a correct FCS. This may or may not be acceptable depending on

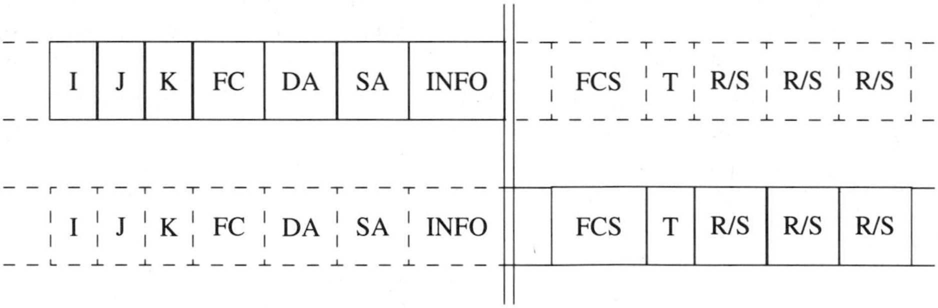

Figure 25.2 Two frames may merge to produce one valid frame.

the frequency of stations going on/off the ring and the number of stations. To avoid frame merging, the FDDI SMT standard requires scrubbing a ring upon station insertion/removal.

25.8 False Ending Delimiter

FDDI uses a frame-ending delimiter of a single symbol T followed by an E-indicator with value R. Thus, to create a false ending delimiter, you need at least two noise events changing two data symbols to a TR pair. There are three possible scenarios for data symbols changing to TR:

1. The T appears in FC, DA, or SA fields. This is counted as a framing violation. The fraction of such *false T* is $130/(F - 50)$, where 130 code bits (13 bytes assuming 12 symbol addresses) of the total $F - 50$ code bits constitute these fields. The remaining 50 code bits are used by the preamble, SD, ED, and FS fields.
2. The T appears in the second symbol of a byte in the INFO field. This results in an odd number of data symbols between SD and ED. This is also counted as frame violation. This fraction is $(F - 180)/2F$. This approximates to about 50%.
3. The T appears in the first symbol of a byte in the INFO field. This will result in a premature termination of the frame. Again, this fraction is $(F - 180)/2F$. In other words, about half of the errors converting a data symbol to T will not be detected by framing violations.

It is also possible that for some of these frames with false ED, the FCS checks out! The probability of this is a product of the probability of the following events:

1. A noise event affects a data symbol.
2. The data symbol is the first symbol of a byte.
3. The data symbol becomes a T.
4. Another noise affects the next data symbol.
5. The second data symbol becomes an R.
6. FCS is correct.

The probability of the second event is 0.5. That of the sixth event is 2^{-32}. The probability of the third event is 4.84% (sum of 3.75% and 1.09% in Table 25.2), and that of the fifth event is 1.25%. (Note that intersymbol errors result in R only if the previous symbol becomes a data symbol; hence, they are not added in this probability.) Thus, the probability of *undetected error* (*UE*) due to false ending delimiter is given by:

$$\begin{aligned} \text{P(UE due to false ED)} &= [\text{P(a data symbol in odd position becoming T)}] \\ &\quad [\text{P(FCS OK)}] \\ &\quad [\text{P(the next data symbol becoming an R)}] \\ &= (0.0484 \times 5p)\left(\frac{F - 180}{5}\right)\left(\frac{1}{2}\right)\left(\frac{L}{2}\right)(2^{-32})(0.0125 \times 5p) \\ &\approx (1.76 \times 10^{-13})p^2 LF \end{aligned}$$

and

$$\text{MT(UE due to false ED)} = \frac{1}{(B/F)(1.76 \times 10^{-13})p^2 LF} = \frac{1}{(1.76 \times 10^{-13})Bp^2 L}$$

For large rings and large frames, the probability of undetected errors is 4.93×10^{-25} and the mean time between undetected errors is 2.31×10^{13} years. This is acceptable for most applications.

25.9 False Starting Delimiter

In FDDI, each frame starts with a J-K symbol pair. It is possible to have two or more noise events and create a valid starting delimiter. Using the percentages specified in Table 25.2 and following a methodology similar to that for the false ED, the probability of undetected errors due to false SD can be computed as follows:

$$\begin{aligned}\text{P(UE due to false SD)} &= (0.0375 \times 5p)(0.05 \times 5p)\left(\frac{L}{2}\right)\left(\frac{F-180}{5}\right)\left(\frac{1}{2}\right)(2^{-32}) \\ &\approx (5.46 \times 10^{-13})LFp^2\end{aligned}$$

and

$$\text{MT(UE due to false SD)} = \frac{1}{(5.46 \times 10^{-13})BLp^2}$$

For large rings and large frames, this probability is 1.53×10^{-24} and the mean time between undetected errors is 7.47×10^{12} years. This may be considered acceptable for most applications. Further, the starting delimiter is actually stronger than this since some of the frames considered valid in this analysis will have nonexistent destination addresses and invalid frame control fields.

The analysis presented here assumes that the J-K code bit pattern "1100010001" appears on a symbol boundary. It does not account for cases in which the pattern may appear at nonboundary positions. The FDDI PHY layer will recognize such nonboundary J-K's and establish a new symbol boundary for the remaining stream. Such nonboundary cases can be caused by a single noise event and are much more likely than boundary cases analyzed here.

25.10 Summary

The numerical results for 4500-byte frames on large FDDI rings with 1000 links each with a noise event probability (BER) of 2.5×10^{-10} are summarized in Table 25.9. By changing each of the three key parameters, namely, noise event probability, number of links, and frame size, by a factor of 10 and recomputing the results as shown in Table 25.9, the sensitivity of the results to these parameters can be seen.

The results of this analysis are as follows:

1. A single noise event that results in misjudging the optical signal level during one code cell always results in two code bit errors. This may result in one or two symbol errors and up to four data bit errors.
2. For large rings, the frame loss rate or token loss rate may be too high for some applications and therefore it may be preferable to use higher quality links, a smaller number of stations, or shorter frames.
3. FCS detects all one or two noise events. Some three noise events may not be detected by the polynomial. For frames of 1553 bytes or shorter, it can protect against all three noise events.
4. A false starting delimiter of J-K can be generated (on a symbol boundary) by two noise events.
5. A false ending delimiter of TR can be generated by two noise events.

Table 25.9 Summary of Error Rates For FDDI Rings*

Quantity	Unit	Large Rings	BER = 2.5×10^{-11}	100 Links	450-Byte Frame
P(Frame error)		1.13×10^{-2}	1.13×10^{-3}	1.13×10^{-3}	1.13×10^{-3}
MT(Frame error)	ms	32.	320.	320.	32.
P(Token loss per token rotation)		7.75×10^{-6}	7.75×10^{-7}	7.75×10^{-7}	7.75×10^{-6}
MT(Token loss on an idle ring)	sec	229.	2288.	229.	229.
P(FCS not detecting 3 noise events)		2.74×10^{-24}	2.74×10^{-27}	2.74×10^{-25}	$0^{\dagger}$
MT(FCS not detecting 3 noise events)	year	4.17×10^{12}	4.17×10^{15}	4.17×10^{13}	∞
P(FCS not detecting 4 noise events)		3.64×10^{-30}	3.64×10^{-34}	3.64×10^{-31}	3.49×10^{-34}
MT(FCS not detecting 4 noise events)	year	3.14×10^{18}	3.14×10^{22}	3.14×10^{19}	3.27×10^{21}
P(UE due to false ED)		4.93×10^{-25}	4.93×10^{-27}	4.93×10^{-26}	4.75×10^{-26}
MT(UE due to false ED)	year	2.31×10^{13}	2.31×10^{15}	2.31×10^{14}	2.40×10^{13}
P(UE due to false SD)		1.53×10^{-24}	1.53×10^{-26}	1.53×10^{-25}	1.47×10^{-25}
MT(UE due to false SD)	year	7.47×10^{12}	7.47×10^{14}	7.47×10^{13}	7.75×10^{12}

*Parameters if unspecified are 1000 links, BER = 2.5×10^{-10}, 4500-byte frames.
†FCS detects all three noise events for frames shorter than 1553 bytes.
Notation: P(.) = probability of, MT(.) = mean time between, UE = undetected error.

25.11 Further Reading

Most of the analysis in this chapter has been reproduced with permission from Jain (1990a). In the initial version of the FDDI MAC standard, all frame status indicators were optional and stations were allowed to reset the E-indicator. The analysis presented here was done originally to quantify the effect of these decisions. As a result of this analysis, the rules for the status indicators were changed by the FDDI standards committee.

Peterson and Weldon (1972) provide a comprehensive discussion of various coding methods for error detection and correction.

The 32-degree FCS polynomial used in FDDI was originally selected by Hammond, Brown, and Liu (1975) after comparing several 32-bit FCS polynomials listed in Peterson and Weldon (1972). It is listed there by its octal representation "40460216667."

For discussions related to errors in IEEE 802 protocols see Lauck (1982), Phinney and Jelatis (1983), and Shoch (1979).

Tables 25.5 and 25.6 are from Phinney (1985). However, in Phinney's paper, the polynomials corresponding to Hamming weights of 8 and 11 are incorrect. The polynomials presented in Table 25.5 are correct.

25.12 Self-Test Exercises

Note: Some exercises have multiple correct answers. See Appendix D for answers.

25.1 How many data bits can be affected by a noise affecting just one code cell in FDDI fiber?

a. 2
b. 4
c. 8

25.2 What is the maximum number of data bit errors that is guaranteed to be detected by the FDDI frame check sequence?

a. 1
b. 2
c. 3
d. 4
e. 5

25.3 What is the maximum number of single-cell noise events that are guaranteed to be detected by the FDDI frame check sequence?

a. 1
b. 2
c. 3
d. 4
e. 5

CHAPTER **26**

Conformance Testing

If you are planning to buy an FDDI product, you probably want to ensure that the equipment follows the standards and that it will interoperate with equipment from other manufacturers. Since most buyers have such questions about conformance and interoperability, ISO and CCITT have attempted to address these issues. The set of notations, specifications, procedures, tests, and forms developed to address the conformance issues are the topics of this chapter.

26.1 What Is Conformance Testing?

Conformance testing helps measure the degree to which a given protocol implementation follows a reference standard. Conformance testing can be used by the implementors for self-testing, by users for validation, and by testing organizations for certification.

Conformance testing must be distinguished from *interoperability testing*, which is done to ensure that two or more implementations can work together in a mixed environment. Although conformance testing increases the probability that different implementations will be able to interoperate, it does not guarantee it. In particular, it is possible for two implementations to be "conformant but not interoperable" or "not conformant but interoperable."

Since 1983, ISO and CCITT have been working together on a series of conformance testing standards. These standards specify a set of test suites for each of the OSI protocols. Since there are so many OSI protocols, ISO has developed a standard notation to specify these tests and a standard methodology to develop such test suites.

ISO conformance test suites are limited to tests involving two systems. More than two systems are not covered. The test suites do not judge the performance, robustness, or reliability of an implementation. They test whether a service is provided but do not care how the service is implemented. The implementation is treated as a black box. Conformance is required only for the external behavior of the implementation even though the protocol standard may define both internal and external behaviors. Internal behavior is normally defined in standards only as an example of implementation.

The two basic concepts introduced in ISO conformance methodology are: *system under test (SUT)* and *implementation under test (IUT)*. The system refers to the complete networking equipment, such as an end-system, bridge, or router. Each system implements many OSI protocols. Conformance testing is generally done for a specific protocol or set of protocols. For example, while talking about FDDI, we are interested in PMD, PHY, MAC, and SMT protocols but may not be interested in LLC, networking, transport, and other higher layer protocols that may be implemented in the system under test. This set of protocol implementations that are under test is called IUT. For FDDI, test suites have been specified separately for PMD, PHY, MAC, and SMT. Thus, an implementation of any of these components of FDDI protocols can be considered an IUT.

26.2 Protocol Implementation Conformance Statement (PICS)

The first step in checking whether an implementation conforms to a standard is to make a list of key specifications in the standard and to ask the implementors whether their implementation satisfies these specifications. The list is called *protocol implementation conformance statement* (*PICS*) proforma and when such a proforma has been filled out by the implementor it is called *protocol implementation conformance statement* (*PICS*). In other words, PICS proforma is a questionnaire, designed by the protocol specifier or conformance test suite specifier, that specifies all mandatory and optional features to be tested in the course of a formal conformance test. The PICS is a statement made by the vendor supplying the implementation under test. It declares the capabilities and options that have been implemented for the system being delivered for testing.

Figure 26.1 shows an example of part of the PICS proforma and a PICS for MAC. The two capabilities addressed by this particular part are whether a station transmits, receives, or forwards restricted and unrestricted tokens. The first column, "Item #," is used to reference this capability in test suites. For example, the MAC conformance test suite may have a test specifically designed to test MAC2.2—whether the station transmits, receives, or forwards restricted tokens. The next column, "Item Name," is a description of the capability. The third column, "Ref #," provides a reference to the base standard section where this capability is described in more detail. The "Status" column indicates whether the capability is mandatory (m), optional (o), conditional (c), prohibited (x), or not applicable (n/a). The entries in the status column are case insensitive. Either uppercase or lowercase

6.3.2 Token Class

Item #	Item Name	Ref #	Status			Support		
			Tx	Rx	Fd	Tx	Rx	Fd
MAC2.1	Unrestricted Token (FC=1000 0000)	8.2.1	m	m	m	Y[ ]N[ ]	Y[ ]N[ ]	Y[ ]N[ ]
MAC2.2	Restricted Token (FC=1100 0000)	8.2.1	c1	o	m	Y[ ]N[ ]	Y[ ]N[ ]	Y[ ]N[ ]

C1. If Rx implemented, then M.

(a) PICS Proforma

6.3.2 Token Class

Item #	Item Name	Ref #	Status			Support		
			Tx	Rx	Fd	Tx	Rx	Fd
MAC2.1	Unrestricted Token (FC=1000 0000)	8.2.1	m	m	m	Y[**X**] N[ ]	Y[**X**] N[ ]	Y[**X**] N[ ]
MAC2.2	Restricted Token (FC=1100 0000)	8.2.1	c1	o	m	Y[ ]N[**X**]	Y[**X**] N[ ]	Y[**X**] N[ ]

C1. If Rx implemented, then M.

(b) PICS

Figure 26.1 Sample part of the MAC PICS proforma and a PICS.

6.4.1 Station Management (SMT) Components

Item #	Item Name	Reference	Status	Support
CFM.1	Single MAC - Dual Attachment Station	5.1	o.1	Y[ ]N[ ]
CFM.2	Dual MAC - Dual Attachment Station	5.1	o.1	Y[ ]N[ ]
CFM.3	Single Attachment Station	5.1	o.1	Y[ ]N[ ]
CFM.4	Dual Attachment Concentrator	5.1	o.1	Y[ ]N[ ]
CFM.5	Single Attachment Concentrator	5.1	o.1	Y[ ]N[ ]
CFM.6	Null Attachment Concentrator	5.1	o.1	Y[ ]N[ ]

o.1 Must specify one of the above FDDI node types.

Figure 26.2 Sample part of the SMT PICS proforma.

letters (m or M) can be used. However, lowercase is more commonly used. The conditions are usually sequentially numbered c1, c2, etc., like footnotes. The final column, "Support," is for answers from the implementor. The standardized symbols for the support column are Y, y, or Yes for implemented capabilities and N, n, or No for capabilities not implemented. In the example shown in Figure 26.1, both status and support columns have been subdivided into three subcolumns corresponding to transmission, reception, and forwarding of tokens. This is simply to save space. An alternative would have been to specify each item as three separate items. The condition c1 as stated implies that if a station receives a restricted token, it must be able transmit it too.

The optional items are sometimes grouped in sets and specified as o.*n*, where *n* is an integer. The implementation is required to support *at least one* or *exactly one* of the group of items numbered o.*n*. The requirement is stated as a footnote. Figure 26.2 shows an example of this notation. Note that o.1 and o1 are different. The first one denotes a set, while the second denotes a specific interpretation explained in a footnote. The dot is used only when there is a group of related options. The absence of a dot means that there is no group.

For some capabilities, support for a default value or range of values is required. These values are specified in a column labeled "STD Type/Range." An example of this notation is shown in Figure 26.3, which shows a portion of the PICS proforma for PMD.

PICS has a number of uses. Protocol implementors can use PICS proforma as a checklist to reduce the risk of failure to conform to the standard through oversight. Buyers and sellers can use

6.1.2 Active Input Interface

Item #	Item Name	Reference	STD Type/range			Status	Support
			MIN	MAX			
PMD2.1	Center Wavelength	8.2	1270	1380	nm	m	Y[ ]N[ ]
PMD2.2	Average Power	8.2	−31	−14	dBm	m	Y[ ]N[ ]
PMD2.3	Rise Time	8.2	0.6	5.0	ns	m	Y[ ]N[ ]
PMD2.4	Fall Time	8.2	0.6	5.0	ns	m	Y[ ]N[ ]
PMD2.5	DCD (P-to-P)	8.2	-	1.0	ns	m	Y[ ]N[ ]
PMD2.6	Random Jitter	8.2	-	0.76	ns	m	Y[ ]N[ ]
PMD2.7	DDJ (P-to-P)	8.2	-	1.2	ns	m	Y[ ]N[ ]

Figure 26.3 Sample part of the PMD PICS proforma.

PICS as a detailed indication of the capabilities of the implementation. Users can use PICS to check initially whether the implementation will work with another implementation. Note that PICS can help find incompatibilities. However, compatibility cannot generally be guaranteed. Protocol testing labs can use PICS to design appropriate tests for conformance.

26.3 Abstract Test Suite (ATS)

An abstract test suite is a set of test cases designed to ensure conformance to the standard. The test cases are *abstract* in the sense that they are independent of any particular implementation. They are expressed only in functional terms, treating the implementation as a black box. For example, the abstract test suite for MAC (MAC-ATS) includes a test to verify that the implementation strips a frame from the ring when it receives a frame with the MAC's own address in the source address field. To execute this test case, the tester will need to learn about a particular implementation and determine how best to conduct this test. The final result, called an *executable test case*, will vary from one implementation to the next. FDDI conformance standard documents specify only abstract test cases. The testing laboratories and the implementors are responsible for translating these abstract cases into executable test cases.

The abstract test suites are designed on the basis of PICS proforma. The tests are designed to test one or more capabilities in the proforma. The PICS as filled out by the implementor helps the testing laboratory to conduct the tests. However, some additional information is usually required to be able to set up tests for a particular implementation. This additional information is called *protocol implementation extra information for testing* (*PIXIT*). A PIXIT proforma is a blank form designed to get the information from the implementor. Figure 26.4 shows an example of a part of PIXIT proforma for MAC.

Figure 26.5 shows a sample abstract test case. This particular test verifies that the implementation strips its own frame from the ring. The test consists of initializing the ring and sending a frame. A timer is started to expire after 1.617 ms (D_max). There are three possible outcomes: (1) The frame is seen and stripped, (2) the frame is seen but not stripped, or (3) the timer expires but the frame is not seen. In the first case, the implementation passes the test and in the other two cases it fails the test. The verdict is indicated by P and F in in the column marked "V" in Figure 26.5. In some cases, a verdict of inconclusive is also possible and is indicated by I. The tests are specified using

⋮

3. The values of timers and parameters to be used by the IUT:

3.1	Target token rotation time to be requested, T_Req	____	μs
3.2	Maximum token rotation time, T_max	____	μs
3.3	Valid transmission timer, TVX	____	μs
3.4	Maximum ring latency, D_Max	____	μs

4. Does the IUT support priority class? Yes____ No____

   If yes, what is the threshold value, T_Pri, of the highest priority class? ____ μs

⋮

Figure 26.4 Sample part of the PIXIT proforma for MAC.

Test Case Dynamic Behavior				
Reference: fddi/MAC/BASIC/STRIP/S_Long_Address				
Identifier: S_Long_Address				
Purpose: Verify that the IUT strips a frame from the ring, when it receives a frame with SA=IUT's address.				
Default:				
Behavior Description	Label	Constraints Reference	V	Comments
+INIT_RING				
!Frame		FRAME_R		(1)
Start D_Max				(2)
?FRAME	L0	FRAME_Strip	P	
?OTHERWISE			F	
?TIMEOUT D_Max			F	
Extended Comments:				
(1) Send frame DA <>IUT's address and SA=IUT's address.				
(2) Wait for frame.				
See 5.4.2: T(10c), p46-47 in ANSI X3.139-1987				

Figure 26.5 A sample abstract test case for MAC.

a *tree and tabular combined notation* (*TTCN*). The name signifies the fact that the test description consists of a tree of tables. Each table defines one aspect of the test suite and contains references to other tables in the suite. For example, the table shown in Figure 26.5 is named S_Long_Address. Its complete reference showing its position in the tree is fddi/MAC/BASIC/STRIP/S_Long_Address. The constraint column defines or limits values of parameters. In the example shown in Figure 26.5, the constraint column makes reference to two other tables, FRAME_R and FRAME_Strip, that define the field values for the frames repeated and stripped, respectively.

Abstract test suites for MAC, PHY, PMD, and SMT are being developed and will be described in four different standard documents abbreviated as MAC-ATS, PHY-ATS, PMD-ATS, and SMT-ATS, respectively.

26.4 International Standardized Profile (ISP)

Most standards contain a number of options and parameters. Two different implementations of the standard may select these options and parameters such that both may conform to the standard but may not interoperate with each other. This problem caused several user groups to develop a list of preferred options and parameters that an implementation should provide. Such lists are called *profiles*. Notable examples of such profiles are *U.S. Government Open Systems Interconnection Profile* (*GOSIP*) used by the U.S. government, *Standards Promotion and Application Group* (*SPAG*) used in Europe, and *Promoting Conformance for OSI* (*POSI*) in Japan. Profiles are also called *functional standards*. Development of numerous regional standards creates confusion. Therefore, ISO has started its own program of developing *international standardized profiles* (*ISPs*). A common classification scheme and notation for developing ISPs has been defined and a number of ISPs either have been developed or are being developed.

Since most users are interested in running their applications on a set of protocol layers and not just one layer, profiles are defined not for individual layers but for a group of layers. An ISP, therefore, is an internationally agreed to, harmonized document that identifies a set of base standards together with options and parameters necessary to accomplish a set of functions. Basically, a profile is a selection of options from the base standards. For each base standard, a choice is made of options that are permitted in that standard and suitable values are chosen for parameters whose allowed ranges are too wide. In this sense, a profile is a limitation of the base standards. The choice of options and parameter ranges in a profile is a proper subset of those allowed by the base standards. The limitation is made to increase the degree of interoperability.

Among the ISPs applicable to FDDI products are two identified as TA54 and RA51.54. A standard method for labeling ISPs has been defined. According to that method, the name TA54, which consists of three parts T-A-54, stands for the transport profile (T) for connection-oriented transport service over connectionless network service (A) over FDDI subnetworks (54). This profile covers the bottom four of the seven layers of the OSI reference model. FDDI has been assigned a subnetwork number of 54. Examples of other subnetworks are 51 (CSMA/CD), 52 (token bus), and 53 (token ring).

Similarly, RA51.54 stands for a relay profile (R) for relaying connectionless network services (A) between CSMA/CD subnetworks (51) and FDDI subnetworks (54). A relay is a general term for bridges and routers. RA is a network layer relay (router). RD is a MAC layer relay (bridge).

Many requirements for the FDDI protocol layers specified in TA54 and RA51.54 are the same. To avoid redundancy, the common part has been specified as ISP 10608-14 and is referenced by other components of TA54 and RA51.54.

Figure 26.6 shows a sample part of the ISP specified for MAC. The letters i, x, and o in the profile feature type column stand for "irrelevant" (out of scope of the profile), excluded (use is prohibited), and optional, respectively. Notice that the delayed token release for SMT frames is allowed by the MAC standard but is excluded by the profile.

ISPs are functional standards. Like other OSI standards, an implementation must be tested for conformance to the ISPs. Therefore, *international standardized profile implementation conformance statement (ISPICS)* proformas have been developed, which like PICS are questionnaires that are

		Base Standard		Profile Feature	
Index	Functions	Clause	Type	Clause	Type
	Token Transmission:				
	Delayed Release	8.1.2			
F221	- SMT Frame		o	5.2.1	x
F4	Ring Scheduling:				
F41	Synch. Service	8.1.4.1	o	5.2.2	i
F42	Async. Service	8.1.4.2			
F4211	Multi Priority Level	7.3.5	o	5.2.3	o
F422	Restricted Token		o	5.2.5	i
F11	Restoring Lost Indicators	8.4.2	o	5.1.4	o

Figure 26.6 Sample part of the MAC ISP.

filled out by the implementors. The completed questionnaires are called ISPICS. ISPICS follow the same conventions and notations that are used for PICS. ISPICS proformas are generally contained in the ISP documents.

26.5 Further Reading

Stallings (1993) provides a good summary of ISO standards related to conformance testing and ISPs.

The general concepts related to development of conformance test suites are covered in ISO 9646-1 through 9646-7.

The PICS for MAC, PHY, PMD, and SMT are covered in CT-PICS (ASC X3T9.5/92-098). The abstract test suites are covered separately in MAC-ATS (ASC X3T9.5/92-101), PHY-ATS (ASC X3T9.5/91-207), PMD-ATS (ASC X3T9.5/92-234), and SMT-ATS (ASC X3T9.5/92-102).

ISO TR 10000-1 and ISO TR 10000-2 cover the framework and taxonomy of ISPs. The TA54 profile is defined in ISO ISP 10608-6. It makes references to ISO ISP 10608-1, 10608-2, and 10608-14. Incidentally, ISP 10608-2 and 10608-6 are currently in the draft and proposed draft stages and are, therefore, referred to as DISP and pdISP, respectively.

Relaying between CSMA/CD networks and FDDI is covered by the RA51.54 profile defined in ISO ISP 10613-6. It makes references to ISO ISP 10613-4 and 10608-14 for FDDI specific parts. ISO DISP 10612 covers transparent bridging among various LANs.

Figures 26.1, 26.2, and 26.3 have been adapted from ASC X3T9.5/92-098. Figures 26.4 and 26.5 are based on ASC X3T9.5/92-101. Figure 26.6 is from ISO/IEC pdISP 10608-14.

26.6 Self-Test Exercises

Note: Some exercises have multiple correct answers. See Appendix D for answers.

26.1 Given that A and B pass the conformance test but C does not, which of the following is true:

a. A and B will interoperate.
b. A and B have a higher performance than C.
c. A and B have a higher reliability than C.
d. A and C will not interoperate.
e. A and B have a higher probability of interoperating than A and C.

26.2 What is PICS?

a. It specifies features of the standard that have been implemented.
b. It specifies features of the profile that have been implemented.
c. It provides additional information required to execute test cases.
d. It is the Picture and Image Communication Standard used for multimedia.

26.3 What is the notation used to specify conformance tests?

a. ATS
b. ISP
c. ISPICS
d. PIXIT
e. TTCN

APPENDIX **A**

Standards Organizations

A number of standards developing organizations have been mentioned throughout this book. This appendix provides brief background information on these organizations. Their addresses are also given here to help you obtain the standards documents.

A.1 International Organization for Standardization (ISO)

The acronym ISO stands for its former name, International Standards Organization. It is the largest standards organization in the world. Its standards cover such diverse areas as agriculture, petrochemicals, environment, and information systems. ISO is not a treaty organization and, therefore, does not require official governmental representation and approval of contributions. It operates on a voluntary basis. Although it is a nongovernmental organization, more than 70% of ISO member bodies are governmental standards institutions or organizations incorporated by public law. The ISO member from the United States is the American National Standards Institute (ANSI). All major industrialized countries have similar standards organizations that represent their national interests in the ISO.

The technical work of ISO is undertaken by *technical committees* (*TCs*) composed of volunteers from manufacturers, suppliers, governments, and major users. These volunteers also represent their national interests. Thus, a delegate from the United States not only brings his or her technical expertise but also represents the United States and ANSI. A TC is composed of several *subcommittees* (*SCs*) and *working groups* (*WGs*), which develop the standards and send it for the approval of the TC. The FDDI standard, for example, is being handled by WG4 of SC25.

In 1977 ISO set up a new subcommittee TC97/SC16 on Open Systems Interconnection (OSI) to investigate and standardize protocols for the interconnection of heterogeneous (or open) computer systems. The committee decided that before developing a set of standards it needed to develop an architectural model of OSI. This resulted in the famous seven-layer reference model that was published in 1984 (ISO 7498:1984).

The *International Electrotechnical Commission* (*IEC*) is also involved in some standards activities similar to that of the ISO. The IEC is concerned primarily with user protection from undesirable side effects of radiation and electrical shock and is, therefore, interested in the physical layer aspects of network cabling. There is an agreement between ISO and IEC to ensure that their work does not overlap. In 1987, ISO and IEC merged their technical committees on information technologies

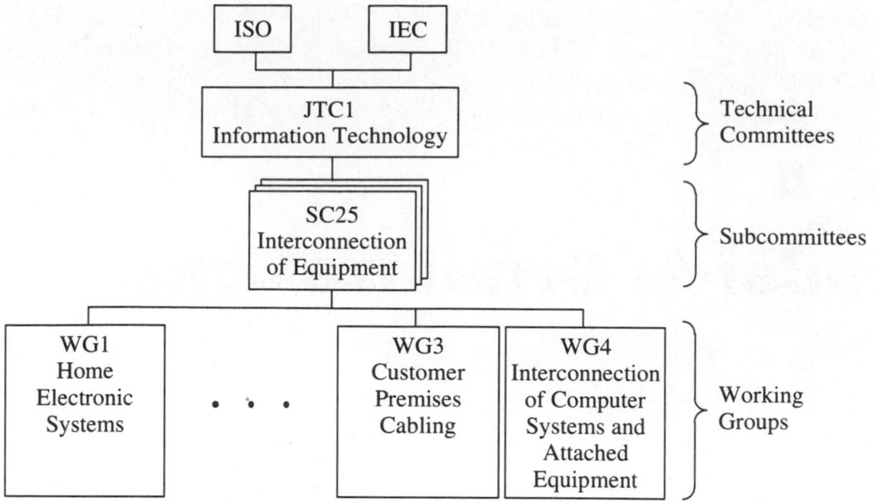

Figure A.1 ISO organizations involved in FDDI standards development.

(ISO TC97, IEC TC83, and IEC SC47B) into a single organization, called ISO/IEC *Joint Technical Committee 1* (*JTC1*). JTC1 is currently handling the network architecture standards including FDDI. Figure A.1 summarizes the organization of ISO.

There are four major stages in the development of a standard. It begins as a *working document* (*WD*) and is assigned a unique number. For example, at one time FDDI PMD standard was referred as ISO WD 9314-3:199x. After the working group or subcommittee considers a draft complete, it is circulated among appropriate TCs, SCs, or WGs as a a *committee draft* (*CD*). [Formerly, the term *draft proposal* (*DP*) was used instead of committee draft.] The CD must receive a substantial level of support from the participating members of the technical committee. This process usually takes several months. After checking for conformity with ISO directives, the secretariat registers the CD as a *draft international standard* (*DIS*). The DIS must be approved by the member bodies of the ISO within six months and must achieve a majority approval by the technical committee members and 75% of all the voting members. The approved DIS, after revisions if necessary, becomes an *international standard* (*IS*). Figure A.2 summarizes the stages in the development of an ISO standard.

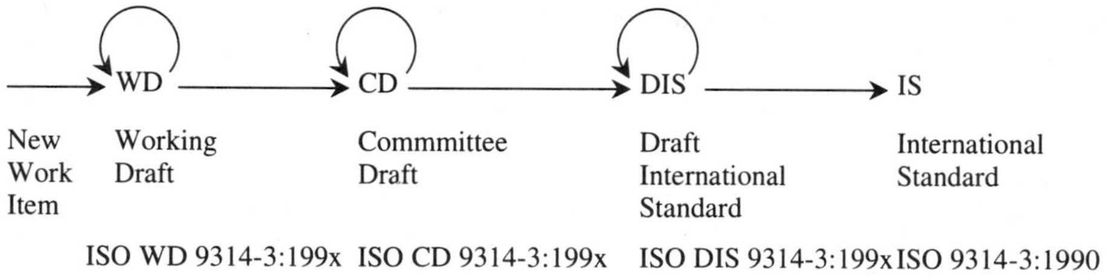

Figure A.2 Stages in the life of an ISO standard.

ISO documents are available from the ISO Office, 1 Rue de Varembé, Case Postale 56, CH-1211, Genève 20, Switzerland. IEC publications may be bought from the Sales Department of the IEC Central Office, P.O. Box 131, 3, Rue de Varembé, 1211 Genèva 20, Switzerland, Phone: +41 (22) 734-0150, Fax: +41 (22) 733-3843. In most countries, the national member committees also sell ISO and IEC documents. For example, in the United States, these documents can be purchased from ANSI.

A.2 The International Telegraph and Telephone Consultative Committee (CCITT)

CCITT is the leading organization for development of standards relating to telephone and other telecommunication services. CCITT is a part of the International Telecommunications Union (ITU), which in turn is a body of the United Nations. In most countries, the government postal, telephone, and telegraph (PTT) organization is the official representative to the CCITT. In the United States, the Department of State is the official representative. The T1 Committee of Exchange Carriers Standards Association (ECSA) supports the Department of State in establishing U.S. positions at CCITT meetings.

CCITT has several study groups, each with responsibilities for a specific area of communications. For example, Study Group XVIII focuses on digital networks and has been active in the development of SONET/SDH and B-ISDN standards.

The plenary assembly of CCITT meets every four years and considers the approval of recommendations produced by the study groups and issues new assignments to them. Thus, CCITT standards are issued at four-year intervals, for example, 1984, 1988, 1992, and so on. This four-year interval has proven too slow for the current rate of change in the telecommunications industry. Therefore, accelerated procedures are being adopted for some specific standards. For example, accelerated development of SDH optical line systems, multiplex equipment, and SDH network management standards was approved by the CCITT plenary in 1988.

CCITT's X-Series Recommendations and Blue Books

CCITT calls the standards it produces *recommendations*. Among its well-known recommendations are the X.25 packet switching interface, X.400 electronic mail services, X.500 directory services, and so on. The X series covers public data networks and services. There are series corresponding to most of the other letters of the alphabet. For example, the D series includes tariff principles and accounting principles for international calls, the E series defines international numbering plan and routing, the F series covers operation and quality of telegraph services, and the Q series describes telephone signaling systems.

CCITT publishes its recommendations at four-year intervals, with the color of the covers changed with each new edition. The color of the set of 1988 CCITT recommendations is blue. The set of the 1988 CCITT recommendations is called the *Blue Book*. The *Blue Book* recommendations will be used until about 1993 after which a new set of books will be issued incorporating revisions until 1992. Since most of the other interesting colors have been used and reused in the last eight editions, the 1992 edition will be white. One of the important items covered by the *White Book* will be broadband ISDN.

CCITT and ISO cooperate and attempt to align their standards so that there is no duplication between them. Standards of mutual interest are generally developed by one organization and then adopted (and published) by both. For example, the OSI reference model was developed by ISO and then published as ISO 7498 as well as CCITT Recommendation X.200. Similarly, the X.400 electronic mail recommendations, developed primarily by CCITT, have been published as ISO/IEC 10021-1 through 10021-7 standards on message oriented text interchange systems.

CCITT documents are available from CCITT General Secretariat, International Telecommunications Union, Sales Section, Place des Nations, CH-1211, Genève 20, Switzerland. In the United States, these documents can also be obtained from the U.S. Department of Commerce, National Technical Information Service (NTIS), 5285 Port Royal Road, Springfield, VA 22161.

In early 1993, ITU was reorganized and the standards-making activities of ITU were consolidated into Telecommunications Standardization Sector (ITU-TS). Thus, the acronym CCITT has been replaced by ITU-TS. CCITT Recommendations X.nnn will now be known as ITU-T Recommendations X.nnn.

A.3 American National Standards Institute (ANSI)

ANSI, created in 1918, is one of the first standards bodies in the United States. ANSI itself does not develop any standards, but it coordinates private sector standards development. It writes the rules for standards bodies to follow and publishes standards produced under its rules. It accredits standards committees, which develop standards in their areas of expertise. When a standards organization is needed for a new work item, ANSI looks for a suitable group willing to sponsor a secretariat. The secretariat provides administrative functions. The major accredited standards committees (ASCs) in the information technology area are JTC1 TAG, X3, and T1. JTC1 TAG is the U.S. technical advisory group (TAG) for ISO/IEC JTC1. It provides U.S. positions on JTC1 standards. ASC X3 produces most of information processing standards. The Computer and Business Equipment Manufacturers Association (CBEMA) supports the secretariat of X3. ASC T1 develops telecommunications standards and is sponsored by the Exchange Carriers Standards Association (ECSA).

X3 was created in 1960 to develop standards in the areas of computers, peripherals equipment, devices, and media. It includes about 40 members. The actual work of X3 is done by its technical committees (TCs). There are more than 40 TCs covering a wide spectrum including programming languages, storage media, databases, graphics, and interconnects. One such TC is X3T9, which is responsible for I/O interfaces. Each TC has several task groups (TGs). For example, X3T9 has three task groups. X3T9.2 is developing **Small Computer System Interface** (**SCSI**) and related standards. X3T9.3 is developing **High-Performance Parallel Interface** (**HIPPI**), **Fiber Channel** (**FC**), and similar standards. X3T9.5 is developing FDDI and related standards.

Data communication standards are normally covered by ASC X3S3. However, FDDI is in X3T9—an I/O oriented committee—purely for historical reasons. It started out as an I/O channel standard (back-end networks). Later its scope was expanded to more general networking but it was left under X3T9.

All proposals for new standards are reviewed by a Standards Planning and Requirements Committee (SPARC). The SPARC also reviews the final standard document to ensure that it complies with the original proposal.

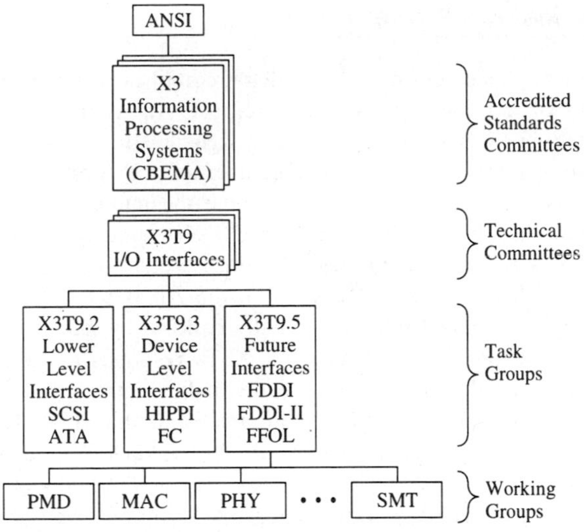

Figure A.3 ANSI organizations involved in FDDI standards development.

Figure A.3 shows the hierarchy of organizations involved in FDDI standards development.

ANSI standards can be purchased from Sales Department, American National Standards Institute, 11 West 42nd Street, New York, NY 10036, Phone: (212)642-4900, Fax: (212)302-1286. Customers in England, Japan, and Canada may purchase ANSI standards from one of ANSI's sales agents:

- American Technical Publishers, Ltd., 27/29 Knowl Place, Wilbury Way, Hertfordshire, SG4 0SX England
- Japanese Standards Association, 1-24, Akasaka, Minato-ku, Tokyo, 107, Japan
- Standards Council of Canada, 350 Sparks, Suite 1200, Ottawa K1P 6N7, Ontario, Canada.

X3T9 and its task groups meet six times a year in February, April, June, August, October, and December. The meetings are held in various cities around the country and usually last one week. The task groups meet on Monday through Thursday, while the X3T9 plenary is held on Friday. The complete X3T9 meeting schedule can be found on the SCSI bulletin board, Phone: (719)574-0424.

X3T9 meetings are open to all and there is usually no fee. All who attend are free to participate in meetings, to make presentations, and to speak on issues. However, only members may vote at the plenaries. Members also receive a mailing containing minutes and copies of all presentations at various working group meetings. These mailings are generally quite voluminous.

Copies of complete ANSI mailings, any submission, or working documents can be purchased from Global Engineering Documents, 2805 McGaw Avenue, Irvine, CA 92714, Phone: (800)854-7179 or (714)261-1455, Fax: (714)261-7892. Global also has branch offices in Clichy, France, and Kowloon, Hong Kong. They also sell standards from numerous organizations including IEC, ISO, CCITT, ECMA, JIS, ANSI, EIA, TIA, and IEEE.

The ANSI Standards Making Process

All standards development processes in ANSI begin with the drafting of a project proposal by a task group. The format of these proposals is described in X3 Standing Document 3. The proposal itself is generally called an SD-3. Any individual or organization can submit a project proposal. However, it is generally prepared by an ad hoc working group of an existing task group that is organized by people interested in a specific topic. The SD-3 must be approved by a task group (X3T9.5 for FDDI-related projects) and X3T9. It is then forwarded to X3 and to X3's SPARC. SPARC reviews the SD-3 and makes a recommendation to X3. If accepted, the X3 secretariat issues a project number. A working group is formed to begin the development of the standard.

Although no technical work should be performed before the project approval, ad hoc working groups often begin technical discussions because project approval can take up to a year.

When a draft standard is completed by a working group, it is presented to the task group (X3T9.5) and a roll call vote is taken. If approved the draft is forwarded to the technical committee (X3T9), which issues a letter ballot to its membership. If a two-thirds majority accepts the draft, it becomes a *draft proposed American National Standard* (*dpANS*). Any comments received during this ballot are carefully considered and resolved if at all possible. The goal is to achieve a consensus of participants rather than a simple majority. If substantive technical changes are made, a new X3T9 letter ballot may be required. In most cases, a roll call vote at the X3T9 meeting is sufficient to make it a dpANS.

The dpANS along with any remaining "no" votes and comments are forwarded to X3 and its SPARC. SPARC reviews the dpANS to ensure that it complies with the authorizing project proposal (SD-3). After SPARC review, the dpANS is assigned a Board of Standards Review (BSR) number of the form X3.999-199x, which will become the number of the final standard. The dpANS then undergoes a public review of four months, which is announced in *Standards Action*, the ANSI publication of record and is finally balloted by X3.

X3T9 responds to the public review and X3 letter ballot comments. If substantive changes are made, another X3T9 letter ballot may be required. The dpANS is then returned to X3 for a second public review of two months. Following resolution of the second public review comments, X3 issues a six weeks letter ballot to determine if the dpANS should be forwarded to the ANSI Board of Standards Review (BSR). Any technical issues raised during the X3 letter ballot are referred back to X3T9 for resolution.

The BSR reviews the dpANS and the procedures related to its handling and ensures that a consensus favoring a standard exists and that the proper procedures were followed. If BSR finds any problems, it returns the standard to X3 for resolution; otherwise, the dpANS is approved as an American National Standard (ANS). The approved standard undergoes a final editing process before it is published as an ANS.

X3T9 generally also sends drafts to ISO at the same time it forwards them for domestic processing. During the first X3 public review, a technical editor appointed by X3T9 and the editorial staff at the ISO secretariat in Geneva conduct a *pre-edit* and convert the document to ISO format. By the time dpANS is balloted by X3, it is generally ready for ISO review procedures.

A.4 Institute of Electrical and Electronics Engineers, Inc. (IEEE)

IEEE is a U.S.-based professional society of electrical and electronic engineers with a worldwide membership of more than 300,000. Its involvement in standards started back in 1890 when the then American Institute of Electrical Engineers (AIEE) proposed the "henry" as the unit of inductance. In 1963, AIEE and the Institute of Radio Engineers (IRE) merged to become the IEEE. Although IEEE was developing standards for quite some time, it formed its first Standards Board in 1973. Work on local area networking standards was started in 1979 in the microprocessor standards working group.

Today IEEE is involved in more than 1400 standards. IEEE operates under ANSI guidelines and passes its recommendations to ANSI for approval as national standards. Some of its standards, notably the IEEE 802 LAN/MAN standards, have been adopted as international standards by ISO/IEC JTC1.

IEEE headquarters are located at 345 E. 47th St., New York, NY 10017, Phone: (212)705-7900, Fax: (212)705-7453.

IEEE standards are available from IEEE Customer Service, 445 Hoes Lane, P.O. Box 1331, Piscataway, NJ 08855-1331, Phone: (800)678-IEEE or (908)981-1392, Fax: (908)562-9667. A set of CD-ROMs containing the full text of 600+ IEEE standards is available from Information Handling Services, 15 Inverness Way East, Englewood, CO 80150, Phone: (800)241-7824 or (303)790-0600. Information Handling Services also supplies standards from several organizations including NEMA and UL on CD-ROMs.

A.5 Electronic Industries Association (EIA)

EIA, founded in 1924 as the Radio Manufacturers Association, is a trade group of U.S. electronic manufacturers. Membership is open to firms who manufacture, produce, or distribute electronic equipment in the United States. It has hundreds of technical committees to develop hardware-oriented standards. Among the well-known EIA standards are the RS-232 and RS-449 interface standards.

EIA has developed a number of building wiring standards that are of interest to FDDI users. These standards have been developed by the TR 41.8 committee, which is subdivided into three ad hoc working groups as follows:

1. *TR-41.8.1*: Working group on commercial and industrial building wiring standard
2. *TR-41.8.2*: Working group on residential and light commercial building wiring standard
3. *TR-41.8.3*: Working group on building telecommunications architecture.

Members of EIA technical committees serve voluntarily and receive no compensation. They represent companies that may or may not be members of EIA. In 1988, the telecommunication sector of the EIA (EIA/ITG) and the U.S. Telephone Suppliers Association merged to become the Telecommunications Industry Association (TIA). While TIA is a separate corporation, it conducts its standards activities through the EIA organization.

EIA/TIA reviews its standards every five years. At that time standards are reaffirmed, rescinded, or revised according to the submitted updates. When a standard is approved as an American National Standard, it is called an ANSI/EIA or ANSI/EIA/TIA standard.

EIA publications can be obtained from EIA Engineering Publications Office, 2001 Pennsylvania Ave., N.W., Washington, DC 20006, Phone: (202)457-4942, Fax: (202)457-4985.

EIA standards and documents can also be obtained from Global Engineering Documents (see address in Section A.3).

A.6 Internet Activities Board (IAB)

IAB manages the TCP/IP protocol suite used on the Internet, which is a collection of several thousand networks from all over the world. In January 1993, more than 137,000 network numbers were assigned for use on the Internet.

The Internet is supported both directly and indirectly by the U.S. government. This started in 1968, when the Advanced Research Project Agency (ARPA), funded the development of an experimental wide area packet-switching network consisting of four nodes. The network was named ARPANET after its sponsor. A working network with about 50 hosts was demonstrated in 1972. Universities and research institutions started joining it in great numbers and the network grew rapidly. In mid-1970s, development of Ethernet and other LANs created a proliferation of networks. Many of these other networks were connected to the ARPANET forming an "Internet." In the early days, only a few researchers worked to develop and test the internet protocols. In 1979, an informal committee, called the Internet Configuration Control Board (ICCB), was formed to guide the technical evolution of the protocols. In January 1983, the Defense Communications Agency reorganized ICCB and named it the Internet Activities Board. In 1992, the Internet Society was created to provide a more formal framework for managing the internet. IAB members were originally appointed by ARPA but now are appointed by the IAB chairman with the advice and consent of the remaining members.

The IAB has two principal subsidiary task forces: the Internet Engineering Task Force (IETF) and the Internet Research Task Force (IRTF). IETF handles short-term practical issues while IRTF handles long-term research issues. Each task force has a number of working groups that handle different issues. IETF meetings are held quarterly and are open to anyone interested in networking issues.

All Internet standards are published in a *Request for Comment* (*RFC*) note series. This archival series was initiated in 1969. All proposed protocols are initially published as *Internet-drafts*, which are available on-line over the Internet. Internet-drafts are discarded automatically after six months if they are not submitted to the RFC editor for publication as an RFC. RFCs are numbered sequentially and new drafts of an RFC are given a new number. There are more than 1400 RFCs but only 100 to 150 of them are standards. Some are earlier versions of a standard and most are just for information—to stimulate discussion. Hence the name "RFC."

When several groups independently implement a protocol proposed in an RFC and test the implementations for interoperability, the RFC may be advanced to a Draft Internet Standard status. Finally, if no further issues exist the RFC may be advanced to the IAB to become an Internet Standard.

RFCs are available in both printed and electronic form. The printed copies of all RFCs and other related documents can be purchased from Network Information Center, 333 Ravenswood Avenue, Menlo Park, CA 94025, Phone: (415)859-3695, Fax: (415)859-6028, E-mail: NIC@NIC.DDN.MIL.

If you are on a system that has FTP access to the Internet, you can obtain RFC via anonymous FTP from NIC.DDN.MIL (192.67.67.20).

If you do not have FTP access to the Internet but can can send and receive mail on the Internet, you can obtain RFCs by mail using an automatic mail service provided by SRI. Address the request to Service@NIC.DDN.MIL and in the subject field indicate the RFC number, for example:

|| Subject: RFC 1340

A reply to your message will contain the desired RFC. To obtain a list of all RFCs, use "RFC Index" on the subject line or get rfc-index.txt via FTP.

A TCP/IP compact disk (CD) containing all the online RFCs, all online Internet Engineering Notes (IENs), For Your Information documents (FYIs), the GOSIP specification, and Berkeley Software Distribution (BSD) networking source code can be purchased from SRI International Network Information Center, Room EJ290, 333 Ravenswood Avenue, Menlo Park, CA 94025, Phone: (415)859-3695, Fax: (415)859-6028, E-mail: NISC@NISC.SRI.COM.

A.7 Other Organizations

A number of standards and rules from other organizations have been referenced in this book. The addresses of these organizations are as follows:

- Bell Communications Research (Bellcore), 60 New England Avenue, Piscataway, NJ 08854-4196, Phone: (800)521-CORE or (908)699-5800, Fax: (908)336-2559.
- Computer and Business Equipment Manufacturers Association (CBEMA), 1250 I Street N.W., Suite 200, Washington, DC 20005-3922, Phone: (202)737-8888, Fax: (202)638-4922, (202)628-2829.
- Exchange Carriers Standards Association (ECSA), 1200 G Street N.W., Suite 500, Washington, DC 20005, (202)628-6380, Fax: (202)393-5453
- Federal Communications Commission (FCC), Washington, DC 20554, Phone: (301)725-1585.
- Institute for Interconnecting and Packaging Electronic Circuits (IPA), 3451 Church Street, Evanston, IL 60203.
- Insulated Cable Engineers Association (ICEA), P.O. Box 440, South Yarmouth, MA 02664, Phone: (508)394-4424.
- National Electrical Manufacturers Association (NEMA), 2101 L Street, Washington, DC 20037, Phone: (202)457-8400. NEMA publications can be obtained from NEMA Publication Distribution Center, P.O. Box 338, Annapolis Junction, MD 20701-0338, Phone: (301)604-8002, Fax: (301)206-9789.
- The National Fire Protection Association (NFPA), 1 Batterymarch Park, Quincy, MA 02269, Phone: (800)344-3555.
- National Technical Information Service (NTIS), 5285 Port Royal Road, Springfield, VA 22161, Phone: (800)553-NTIS, (703)487-4650, Fax: (703)321-8547.
- Telecommunications Industry Association (TIA), 150 N. Michigan Ave., Suite 600, Chicago, IL 60601, Phone: (312)782-8597.
- Underwriters Laboratories, Inc. (UL), 333 Pfingsten Road, Northbrook, IL 60062-2096, Phone: (708)272-8800. UL Standards for Safety are available on CD-ROM from Information Handling Services (see address in Section A.4).

A.8 Further Reading

Judge (1991) and Minoli (1991) provide good descriptions of various standards organizations. RFC 1160 provides a history and description of the IAB and its subsidiary organizations. Burr (1992) provides a summary of ASC X3T9 standards.

A.9 Self-Test Exercises

Note: Some exercises have multiple correct answers. See Appendix D for answers.

A.1 What is an ISO CD?

a. A completed draft that is circulating in a technical committee
b. A certificate of deposit issued by ISO
c. A document stage between the draft international standard (DIS) and IS

A.2 What is the function of ANSI?

a. To develop new standards
b. To accredit groups that develop standards
c. To enforce standards

A.3 The secretariat that is developing FDDI standards is sponsored by:

a. ANSI
b. CBEMA
c. CCITT
d. IEC
e. IEEE
f. ISO

APPENDIX **B**

Sources for Further Information

B.1 FDDI Standards

Published ANSI standards can be obtained from ANSI (see address in Section A.3). Published ISO standards can be purchased from ISO or your national standards organizations. (see Section A.1).

Draft proposed FDDI standards and copies of all documents presented at X3T9.5 meetings can be purchased from Global Engineering Documents (see address in Section A.3).

Many of the FDDI working documents are also available on-line by anonymous FTP from nis.nsf.net (35.1.1.48) in the "working.groups/fddi" directory. The files are of the format *.txt, *.ps, or *.ps.zip. The file INDEX.fddi contains a description of what is in the directory.

Minutes of FFOL meetings and a list of FFOL documents are available via anonymous FTP from ffol.lbl.gov in the ffol directory.

The Internet news group comp.dcom.lans.fddi is devoted to discussion of FDDI issues. If you want to know more about news groups and how to access them, see Krol (1992).

B.2 Product Buyers' Guides

A number of buyer's guides listing all networking or fiber optic products are published annually and quarterly.

Computer Select is a CD-ROM containing the latest industry news, product information, and company information. It includes information about FDDI adapters, bridges, routers, fiber cables, and numerous other products. It is published quarterly by Computer Library, One Park Avenue, New York, NY 10016, Phone: (800)827-7889 or (212)503-4400.

Data Sources is a comprehensive guide to available data communications equipment software and companies. It is published by Ziff Communications Company, One Park Avenue, New York, NY 10016, Phone: (212)503-5398.

Communications and Networking Solutions, Volume 1: LANs & Internetworking contains a comprehensive list of adapters, concentrators, bridges, and router products. It is published by Datapro Information Services Group, 600 Delran Parkway, P.O. Box 1066, Delran, NJ 08075, Phone: (800)328-2776 or (609)764-0100, Fax: (609)764-2814.

Many magazines publish an annual product guide. For example, *Fiberoptic Product News*, a monthly trade publication, has a special issue in October every year. This annual buyers' guide and directory issue lists all fiber optic components and cable manufacturers. The magazine and the special issue are available free to qualified subscribers in the United States and Canada. It is published by Gordon Publications, 301 Gibraltar Drive, Box 650, Morris Plains, NJ 07950, Phone: (201)292-5100, Fax: (201)898-9281.

Fiber Optics Directory is another annual guide listing suppliers of fibers, cables, and other optical components. It can be purchased from Phillips Publishing, Inc., 7811 Montrose Road, Potomac, MD 20854, Phone: (800)722-9120, Fax: (301)424-4297.

B.3 Magazines

Many trade magazines and newsletters cover announcements about FDDI products and architectures. In particular, *FDDI News* is a monthly newsletter devoted exclusively to developments in FDDI. It is published by Information Gatekeepers, Inc., 214 Harvard Ave., Boston, MA 02134, Phone: (800)323-1088 or (617)232-3111, Fax: (617)734-8562. In Europe, contact IGI Europe, Inc., c/o AKM AG, P.O. Box 6, CH-4005 Basel, Switzerland, Phone: +41 61 691 8888, Fax: +41 61 691 8189. They publish a number of other newsletters related to fiber optics, conduct the FOC/LAN and EFOC/LAN conferences and exhibitions, and have published a number of marketing and technology assessment studies.

B.4 Conferences

In the bibliography, you will find references to a number of proceedings of symposia and conferences. In particular, the conferences conducted by the following organizations have been referenced frequently:

- IEEE: See address in Section A.4.
- ACM: ACM Member Service Department, P.O. Box 12115, Church Street Station, New York, NY 10249, Phone: (212)626-0500, Fax: (212)944-1318, E-mail: ACMHELP@ACMVM.BITNET
- SPIE: The International Society for Optical Engineering, P.O. Box 10, Bellingham, WA 98227-0010, Phone: (206)676-3290, Fax: (206)647-1445, E-mail: spie@mom.spie.org.
- EFOC/LAN and FOC/LAN conferences are organized annually by Information Gatekeepers. See Section B.3 for their address.

InterOp conferences, held twice each year, are a major source of information about new networking products. Several hundred vendors exhibit their new products. For more information contact: InterOp, Inc., 480 San Antonio Road, Suite 100, Mountain View, CA 94040, Phone: (800)468-3767 or (415)941-3399, Fax: (415)949-1779.

Another conference with heavy coverage of FDDI-related topics is the IEEE Local Computer Networking conference held once each year in Minneapolis, MN. Further information can be obtained from the IEEE.

B.5 Manufacturers' Documentation

Most manufacturers of FDDI equipment and chip sets have published some literature on FDDI and building wiring, which they are willing to share with (or sell to) prospective buyers. If you are in the market to buy FDDI equipment, you should check with the manufacturers about literature available from them.

APPENDIX **C**

List of Symbols

Table C.1 List of Symbols

Symbol	Meaning
A	Amplitude of the clock signal
α	Total relative synchronous bandwidth allocation (SBA)
	Total SBA = αT
a	Core radius of a fiber
A_C	Maximum cycle clock jitter
α_i	Relative SBA for ith station
	SBA for ith station = $\alpha_i T$
A_S	Amplitude of the cycle using sinusoidal approximation
$A_{\text{SP-P}}$	Peak-to-peak jitter using sinusoidal approximation
A_T	Amplitude of the cycle using triangular approximation
$A_{\text{TP-P}}$	Peak-to-peak jitter using triangular approximation
b_i	Coefficient of x^i in the CRC polynomial
B	Media bandwidth in code bits/second = 1.25×10^8 for FDDI (Chapters 24 and 25)
B_x	x bandwidth, x = 3-dB electrical, 3-dB optical, channel, chromatic, electrical, fiber, link, modal, source, or system
C	Average token rotation time
c	Velocity of light in vacuum
c_i	Token rotation time in ith rotation
D	Ring latency
d	Length of a data bit pattern
Δ	Source spectral width in nm
$D_{\text{chromatic}}$	Chromatic dispersion
D_{eff}	Effective dispersion
dx	Differential of x
e	Base of natural logarithm
erf(x)	Error function of x
$E[x]$	Expected value of x
F	Frame size in code bits (Chapters 24 and 25)

Table C.1 (*Cont.*)

Symbol	Meaning
F	Frame transmission time (Chapter 22)
f	Frequency
F_0	Nominal frequency of the clock
F_a	Average frequency of the clock
F_J	Frequency of the jitter
F_Max	Maximum frame time
$FT[x]$	Fourier transform of x
$g(x)$	CRC polynomial
h	Frame transmission time (a random variable)
$\bar{h}$	Mean frame transmission time
$\ddot{h}$	Second moment of frame transmission time
$h(f)$	Frequency response
h_{large}	Frame transmission time for large frames
h_{small}	Frame transmission time for small frames
i	Generic index variable
j	Generic index variable
k	Number of frames transmitted by ith station during a cycle
k_i	Number of frames transmitted by ith station during first token rotation
L	Number of links in the ring (Chapter 25)
L	Length of a fiber link (Chapter 20)
l	Number of links between the source and destination of a frame
λ	Wavelength
λ	Total frame arrival rate (Chapter 24)
λ_0	Zero-dispersion wavelength
λ_c	Center wavelength
l_f	Length of a fiber link
λ_i	Frame arrival rate at ith station
l_r	Length of a fiber reel
M	Bandwidth-distance product for a fiber
m	Generic index variable
m	Token count (Chapter 23)
μ_i	Average attenuation of ith component
MT(x)	Mean time between events x
N	Number of error events (Chapter 11)
n	Number of active stations (Chapter 22)
n	Number of bits per cycle (Chapter 15)
n	Refractive index (Chapter 4)
n_1	Refractive index of the core
n_2	Refractive index of the cladding
NA	Numerical aperture
n_{eff}	Effective number of active stations
n_i	Number of ith components
n_s	Number of splices

Table C.1 (*Cont.*)

Symbol	Meaning
P	Power
ϕ	Phase of the clock
p	Noise event probability per link (link BER)
ϕ_a	Average phase
P_a	Power level for signal detect assertion
ϕ_a	Average phase of the clock
P_{Avg}	Average of power during low and high signal states
P_b	Power level at which signal detect BER is 1%
P_d	Power level for signal detect deassertion
P_e	Power level for signal deassertion timing test
P_{High}	Power output during high signal state
P_{in}	Input power
$P_{\mathrm{in}}(t)$	Input pulse shape
$P_{\mathrm{link}}(f)$	Frequency response of the link
P_{Low}	Power output during low signal state
P_{Min}	Minimum power required at the receiver
P_{out}	Output power
$P_{\mathrm{out}}(t)$	Output pulse shape
$\phi(t)$	Instantaneous phase of the clock
$\mathrm{P}(x)$	Probability of event x
q	Exponent used in computing modal bandwidth
Q_i	Average queue length at a station
R	Response time
r	Radius of the ring
R_1	Response time for the first frame
$R_{\mathrm{exhaustive}}$	Response time for exhaustive service
R_{FDDI}	Response time for FDDI
R_i	Response time at ith station
r_i	Load share of the ith station
R_{limited}	Response time for limited service
r_{max}	Maximum load share
S	Slope of the dispersion curve at λ_0
σ	Standard deviation
σ_i	Standard deviation of attenuation of ith component
σ_λ	Standard deviation of the wavelength
σ_{link}	Shape parameter for the link frequency response
σ_F	Standard deviation of frame size
σ_w	Standard deviation of interstation delay
Synch_i	Synchronous bandwidth allocated to ith station
T	Period of the clock cycle (only in Chapter 15)
T	Target token rotation time (TTRT)
t	Time
τ	Monitoring interval

Table C.1 (*Cont.*)

Symbol	Meaning
θ	Entrance angle
$\theta_{\max}$	Maximum entrance angle
T_0	Nominal period of the clock
T_b	Period of the bit clock = bit duration
T_C	Period of Cycle clock = cycle duration
T_i	Average data transmission time per rotation at *i*th station
t_i	Rise time contribution of *i*th component
t_i	Time of *i*th event
t_{ij}	Propagation delay between stations *i* and *j*
T_J	Period of the jitter
T_Pri*i*	Token rotation time threshold for *i*th priority
t_x	Rise time of *x*, *x* = fiber, link, source, total
U_a	Throughput for asynchronous traffic
U_i	Throughput of *i*th station
$U_{\max}$	Maximum possible utilization
U_s	Throughput for synchronous traffic
V	Normalized frequency
v	Velocity of light in fiber
w	Token walk time between successive stations
$\bar{w}$	Mean token walk time
$\ddot{w}$	Second moment of token walk time
W_{FWHM}	FWHM pulse width
W_{rms}	rms pulse width
x	Any random variable
$\bar{x}$	Mean of *x*
$\ddot{x}$	Second moment of *x*

APPENDIX **D**

Solutions to Self-Test Exercises

1.1 d

1.2 c

1.3 c

1.4 c

1.5 c

1.6 a. Otherwise, there would not be any trees.

1.7 g. Consider rings with two SASs or with two DASs.

2.1 e

2.2 d

2.3 a and e

2.4 e

2.5 c

2.6 e. Some bridges can set the C-indicator.

2.7 d and e

2.8 c

2.9 c

2.10 b

2.11 c. The addresses are defined as bit strings. There is no standard about how these bit strings are stored in the adapter ROM. Some adapters store it in msb order, others in lsb order.

2.12 d. In particular, the transmission order of the multibyte protocol data is determined by the protocol and not by the system.

2.13 a

2.14 b

2.15 c

3.1 g. The number of bits deleted also depends on the clock rate of the previous station. The previous station may not be properly functioning.

3.2 a

3.3 b

3.4 f

3.5 f

3.6 a

3.7 d

3.8 d. It may not be able to add if it is fully extended.

4.1 a

4.2 b. Electrons travel at the speed of 250 m/μs, while photons in a fiber travel only 200 m/μs (refractive index = 1.5).

4.3 c

4.4 c

4.5 d

4.6 a. At lower wavelengths, the number of modes increases.

4.7 d

4.8 a. Current is proportional to power in milliwatts.

5.1 b

5.2 a

5.3 c

5.4 a, b, and c

6.1 e

6.2 e

6.3 b. Others may require an attenuator.

6.4 d

6.5 b

7.1 d

7.2 b. Duplex-ST is allowed but not without polarity keying.

8.1 c

8.2 b. Also c if you include scrambling as part of the coding.

9.1 b. CCITT standard SDH is slightly different from SONET.

9.2 b

9.3 d

9.4 d

10.1 b

10.2 d

10.3 a, b, and e

11.1 b

11.2 b

11.3 b or c

11.4 b

11.5 d

11.6 a

11.7 d

11.8 a

12.1 b

12.2 b

12.3 b

13.1 a

13.2 c

13.3 b and d

13.4 d

13.5 c

13.6 c

13.7 c

14.1 b

14.2 a

14.3 b

15.1 b and c

15.2 b

16.1 a, b, c, and d. SONET rates do not include 1.00 Gbps.

16.2 b

17.1 e

17.2 a, b, and c

17.3 a and d

18.1 a

18.2 a. This is also known as canonical representation.

18.3 b and c

18.4 i

19.1 b and c

19.2 c

19.3 a and b

19.4 a and c

19.5 a, b, c, and d

20.1 a

20.2 a

20.3 a

20.4 c

21.1 a, b, c, and d

21.2 b and c

21.3 e

21.4 a, b, and d

21.5 b

21.6 a

21.7 a and c

21.8 b, c, and d

22.1 a

22.2 d

23.1 c

23.2 b

23.3 b

23.4 a

23.5 c

24.1 b

24.2 c

25.1 b

25.2 c

25.3 b

26.1 e

26.2 a

26.3 e

A.1 a

A.2 b

A.3 b

APPENDIX **E**

Status of FDDI Standards

Table E.1 Status of FDDI Documents (as of October 1993)

Document	ANSI Reference ISO/IEC Reference	Status
Media Access Control (MAC)	ANSI X3.139-1987	Published.
	ISO 9314-2:1989	Published.
Physical Layer Medium Independent (PHY)	ANSI X3.148-1988	Published.
	ISO 9314-1:1989	Published.
Enhanced Media Access Control (MAC-2)	ANSI X3.239-199x	X3 public review ended July 17, 1993 with no comments.
	ISO/IEC WD 9314-8	CD letter ballot to be issued.
Enhanced Physical Layer Protocol (PHY-2)	ANSI X3.231-199x	X3 letter ballot to be issued.
	ISO/IEC WD 9314-7	CD letter ballot to be issued.
Physical Layer Medium Dependent (PMD)	ANSI X3.166-1990	Published.
	ISO/IEC 9314-3:1990	Published.
Station Management (SMT)	ANSI dpANS X3.229-199x	X3 letter ballot to be issued.
	ISO/IEC WD 9314-6	CD letter ballot to be issued.
Hybrid Ring Control (HRC)	ANSI dpANS X3.186-1992	To be published as an ANSI Standard.
	ISO/IEC DIS 9314-5	To be published as international standard.
Single-Mode Fiber PMD (SMF-PMD)	ANSI X3.184-199x	Approved. To be published as an ANSI standard.
	ISO/IEC CD 9314-4	DIS letter ballot to be issued.
Low-Cost Fiber PMD (LCF-PMD)	ANSI X3.237	X3 public review ended May 8, 1993, with no comments.
	ISO/IEC WD 9314-9	CD letter ballot to be issued.
Twisted-Pair (copper) PMD (TP-PMD)	ASC X3T9.5/93-022	Under development.
Enhanced Station Management Common Services (SMT-2-CS)	ASC X3T9.5/92-299	X3T9 letter ballot in process.

Table E.1 (*Cont.*)

Document	ANSI Reference ISO/IEC Reference	Status
Enhanced Station Management Packet Services (SMT-2-PS)	ASC X3T9.5/92-297	X3T9 letter ballot in process.
Enhanced Station Management Isochronous Services (SMT-2-IS)	ASC X3T9.5/92-298	X3T9 letter ballot in process.
SONET Physical Layer Mapping (SPM)	ANSI T1.105a-1991	Published.
Conformance Test PICS Proforma for FDDI (CT-PICS)	ASC X3T9.5/92-098	X3T9 letter ballot ended April 1993. Comments resolved.
Abstract Test Suite for MAC (MAC-ATS)	ASC X3T9.5/92-101	X3 public review in process.
Abstract Test Suite for PHY (PHY-ATS)	ASC X3T9.5/91-207	X3 public review in process.
Abstract Test Suite for PMD (PMD-ATS)	ASC X3T9.5/92-234	X3T9 letter ballot ended in October 1993.
Abstract Test Suite for SMT (SMT-ATS)	ASC X3T9.5/92-102	Under development.

Notation: WD = Working document
CD = Committee draft
DIS = Draft International Standard
BSR = ANSI Board of Standards Review

APPENDIX **F**

Addresses of Manufacturers

3Com Corp., P.O. Box 58145, 5400 Bayfront Plaza, Santa Clara, CA 95052-8145, Phone: (800)638-3266, (408)764-5000, Fax: (408)764-5001; *Adapters (ISA/EISA), Concentrators, Bridges (IEEE 802.3, IEEE 802.5), Routers, Management software*

3M Telecom Systems Group, 6801 River Place Blvd., Austin, TX 78726-9000, Phone: (512)984-1800, (800)426-8688, Fax: (800)626-0329; *Cables and accessories*

Addax Computers, 3054 Lawrence Expwy., Santa Clara, CA 95051, Phone: (800)333-1944, (408)245-2144, Fax: (408)245-0822; *Adapters*

Advanced Computer Communications, 315 Bollay Dr., Santa Barbara, CA 93117, Phone: (800)444-7854, (805)685-4455, Fax: (805)685-4465; *Bridges, Routers, Networking software*

Advanced Micro Devices, 901 Thompson Place, P.O. Box 3453, Sunnyvale, CA 94088, Phone: (408)987-2382, Fax: (408)987-2800; *FDDI chip set and evaluation boards*

AG Communications Systems Corp., Publications Manager, 2500 West Utopia Road, Phoenix, AZ 85027, Phone: (602)581-4225, Fax: (602)582-7009; *Building wiring documentation*

ALANTEC, Inc., 2380 E. Bering Dr., San Jose, CA 95131, Phone: (800)ALANTEC, (408)955-9000, Fax: (408)955-9500; *Concentrators, Bridges, Routers*

ALCATEL Cable Systems, Inc., P.O. Box 39, Claremont, NC 28610-0039, Phone: (704)459-9787, Fax: (704)459-9312; *Copper/fiber cables and accessories*

ALFA, Inc., 110 Breeds Hill Road, Hyannis, MA 02601, Phone: (508)790-6901, Fax: (508)790-6903, E-mail: scoop4@AOL.com; *Adapters (ISA/EISA, Sbus, Nubus) with synchronous services, Concentrators*

AMP Inc., P.O. Box 3608, Harrisburg, PA 17105-9964, Phone: (800)522-6752, (717)564-0100, Fax: (510)657-4110; *Fiber cables and accessories, Optoelectronic components, Bypass switches*

Amphenol Corporation, 1925 Ohio Street, Lisle, IL 60532, Phone: (312)810-5636; *Cables and accessories*

Anixter Bros., Inc., 4711 Golf Road, Skokie, IL 60076-9723, Phone: (708)677-2600; *Cables and accessories*

Apple Computer, Inc., 20525 Mariani Ave., Cupertino, CA 95014, Phone: (800)776-2333, (408)996-1010, Fax: (408)974-6412; *Adapters*

Applitek Corp., 107 Audubon Rd., Wakefield, MA 01880, Phone: (617)246-4500, Fax: (617)245-7340; *Bridges, Gateways*

Artel Communications Corp., 22 Kane Industrial Dr., Hudson, MA 01749-2906, Phone: (800)225-0228, (508)562-2100, Fax: (508)562-6942; *Bridges, Routers*

Ascom Timeplex, Inc., 400 Chestnut Ridge Rd., Woodcliff Lake, NJ 07675, Phone: (800)669-2677, (201)391-1111, Fax: (201)573-6470; *Concentrators, Bridges (IEEE 802.3, IEEE 802.5, T1), Routers, Management software*

AT&T Customer Information Center, Commercial Sales Representative, P.O. Box 19901, Indianapolis, IN 46219, Phone: (800)432-6600, (317)322-6557, Fax: (317)322-6484; *Building wiring documentation*

AT&T Microelectronics, Lightwave Headquarters, 9999 Hamilton Boulevard, Breinigsville, PA 18031, Phone: (800)372-2447, (215)391-2511, Fax: (215)391-2546; *Optoelectronic components, FDDI chip set*

AT&T Network Systems, 505 North 51 Avenue, Phoenix, AZ 85043, Phone: (800)344-0223, (602)233-5855, Fax: (602)233-5004; *Adapters, Bridges, Routers, Fiber cables and accessories*

BBN Communications, 150 Cambridge Park Dr., Cambridge, MA 02140, Phone: (800)765-4441, (617)873-4000, Fax: (617)354-1349; *Bridges, Routers*

Belden Wire and Cable, P.O. Box 1980, Richmond, IN 47375, Phone: (800)BELDEN-2, (317)983-5200, Fax: (317)983-5294; *Cables and accessories*

BT&D Technologies, Ltd., White House Road, Ipswitch, Suffolk IP1 5PB, UK; *Adapters*

Cable Technology Group, 55 Chapel St., Newton, MA 02160, Phone: (617)969-8552, Fax: (617)964-1432; *Management software*

Cabletron Systems, Inc., 35 Industrial Way, P.O. Box 5005, Rochester, NH 03867-5005, Phone: (603)332-9400, Fax: (603)332-4616; *Adapters (ISA/EISA, Sbus, Micro Channel, NuBus), Bridges (IEEE 802.3), Concentrators, Management software, Fiber cables and accessories, Optoelectronic components*

CACI Products Co., 3344 N. Torrey Pines Court, La Jolla, CA 92037, Phone: (619)457-9681, Fax: (619)457-1184; *FDDI simulation and modeling software*

Canoga-Perkins, 21012 Lassen St., Chatsworth, CA 91311, Phone: (818)718-6300, Fax: (818)718-6312; *Bridges, Routers*

Chipcom Corp., 118 Turnpike Rd., Southborough Office Park, Southborough, MA 01772-1886, Phone: (800)228-9930, (508)460-8900, Fax: (508)460-8950; *Concentrators*

Cisco Systems, Inc., 1525 O'Brien Dr., Menlo Park, CA 94025, Phone: (800)553-6387, (415)326-1941, Fax: (415)326-1989; *Bridges (IEEE 802.3, IEEE 802.5, T1, T3), Routers, Management software*

Codenoll Technology Corp., 1086 N. Broadway St., Yonkers, NY 10701, Phone: (914)965-6300, Fax: (914)965-9811; *Management software, Concentrators, Adapters*

Computer Technology Group, 750 Lake Cook Rd., Buffalo Grove, IL 60089, Phone: (800)837-8649, (708)808-4044, Fax: (708)808-4003; *Education/Training*

Concurrent Computer Corp., 2 Crescent Place, Oceanport, NJ 07757, Phone: (800)631-2154, (908)870-4500, Fax: (908)870-5976; *Adapters (VME)*

Control Data Systems, Inc., 4201 Lexington Ave., N, Arden Hills, MN 55126-6198, Phone: (800)257-OPEN, (612)482-6736, Fax: (612)482-2791; *Adapters*

Coral Network Corp., 734 Forrest St., Marlborough, MA 01752, Phone: (800)424-3579, (508)460-6010, Fax: (508)481-6258; *Bridges, Routers*

Corning, Inc., Telecommunications Products Div., Corning, NY 14831, Phone: (607)974-7914, Fax: (617)974-7522; *Fiber cables and accessories*

COSMIC, University of Georgia, 382 E. Broad St., Athens, GA 30602, Phone: (706)542-3265, Fax: (706)542-4807; *FDDI simulation and modeling software*

Cray Communications, Inc., 9020 Junction Dr., Annapolis Junction, MD 20701, Phone: (800)424-4451, (301)317-7710, Fax: (301)317-7487; *Concentrators, Bridges, Routers*

Cray Research, Inc., 655A Lone Oak Dr., Eagan, MN 55121, Phone: (800)284-2729, (612)683-7100, Fax: (612)683-7199; *Adapters*

Crescendo Communications, Inc., 710 Lakeway Dr., Suite 200, Sunnyvale, CA 94086-4058, Phone: (800)238-CDDI, (408)732-4400, Fax: (408)732-4604; *Adapters (Sbus, EISA, Micro Channel), Concentrators, Management software, Fiber cables and accessories, Fiber to copper media translators*

Data General Corp., 4400 Computer Dr., Westboro, MA 01580, Phone: (800)343-8842, (508)366-8911, Fax: (508)366-1319; *Adapters*

DAVID Systems, Inc., 701 E. Evelyn Ave., Sunnyvale, CA 94088-3718, Phone: (800)762-7848, (408)720-8000, Fax: (408)720-1337; *Concentrators*

Desknet Systems, Inc., 244 Westchester Ave., Suite 209, White Plains, NY 10604, Phone: (800)892-7464, (914)428-7464, Fax: (914)428-7597; *Monitoring and testing equipment*

DiCon Fiberoptics, Inc., 950-C Gilman St., Berkeley, CA 94710, Phone: (415)528-0427; *Optical bypasses*

Digital Equipment Corp., 146 Main St., Maynard, MA 01754-2571, Phone: (800)332-4636, (508)493-5111, Fax: (508)493-8780; *Adapters (ISA/EISA, TurboChannel, Qbus, XMI), Concentrators, Bridges (IEEE 802.3), Routers, Management software, Fiber cables and accessories*

Digital Technology, Inc., 2300 Edwin C. Moses Blvd., Dayton, OH 45408, Phone: (800)852-1252, (513)443-0412, Fax: (513)226-0511; *Monitoring and testing equipment*

Distributed Systems International, Inc., 531 W. Roosevelt Rd., Suite 2, Wheaton, IL 60187-5057, Phone: (708)665-4639, Fax: (708)665-4706, E-mail: Mark1@dsiinc.com; *Adapter (ISA/EISA), Concentrators, SMT software*

DY 4 Systems, Inc., 21 Fitzgerald Road, Nepean, Ontario K2H 9J4, Canada, Phone: (613)596-9911, Fax: (613)596-0574; *Adapters (VME)*

EEC Systems, Inc., 327/E Boston Post Rd., Sudbury, MA 01776, Phone: (800)388-TURBO, (508)443-5106, Fax: (508)443-9997; *FDDI cluster caching software*

Encore Computer Corp., 6901 W. Sunrise Blvd., Ft. Lauderdale, FL 33313-4499, Phone: (800)933-6267, (305)587-2900, Fax: (305)797-5793; *Adapters*

Ensign-Bickford Optics Company, 16 Ensign Drive, P.O. Box 1260 Avon, CT 06001, Phone: (203)678-0371, Fax: (203)674-8818; *Fiber cables and accessories*

FiberCom, Inc., 3353 Orange Ave., Roanoke, VA 24012, Phone: (800)537-6801, (703)342-6700, Fax: (703)342-5961; *Concentrators, Bridges (IEEE 802.3, IEEE 802.5, T1), Routers*

Fibermux Corp., 9310 Topanga Canyon Blvd., Chatsworth, CA 91311, Phone: (800)800-4624, (818)709-6000, Fax: (818)709-1556; *Bridges, Routers*

FiberNet Research, Inc., 1 Tara Blvd., Nashua, NH 03062, Phone: (603)891-2600, Fax: (603)891-4242; *Bridges (IEEE 802.3)*

Fibronics International Inc., 33 Riverside Dr., Pembroke, MA 02359-1978, Phone: (800)553-1552, (617)826-0099, Fax: (617)826-7745; *Concentrators, Bridges (IEEE 802.3, IEEE 802.5), Routers, Management software, Fiber cables and accessories*

Formation, Inc., 121 Whittendale Dr., Moorestown, NJ 08057, Phone: (800)220-1209, (609)234-5020, Fax: (609)234-4252; *Adapters*

FUJITSU Limited, Lightwave Semiconductor Marketing, Furukawa Sogo Bldg., 6-1, Marunouchi 2-chome, Chiyoda-ku, Tokyo 100, Japan, Phone: (03)216-3211, Fax: (03)216-9771; *Fiber optic components*

Gould, Fiber Optics Operations, 6730 Baymeadow Drive, Suite D, Glen Burnie, MD 21061, Phone: (800)54-GOULD; *Fiber cables and optical components*

Harris Corp., 1691 Bayport Ave., San Carlos, CA 94070-5307, Phone: (800)327-4666, (415)594-3000, Fax: (415)594-3110; *Adapters*

Hewlett-Packard Co., 3000 Hanover St., Palo Alto, CA 94304, Phone: (800)452-4844, (415)857-1501; *Adapters, Fiber cables and accessories, Monitoring and testing equipment*

Honeywell, 830 East Arapaho Road, Richardson, TX 75081, Phone: (800)367-6786, (214)470-4271; *Adapters, Optical components*

Hughes LAN Systems, Inc., 1225 Charleston Rd., Mountain View, CA 94043, Phone: (800)732-4252, (415)966-7300, Fax: (415)960-3738; *Concentrators*

International Business Machines Corp., Old Orchard Rd., Armonk, NY 10504, Phone: (800)426-3333, (914)765-1900; *Adapters (Micro Channel), Concentrators, Routers, Network Monitors, Management software, Fiber cables and accessories*

Impulse Technology, 210 Dahlonega St., Suite 205, Cumming, GA 30130, Phone: (404)889-8294, Fax: (404)781-8738; *Concentrators, Adapters*

IN-NET Corp., 15150 Avenue of Science, Suite 100, San Diego, CA 92128-3495, Phone: (800)283-FDDI, (619)487-3693, Fax: (619)487-3697; *Networking software, Channel extenders*

Intel Supercomputer Systems, 15201 N.W. Greenbrier Pkwy., Beaverton, OR 97006, Phone: (503)629-7835, Fax: (503)629-9147; *Adapters*

Interphase Corp., 13800 Senlac, Dallas, TX 75234, Phone: (214)919-9000, Fax: (214)919-9200; *Adapters (VMA, EISA, Sbus, Multibus), Concentrators*

Kardios Systems Corp., 26 N. Summit Ave., Gaithersburg, MD 20877, Phone: (301)840-9225, Fax: (301)990-6378; *Network management*

LANNET Data Communications Ltd., ATIDIM Technological Park, Building #3, Tel Aviv 61131, Israel, Phone: +972 (3)645-8458, Fax: +972 (3)544-7146; *Concentrators, Bridges (IEEE 802.3), Routers, Network monitors, Management software, LAN switches*

Madge Networks, 2310 North First Street, San Jose, CA 95131-1011, Phone: (408)955-0700, (800)876-2343, Fax: (408)955-0970; *Adapters (ISA/EISA), Routers*

Math Associates, Inc., 2200 Shames Drive, Westbury, NY 11590, Phone: (516)334-6800, Fax: (516)334-6473; *Fiber cables and accessories*

McDonnell Douglas Aerospace, MIDOCS Program Office, 1801 E. St. Andrew Place, Santa Ana, CA 92705, Phone: (800)234-2772, (714)566-4560, Fax: (714)566-4557; *Secure FDDI repeater*

Metrix Network Systems, Inc., One Tara Blvd., Nashua, NH 03062, Phone: (603)888-7000, Fax: (603)891-2796; *Networking software*

Microdyne Corp., 207 S. Peyton St., Alexandria, VA 22314, Phone: (800)255-3967, (703)739-0500, Fax: (703)739-0572; *Adapters*

Mitsubishi Electric Corp., Semiconductor Marketing Division, 2-3, Marunouchi 2-chome, Chiyoda-ku, Tokyo 100, Japan, Phone: +81 (03)218-3473, Fax: +81 (03)218-5570; *Optical components*

Modular Computer Systems, Inc. (MODCOMP), 1650 W. McNab Rd., P.O. Box 6099, Ft. Lauderdale, FL 33340-6099, Phone: (305)974-1380, Fax: (305)977-1900; *Adapters*

Motorola, Inc., Data Communications Operation, 6501 William Cannon Dr., Austin, TX 78735-8598, Phone: (512)891-3823, Fax: (512)891-8807; *FDDI chip set*

Motorola, Inc., GSTG, 8201 E. McDonnel Road, Scottsdale, AZ 85252, Phone: (602)441-3686, Fax: (602)441-2368; *Network encryption systems*

National Semiconductor Corp., 2900 Semiconductor Drive, P.O. Box 58090, Santa Clara, CA 95052-8090, Phone: (408)721-5000, Fax: (910)339-9240; *FDDI chip set and evaluation kits*

NCR Corp., 1700 S. Patterson Blvd., Dayton, OH 45479, Phone: (800)CALL-NCR, (513)445-5000, Fax: (513)445-4184; *Concentrators, Bridges, Routers*

NEC America, Inc., 110 Rio Robles, San Jose, CA 95134-1899, Phone: (800)222-4NEC ext. 1277, (408)433-1250, Fax: (408)433-1239; *Bridges, Routers*

Network General Corp., 4200 Bohannon Dr., Menlo Park, CA 94025, Phone: (800)695-8251, (415)688-2700, Fax: (415)321-0855; *Monitoring and testing equipment*

Network Peripherals, Inc., 1371 McCarthy Blvd., Milpitas, CA 95035, Phone: (408)321-7300, Fax: (408)321-9218, E-mail: Info@fastnet.com; *Adapters (VME, ISA, EISA, Sbus, Micro Channel), Concentrators, Bridges (IEEE 802.3)*

Network Systems Corp., 7600 Boone Ave., N, Minneapolis, MN 55428, Phone: (800)338-0122, (612)424-4888, Fax: (612)424-2853; *Bridges, Routers, Adapters, Concentrators, LAN repeaters*

NetWorth, Inc., 8404 Esters Rd., Irving, TX 75063, Phone: (800)544-5255, (214)929-1700, Fax: (214)929-1720; *Concentrators*

Newbridge Networks Corp., 593 Herndon Pkwy., Herndon, VA 22070-5421, Phone: (800)343-3600, (703)834-3600, Fax: (703)471-7080; *Bridges, Routers*

Newport Corp., 18235 Mt. Baldy Cir., Fountain Valley, CA 92708, Phone: (714)965-5406; *Fiber optic instruments and tools*

Novell, Inc., 122 East 1700 South, Provo, UT 84606-6194, Phone: (800)NETWARE, (801)429-7000, Fax: (801)429-5775; *Networking software*

Optical Cable Corp., P.O. Box 999, 870 Harrison Ave., Salem, VA 24153-0990, Phone: (703)389-9900; *Optical cable*

Optical Data Systems (ODS), Inc., 1101 E. Arapaho Rd., Richardson, TX 75081-2336, Phone: (214)234-6400, Fax: (214)234-1467; *Adapters (VME, ISA/EISA, Sbus, Micro Channel), Concentrators, Bridges, Routers, Management software, Fiber cables and accessories, Optoelectronic components*

Ortronics, Inc., 595 Greenhaven Road, Pawcatuck, CT 06379, Phone: (800)356-7785, (203)599-1760, Fax: (203)599-1774; *Fiber cables and accessories*

PC Office, Inc., 4901 Morena Blvd., Suite 805, San Diego, CA 92117, Phone: (619)273-1442, Fax: (619)273-2706; *Adapters*

PCO, Inc., 20200 Sunburst St., Chatsworth, CA 91311, Phone: (818)700-1233, Fax: (818)882-7041; *FDDI optical components*

Penril DataComm Networks, 1300 Quince Orchard Blvd., Gaithersburg, MD 20878-4106, Phone: (800)4-PENRIL, (301)921-8600, Fax: (301)921-8376; *Bridges, Routers*

Plexcom, Inc., 2255 Agate Court, Simi Valley, CA 93065, Phone: (805)522-3333, Fax: (805)583-4764; *Adapters*

PlusNet Corp., 21630 North 19th Ave., Suite B-16, Phoenix, AZ 85027, Phone: (800)468-9032, (602)581-6771, Fax: (602)581-8545; *Adapters, Concentrators*

Proteon, Inc., 9 Technology Dr., Westborough, MA 01581-1799, Phone: (800)545-7464, (508)898-2800, Fax: (508)366-8901; *Bridges, Routers*

Racal-Datacom, Inc., 1601 N. Harrison Pkwy., Sunrise, FL 33323-2899, Phone: (800)RACAL-55, (305)846-1601, Fax: (305)846-5510; *Bridges, Routers*

RAD Data Communications, 8 Hanechoshet St., Tel Aviv 69710, Israel, Phone: +972 3 6458181, (201)529-1100 in USA, Fax: +972 3 498250; *Adapters (ISA/EISA, Sbus), Concentrators, Bridges (IEEE 802.3)*

Radiant Communications Corp., P.O. Box 867, South Plainfield, NJ 07080, Phone: (800)WOW-FIBR, (201)757-7444, Fax: (201)757-8666; *Fiber cables and accessories*

Raycom Systems, Inc., 16525 Sherman Way, Bldg. C-8, Van Nuys, CA 91406, Phone: (800)288-1620, (818)909-4186, Fax: (818)909-4190; *Bridges, Routers*

Retix Corp., 2401 Colorado Ave., Santa Monica, CA 90404-3563, Phone: (800)255-2333, (310)828-3400, Fax: (310)828-2255; *Bridges, Routers*

Rockwell International Corp., 125 Cremona Dr., Santa Barbara, CA 93117, Phone: (800)262-8023, (805)968-4262, Fax: (805)968-6478; *Networking software, Adapters*

SBE, Inc., 2400 Bisso Lane, Concord, CA 94520, Phone: (800)347-2666, (510)680-7722, Fax: (510)680-1427; *Adapters*

Siecor Corp., 489 Siecor Park, P.O. Box 489, Hickory, NC 28603-0489, Phone: (800)FON-SIEC, (704)327-5000, Fax: (704)327-5973; *Fiber cables and accessories*

SIEMENS, Fiber Optic Components, Group of Potter & Brumfield, P.O. Box 4757, 3846 First Avenue, Evansville, IN 47710, Phone: (812)422-2322; *Fiber optic components*

SIGMA Networking Systems, Inc., 25 Walkers Brook Dr., Reading, MA 01867, Phone: (800)64-SIGMA, (617)942-0200, Fax: (617)942-0825; *Bridges, Routers*

Silicon Graphics, Inc., 2011 N. Shoreline Blvd., PO Box 7311, Mountain View, CA 94039-7311, Phone: (800)800-4744, (415)960-1980, Fax: (415)961-0595; *Adapters, Networking software*

Simple Net Systems, Inc., 545 West Lambert Road, Suite A, Brea, CA 92621, Phone: (714)529-8850; *Adapters*

Star-Tek, Inc., 71 Lyman St., Northboro, MA 01532, Phone: (800)225-8528, (508)393-9393, Fax: (508)393-6934; *Concentrators*

Storm Products Co., 116 Shore Drive, Hinsdale, IL 60521, Phone: (708)323-9121, Fax: (708)323-9398; *Fiber optic cables and supplies*

Sumitomo Electric, 551 Madison Avenue, New York, NY 10022, Phone: (212)308-6444, Fax: (212)308-6575; *Adapters, Routers, FDDI chip set, Optical components*

Sun Microsystems, Inc., 2550 Garcia Ave., Mountain View, CA 94043, Phone: (800)241-CONX, (415)960-1300; *Networking software, Adapters*

Synernetics, Inc., 85 Rangeway Rd., North Billerica, MA 01862, Phone: (508)670-9009, Fax: (508)670-9015; *Bridges, Routers, Concentrators*

SynOptics Communications, Inc., P.O. Box 58185, 4401 Great America Pkwy., Santa Clara, CA 95052-8185, Phone: (800)776-6895, (408)988-2400, Fax: (408)988-5525; *Concentrators, Bridges (IEEE 802.3, IEEE 802.5), Routers, Management software, Fiber cables and accessories*

SysKonnect, Inc., 12930 Saratoga Ave., Suite D-1, Saratoga, CA 95070-4669, Phone: (800)SK2-FDDI, (408)725-4650, Fax: (408)725-4654; *Adapters (ISA/EISA, Micro Channel, NuBus), Concentrators, Internetworking software*

Technitrol, Inc., 1952 E. Allegheny Ave., Philadelphia, PA 19134, Phone: (215)426-9105, Fax: (215)426-2836; *STP and UTP transceivers*

Tekelec, 26580 W. Agoura Rd., Calabasas, CA 91335, Phone: (800)TEK-ELEC, (818)880-5656, Fax: (818)880-6993; *Monitoring and testing equipment*

Tektronix, Inc., P.O. Box 1197, Redmond, OR 97756, Phone: (800)833-9200, (503)923-0333, Fax: (503)923-4434; *Monitoring and testing equipment*

Telecommunications Techniques Corp., 20410 Observation Dr., Germantown, MD 20876, Phone: (800)638-2049, (301)353-1550, Fax: (301)353-0734; *Monitoring and testing equipment*

Thinking Machines Corp., 245 First St., Cambridge, MA 02142-1214, Phone: (617)876-1111, Fax: (617)234-4444; *Adapters*

Thomson Electron Tubes and Devices, 550 Mount Pleasant Ave., Dover, NJ 07801, Phone: (201)328-1400; *Optical transceivers*

Trellis Communications Corp., 749 E. Industrial Park Dr., Manchester, NH 03109, Phone: (603)668-1213, Fax: (603)668-9211; *Monitoring and testing equipment*

Ungermann-Bass, Inc., P.O. Box 58030, 3900 Freedom Circle, Santa Clara, CA 95052-8030, Phone: (800)777-4LAN, (408)496-0111, Fax: (408)970-7300; *Concentrators, Bridges, Routers*

UNISYS Corp., P.O. Box 500, Suite S2, Blue Bell, PA 19424-0001, Phone: (800)448-1424, (215)986-4011, Fax: (215)986-2312; *Adapters, Concentrators, Gateways*

Universal Fiber Optics, Inc., 215 W. 4th Street, P.O. Box 1909, Salem, VA 24153, Phone: (703)389-9844, Fax: (703)389-4408; *Fiber cables and accessories*

Vitalink Communications Corp., 48761 Kato Rd., Fremont, CA 94538, Phone: (800)443-5740, (510)226-6500, Fax: (510)440-2380; *Bridges, Routers*

Vortech Data, Inc., 10700 Parkridge Blvd., Reston, VA 22091, Phone: (800)869-9998, (703)264-0020, Fax: (703)264-1941; *Text/image management systems*

Wandel & Goltermann Technologies, Inc., 1030 Swabia Court, P.O. Box 13585, Research Triangle Park, NC 27709-3585, Phone: (800)277-7404, (919)941-5730, Fax: (919)941-5751; *Monitoring and testing equipment*

Wang Laboratories, Inc., One Industrial Ave., Lowell, MA 01851, Phone: (800)835-9264, (508)459-5000; *Adapters*

Wellfleet Communications, Inc., 2 Federal Street, Billerica, MA 01821, Phone: (800)448-3400; (508)663-6676; Fax: (508)670-5747; *Routers*

XLNT Designs, Inc., 15050 Avenue of Science, Suite 106, San Diego, CA 92128, Phone: (619)487-9320, Fax: (619)487-9768, E-mail: marcom@xlnt.com; *SMT software, Special function FDDI chips, Product development contract engineering services*

Xylogics, Inc., 53 Third Ave., Burlington, MA 01803, Phone: (800)225-3317, (617)272-8140, Fax: (617)273-5392; *Terminal servers, Peripheral controllers*

References

ANSI T1.105-1991. *Digital Hierarchy—Optical Interface Rates and Formats Specifications (SONET)*, 2 July 1991. ANSI T1.105-1991 includes supplement ANSI T1.105a-1991.

ANSI T1.105a-1991. *Digital Hierarchy—Optical Interface Rates and Formats Specifications (SONET) (FDDI and STS path signal level)*, Supplement to ANSI T1.105-1991, 20 November 1991, 5.

ANSI T1.106-1988. *Telecommunications—Digital Hierarchy Optical Interface Specifications (Single Mode)*.

ANSI X3.139-1987. *Information Systems—Fiber Distributed Data Interface (FDDI)—Token Ring Media Access Control (MAC)*. See also ISO 9314-2:1989.

ANSI X3.148-1988. *Information Systems—Fiber Distributed Data Interface (FDDI)—Token Ring Physical Layer Protocol (PHY)*. See also ISO 9314-1:1989.

ANSI X3.166-1990. *Information Systems—Fiber Distributed Data Interface (FDDI)—Token Ring Physical Layer Medium Dependent (PMD)*. See also ISO/IEC 9314-3:1990.

ANSI X3.184-199x. *Information Processing Systems—Fiber Distributed Data Interface (FDDI) Part 4: Single-Mode Fiber PMD (SMF-PMD)*, ASC X3T9/89-080, Rev 4.2, December 7, 1992, ISO/IEC CD 9314-4:199x.

ANSI dpANS X3.186-199x. *Information Processing Systems—Fiber Distributed Data Interface (FDDI) Part 5: Hybrid Ring Control (HRC)*, ASC X3T9.5/87-10, Rev. 6.3, ISO/IEC DIS 9314-5:199x, May 28, 1992.

ANSI dpANS X3.229-199x. *Information Processing Systems—Fiber Distributed Data Interface (FDDI) Part 6: Token Ring Station Management (SMT)*, ASC X3T9.5/84-49, Rev. 7.2, ISO/IEC CD 9314-6:199x, June 25, 1992.

ANSI X3.231-199x. *Information Processing Systems—Fiber Distributed Data Interface (FDDI) Part 7: Token Ring Physical Layer Protocol (PHY-2)*, Rev. 5.2, November 1, 1993, ISO/IEC 9314-7, 51 pp.

ANSI X3.237-199x. *FDDI Low-Cost Fibre Physical Layer Medium Dependent (LCF-PMD)*, ASC X3T9.5/92-155, Rev. 1.3, September 1, 1992, ISO/IEC CD 9314-9:199x, 50 pp.

ANSI X3.239-199x. *Enhanced Media Access Control (MAC-2)*, Rev. 4.1, September 3, 1992, ISO/IEC CD 9314-8:199x.

ANSI Z136.1-1993. *American National Standard for the Safe Use of Lasers*, 92 pp.

ANSI Z136.2-1988 *American National Standard for the Safe Use of Optical Fiber Communications Systems Utilizing Laser Diode and LED Sources*, 36 pp.

ANSI/EIA. See also EIA.

ANSI/EIA/TIA 492AAAA-1989. *Specification for 62.5 μm Core Diameter/125 μm Cladding Diameter Class 1a Multimode Graded-index Optical Waveguide Fibers.*

ANSI/EIA/TIA 568-1991. *Commercial Building Telecommunications Wiring Standard*, 71 pp.

ANSI/EIA/TIA 569-1990. *Commercial Building Standard for Telecommunications Pathways and Spaces.*

ANSI/EIA/TIA 570-1991. *Residential and Light Commercial Telecommunications Wiring Standard.*

ANSI/ICEA S-80-576-1990. *Telecommunications Wire and Cable for Wiring of Premises.*

ANSI/ICEA S-83-596-1988. *Fiber Optic Premises Distribution Cable.*

ANSI/IEEE. See also IEEE and ISO 8802.

ANSI/IEEE 802.1a-1990. *Local Area Network and Metropolitan Area Network—Overview and Architecture*. See also IEEE 802-1990.

ANSI/IEEE 802.1d-1990. *Local Area Network MAC (Media Access Control) Bridges*. See also IEEE 802.1D-1990.

ANSI/IEEE 802.3-1992. Same as ISO/IEC 8802-3:1992.

ANSI/IEEE 802.6-1991. *Distributed Queue Dual Bus (MAN).*

ASC X3T9.5/84-49. See ANSI dpANS X3.229-199x.

ASC X3T9.5/91-207. *Abstract Test Suite for FDDI Physical Layer Protocol Conformance Testing (FDDI PHY ATS)*, Rev 2.5, February 22, 1993, 13 pp.

ASC X3T9.5/92-098. *Conformance Test Protocol Implementation Conformance Statement Proforma (CT-PICS) for ANSI X3T9.5 FDDI Standards*, Rev 3.4, October 12, 1993, 38 pp.

ASC X3T9.5/92-101. *Abstract Test Suite for FDDI Media Access Control Conformance Testing (FDDI MAC ATS)*, Rev 2.2, February 18, 1993, 81 pp.

ASC X3T9.5/92-102. *Abstract Test Suite for FDDI Station Management (FDDI SMT ATS)*, June 2, 1992, 44 pp.

ASC X3T9.5/92-155. See ANSI X3.237-199x.

ASC X3T9.5/92-234. *Abstract Test Suite for FDDI Physical Media Dependent Conformance Testing (FDDI PMD ATS)*, Rev 2.4, August 20, 1993, 28 pp.

ASC X3T9.5/92-297. *FDDI Station Management-2 Packet Services (SMT-2-PS)*, Rev 2.1, August 31, 1993, 119 pp.

ASC X3T9.5/92-298. *FDDI Station Management-2 Isochronous Services (SMT-2-IS)*, Rev 2.3, August 31, 1993, 105 pp.

ASC X3T9.5/92-299. *FDDI Station Management-2 Common Services (SMT-2-CS)*, Rev 2.1, September 1, 1993, 162 pp.

ASC X3T9.5/93-022. *FDDI Twisted Pair Physical Layer Medium Dependent (TP-PMD)*, Rev. 1.1, October 14, 1993, 69 pp.

Annamalai, K. (1988). FDDI physical layer implementation considerations, Proc. SPIE Conf. on Optic Datacom and Computer Networks, Boston, MA, **991**, 88–95.

Architecture Technology Corp. (1990). *Fiber Distributed Data Interface (FDDI) Technology Report,* 155 pp.

Arnoff, R., K. Brady, M. Chernick, et al. (1992). *Government Network Management Profile (GNMP): Public Review Version of Proposed FIPS*, NIST Internal Report, NISTIR 4651. Available from NTIS, Springfield, VA.

Basch, E. (Ed.) (1986). *Optical-Fiber Transmission*, Howard W. Sams & Co., Indianapolis, IN, 542 pp.

Bell, G. (1992). Ultracomputers: A teraflop before its time, *CACM*, **35**(8), 26–47.

Bellamy, J. (1991). *Digital Telephony*, Wiley, New York, 572 pp.

Bellcore TA-NWT-000253 (1990). *Synchronous Optical Network (SONET) Transport Systems: Common Generic Criteria*, Issue 6.

Bellcore TR-TSY-0000020 (1989). *Generic Requirements for Optical Fiber and Optical Fiber Cable*, Issue 4, March 1989.

Black, U. (1992). *Network Management Standards: The OSI, SNMP and CMOL Protocols*, McGraw-Hill, New York, 336 pp.

Boston, T. (1988). FDDI-II: A high speed integrated service LAN, Proc. EFOC/LAN'88, Amsterdam, Netherlands, Information Gatekeepers, Boston, MA, 312–315.

British Standards Institution, BS6527. *Limits and Methods of Measurement of Radio Interference Characteristics of Information Technology Equipment*. Available from BSI, Marylands Avenue, Hemel Hempstead, Herts, England.

Brooks, C. and Yue, O. (1989). Effect of the token holding timer on map performance, Proc. IEEE INFOCOM'89, Ottawa, Ont., Canada, 342–347.

Burr, W. (1986). The FDDI optical data link (fibre distributed data interface), *IEEE Commun. Mag.*, **24**(5), 18–23.

Burr, W. (1989). *FDDI Transparent Bridge Issues*, Presentation to ASC X3T9.5 FDDI SMT working group, SMT-311, March 6, 1989, 8 pp.

Burr, W. (1990). *Architectures for Future Multigigabit Lightwave Networks*, Technical Report, National Bureau of Standards, 63 pp.

Burr, W. (1992). *An Introduction to X3T9 and I/O Interface Standards*, Presentation ASC X3T9.5/92-151, 4 May 1992, 28 pp.

Burr, W. and F. Ross (1984). The fiber distributed data interface: A proposal for a standard 100 Mbit/s, fiber optic token ring network, Proc. FOC/LAN'84, Las Vegas, NV, Information Gatekeepers, Boston, MA, 254–257.

W. Bux (1989). Token-ring local-area networks and their performance, *Proceedings of the IEEE*, **77**(2), 238–256.

Bux, W. and H. Truong (1983). Mean-delay approximation for cyclic-service queueing systems, *Performance Evaluation*, **3**, 187–196.

CCITT Recommendation G.703 (1988). Physical/electrical characteristics of hierarchical digital interfaces, *Blue Book Fascicle III.4*, 45–75.

CCITT Recommendation G.732 (1988). Characteristics of primary PCM multiplex equipment operating at 2048 kbit/s, *Blue Book Fascicle III.4*, 375–381.

CCITT Recommendation G.957 (1990). Optical interfaces for equipment and systems relating to the synchronous digital hierarchy.

Calvo, R. and M. Teener (1990). FDDI-II architectural and implementation examples, Proc. EFOC/LAN'90, Munich, Germany, Information Gatekeepers, Boston, MA, 76–86.

Case, J. (1990). Management of high speed networks with the simple network management protocol (SNMP), Proc. IEEE LCN'90, Minneapolis, MN, 195–199.

Case, J., K. McCloghrie, M. Rose, and S. Waldbusser (1992). The Simple Management Protocol and Framework: Managing the evolution of SNMP, *ConneXions*, **6**(10), 16–23.

Caves, K. (1987). FDDI-II: A new standard for integrated services high-speed LANs, *Telecommunications*, **21**(9), 91–2, 95-6, 100.

Caves, K. and A. Flatman (1986). FDDI-II: A new standard for integrated services high speed LANs, Proc. International Conference on Wideband Communications, Online Publications, Pinner, Middx., England, 81–91.

Cherin, A. (1983). *An Introduction to Optical Fibers*, McGraw-Hill, New York, 326 pp.

Chown, D., R. Musk, R. Plumb, J. Somerville, and M. Kaplit (1988). ELED as a source for FDDI networks, Proc. SPIE Conf. on Optic Datacom and Computer Networks, Boston, MA, **991**, 69–76.

Ciarfella, P., D. Benson, and D. Sawyer (1991). An overview of the common node software, *Digital Technical Journal*, **3**(2), 42–52.

Cohen, D. (1981). On holy wars and a plea for peace, *IEEE Computer Magazine*, **14**(10), 48–54.

Comer, D. (1990). *Internetworking with TCP/IP*, Ed. 2, Prentice Hall, Englewood Cliffs, NJ, 547 pp.

Computer Technology Research Corporation (1991). *FDDI Technology Report*, Computer Technology Research Corporation, Charleston, SC.

Davids, P. and T. Meuser (1991). FDDI-II and DQDB under heavy load, Proc. EFOC/LAN'91, London, UK, Information Gatekeepers, Boston, MA, 28–32.

Davidson, R. and N. Muller (1991). *The Guide to SONET: Planning, Installing & Maintaining Broadband Networks*, Telecom Library, New York, 215 pp.

Davies, P., Ed. (1981). *The American Heritage Dictionary of the English Language*, Dell Publishing, New York, 820 pp.

Digital Equipment Corporation (1990). *DECconnect System: Fiber Optic Planning and Configuration*, EK-DECSY-FP-001.

DIN VDE 0878 Part 3. *Electromagnetic Compatibility of Information Technology and Telecommunications Equipment; Limits and Methods of Measurement of Radio Interference Characteristics of Information Technology Equipment* (CISPR 22, modified). Available from VDE-Verlag GmbH, 1 Berlin 12, Germany.

DIN VDE 0878 Part 30. *Electromagnetic Compatibility of Information Technology and Telecommunications Equipment; Limits and Methods of Measurement of Radio Interference Characteristics of Information Technology Equipment; Supplement to DIN VDE 0878 Part 3.*

Dodds, D. and J. Hingston (1987). Point to point clocking for FDDI fiber optic data rings, Proc. IEEE Pacific Rim Conference on Communications, Computers and Signal Processing, 323–326.

Dykeman, D. and W. Bux (1987). An investigation of the FDDI media-access control protocol, Proc. EFOC/LAN'87, Basel, Switzerland, Information Gatekeepers, Boston, MA, 229–236.

Dykeman, D. and W. Bux (1988). Analysis of tuning of FDDI media access control protocol, *IEEE J. Sel. Areas Commun.*, **6**(6), 997–1010.

Eberle, J. (1991). *Duplex Push-pull SC Receptacle & Connector System*, Presentation to ASC X3T9.5 FDDI LCF-PMD working group, LCF-PMD/045, October 14, 1991, 62 pp.

EEC Directive 89/336. *Council Directive of 3 May 1989 on the Approximation of the Laws of the Member States Relating to Electromagnetic Compatibility.*

EIA/IS-43 (1987). *Omnibus Specification—Local Network Twisted Pair Data Communications Cable.*

EIA/TIA TSB-36 (1991). *Additional Cable Specifications for Unshielded Twisted Pair Cables.*

EIA/TIA TSB-40 (1992). *Additional Transmission Specifications for Unshielded Twisted-Pair Connecting Hardware.*

EIA/TIA. See also ANSI/EIA/TIA.

FCC (1989). *FCC Rules and Regulations, Part 15: Radio Frequency Devices*, FCC CFR 47, Available from the U.S. Government Printing Office, Washington, DC.

Farber, D. et al. (1973). The distributed computing system, Proc. 7th Annual IEEE Computer Society International Conference (COMPCON'73), San Francisco, CA, 31–34.

Farmer, W. and E. Newhall (1969). An experimental distributed switching system to handle bursty computer traffic, Proc. ACM Symp. Problems Optim. Data Compm. Syst., 1–33.

Federal Information Processing Standards (FIPS) Publication 146-1 (1991). *U.S. Government Open Systems Interconnection Profile (GOSIP)*, Version 2, April 3, 1991. Available from NTIS, Springfield, VA.

Field, J. (1986). Logical Link Control, Proc. IEEE INFOCOM'86, Miami, FL, 331–336.

Fink, R. and F. Ross (1992). FFOL and its relationship to the MAN/WAN environment, *Computer Communications*, **15**(9), 603–606.

Franzen, M. (1991). FDDI concentrators and how they work together with other FDDI network components, *Computer Networks and ISDN Systems*, Proc. 2nd Joint European Networking Conference, Blois, France, **23**(1–3), 51–55.

Ginzburg, S., W. Mallard, and D. Newman (1990). FDDI over unshielded twisted pairs, Proc. IEEE LCN'90, Minneapolis, MN, 395–398.

Ginzburg, S. and J. Rieger (1988). FDDI physical channel: Jitter-bandwidth budget and experimental results, Proc. SPIE Conf. on Optic Datacom and Computer Networks, Boston, MA, **991**, 52–55.

Ginzburg, S., J. Rieger, and C. Baldwin (1988). A new parameter for characterizing the step response of a high speed fiber optic transmission channel with LED source (FDDI), Proc. SPIE Conf. on Fiber Optic Networks and Coherent Technology in Fiber Optic Systems II, San Diego, CA, **841**, 70–73.

Goyal, A. and D. Dias (1987). Performance of priority protocols on high speed token ring networks, Proc. 3rd IFIP TC 6/WG 7.3 Conf. on Data Communication Systems and Their Performance, Rio de Janeiro, Brazil, 13–23.

Green, L. (1987a). Application of FDDI: A 100 Mbit token ring, Proc. Interface'87, McGraw-Hill, New York, I–IV.

Green, L. (1987b). Performance analysis of FDDI (fiber distributed data interface), Proc. IEEE COMPCON Spring'87, 441–443.

Green, P. (1989). Transparent and source routing FDDI bridges, Proc. Broadband (FOC/LAN)'89, San Fransisco, CA, Information Gatekeepers, Boston, MA, 91–96.

Green, Jr., P. (1992). *Fiber Optic Networks*, Prentice-Hall, Englewood Cliffs, NJ, 513 pp.

Grow, R. (1982). A timed-token protocol for local area networks, Proc. Electro'82, Paper 17/3.

Grow, R. (1989). *A Functional Analysis of Network Management*, Presentation to X3T9.5, October 14, 1989, 11 pp.

Grow, R. (1990). FDDI follow-on status, Proc. IEEE LCN'90, Minneapolis, MN, 45–48.

Hammond, J., J. Brown, and S. Liu (1975). *Development of a Transmission Error Model and an Error Control Model*, Rome Air Development Center, Technical Report, RADC-TR-75-138, 141 pp.

Hammond, J. and P. O'Reilly (1986). *Performance Analysis of Local Computer Networks*, Addison-Wesley, Reading, MA, 411 pp.

Hamstra, J. (1988). FDDI design tradeoffs, Proc. IEEE LCN'88, Minneapolis, MN, 297–300.

Hamstra, J. and R. Fink (1992). FFOL transmission services-issues for a PHY physical layer protocol, *Computer Communications*, **15**(5), 305–310.

Hamstra, J. and R. Moulton (1985). *Group Coding System for Serial Data Transmission*, U.S. Patent #4,530,088, Sperry Corporation, New York.

Hanson, D. and J. Hutchison (1987). LED source and fiber specification issues for the FDDI network, Proc. Compcon Spring'87, San Fransisco, CA, 24–40.

Hartmann, M., B. Chen, and T. Muoi (1986). Integrated optical transmitter and receivers for FDDI-LAN applications, Proc. SPIE Conf. on Fiber Telecommunications and Computer Networks, Cambridge, MA, **715**, 80–88.

Hawe, W., R. Graham, and P. Hayden (1991). Fiber distributed data interface overview, *Digital Technical Journal*, **3**(2), 10–18.

Hayes, J. (1990). Examining cable plant bandwidth for FDDI, Proc. SPIE Conf. on FDDI, Campus-Wide, and Metropolitan Area Networks, San Jose, CA, **1364**, 115–119.

Hentschel, C. (1989). *Fiber Optics Handbook*, Hewlett-Packard GmbH, Germany, 238 pp.

Hiles, W. and D. Marlow (1992). Approaches for survivability in FDDI networks, Proc. IEEE LCN'92, Minneapolis, MN, 178–185.

Hills, A. (1991). FDDI-II—An implementor's perspective, Proc. EFOC/LAN'91, London, UK, Information Gatekeepers, Boston, MA, 194–200.

Horvath, S. (1991). *Multimedia Applications & Their Impact on the FFOL Design*, Presentation to ASC X3T9.5 ad hoc working meeting on FDDI Follow-On LAN, FFOL-055, December 10, 1991, 8 pp.

Hoss, R. (1990). *Fiber Optic Communications Design Handbook*, Prentice-Hall, Englewood Cliffs, NJ, 384 pp.

Hotard, E. (1990). FDDI concentrator design issues, Proc. IEEE LCN'90, Minneapolis, MN, 388–394.

Huber, M., K. Sauer, and W. Schödl (1988). QPSX and FDDI-II performance study of high speed LAN's, Proc. EFOC/LAN'88, Amsterdam, Netherlands, Information Gatekeepers, Boston, MA, 316–321.

Hutchison, J. (1989). The role of concentrators in FDDI rings Proc. IEEE LCN'89, Minneapolis, MN, 24–40.

Hutchison, J., C. Baldwin, and B. Thompson (1991). Development of the FDDI physical layer, *Digital Technical Journal*, **3**(2), 19–30.

Hutchison, J. and D. Knudson (1986). Developing standards for a fiber optic LAN - FDDI, Proc. SPIE Conf. on Fiber Telecommunications and Computer Networks, Cambridge, MA, **715**, 72–77.

Hutchison, J. and H. Yang (1991). Control of duplicate addresses for FDDI, Proc. IEEE LCN'91, Minneapolis, MN, 473–484.

IBM (1987). *IBM Cabling System Planning and Installation Guide*, Publication No. GA27-3361-7.

IEC 825:1984. *Radiation Safety of Laser Products, Equipment Classification, Requirements and User's Guide*, 137 pp. Also Amendment No. 1 (1990), 53 pp.

IEEE. See also ANSI/IEEE and ISO 8802-x.

IEEE 802-1990. *IEEE Standards for Local and Metropolitan Area Networks: Overview and Architecture*. See also ANSI/IEEE 802.1a-1990.

IEEE 802.1D-1990. *IEEE Standards for Local and Metropolitan Area Networks: Media Access Control (MAC) Bridges*. See also ANSI/IEEE 802.1d-1990. IEEE 802.1D-1990 now includes supplement IEEE 802.1i-1992.

IEEE 802.1G. *Remote MAC Bridging*. P802.1G/D7 draft of December 30, 1992.

IEEE 802.1H. *Media Access Control (MAC) Bridging of Ethernet V2.0 in 802 Local Area Networks*. P802.1H/D4 draft of January 12, 1993.

IEEE 802.1i-1992. *Supplement to Media Access Control (MAC) Bridges: Fiber Distributed Data Interface (FDDI).*

IEEE 802.2 Working Draft 91/6 (1991). *Information processing systems—Local area networks, Part 2: Logical Link Control. Working Draft 1.0: High Speed Transfer Service and Protocol, Type 4 Operation.*

Info Gatekeepers (1989). *FDDI Markets and Trends*, 309 pp.

Info Gatekeepers (1990). *FDDI*, 384 pp.

ISO/IEC 7498-4:1989. *Information Processing Systems—Open Systems Interconnection—Basic Reference Model—Part 4: Management Framework*, 9 pp.

ISO 7498:1984. *Information Processing Systems—Open Systems Interconnection—Basic Reference Model*, Ed. 3, 40 pp.

ISO 8473:1988. *Information Processing Systems—Data Communications—Protocol for Providing the Connectionless-mode Network Service*, 51 pp.

ISO 8473:1989/AM3. *Information Processing Systems—Data Communications—Protocol for Providing the Connectionless-mode Network Service, Amendment 3*, 2 pp.

ISO 8802-x. See also ANSI/IEEE and IEEE.

ISO 8802-2:1989 *Information Processing Systems—Local Area Networks, Part 2: Logical Link Control*, 117 pp.

ISO/IEC 8802-2:1989/AM2 (1989). *Information processing systems—Local Area Networks, Part 2: Logical Link Control. Amendment 3: Acknowledged Connectionless-mode Service and Protocol, Type 3 Operation.*

ISO/IEC 8802-3:1992 *Information Technology—Local and Metropolitan Area Networks—Part 3: Carrier Sense Multiple Access with Collision Detection (CSMA/CD) Access Method and Physical Layer Specifications*, Ed. 3, 320 pp.

ISO/IEC 8802-4:1990 *Information Processing Systems—Local and Metropolitan Area Networks—Part 4: Token Passing Bus Access Method and Physical Layer Specifications*, 288 pp.

ISO/IEC 8802-5:1992 *Information Processing Systems—Local and Metropolitan Area Networks—Part 5: Token Ring Access Method and Physical Layer Specifications*, 112 pp.

ISO 8824:1990. *Information Technology—Open Systems Interconnection—Specification of Abstract Syntax Notation One (ASN.1) Ed. 2*, 51 pp.

ISO 8825:1990. *Information Technology—Open Systems Interconnection—Specification of Basic Encoding Rules for Abstract Notation One (ASN.1), Ed. 2*, 17 pp. See also CCITT Recommendation X.208.

ISO/IEC 8880-1:1990. *Information Technology—Telecommunications and Information Exchange Between Systems—Protocol Combinations to Provide and Support the OSI Network Service—Part 1: General Principles*, 4 pp.

ISO/IEC 8880-2:1990. *Information Technology—Telecommunications and Information Exchange Between Systems—Protocol Combinations to Provide and Support the OSI Network Service—Part 2: Provision and Support of the Connection-mode Network Service*, 5 pp.

ISO/IEC 8880-3:1990. *Information Technology—Telecommunications and Information Exchange Between Systems—Protocol Combinations to Provide and Support the OSI Network Service—Part 3: Provision and Support of the Connectionless-mode Network Service*, 5 pp.

ISO 9314-1:1989, *Information Processing Systems—Fiber Distributed Data Interface (FDDI) Part 1: Token Ring Physical Layer Protocol (PHY)*, 31 pp.

ISO 9314-2:1989, *Information Processing Systems—Fiber Distributed Data Interface (FDDI) Part 2: Token Ring Media Access Control (MAC)*, 67 pp.

ISO/IEC 9314-3:1990. *Information Processing Systems—Fiber Distributed Data Interface (FDDI) Part 3: Token Ring Physical Layer Medium Dependent (PMD)*, 47 pp.

ISO/IEC CD 9314-4:199x. See ANSI X3.184-199x.

ISO/IEC DIS 9314-5:199x. See ANSI X3.186-199x.

ISO/IEC WD 9314-6:199x. See ANSI X3.229-199x.

ISO/IEC WD 9314-7:199x. See ANSI X3.231-199x.

ISO/IEC WD 9314-8:199x. See ANSI X3.239-199x.

ISO/IEC WD 9314-9:199x. See ANSI X3.237-199x.

ISO 9542:1988. *Information Processing Systems—Telecommunications and Information Exchange Between Systems—End System to Intermediate System Routing Exchange Protocol for Use in Conjunction with the Protocol for Providing the Connectionless-mode Network Service (ISO 8473)*, 30 pp.

ISO/IEC TR 9577:1990. *Information Technology—Telecommunications and Information Exchange Between Systems—Protocol Identification in the Network Layer*, 11 pp.

ISO/IEC 9595:1991. *Information Technology—Open Systems Interconnection—Common Management Information Service Definition*, Ed. 2, 28 pp.

ISO/IEC 9596-1:1991. *Information Technology—Open Systems Interconnection—Common Management Information Protocol—Part 1: Specification*, Ed. 2, 34 pp.

ISO/IEC 9646-1:1991. *Information Technology—Open Systems Interconnection—Conformance Testing Methodology and Framework—Part 1: General Concepts*, 31 pp.

ISO/IEC 9646-2:1991. *Information Technology—Open Systems Interconnection—Conformance Testing Methodology and Framework—Part 2: Abstract Test Suite Specification*, 28 pp.

ISO/IEC 9646-3:1992. *Information Technology—Open Systems Interconnection—Conformance Testing Methodology and Framework—Part 3: The Tree and Tabular Combined Notation (TTCN)*.

ISO/IEC 9646-4:1991. *Information Technology—Open Systems Interconnection—Conformance Testing Methodology and Framework—Part 4: Test Realization*, 10 pp.

ISO/IEC 9646-5:1991. *Information Technology—Open Systems Interconnection—Conformance Testing Methodology and Framework—Part 5: Requirements on Test Laboratories and Clients for the Conformance Assessment Process*, 25 pp.

ISO/IEC 9646-6:199x. *Information Technology—Open Systems Interconnection—Conformance Testing Methodology and Framework—Part 6: Protocol Profile Test Specification.*

ISO/IEC WD 9646-7:199x. *Information Technology—Open Systems Interconnection—Conformance Testing Methodology and Framework—Part 7: Implementation Conformance Statements - Requirements and Guidance on ICS and ICS Proformas*, November 1992.

ISO/IEC TR 10000-1:1990. *Information Technology—Framework and Taxonomy of International Standardized Profiles—Part 1: Framework*, 22 pp.

ISO/IEC TR 10000-2:1990. *Information Technology—Framework and Taxonomy of International Standardized Profiles—Part 2: Taxonomy of Profiles*, 14 pp.

ISO/IEC 10040:1991. *Information Technology—Open Systems Interconnection—Systems Management Overview.*

ISO/IEC 10165-1:1991. *Information Technology—Open Systems Interconnection—Management Information Services—Structure of Management Information—Part 1: Management Information Model.*

ISO/IEC 10165-2:1991. *Information Technology—Open Systems Interconnection—Structure of Management Information—Part 2: Definitions of Management Information.*

ISO/IEC 10165-4:1992. *Information Technology—Open Systems Interconnection—Structure of Management Information—Part 4: Guidelines for the Definition of Managed Objects,* 50 pp.

ISO/IEC DIS 10165-5 (1992). *Information Technology—Open Systems Interconnection—Structure of Management Information—Part 5: Generic Management Information,* ISO/IEC JTC1/SC21 N6752, February 20, 1992.

ISO/IEC CD 10165-6 (1992). *Information Technology—Open Systems Interconnection—Structure of Management Information—Part 6: Requirements and Guidelines for Implementation Conformance Statement Proformas Associated with Management Information.*

ISO/IEC TR 10178:1992. *Information Technology—Telecommunications and Information Exchange Between Systems—The Structure and Coding of Logical Link Control Addresses in Local Area Networks,* 12 pp.

ISO/IEC 10589:1992. *Information Technology—Telecommunications and Information Exchange Between Systems—Intermediate System to Intermediate System Intra Domain Routing Exchange Protocol for Use in Conjunction with the Protocol for Providing the Connectionless-mode Network Service (ISO 8473),* 150 pp.

ISO/IEC pdISP 10608-1:199x. *Information Technology—International Standardized Profile TA—Connection-mode Transport Service over Connectionless Network Service—Part 1: General Overview and Subnetwork-Independent Requirements.*

ISO/IEC DISP 10608-2:199x. *Information Technology—International Standardized Profile TA—Connection-mode Transport Service over Connectionless Network Service—Part 2: TA51 Profile Including Subnetwork-Dependent Requirements for CSMA/CD Local Area Networks (LANs).*

ISO/IEC pdISP 10608-6. *Information Technology—International Standardized Profile TAnnnn—Connection-mode Transport Service over Connectionless Network Service—Part 6: Definition of Profile TA54 for Operation over an FDDI LAN Subnetwork,* October 20, 1992, 8 pp.

ISO/IEC pdISP 10608-14. *Information Technology—International Standardized Profile TAnnnn—Connection-mode Transport Service over Connectionless Network Service—Part 14: MAC/PHY and PMD Sublayer Dependent Requirements and Station Management Requirements for an FDDI LAN Subnetwork,* October 20, 1992, 43 pp.

ISO/IEC DISP 10612-1. *Information Technology—International Standardized Profile RD5p.5q—Relaying the MAC Service Using Transparent Bridging—Part 1: Subnetwork-independent Requirements.*

ISO/IEC DISP 10612-2. *Information Technology—International Standardized Profile RD5p.5q—Relaying the MAC Service Using Transparent Bridging—Part 2: CSMA/CD LAN Subnetwork-dependent, Media-dependent Requirements.*

ISO/IEC pdISP 10612-3. *Information Technology—International Standardized Profile RD5p.5q—Relaying the MAC Service Using Transparent Bridging—Part 3: Token Ring LAN Subnetwork-dependent, Media-dependent Requirements,* September 9, 1993, 7 pp.

ISO/IEC pdISP 10612-4. *Information Technology—International Standardized Profile RD5p.5q—Relaying the MAC Service Using Transparent Bridging—Part 4: Profile RD51.51 (CSMA/CD LAN - CSMA/CD LAN).*

ISO/IEC pdISP 10612-5. *Information Technology—International Standardized Profile RD5p.5q—Relaying the MAC Service Using Transparent Bridging—Part 5: Profile RD51.54 (CSMA/CD-FDDI)*, September 9, 1993, 5 pp.

ISO/IEC pdISP 10612-6. *Information Technology—International Standardized Profile RD5p.5q—Relaying the MAC Service Using Transparent Bridging—Part 6: Profile RD54.54 (FDDI-FDDI)*, September 9, 1993, 5 pp.

ISO/IEC pdISP 10612-7. *Information Technology—International Standardized Profile RD5p.5q—Relaying the MAC Service Using Transparent Bridging—Part 7: Profile RD51.53 (CSMA/CD LAN - Token Ring LAN)*, September 9, 1993, 5 pp.

ISO/IEC pdISP 10612-8. *Information Technology—International Standardized Profile RD5p.5q—Relaying the MAC Service Using Transparent Bridging—Part 8: Profile RD53.53 (Token Ring LAN - Token Ring LAN)*, September 9, 1993, 5 pp.

ISO/IEC pdISP 10612-9. *Information Technology—International Standardized Profile RD5p.5q—Relaying the MAC Service Using Transparent Bridging—Part 9: Profile RD53.54 (Token Ring LAN - FDDI LAN)*, September 9, 1993, 5 pp.

ISO/IEC pdISP 10613-4. *Information Technology—International Standardized Profile RAp.q—Relaying the Connectionless-mode Network Service Part 4: FDDI LAN Subnetwork-Dependent Media-Dependent Requirements*, February 18, 1993, 8 pp.

ISO/IEC pdISP 10613-6. *Information Technology—International Standardized Profile RAp.q—Relaying the Connectionless-mode Network Service Part 6: Profile RA51.54*, February 18, 1993, 7 pp.

ISO/IEC JTC1/SC25 N106. *Generic Cabling for Customer Premises*, October 12, 1992.

Ichihashi, T., K. Koui, Y. Yokoyama, K. Hiramatsu (1992). Implementing models of the FDDI-II cycle synchronization technique, *Computer Communications (UK)*, **15**(3), 169–176.

Ichihashi, T., Y. Yokoyama, K. Hiramatsu, et al. (1991). Evaluation of FDDI-II cycle synchronization mechanisms, Proc. IFIP TC6/WG6.4 Conference on High Speed Networking III, Berlin, Germany, North-Holland, Amsterdam, Netherlands, 91–108.

Infonetics Research Institute (1990). *FDDI: User Requirements and Buying Plans*, Infonetics, San Jose, CA, 133 pp.

Iyer, V. and S. Joshi (1985). FDDI's 100M-bps protocol improves on 802.5 spec's 4M-bps limit, *EDN*, May 2, 151–160.

Jain, R. (1990a). Error characteristics of fiber distributed data interface (FDDI), *IEEE Trans. Commun.*, **38**(8), 1244–1252.

Jain, R. (1990b). Performance analysis of FDDI token ring networks: Effect of parameters and guidelines for setting TTRT, Proc. ACM SIGCOMM'90, Philadelphia, PA, 264–275. Also in *IEEE LTS Magazine*, May 1991, and in *Digital Technical Journal*, **3**(3), 78–88.

Jain, R. (1991). *The Art of Computer Systems Performance Analysis*, Wiley, New York, 720 pp.

Johnson, M. (1986). Reliability mechanisms of the FDDI high bandwidth token ring protocol, *Comput. Networks & ISDN Syst. (Netherlands)*, **11**(2), 121–131, also in Proc. IEEE LCN'85, Minneapolis, MN, 124–133.

Johnson, M. (1987). Proof that timing requirements of the FDDI token ring protocol are satisfied, *IEEE Trans. Commun.*, **COM-35**(6), 620–625.

Johnson, M. (1988). Performance analysis of FDDI, Proc. EFOC/LAN'88, Amsterdam, Netherlands, Information Gatekeepers, Boston, MA, 295–300.

Joshi, S. (1986). The fiber distributed data interface: A bright future ahead, Proc. IEEE FJCC'86, 504–512.

Ju, R. and K. Jabbour (1989). Estimation of propagation time and bit error rate in point-to-point physical layer channel of 100 Mbps FDDI network, Proc. 23rd IEEE Annual Asilomar Conference on Signals, Systems & Computers, Pacific Grove, CA, **2**, 908–913.

Judge, P. (1991). *Guide to IT Standards Makers and Their Standards*, Technology Appraisals Ltd., Isleworth, UK, 241 pp.

Kajos, G. and D. Hunt (1989). FDDI link error rate monitor, Proc. IEEE LCN'89, Minneapolis, MN, 347–357.

Kalkunte, R. (1991). Performance analysis of a high-speed FDDI adapter, *Digital Technical Journal*, **3**(3), 64–77.

Kao, K. and G. Hockham (1966). Dielectric-fibre surface waveguide for optical frequency, *Proceedings of IEE*, **113**(7), 1151.

Karvelas, D. and A. Leon-Garcia (1987). A performance comparison of voice/data token ring protocols, Proc. IEEE INFOCOM'87, San Francisco, CA, 846–855.

Karvelas, D. and A. Leon-Garcia (1988). Performance analysis of the medium access control protocol of the FDDI token ring network, Proc. IEEE Globecom'88, **2**, 1119–1123.

Katz, D. (1990a). The use of connectionless network layer protocols over FDDI networks, *Computer Communications Review*, **3**, 32–45.

Katz, D. (1990b). The use of DoD IP over FDDI networks, Proc. BROADBAND'90, Baltimore, MD, Information Gatekeepers, Boston, MA, 28–33.

Katz, D. (1990c). Everything you always wanted to know about FDDI basics, *ACM SIGUCCS Newsletter*, **20**(4), 24–25.

Keiser, G. (1991). *Optical Fiber Communications*, Ed. 2, McGraw-Hill, New York.

Khan, A. (1989). FDDI interoperability between vendors, Proc. SPIE Conf. on Networking and Telecommunications, Boston, MA, **1179**, 266–275.

Kimball, R. (1989). Optical performance models for FDDI links, Proc. SPIE Conf. on Networking and Telecommunications, Boston, MA, **1179**, 252–265.

Kochem, R., J. Hiscock, and B. Mayo (1991). Development of the DECbridge 500 Product, *Digital Technical Journal*, **3**(2), 53–63.

Krol, E. (1992). *The Whole Internet User's Guide & Catalog*, O'Reilly Associates, Sebastopol, CA, 376 pp.

LaMaire, R. (1991a). FDDI performance at 1 Gbits/s, Proc. IEEE ICC'91, Denver, CO, 1043–1048.

LaMaire, R. (1991b). An M/G/1 vacation model of an FDDI station, *IEEE J. Sel. Areas Commun.*, **9**(2), 257–264.

LaMaire, R. and E. Spiegel (1990). FDDI performance analysis: Delay approximations, Proc. IEEE Globecom'90, San Diego, CA, **3**, 1838–1845.

Lauck, A. (1982). An Analysis of CSMA/CD Undetected Error Rates, Presentation to IEEE Project 802 Committee, 7 pp.

Le, M. (1989). *Fault Detection & Recovery Mechanism*, Presentation to ASC X3T9.5 FDDI SMT working group, SMT-288, 20 February 1989, 8 pp.

Levenson, H. (1988). *Link Error Monitor (LEM)*, Presentation to ASC X3T9.5 FDDI SMT working group, SMT-255, 10 October 1988, 8 pp.

Li, G. (1988). A Symbol wide smoothing algorithm and an analysis on the interoperability with a byte wide smoother in a FDDI token ring network, Proc. MFOC'88, Arlington, VA, Information Gatekeepers, Boston, MA.

Logothetis, D. and K. Trivedi (1991). Reliability analysis of the FDDI token ring, Proc. IEEE LCN'91, Minneapolis, MN, 41–51.

Lundy, G. and I. Akyildiz (1991). Specification and analysis of the FDDI network protocol, Proc. EFOC/LAN'91, London, UK, IGI Europe, Boston, MA, 206–214.

Mahlke, G. and P. Gössing (1987). *Fiber Optic Cables*, Wiley, Chichester, UK, 253 pp.

Manning, E. and R. Peebles (1977). A homogeneous network for data sharing, *Computer Networks*, **1**, 211–224.

Market Intelligence Research Corporation (1992). *World FDDI, SONET, and 802.6 MAN Equipment Markets*, 249 pp.

Martini, P. and T. Meuser (1990). Service integration in FDDI, Proc. IEEE LCN'90, Minneapolis, MN, 23–32.

Martini, P. and T. Meuser (1991). Real-time traffic in FDDI-II packet switching vs. circuit switching, Proc. IEEE INFOCOM'91, Bal Harbour, FL, **3**, 1413–1420.

McClimans, F. (1990). *Communications Wiring and Interconnection*, McGraw-Hill, New York, 354 pp.

McClure, R. B. (1987). Management services for FDDI systems, Proc. FOC/LAN'87 and MFOC-WEST, Anaheim, CA, Information Gatekeepers, Boston, MA, 57–64.

McClure, R. B. (1989). Standards for robust second generation LAN management, Proc. IEEE LCN'89, Minneapolis, MN, 133–142.

McCool, J. (1987). The emerging FDDI standard, *Telecommunications*, **21**(5), 50, 52, 54, 56, 58.

McIntosh, T. (1989). Engineering building and campus networks for fiber distributed data interface (FDDI), Proc. SPIE Conf. on Networking and Telecommunications, Boston, MA, **1179**, 240–251.

Mettler, S. (1979). A general characterization of splice loss for multimode optical fibers, *Bell Systems Technical Journal*, December, 2163–2182.

Michael, W., W. Cronin, Jr., and K. Pieper (1993). *FDDI: An Introduction to Fiber Distributed Data Interface*, Digital Press, Burlington, MA, 220 pp.

Miller, R. (1986). Optical requirements for the fiber distributed data interface (FDDI), Proc. SPIE Conf. on Fiber Telecommunications and Computer Networks, Cambridge, MA, **715**, 66–70.

Miller, S. and I. Kaminow (Eds) (1988). *Optical Fiber Telecommunications*, **II**, Academic Press, New York, 768 pp.

Milligan, G. (1988). FDDI emerges as a high-speed fiber LAN, *TPT*, **6**(4), 43–45.

Milligan, G. (1989). FDDI standard fosters improved interoperability, *Network Management*, **7**(9), 66, 68, 70, 72.

Minoli, D. (1991). *Telecommunications Technology Handbook*, Artech House, Boston, MA.

Mityko, G. (1991). The FDDI follow-on LAN, Proc. EFOC/LAN'91, London, UK, Information Gatekeepers, Boston, MA, 201–205.

Mogul, J. (1991). Applications and techniques for LAN monitoring, *ConneXions*, **5**(10), 36–45.

Moore, G. and R. Weber (1987). Evolution of the FDDI connector, Proc. FOC/LAN'87 and MFOC-WEST, Anaheim, CA, Information Gatekeepers, Boston, MA, 311–315.

Motteler, H. and D. Sidhu (1992). Components of OSI: Abstract Syntax Notation One (ASN.1), *ConneXions*, **6**(1), 2–19.

Myles, A. (1988). *FDDI Topology*, Presentation to ASC X3T9.5 FDDI SMT working group, SMT-173, 21 April 1988, 8 pp.

National Fire Protection Agency (NFPA) (1993a). *National Electrical Code 1993.*

National Fire Protection Agency (NFPA) (1993b). *NEC Handbook 1993.*

Ocheltree, K. (1990). Using redundancy in FDDI networks, Proc. IEEE LCN'90, Minneapolis, MN, 261–267.

Ocheltree, K., S. Horvath, and G. Mityko, (1990). *Requirements and Design Considerations for the FDDI Follow-On LAN (FDDI-FO)*, Version 2.0, Presentation to ASC X3T9.5 ad hoc working meeting on FDDI Follow-On LAN, FFOL-007, X3T9.5/90-068, 17 May 1990, 5 pp.

Ocheltree, K. and R. Montalvo (1989). FDDI ring management, Proc. IEEE LCN'89, Minneapolis, MN, 18–23.

Paige, J. and E. Howard (1990). SAFENET II—the Navy's FDDI-based computer network standard, Proc. SPIE Conf. on FDDI, Campus-Wide and Metropolitan Area Networks, San Jose, CA, **1364**, 7–13.

Pang, J. and F. Tobagi (1988). Throughput analysis of a timer-controlled token-passing protocol under heavy load, Proc. IEEE INFOCOM'88, New Orleans, LA, 8B.1.1–8B.1.9.

Pang, J. and F. Tobagi (1989a). Generalized access control strategies for token passing systems, Proc. IEEE INFOCOM'89, Ottawa, Ont., Canada, 332–341.

Pang, J. and F. Tobagi (1989b). *Throughput approximation for the generalized timer based protocol for token passing systems*, Technical Report CSL-TR-89-375, Stanford University, Palo Alto, CA, 28 pp.

Pang, J. (1989). *Access Control Strategies for Token Passing Integrated Services Networks*, Technical Report CSL-TR-89-377, Stanford University, Palo Alto, CA, 139 pp.

Parker, K. (1989). Designing an FDDI network to maximize network availability, Proc. Wescon'89, San Francisco, CA, Electron. Conventions Manage., Ventura, CA, 668–670.

Patel, B., A. Ruiz, F. Schaffa, and M. Willebeek-LeMair (1992). Graceful insertion and removal approaches for FDDI-II, Proc. IEEE LCN'92, Minneapolis, MN, 134–138.

Peden, J. and A. Weaver (1988a). The utilization of priorities on token ring networks, Proc. IEEE LCN'88, Minneapolis, MN, 472–478.

Peden, J. and A. Weaver (1988b). An intuitive approach to priority operation on token ring networks, *Transfer*, Protocol Engines, Inc., **1**(5), 5–8.

Peterson, W. and E. Weldon (1972). *Error-Correcting Codes*, The MIT Press, Cambridge, MA.

Phinney, T. (1985). *Hamming Distances of IEEE 802's 32-bit FCS Mechanism*, Presentation to IEEE Project 802 Executive Committee, June 18, 1985, 2 pp.

Phinney, T. and G. Jelatis (1983). Error handling in the IEEE 802 token-passing bus LAN, *IEEE J. Sel. Areas Commun.*, **SAC-1**(5), 784–789.

Pieper, K. (1991). FDDI over non-fiber media, *Bus. Commun. Rev.*, **21**(6), 22, 24, 26.

Pyykkonen, M. (1987). The upside and downside potential for fiber optics in local area networks, Proc. FOC/LAN'87 and MFOC-WEST, Anaheim, CA, Information Gatekeepers, Boston, MA, 48–49.

RFC 791 (1981). *Internet Protocol*, by J. Postel, 45 pp.

RFC 826 (1982). *An Ethernet Address Resolution Protocol: Or Converting Network Protocol Addresses to 48.bit Ethernet Address for Transmission on Ethernet Hardware*, by D. Plummer. 10 pp.

RFC 903 (1984). *Reverse Address Resolution Protocol*, by R. Finlayson, T. Mann, J. Mogul, and M. Theimer, 4 pp.

RFC 1028 (1987). *Simple Gateway Monitoring Protocol*, by J. Davin, J. Case, M. Fedor, and M. Schoffstall, 38 pp.

RFC 1052 (1988). *IAB Recommendations for the Development of Internet Network Management Standards*, by V. Cerf, 14 pp.

RFC 1058 (1988). *Routing Information Protocol*, by C. Hedrick, 33 pp.

RFC 1155 (1990). *Structure and Identification of Management Information for TCP/IP-Based Internets*, by M. Rose and K. McCloghrie, 22 pp.

RFC 1156 (1990). *Management Information Base for Network Management of TCP/IP-based Internets*, K. McCloghrie and M. Rose, 91 pp.

RFC 1157 (1990). *Simple Network Management Protocol (SNMP)*, by J. Case, M. Fedor, M. Schoffstall, and C. Davin, 36 pp.

RFC 1160 (1990). *The Internet Activities Board*, by V. Cerf, 11 pp.

RFC 1189 (1990). *Common Management Information Services and Protocols for the Internet (CMOT and CMIP)*, by U. Warrier, L. Besaw, L. LaBarre, and B. Handspicker, 15 pp.

RFC 1212 (1991). *Concise MIB Definitions*, by M. Rose and K. McCloghrie, 19 pp.

RFC 1213 (1991). *Management Information Base for Network Management of TCP/IP-Based Internets: MIB-II*, by K. McCloghrie and M. Rose, 70 pp.

RFC 1227 (1991). *SNMP MUX protocol and MIB*, by M. Rose, 13 pp.

RFC 1228 (1991). *SNMP-DPI: Simple Network Management Protocol Distributed Program Interface*, by G. Carpenter and B. Wijnen, 50 pp.

RFC 1229 (1991). *Extensions to the Generic-Interface MIB*, by K. McCloghrie, 16 pp.

RFC 1230 (1991). *IEEE 802.4 Token Bus MIB*, by K. McCloghrie, R. Fox, and E. Decker, 23 pp.

RFC 1231 (1991). *IEEE 802.5 Token Ring MIB*, by K. McCloghrie, R. Fox, and E. Decker, 23 pp.

RFC 1238 (1991). *CLNS MIB for Use with Connectionless Network Protocol (ISO 8473) and End System to Intermediate System (ISO 9542)*, by G. Satz, 32 pp.

RFC 1239 (1991). *Reassignment of Experimental MIBs to Standard MIBs*, by J. Reynolds, 2 pp.

RFC 1247 (1991). *OSPF Version 2*, by J. Moy, 189 pp.

RFC 1269 (1991). *Definitions of Managed Objects for the Border Gateway Protocol: Version 3*, by S. Willis and J. Burruss, 13 pp.

RFC 1270 (1991). *SNMP Communications Services*, by F. Kastenholz, 11 pp.

RFC 1283 (1991). *SNMP over OSI*, by M. Rose, 8 pp.

RFC 1284 (1991). *Definitions of Managed Objects for the Ethernet-Like Interface Types*, by J. Cook, 21 pp.

RFC 1285 (1992). *FDDI Management Information Base*, by J. Case, 46 pp. Updated by RFC 1512.

RFC 1286 (1991). *Definitions of Managed Objects for Bridges*, by E. Decker, P. Langille, A. Rijsinghani, and K. McCloghrie, 40 pp.

RFC 1289 (1991). *DECnet Phase IV MIB Extensions*, by J. Saperia, 64 pp.

RFC 1300 (1992). *Remembrances of Things Past*, by S. Greenfield, 4 pp.

RFC 1303 (1992). *Convention for Describing SNMP-based Agents*, by K. McCloghrie and M. Rose, 12 pp.

RFC 1315 (1992). *Management Information Base for Frame Relay DTEs*, by C. Brown, F. Baker, C. Carvalho, 19 pp.

RFC 1316 (1992). *Definitions of Managed Objects for Character Stream Devices*, by B. Stewart, 17 pp.

RFC 1317 (1992). *Definitions of Managed Objects for RS-232-like Hardware Devices*, by B. Stewart, 17 pp.

RFC 1318 (1992). *Definitions of Managed Objects for Parallel-Printer-Like Hardware Devices*, by B. Stewart, 11 pp.

RFC 1329 (1992). *Thoughts on Address Resolution for Dual MAC FDDI Networks*, by P. Kuehn, 28 pp.

RFC 1340 (1992). *Assigned Numbers*, by J. Reynolds and J. Postel, 139 pp. This RFC is updated frequently. Consult the Internet RFC index (rfc-index.txt) for the latest RFC with this title.

RFC 1351 (1992). *SNMP Administrative Model*, by J. Davin, J. Galvin, and K. McCloghrie, 35 pp.

RFC 1352 (1992). *SNMP Security Protocols*, by J. Galvin, K. McCloghrie, and J. Davin, 41 pp.

RFC 1353 (1992). *Definitions of Managed Objects for Administration of SNMP Parties*, by K. McCloghrie, J. Davin, and J. Galvin, 26 pp.

RFC 1390 (1993). *Transmission of IP and ARP over FDDI Networks*, by D. Katz, 11 pp.

RFC 1512 (1993). *FDDI Management Information Base*, by J. Case and A. Rijsinghani, 51 pp. This RFC updates RFC 1285.

Ramakrishnan, K., (1993). Performance considerations in designing network interfaces, *IEEE J. Sel. Areas Commun.*, **11**(2).

Refi, J. (1988). Determining the zero dispersion wavelength and dispersion slope of fibers used for the fiber distributed data interface (FDDI), Proc. SPIE Conf. on Fiber Optic Networks and Coherent Technology in Fiber Optic Systems II, San Diego, CA, **841**, 66–69.

Rege, S. (1991). The architecture and implementation of a high-performance FDDI adapter, *Digital Technical Journal*, **3**(3), 48–63.

Rigsbee, E., (1990a). *Proposed Super-Rate Mapping for ASC X3T9.5 (FDDI)*, Presentation to T1X1.5 Optical Hierarchical Interfaces Working Group, ASC T1X1.5/90-029, also ASC X3T9.5/90-004, February 19, 1990, 4 pp.

Rigsbee, E. (1990b). SONET scrambler interference analysis of ASC X3T9.5 (FDDI) mapping data, Presentation to ASC X3T9.5 working group on FDDI/SONET Phy-layer Mapping, SPM/90-011,

Rising Star Research (1992). *FDDI Market Research Study 1992*, Rising Star Research, Van Nuys, CA.

Ritchie, G. (1991). SONET: No longer just a concept, *IEEE LTS*, **2**(4).

Rocher, E. (1988). Singlemode fiber distributed data interface (FDDI), Proc. SPIE Conf. on Optic Datacom and Computer Networks, Boston, MA, **991**, 56–60.

Rose, M. (1991). *The Simple Book—An Introduction to Management of TCP/IP-based Internets*, Prentice Hall, Englewood Cliffs, NJ, 347 pp.

Ross, F. (1986a). FDDI—A tutorial (fibre distributed data interface), *IEEE Commun. Mag.*, **24**(5), 10–17.

Ross, F. (1986b). FDDI—Fiber, farther, faster (fiber distributed data interface), Proc. IEEE INFOCOM'86, Miami, FL, 323–330.

Ross, F. (1987). FDDI—An overview (fibre distributed data interface a 100 Mb/ s token ring), Proc. IEEE COMPCON Spring'87, 434–440.

Ross, F. (1989a). Fiber distributed data interface—An overview, Proc. IEEE LCN'89, Minneapolis, MN, 5–8.

Ross, F. (1989b). Overview of FDDI: The fiber distributed data interface, *IEEE J. Sel. Areas Commun.*, **7**(7), 1043–1051.

Ross, F. (1991a). Fiber distributed data interface: An overview and update, *Fiber Optics Magazine*, July-August, 12–16.

Ross, F. (1991b). Get ready for FDDI-II, *Networking Management*, **9**(8), 54, 56–58.

Ross, F. and R. Fink, (1992). Overview of FFOL—FDDI Follow-On LAN, *Computer Communications*, **15**(1), 5–10.

Ross, F. and R. Moulton (1984). FDDI overview—A 100 megabit per second solution, Proc. Wescon'84, Electron. Conventions Manage., Los Angeles, CA.

Sachs, S., K. Kan, and J. Silvester (1985). Token-bus protocol performance analysis and comparison with other LAN protocols, Proc. IEEE Globecom'85, New Orleans, LA, 1492–1498.

Saltzer, J., D. Clark, and K. Progran (1981). Why a ring?, Proc. 7th Data Communications Symposium, Mexico City, Mexico, 211–217.

Saltzer, J. and K. Progran (1980). A star-shaped ring network with high maintainability, *Computer Networks*, **4**, 239–244.

Salwen, H. (1984). A comparison of bypassing methods in high data rate fiber optic LAN's, Proc. FOC/LAN'84, Las Vegas, NV, Information Gatekeepers, Boston, MA, 258–261.

Schicketanz, D. and W. Jackman (1986). Effective fiber bandwidths in LED-based systems, Proc. Symposium on optical fiber measurements, Boulder, CO, NBS speical publication 720, 93–96.

Schill, A. and M. Zieher (1987). Performance analysis of the FDDI 100 Mbit/s optical token ring, Proc. IFIP TC6/WG 6.4 International Workshop on High Speed Local Area Networks, North-Holland, Amsterdam, Netherlands, 53–74.

Schödl, W. and M. Tangemann (1990). Strategies for interconnecting HSLANs to B-ISDN and their performance, Proc. 10th International Conference on Computer Communication, New Delhi, India, 442–449.

Sevcik, K. and M. Johnson (1987). Cycle time properties of the FDDI token ring protocol, *IEEE Trans. Software Engineering*, **SE-13**(3), 376–385. Also in Proc. ACM SIGMETRICS'86, Raleigh, NC, 109–110.

Shah, A., D. Staddon, I. Rubin, and A. Ratkovic (1992). Multimedia over FDDI, Proc. IEEE LCN'92, Minneapolis, MN, 110–124.

Shoch, J. (1979). *Reliability and Errors in Ethernet*, Chap. 5, Ph.D. Dissertation, Stanford University, Palo Alto, CA. Available from University Microfilms International, Ann Arbor, MI.

Sinkewicz, U., C. Chang, L. Palmer, et al. (1991). ULTRIX fiber distributed data interface networking subsystem implementation, *Digital Technical Journal*, **3**(3), 85–93.

Slawson, M. (1987). Surface acoustic wave (SAW) technology for clock recovery in the fiber distributed data interface (FDDI), Proc. SPIE Conf. on Optic Networks and Coherent Technology in Fiber Optic Systems II, San Diego, CA, **841**, 74–79.

Spiegel, E. (1991). Performance analysis of the timed-token protocol: A vacation model, Proc. IFIP TC6/WG6.4 Conference on High Speed Networking III, Berlin, Germany, North-Holland, Amsterdam, Netherlands, 109–124.

Stallings, W. (1992). *ISDN and Broadband ISDN*, MacMillan, New York, 633 pp.

Stallings, W. (1993). *Networking Standards: A Guide to OSI, ISDN, LAN, and MAN Standards*, Addison-Wesley, Reading, MA, 646 pp.

Sterling, Jr., D. (1987). *Technician's Guide to Fiber Optics*, Delmar Publishers Inc., Albany, NY, 242 pp.

Stevens, R. (1990). FDDI network cabling, Proc. SPIE Conf. on FDDI, Campus-Wide, and Metropolitan Area Networks, San Jose, CA, **1364**, 101–114.

Swastek, M., D. Vereeke, and D. Scherbarth (1989). Migrating to FDDI on your next big LAN installation, *Data Communications*, June 21, 35–43.

Takagi, H. (1988). Queueing analysis of polling models, *ACM Computing Surveys*, **20**(1), 5–28.

Teener, M. and R. Gvozdanovic (1989). FDDI-II operation and architectures, Proc. IEEE LCN'89, Minneapolis, MN, 49–61.

Tiffany, W., P. Koning, and J. Kuenzel (1991). The DECconcentrator 500 product, *Digital Technical Journal*, **3**(2), 64–75.

Torgerson, J. (1989). FDDI MAC services design considerations, Proc. IEEE LCN'89, Minneapolis, MN, 41–48.

Tosco, F., Ed., (1990). *Fiber Optic Communications Handbook*, TAB Books, Blue Ridge Summit, PA.

UL 910 (1991). *Test Method for Fire and Smoke Characteristics of Electrical and Optical-Fiber Cables Used in Air-Handling Spaces.*

UL 1581 (1991). *Reference Standard for Electrical Wires, Cables, and Flexible Cords.*

UL 1666 (1990). *Flame Propagation Height of Electrical and Optical-Fiber Cables Installed Vertically in Shafts.*

Ulm, J., (1982). A timed-token ring local area network and its performance characteristics, Proc. IEEE LCN'82, Minneapolis, MN, 50–56.

U.S. Department of Health and Human Services (1985). *Laser Product Performance Standard, Code of Federal Regulations,* Title 21, Subchapter J, part 1040, Federal Register, Vol. 50, No. 161, August 20, 1985.

Venture Development Corporation (1988). *FDDI: The Emerging Standard for High Speed Fiber Optic Communication and Networking*, VDC, Natick, MA, 89 pp.

Watson, K. (1984). Performance evaluation of cyclic service strategies—a survey, Proc. Performance'84, North-Holland, Amsterdam, Netherlands, 521–533.

Watson, R. and S. Ward (1991). Performance of the FDDI prioritisation scheme using fixed and adaptive timer threshold selections, Proc. 3rd Bangor Symposium on Communications, Bangor, UK, Univ. Wales, Bangor, UK, 355–358.

Watson, R. and S. Ward (1994). Prioritisation in FDDI networks, *Computer Communications (UK)*, to appear.

Weber, R. (1986). The evolution of the duplex connector system for ANSI X3T9.5 FDDI (fiber distributed data interface), Proc. SPIE Conf. on Components for Fiber Optic Applications, Cambridge, MA, **722**, 134–139.

Weik, M. (1989). *Fiber Optics Standard Dictionary*, Van Nostrand Reinhold, 352 pp.

Welzel, T. (1989). FDDI and BWN backbone networks: A performance comparison based on simulation, Proc. 8th Annual IEEE International Phoenix Conference on Computers and Communications, Scottsdale, AZ, 190–194.

Welzel, T. (1990). Performance analysis of token rings as high speed backbone networks, Proc. IEEE INFOCOM'90, San Francisco, CA, 23–29.

Willebeek-LeMair, M., F. Schaffa, and B. Patel (1992). Isochronous versus synchronous traffic in FDDI, Proc. IEEE LCN'92, Minneapolis, MN, 100–109.

Yang, H. and K. Ramakrishnan (1990). Frame content independent stripping for token rings, Proc. ACM SIGCOMM'90, Philadelphia, PA, 276–286.

Yang, H. and K. Ramakrishnan (1991). A ring purger for the FDDI token ring, Proc. IEEE LCN'91, Minneapolis, MN, 503–514.

Yang, H., K. Ramakrishnan, B. Spinney, and R. Jain (1989). Frame removal mechanism for token ring networks, U.S. Patent filed February 1989.

Yang, H., B. Spinney, and S. Towning (1991). FDDI data link development, *Digital Technical Journal*, **3**(2), Spring 1991, 31–41.

Yoneda, K. and T. Kaji (1986). On a preamble size for FDDI-II network distributed clocking, *Trans. Inst. Electron. & Commun. Eng. Jpn. Sect. E (Japan)*, **E69**(11), 1157–1160.

Yue, O. and C. Brooks, (1990). Performance of the timed token scheme in MAP, *IEEE Trans. Commun.*, **38**(7), 1006–1012.

Index

-G-

-M-